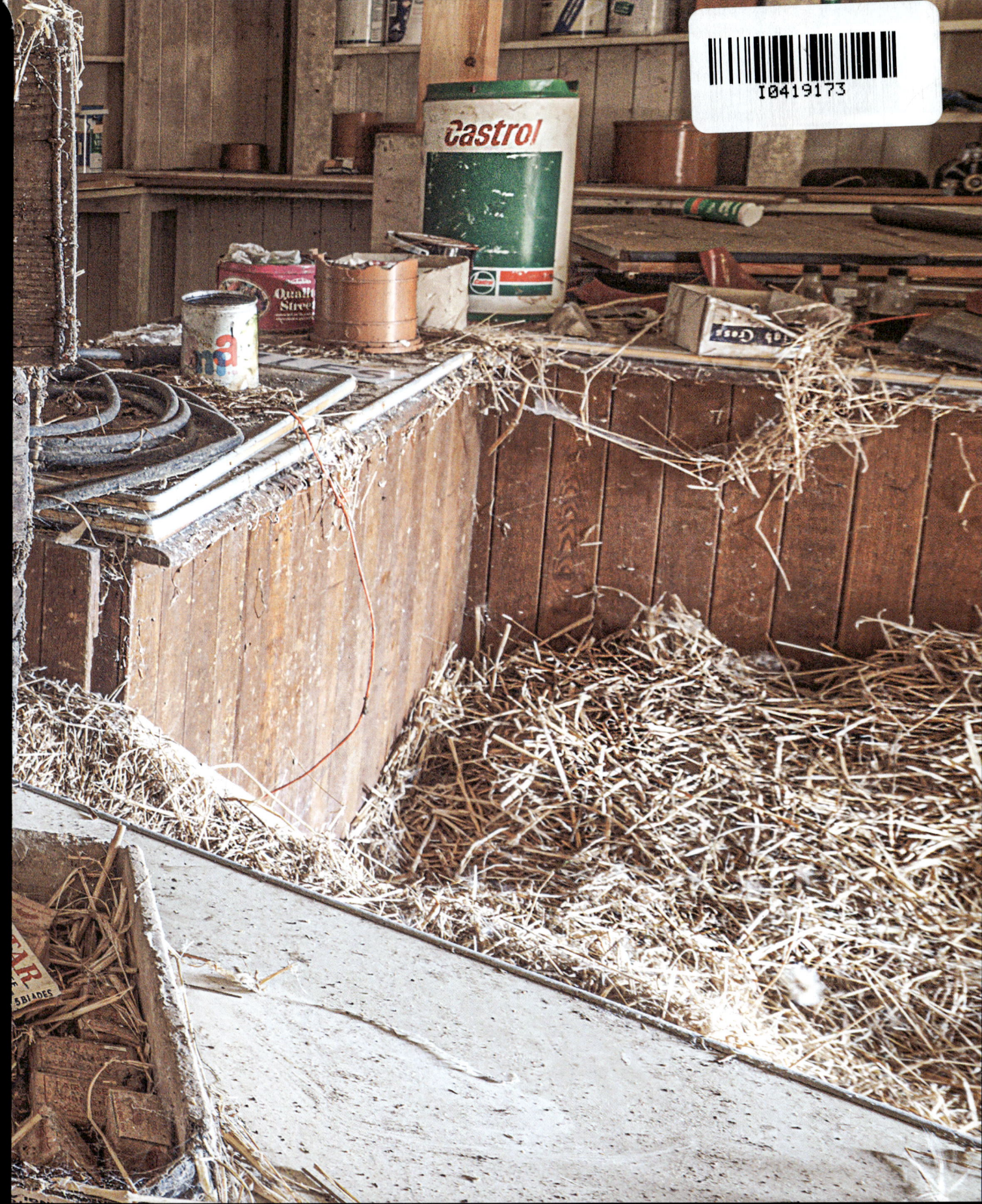

# ABANDONED IRELAND 2

**Rebecca Brownlie** grew up in a small rural village in Co. Down, Northern Ireland. When she was just twelve years old, she won her first camera on a TV show and, from that day, a camera has rarely been far from her side. Her passion for abandoned buildings and her love of photography have led her to appear on several local television shows featuring some of Ireland's lost buildings. She is an avid adventurer and can regularly be found hiking up mountains with her four-legged friend and children in tow.

# ABANDONED IRELAND 2

Rebecca Brownlie

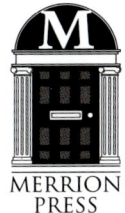

MERRION
PRESS

First published in 2024 by
Merrion Press
10 George's Street
Newbridge
Co. Kildare
Ireland
www.merrionpress.ie

© Rebecca Brownlie, 2024

9781785375262 (Hardback)
9781785375361 (Ebook)

A CIP catalogue record for this book is available from the British Library.

Typeset in PSFournier and Operetta

Cover design by riverdesignbooks.com

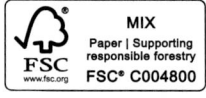

Printed in Dubai.

Merrion Press is a member of Publishing Ireland.

# CONTENTS

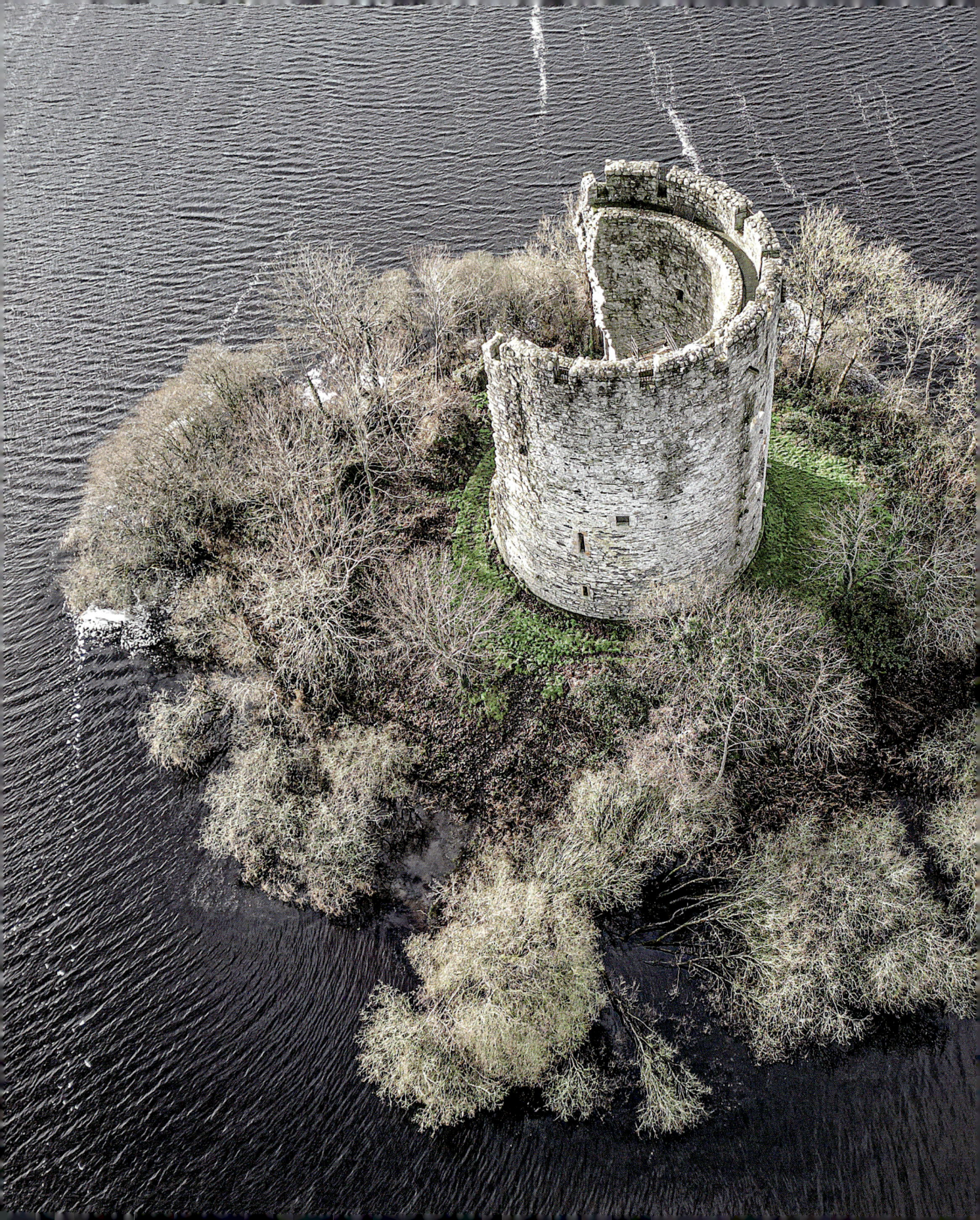

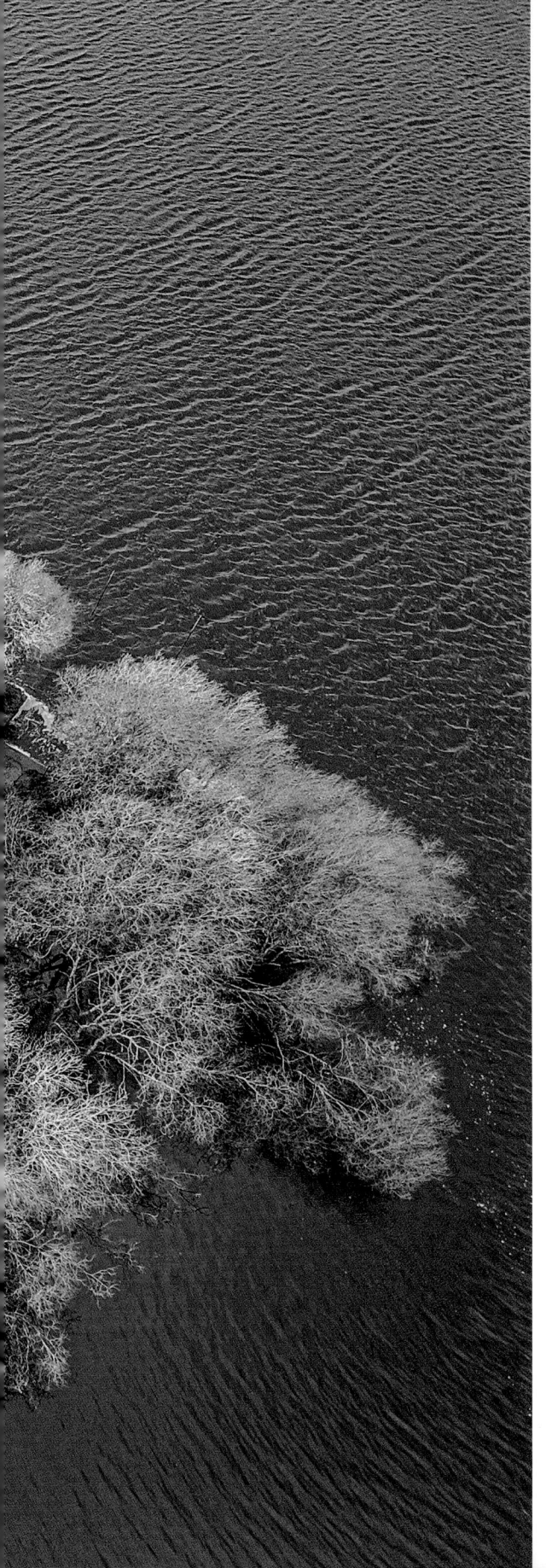

# INTRODUCTION

For those who have not read *Abandoned Ireland*, my first book, I wanted to provide a brief introduction to what inspires me to travel this country recording the fascinating and often beautiful pieces of our heritage that have been left to fall into ruin and decay. Places like Clough Oughter, built on a man-made island on Lough Oughter as early as the thirteenth century and inhabited for centuries by the O'Reilly clan. Then, following the plantation of Ulster and subsequent land confiscations in 1610, it was granted to Captain Hugh Culme. However, during the Irish Rebellion in 1641, local MP for Cavan Philip O'Reilly, a key leader, took control of Clough Oughter and used it as a prison. He retained ownership of the castle until 1653, when it fell to Cromwell's cannons, and what remains today is largely what was left after that destruction. The island and castle were never again inhabited.

My interest in such places was initially aroused when I joined a paranormal group led by Mike Hirons called 'Paranormal Ulster' in the early 2000s. I became the team photographer and location finder, and started discovering interesting buildings to investigate. But beyond the paranormal I soon found myself intrigued by the history of the buildings themselves – why were they left empty, who were the previous occupants and what were their lives like?

Soon my focus shifted away from the paranormal and became solely concentrated on abandoned photography. I first discovered my love for photography as a young teenager. Like many my age, I was a fan of a local Saturday-morning TV show called *SUS*, hosted by Patrick Kielty, who now hosts *The Late Late Show*. I remember phoning in one morning to participate in a competition, although I can't recall the exact question I had to answer – most likely it had something to do with New Kids on the Block, with whom I was completely obsessed at the time. To my excitement, I answered correctly and won a new camera. This moment marked the beginning of my passion for photography and I quickly became the designated photographer among my friends. Thankfully, most of my early photos never made it to the darkroom!

Once I started to concentrate on documenting our abandoned buildings, I created a Facebook page called Abandoned N.I., which was soon followed by a website. The feedback I started getting from people visiting my site was overwhelming, and I was thrilled to see that so many shared the same interest in these properties and their history as I did.

And soon that interest began to branch beyond buildings to include other types of objects. One memorable find came from County Meath, where a plane is just sitting beside a car park at an activity centre, abandoned and unlikely to fly again. This was a Hunter F.51 fighter jet retired from the Danish Air Force in 1976. It was on display in a small number of English museums before it made its way to Meath, where it has been resting ever since. It's unclear what will happen to this jet in the long run, but what a sight it is. To get the best view I used a drone, a developing technology that has made it possible for me to record the sites I visit in all their glory, from above as well as from the ground.

Another unusual find was one of Ireland's handful of pyramids. Hidden away in Garvagh forest, this one was commissioned in the nineteenth century by the first Baron Garvagh, George Canning, after he had taken a grand tour of Egypt. Like the pharaohs of old, he had decided that he wanted to be buried in a grand mausoleum when the time came, and so he chose to have his own pyramid constructed for the purpose. Unfortunately for Lord Garvagh, his wishes were not granted after he died in Paris in 1840, and he was instead buried in Derry. His wife, who outlived him by many years, chose not to

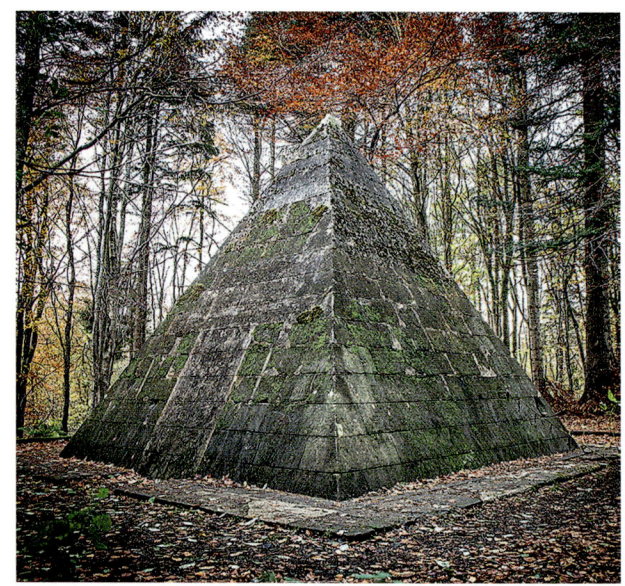

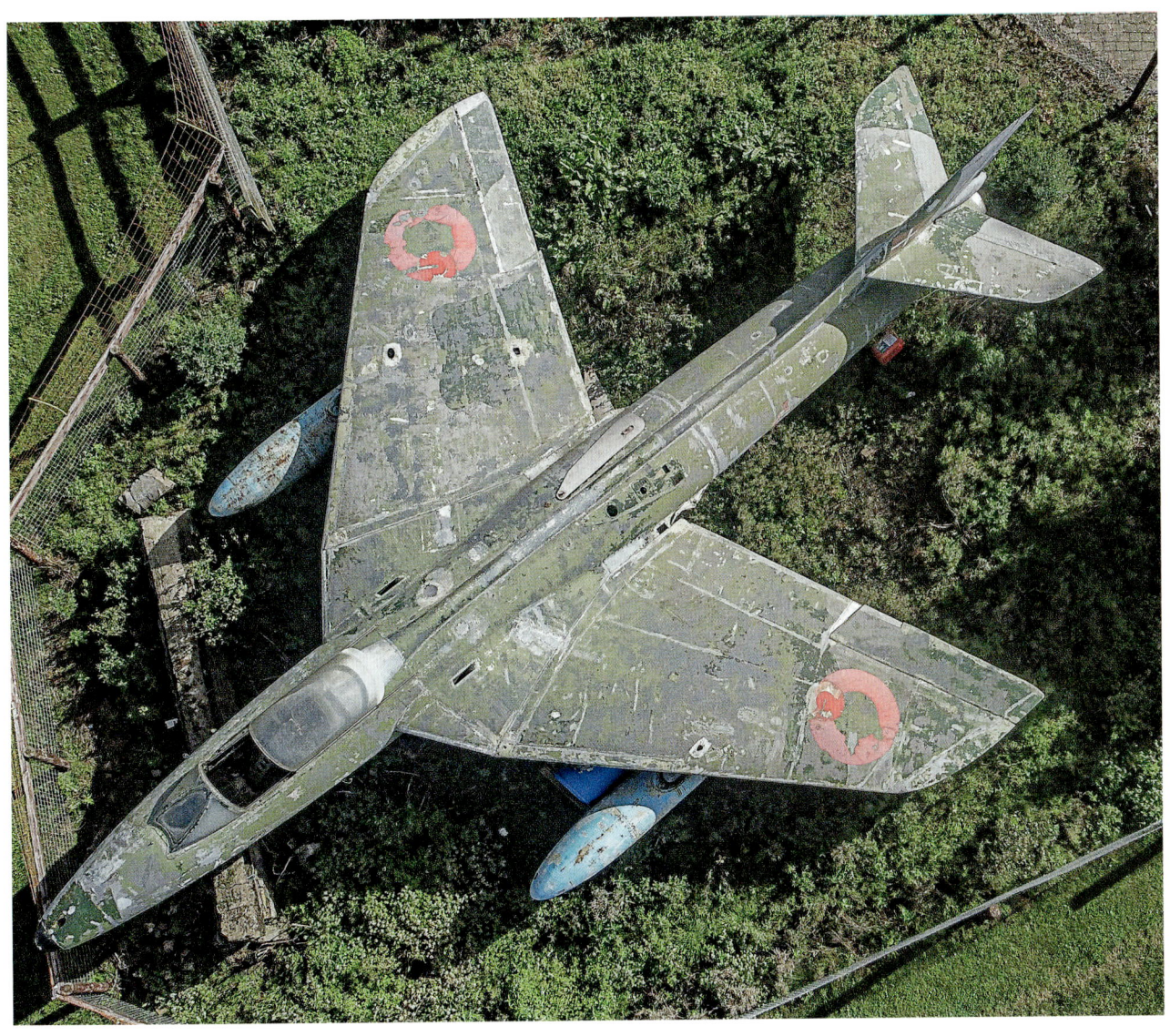

use the pyramid as her final resting place either, and eventually it was closed up and sealed forever.

The pyramid is accessible to the public in Garvagh forest, but many of the places I visit are much harder to get to and permission is needed from the current owner or landowner. Liscloon House is one such place. This impressive Gothic ruin, also known as Ogilby's Castle, has its own tragic love story attached to its history, as do many Irish castles. Built in 1860 by William Ogilby, a zoologist from London, the castle served as a project for him to work on while pursuing his dream of writing a book. The castle was made entirely of Irish cut stone transported by horse and cart from nearby Dungiven. Upon completion, it was considered a marvel of modernity for its time. The banquet hall was renowned as one of the finest in all of Ireland, hosting elaborate dinner parties attended by high-ranking bishops and politicians from London, Dublin and Belfast.

Shortly after William completed the castle, he passed away, leaving the estate to his son Claude. Known for his heavy drinking, Claude succumbed to kidney failure at the age of forty-three in 1875. It was reported that he had abandoned the castle six years prior to his death, and by 1909 the castle was considered a ruin.

The love story concerns another of William's seven children, James, who fell in love with a local seamstress named Mary when he was twenty-seven and she was just sixteen. Despite concerns about their differing social statuses, they pursued a passionate romance, leaving love letters for each other in a nearby tree. When James' family learned of the relationship, they forbade him from marrying Mary and he was sent to America to study wildlife, where he focused on cataloguing birds in Navarro, Texas, for *The Scientific Transactions of the Royal Dublin Society*.

However, James never forgot Mary, and seven years later he travelled back to Ireland in search of her. The two finally married in 1884 in Donagheady, without either of their families in attendance. They left for Australia to start anew, leaving Ogilby's Castle and their past behind them. James worked tirelessly and excelled in his field of zoology, earning recognition from the prestigious Linnea Society of London as a Fellow in 1887.

The couple's happiness was not to last. Tragically, Mary contracted tuberculosis and passed away at the young age of twenty-nine, leaving James heartbroken. They had no children. Devastated by her death, James turned to alcohol and eventually lost his job. Despite this setback, he continued to pursue his passion for science and became the author of numerous scientific papers on reptiles. He even discovered new species of turtles and lizards. James passed away in a hospital in Brisbane in 1925 at the age of seventy-two, leaving behind a legacy of scientific discovery and a bittersweet love story that defined his life.

Stories such as these were what spurred on my interest in the places I was recording. In 2022 I released my first book, and the overwhelmingly positive response to that has led to this second work. One question that came up a lot when *Abandoned Ireland* came out was why I hadn't identified where most of the places were. My answer is that these places need to be protected, and too often if their location is disclosed they become a target for vandalism. So I have continued that trend in most cases for this book too, unless they are well-known properties – I hope the reader will forgive me!

When I started out on this journey, I could never have imagined how far it would take me, from the books to TV shows, such as the BBC's *Barra on the Foyle*, *Tréigthe* (Abandoned) with Doubleband Films and UTV's *Hidden NI*, as well as radio interviews and

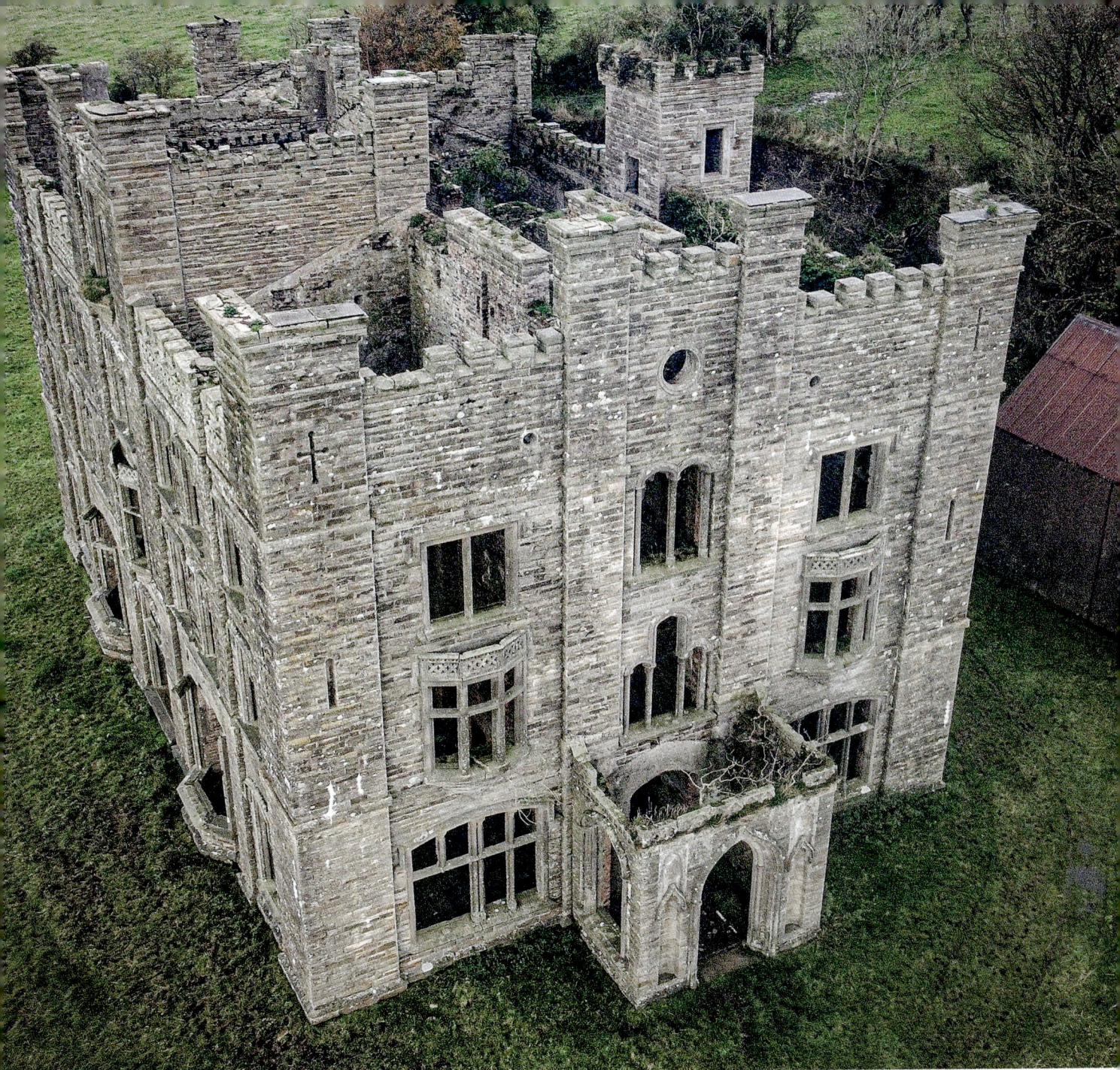

podcasts. But I find that once I start talking about this subject, I just can't seem to stop. Can you tell?

Finally, I want to thank you, the reader, for supporting me on this incredible journey. I hope you enjoy this second book as much as I enjoyed putting it together. All that remains now for me is to ask myself: where to next?

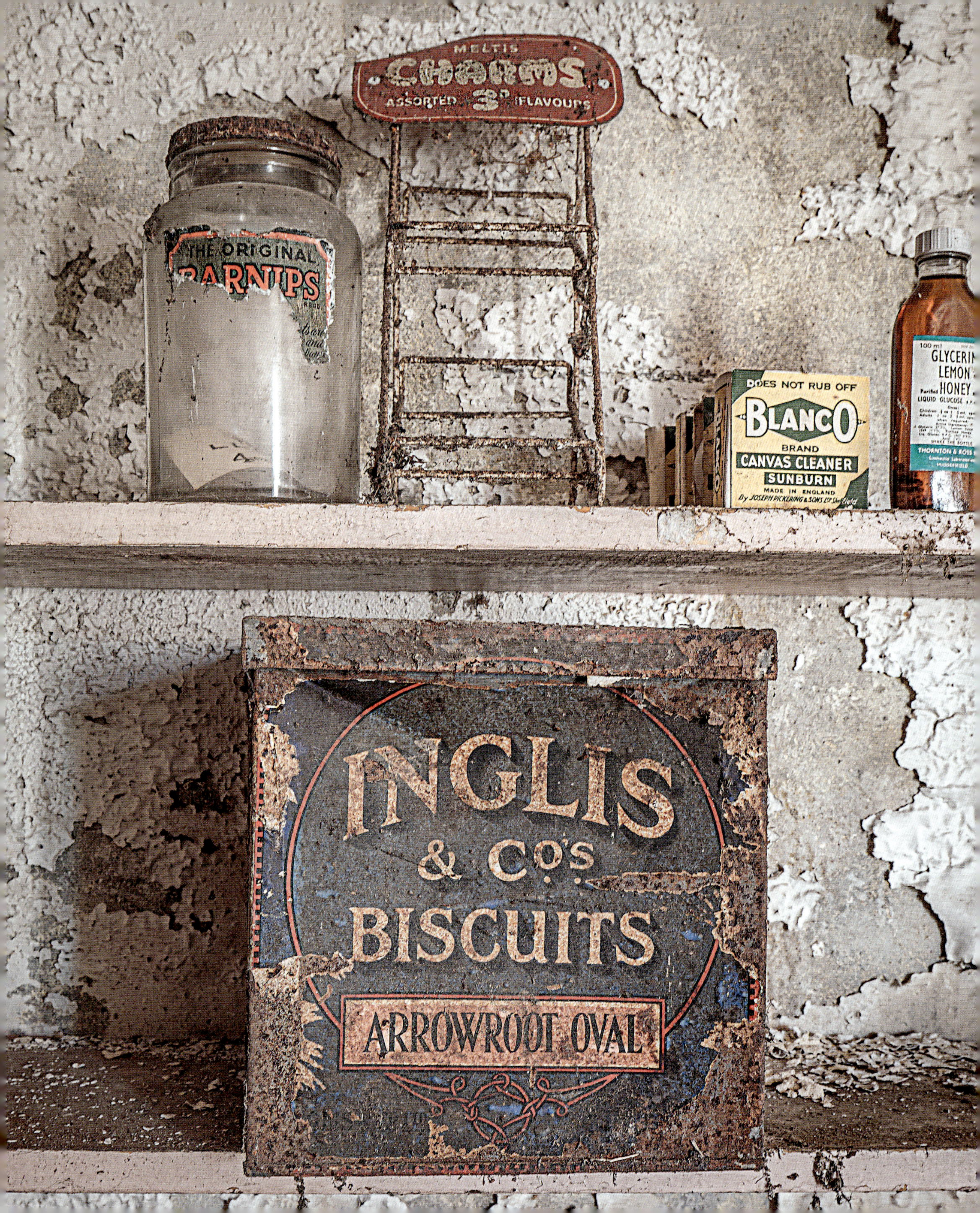
MELTIS
CHARMS
ASSORTED 3D FLAVOURS
THE ORIGINAL
DOES NOT RUB OFF
BLANCO
BRAND
CANVAS CLEANER
SUNBURN
MADE IN ENGLAND
LEMON
HONEY
INGLIS
& Co's
BISCUITS
ARROWROOT OVAL

# ASHFIELD STORE

Back in the summer of 2023 I was woken up in the middle of the night by strong winds and the fact that I'm a light sleeper, which can be a curse, but not on this night.

Unable to get back to sleep, I checked my phone and noticed that an email had arrived at around 2 a.m. through my website. Intrigued, I decided to read it. The message was from someone called

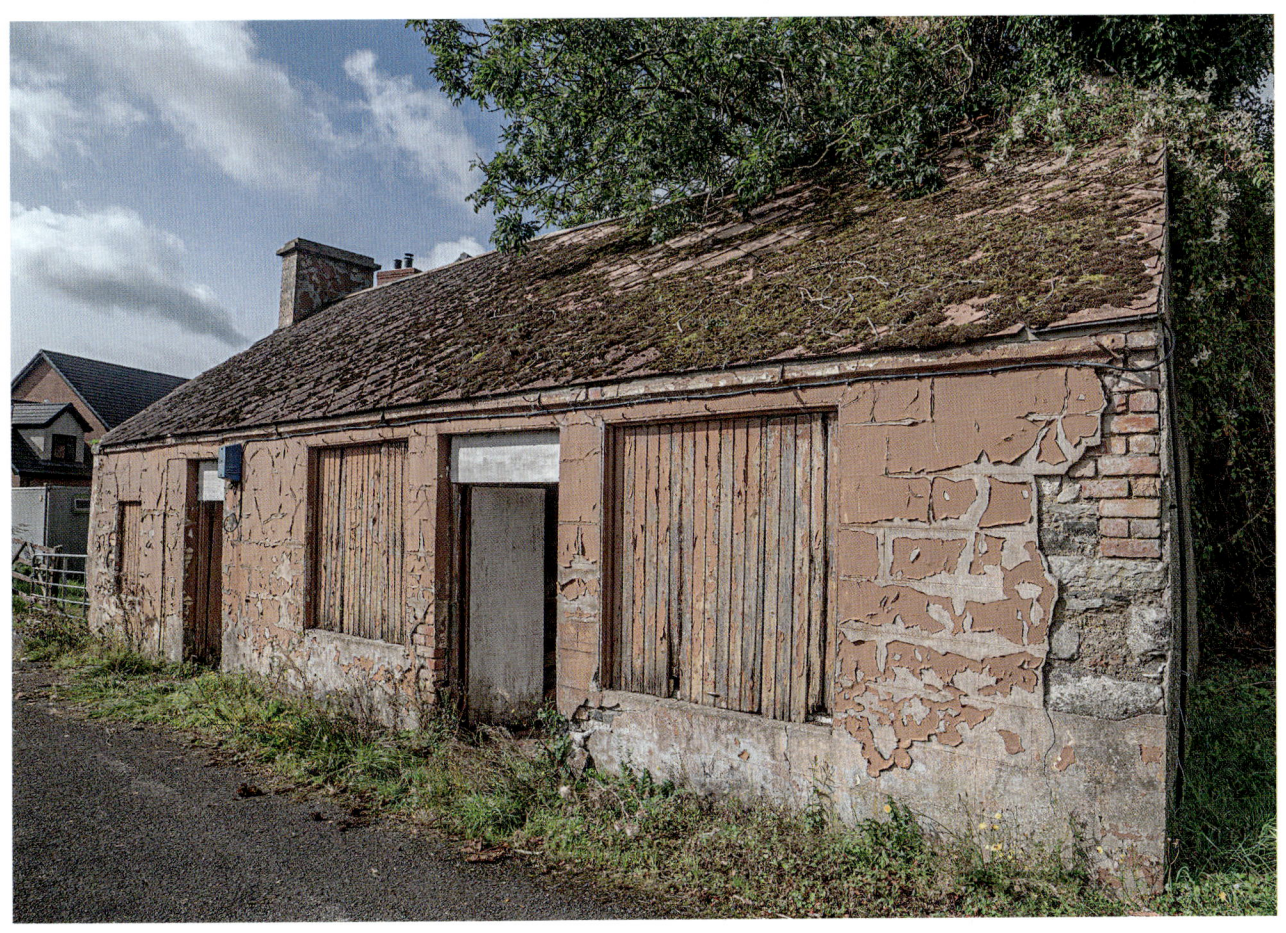

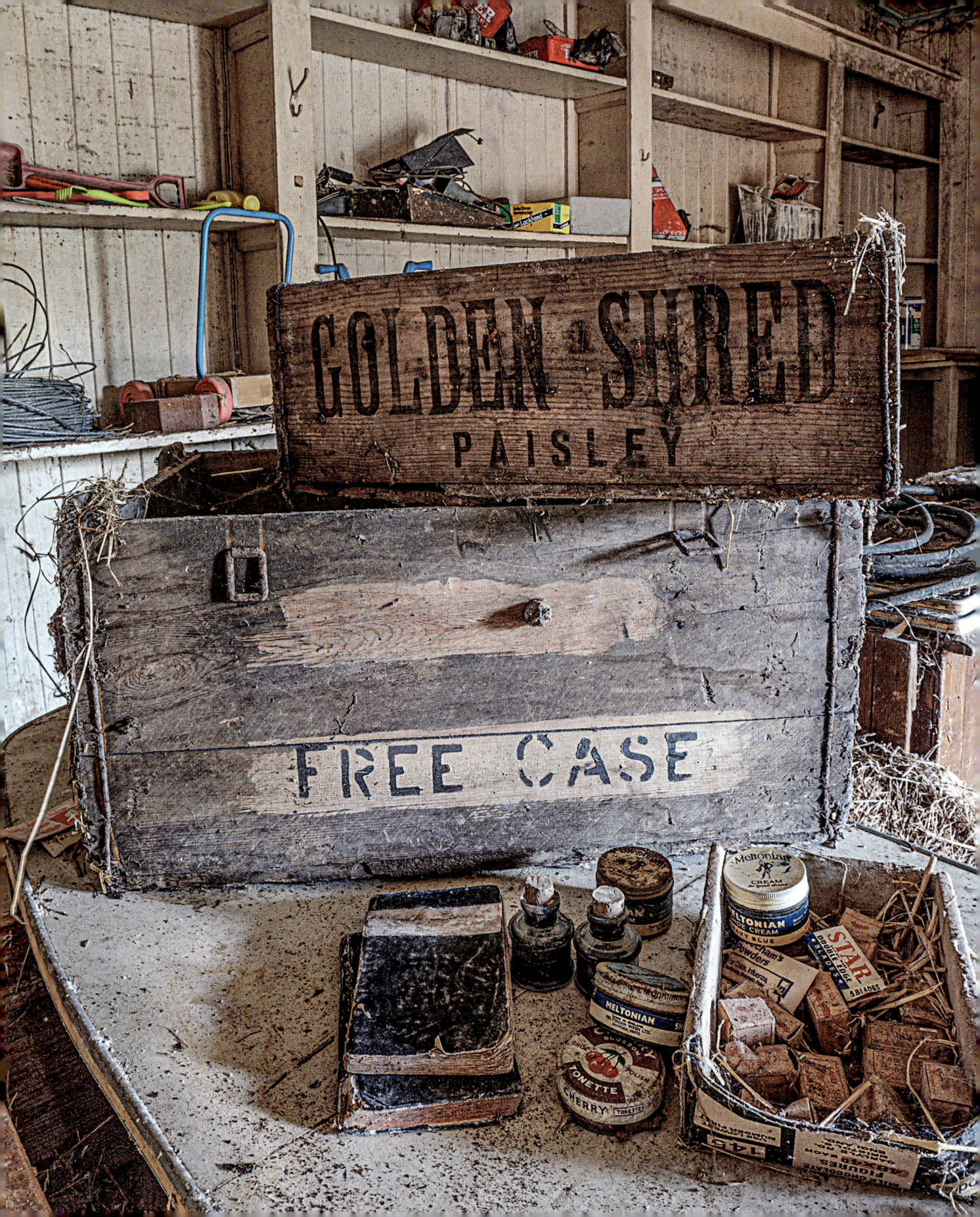

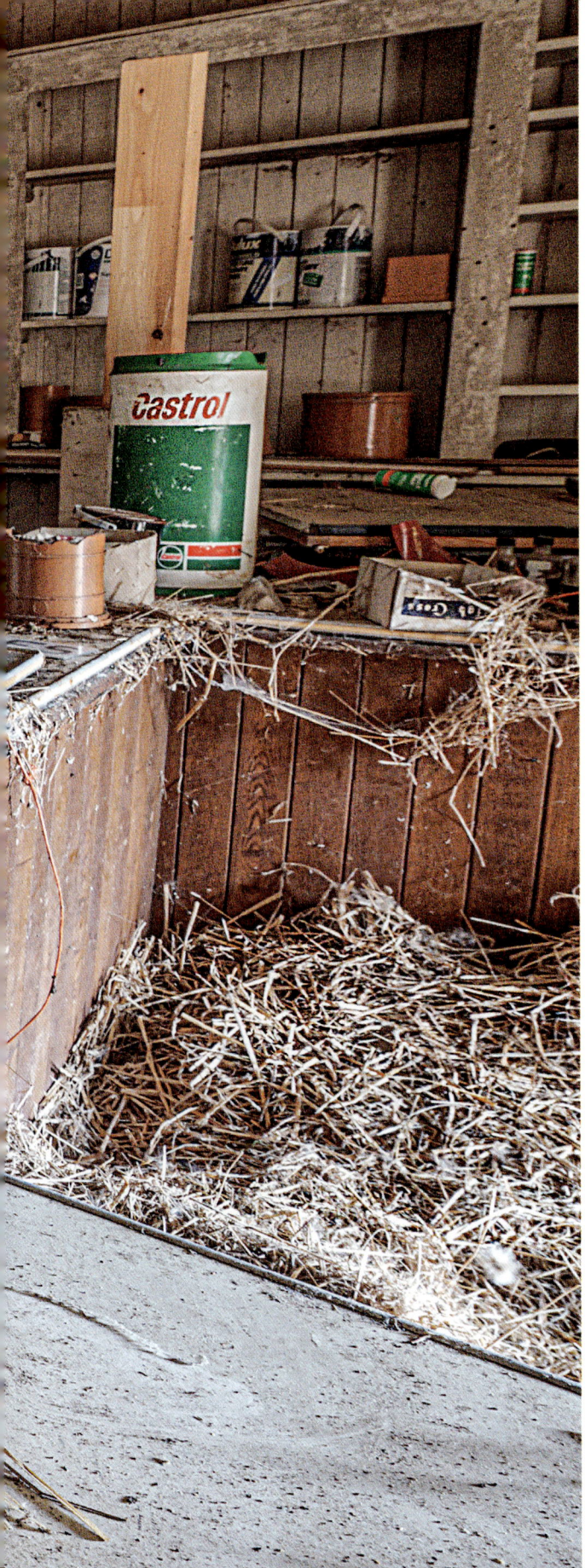

Elaine, telling me about an old shop in Ashfield, Dromore, near Ashfield House, that was scheduled to be demolished the following day. She asked if I could come and document it before that happened. Without hesitation, I responded, arranging to meet her on site just after 9 a.m. I couldn't bear the thought of missing out on this opportunity and spent a while worrying that the building might be gone by the time I got there.

A few hours later, I arrived at the site and met Elaine. From the outside, the shop appeared very unassuming and, looking at it, I could never have imagined it serving that purpose. Elaine briefly recounted the building's history as we stood at the roadside. She explained that her three great-aunts had owned and operated the shop, which was now being demolished to make room for houses.

On opening the door, I noticed numerous old ceramic tins, bottles and some well-kept old crates on the shelves. As I began to move around and snap some pictures, I asked Elaine if she had any more historical information on the place. She told me that the shop was established in 1903 and had served as a general store for the local community. It stocked sweets, boot polish, washing powder, engine oil, clothes and even food – truly a one-stop shop catering for everyone, far and wide. Her aunts treated every customer as a friend, making the shop more of a social hub than a simple business. After closing its doors in 1989, when the aunts got too old to keep running it, the shop remained largely untouched, although it was used occasionally as a hay store.

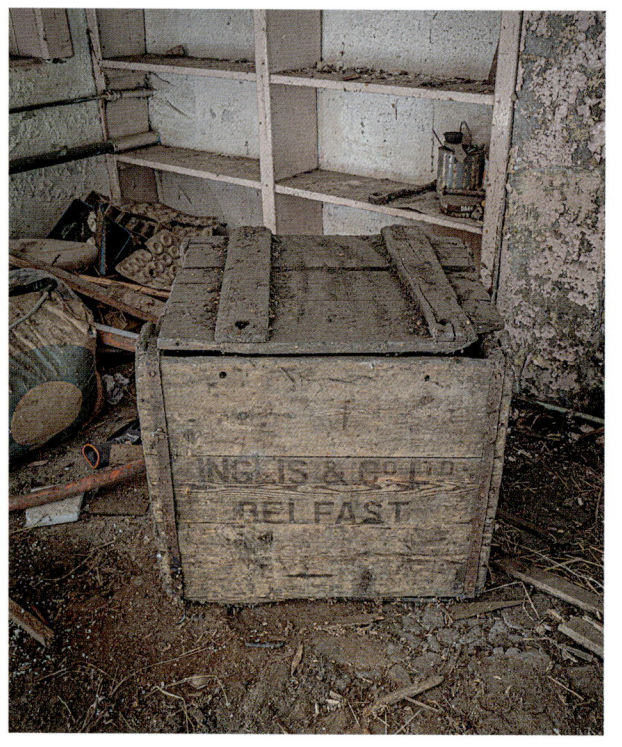

While wandering around and looking at the shelves, I stumbled upon some old ledgers dating back to 1922. The beautiful handwriting was a sight to behold. The shop held a treasure trove of items including polish tins, sweet jars, iodine, a bottle of disinfectant and bread tins. The labels on display are all now extinct, but I loved seeing the old-style fonts and designs; everything had so much detail.

There were two rooms to the shop, with the second room still showcasing the wrap-around counter. Elaine recalled one of her aunts standing beneath the doorway behind the counter, a poignant memory she was able to share through a photograph.

The shop also featured a small staircase leading up to an attic with old chests, though I decided not to explore up there due to safety concerns. Despite being insured, I never take unnecessary risks for a

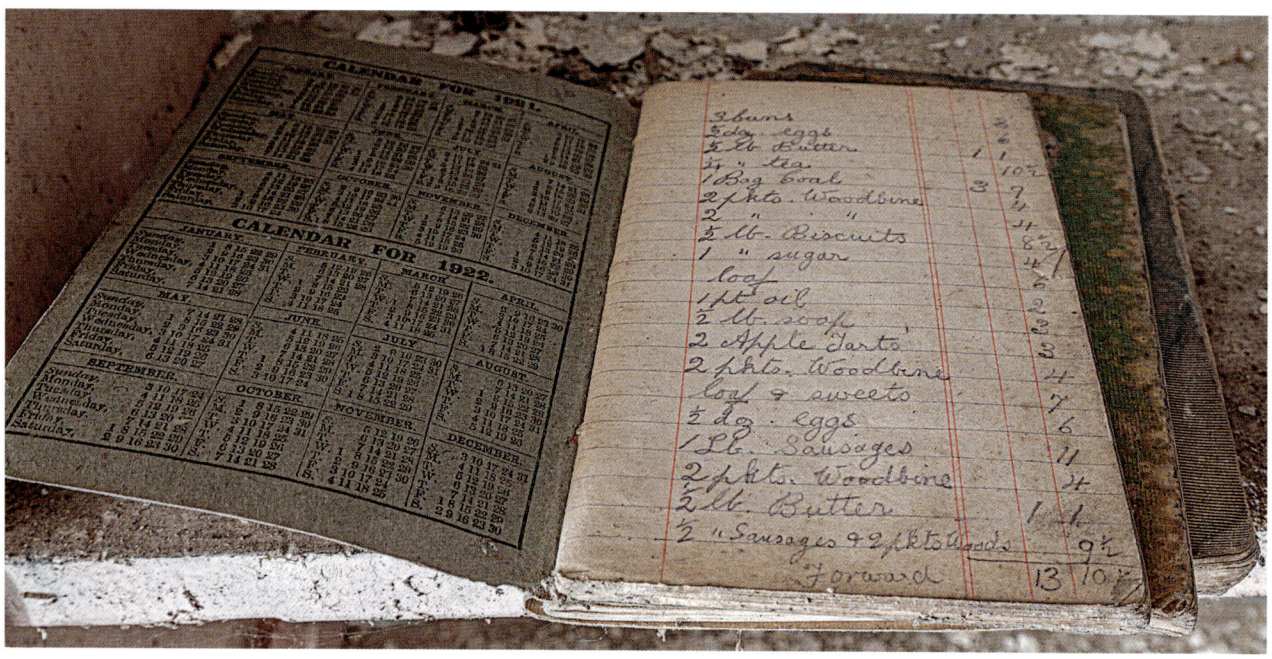

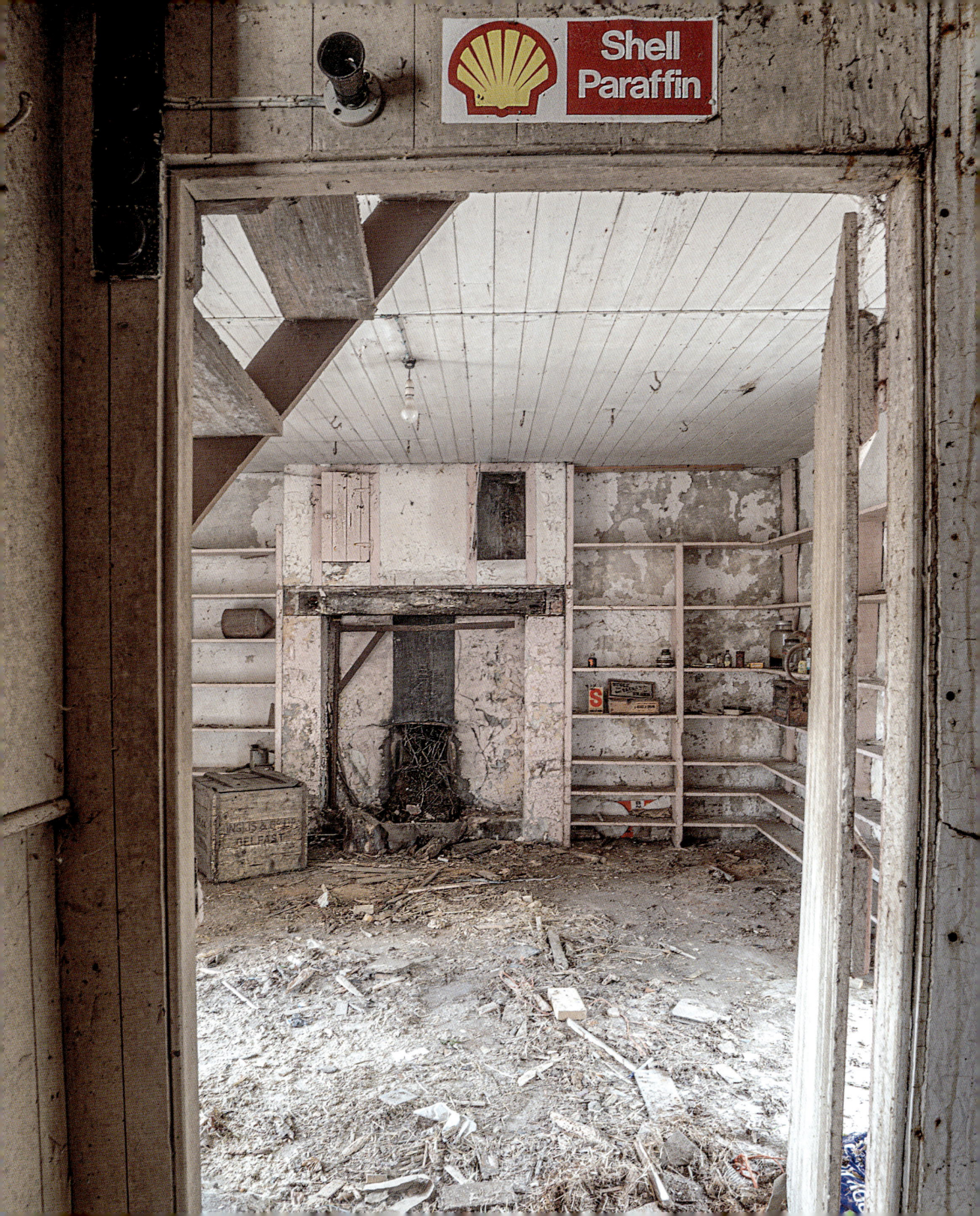

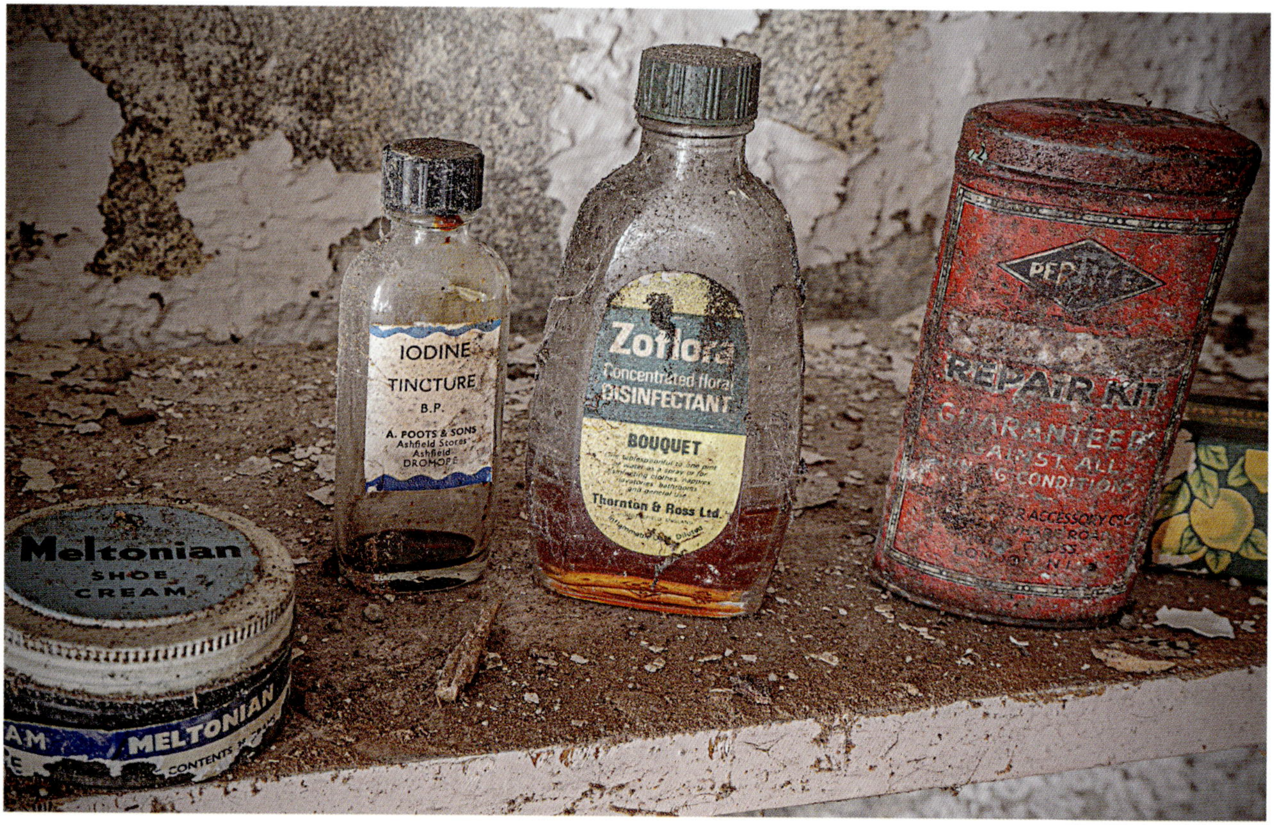

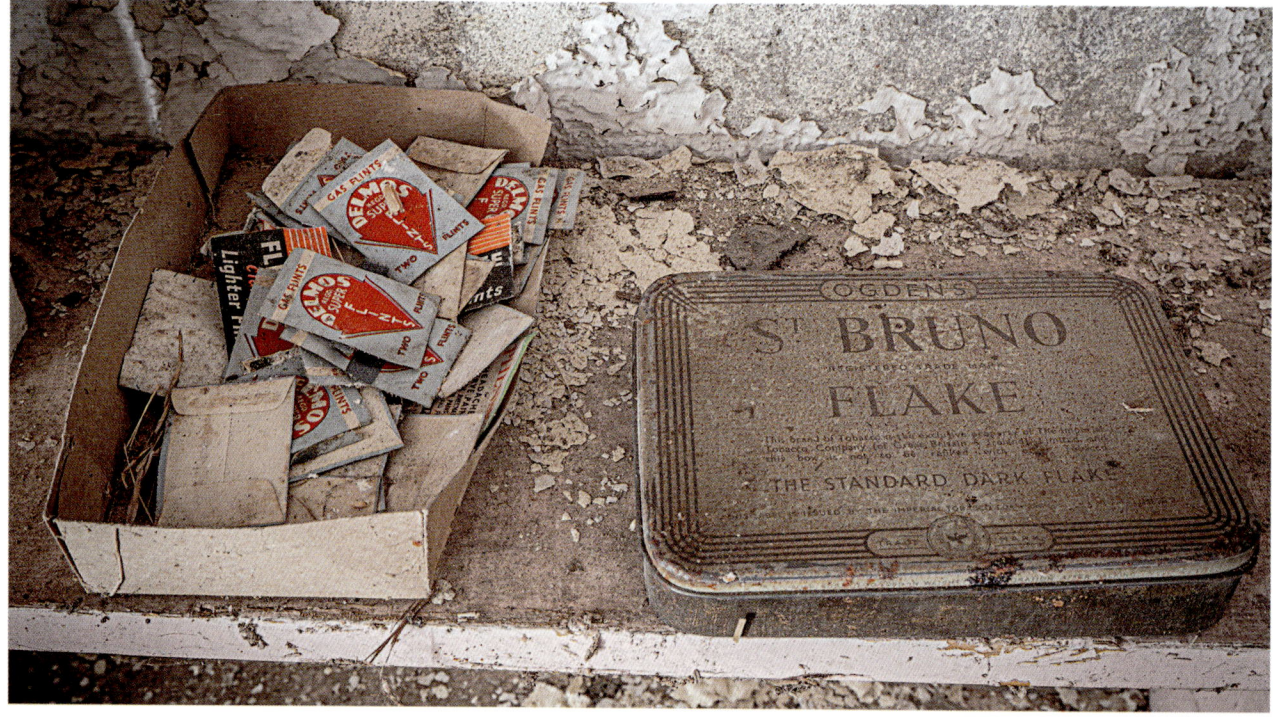

photograph. After wrapping up the exterior shots, I bid farewell to Elaine.

As I drove away, I took a final glance in the rear-view mirror, realising it was both the first and last time I would see Ashfield Store – an unforgettable example of days gone by.

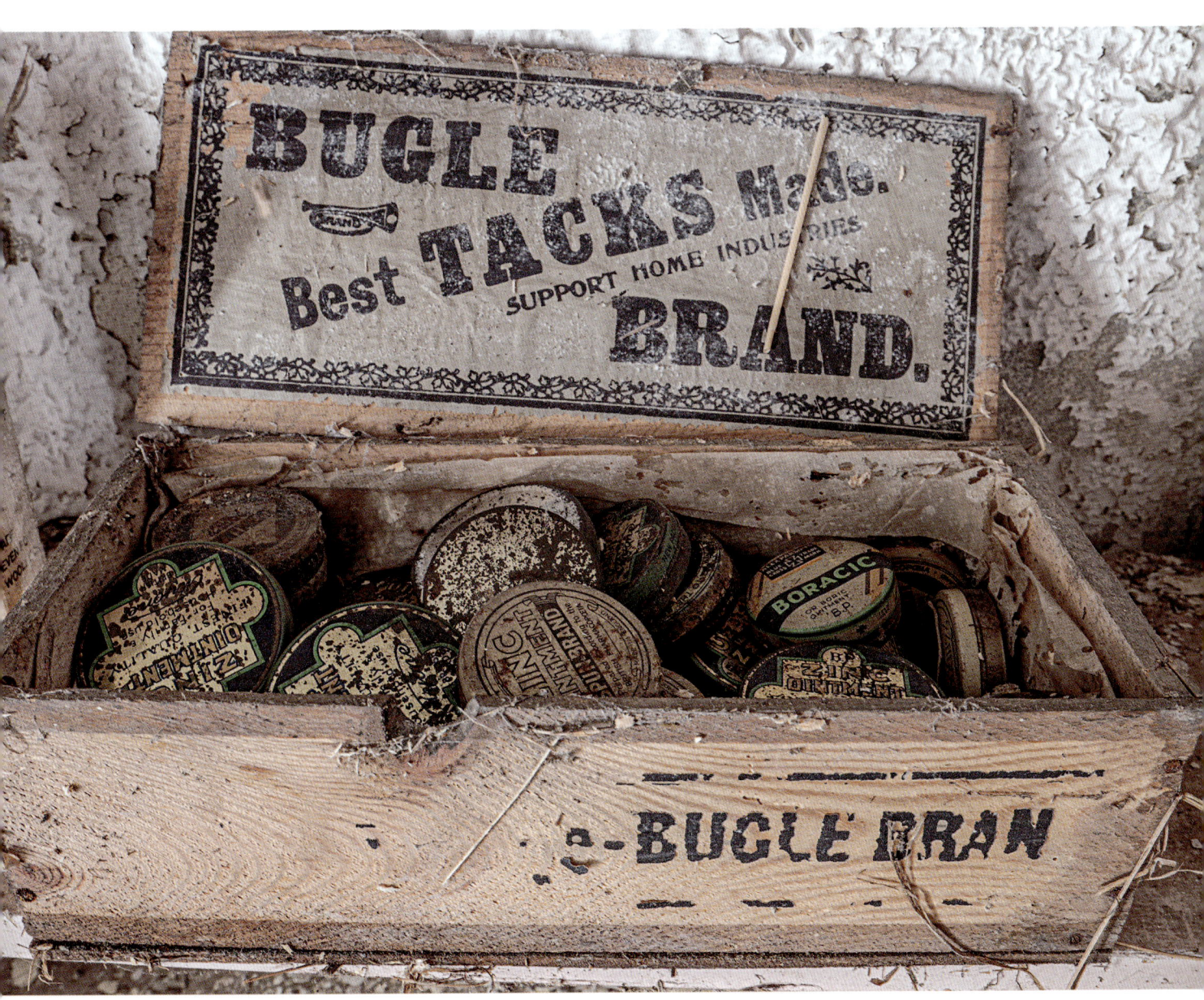

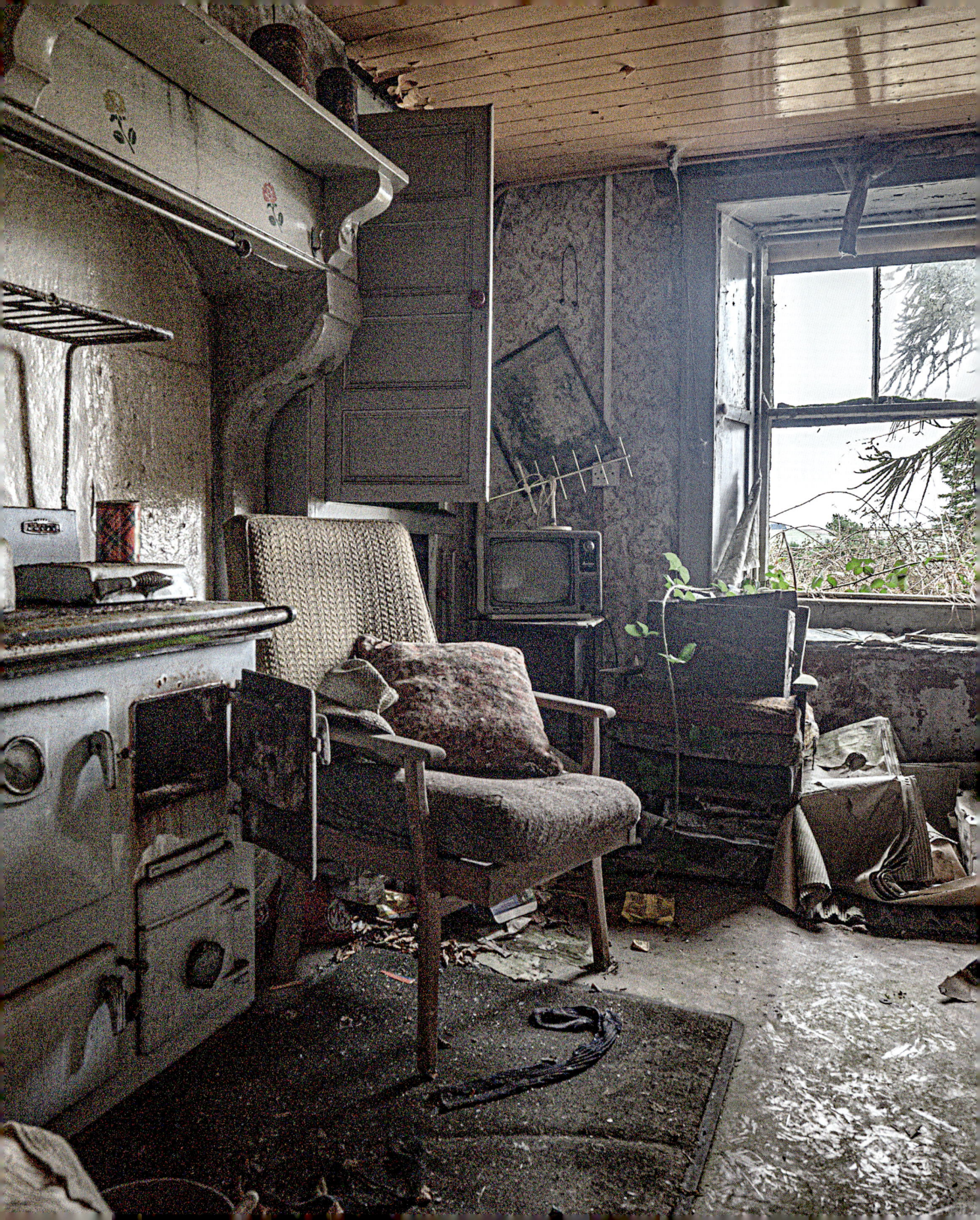

# BOBBY'S PLACE

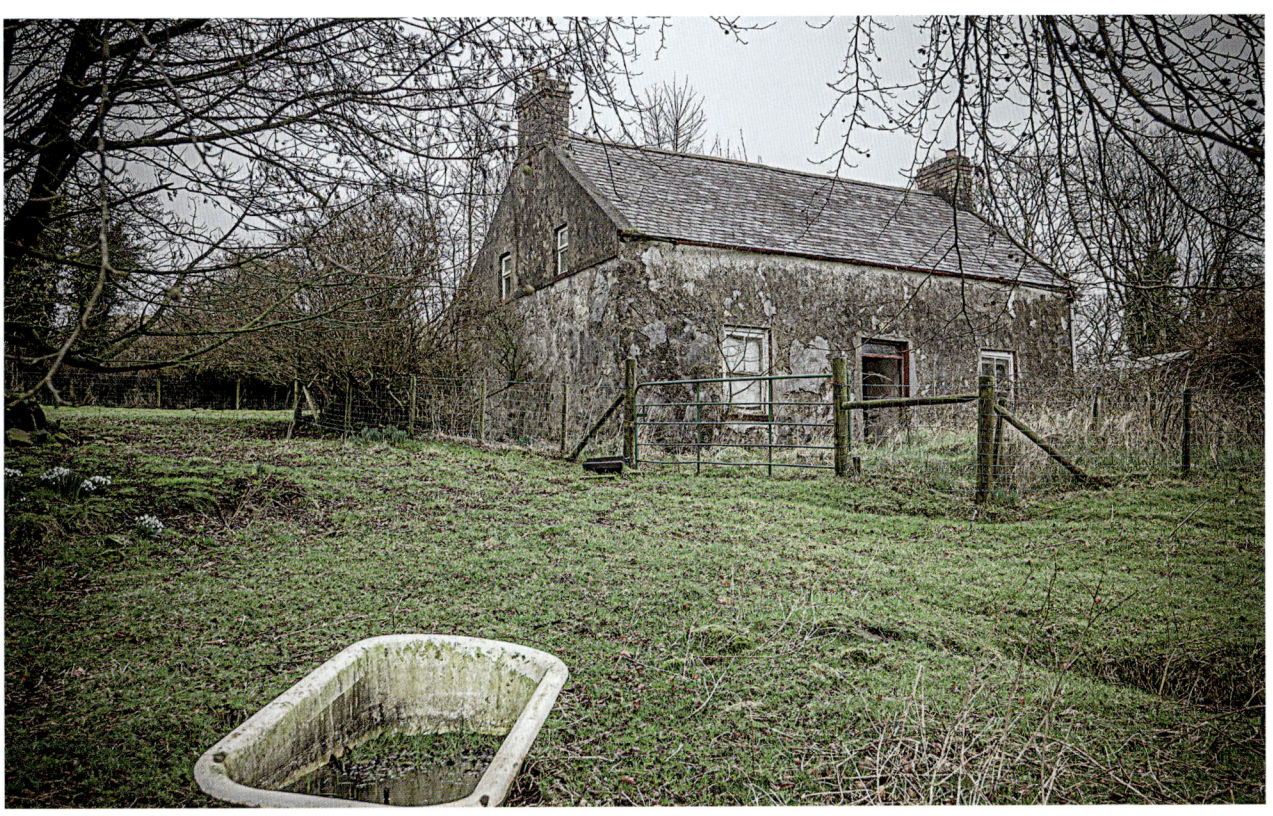

After releasing my first book, I received a phone call from a lady who recommended a house that might be worth investigating. She explained that while working at a corner shop, she had a customer named Bobby who used to come in many years ago. Bobby would purchase items ranging from a pint of milk to a gallon of oil. Despite not owning a car, he travelled around on his tractor, a Massey Ferguson. Bobby had no family and lived alone in a house not far from the shop. The lady provided directions and suggested I should check if it was still intact. Without hesitation, I set off to visit Bobby's place.

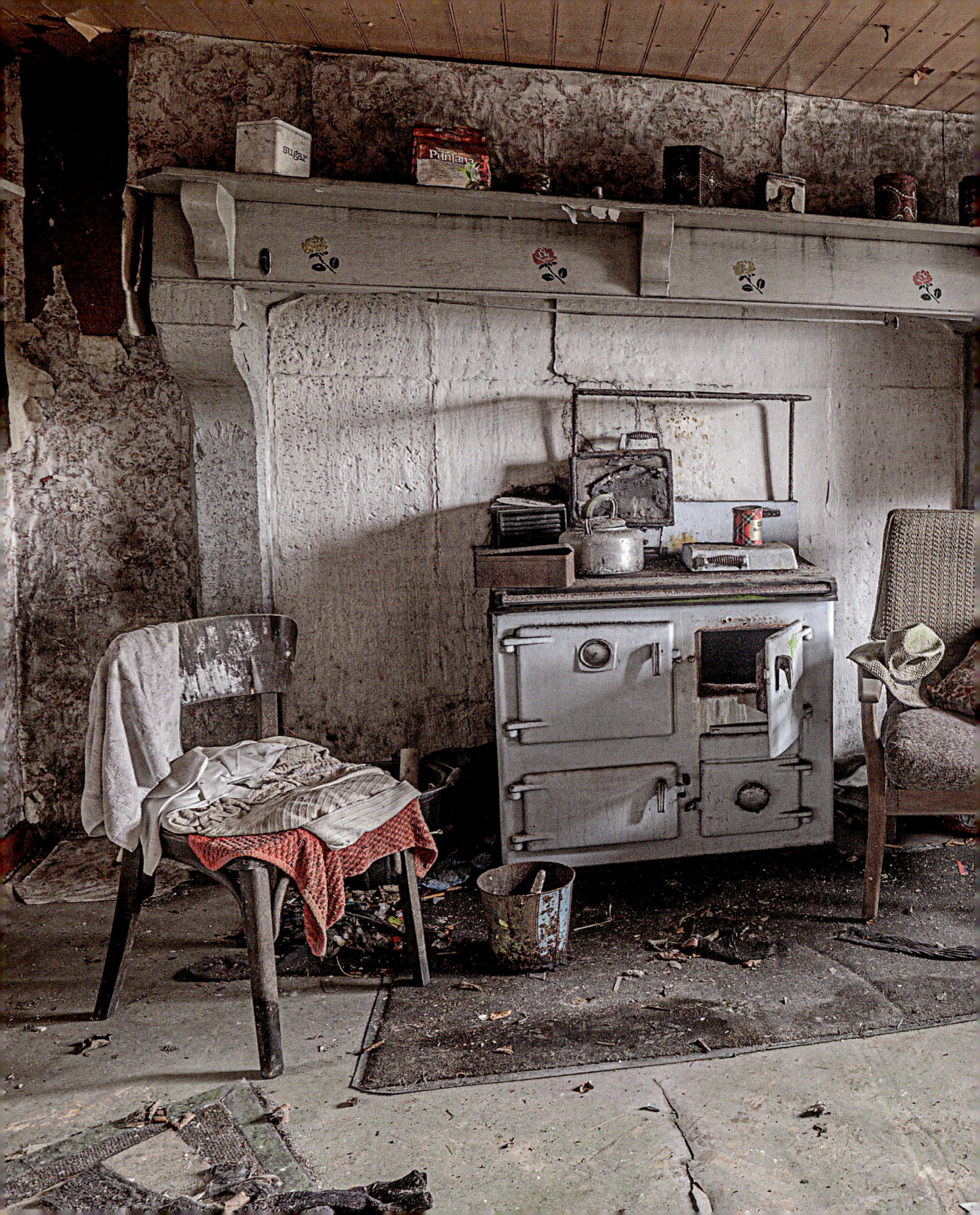

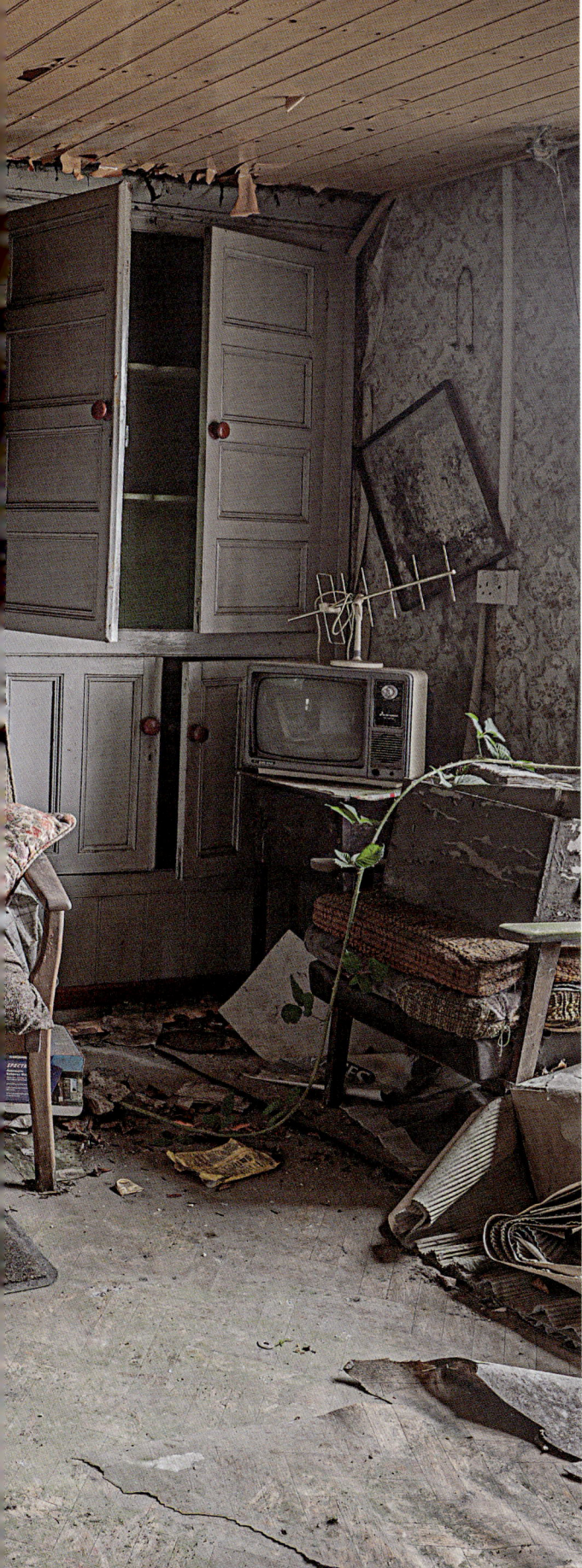

I approached the house up the overgrown drive. A gigantic monkey puzzle tree stood in the garden, towering over the single-storey cottage. An old bathtub filled with murky water sat beneath the tree, likely once used as a water trough for animals such as cattle or sheep.

As I neared the entrance, I noticed the derelict state of the house. Overgrown drainpipes, broken windows and a front door barely hanging on by one hinge greeted me. Stepping inside, the first thing I saw were overcoats swaying in the howling wind coming through the open windows. In the sitting room, a beautiful pale-blue stove caught my eye. Two chairs sat beside it, as if two friends had just finished a conversation.

I entered the room and was struck by the plethora of items that filled the space. The stove was adorned with an old kettle and some tin containers, and a weathered sun hat lay on one of the chairs. In the corner sat a small black-and-white portable TV with an aerial caked in dust. Bobby must have been a religious man, judging by the scripture-based pictures around the house, one of which said, 'God Bless This Home'.

I marvelled at the time capsule that was Bobby's home. According to the woman who reached out to me, he had passed away twenty years earlier, and it seemed like the house had been left untouched since then.

My attention shifted to a staircase that I had missed upon first entering. I climbed up with

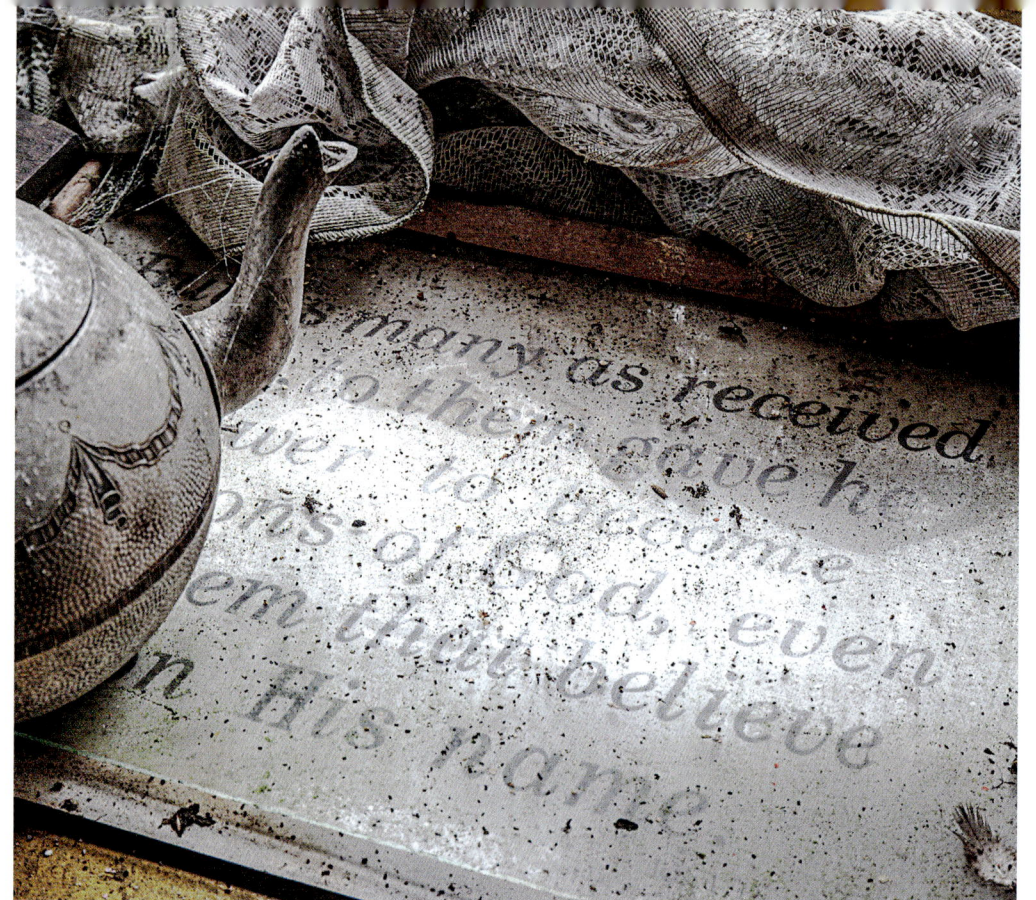

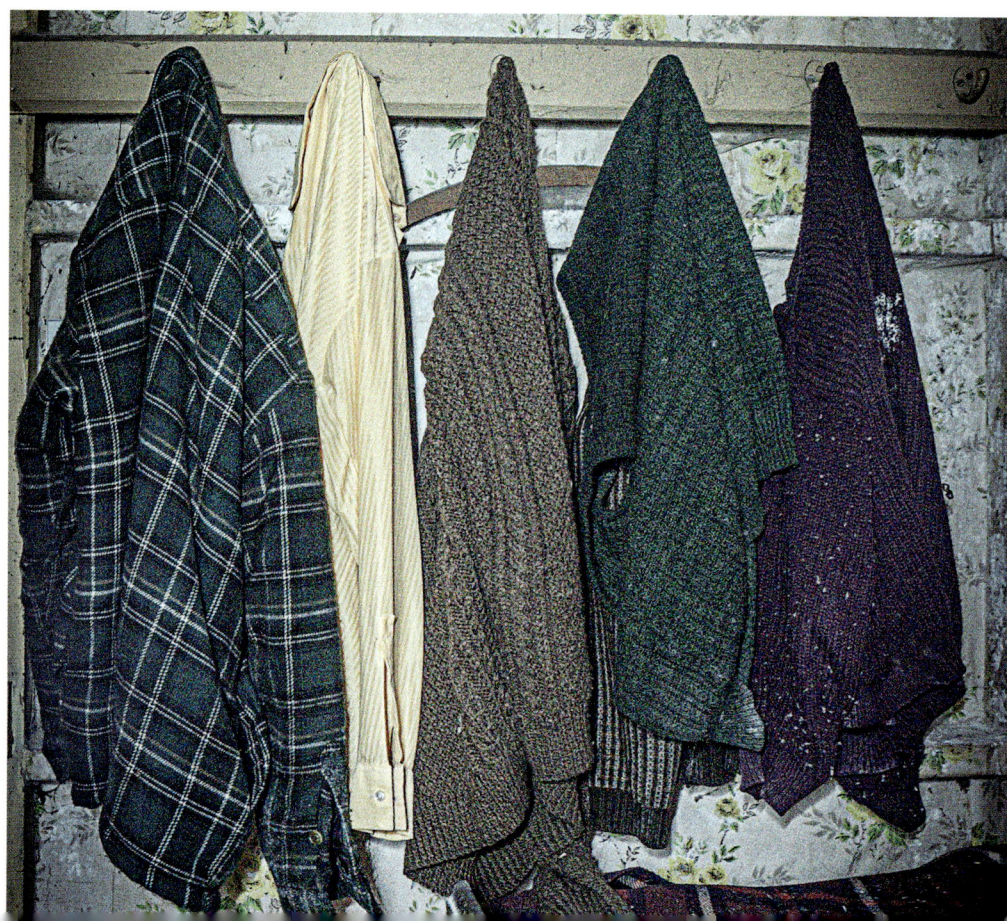

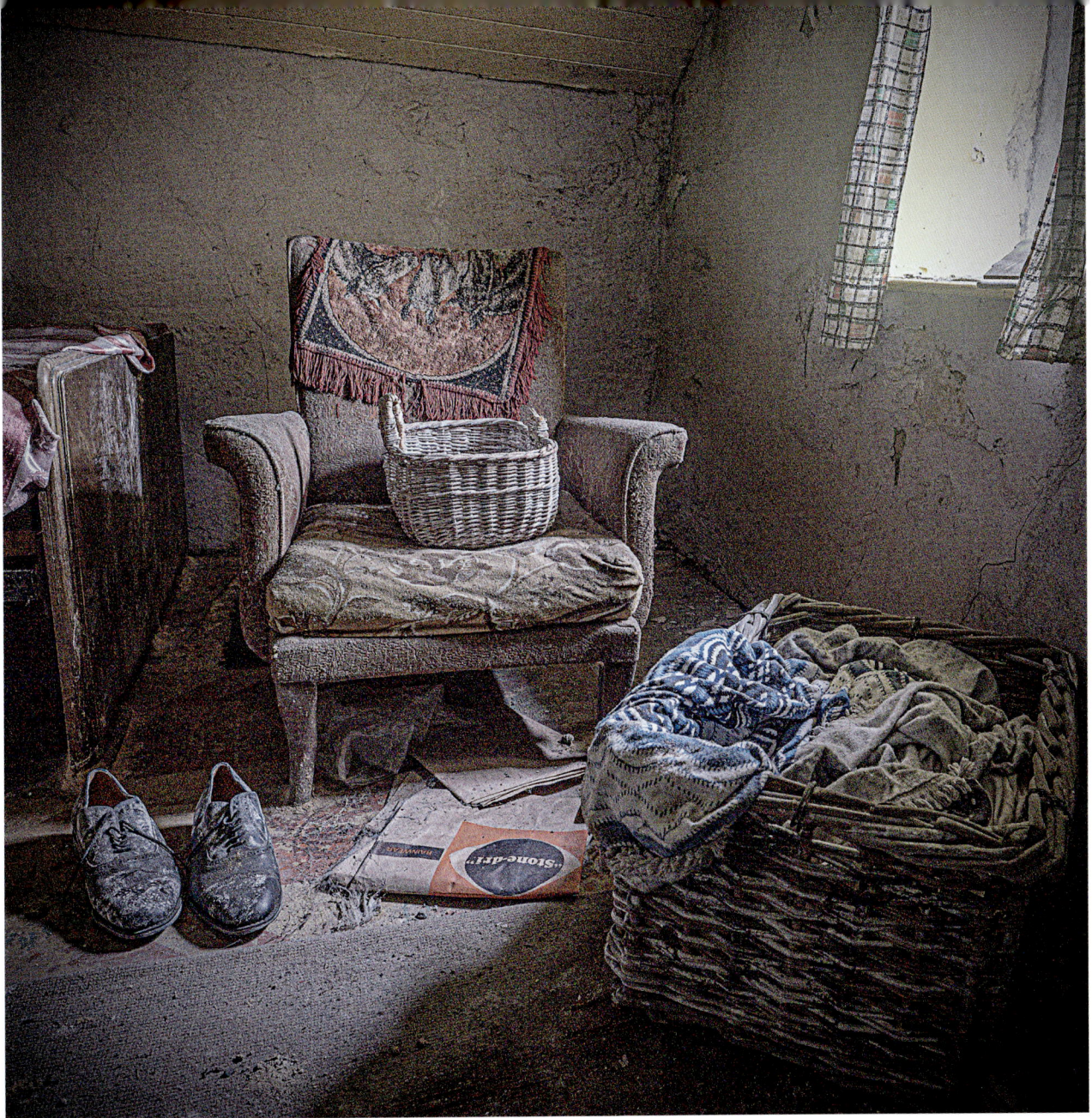

caution, eager to explore the rest of the house. And I was not disappointed. Four bedrooms, with perfectly made beds, wardrobes full of clothes, and bookshelves covered in cobwebs greeted me. In one of the rooms hung a red dressing gown that was noticeably smaller, most likely worn by a female, possibly Bobby's mum or sister. The shoes and slippers in the room led me to believe that Bobby had grown up in the house and left his parents' and siblings' rooms untouched after they passed or left.

As I departed the house, I felt a sense of pride in documenting this piece of history. Although I knew little about Bobby's life, the house was able to tell at least some of his story.

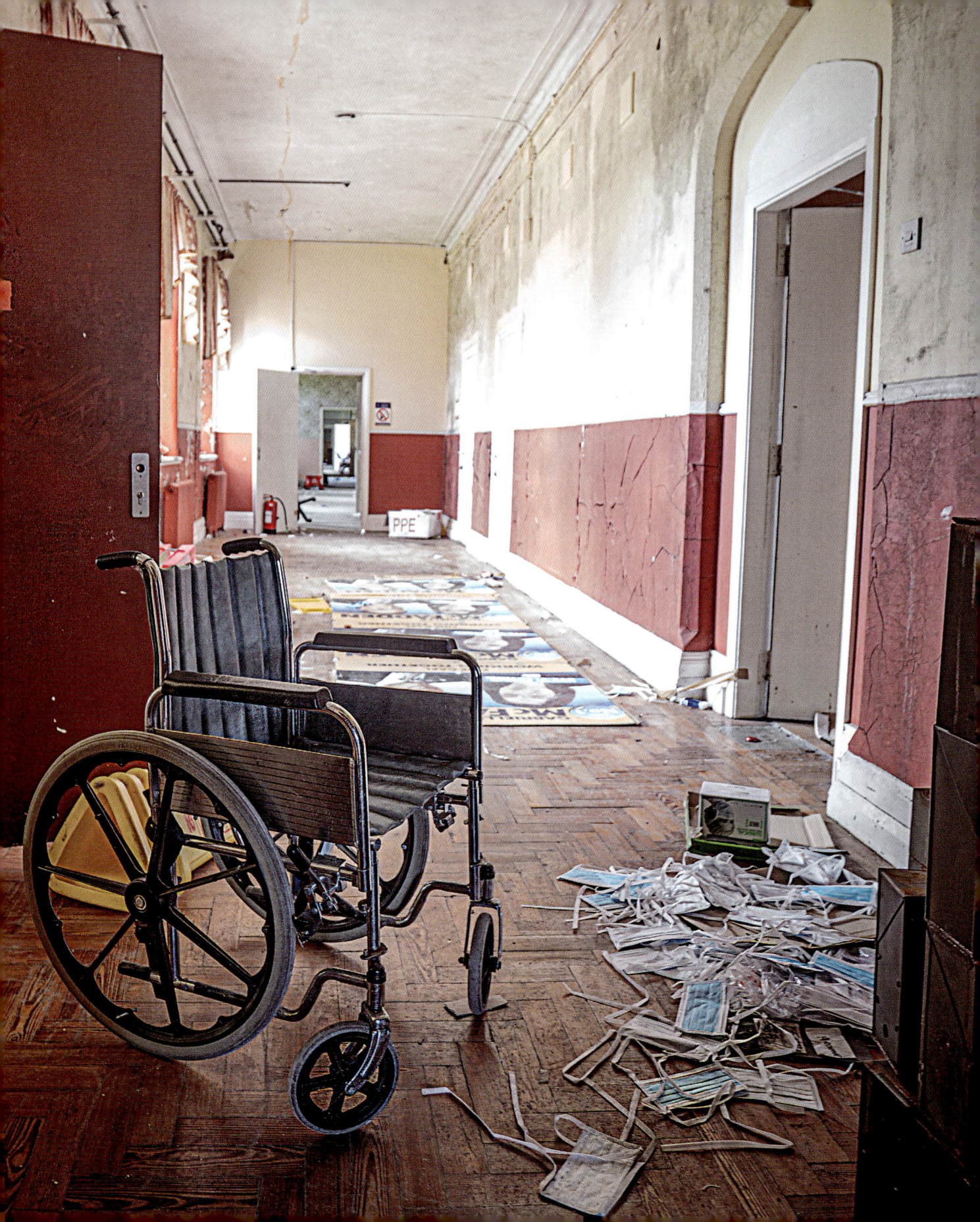

# A SHAMEFUL ASYLUM

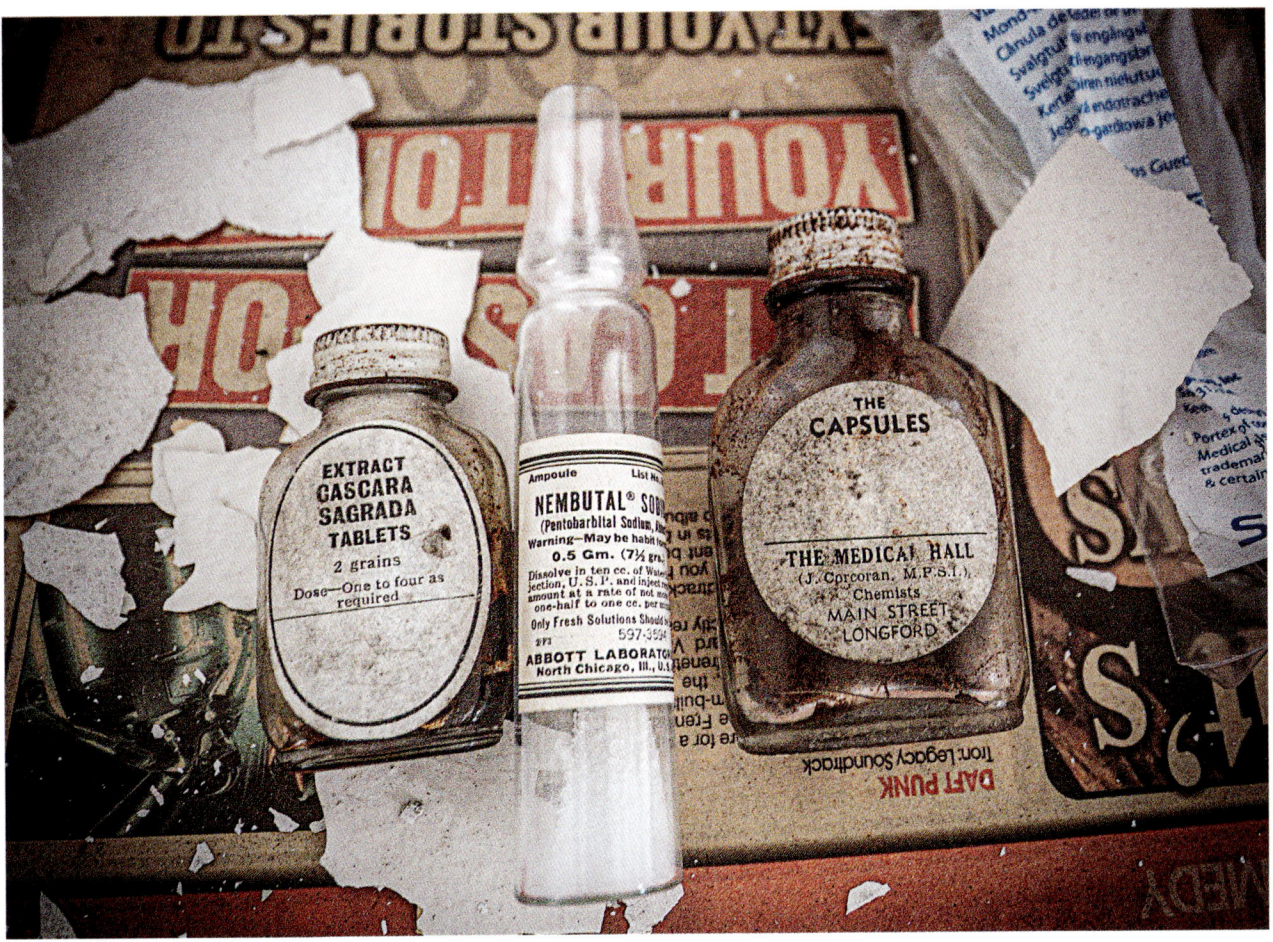

The 1821 Lunacy (Ireland) Act provided a network of lunatic asylums across Ireland and the landscape is marred by the remains of these buildings. In the past, these were places where individuals could be sent for the smallest of reasons often far removed from any legitimate need for mental health support.

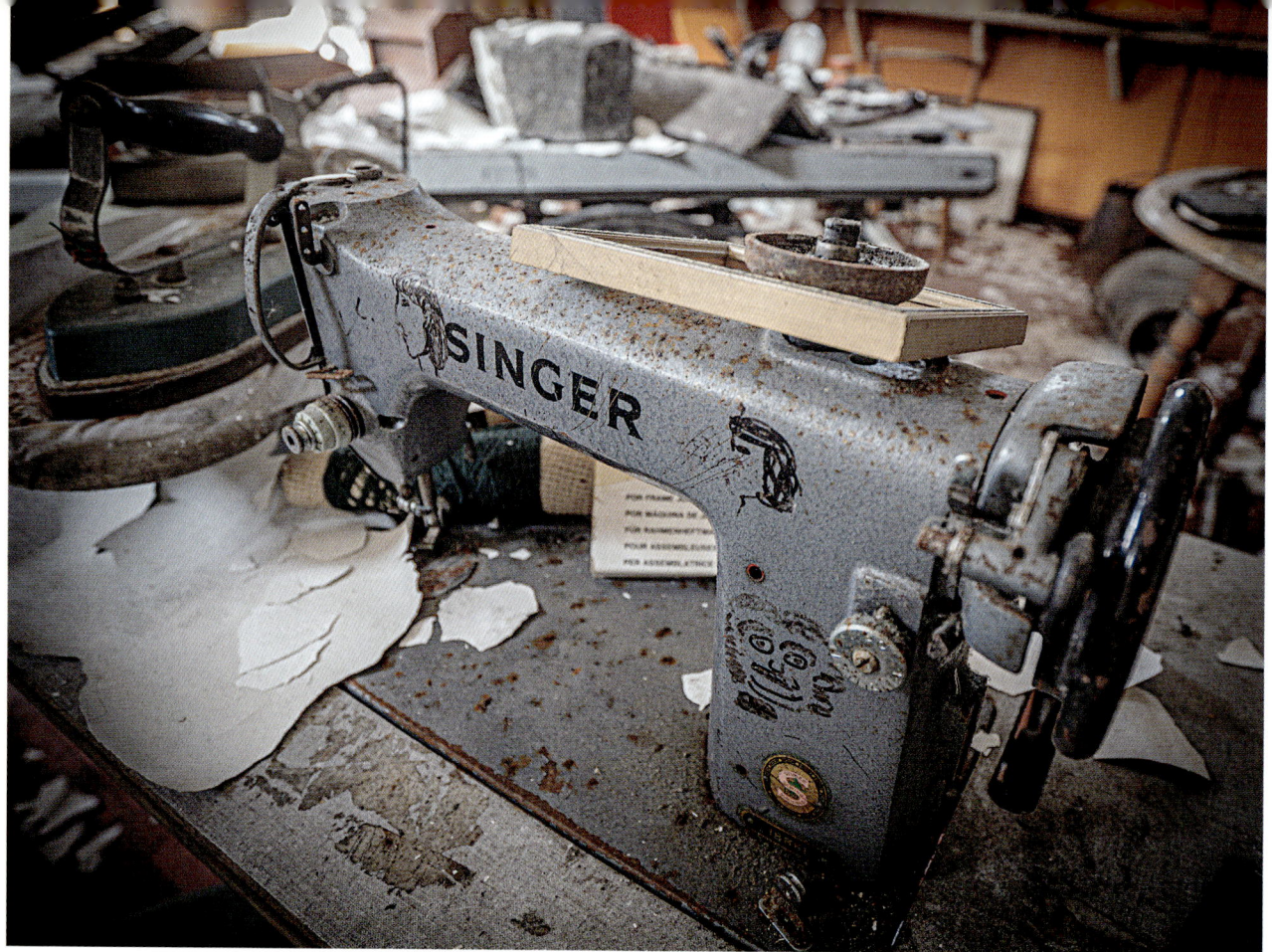

Such individuals were referred to as 'lunatics', a term that I find unsettling. A report from 1958 detailed how 21,000 patients, 0.7 per cent of the population, were confined in mental hospitals throughout Ireland at that time.

The Victorian institution pictured here was established in 1848 and welcomed its first patients a year later. It was constructed at a cost of £35,000, equivalent to around 4.5 million in today's currency. In 2007 the Inspector of Mental Health released a report which included the recommendation that the asylum be closed immediately. The Inspector described the conditions as 'deplorable', stating that every possible effort should be made to shut it down without delay.

The mortality rate in such institutions was alarmingly high, with over 11,000 deaths recorded countrywide in every decade from 1920 to 1960. Shockingly, there are 1,304 bodies documented to have been buried on the grounds of this asylum, with the most recent burial occurring in 1970. It is unsettling to note that these graves are unmarked – the numbered crosses that once marked them are now stored in an outbuilding, having been removed for the purpose of cutting the grass over the graves.

For much of their history, the treatment provided at such asylums was horrifying, with little regard for human life. Sadly, it was rare for individuals admitted to these institutions to ever leave. The documented accounts of those who were held captive in this

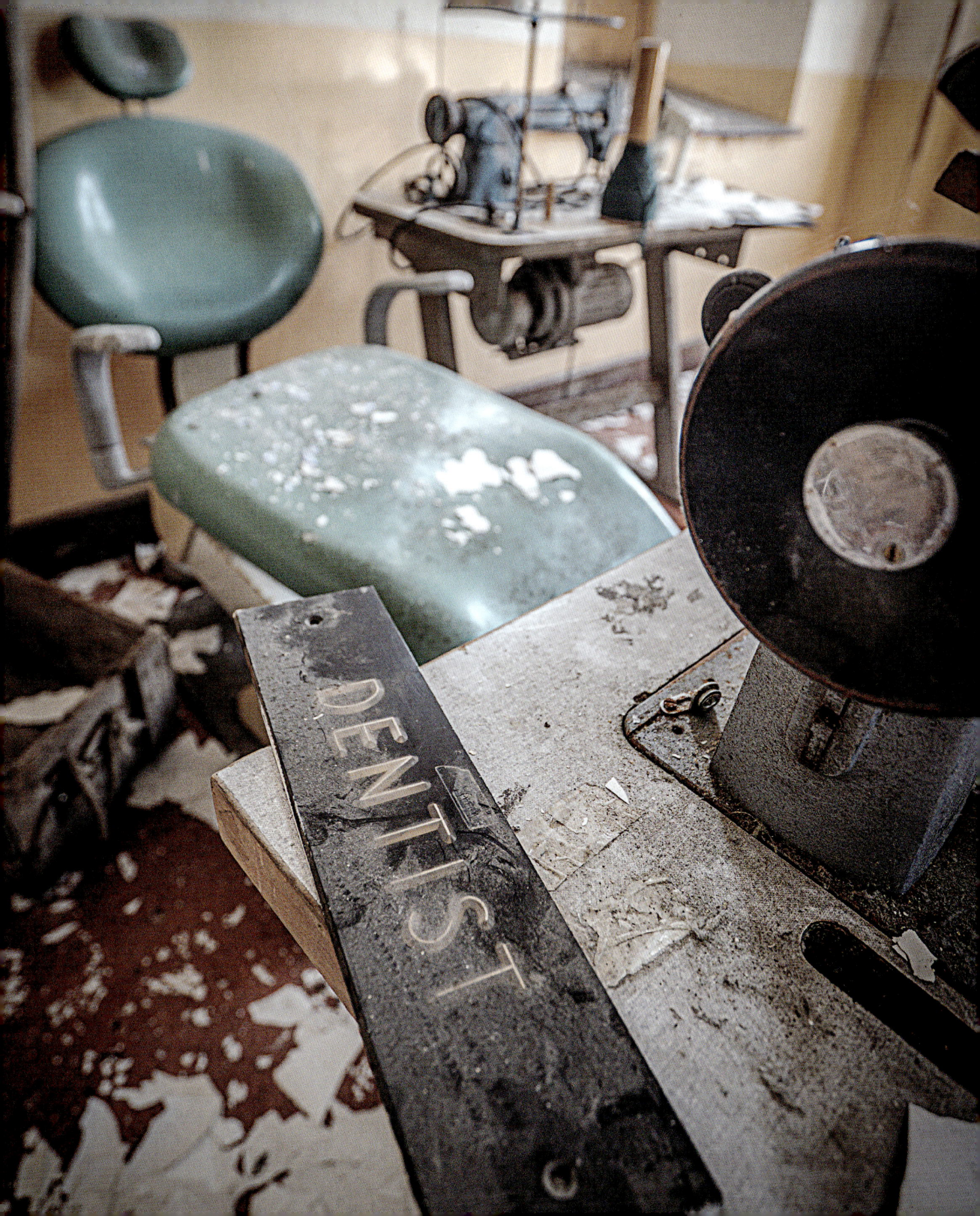

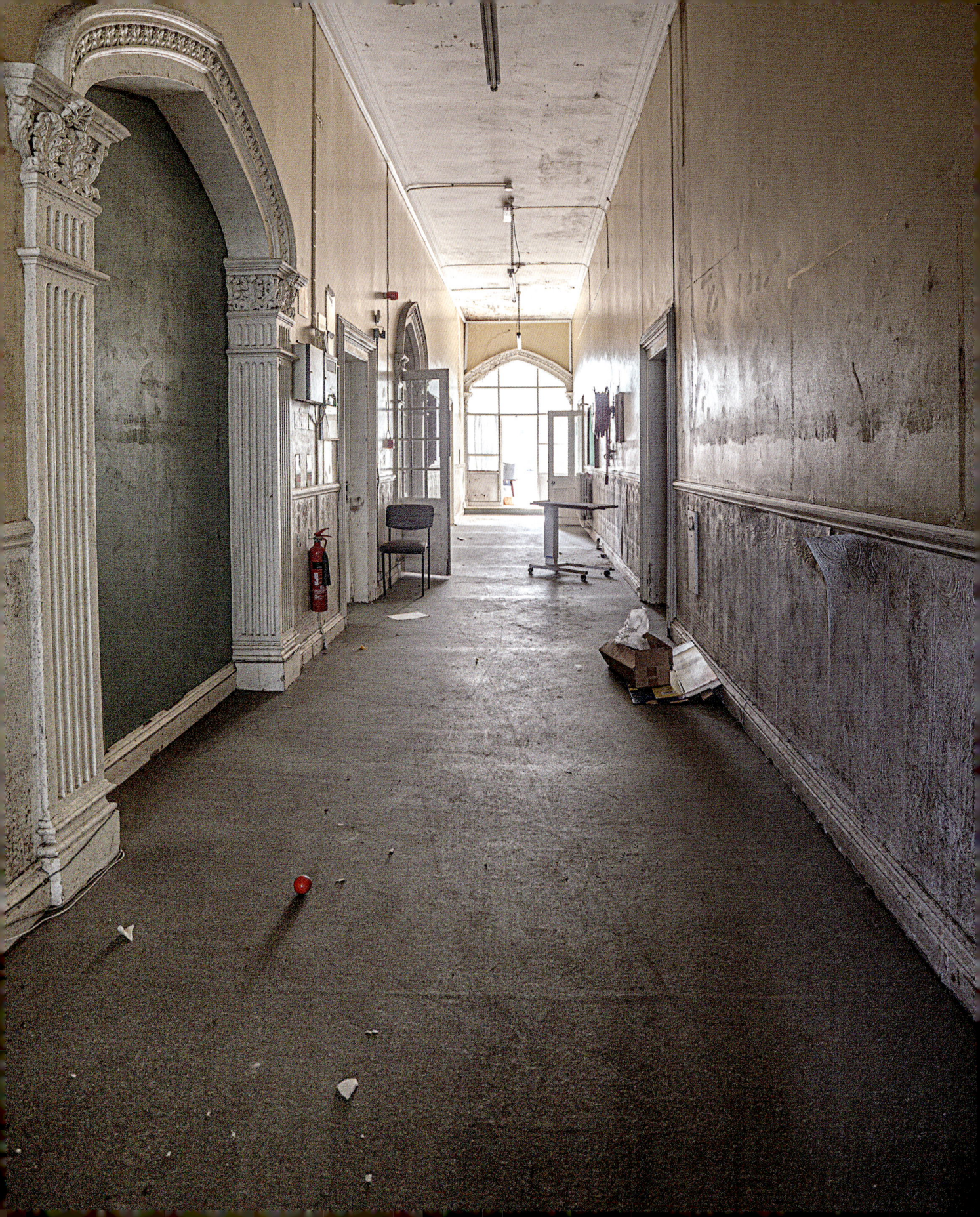

facility are difficult for us to understand in the light of modern medical care, but it is essential for us all to be aware of them.

One of the tragic stories that I came across was that of Julia Caffrey Leonard, who was involuntarily admitted in 1895. She was pregnant with her sixth child at the time and suspected her husband, Christopher, of having an affair (she was later proven correct). After she threw a cup of hot tea at him during an argument, Christopher talked to their doctor and obtained the medical certificate necessary to commit Julia. As a result, she was sent to this institution, leaving her five children behind. Nine months later she gave birth to her sixth child in the asylum. Julia spent the next twenty-two years of her life there, until she passed away of heart failure in 1919 at the age of fifty-four. Her great-granddaughter, Julianne Clarke, is now advocating for the marking and restoration of all the unmarked graves at this asylum, including Julia's.

Hanna Greally entered this institution in 1943 at the age of nineteen, seeking a short respite. She was the primary carer for her sick mother but was unable to look after her due to exhaustion. In the end she was left there for nearly twenty years, during which time she sent desperate letters to her family begging for release. She also attempted to escape multiple times from what locals referred to as 'the big house'. Throughout her time in confinement, Hanna endured electroconvulsive therapy, sedation, seclusion and confinement. Finally, in the late 1950s, she was moved to a newly established rehabilitation centre in Longford. There she trained to become

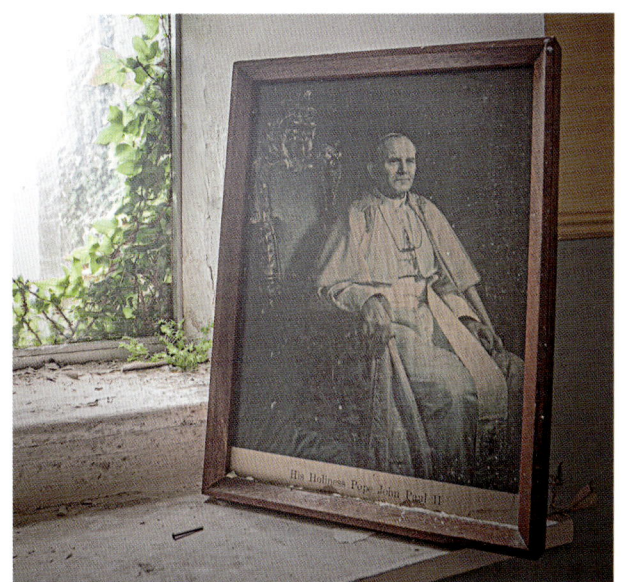

a housekeeper and was eventually discharged in 1962. Hanna then travelled to England to work for a retired doctor, saving enough money to purchase her own home in Roscommon, where she lived out the remainder of her days. She passed away in 1987 aged sixty-two.

The asylum finally closed in 2013. It currently stands empty, waiting for the next chapter in its story.

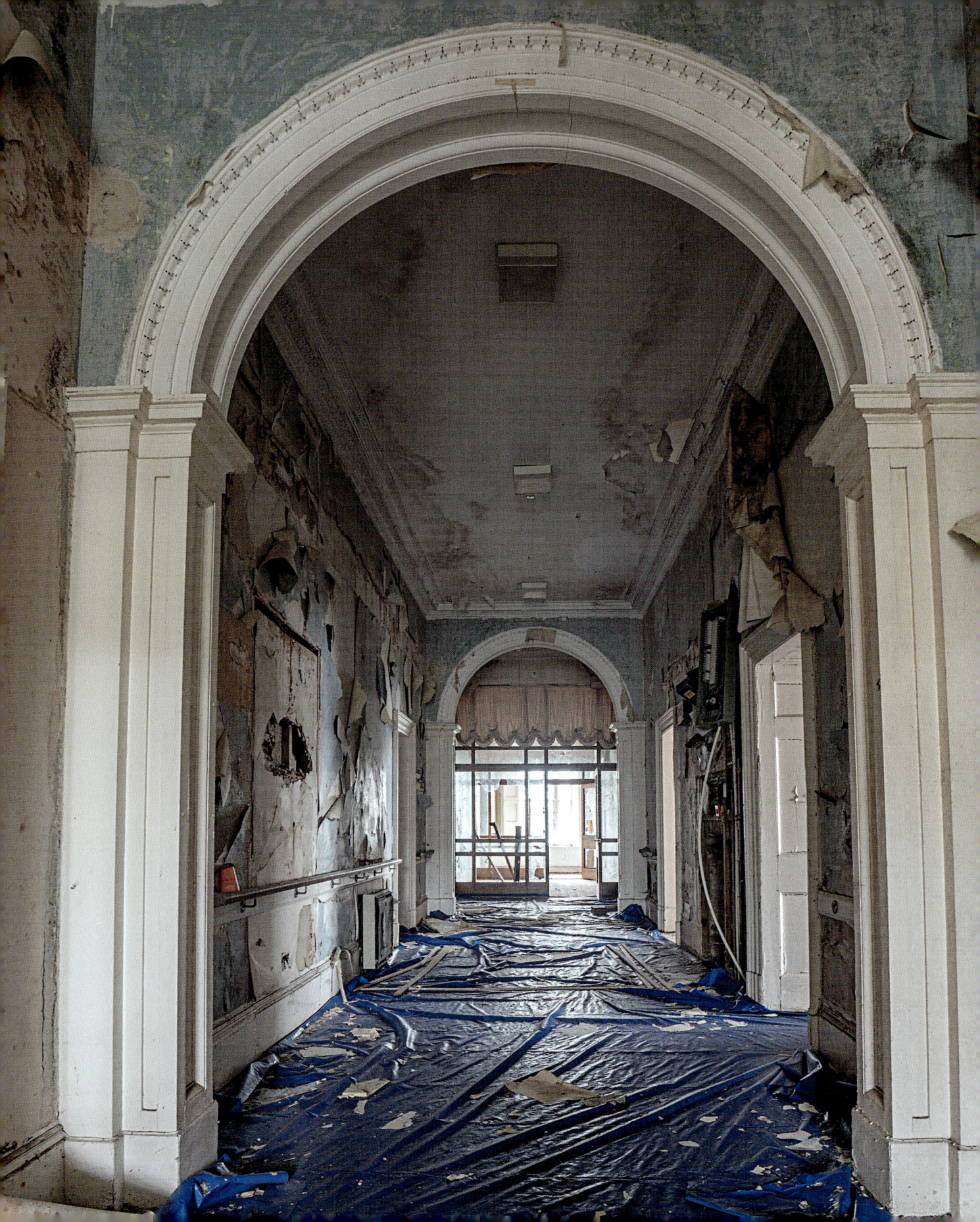

# CASTLEDILLON

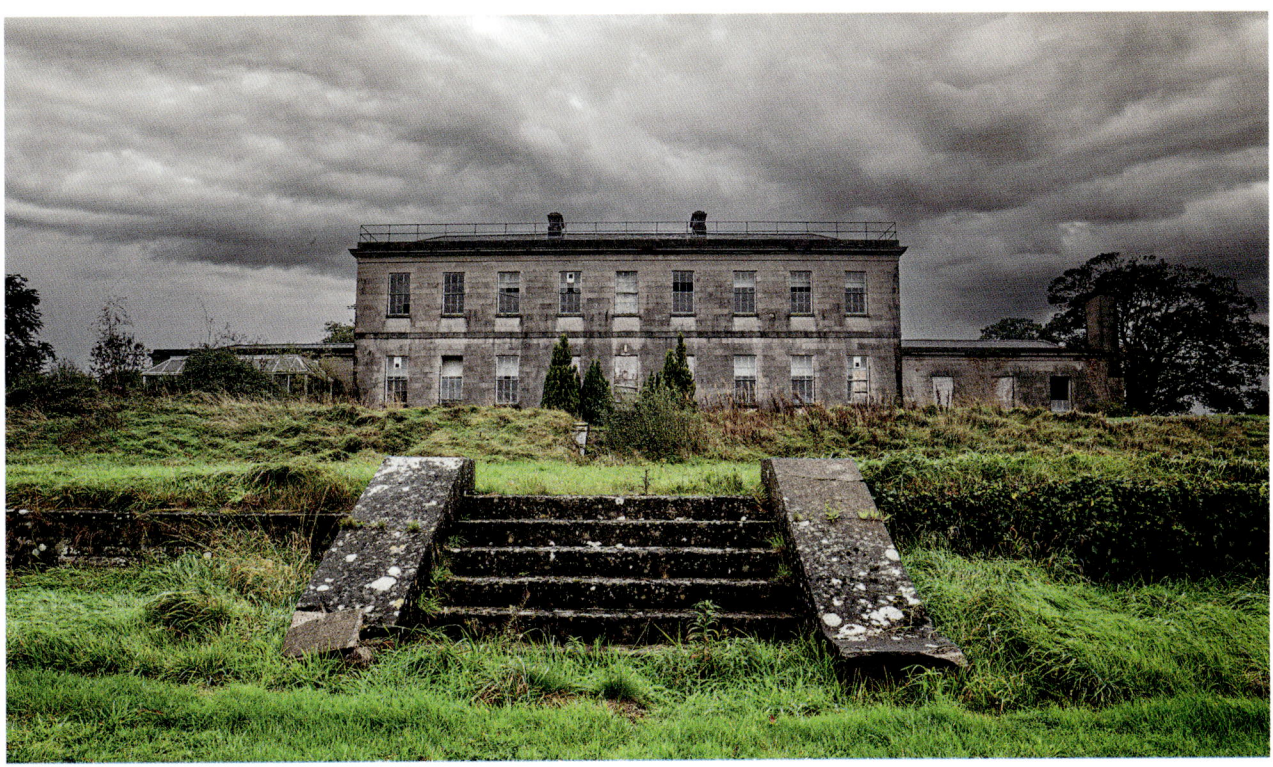

When I first started my hobby of documenting these abandoned beauties over a decade ago, I was told about Castledillon house by my friend Catherine, who lived near to it. She explained that it had been used by American soldiers in the Second World War and in later years was a nursing home. I'd never heard of it and, naturally, I couldn't wait to see it.

The house sits in a massive estate at the end of a lengthy driveway – once you round the last bend you can see the austere mansion in front of you. When we first visited it looked very neglected; just how I like them! All the windows were broken and there was a conservatory at the back that had also been smashed up. We took a quick look inside but

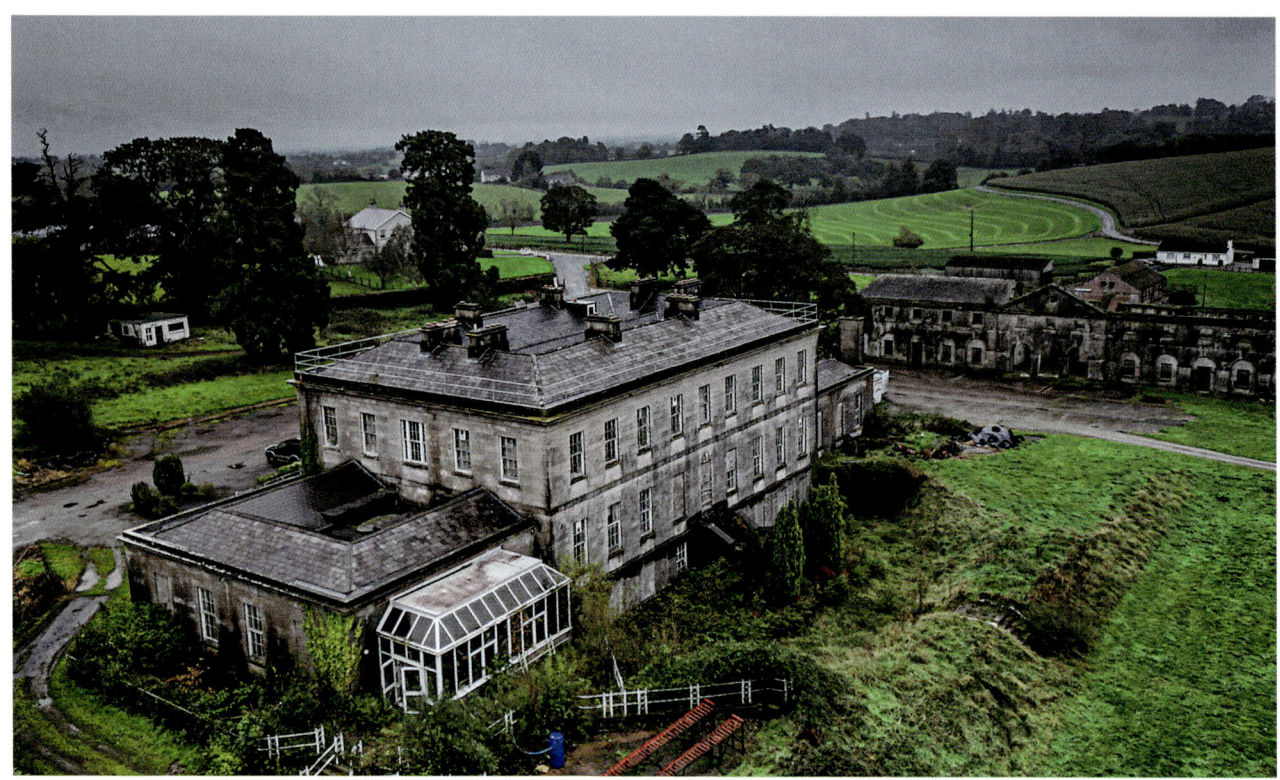

didn't stay long as it was so damaged by vandalism it wasn't really worth taking out the camera. Old hospital beds, Zimmer frames and what looked like medical equipment lay amongst smashed-up toilet bowls, and there were even holes punched through walls. I left disappointed.

When I decided to write a second book, I knew I wanted Castledillon to have a chapter, so I set out to find the owner. Sometimes this process can be lengthy, but luckily I was able to locate Colin and he graciously gave me permission to visit. In 2023 I returned to Castledillon with Catherine. The house now has a caretaker, whom I met on site, and he gave us a tour while sharing its history and updates on the work. Colin had purchased the house shortly after my first visit and, since then, he has done great

work, even replacing the roof, which was leaking due to the theft of lead – always a significant issue for these old buildings. All the old equipment had been removed and the place was looking in much better shape, though there is still some work to be done.

There was originally a castle on this site, constructed in the early 1600s by John Dillon, a native of Staffordshire. It was destroyed by fire in 1641, and the site, along with a 6,000-acre estate and its private lake, was acquired in 1664 by Samuel Molyneux, the chief engineer of Ireland at the time. The stable block, added in the 1720s, was designed by London-born architect Thomas Cooley, who was also responsible for buildings like St Patrick's Cathedral, Caledon House and the Royal School, Armagh. The current large country mansion was built in 1845 and

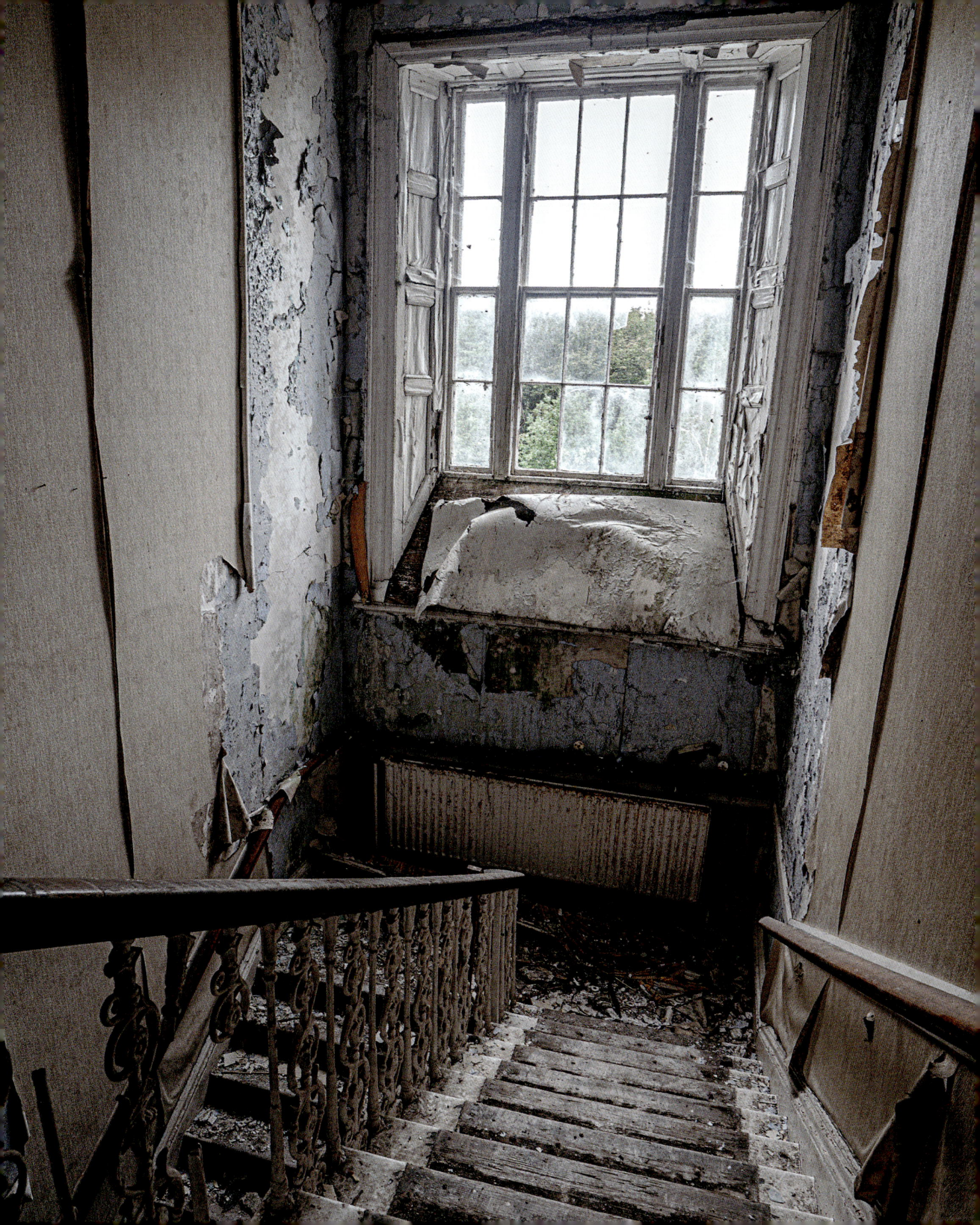

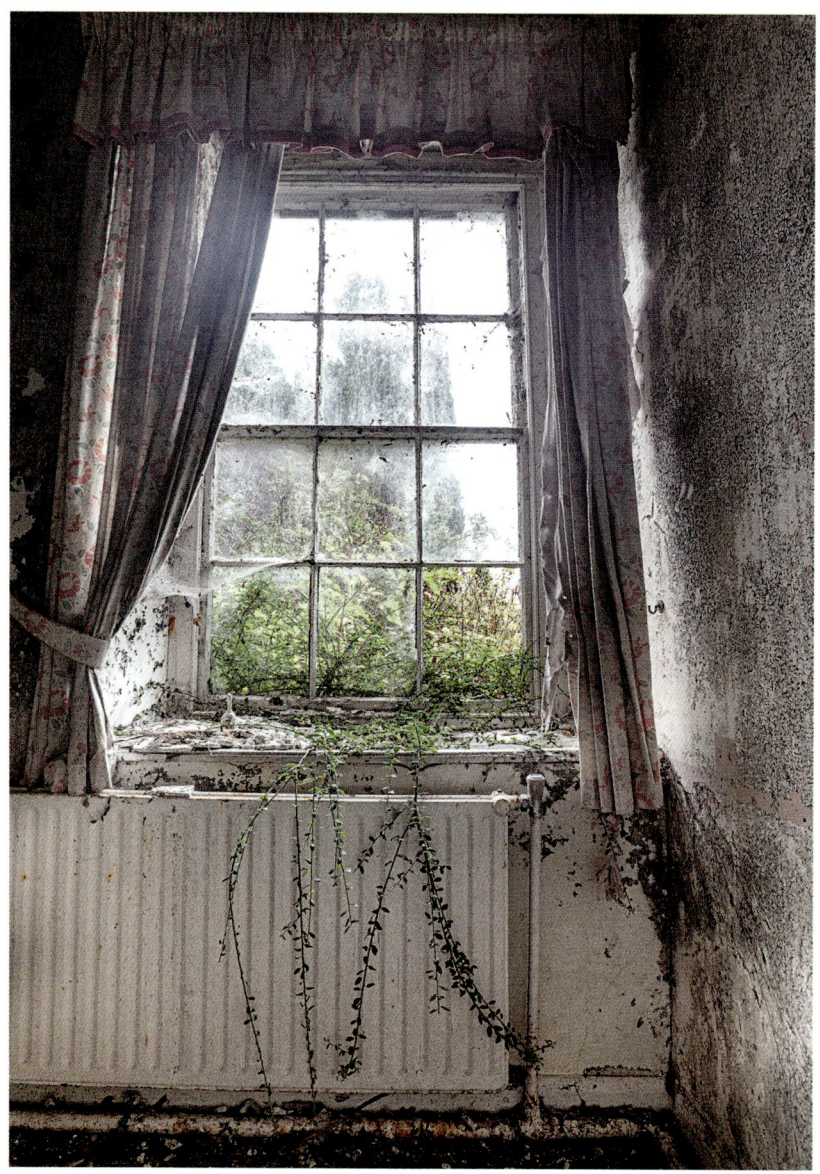

designed by William Murray, known for his work on Armagh Gaol and St Brigid's Asylum, both of which feature in my first book.

During the Second World War, Castledillon was used by the British Army and for training by American and Belgian troops. I've been told that initials written in the stable block were left by soldiers. Subsequently, the house served as a nursing home.

At the time of its closure, in the early 2000s, it had twenty-one bedrooms, multiple reception rooms, bathrooms, kitchens, a basement and a lift.

At present it is used for duck hunting and is undergoing total refurbishment and repair. Firm plans have not been made for the mansion, but things are heading in the right direction and I'm so happy it's been saved.

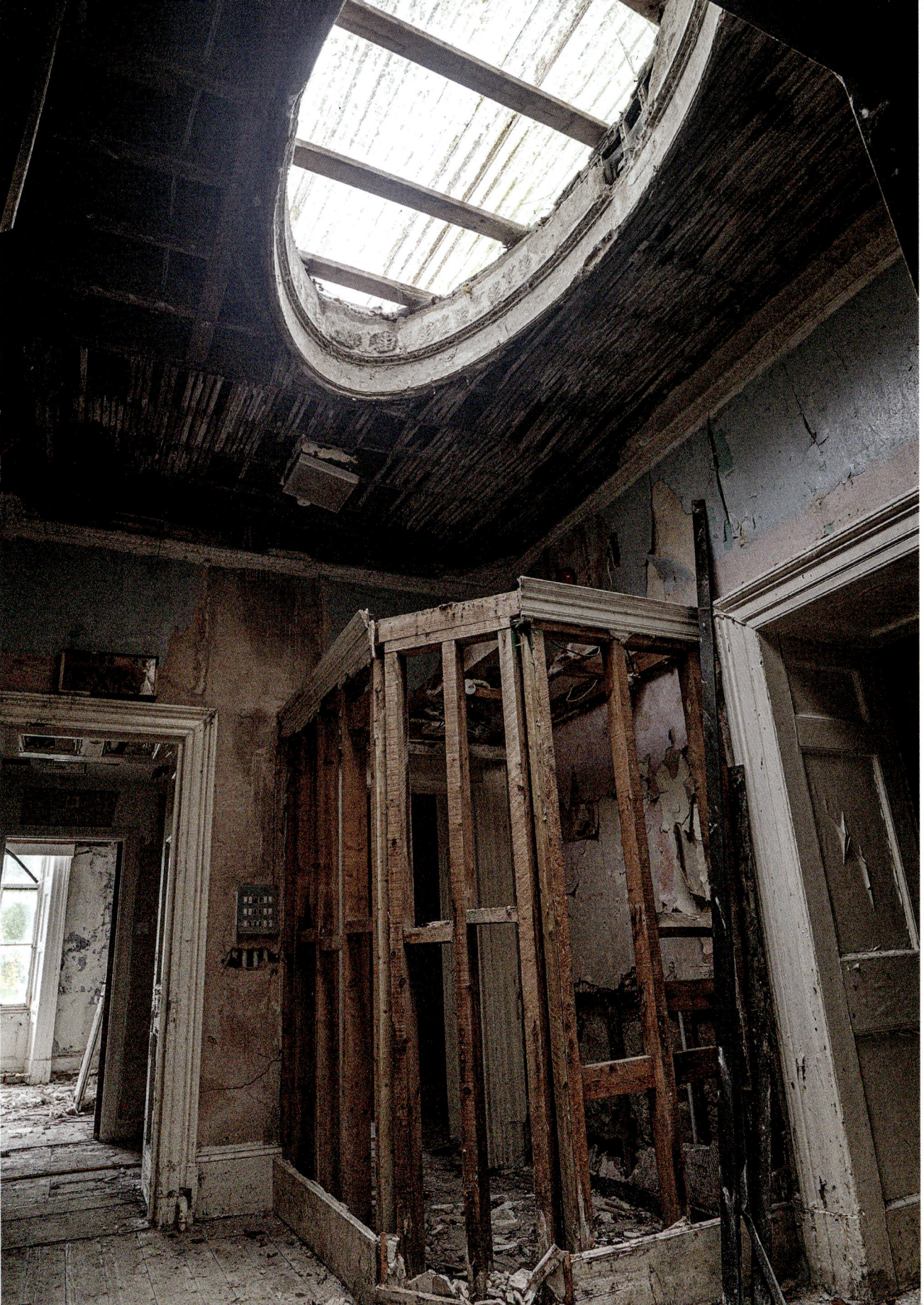

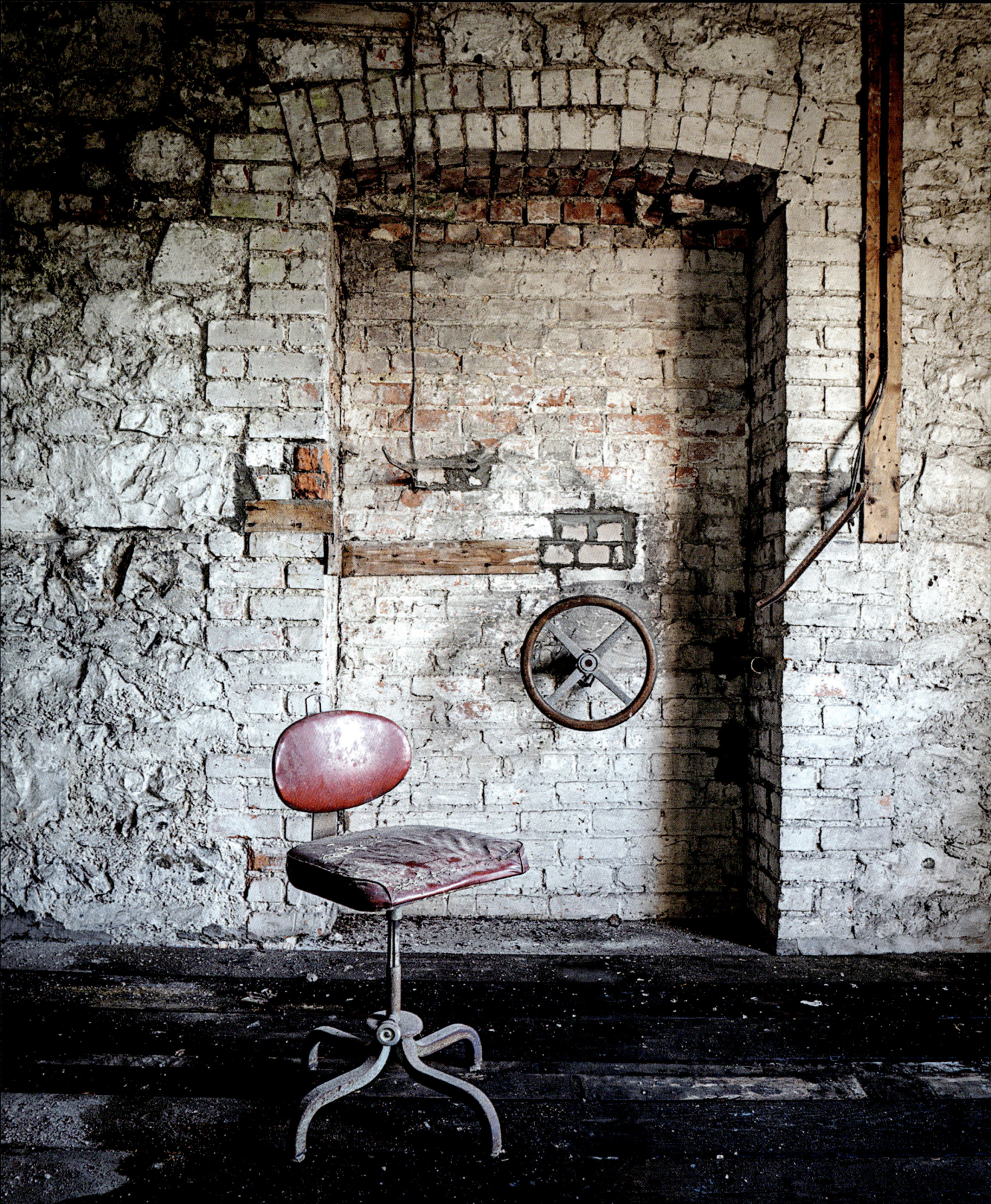

# THE BEETLING MILL

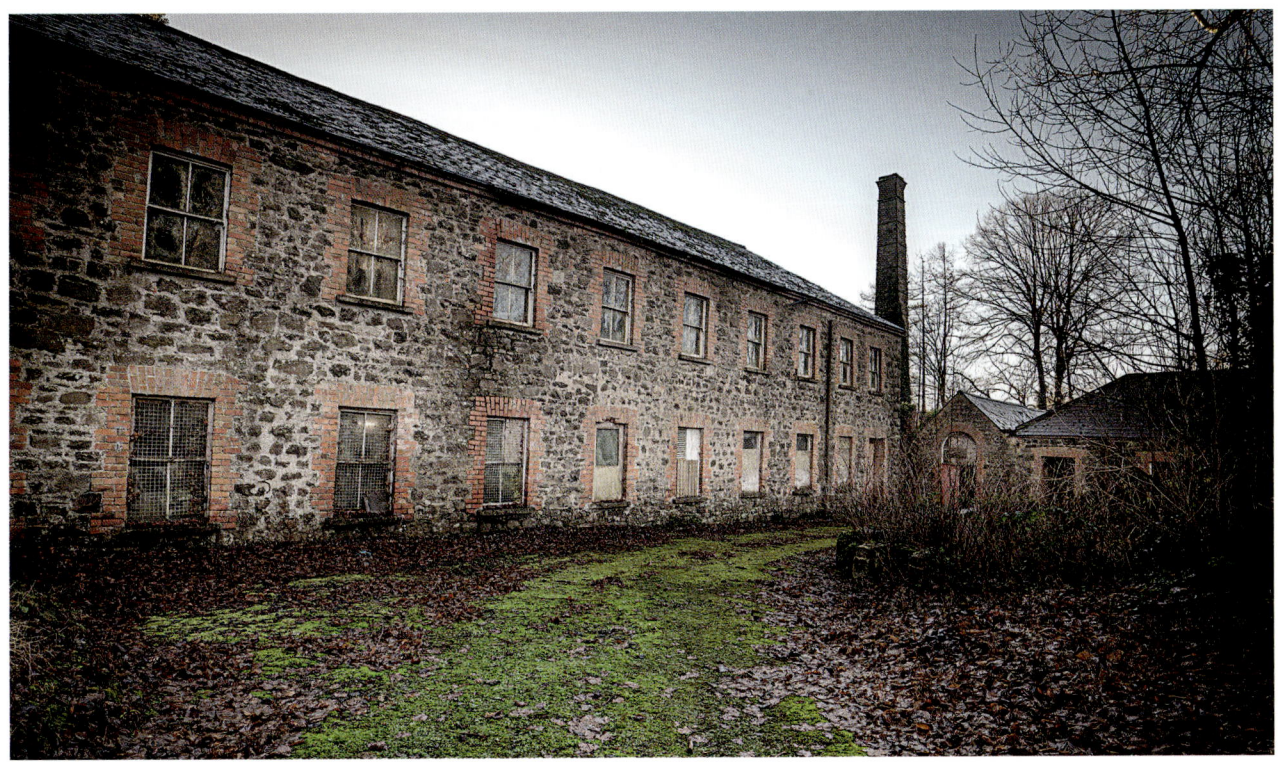

I never refuse an invitation to document an abandoned property, especially a complex like this. Most of the mills I have documented are ones I have heard of over time, but not this one. I was quite surprised that it was not on my radar until I was contacted about it. Possibly this was because the site is very remote – you have to cross a private bridge to reach it and it feels almost like crossing onto a private island.

This mill complex first appeared on maps as early as 1780, where it is shown as a bleach works. The beetling mill and warehouse were added later, in 1888. There are also some houses on the site where the McClures, the owners of the beetling mill,

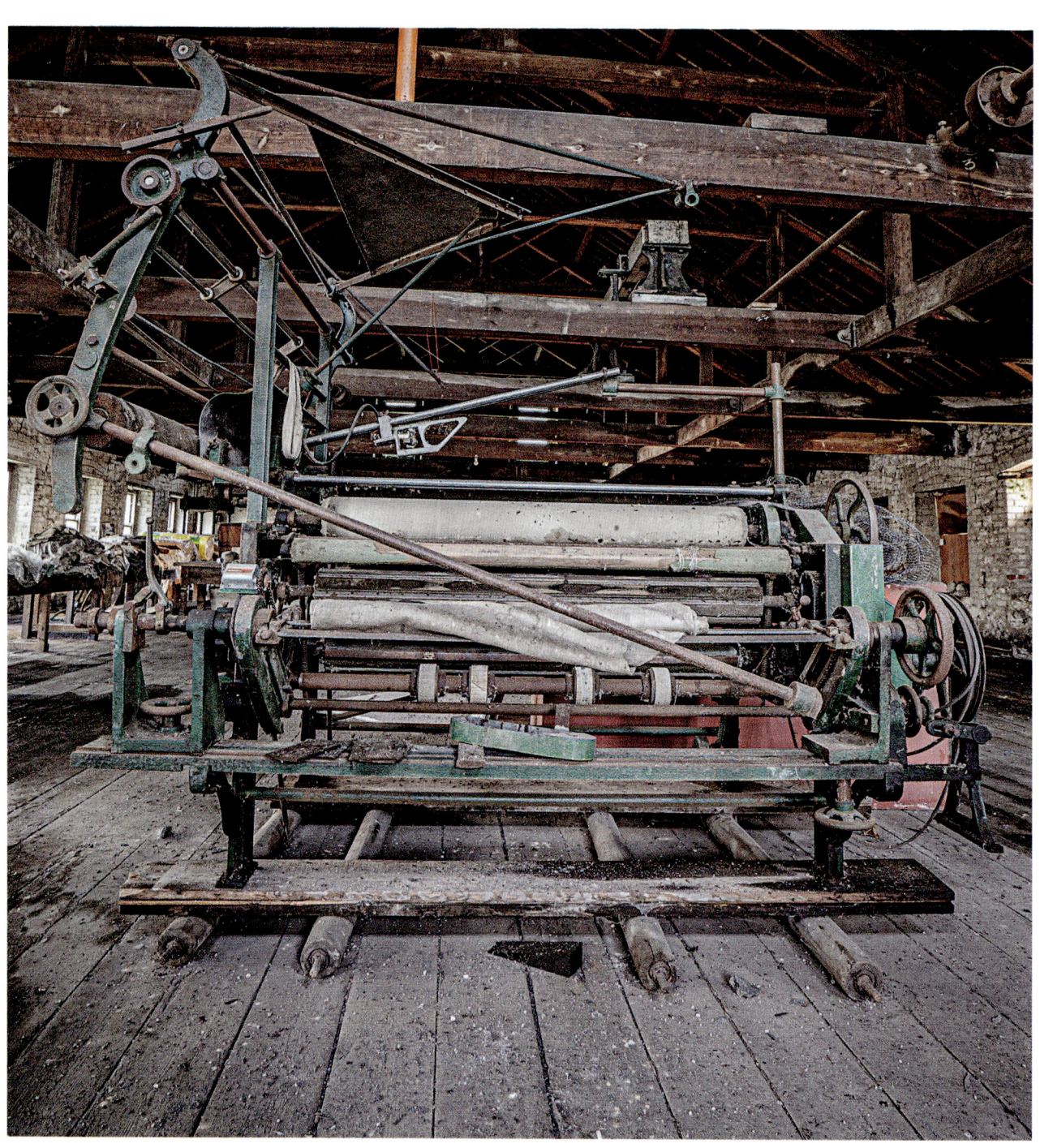

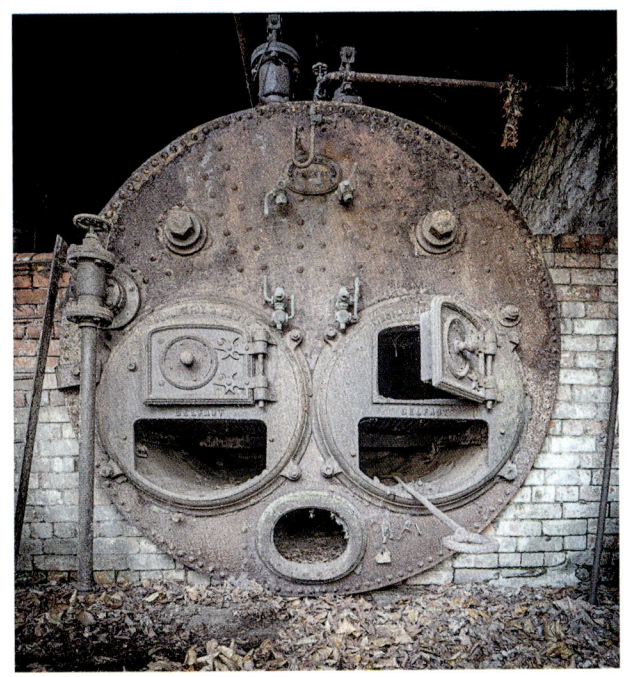

The mill also had dyeing pits, which are still visible today. Workers would have gone into the pits barefoot to mix the dye into the cloth. The finished linen was shipped all around the world, as far afield as India.

The huge boilers that were used to generate heat in the complex are still there, and upon closer inspection I saw they had the name McIlwaine & Lewis on them. After some research, I learned that this was a largely forgotten shipyard in Belfast and one of the things it produced was these boilers.

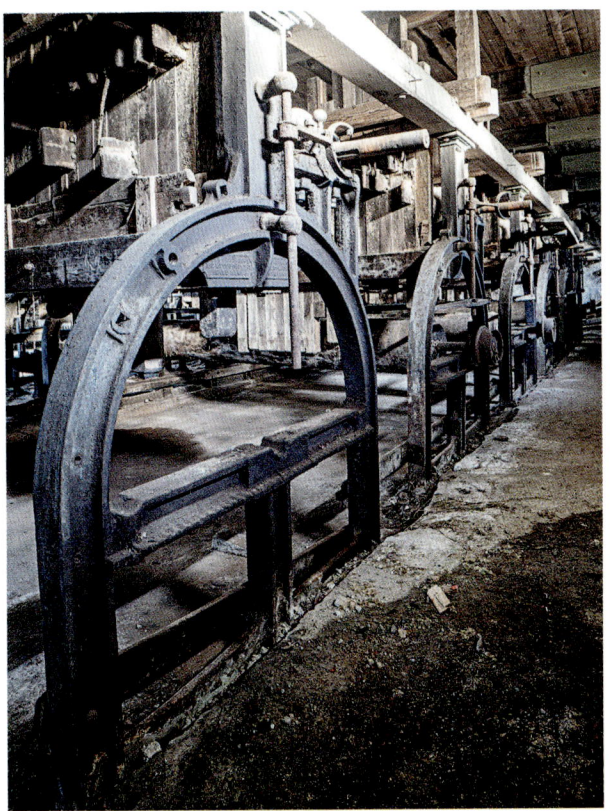

lived. The mill would have operated twenty-four hours a day for six months of the year, and for the remainder of the year it would have been working for ten hours a day.

I had never seen beetling machines before, but there are lots of them left in this mill, still in position from the last run of linen they smashed. The beetling process was the last finishing method that the linen would have gone through. The teeth on the machines would repeatedly smash down on the linen, giving it a lustrous finish. As they are on the lower level of the mill, with the factory floor above, it made me think of being in the bowels of a ship and I could imagine how loud it must have been when the machines were working.

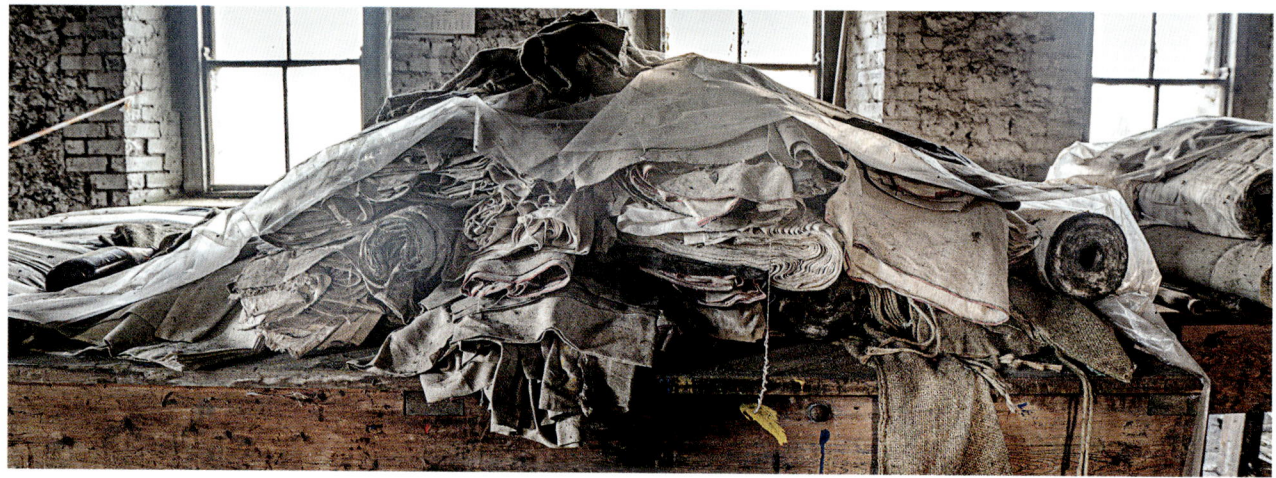

The Lewis name comes from Richard Lewis, the grandfather of C.S. Lewis, author of *The Chronicles of Narnia*.

Throughout the mill's history, there were fires in the complex, notably a large one in 1896. After the damage that caused, the owners rebuilt and extended the mill, doubling its size. However, the linen industry began to struggle in the twentieth century, with the rise of cotton and later man-made fibres, and demand for their product declined, which may have led to the closure of this mill in 1934.

This was not the end of its story, however. During the Second World War, James Mackie and Company used the mill and warehouse to produce ammunition and machine tools. Post-war, the Ministry of Food used the warehouses to store food until 1955. The mill and machinery were then used for one last time before closing for good in the 1980s.

The site is now owned by a property developer and there are plans in place to turn the buildings into apartments, while keeping the machinery below with glass casing for viewing purposes. It's a fantastic idea and something unique. While documenting the site, I noticed how serene it was, with the fast-flowing river beside me. I would love to live in a place like this; maybe one day!

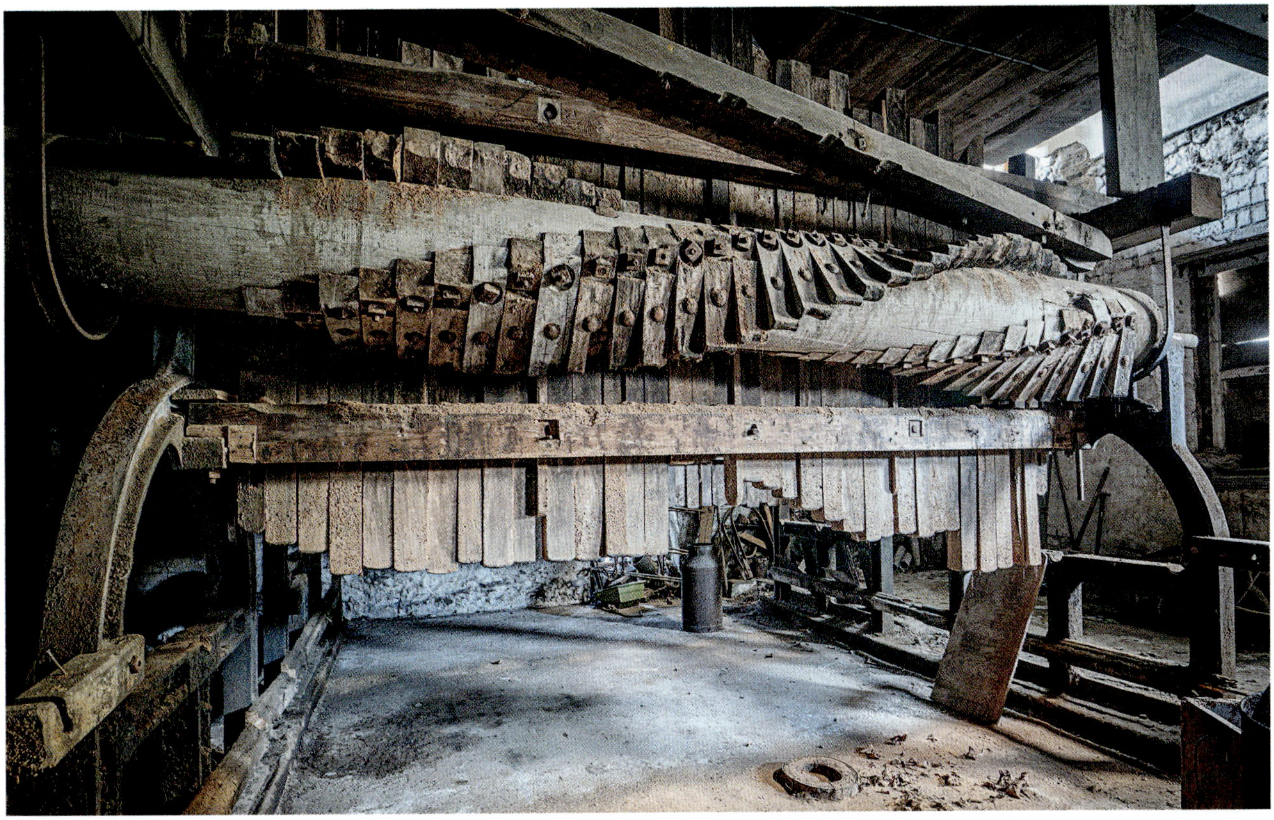

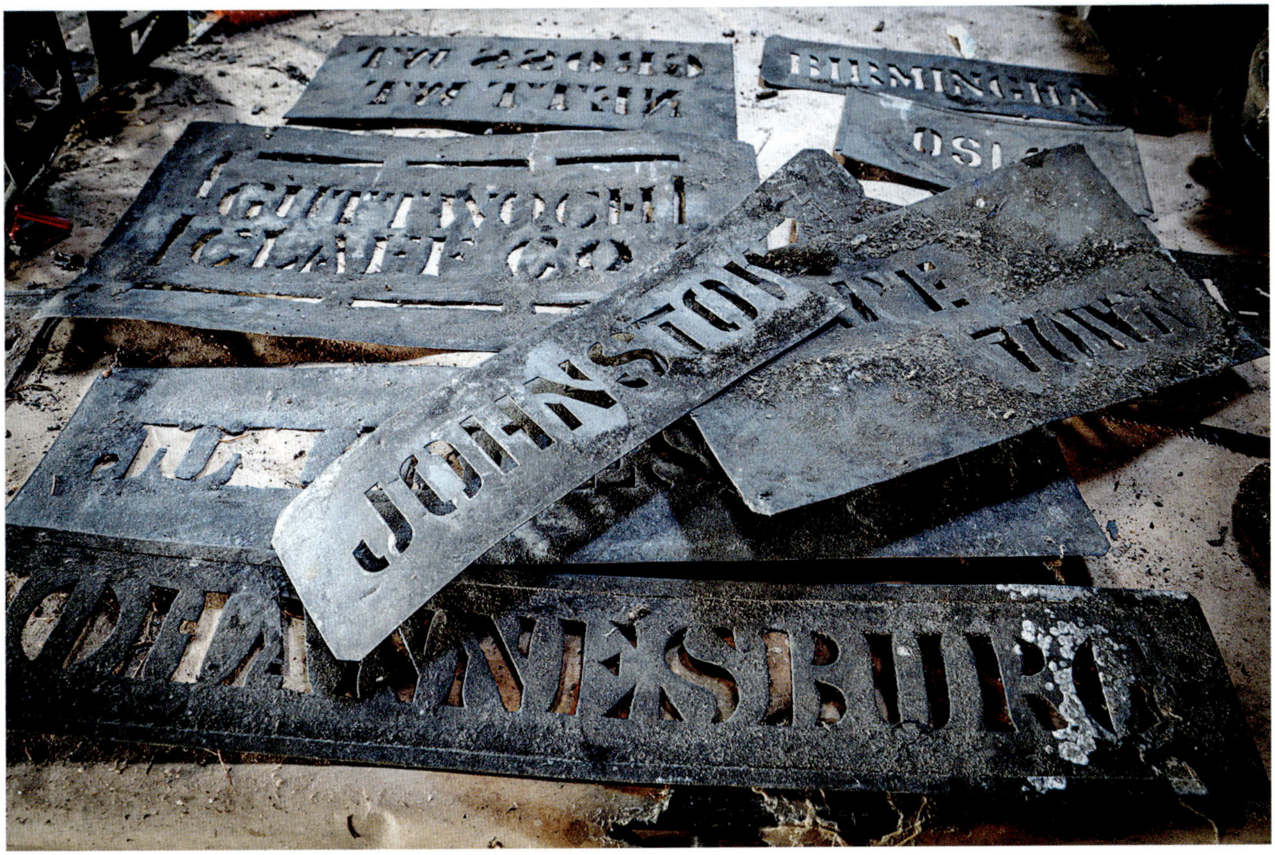
BIRMINGHA
JOHNSTO

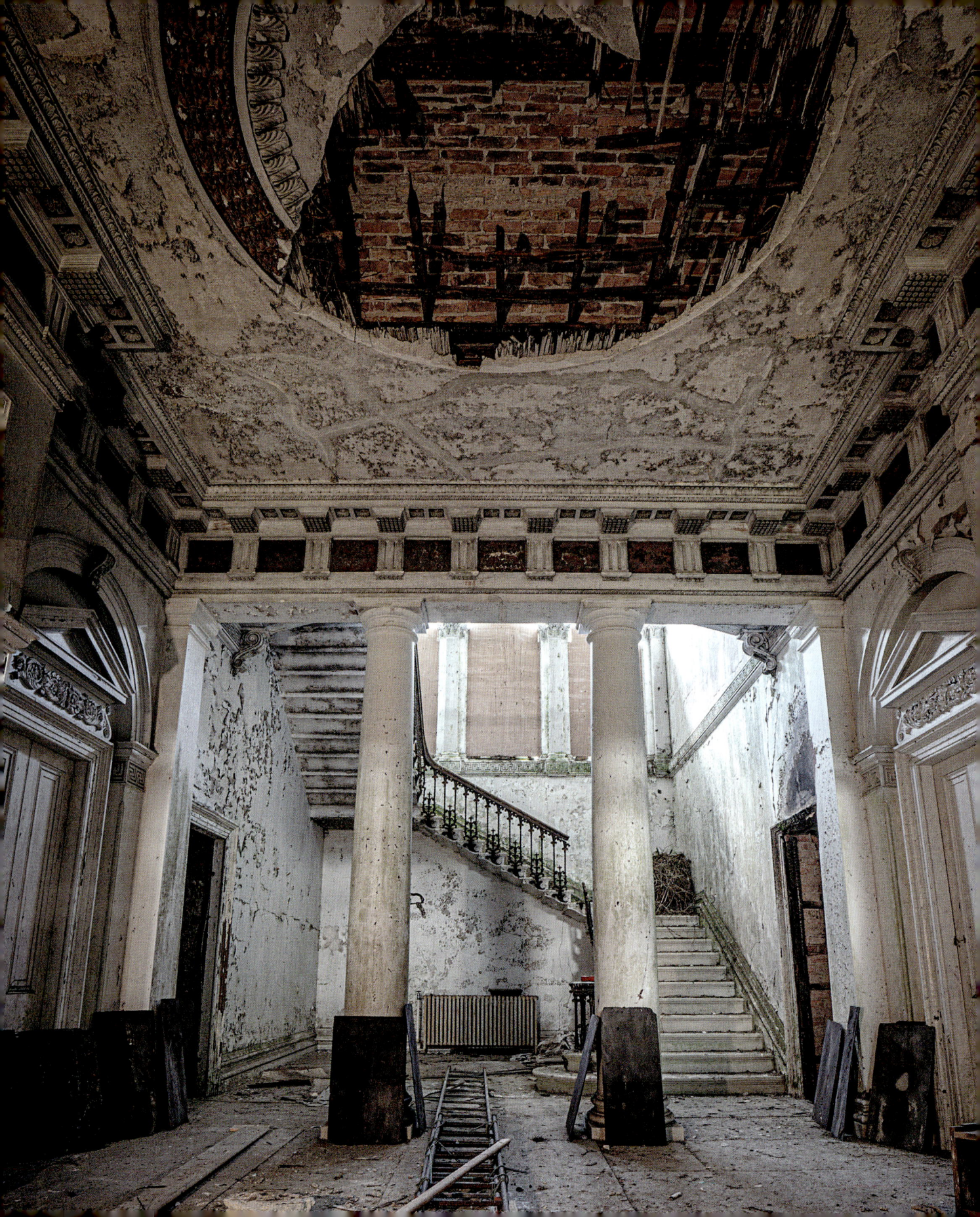

# WOODLAWN HOUSE

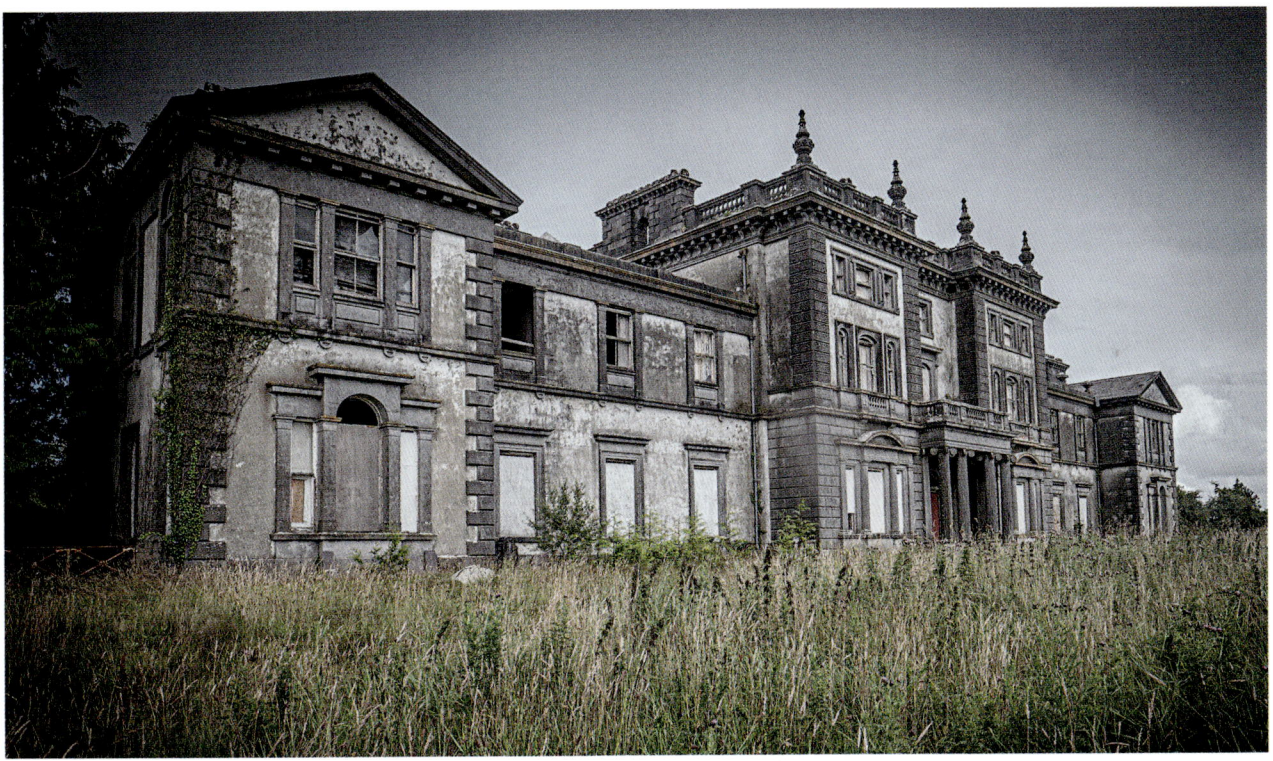

This sprawling mansion had been on my bucket list for as long as I could remember, and when I finally saw it with my own eyes, it did not disappoint. I had seen many images of it online, but they could not compare to actually witnessing it in person. I had also heard rumours that the house was haunted, but all was quiet on my visit, thankfully!

When I delved deeper into the mansion's history, I was surprised by some of the information I uncovered. It is a massive 30,000 square feet, with 365 windows, one for each day of the year, making it one of Ireland's largest houses. The estate it sits in spans 115 acres and includes stables, a greenhouse, a guest house, a church, a mausoleum and several

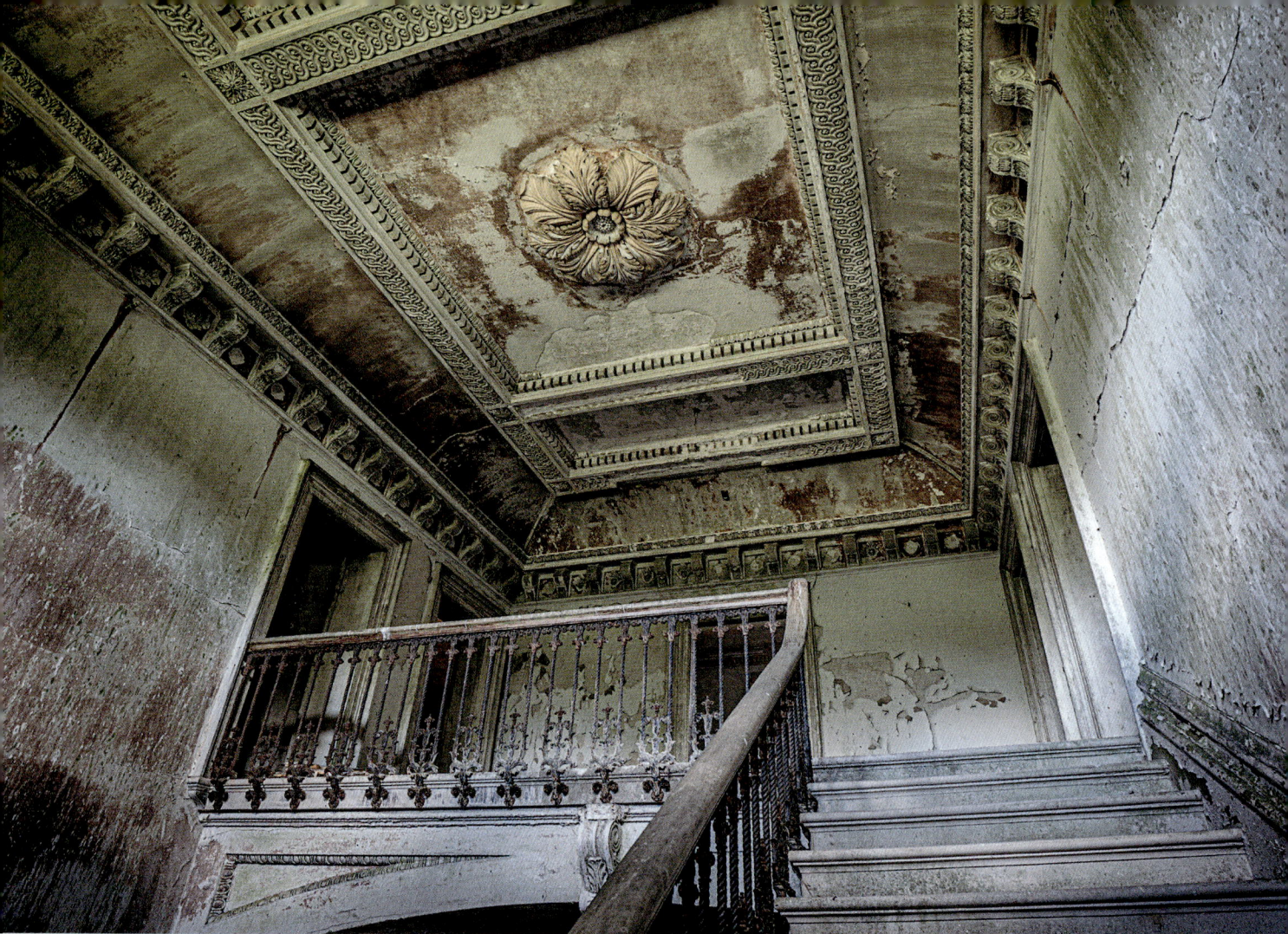

workers' cottages. Additionally, it boasts its own train station, which is still in use.

The house was constructed in the 1800s by Frederic Trench, the first Baron Ashtown and an Irish politician who had enough influence to have a new train line redirected through his lands to accommodate the station. A significant staff was needed to manage both the estate and the house. According to the 1901 census, there were fourteen servants living there.

The mansion underwent renovation in the mid-nineteenth century, carried out by Frederick Mason Trench, the 2nd Baron and the nephew of the mansion's original builder. His grandson, Frederick Oliver Trench, became the 3rd Baron in 1880 and inherited Woodlawn, along with over £1 million, at the young age of twelve. After completing his education at Eton, he returned to take over the management of the estate, but decisions he made led to changes that negatively affected the livelihoods of estate workers, causing them to strike and boycott Woodlawn. Undeterred by this backlash, Trench hired in workers from Scotland instead of relying on the loyal families. As a staunch unionist,

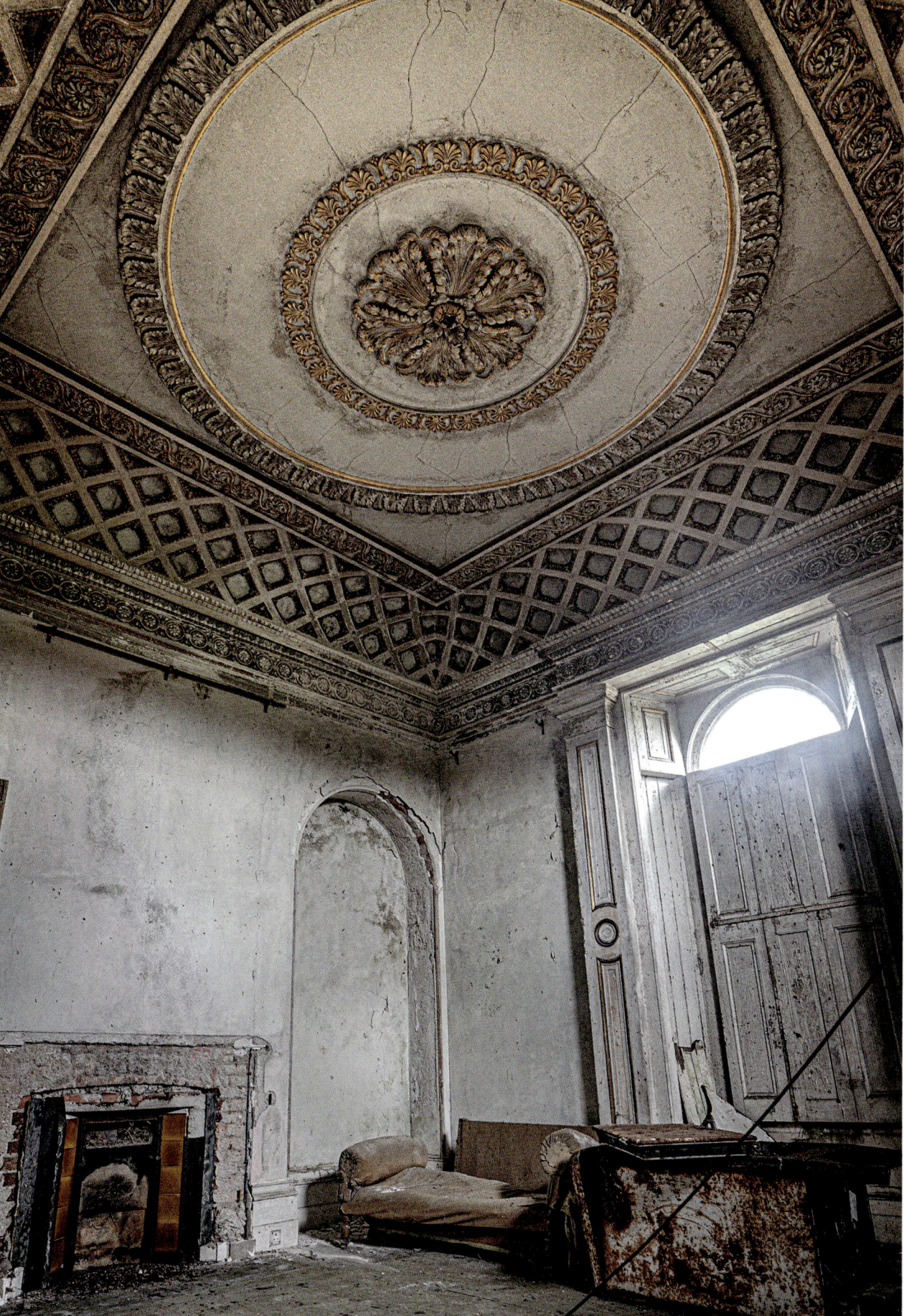

he edited a monthly magazine called *Grievances from Ireland* to express his views, further alienating himself from the local people.

Trench also owned a lodge in Co. Waterford, which was bombed and set on fire in 1904 – he claimed that this was carried out by disgruntled former staff. However, local law enforcement believed it was a publicity stunt. Ashtown was tried for orchestrating the incident, but lack of evidence led to the case being dismissed.

In 1921 Ashtown was making a lot of noise politically and this made him a serious target for republicans. He received a letter from the IRA demanding his departure from Ireland. Frederick went into hiding, fleeing to London. The IRA confiscated Woodlawn house, which was used to house Catholic refugees from Belfast; soon afterwards its contents were auctioned off. Frederick returned after the Irish Civil War had ended, only to find Woodlawn ransacked and vandalised. Despite this, he continued to live on the estate in a reduced capacity until infirmity forced him to move to a nursing home, where he died in 1946.

Just over a year later, Woodlawn was acquired by a family cousin, Derek Le Poer Trench, who lived there until 1973 when, facing financial troubles, he sold the mansion and then tragically took his own life.

Woodlawn has changed hands a few times since then, and the new owner has begun restoration work. I am thrilled that the mansion is being saved and can imagine it will stand for at least another 200 years.

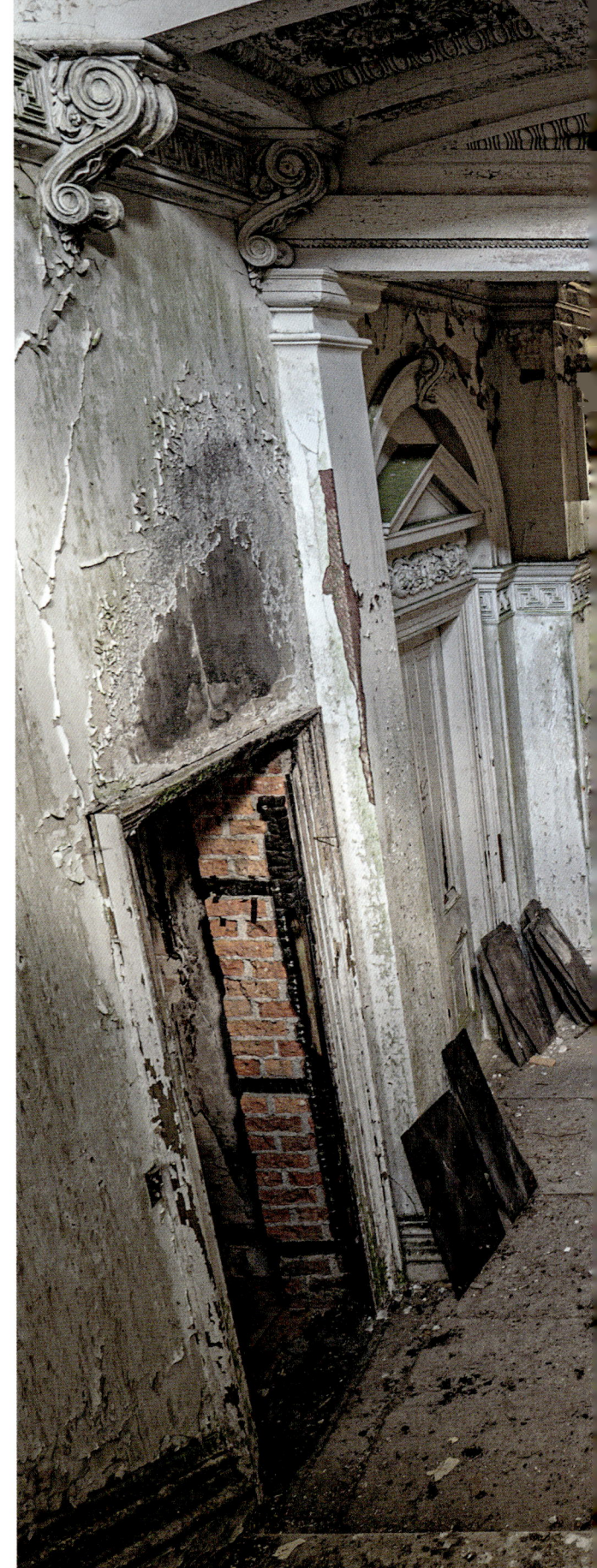

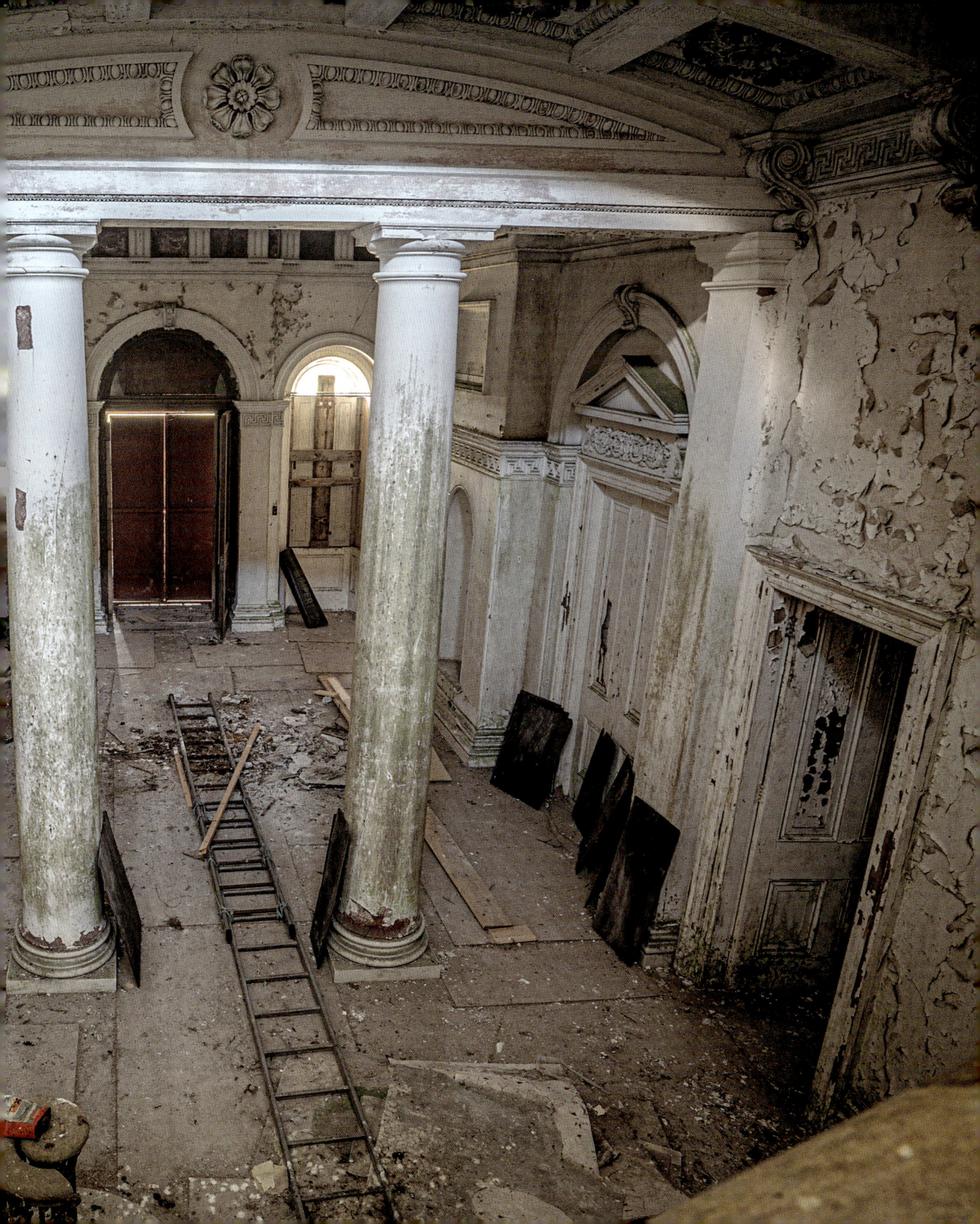

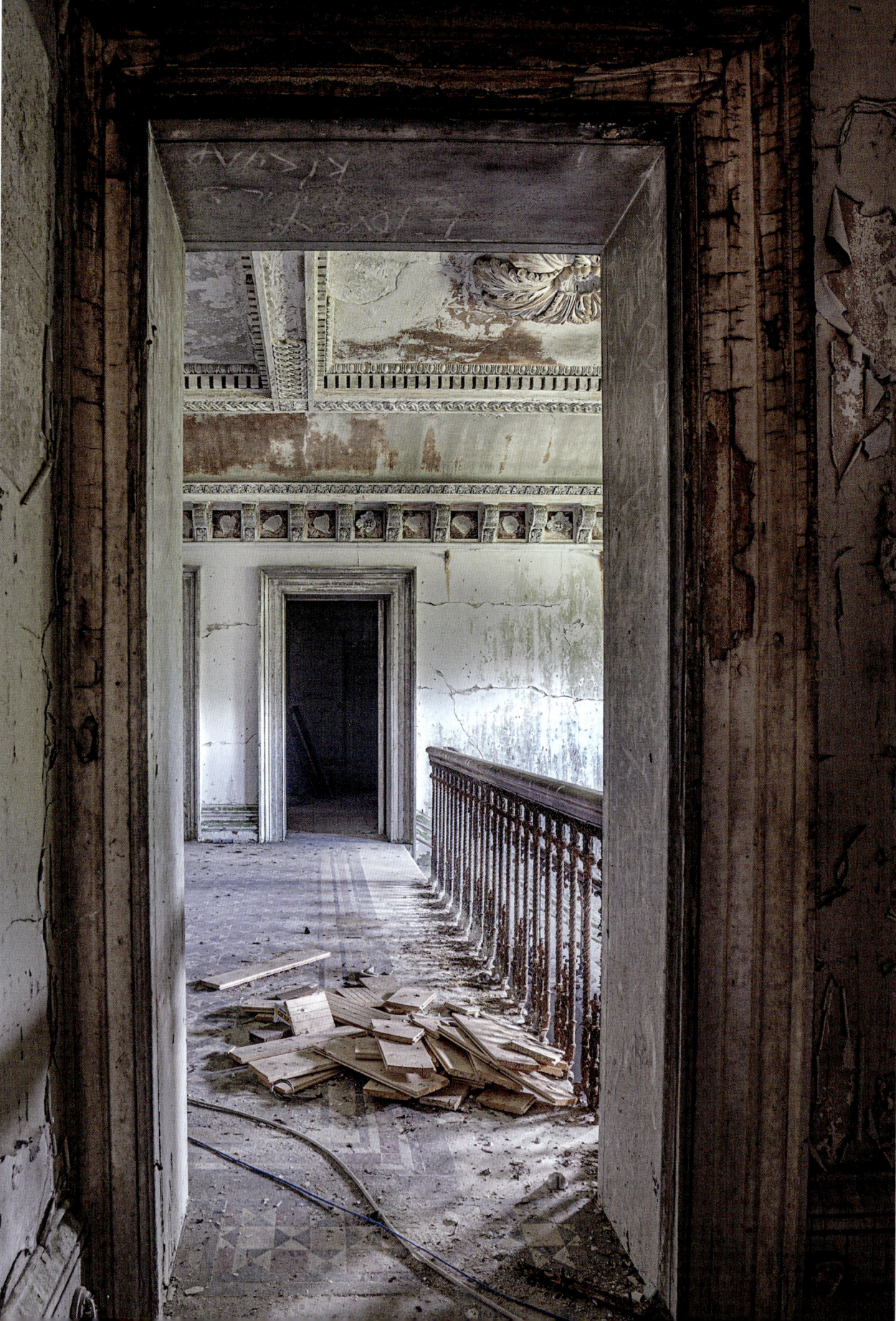

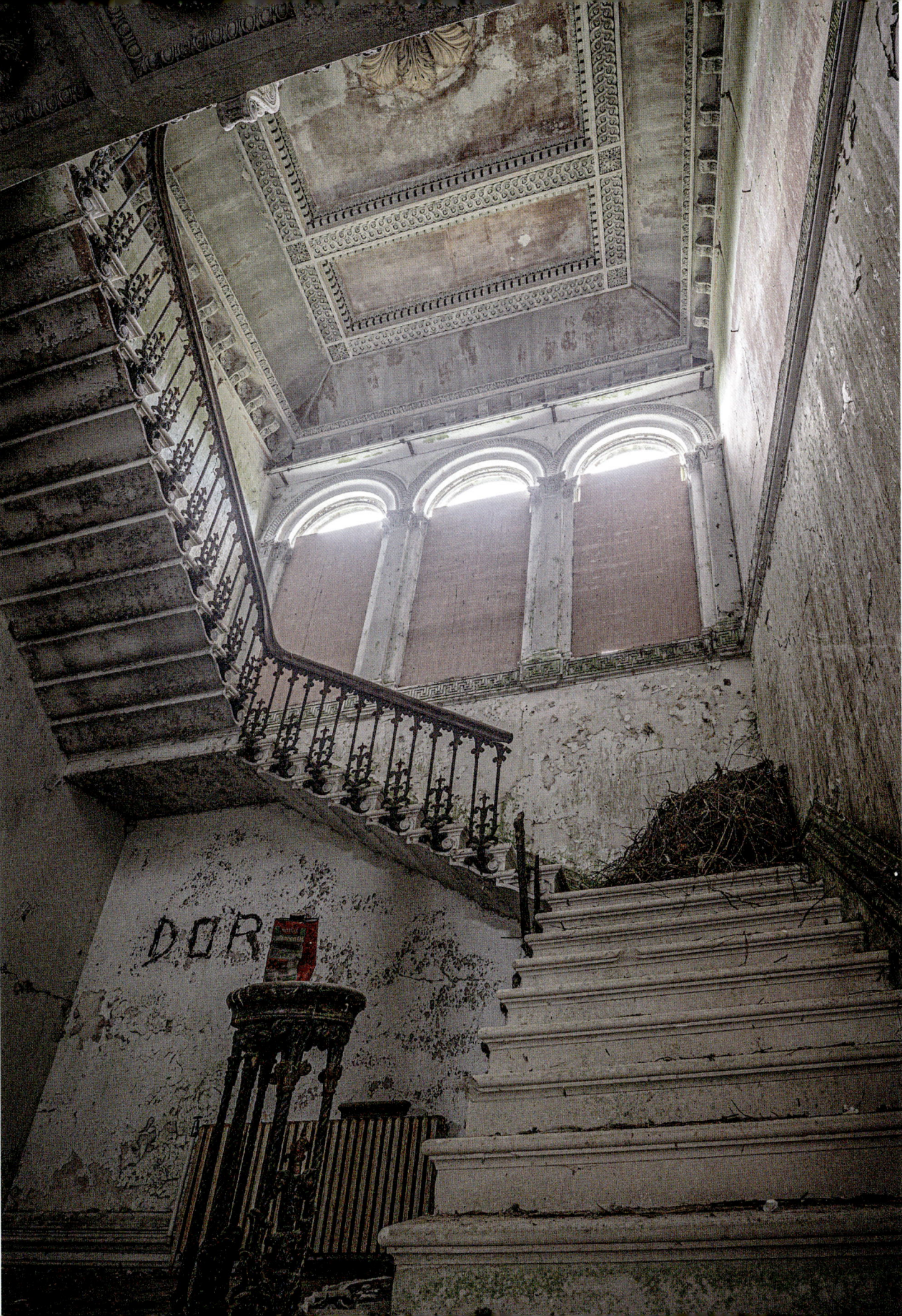

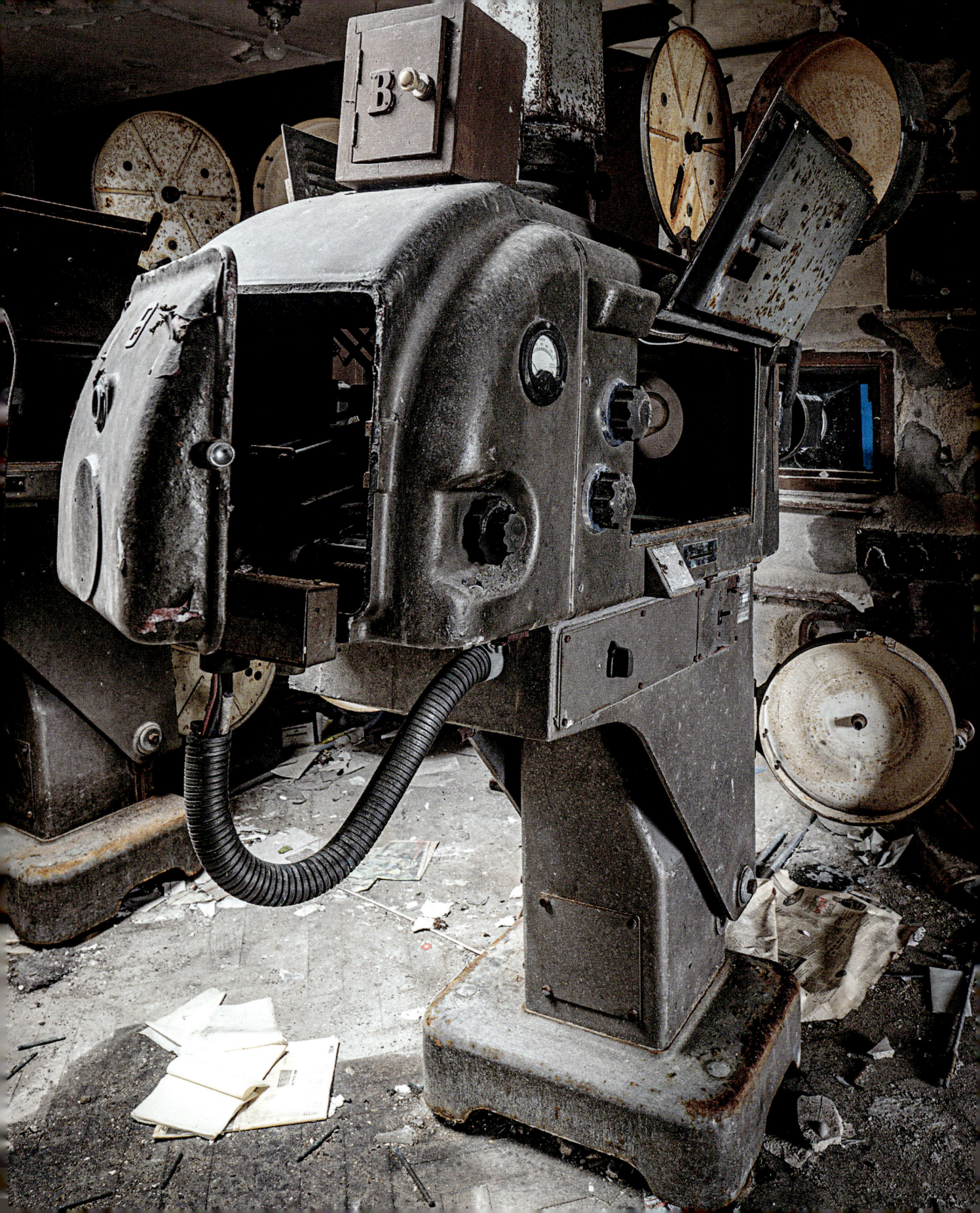

# THE SCALA CINEMA

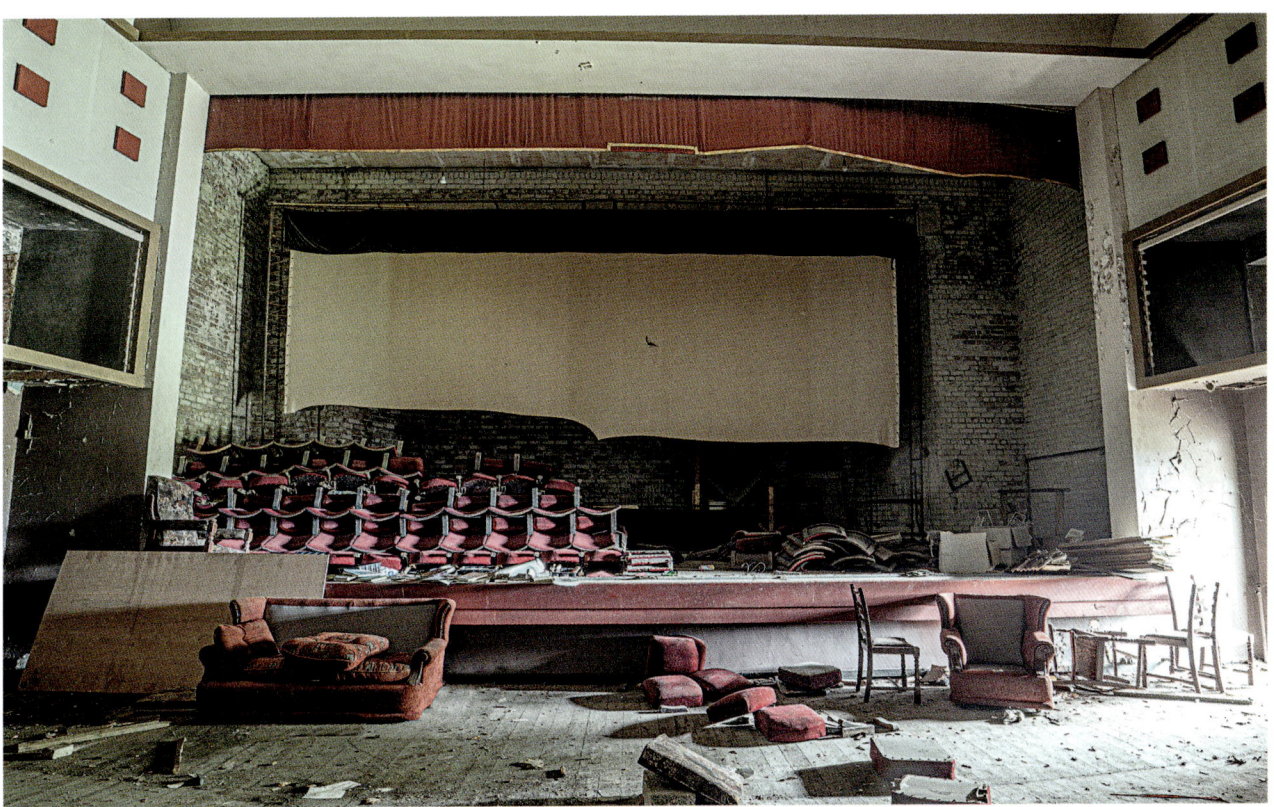

There are few cinemas like this left on the island of Ireland, which is why I was so delighted to have the opportunity to see it first-hand. The Scala opened its doors in 1953, and the first film shown there was *The Robe*, a biblical epic starring Richard Burton and Jean Simmons. It quickly became the busiest venue in Keady town. In its heyday, the cinema boasted 400 seats, and some of them are still in place today. I was surprised to see just how small they are in comparison to the seats in modern cinemas.

Venturing upstairs, I found the projectors still in place. These huge pieces of equipment take up

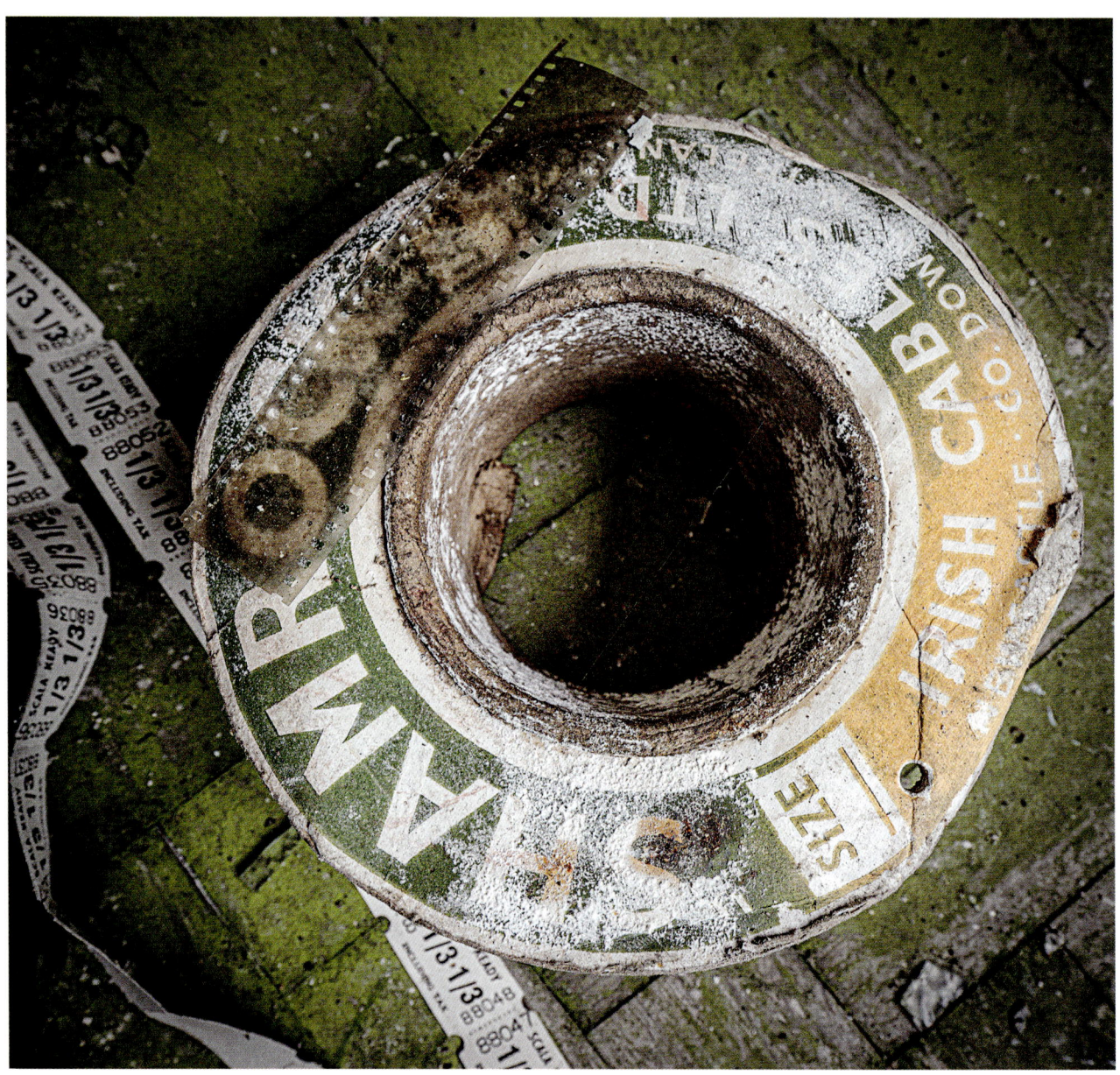

lots of space in the small room. The projectors ran films on twenty-minute reels, which would have to be changed as the film progressed. More than one projector would be used so that there was no break in the film. A cue mark at the end of each reel would tell the projectionist when to start the second projector. Some of the old reels are still there, giving the visitor a sense of being in a time warp.

When the movies were running the room would have been in darkness and I imagine those working

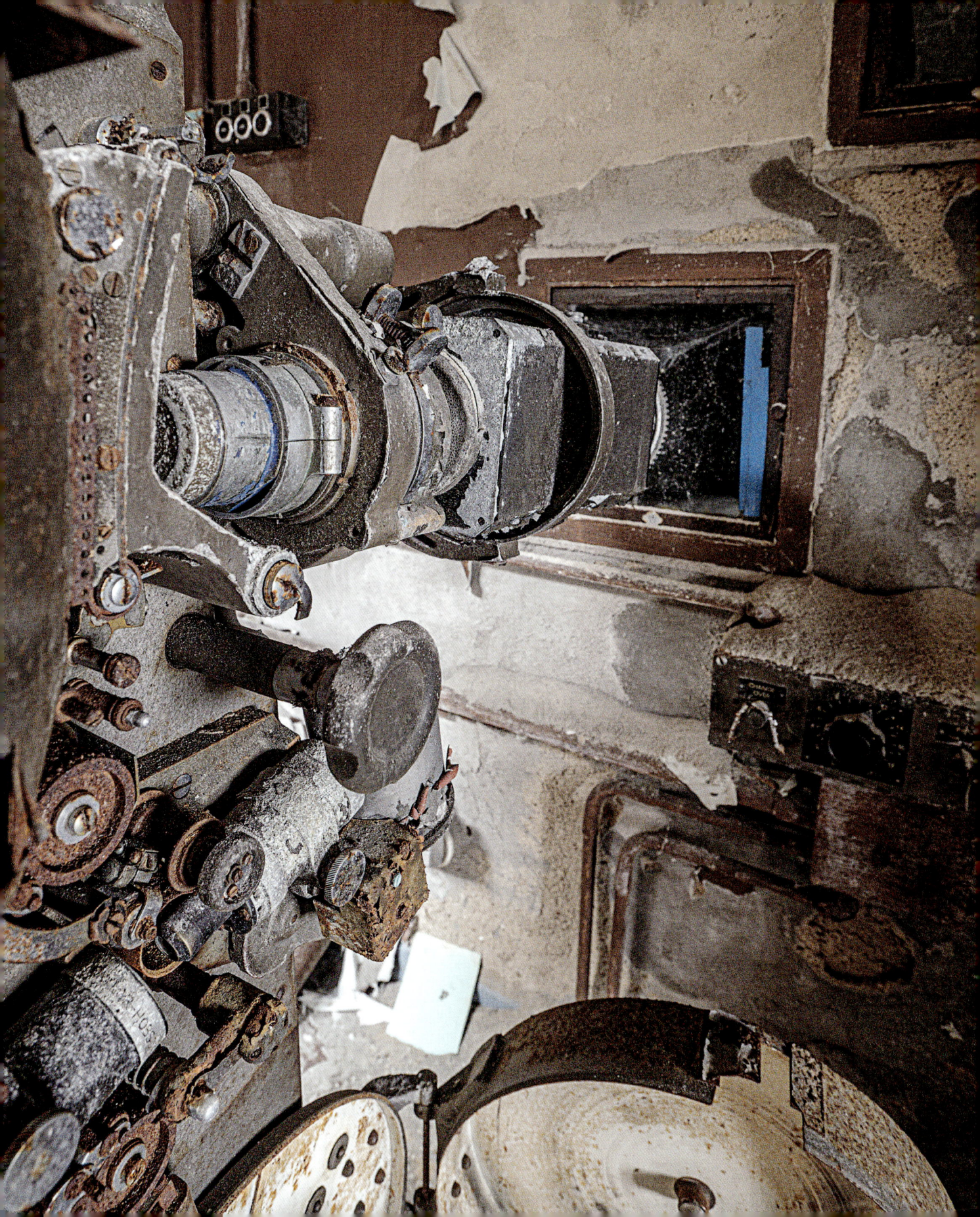

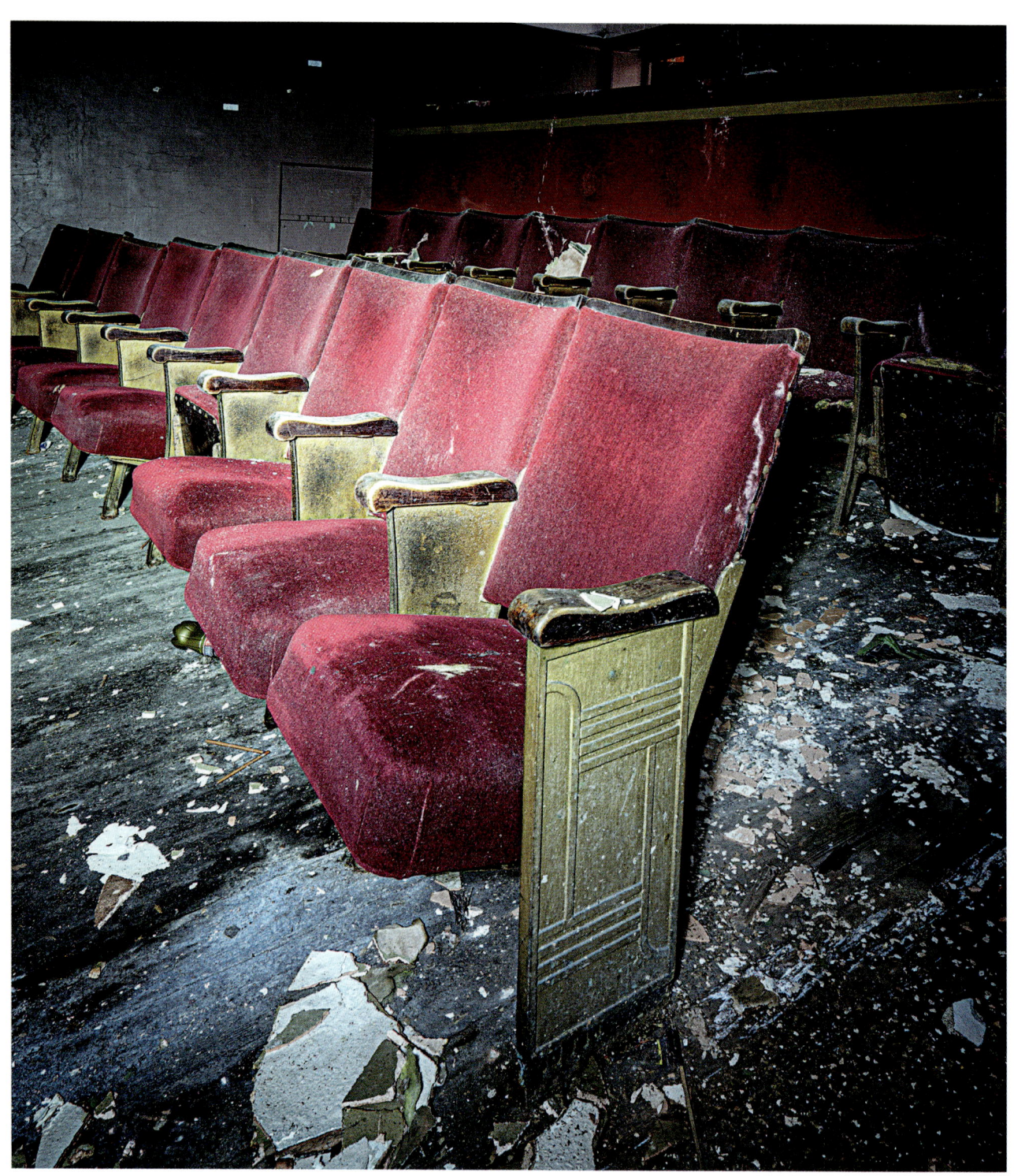

there would have needed to take care during the process! But I also think the projectionist must have felt a sense of calm watching the crowd below become immersed in the film.

Looking down from the projector room, the view of the cinema is breathtaking. I can imagine the light from the projector shining through and hitting the cloth screen, which was revealed as the large curtains in front of it swept open. The atmosphere must have been electric back in those early days, when going to the cinema was viewed as a grand night out. People got dressed up specifically to go to see their chosen movie – it was a big deal then. It was also a popular venue for first dates, the dark room being perfect for a furtive kiss or two.

Sadly, smaller cinemas like this couldn't compete with the bigger, more modern chains that have opened venues all over the country in more recent times, with their massive screens and surround sound. The Scala closed its curtains for the final time in 1990. The owner plans to restore the building and use it for shop units in the future, with work due to start soon. When it does, another small piece of Ireland's entertainment history will be lost.

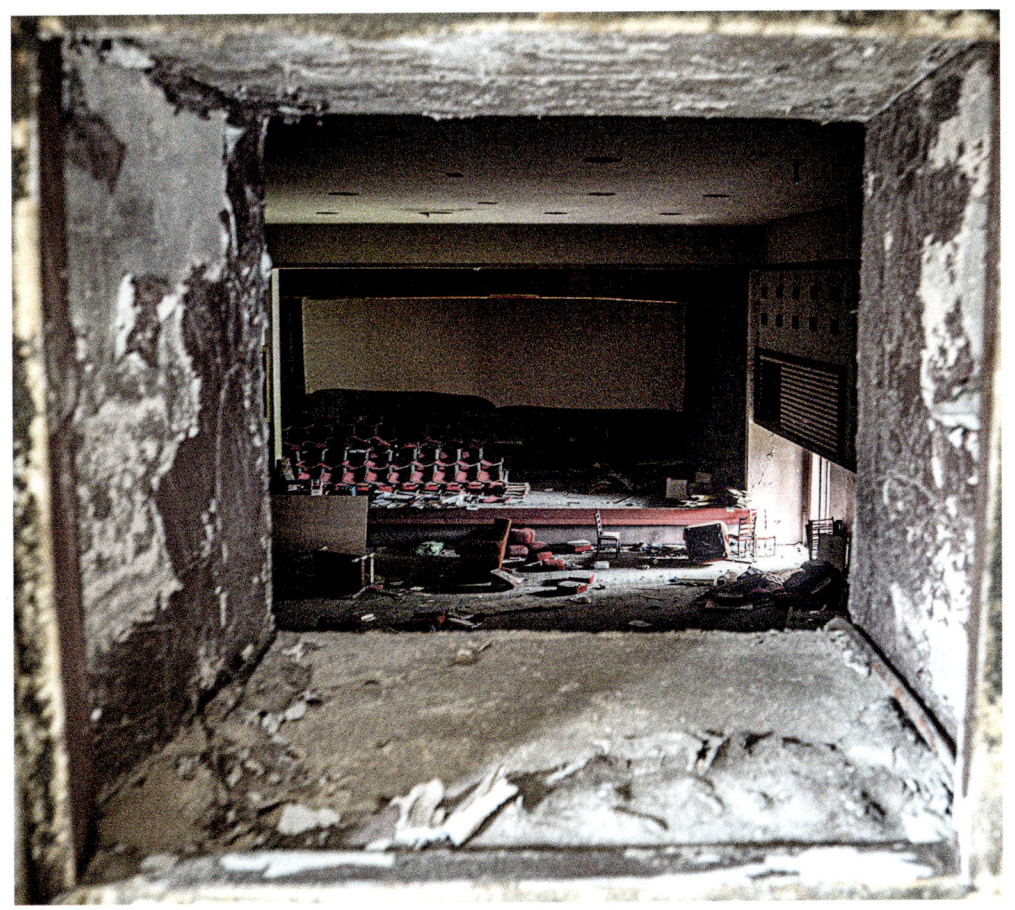

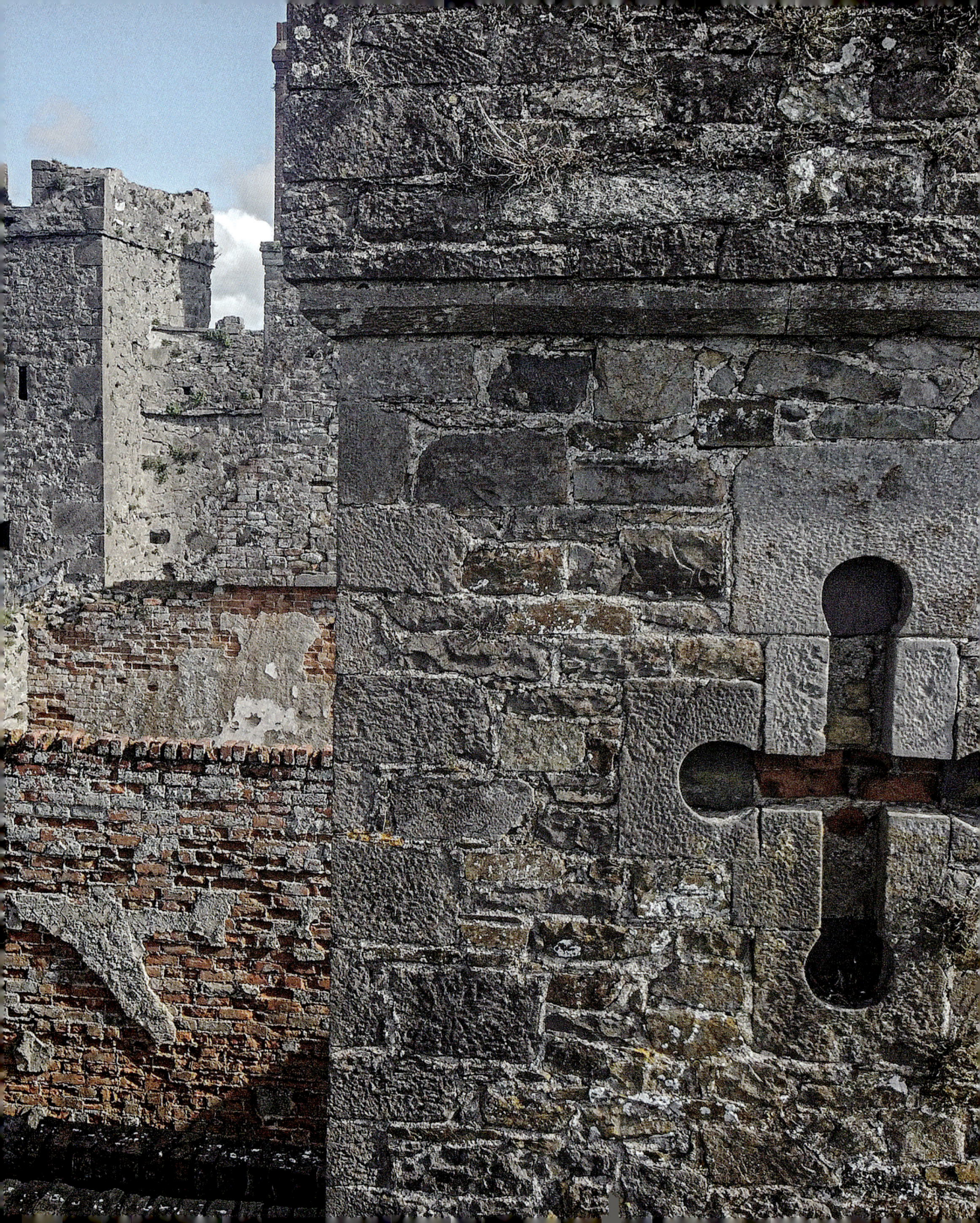

# ATHCARNE CASTLE

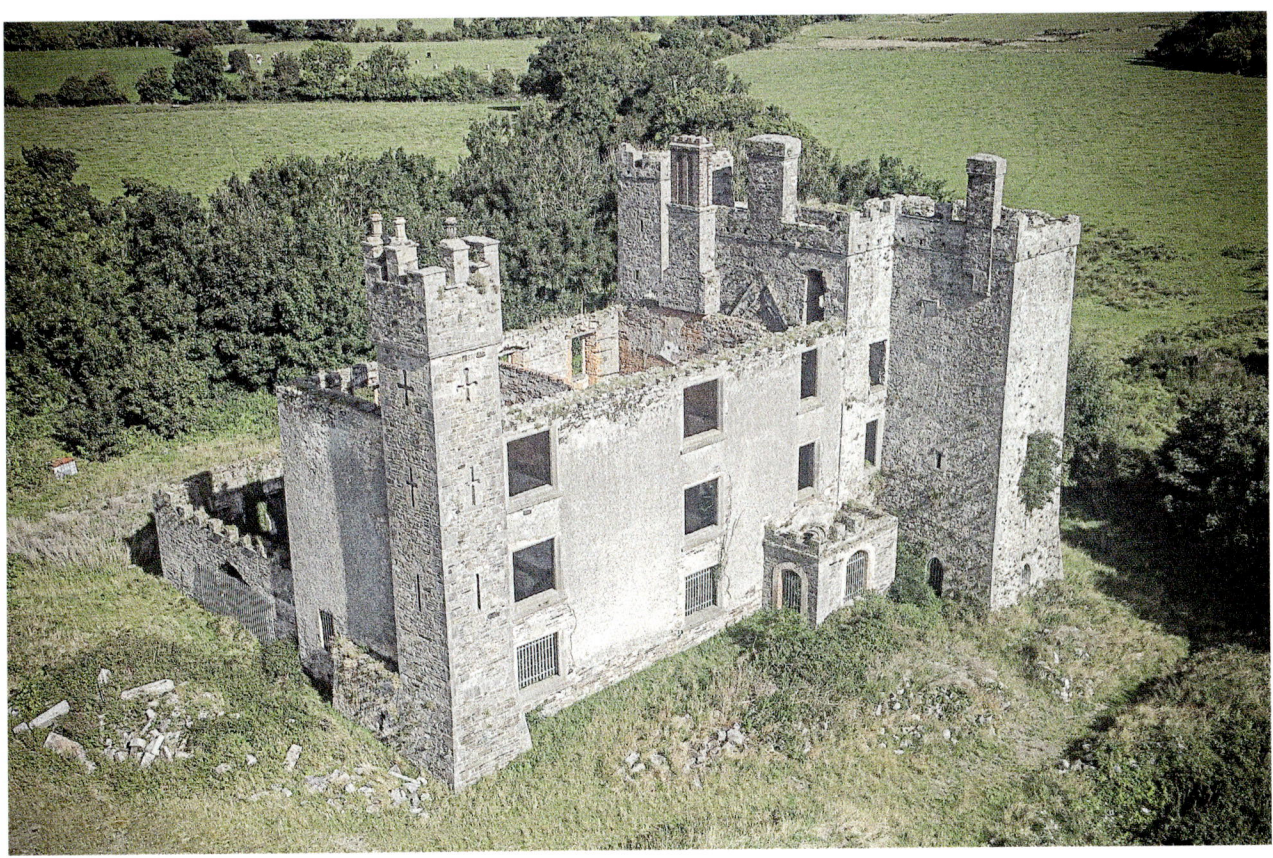

Ireland has castles everywhere, many of them derelict. You could be driving down an unassuming country lane when suddenly a beautiful stone castle pops into view. Such places have layers and layers of stories waiting to be retold. This one is no different.

Athcarne Castle, built in 1590, has a rich and colourful history. The original Elizabethan structure consisted of a three-storey mansion with a corner turret. It was constructed by Sir William Bathe, a high court judge, who passed away shortly after its completion, leaving the house to his brother James.

In 1649 the castle was witness to some dramatic events and underwent a change of ownership. Oliver Cromwell marched with his army from Dublin and besieged the mansion, along with three other surrounding castles, in order to gain full control of the strategically important crossing point on the nearby River Nanny. He then transferred ownership of the property to one of his commanders, forcing Bathe and his family to flee.

In 1660 James passed away, leaving his son Luke to try to reclaim the family home. Despite his petitions for the return of the lands, Athcarne and other estates seized by Cromwell were transferred to the Duke of York (the future King James II). The Duke eventually allowed the Bathe family to return to Athcarne in 1668, granting them a 99-year lease for a peppercorn rent of £430. Legend has it that the night before the Battle of the Boyne, King James stayed at Athcarne (located only six miles from the battlefield).

By the following century the Bathe family had vacated the castle and it was inhabited by the Garnett family. In 1830 they moved away and the property was purchased by the Gernon family. The Gernons undertook extensive renovations to the building, demolishing the mansion but preserving the tower and transforming it into the castellated three-storey construction we see today. Unfortunately, they later faced some financial difficulties and had to sell off the castle due to the high upkeep costs. Its contents were auctioned off in 1939 and the building offered for sale by the Land Commission. Initially, there were proposals to demolish the castle and use the rubble for road repairs and extensions, but this plan did not come to fruition, much to the relief of many.

According to documented stories, during a nearby battle of an unspecified time an Irish fighter hid in a pile of hay, waiting to ambush some English soldiers. When they approached his hiding spot he opened fire, but soon ran out of ammunition. The English set fire to the hay, forcing him out, and he was captured and killed on the spot. His may be one of the ghosts said to haunt the castle to this very day.

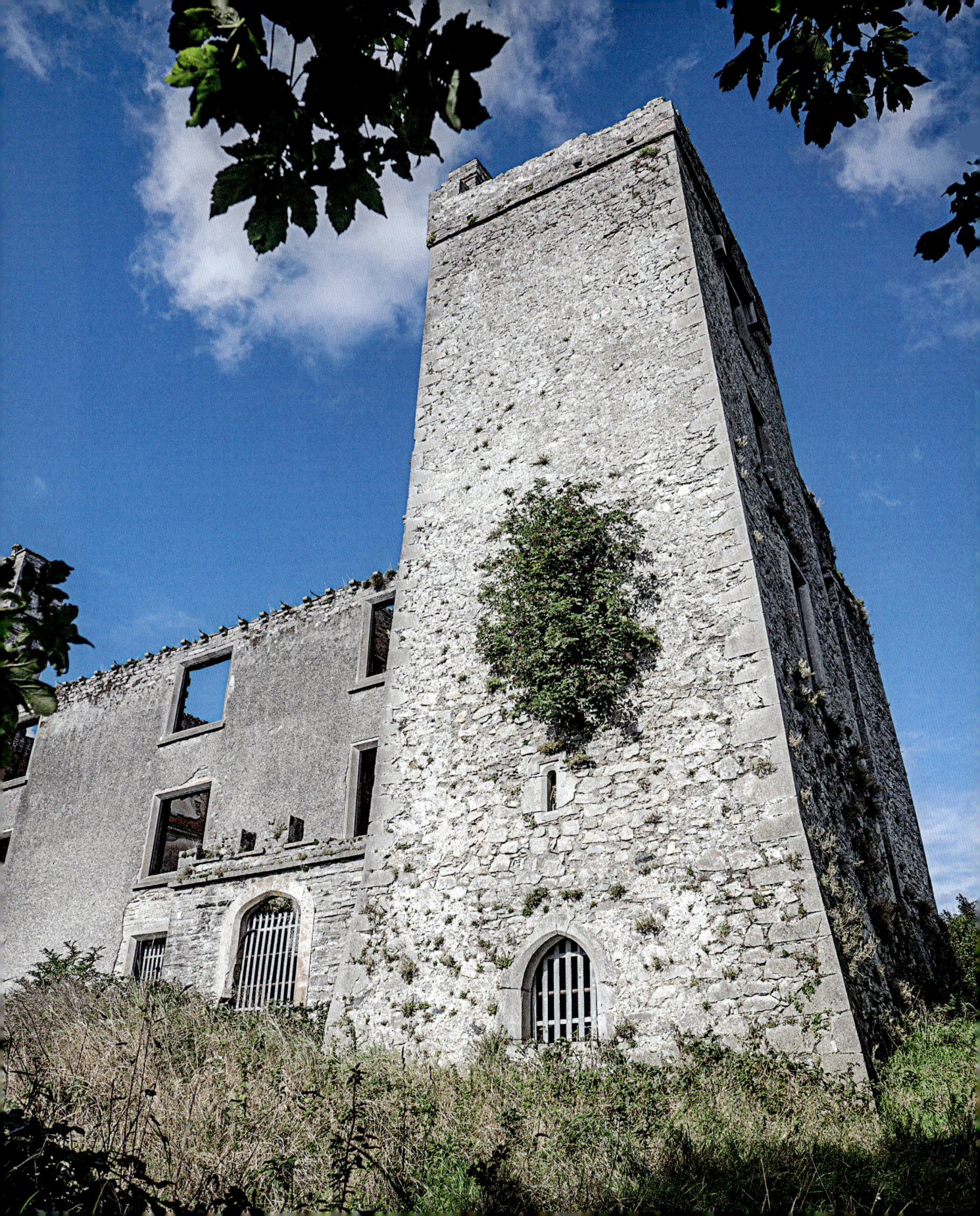

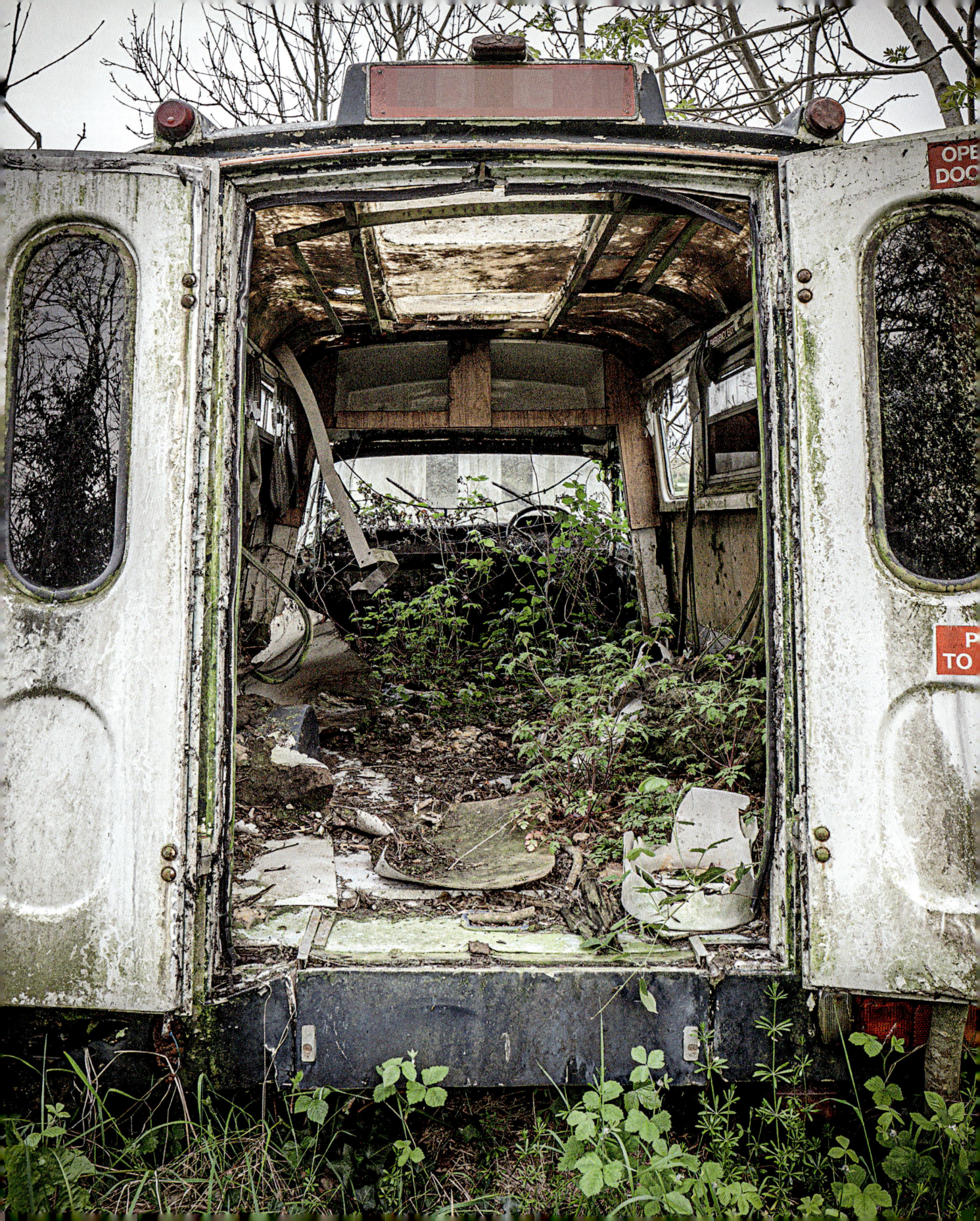

# THE CAR GRAVEYARD

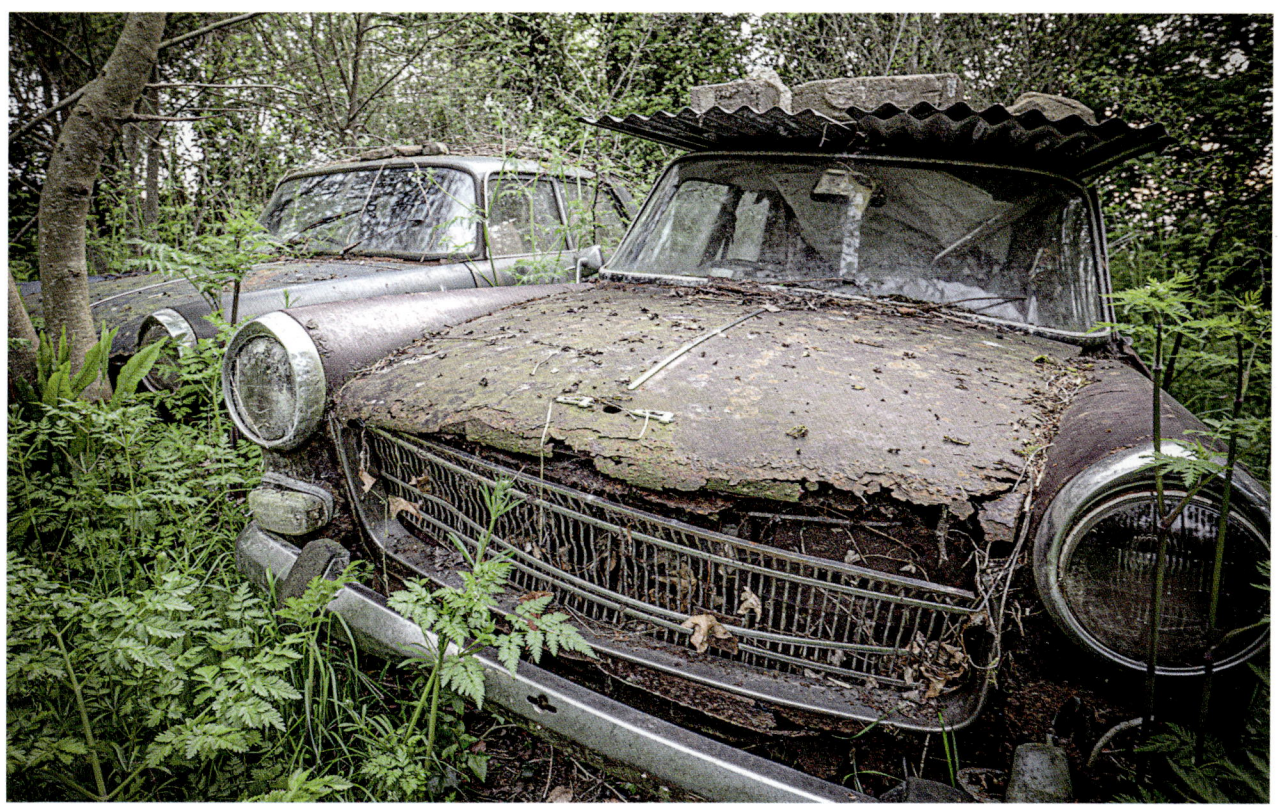

During the early days of urbexing (the recreational activity where people explore derelict, mostly urban, structures), a new location drew the attention of those involved. The discovery of a car graveyard in the heart of Ireland sparked widespread interest. Allegedly filled with vintage vehicles aban-doned for decades in a remote field, it became a must-see spot.

After seeing some online posts and intrigued by the stories, I decided to investigate this location for myself. On a sunny day, I made the two-hour drive to reach the site. I roamed around and spotted

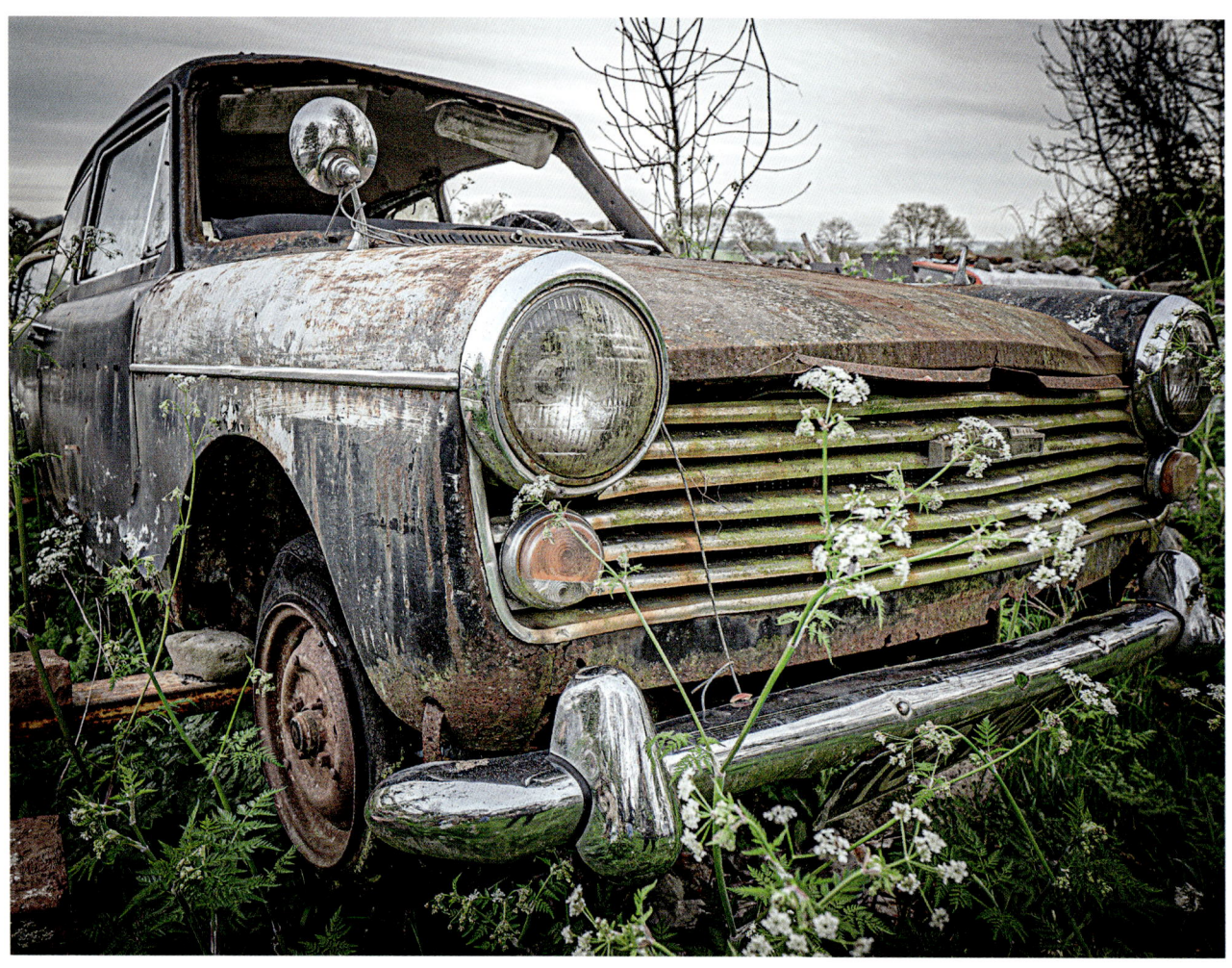

several cars that, had they been taken care of, might be worth a fortune today! Sadly, they were now in terrible condition: rusted, battered and desolate-looking. However, I still found them beautiful.

There were plenty of treasures to be discovered, from Jeeps, Land Rovers, vintage box vans, ambulances and sports cars to one or two tractors. Recently, on a return visit, I noticed that most of the cars now had bricks piled up on their roof or bonnets. I'm unsure why someone would do this – perhaps to deter thieves?

To date this is the only car graveyard in Ireland that I've come across.

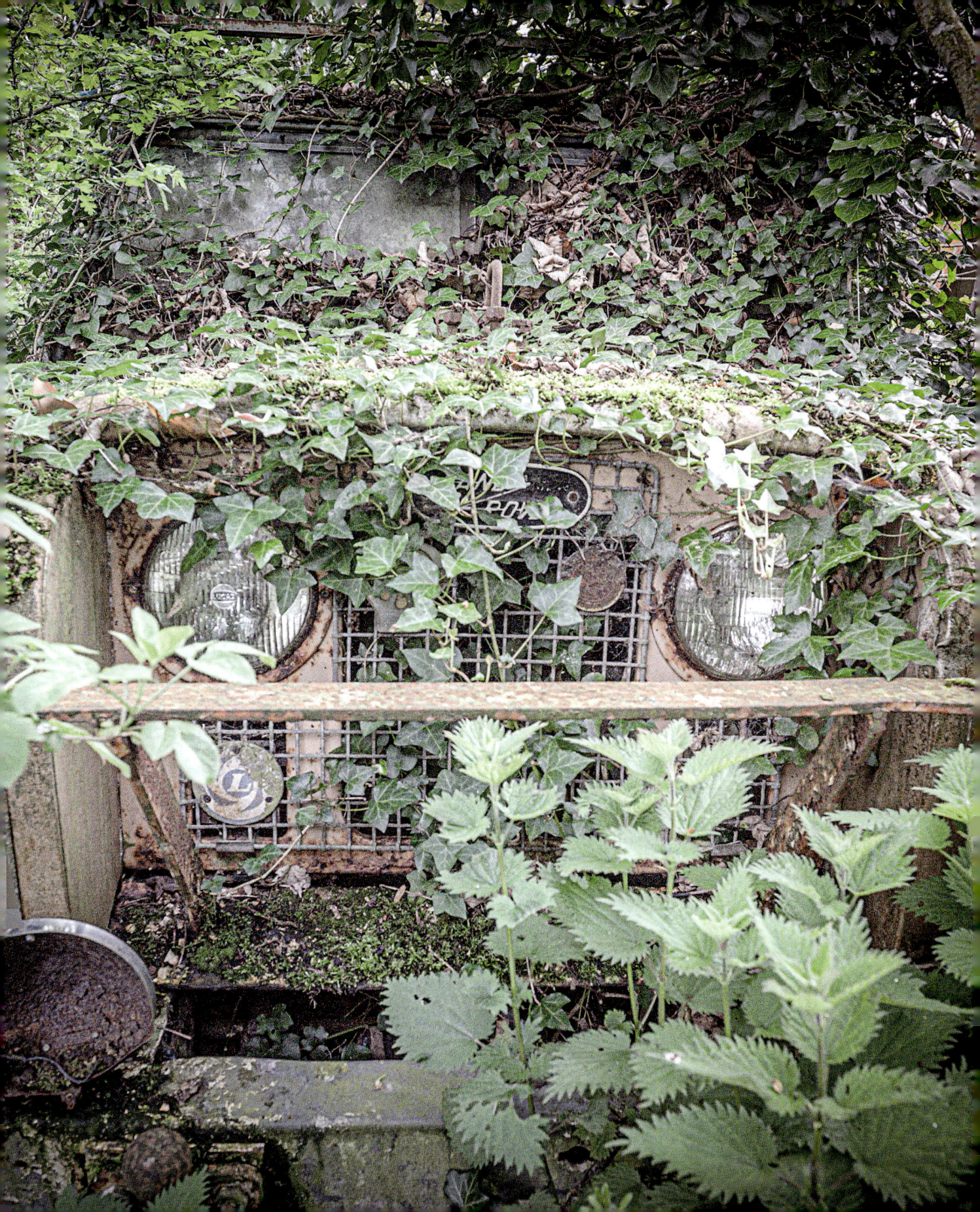

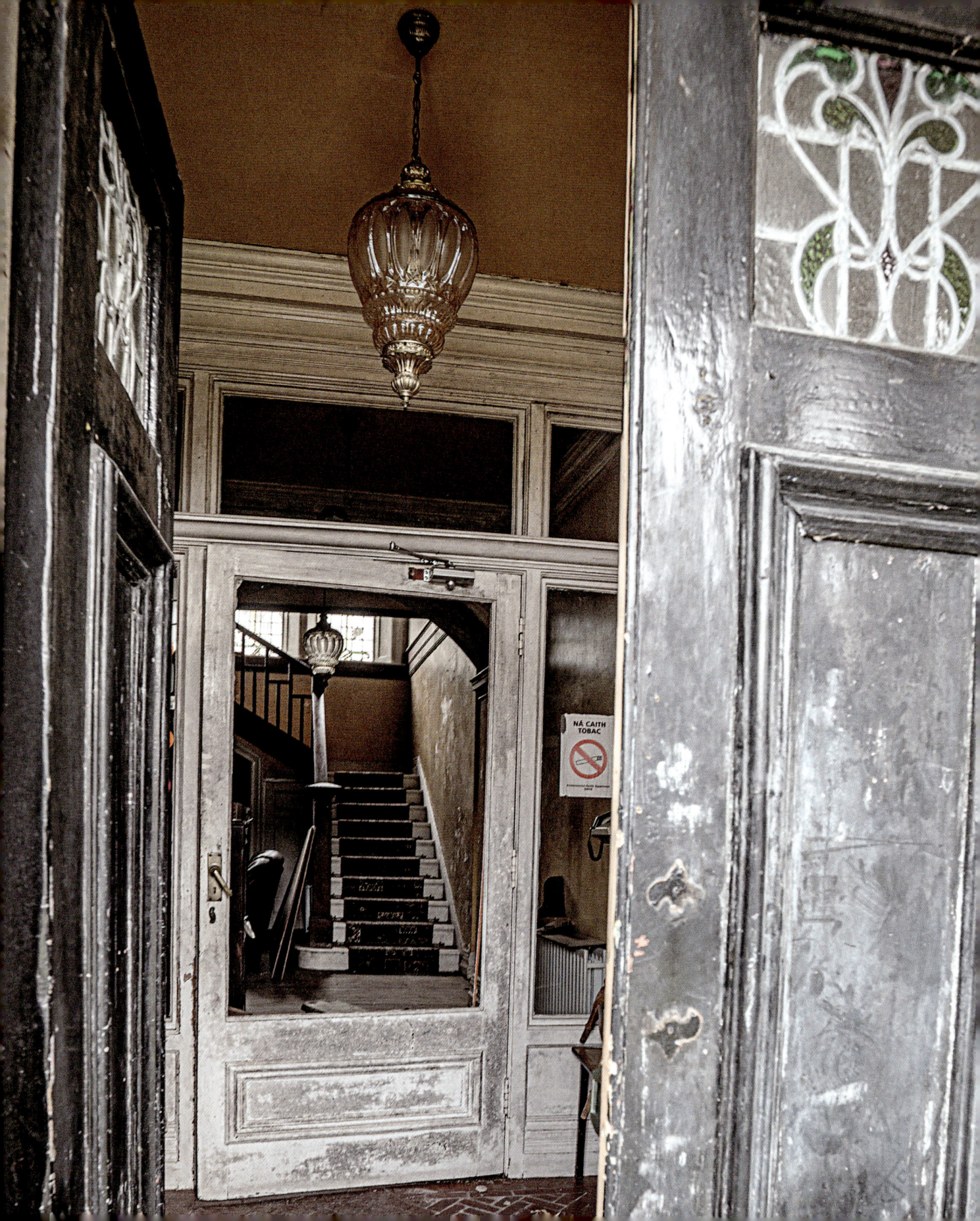

# THE HUNTING LODGE

Set deep within a dense forest, this impressive Tudoresque lodge is part of a larger 55-acre estate that includes its own lakes and boasts of having the best salmon in the world. As I walked up the driveway, I was truly captivated by the views of the surrounding lakes and mountains, as well as the

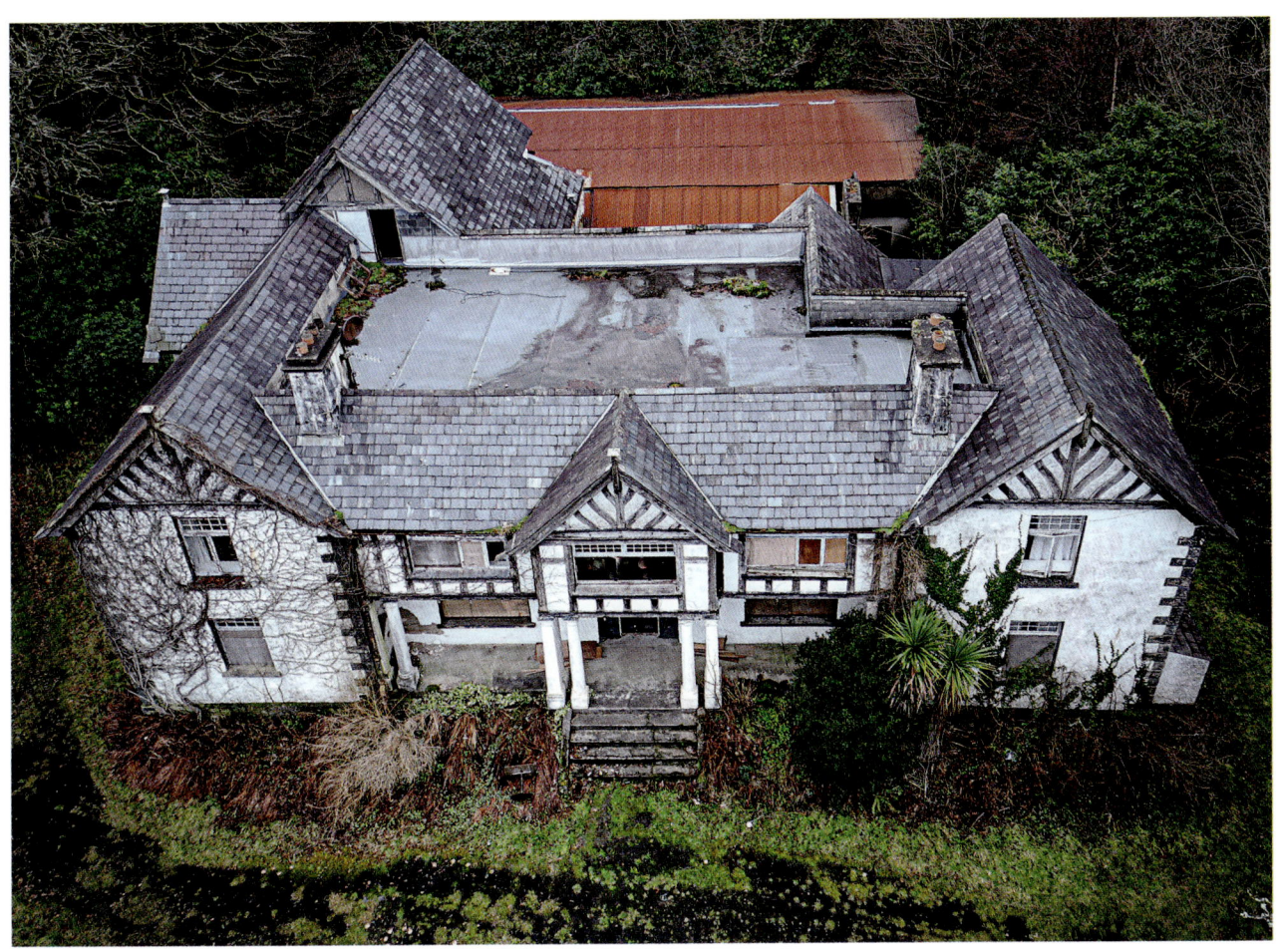

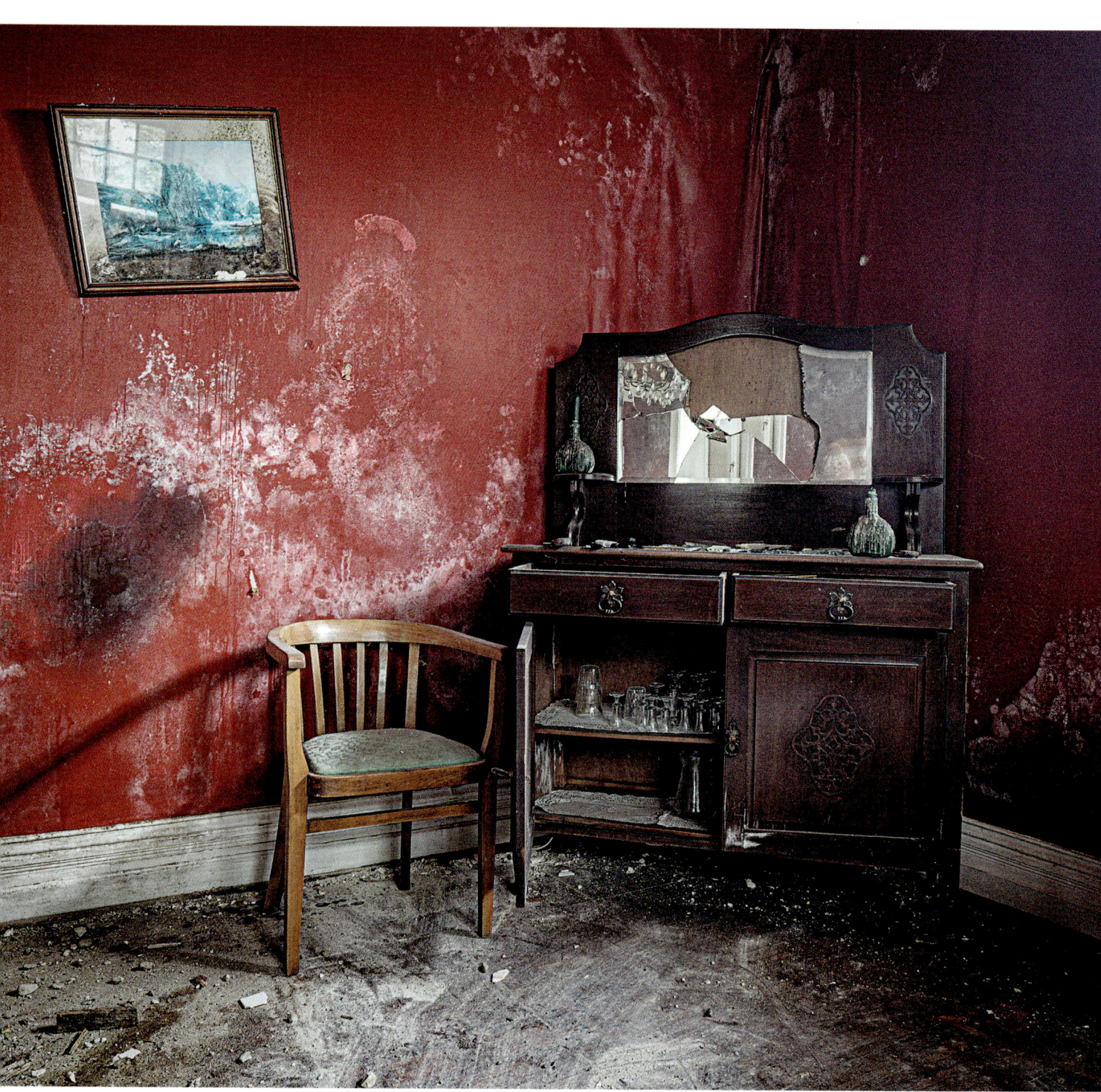

peacefulness of the place. It almost felt like a sanctuary, perfect for retreats of all kinds and not just as a base for salmon fishing, which it was previously used for.

The house is recorded as being built or heavily rebuilt around 1911, after a massive fire ripped through the previous building on the site. It is thought that part of the original dwelling may have been incorporated into the current structure, as it stands on the same site and the same axis according to the depiction of the previous building on the Ordnance Survey map of 1904.

There has been a house on this site since at least the mid-eighteenth century, and over the years it has been home to various gentry, a magistrate and even a captain who established a successful agricultural school on the estate in the mid-1800s. Having changed ownership several times, in its last iteration it became a fishing lodge, with twelve bedrooms, a bar and restaurant facilities. It was a popular weekend destination for fishing enthusiasts looking to catch the exquisite salmon from the local rivers.

However, in 2017 it closed its doors. Local rumour has it that Simply Red singer Mick Hucknall expressed an interest in purchasing the lodge, but that was not to be and it is now under new ownership. Plans for redevelopment have been approved to restore the protected structure, turning it into a thirty-four-bedroom, 5-star hotel with conference facilities. Additionally, a new five-bed fisherman's lodge will be added. Truly something for everyone!

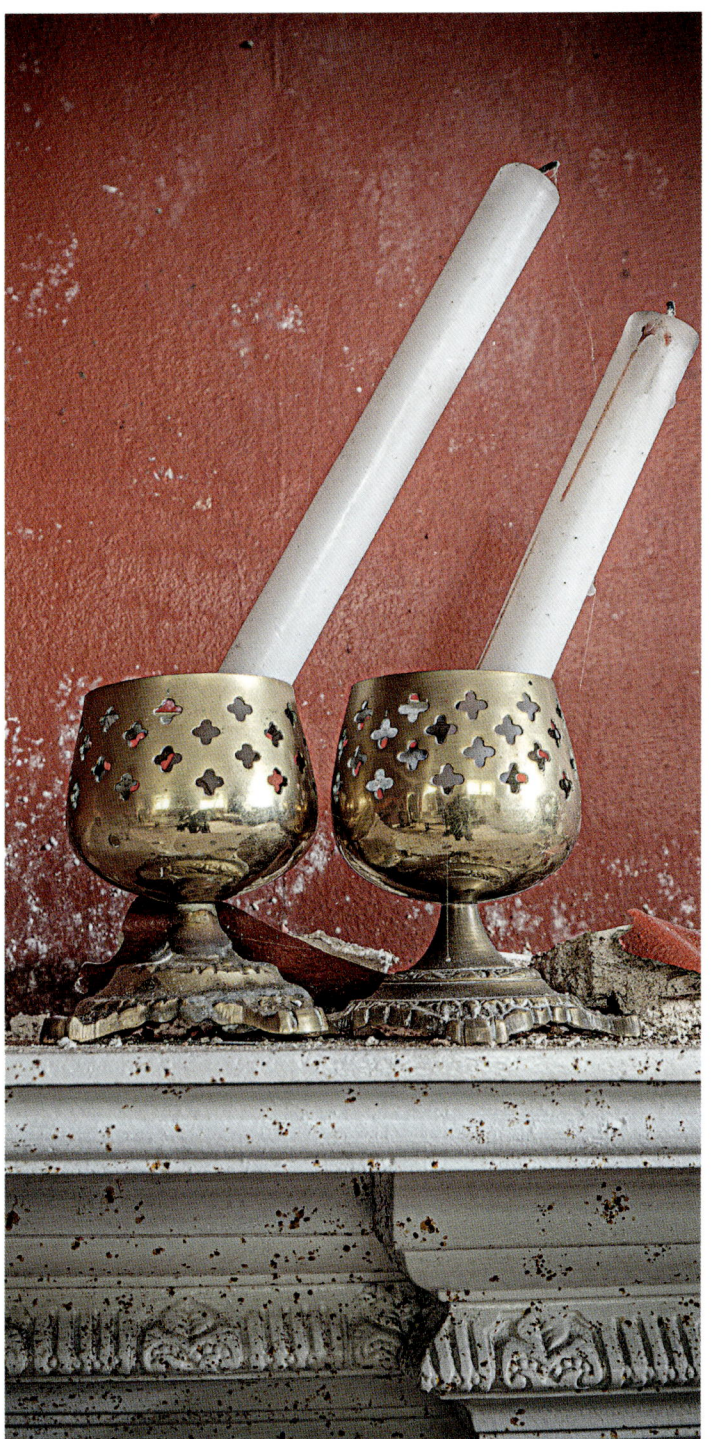

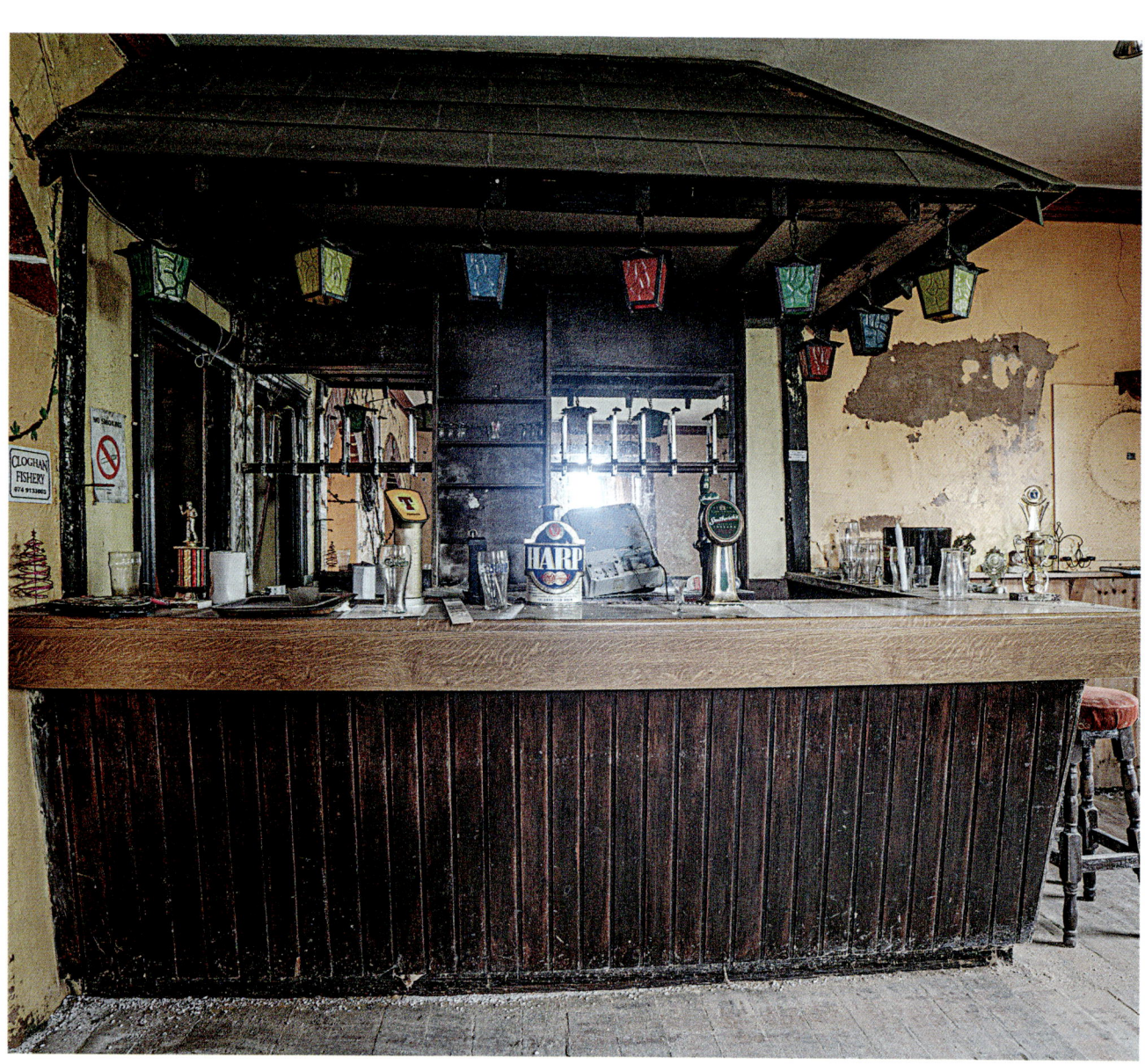

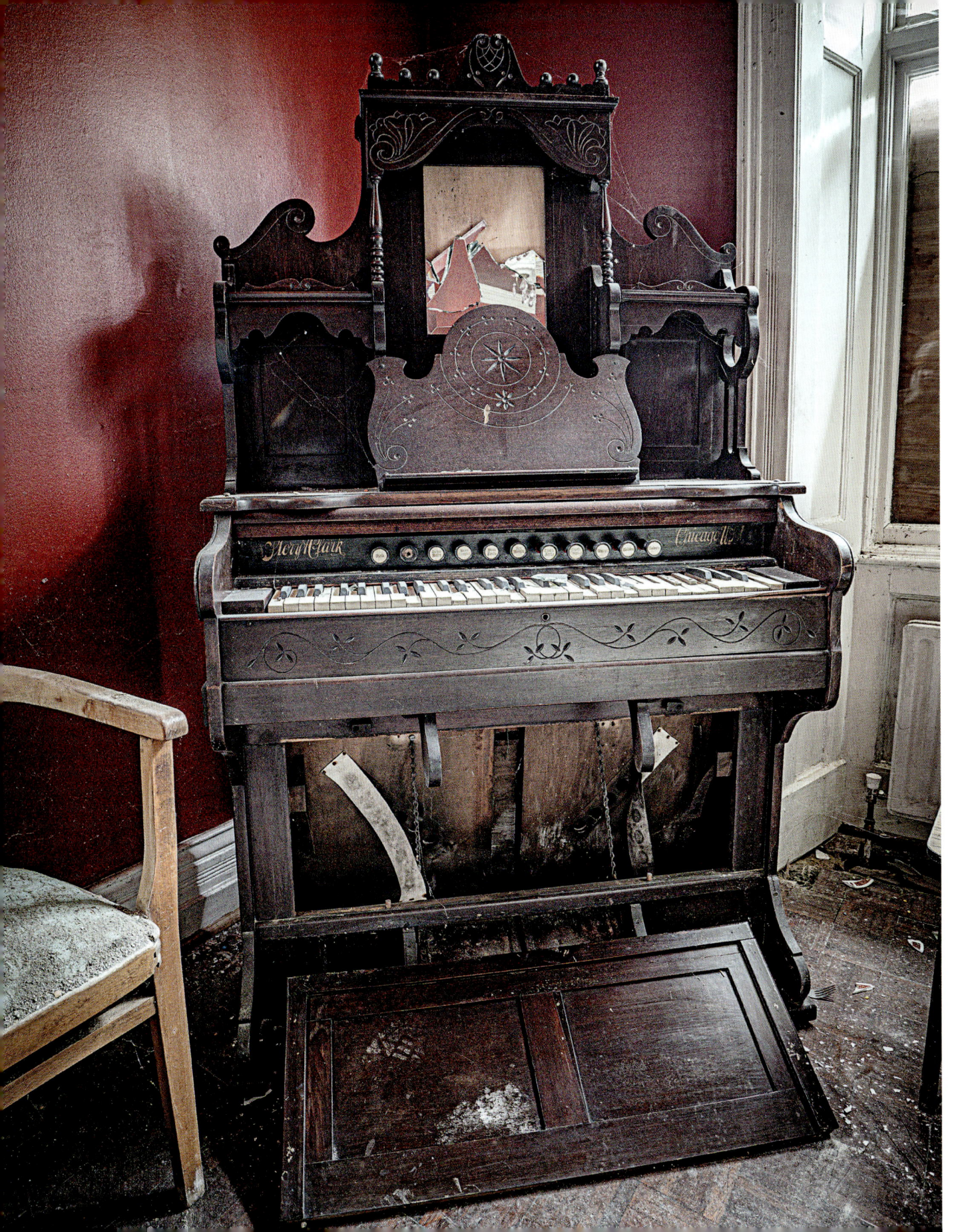

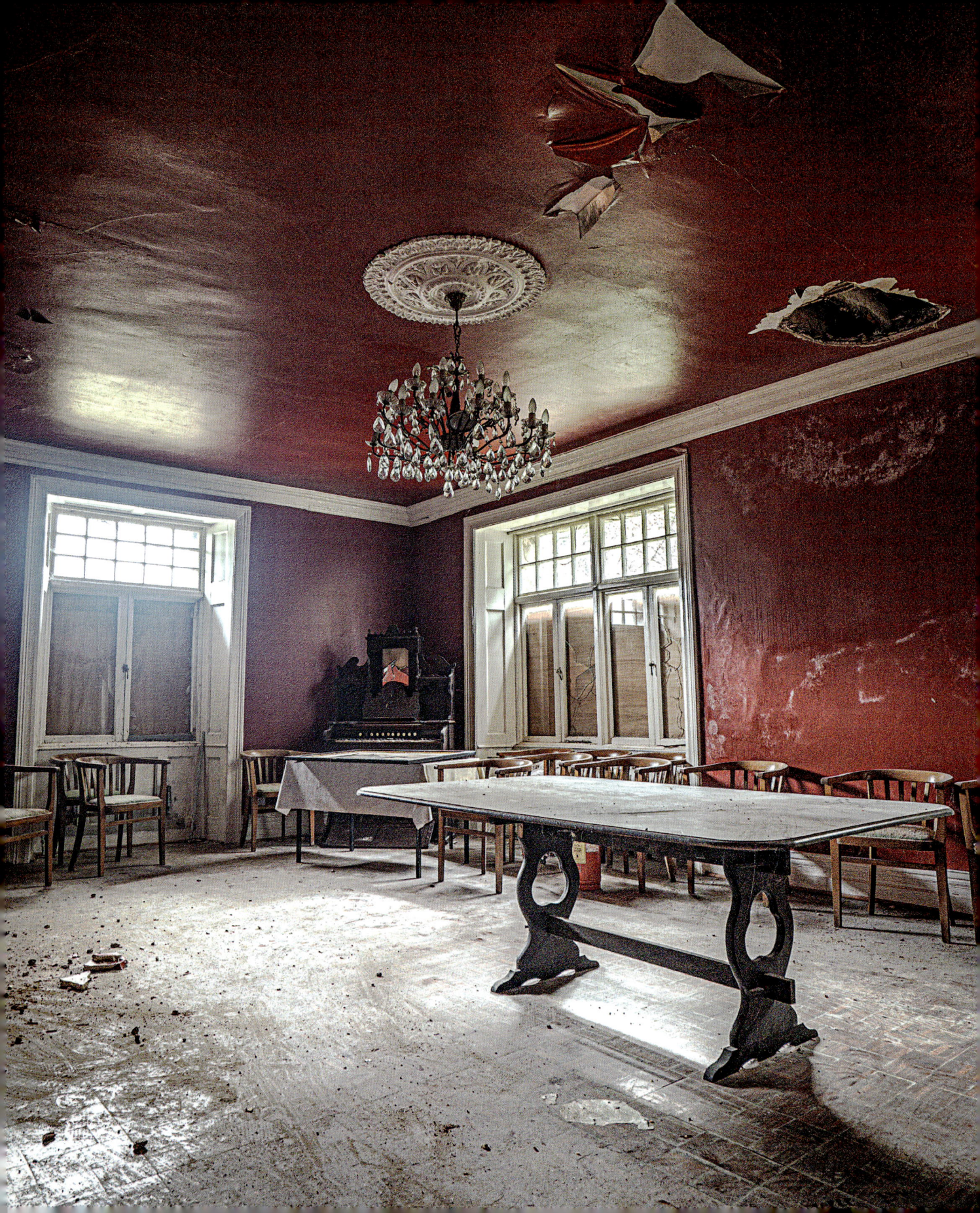

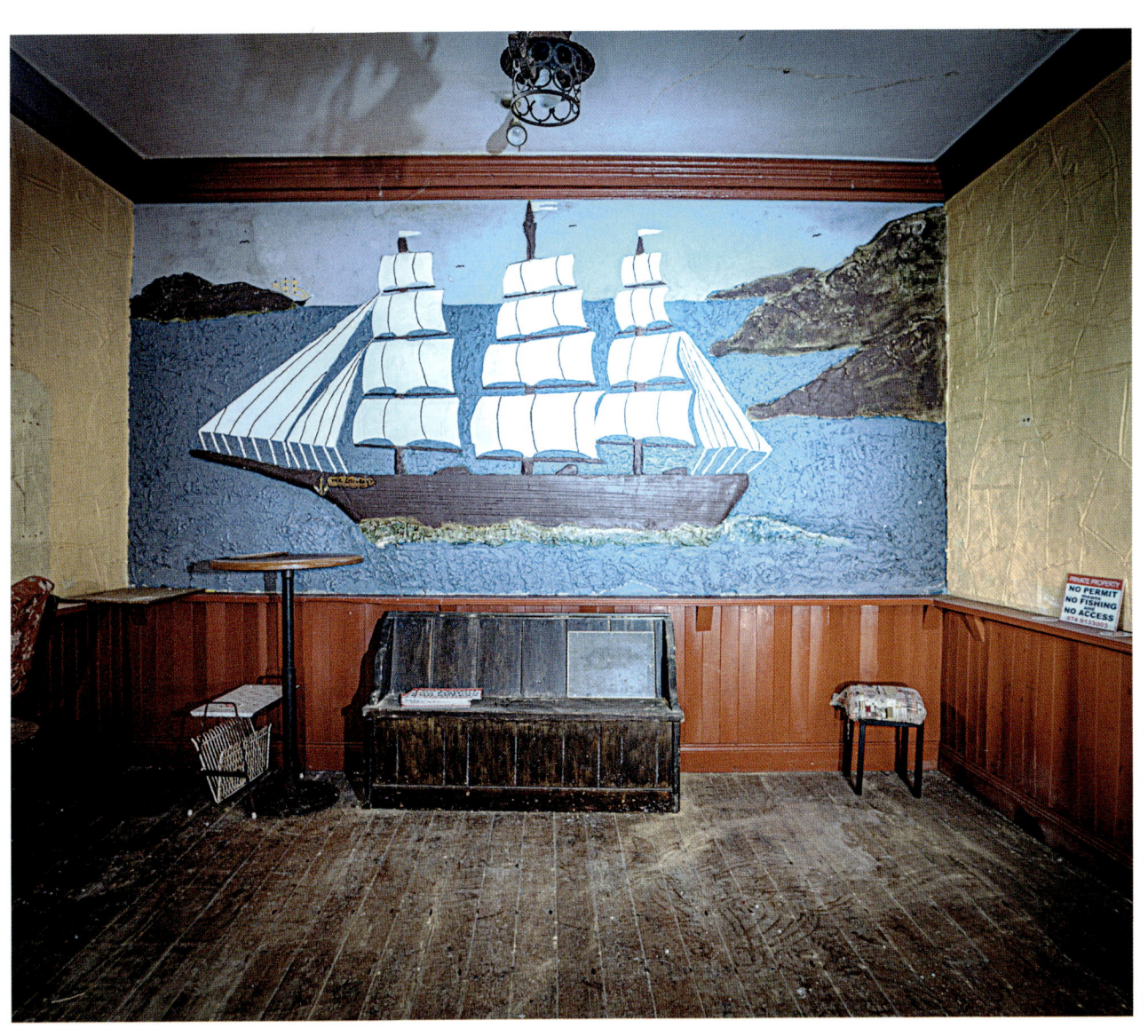

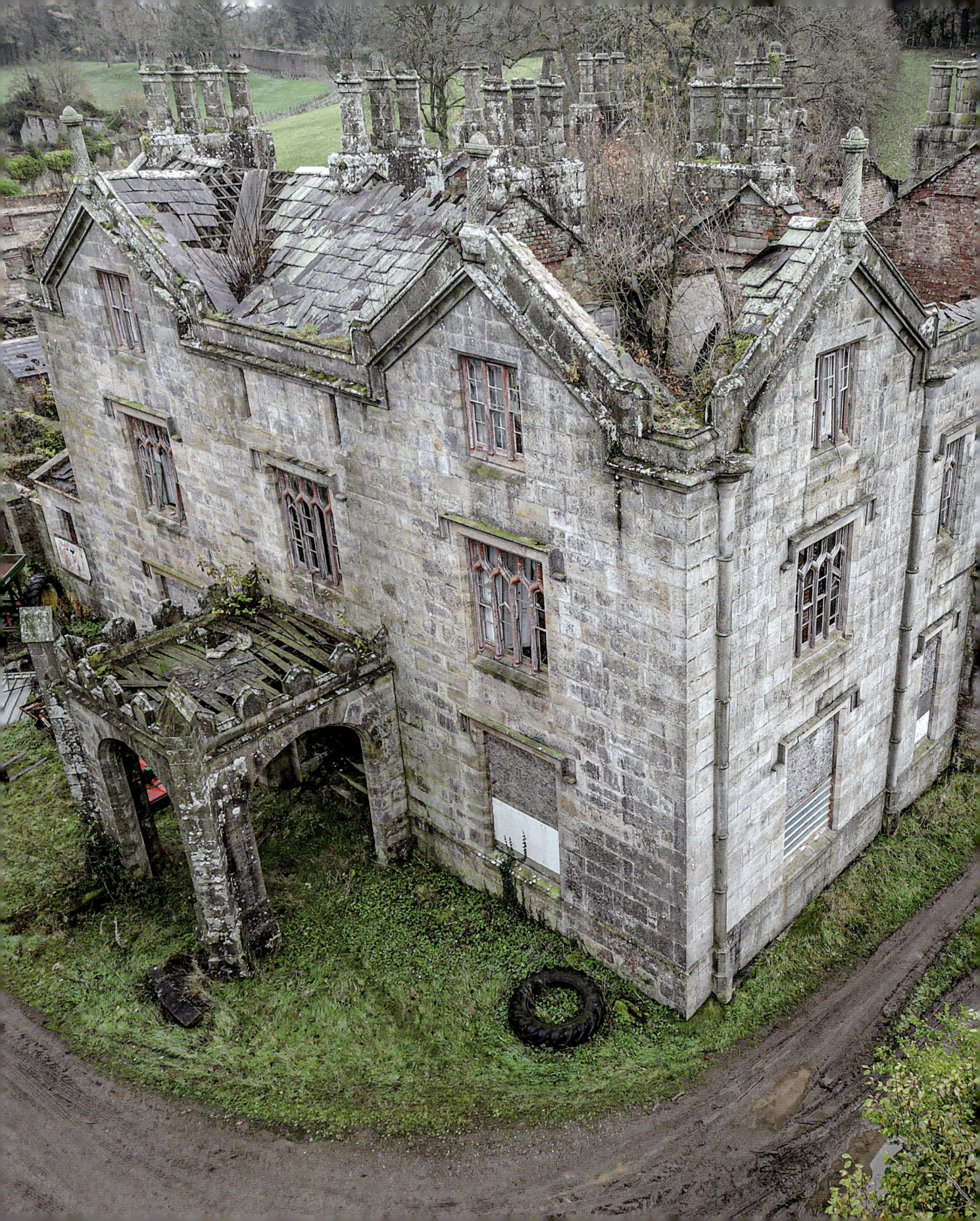

# A ROYAL FAVOUR

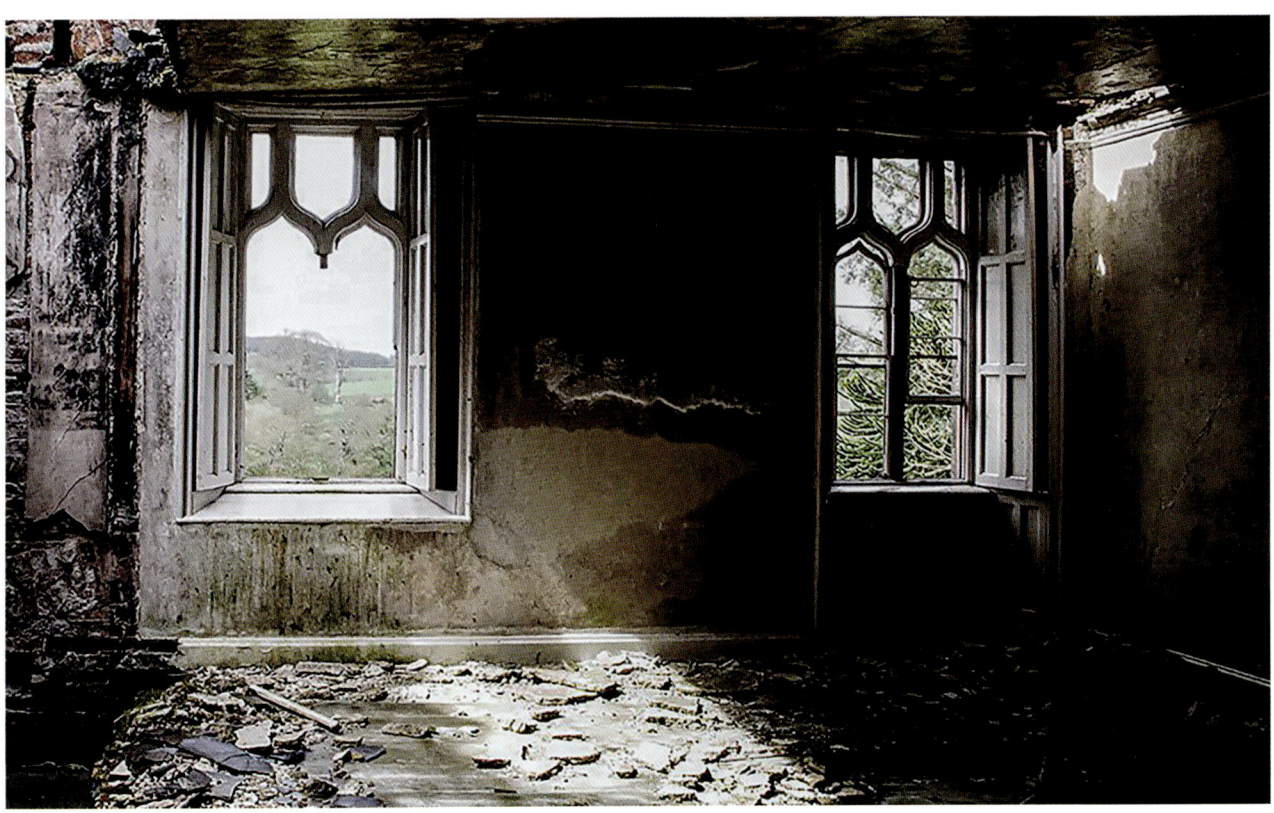

Favour Royal sits beside the River Blackwater, shrouded by forest. It caught my attention a few times over the years and I first documented the house in the early 2000s. An earlier fire had damaged most of the upper floors, making them inaccessible, but even then you could see the grandeur of the original house, with its flamboyant stone staircase flanked by a large Gothic arched window frame that must have held brightly coloured stained glass at one point. I could imagine walking down it and seeing the morning sunshine flood through, illuminating the stairs – what a sight that must have been!

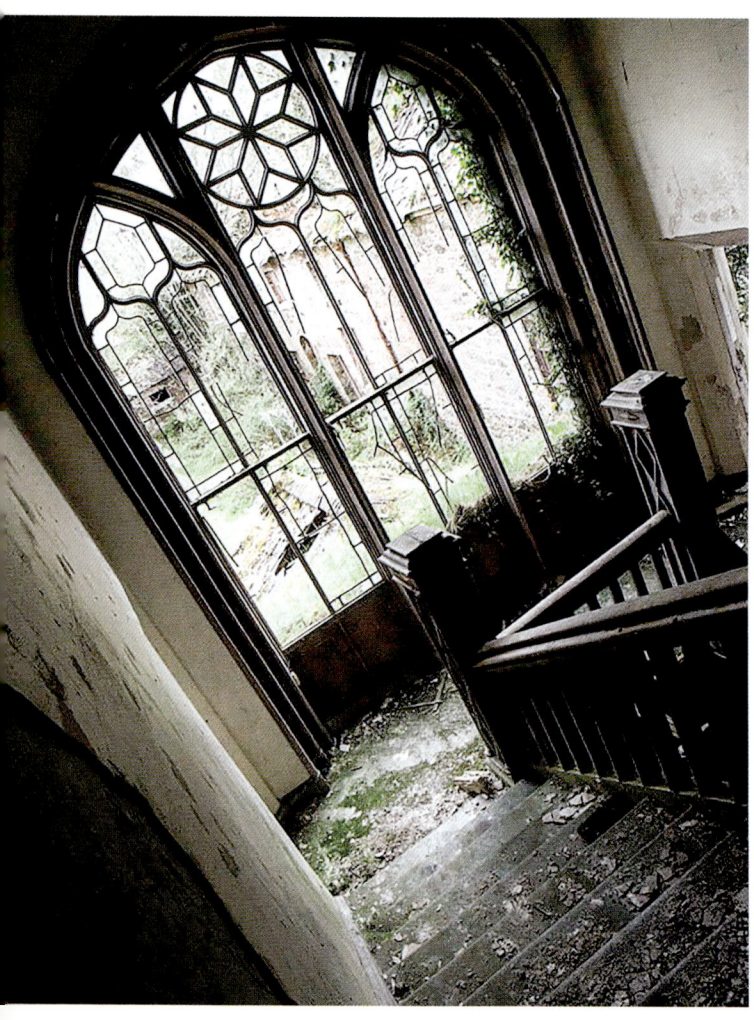

After this sale it was discovered that a mistake had been made in the original land grant to Ridgeway, so King Charles I regranted the land as a favour to Erskine, who renamed the estate Favour Royal in acknowledgement. The estate was later divided between Erskine's two granddaughters, with Favour Royal on one part and Augher Castle on the other. It was after this that the original house at Favour Royal was constructed, in 1670.

John Moutray married one of the Erskine granddaughters, Ann, and became the heir of Favour Royal. In 1816 the Moutrays hired a local boy, John Hughes, who came from a poor farming family, as their gardener. Hughes would later emigrate to America following his father and he went on to become the Catholic Archbishop of New York in 1842. John is responsible for building St Patrick's Cathedral on Fifth Avenue.

The original house at Favour Royal was destroyed by a fire in 1823 and replaced by Captain John Corry Moutray, who had John Hargrave design the new building in the Tudor revival style. It was completed in 1825. The house remained in the Moutray family until 1976, when it was sold along with its contents. Although occupied until the 1990s, the house has since been abandoned and left in a state of disrepair. During a recent visit in 2023 I flew my drone over the property to check on its condition. Unfortunately, it was not holding up well – the roof was completely gone, and all that remained was the shell of the building.

The history of Favour Royal is quite fascinating. In 1610 the estate, then known as 'Portclare', was granted by King James I to Sir Thomas Ridgeway, the 'Treasurer of Wars' in Ireland. Sir Thomas played a significant role in the plantation of Ulster, and grants of land were common practice at that time for repaying services rendered. In 1613 Sir Thomas built the nearby Augher Castle; then in 1622, he sold the entire Portclare estate to Sir James Erskine.

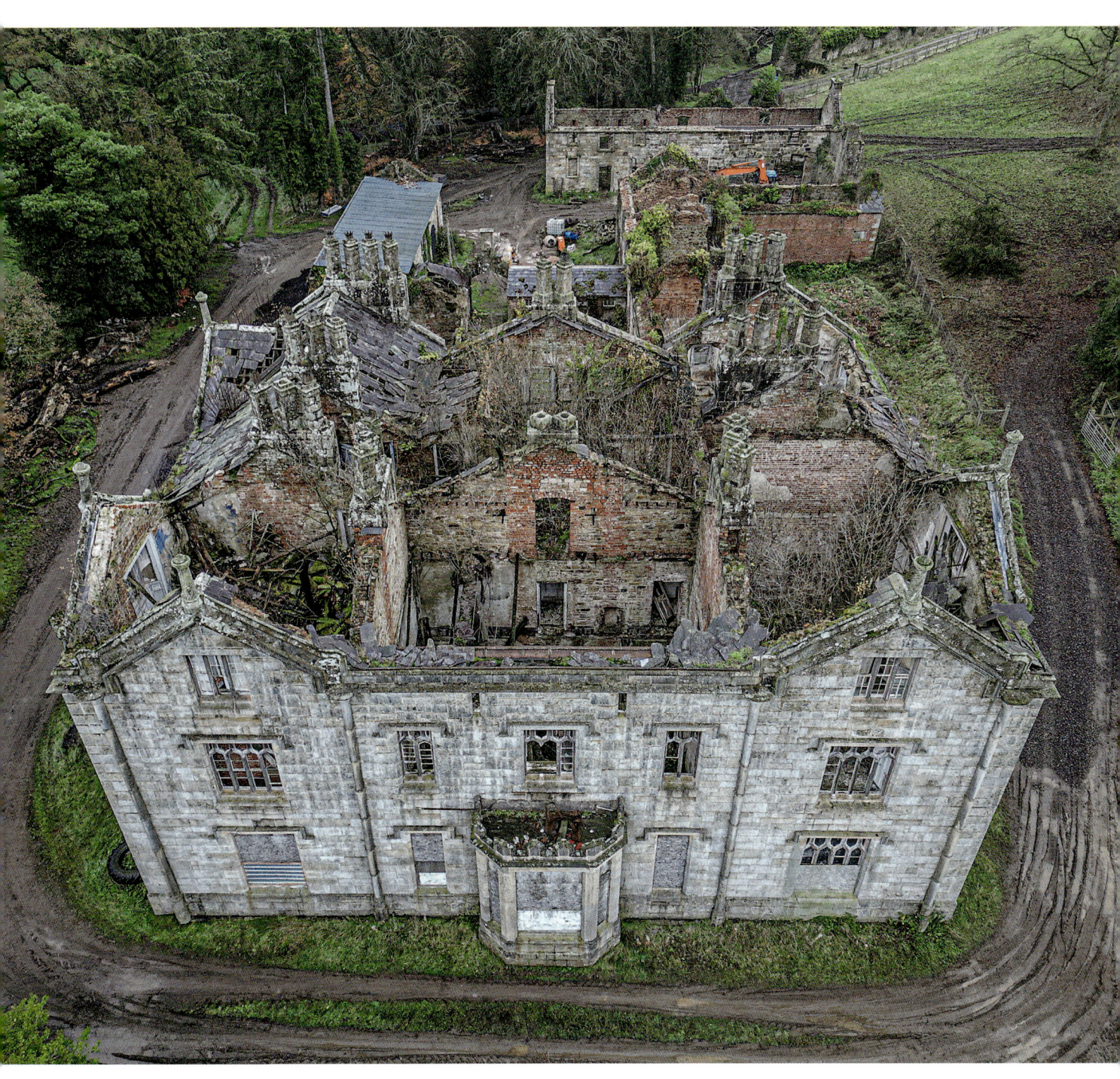

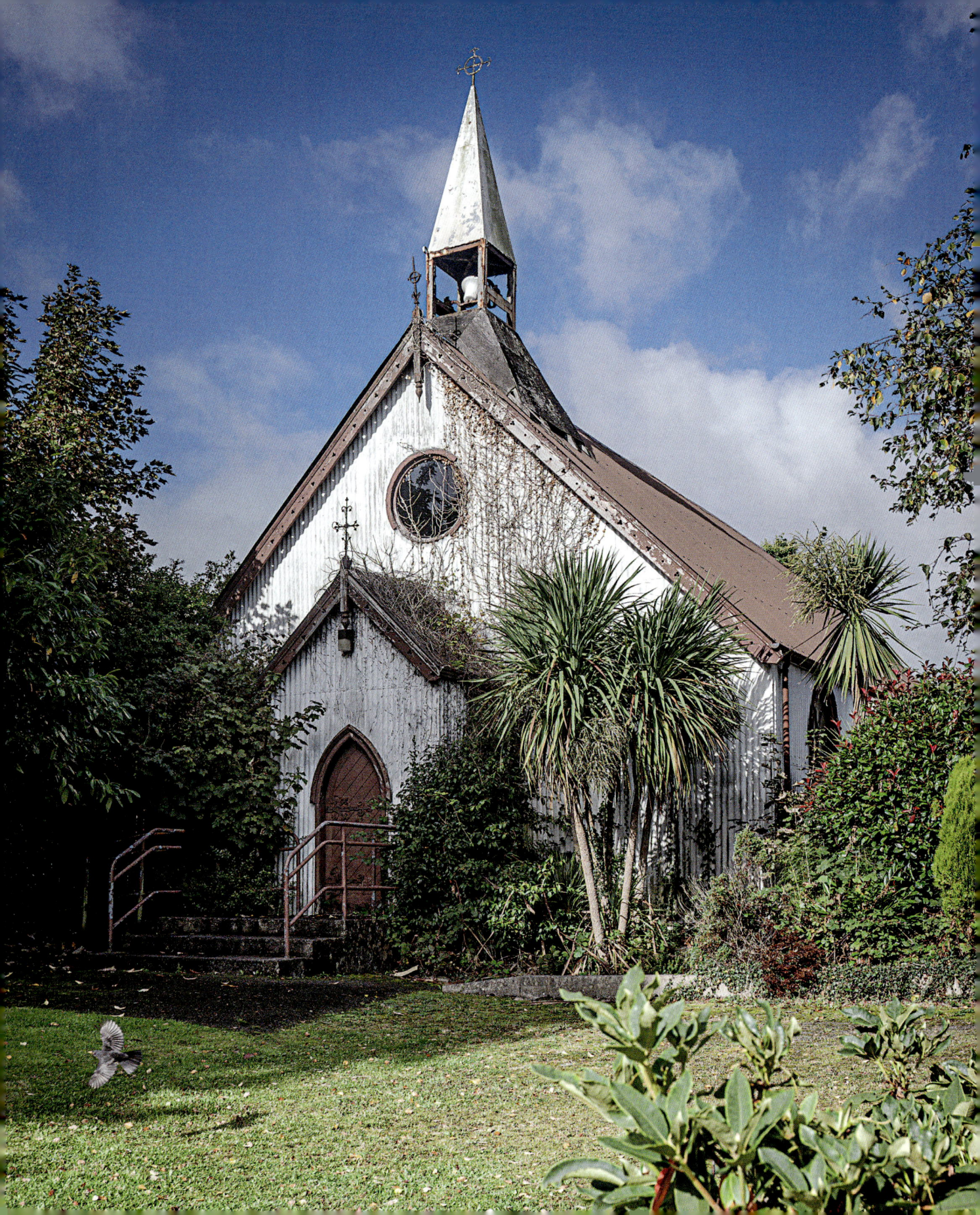

# THE WEE TIN CHURCH

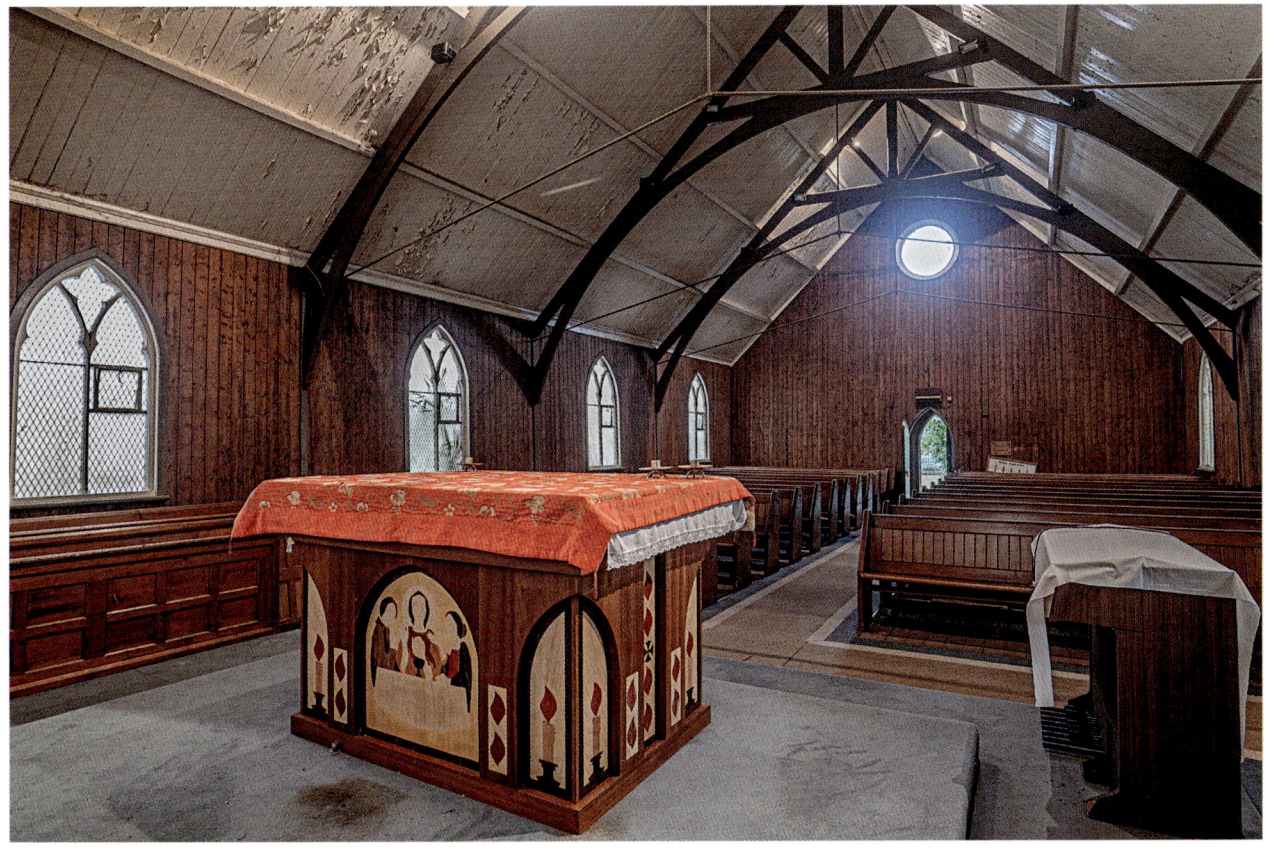

Known by locals as the 'wee tin church', you might mistake this as something from a scene in America or the set of *Little House on the Prairie*. However, this abandoned church is actually located in Belfast.

What makes this church unique is that it is made entirely of tin, one of only a few remaining in Ireland. Another notable example is St Peter's in Co. Monaghan, which is still fully operational. In the 1800s it was a popular trend to build tin structures, including churches, from flat-packed kits.

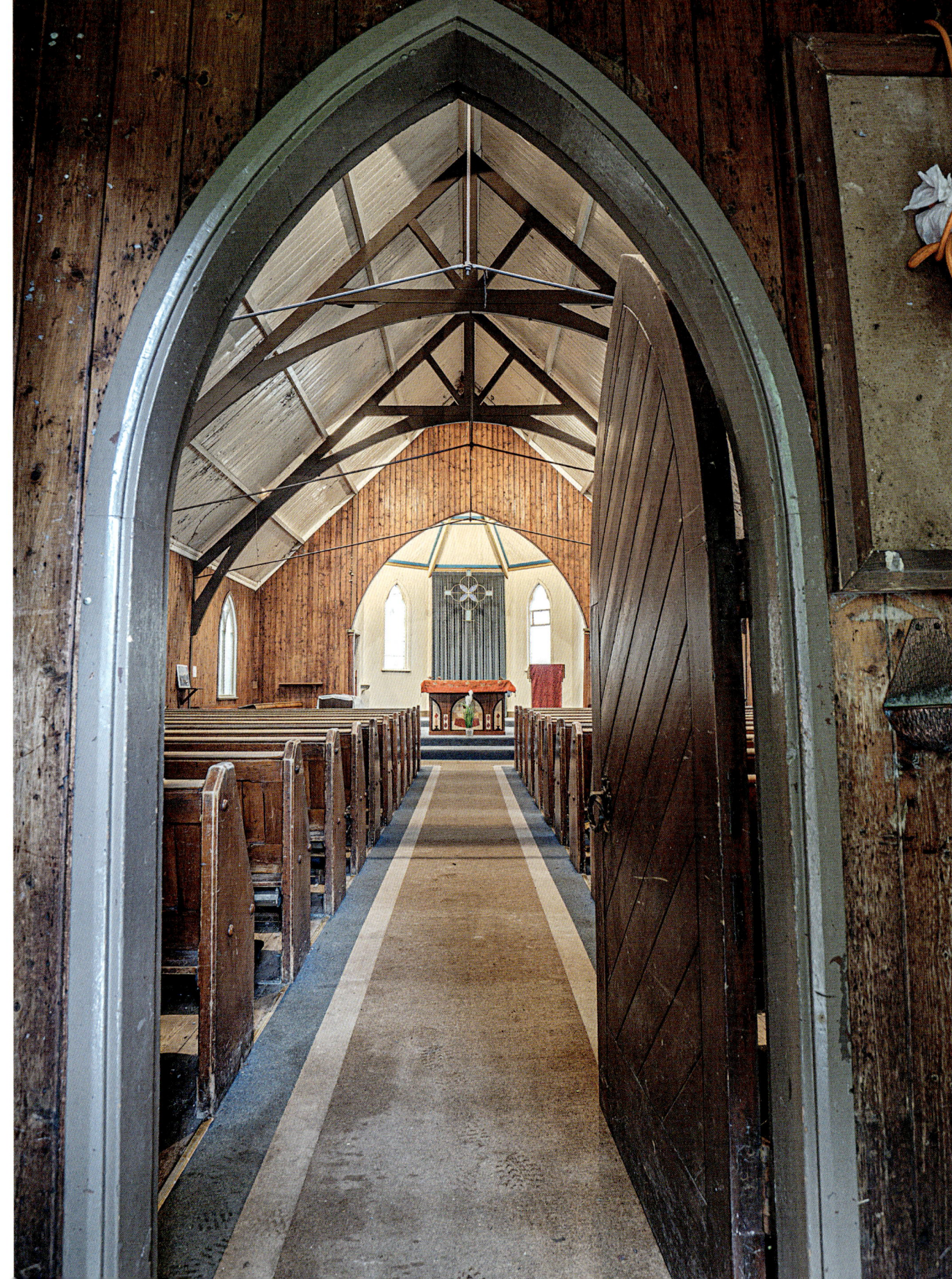

This made them relatively affordable and easy to assemble. Shipyards such as Harland & Wolff, which was responsible for building *Titanic*, produced these kit buildings, which were shipped worldwide and proved especially popular in America.

This church first opened for worship in 1892 as a Church of Ireland and was initially named St Luke's. The church was closed in 1969 due to changing demographics and then, in February 1970, was reconsecrated as a Catholic church and renamed St Matthias'. The church was a popular venue for weddings, for both parishioners and those living outside the parish. This was probably because the quaint little building with its small bell tower would make a great backdrop for any wedding photo.

In 2004 a newer, more modern church was built to accommodate a growing congregation and to provide a modern church for future generations. There were also concerns about the deterioration of the tin structure. Opposition to plans to demolish it means the 'wee tin church' remains on site to serve as a permanent reminder of the history of the parish.

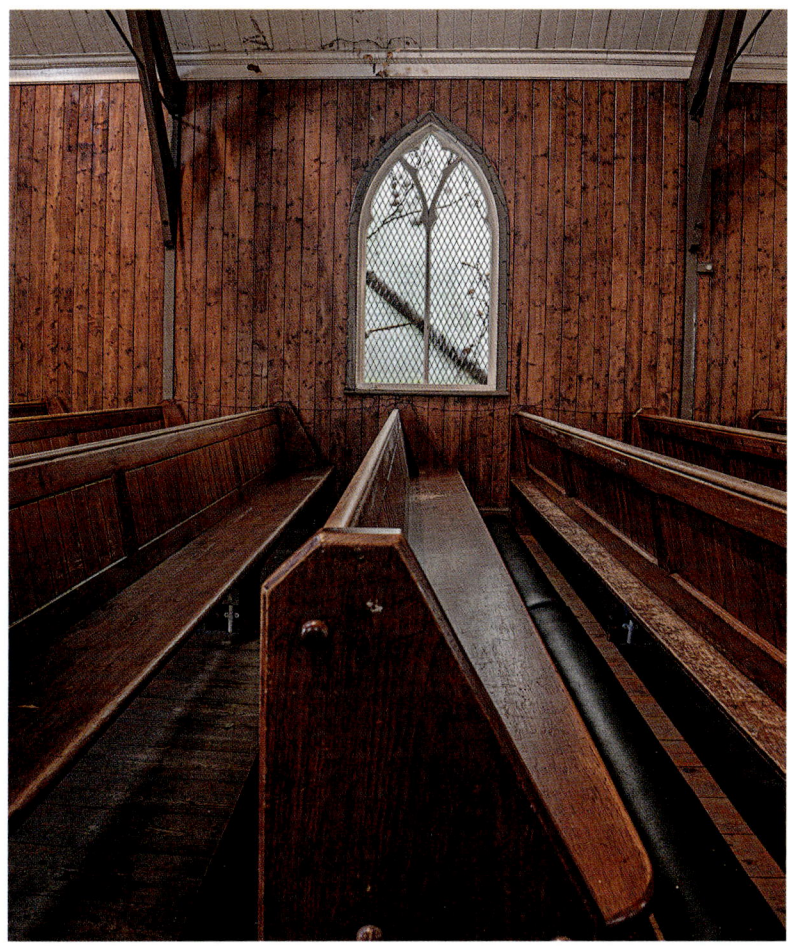

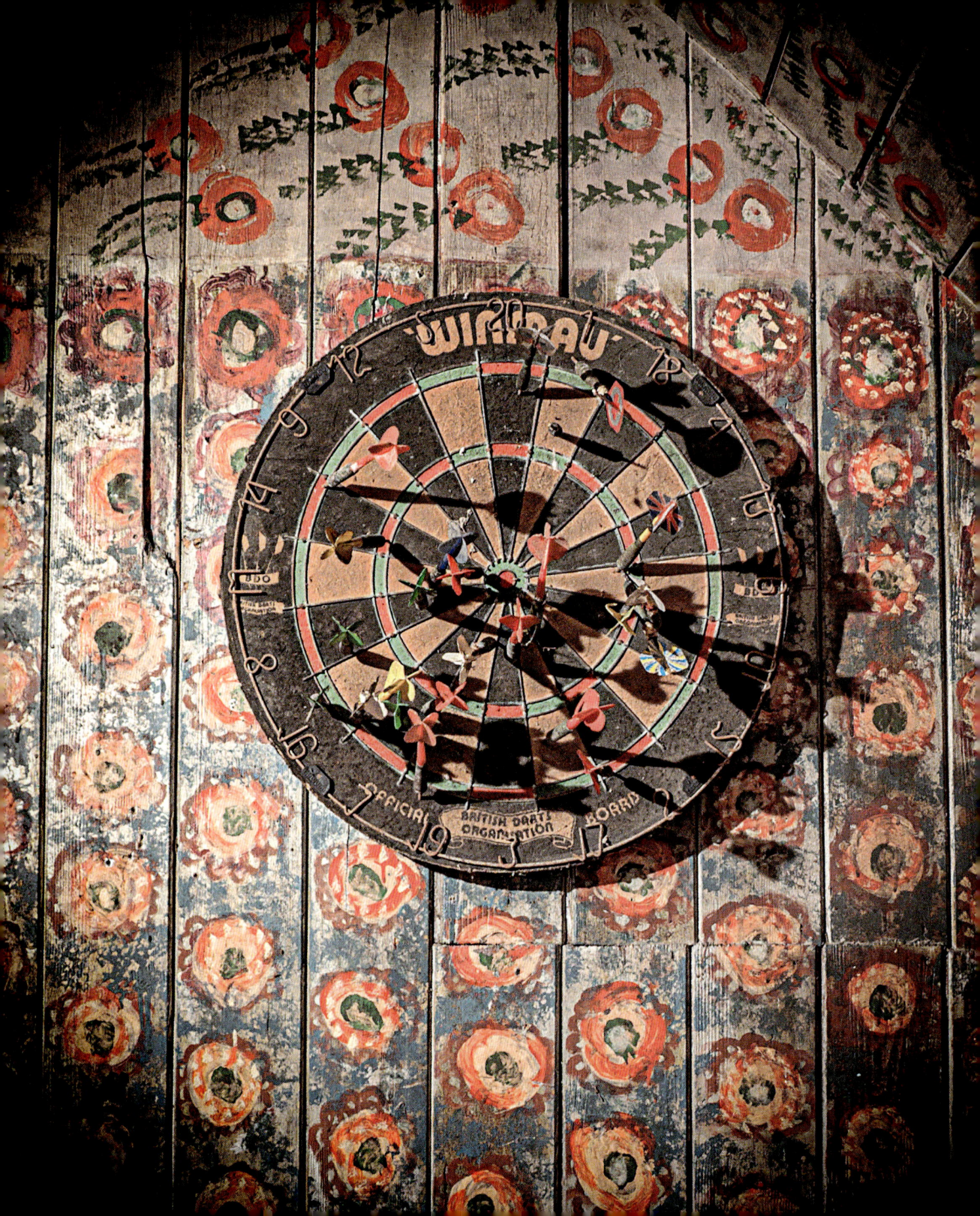

# MICK MURPHY'S COTTAGE

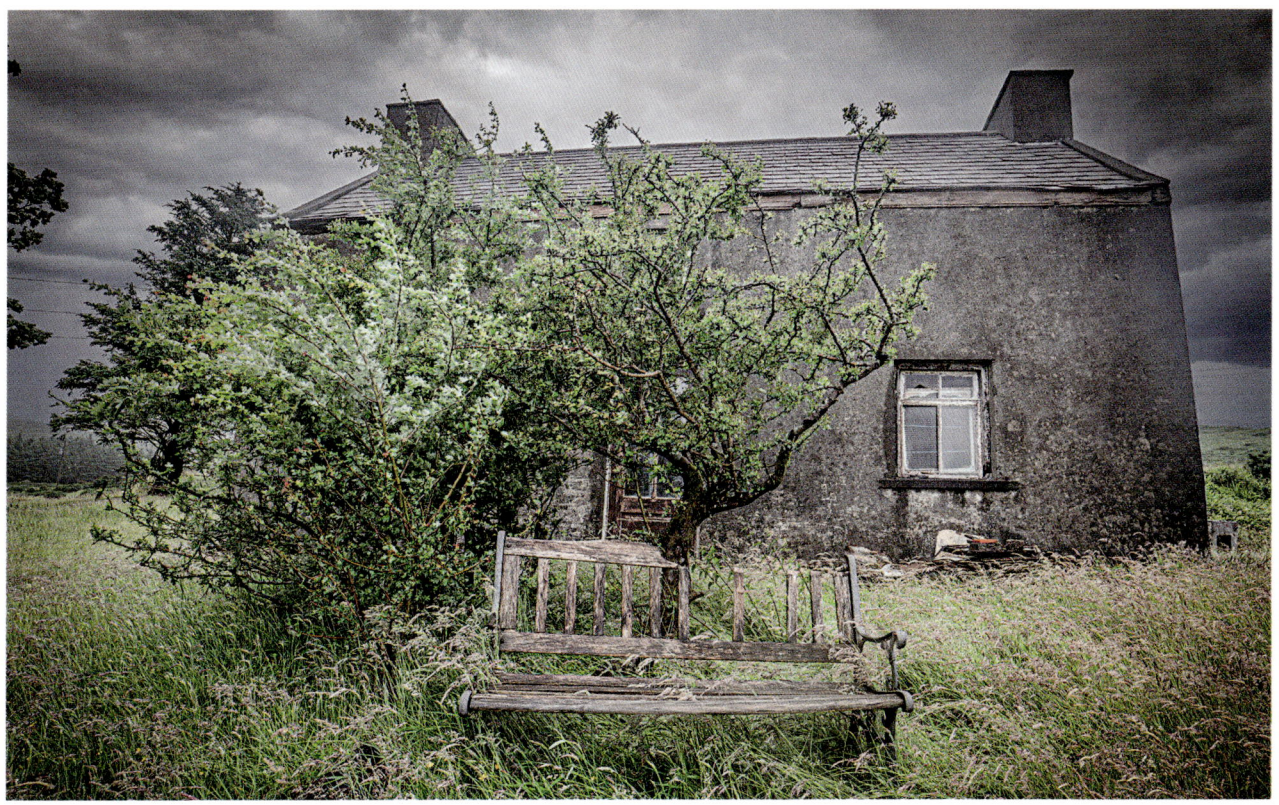

If there ever was a house that could inspire me to write a book, it would be this one, and that is all to do with its owner, Mick Murphy. I first heard about Mick one day when I was in Bridge Books in Dromore, Co. Down, signing copies of my first book. A man came into the shop and introduced himself to me as Kieran Murray. As we chatted, Kieran mentioned a man from Co. Kerry whom he had photographed years ago, known as the 'Iron Man'. He told me that this man had won the Irish cycling race the Rás Tailteann back in the 1950s and had a unique training regimen that involved

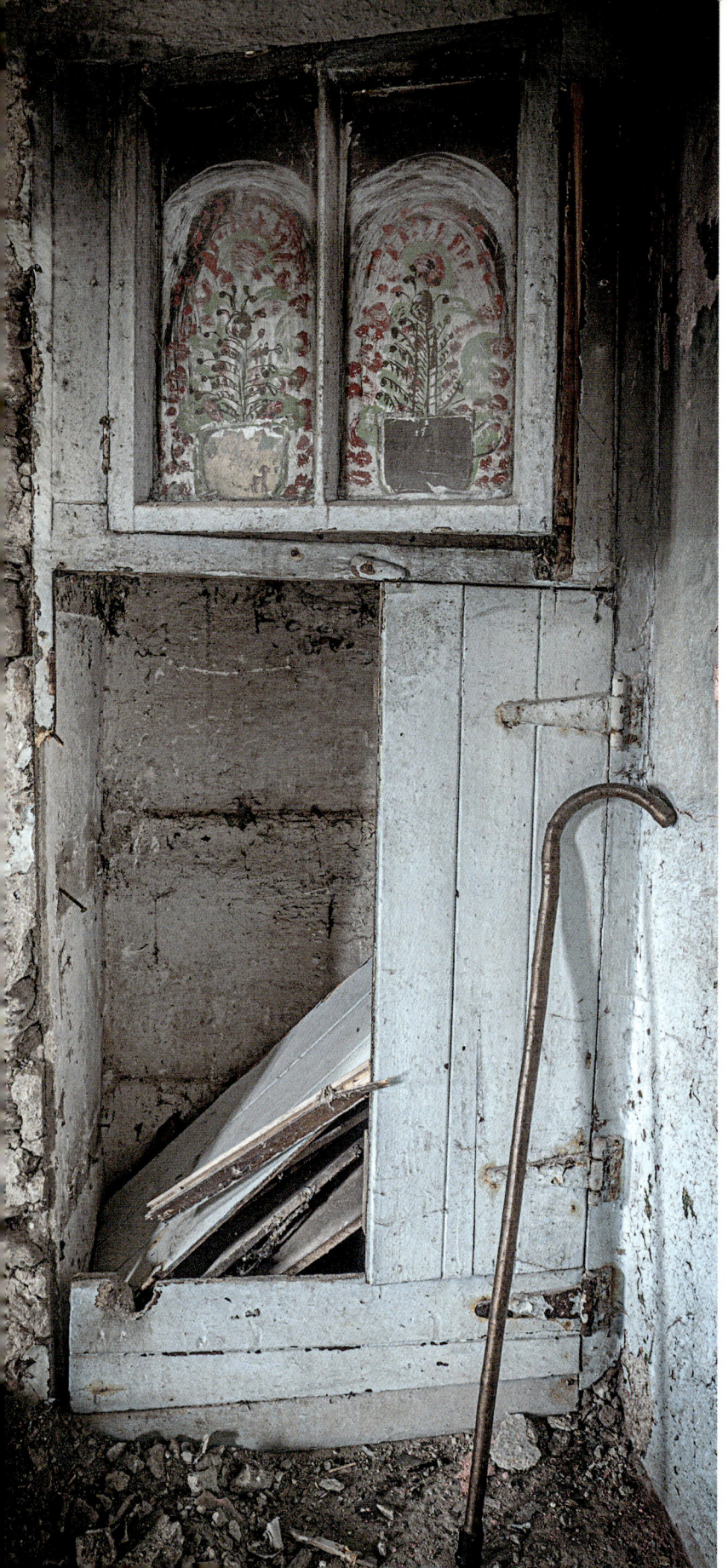

drinking cow's blood by nicking the animal's vein with his penknife and drinking it straight from the source.

I was intrigued. It transpired that Mick had passed away a few years earlier, but we thought it would be worth contacting his family to see if his house was still standing and if I could visit and learn more about Mick.

Having been given his details, I reached out to Mick's cousin Ciaran. He was able to tell me that Mick's house was indeed still standing, and that he owned it. I explained what I wanted to do and asked if I could meet him to discuss photographing the house. He seemed a bit unsure at first, but eventually agreed, for which I was extremely grateful.

I had never been to that part of Kerry and the scenery was absolutely breathtaking, with the sea and mountains creating a stunning backdrop. The air felt different, almost otherworldly. When I met Ciaran at the local marina, I showed him my book and the other places I had documented. This seemed to put his mind at ease as he began to understand the vision I had for the project involving Mick. He mentioned that the house had been emptied, with Mick's belongings stored away safely. He said that I could look at the house that day, but return at a later date to do the documentation. This would allow him time to place some items back in the house as they were when Mick was alive. This made my day!

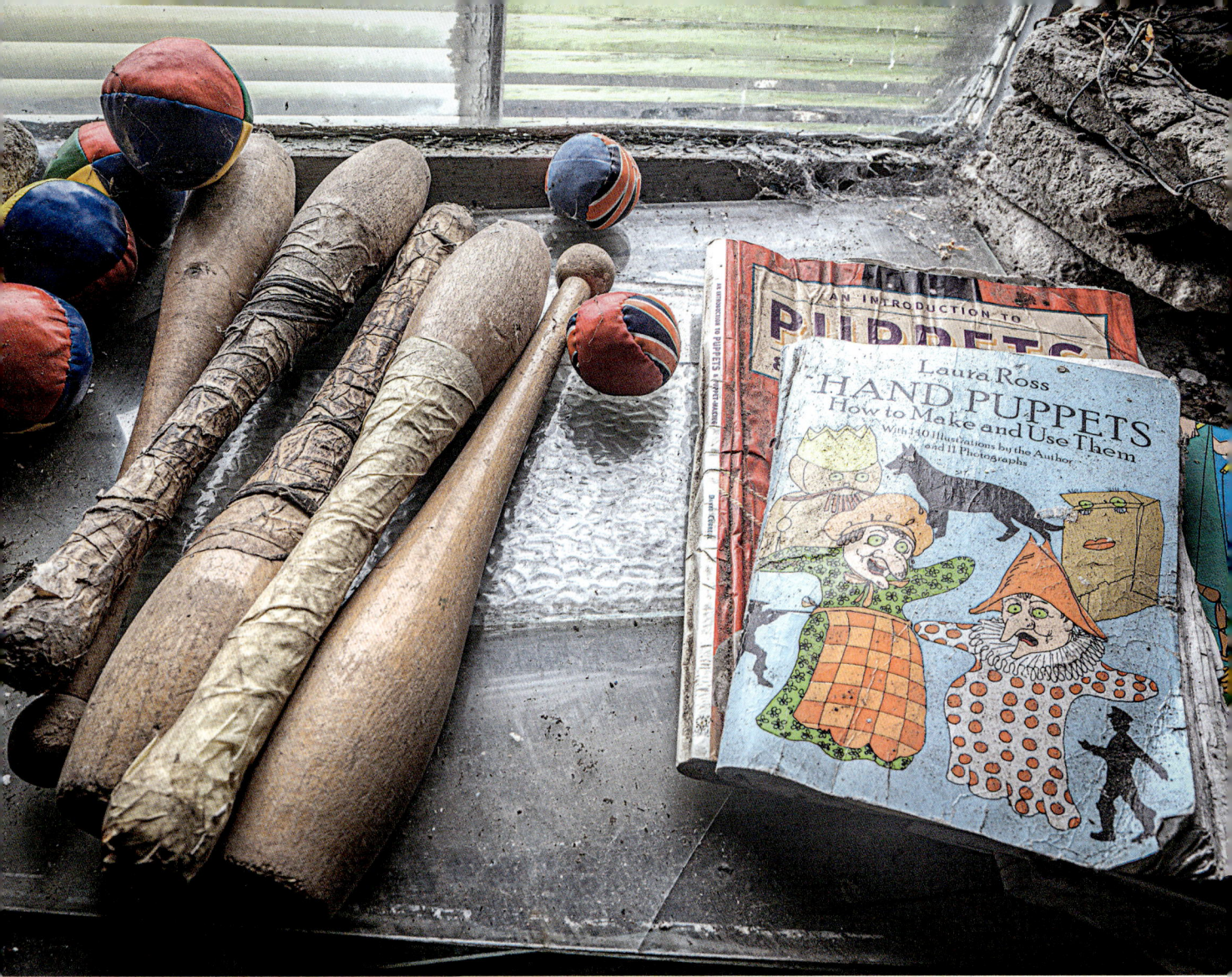

We took a short trip on winding mountain roads to Mick's house. I had read a lot about him online and felt a little emotional when we arrived at his cottage. When you research these properties you can't help but feel a connection to the lives and stories behind them. We stood outside the gate for a while as Ciaran shared stories about his cousin.

Mick had grown up in the house with his parents and a younger brother, who tragically passed away at a young age. His mother homeschooled him, teaching him how to read and write. Mick developed a love for reading, spending hours immersed in books. He was a jack of all trades, teaching himself various skills, including farming, juggling, fire-eating, cycling, wrestling, boxing, running and bricklaying. Whatever he learned, he mastered. As I listened to Ciaran's tales, I absorbed every detail, eager to learn more. I regretted not having had the chance to meet Mick in person, a common feeling when documenting a house.

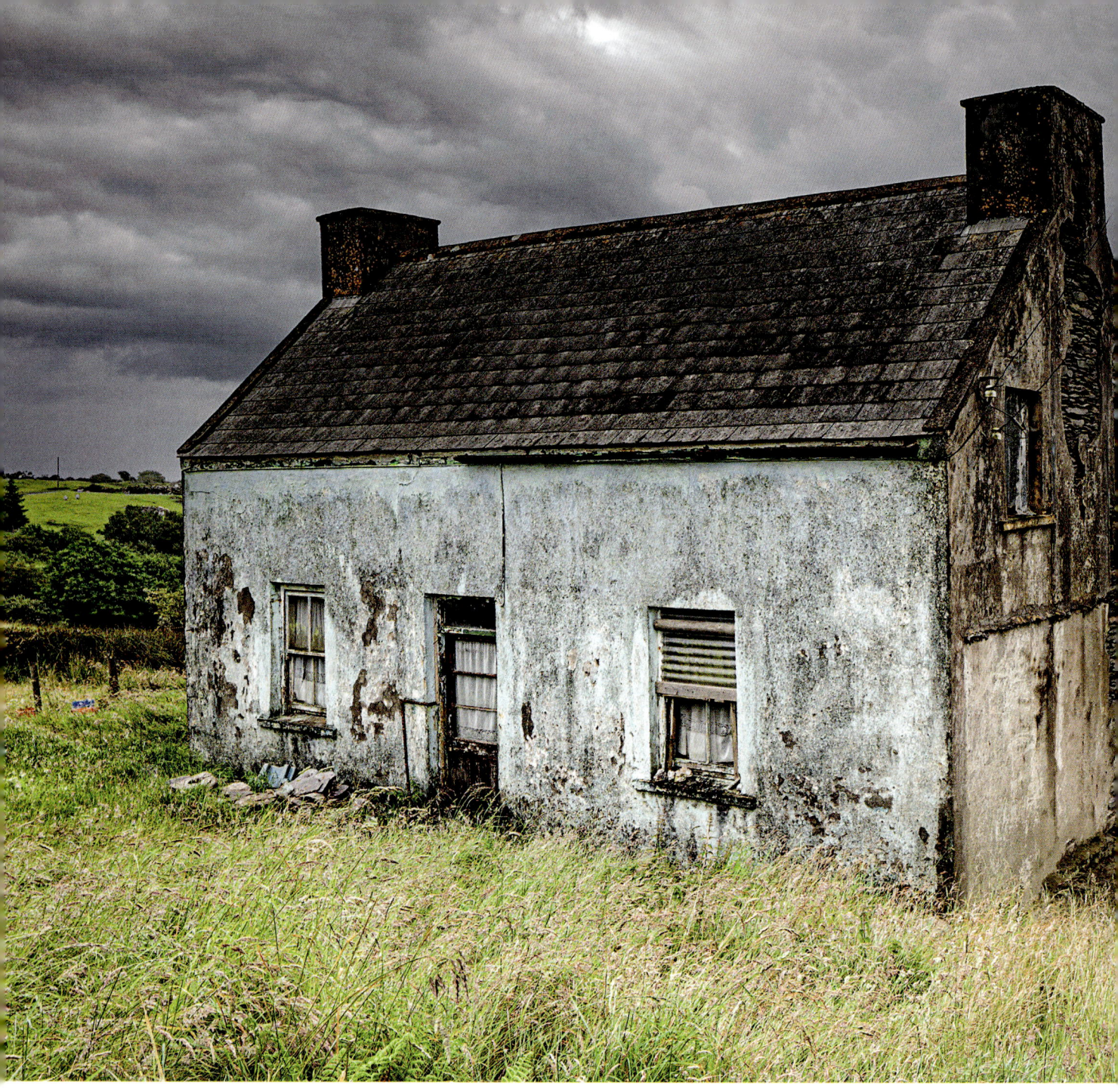

In June, I made my second trip to west Kerry, filled with anticipation. I met Ciaran at Mick's house. As I gazed at some hand-painted designs on the low garden wall, I asked if Mick was the artist, but Ciaran informed me that it was actually Mick's mother who had covered both external and internal walls with her beautiful creations. Intrigued, I couldn't wait to see more.

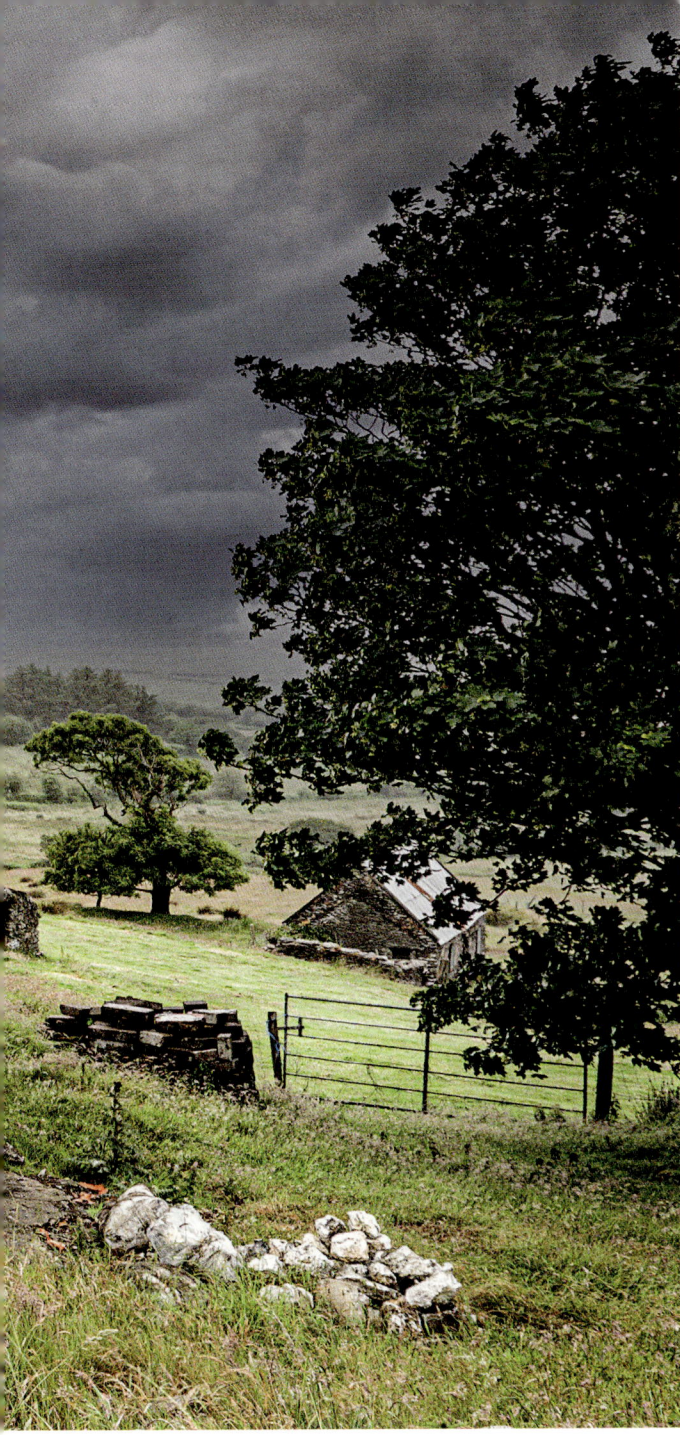

I noticed weights in the living room and various items scattered around, such as books, pictures, a dartboard, juggling sticks and circus balls. It was clear that Mick had a rich and colourful past.

One story that truly showcased Mick's determination and grit was his experience in the famous Rás Tailteann. A talented cyclist, he was leading the 1958 race when his front wheel gave out, forcing him to stop and allowing him to be overtaken by the others. Undeterred, Mick lifted his bike onto his shoulder and began running after the pack. When he came upon a farmer who was watching the race at the side of the road and holding a bike, Mick set down his own damaged vehicle and hopped onto the farmer's. He later said it was a big, awkward, girly-looking bike, but that didn't stop him; he pedalled furiously to catch up with his competitors. He made it to Cork, where his team car met him and he was able to swap the bike for the team spare. With forty miles to go, Mick caught the rest of the pack and crossed the finishing line without losing any time.

But there's more to the story. The following day Mick suffered a serious crash during the fourth stage of the race. He was speeding downhill at 50mph when he hit a bridge and came flying off the bike, injuring his shoulder and suffering a concussion. Another rider offered his bike to Mick, gave him a slap on the chin and said, 'Get on it,' urging him to continue the race. Mick not only finished, but went on to win the race.

I asked Ciaran how Mick had passed. He shared the story with me, and I was not prepared for what

Ciaran opened the door and we stepped inside the modest cottage. Despite its small exterior, the inside was surprisingly spacious. The ground floor had two rooms, with a flight of stairs leading up.

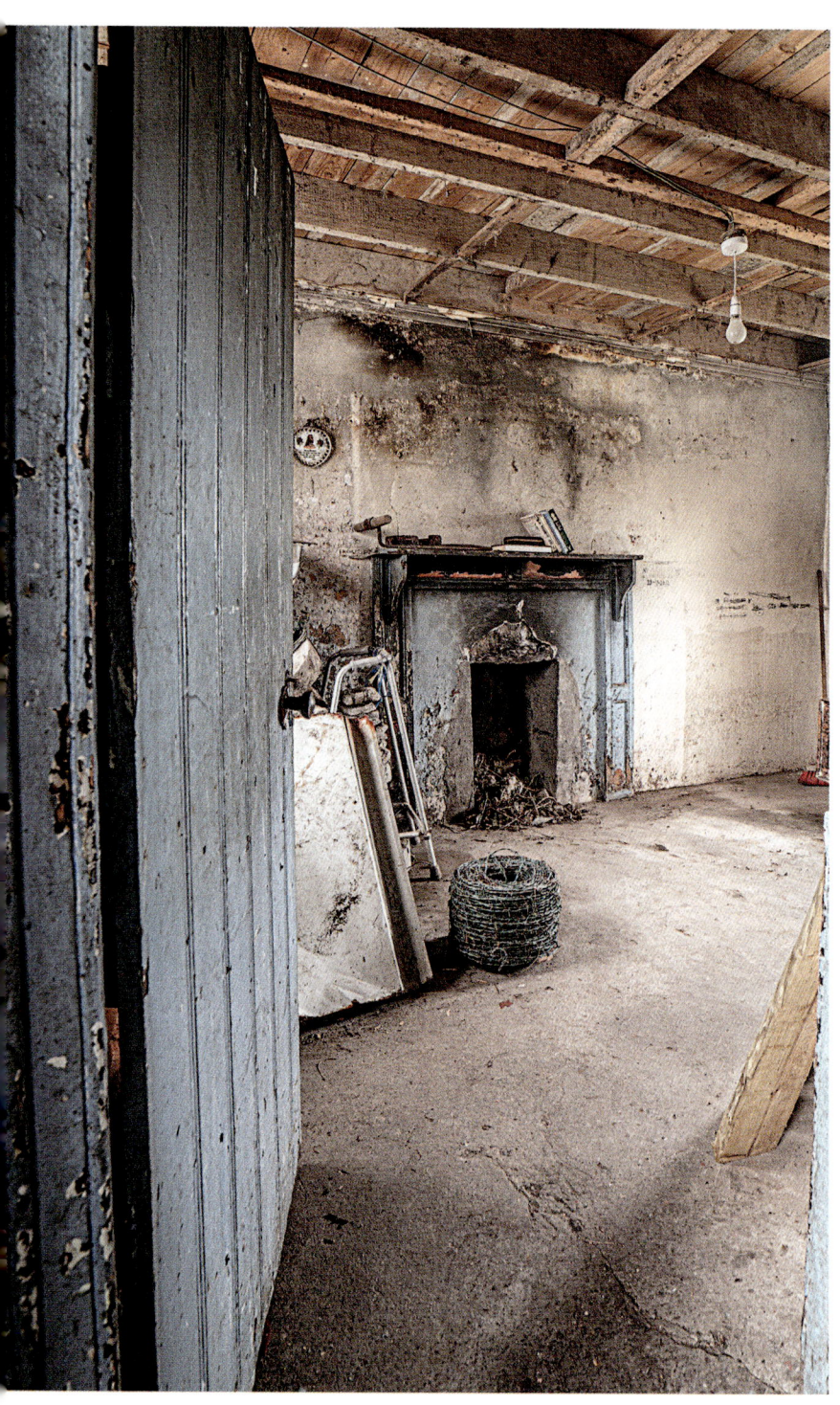

I heard. Mick was best friends with Ciaran's father – they grew up together and were cousins. When Ciaran's father passed away unexpectedly, he drove over to tell Mick the news. Mick was devastated.

On the morning of the funeral Ciaran arrived to pick up Mick, but the front door of the house was slightly ajar and he was nowhere to be found. Despite Ciaran's efforts to locate him, there was no sign of Mick, and the funeral proceeded without him. Ciaran was deeply worried, as this was very unlike Mick, and he called again to the house once the funeral was over. He even phoned the local gardaí to ask if they'd seen him.

Across from Mick's house is a small ruin of a stone house. Ciaran noticed the field gate to this was wide open. His suspicions led him there and he discovered Mick lying behind the stones. He was wearing the same clothes as he'd had on the day he'd heard about Ciaran's father. It seems Mick had gone there after receiving the news and passed away from a broken heart. He was buried near the house in his parents' grave. I paid my respects before leaving.

Visiting Mick's house and learning about his life was an honour, and the experience will stay with me forever. He was truly inspirational; individuals like him are rare indeed. I will always remember my visit to Kerry, and the hospitality and kindness shown to me by Ciaran.

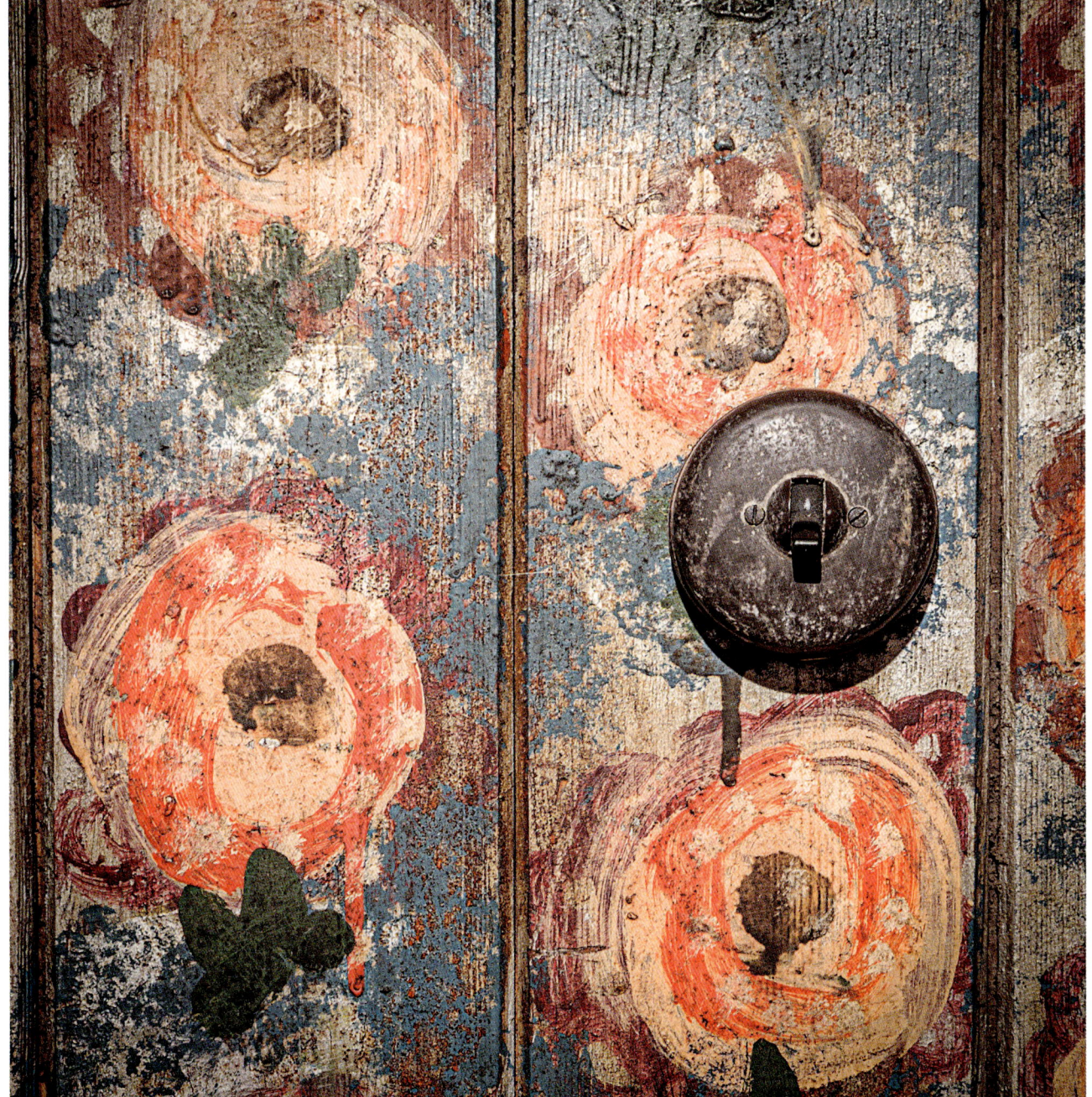

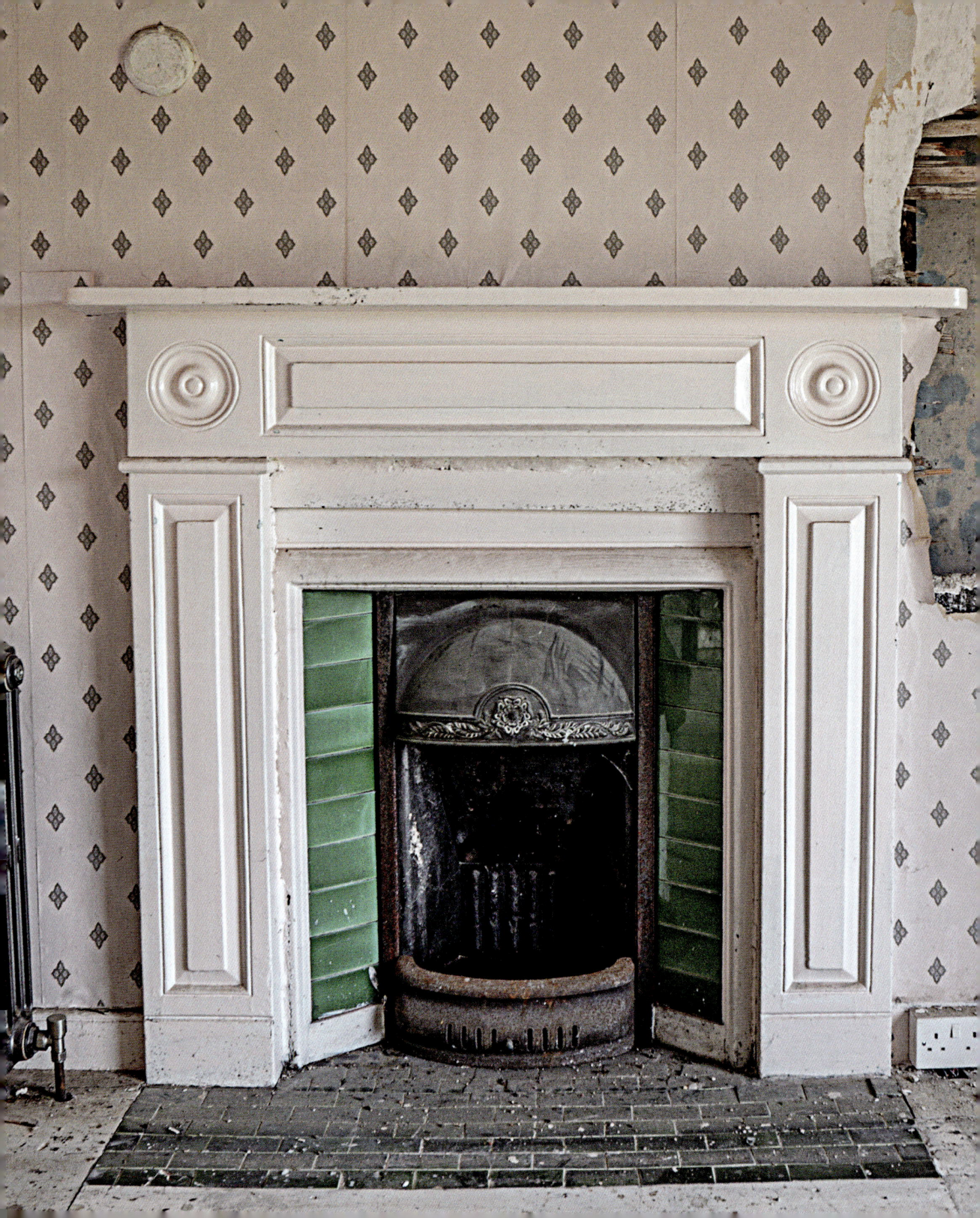

# ASHFIELD HOUSE

Social media, with all its flaws, does have its positive moments. One of those is when the owners of captivating properties reach out to me to document their buildings. It's a chance to capture the essence of a place before it is either demolished or transformed through renovation. Ashfield House was one of those remarkable places.

In early 2023 Judith and Mark Armstrong contacted me through Instagram. They were hoping to acquire a charming period farmhouse in Dromore,

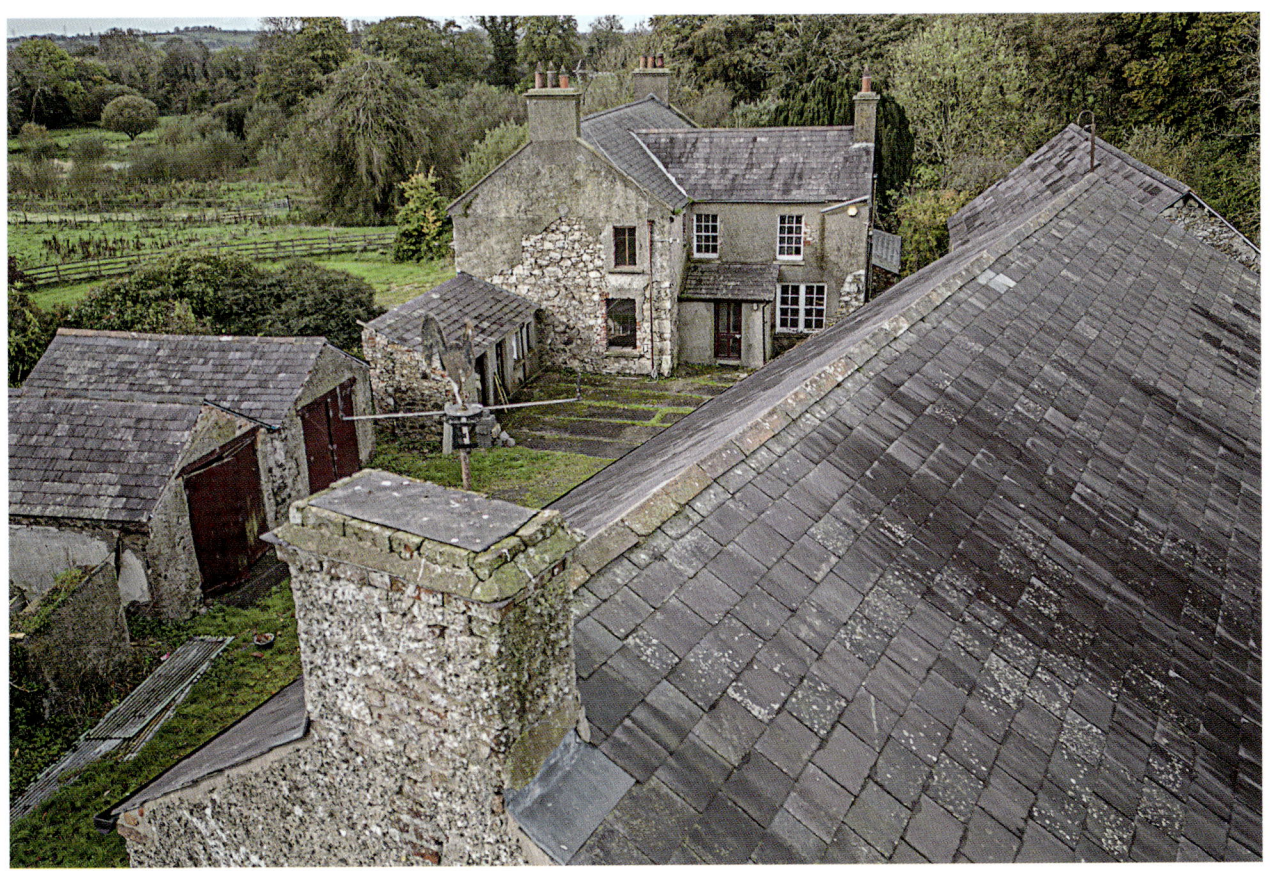

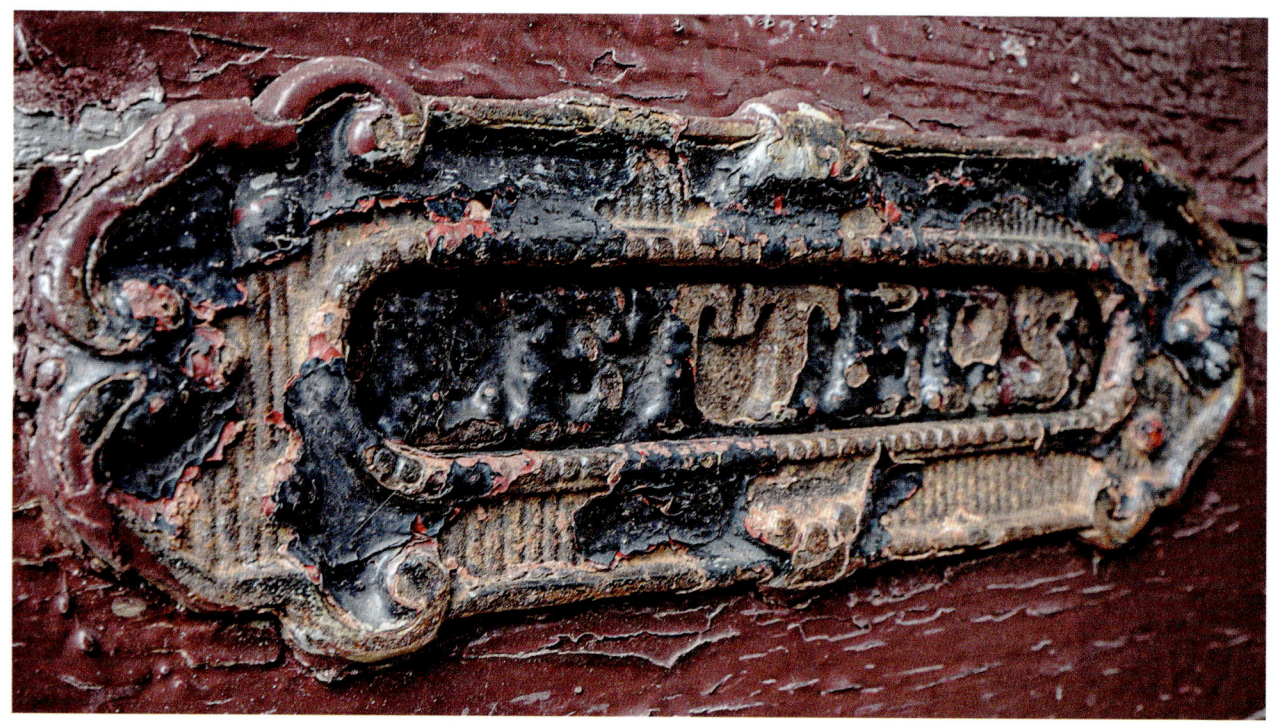

Co. Down, and suggested that if the sale were successful, I could document the property before any work commenced. How could I possibly resist?

Fast forward to a few months later, and the keys to the farmhouse were finally in Judith and Mark's possession. I packed my gear, eager to uncover the mysteries that awaited me at Ashfield. Adding an extra layer of excitement to this endeavour was the fact that I was familiar with the house and its neighbouring mill, which were not far from my childhood home. For years, I had strained my neck to catch a glimpse of Ashfield as I passed by, hoping someday for an opportunity to set foot inside.

As I arrived at the estate, camera gear in hand, I met Judith at the entrance, ready to embark on our journey through its rooms. Remarkably, the house had been abandoned for a mere two years, but the previous owner had stripped it down to its very core, leaving only the bare bricks and exposing the earth below by removing the floors. It seemed as though plans for renovation had been in progress but weren't seen through. This led Judith and Mark to take on the challenge and forge their own path for Ashfield.

As Judith and I made our tour of the house, she unveiled its fascinating history. According to records, the house was constructed before 1760 by David Lindsay, a prominent figure in the Upper Bann's linen industry. Lindsay's family came from Scotland and were direct descendants of men who had been sent as part of General Monro's army to fight against the Irish in the rebellion

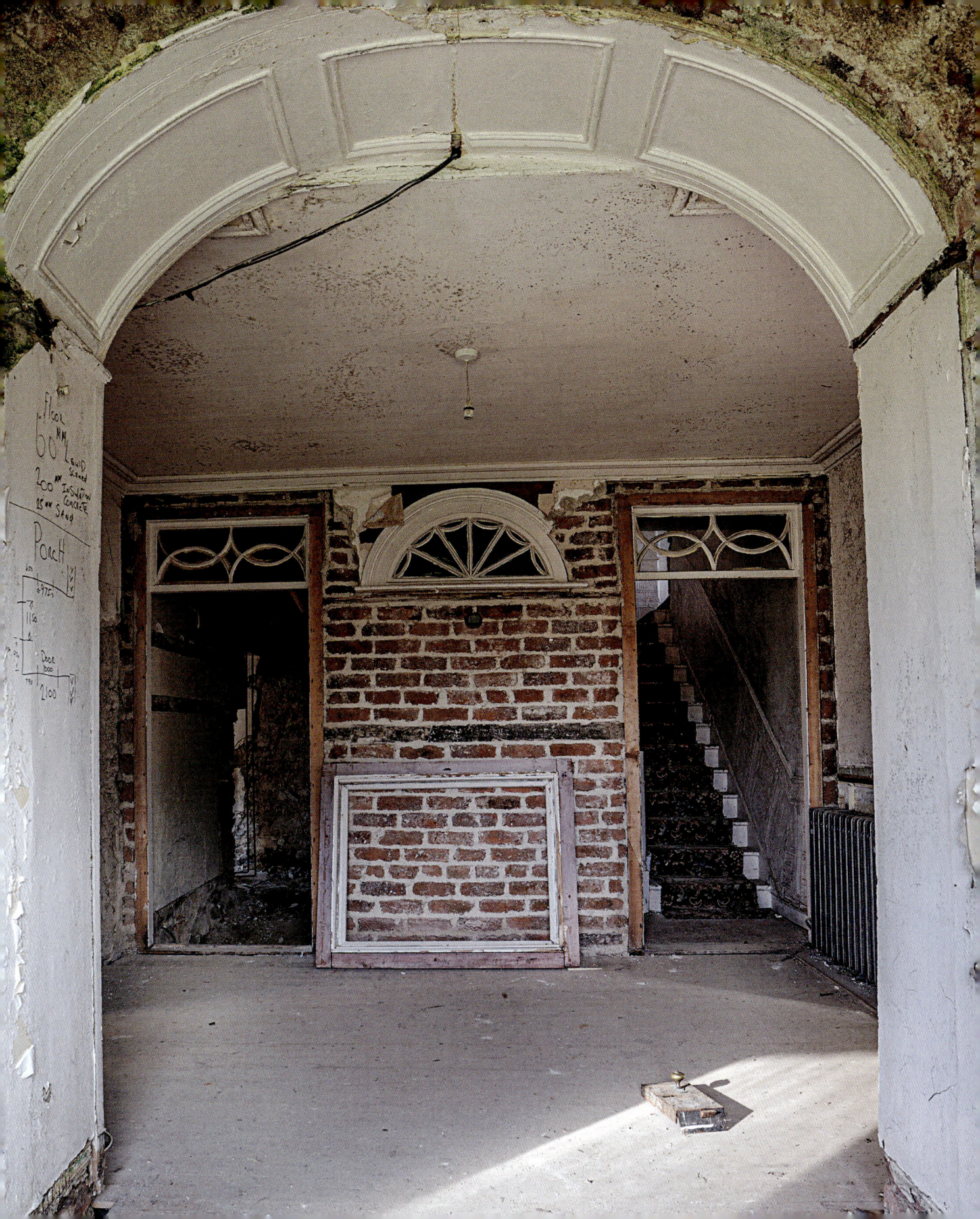

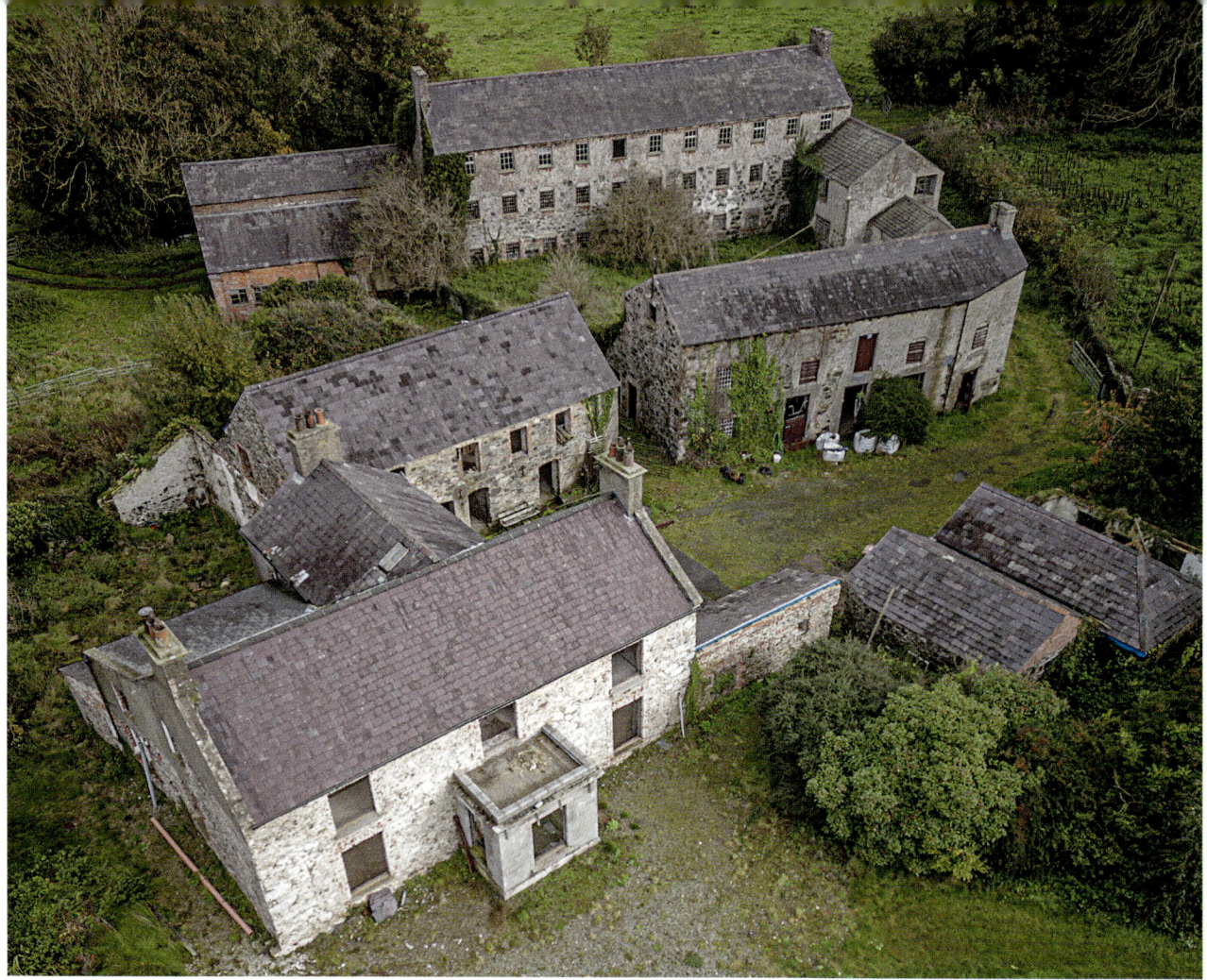

that began here in 1641. After Lindsay's death, the estate passed to his son, Maurice, an entrepreneur with a keen eye for business, who had established a thriving textile enterprise in the early 1820s. Maurice specialised in crafting heavy fabrics using traditional hand looms, employing a vast workforce of weavers who predominantly worked locally from their own homes.

However, it wasn't long before Maurice recognised the need for expansion. Hence, a magnificent three-storey mill was constructed directly behind the house, which became renowned for its expertise in the art of 'hemstitching'. This innovative establish-

ment quickly became the talk of Dromore, capturing the attention of locals and visitors alike.

Regrettably, fate would take a sombre turn a couple of decades later when Maurice passed away, leaving his grand estate up for auction. This took place at the Downshire Arms in Banbridge, a venue that still thrives today, and as a result the site would find a new guardian in a man named John Moore. Down went the hammer and the baton was passed; a new chapter in the house's story began.

John was a widower and he lived on the estate with one of his daughters. He served as a justice of the peace for County Down and was responsible for the addition of a small holding cell at the back of the property. The estate boasted not only the holding cell, but also two cow houses, a dairy, piggery, barn, forge and laundry room. By 1922 John had passed away, leaving the house to one of his daughters.

Ashfield house and mill then came under the ownership and occupation of Captain George Coey. Coey was also a justice of the peace and it can be assumed that he made good use of the holding cell and the stables, given his impressive skills as a horseman. In fact, he even met his wife at a local hunt. Coey passed away in 1969 and left the estate to his daughter, Mary, who had married a respected doctor named McBride. The couple and their son, John, lived happily on the estate for many years.

Ashfield is now at the start of another exciting chapter in its history, with the Armstrongs at the reins.

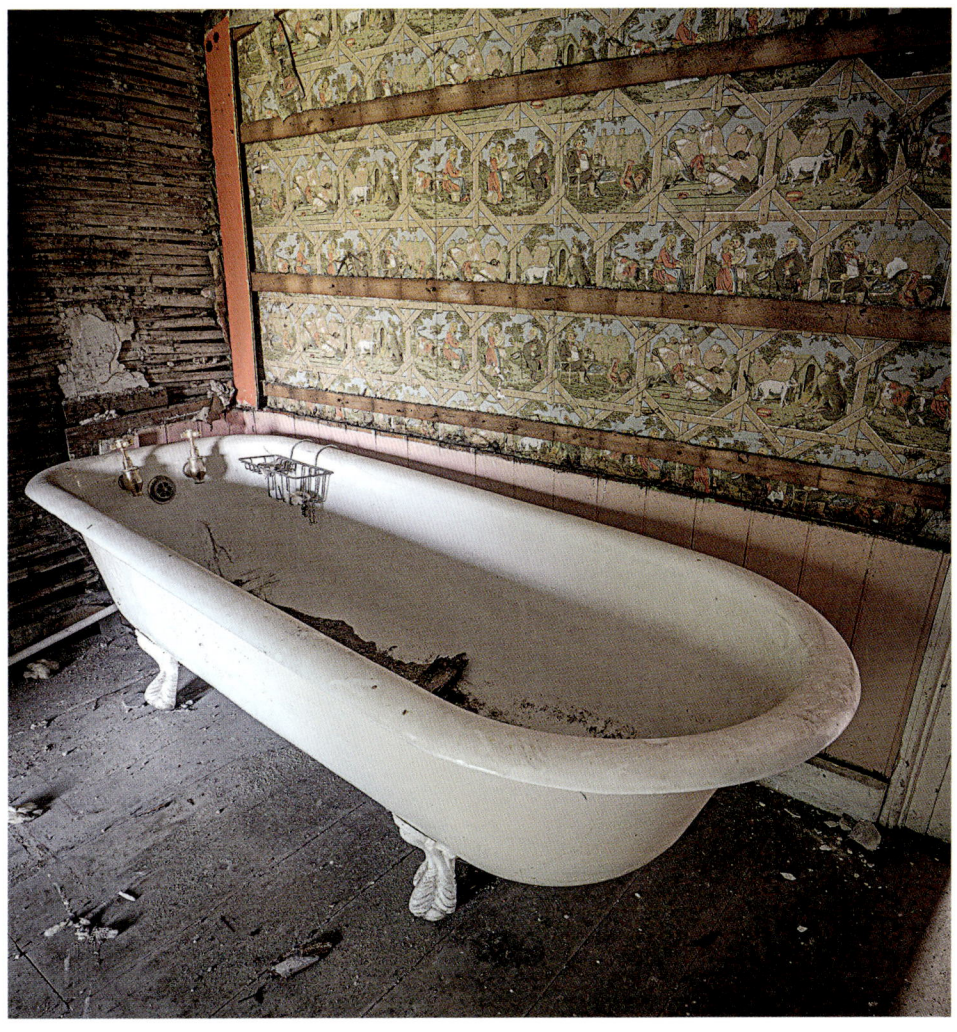

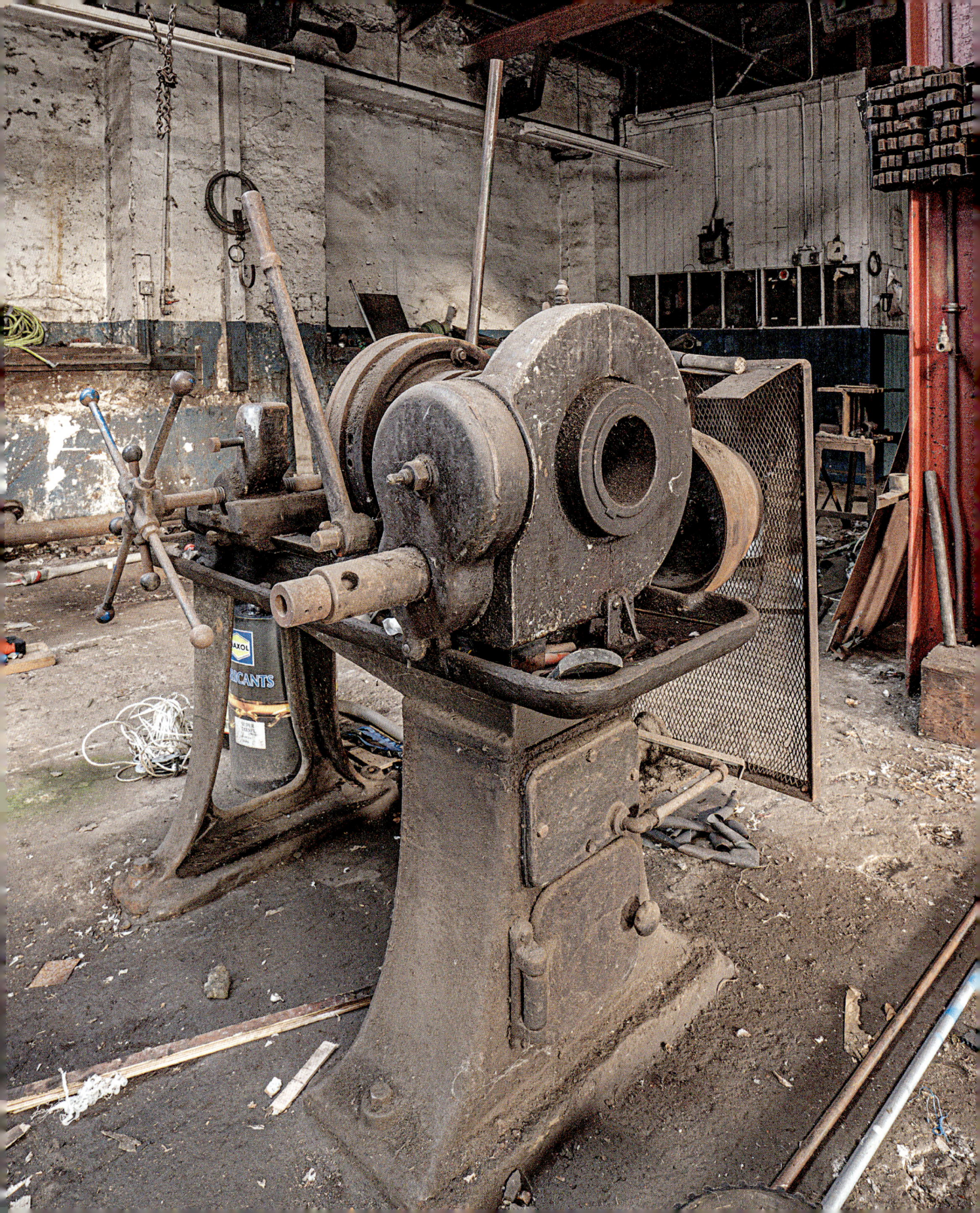

# CLARK'S MILL

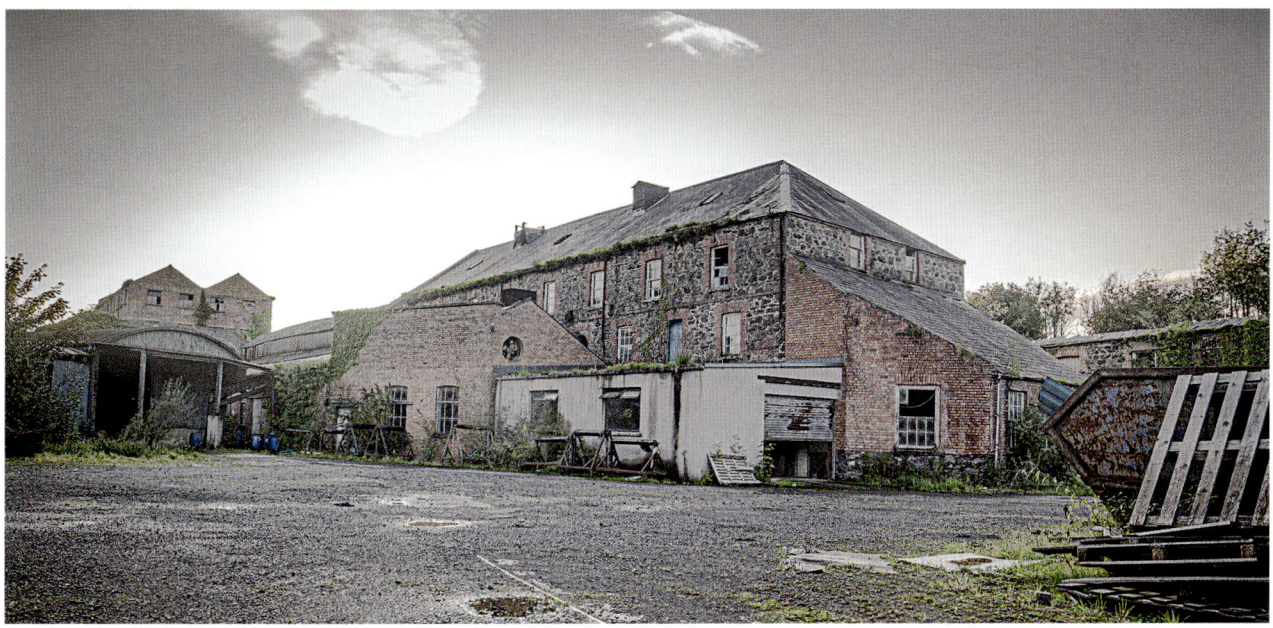

I am always discovering new mills to document and explore, probably because Ireland was one of the largest exporters of linen in the world. We were renowned for our production, with many families and homes relying on the industry for employment at some point. These mills are a crucial part of our heritage and were once the backbone of our industry. It is a particular joy for me to have the opportunity to record as many of them as possible.

This particular example is located between two dams and is recognised as one of the oldest mills in Ireland, dating back to 1736. It all began with a chance visit to Upperlands by innovator Jackson Clark, who noticed a fast-flowing river that would be an ideal spot for a waterwheel to power a new machine known as the beetling engine. Beetlings, equipped with wooden paddles, would hammer down on the linen to give it a lustrous finish and absorbent effect, perfect for linen dishcloths.

The flax plant thrives in Ireland's wet, fertile

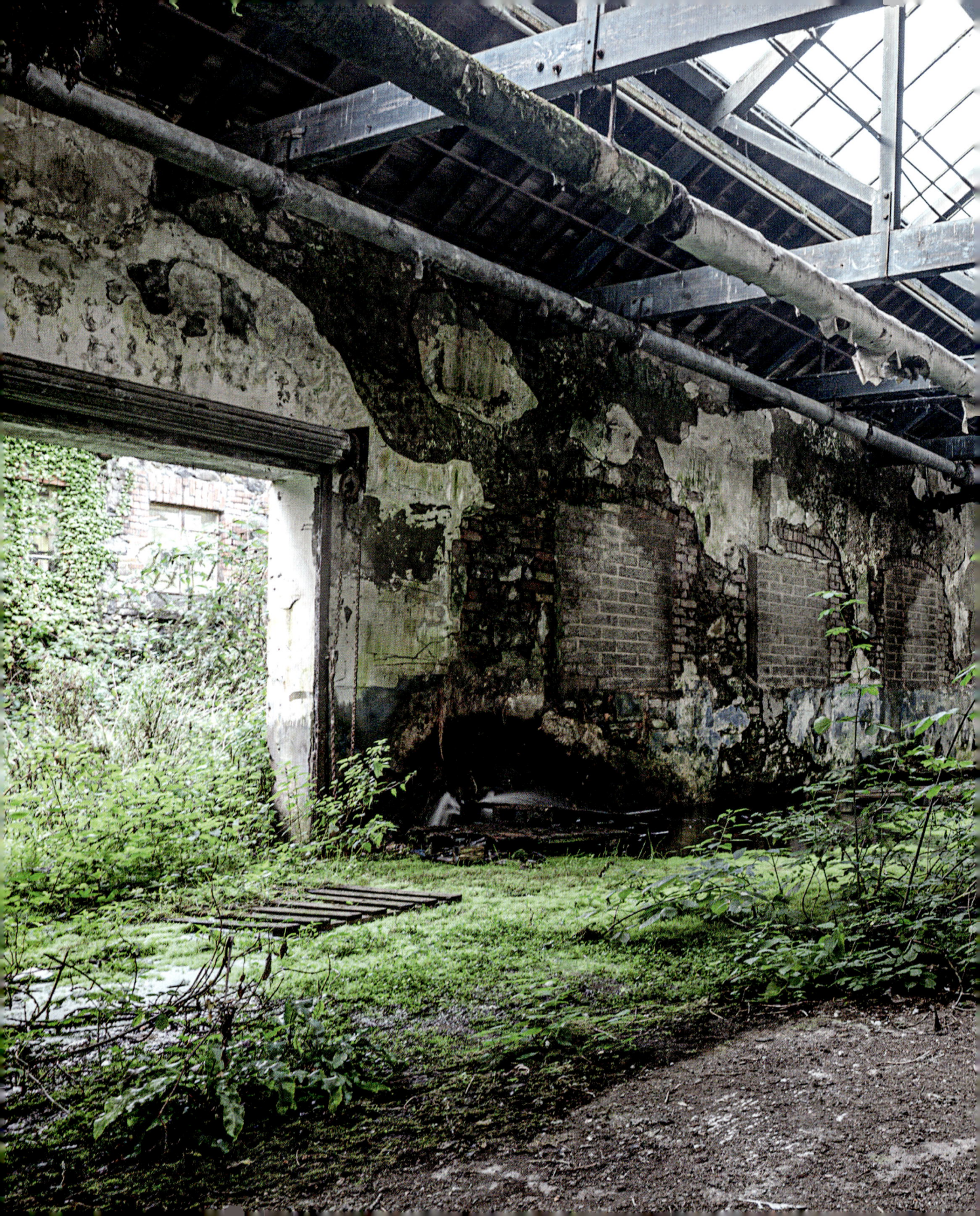

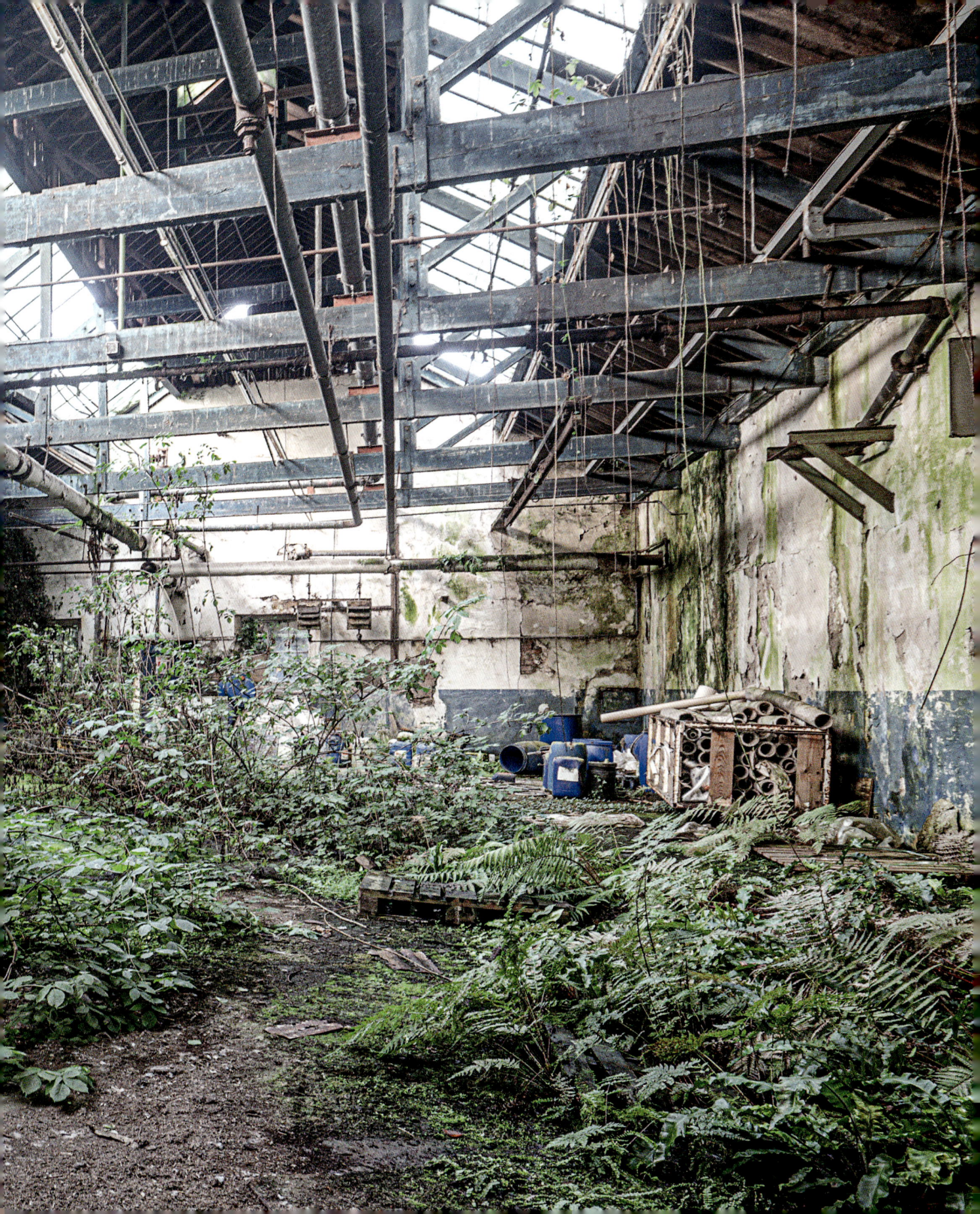

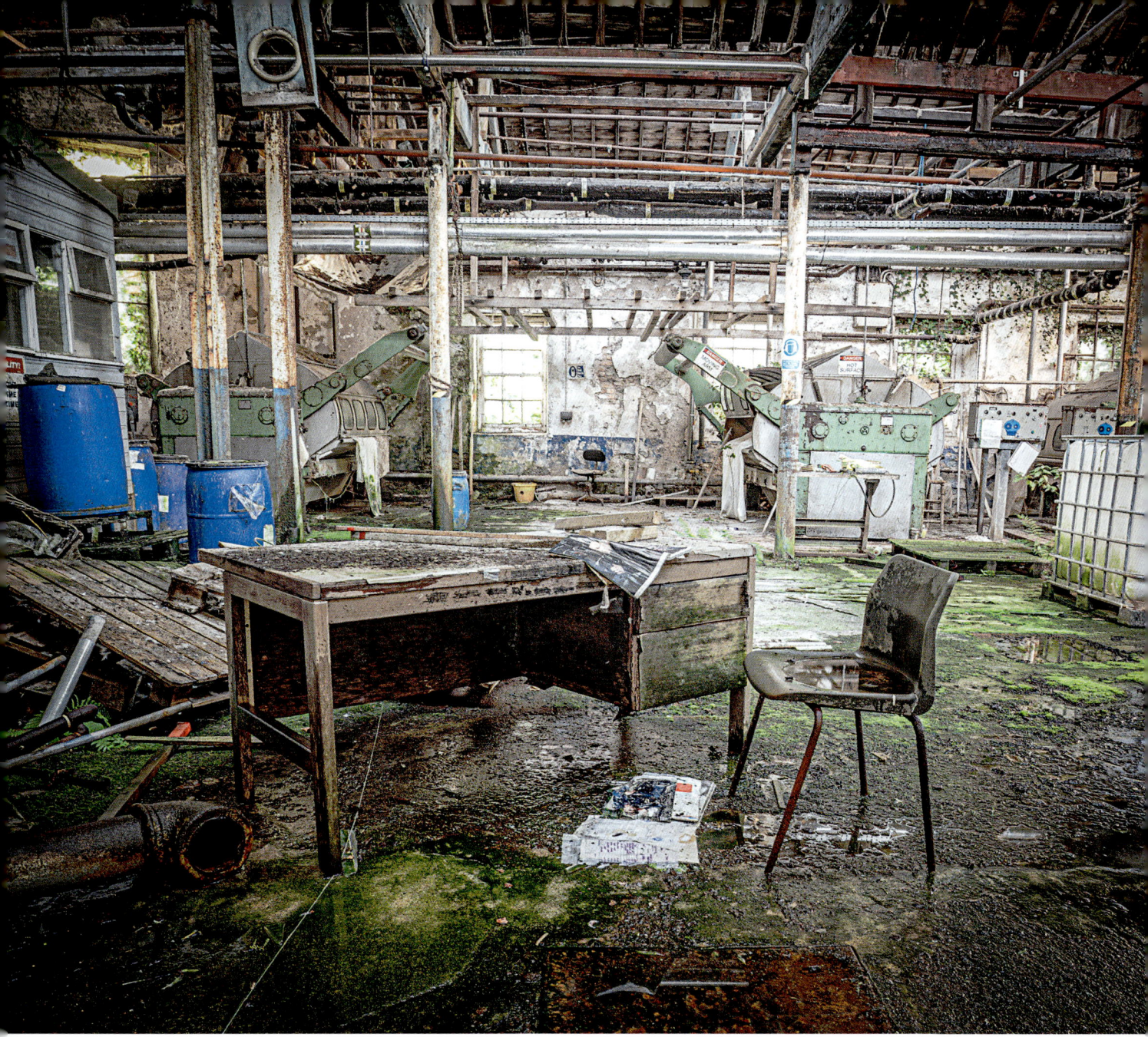

soil, making it the perfect location for linen production. By the late eighteenth century, the linen trade was booming, and the material had become the country's main export. A significant portion of the linen spinning mills were located in Belfast, with the two major mills on York Street and Brookfield accounting for over half of Ireland's linen output and a third of the world's linen supplies.

An intriguing story from Clark's mill involves its chairman of the late 1880s, Henry Jackson, also known as 'Old Harry'. At the tender age of eighteen he ran away to America in search of his fortune but was then persuaded by his father to represent Upperlands linen there. He agreed and secured hundreds of orders, while also embarking on various adventurous escapades, including meeting with an Indian chief, bear-hunting in Quebec and getting to meet President Cleveland in the White House. Upon his return to Ireland, he took charge of the newly established American department, which became instrumental in the growth of the business.

By 1903 the bleaching business had been operating for over 150 years, with continuous improvements. The business had grown to include twenty buildings and had hundreds of local employees. As business boomed, houses were constructed on the surrounding land, forming a community with the mill at its heart. The Clark family lived in residences known as 'the Castles', though they were far from luxurious.

After the Second World War, the linen industry faced challenges, such as competition from synthetic materials and foreign competitors, and rising costs, leading to its decline. However, Clark's remains a successful linen business to this day, now operating from new premises. The Clark's site has recently received approval for planning for a heritage-led project involving renovating the mill buildings and adding some new homes. I'm glad I have this record of the mill and its buildings before work begins.

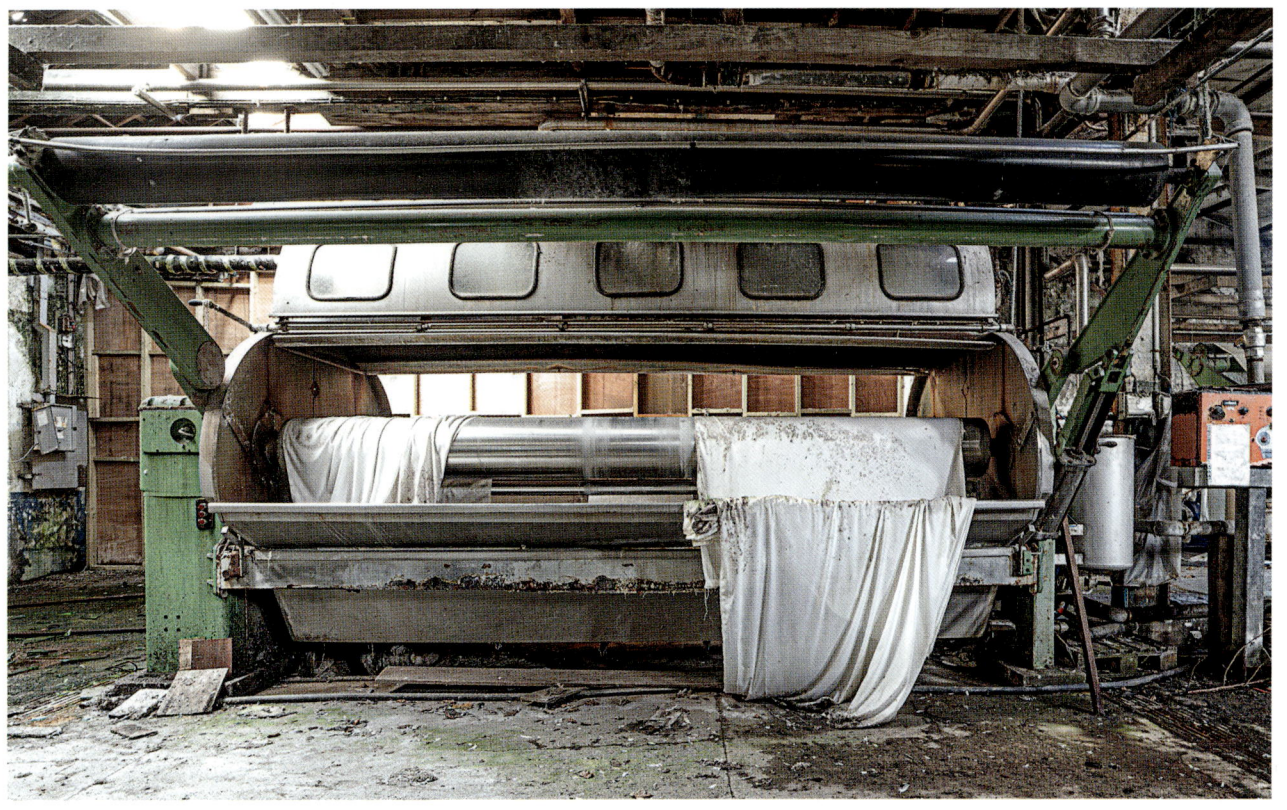

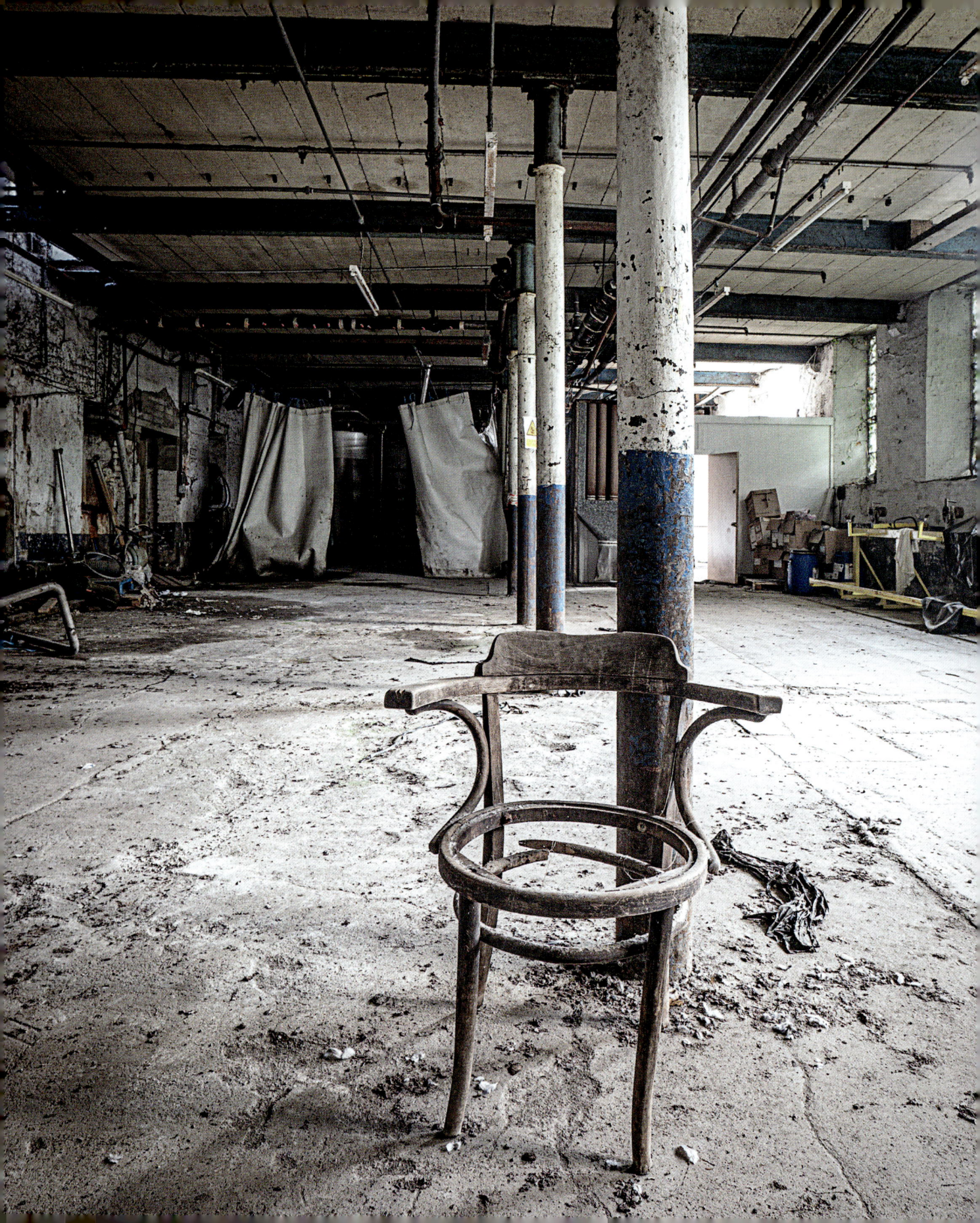

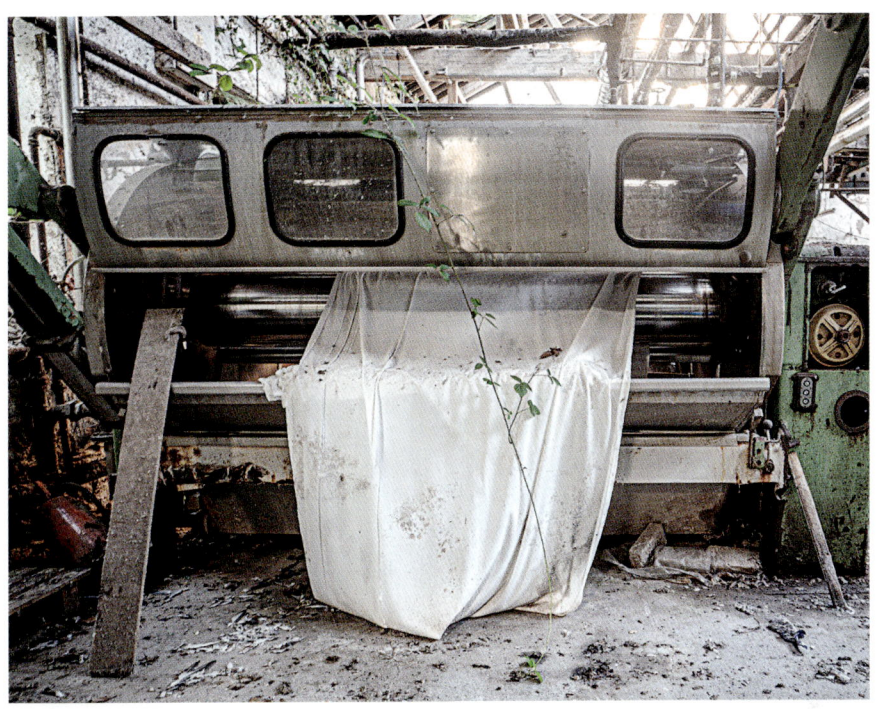

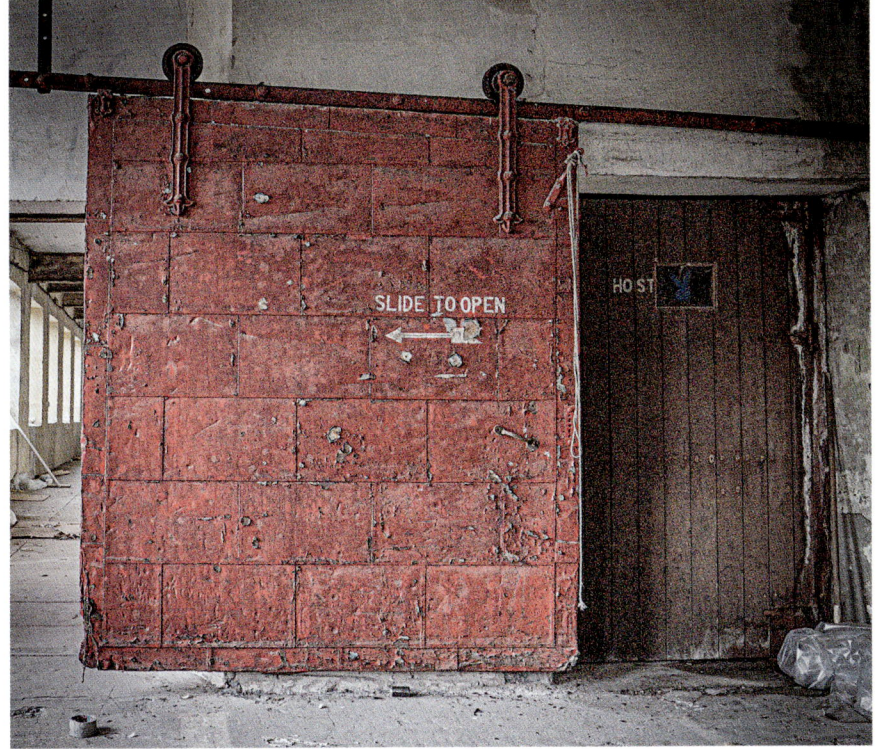

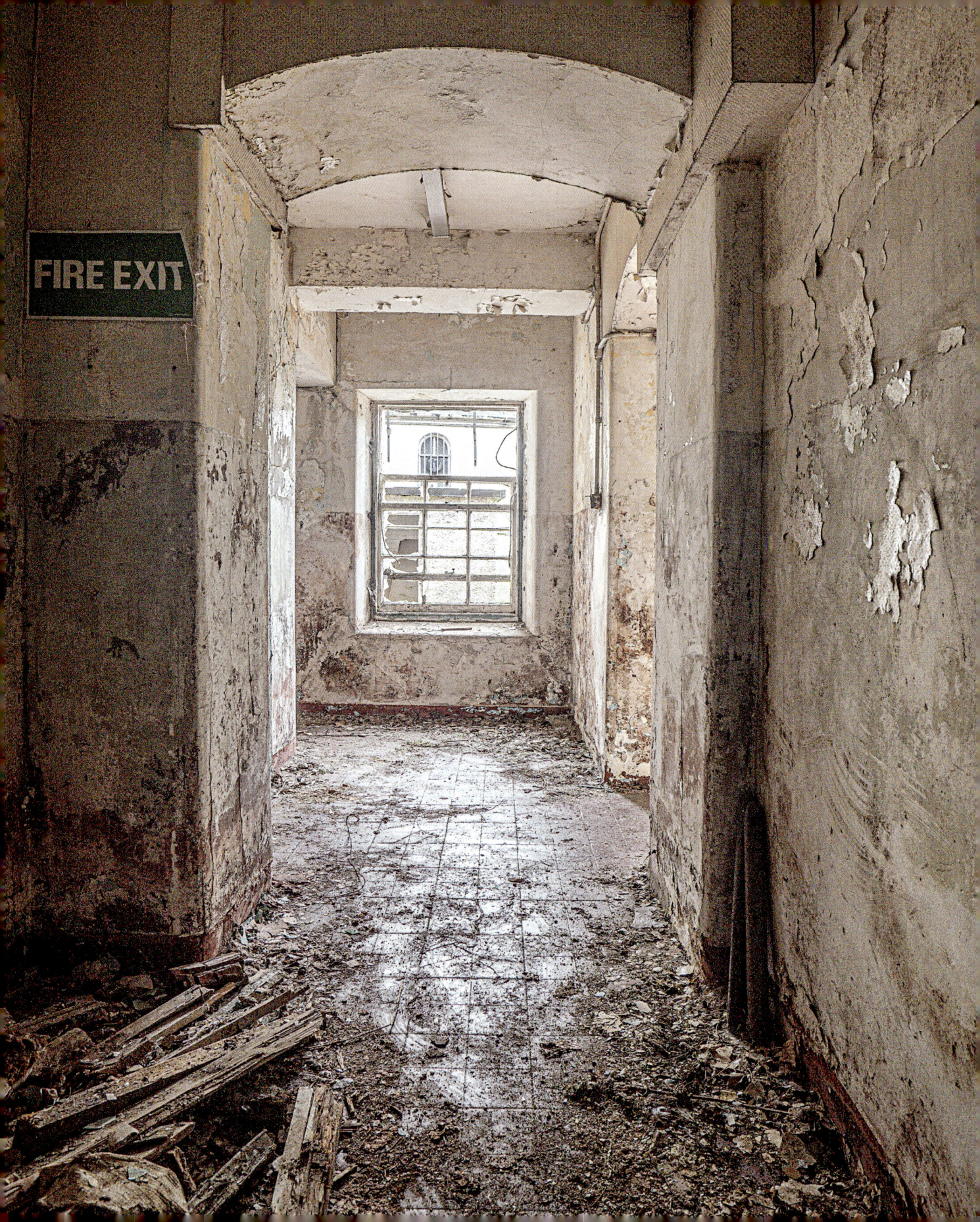

# BANBRIDGE POLICE STATION

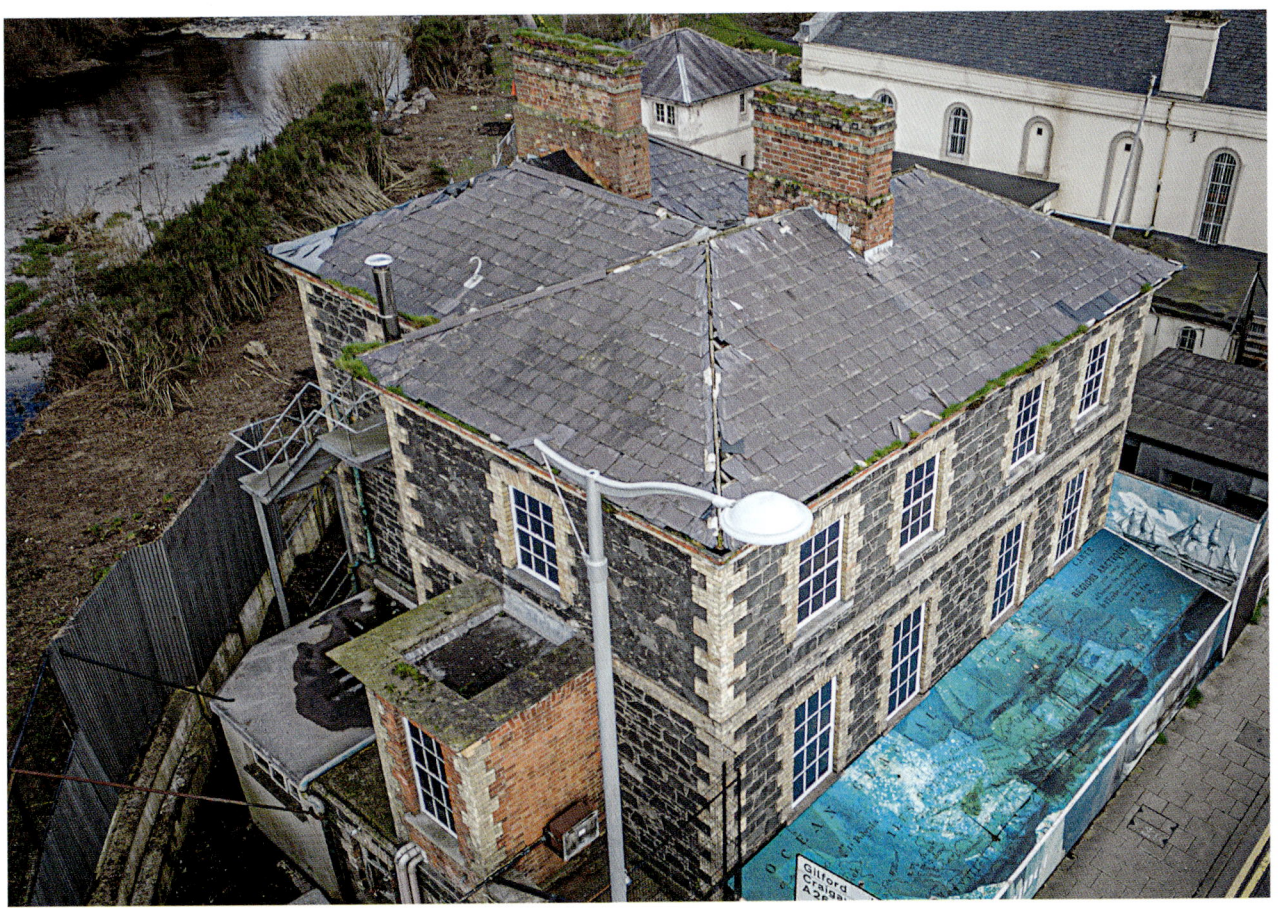

I have driven past the former police station in Banbridge many times. In fact, I remember when it was operational, and during the Troubles it was a hotbed of activity. In the 1990s two nightclubs were opened within a stone's throw of the building – The Coach and Circus Circus. The station would undoubtedly have held a few party-goers from those establishments overnight on occasion!

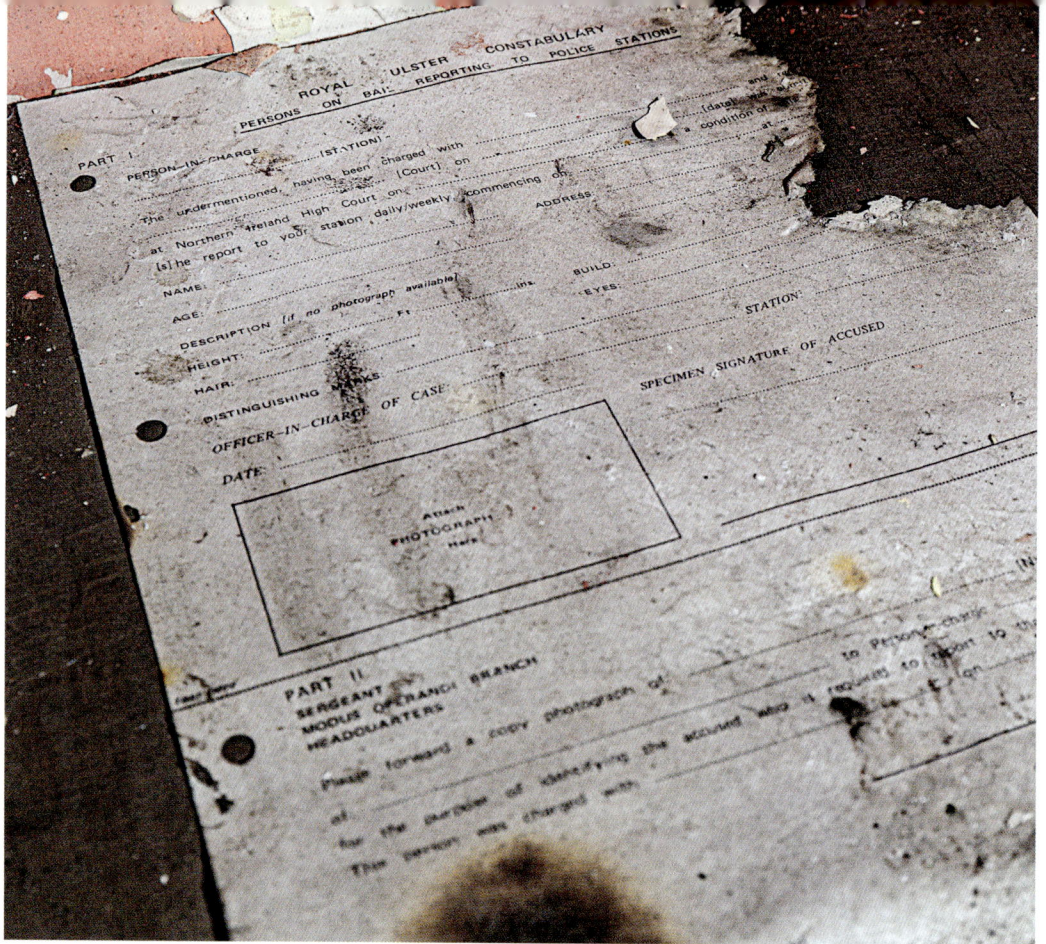

In recent years it became obvious that the building was derelict. I once ventured inside to see if it would be worth photographing but left quickly due to the extensive vandalism; the building just didn't seem safe and was becoming an eyesore.

In early 2023 I saw that the barracks had been purchased and renovation work had begun. I took this as a sign and thought it would be a good time to revisit it and take some pictures before major construction began. I got chatting online to the new owner, a local man named Stephen. I explained to him what I do and asked if I could get in to take some pictures before any more work took place. Thankfully he agreed, and I called down a few days later.

Every weekend Stephen and his brother work on the building. They've already cleaned much of it out and it was in much better shape than when I first visited. When I arrived, Stephen told me about his plans for the building. The first stage is clearing it out and making it waterproof; then it will be fixed within regulations – as a listed building, renovations have to be done to certain specifications. Ideas for its final use include an Airbnb, possibly with a café on street level and the lower cells employed as particularly authentic escape rooms.

The main structure of three storeys was built around 1860, with additional modifications made in 1927. Originally a police barracks with living quarters and cells, the location also served for a time as the estate offices of the Marquess of Downshire, a prominent figure and landowner who played a significant role in the development of Banbridge.

As I walk through the barracks, absorbing what's around me, I still get the feeling of a police station. Counters remain in place, gun cabinets on the walls, and in one room a huge map of Northern Ireland is pinned to a whiteboard and has 'Under UVF' spray-painted over it. Graffiti like this is commonplace and a reminder of days not so distant. In one room there is a set of pigeon holes, each with a specific offence marked on it, such as 'Def. Tyres' (defective tyres) and 'FLG Med. Exam' (failing medical exam). One which I found very interesting was 'Allowing oneself to be carried'. According to a policeman who wrote to my website, this means being transported in a vehicle while the driver is under the influence.

In a cabinet I see some burned paperwork. On closer inspection I can see the header 'Royal Ulster Constabulary' and realise this was paperwork used to check people in, recording detailed information of the detainee including name, age, description, height and hair colour.

Beneath the barracks, unused rails lead to a hidden passageway, showcasing impressive ironwork and clawed feet. The passageway is blocked off with heavy stone, so it is unclear where it might have led and what it was used for.

I leave the barracks happy that I've captured it before serious work commences. Stephen is unsure when the work will be completed, but I still regularly check the Instagram page to see the progress.

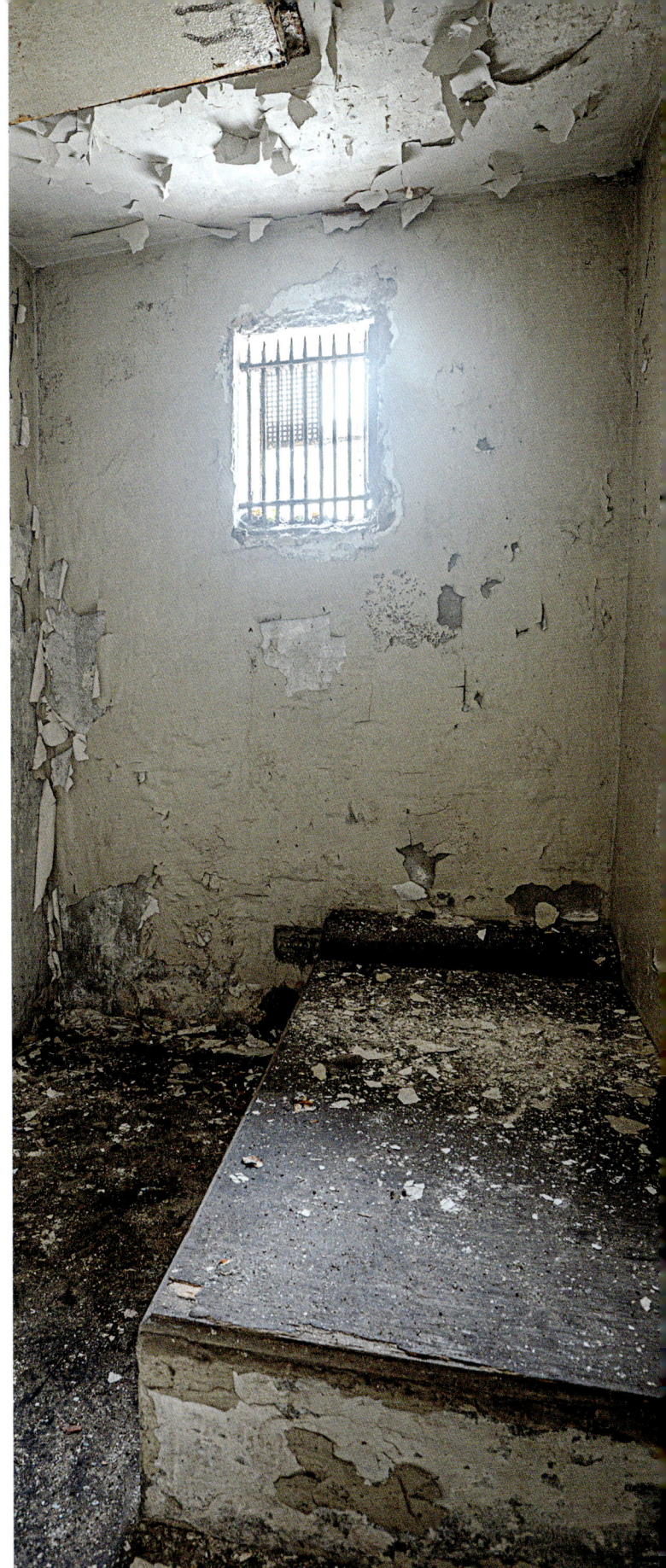

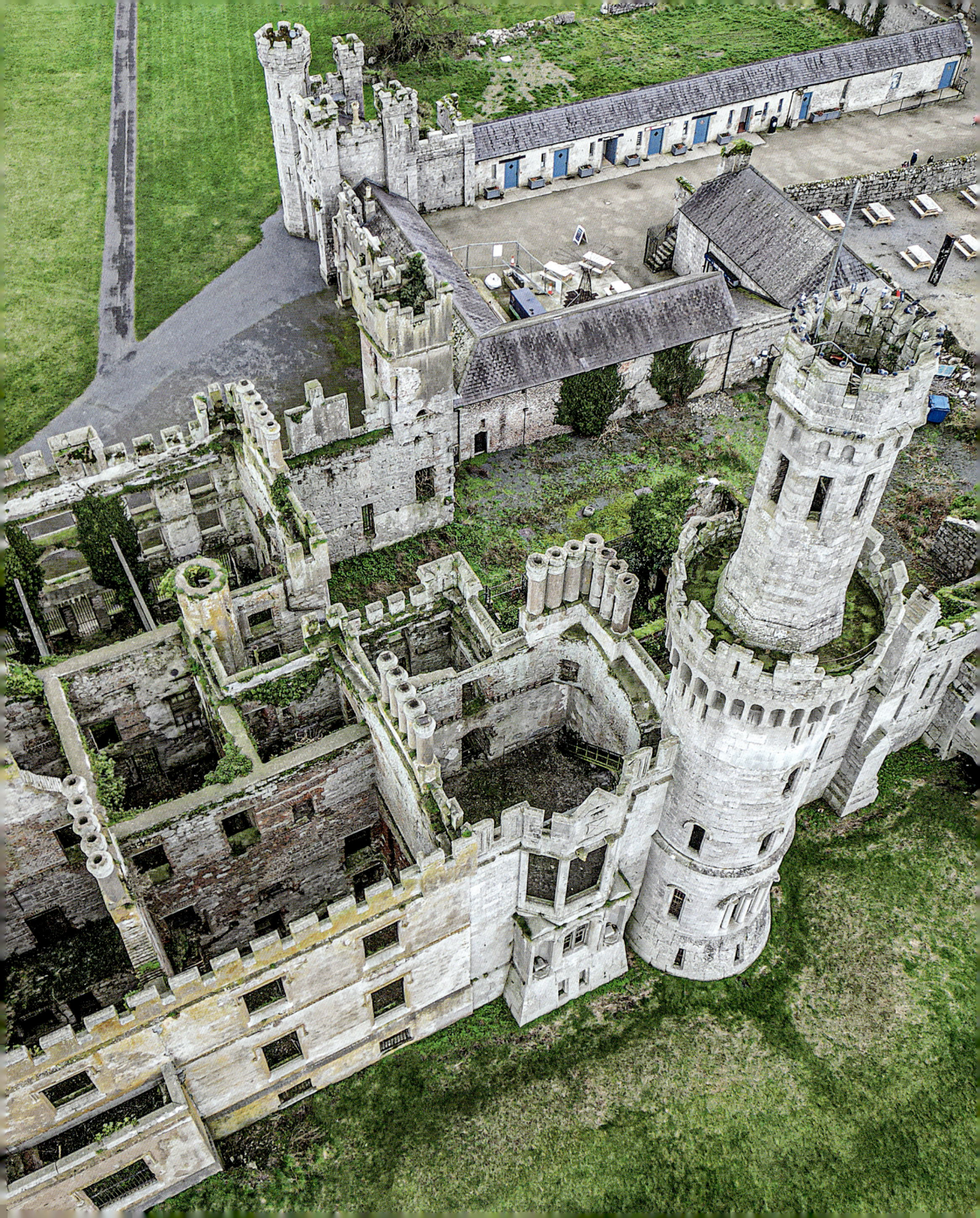

# DUCKETT'S GROVE

This historic ruin has been on my bucket list for as long as I can remember, and when I had the opportunity to visit recently I was not disappointed!

I was given a wonderful tour by Danny, who is incredibly knowledgeable and passionate about the place. He explained that originally the house was built around 1745 as a three-storey Georgian manor house with a basement. Nearly a century later, it was extended and remodelled by British architect Thomas A. Cobden at the request of John (Dawson) Duckett. This is when the Gothic style was incorporated, including the arches, gargoyles and turrets that are still visible today. It was considered a vanity project, used to show off the wealth and prosperity of the Duckett family.

The work did not end there. In 1845 Sligo architect John Macduff Derick made further additions, which included an elaborate granite ashlar viewing tower, additional turrets, entrance screens and a stable complex at the back of the property. The viewing tower, one

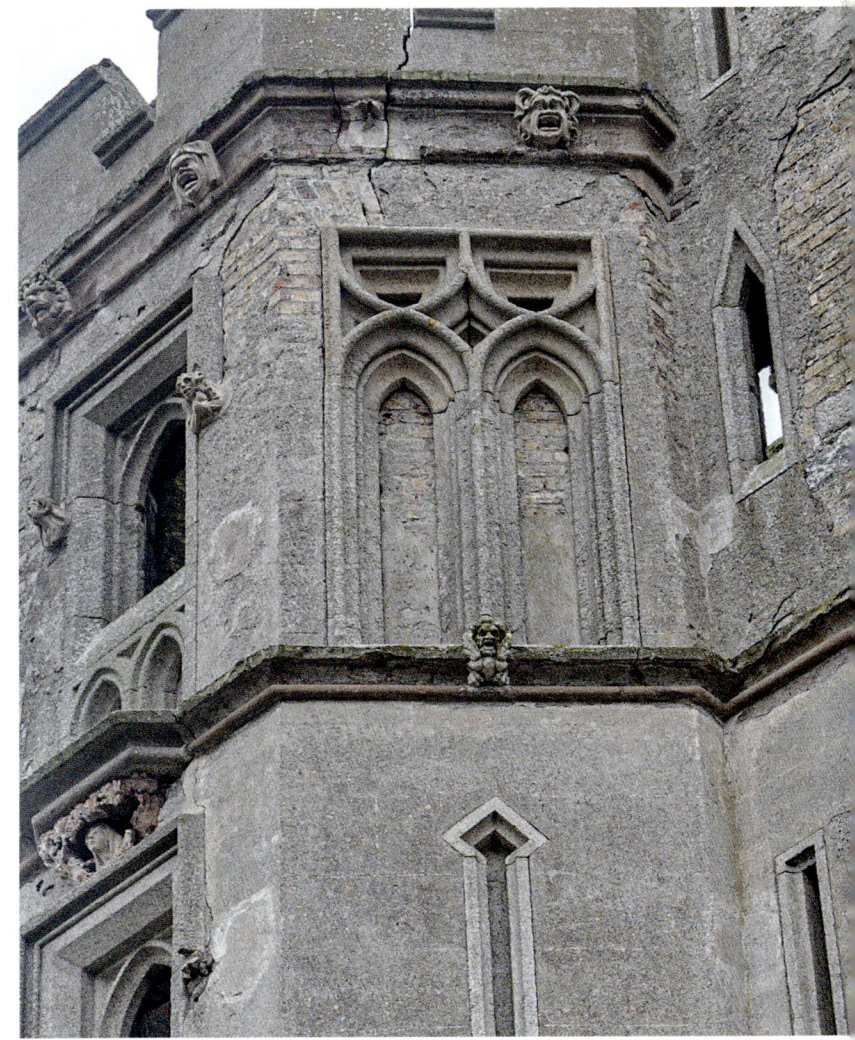

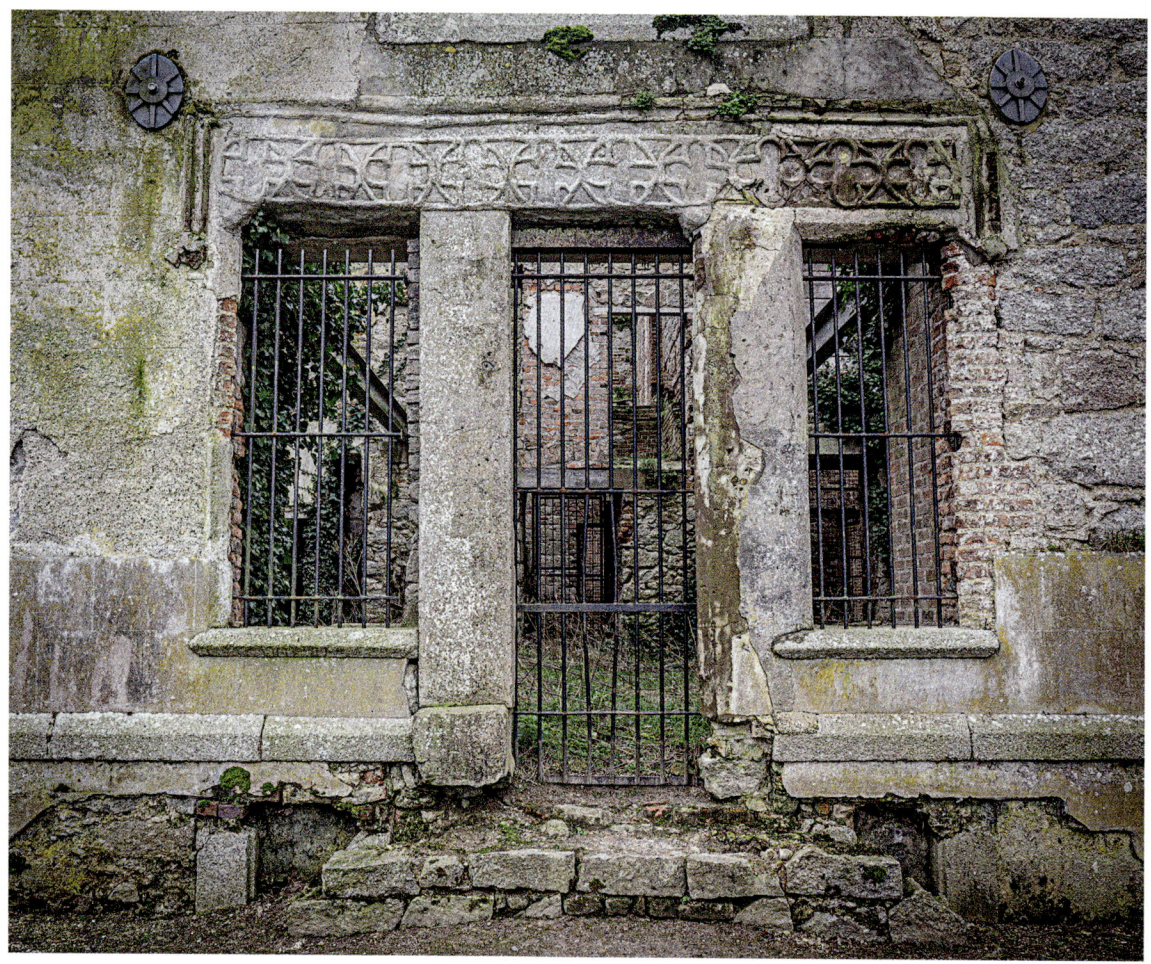

of the building's most distinctive features, offered a 360-degree view of the grounds, including the walled gardens.

The lineage of the Ducketts can be traced back to William the Conqueror and King Edward I. Sir George Duckett, the first member of the family to arrive in Ireland, came over during the Cromwellian period in the 1650s. But it was Thomas Duckett who purchased 500 acres of land in Rainestown and Palatine in County Carlow from British landlord

Thomas Costhwaite, and during the 1700s built the Georgian manor house, replacing a smaller house that stood where Duckett's Grove is located today.

The last Duckett to reside in the Grove was William, who was born in 1822 and died in 1908. He held the position of high sheriff in Carlow and later in Queen's County. William threw extravagant parties at the Grove, inviting high-ranking socialites from Dublin to mingle with the local gentry. As a Quaker, he also showed kindness and generosity to his tenants and workers. Although his second wife, Maria, a Protestant, held deep-seated animosity towards Catholics and their religion, William ensured that his servants were outfitted with new clothes and boots and received Christmas bonuses. He also made a point to give gifts to their children at Christmas, a gesture that was uncommon in those times.

It was said that with William's death, the essence of the estate perished as well, as he was the heart and soul of Duckett's Grove. Maria and her daughter from a previous marriage, Olive, lived on the estate until 1916. In that year Maria left and moved to Dublin. She had become estranged from Olive and, in a bitter turn of events, disinherited her daughter. On Maria's death in 1937, the Duckett's Grove estate was valued at £97,000 (equivalent to over €2 million today), but she only left Olive what was known as 'the angry shilling' (one shilling). Olive contested this in court and eventually received a cash settlement.

The house was purchased by a farmers' collective, but a default in payment led the Land Commission to step in and take over the property. During the War of Independence, the IRA seized control of the house, using it as a command centre and training camp. The watchtower provided them with a strategic advantage, allowing them to scan for incoming attacks from miles away. Linda Kearns, Eithne Ní Chumhaill and May Burke, members of Cumann na mBan, sought refuge there after they escaped from Mountjoy

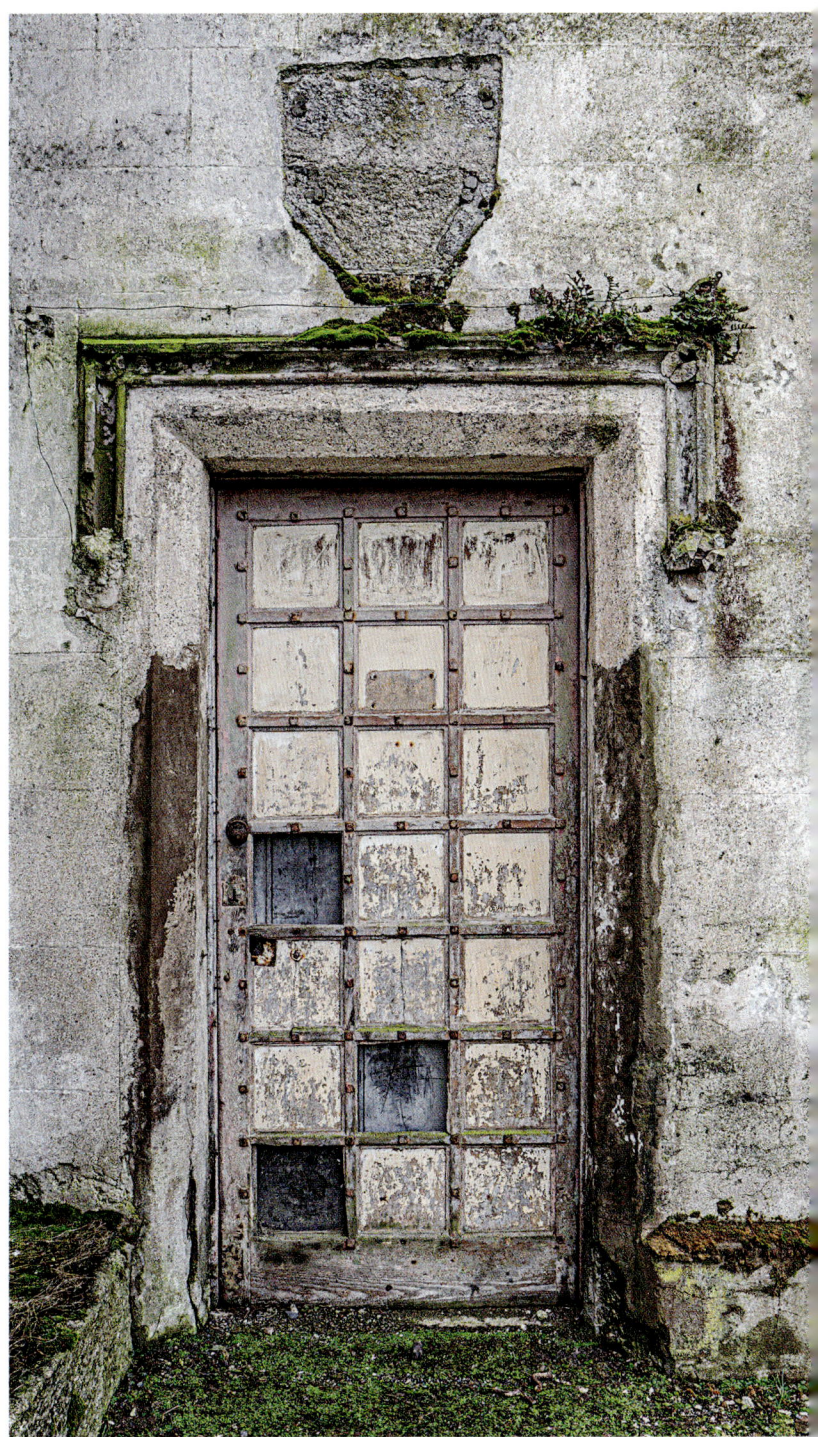

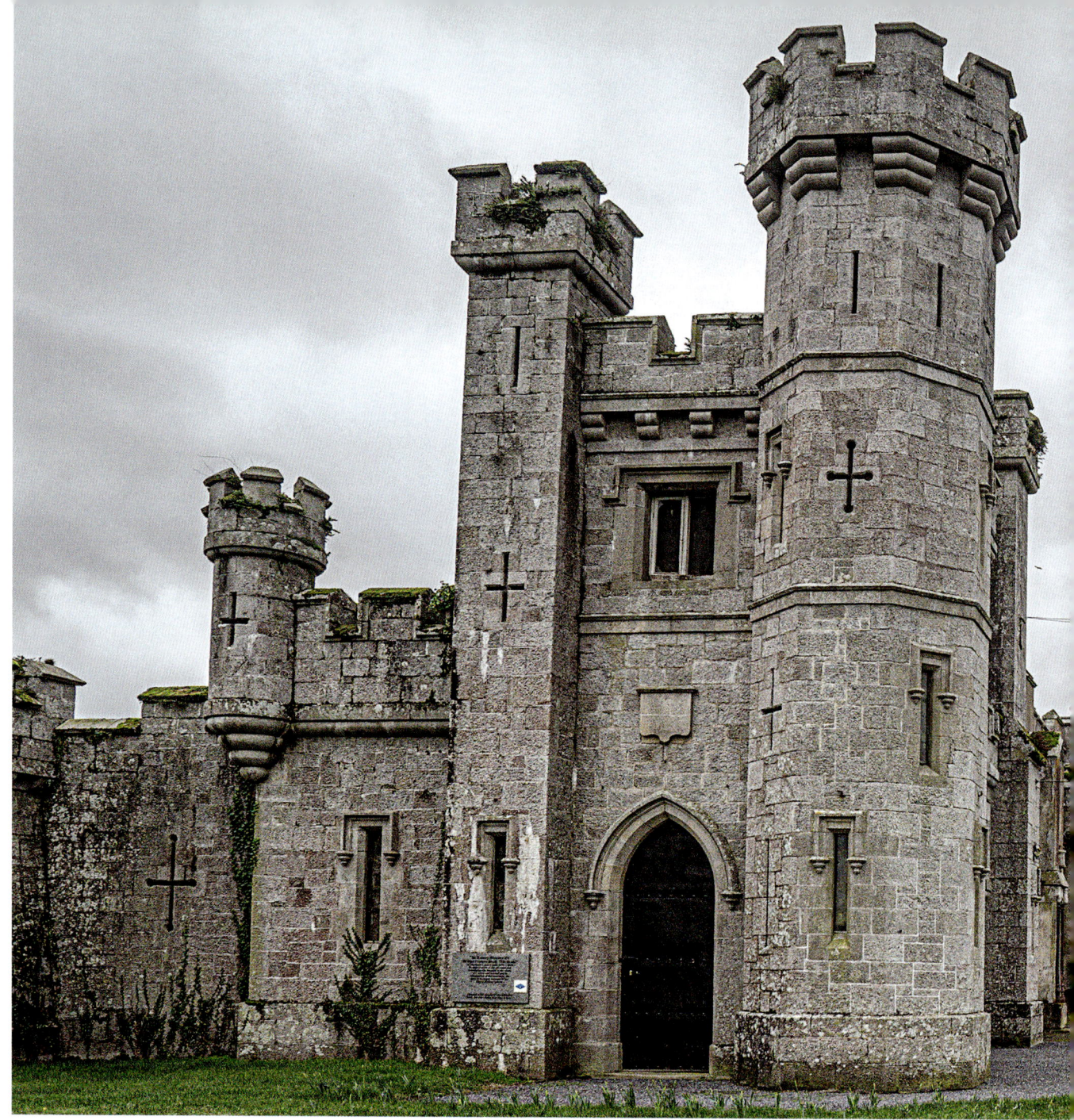

Prison in Dublin in October 1921. The IRA kept the house well maintained, and upon their departure the interiors and furniture were left intact.

In 1933 the house was severely damaged by a major fire, the cause of which was never deter-

mined. A minor fire there a week prior, which was extinguished, led to speculation about arson. It remained vacant and neglected until 1976, when a Miss Frances Brady started to squat in the house. She then declared it as her own, residing in a room

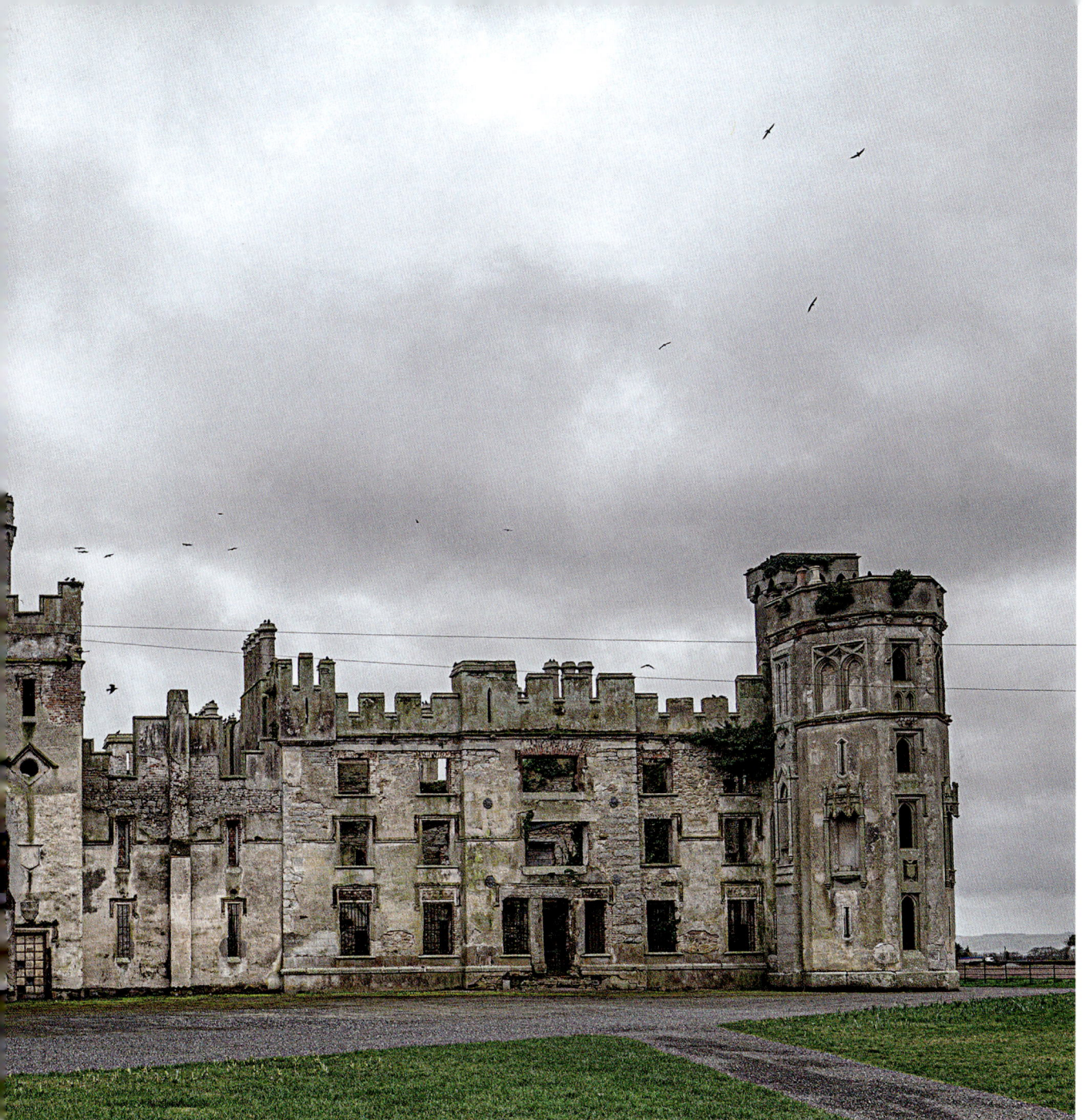

above the archway of the courtyard. During her time there, she turned the estate into an animal sanctuary and horse-riding school, where she instructed numerous local children. Frances shared her passion for wildlife and the natural world with all who visited until her passing in 2004. In 2005 Carlow Council took ownership of Duckett's Grove and began the restoration of its two walled gardens. In 2007 the estate was officially opened as a public park.

I highly recommend a visit.

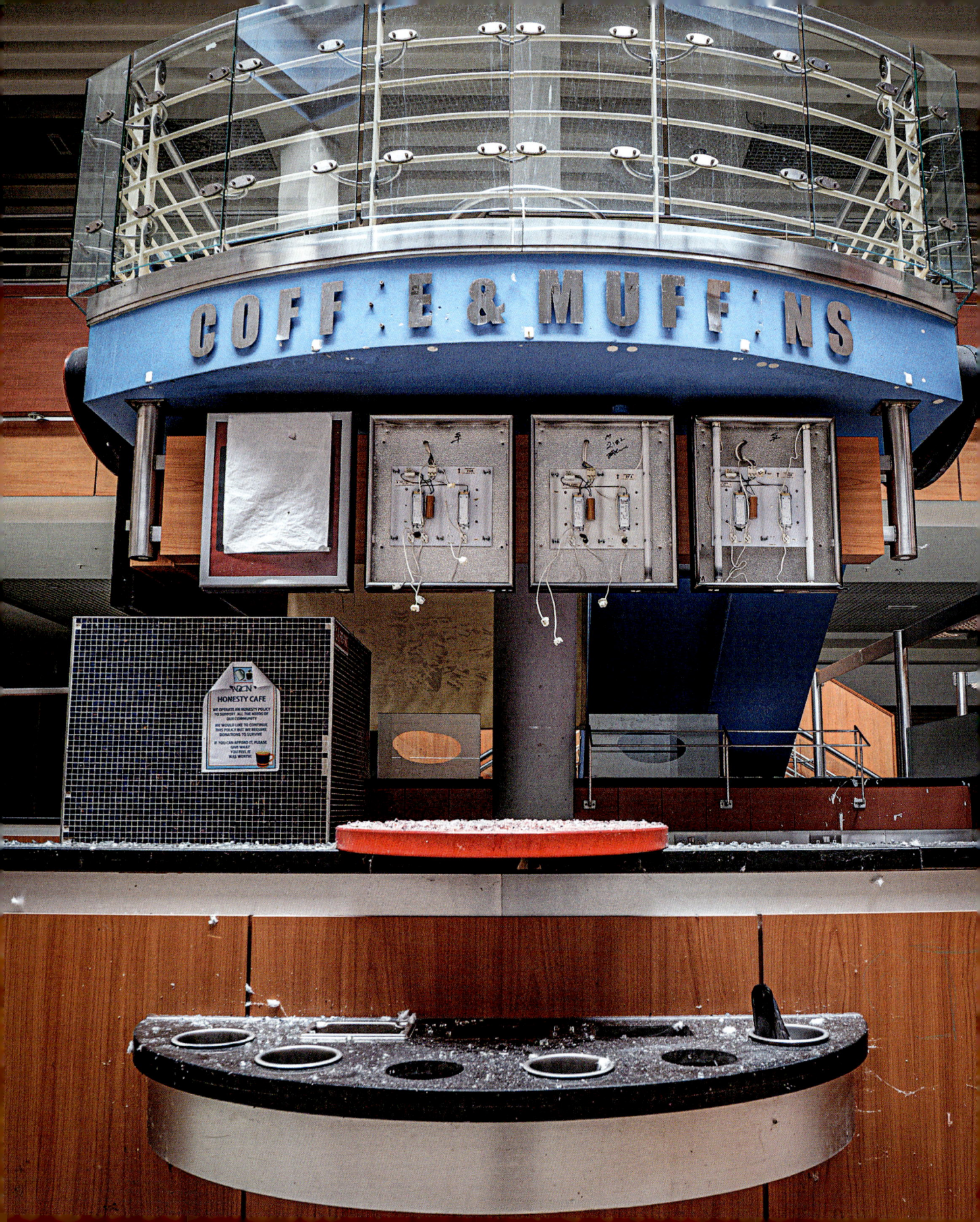

# FLAGSHIP SHOPPING CENTRE

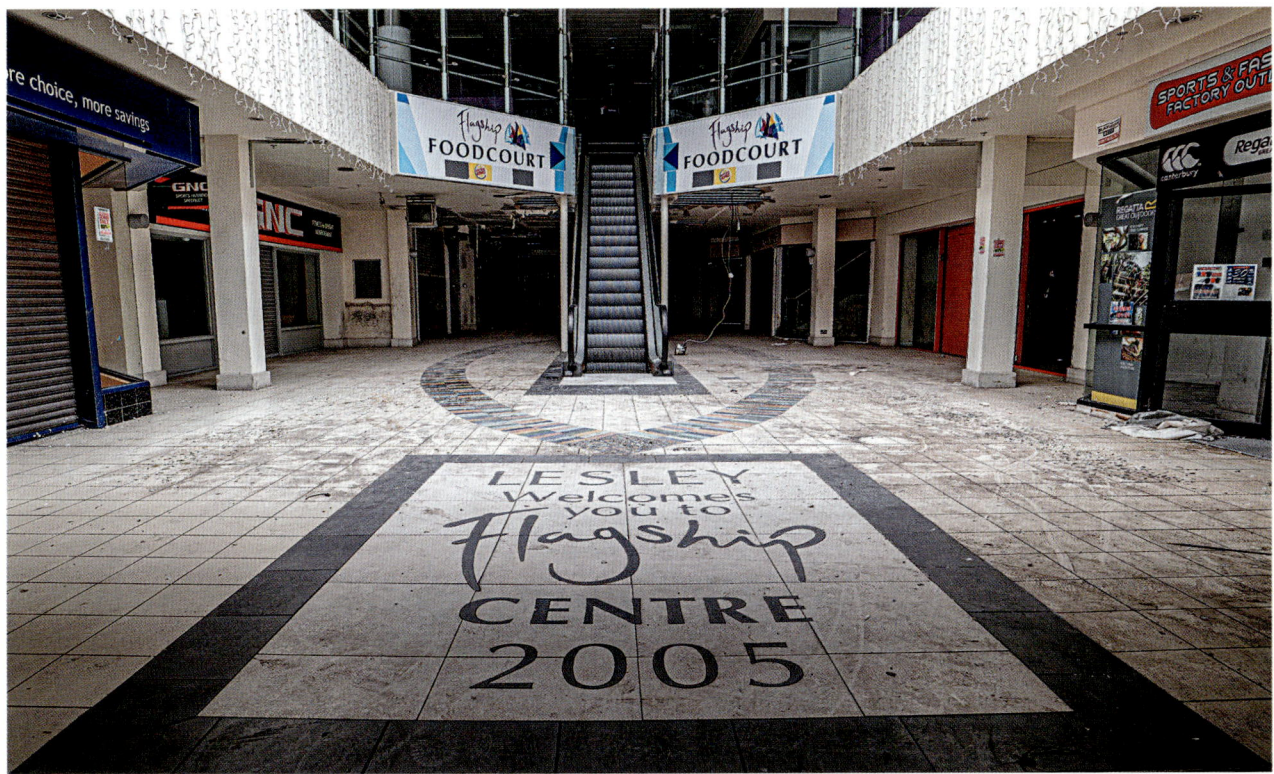

Opened in the early 1990s, this 206,500-square-foot shopping centre was a huge success upon its initial launch. It boasted a variety of shops, including well-known supermarkets and a mix of local stores. In 1999 it was sold for a modest £15 million and was reportedly generating £1.1 million in rent annually.

However, its long corridors and shopfronts now sit vacant, with only pigeons inhabiting the space they consider home.

The shopping centre was prominently situated on the main street in Bangor, but competition from larger out-of-town centres, which offer free

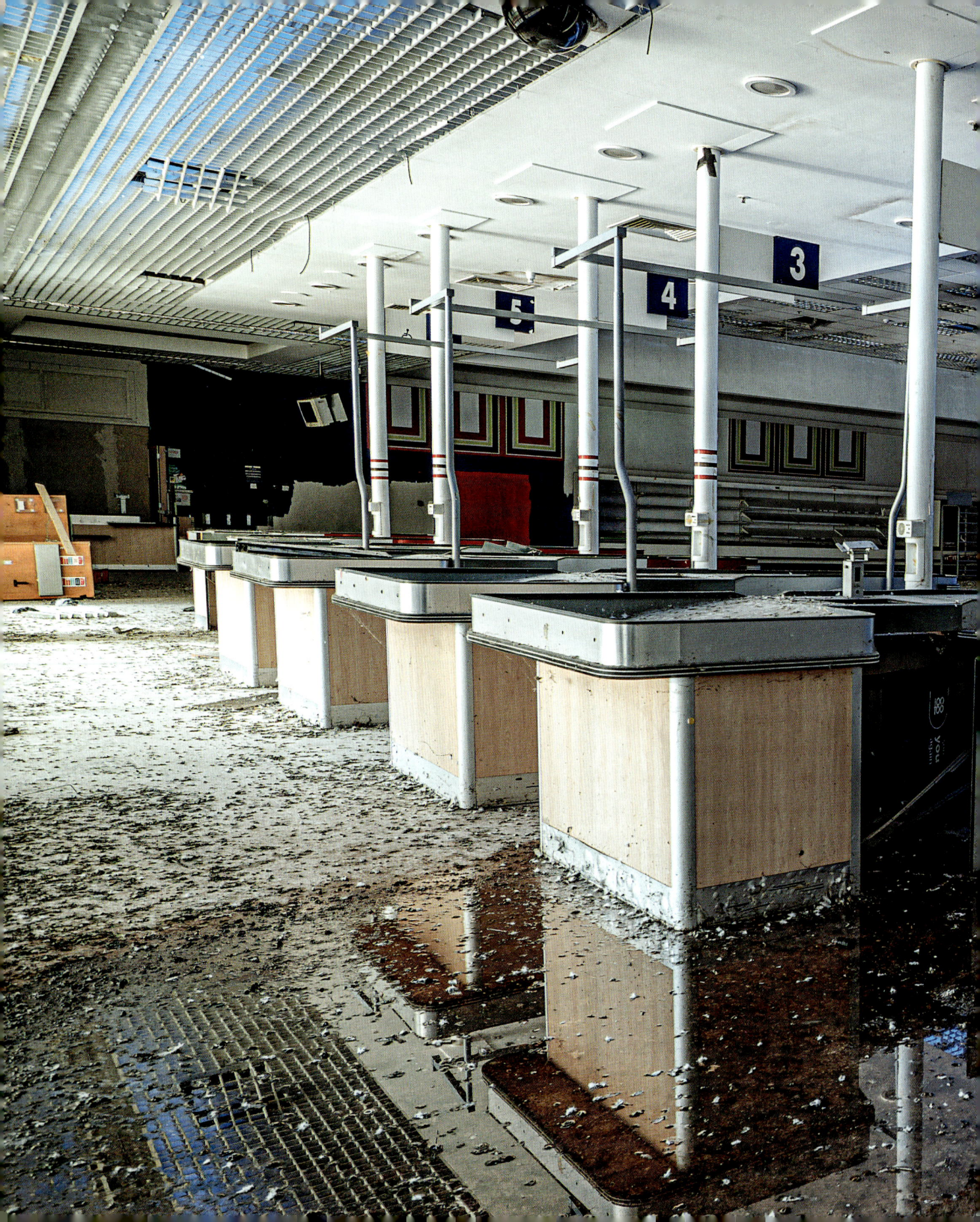

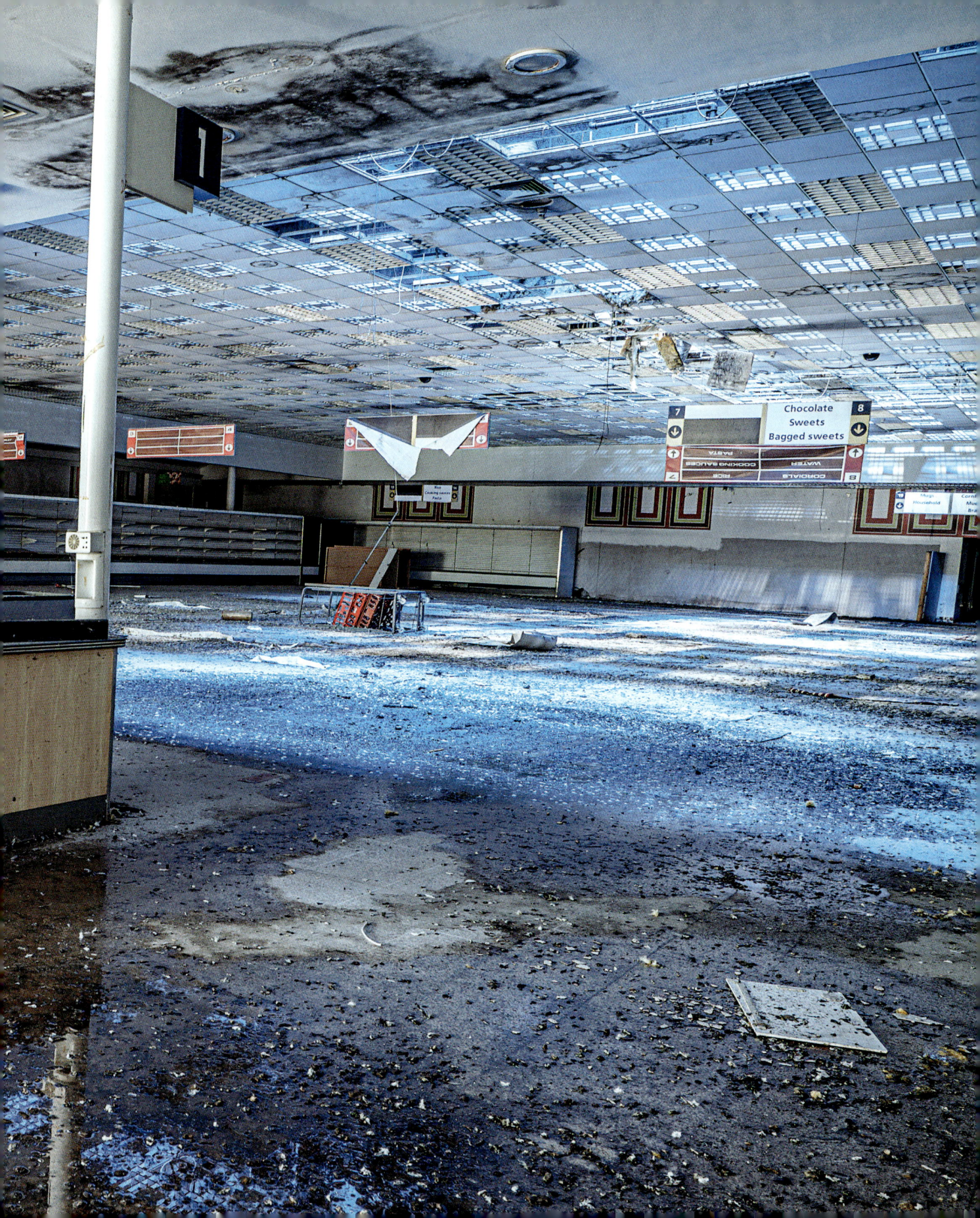

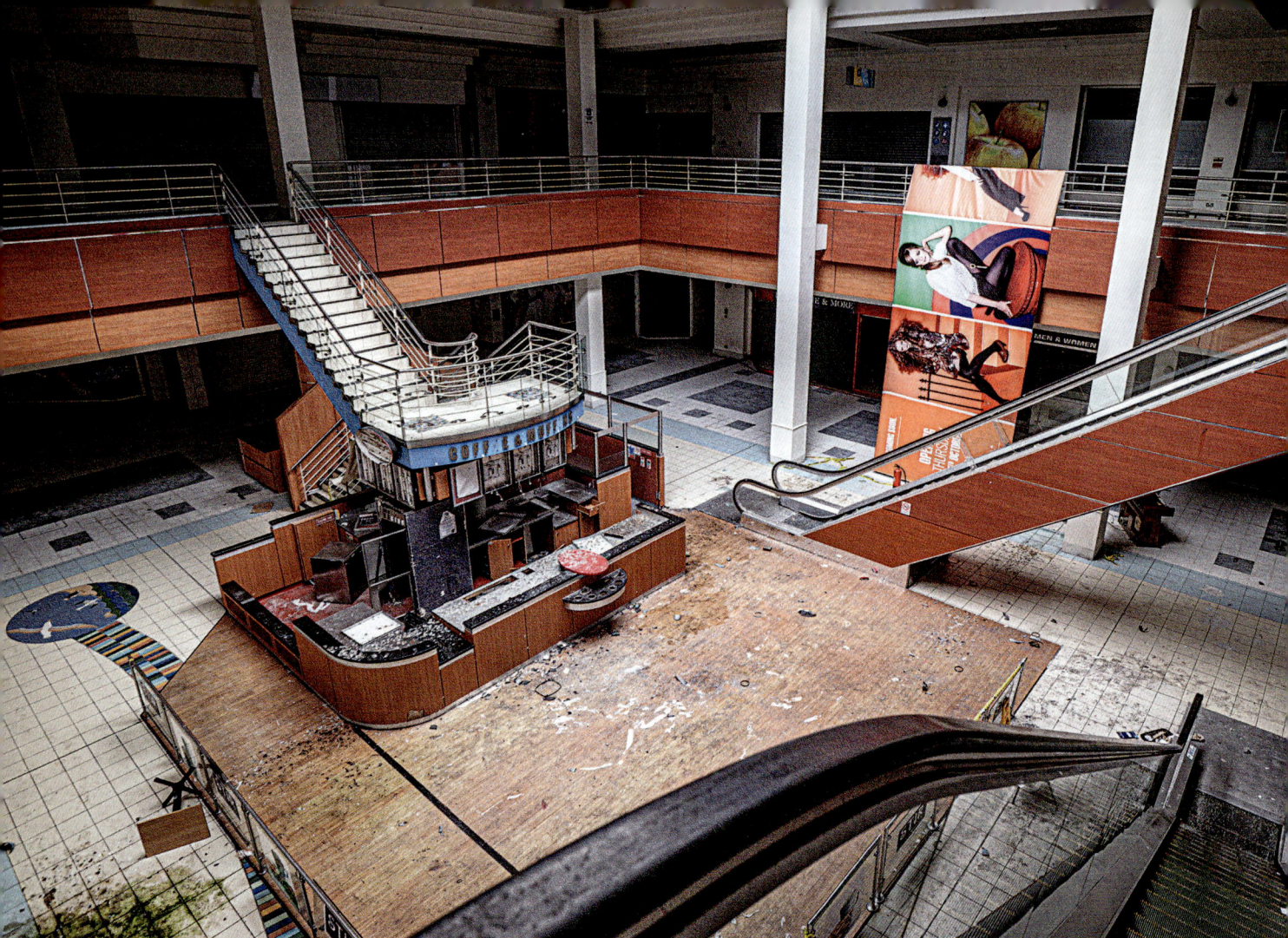

parking, coupled with the rise of online shopping, led to a severe decline in foot traffic. Following the 2008 economic downturn, a mass exodus of retail tenants who had been present since the opening of the centre ensued, ultimately resulting in its closure in 2019.

I was thrilled to be asked to document the arcade on behalf of the new owner, who has ambitious plans for revitalising the abandoned complex. These plans involve subdividing units for local businesses to expand into larger spaces in a prime location. Additionally, there are proposals for incorporating

entertainment and restaurant amenities, offering endless possibilities for the site's future.

Documenting an abandoned shopping centre was a first for me, and its vastness only amplified the sense of desolation. It felt as though I had stepped into a scene from a post-apocalyptic TV show like *The Last of Us*. Hopefully, the shopping centre will soon reopen and see life brought back within its walls.

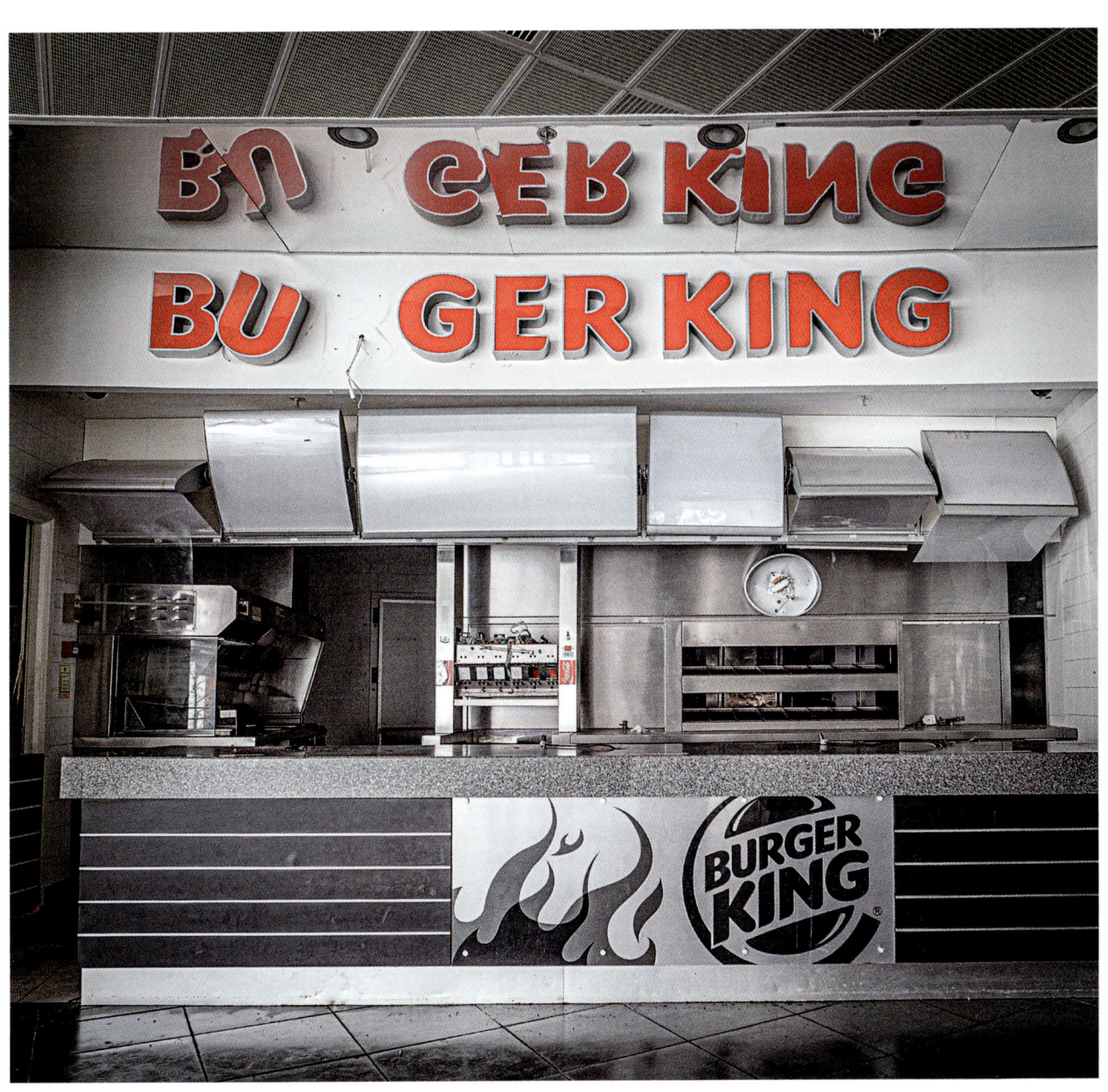

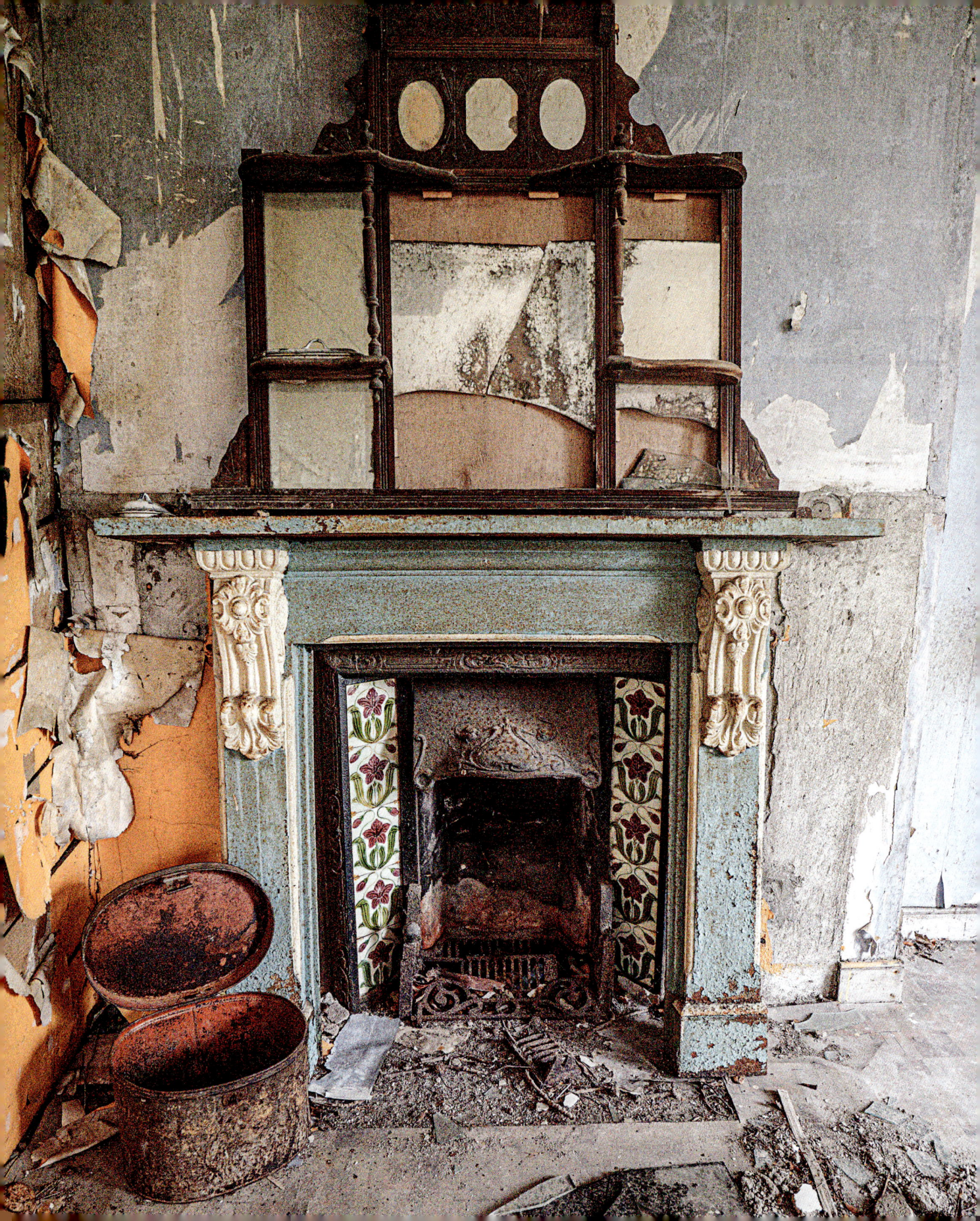

# GARLIC HOUSE

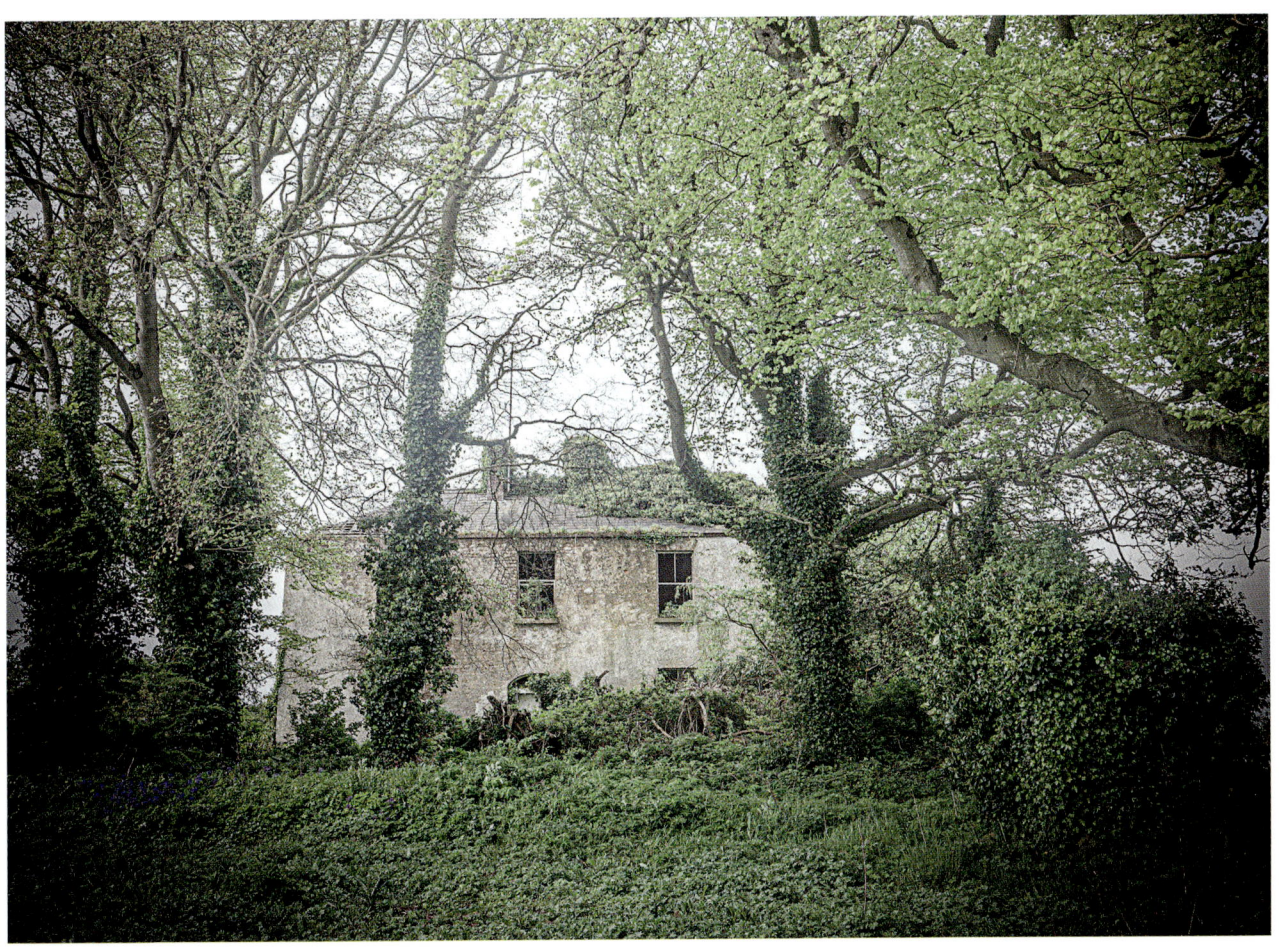

This abandoned house is a perfect time capsule. At first glance it looks like a normal, modest farmhouse, but when you look closer, the bars on the lower windows suggest something unusual. Peter, the present owner of the house, explains that these security measures were installed in the mid-1800s to

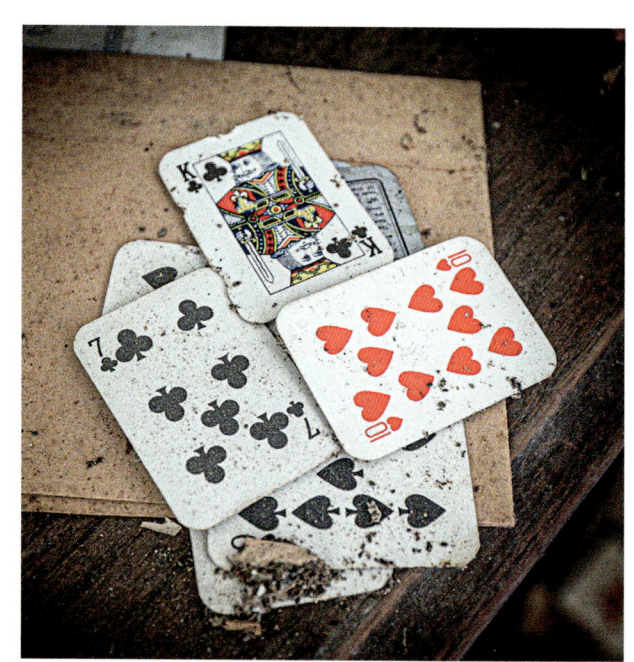

prevent break-ins during the Great Famine period, when local people would have resorted to desperate measures to try to find food.

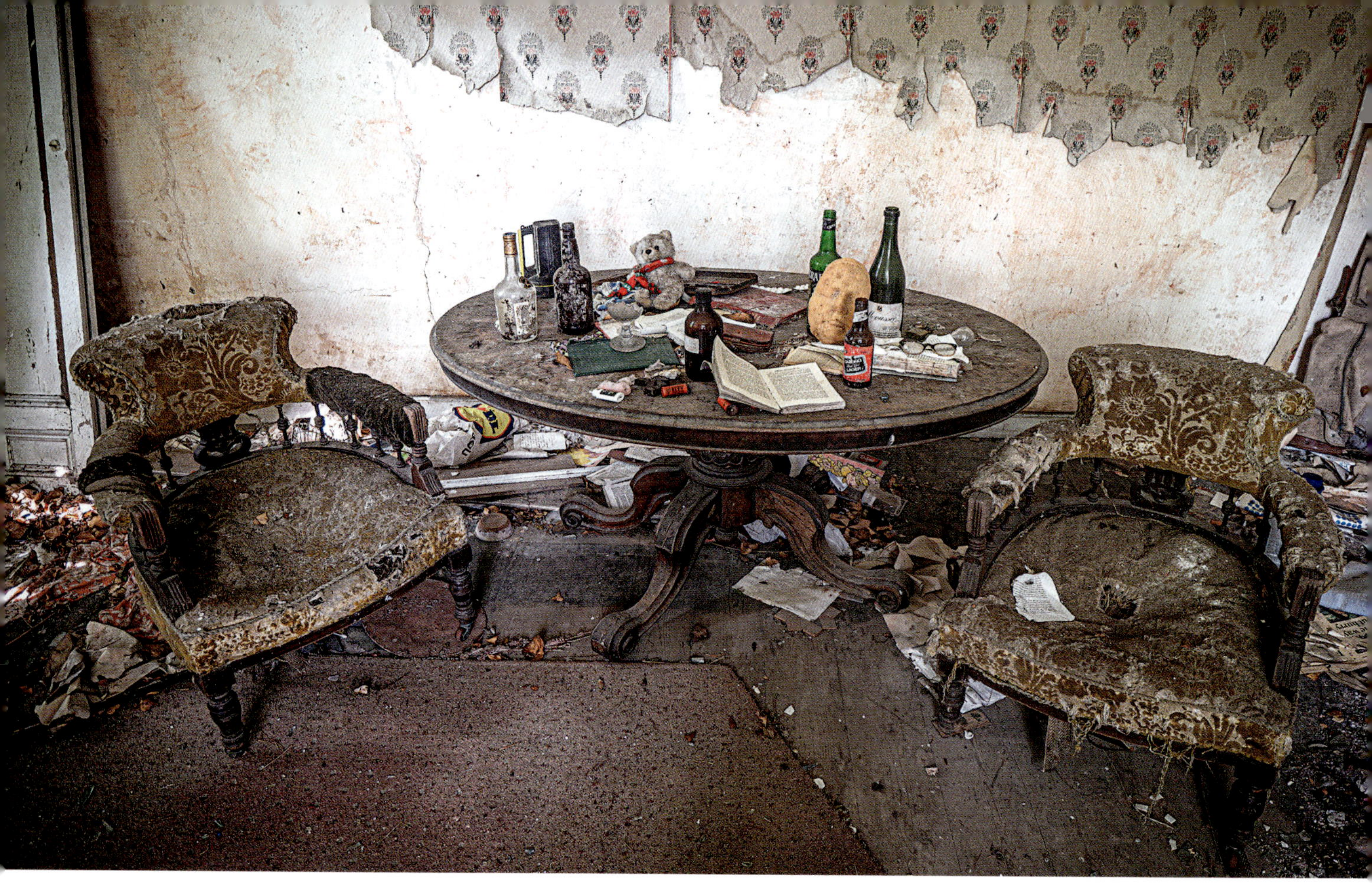

The house is situated on a sprawling 100-acre farm that has been in Peter's family since the 1850s. Across from it, remnants of a walled garden and stables can still be seen. The garden is dotted with impressive mature trees, which provide both shelter from the wind and privacy from passers-by.

On entering the house, I am struck by the amount of furniture that has been left there. While it may be old now, back in the day these pieces would have been considered luxurious and expensive, yet they are now slowly decaying after being abandoned. A beautiful piano catches my eye, surrounded by

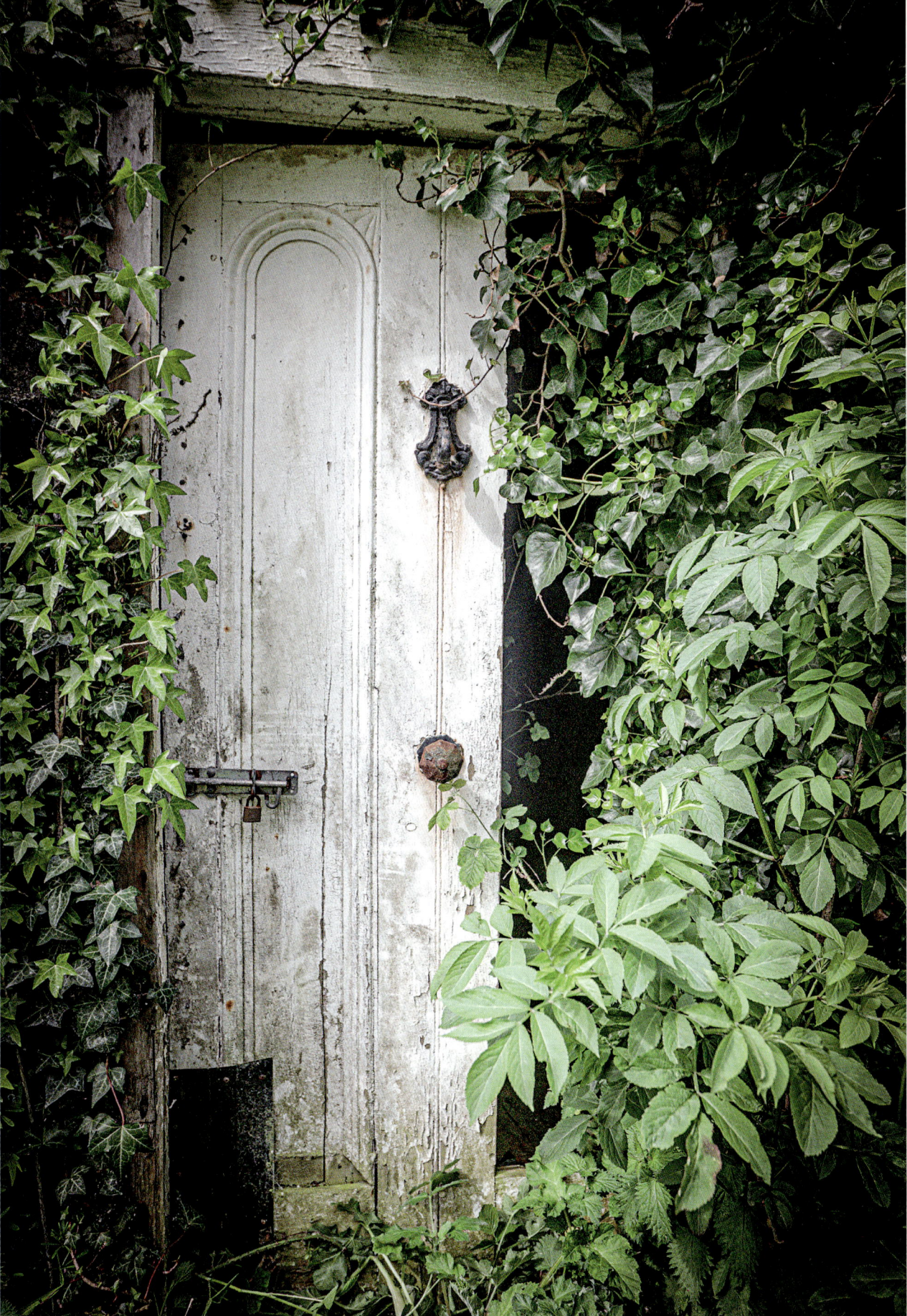

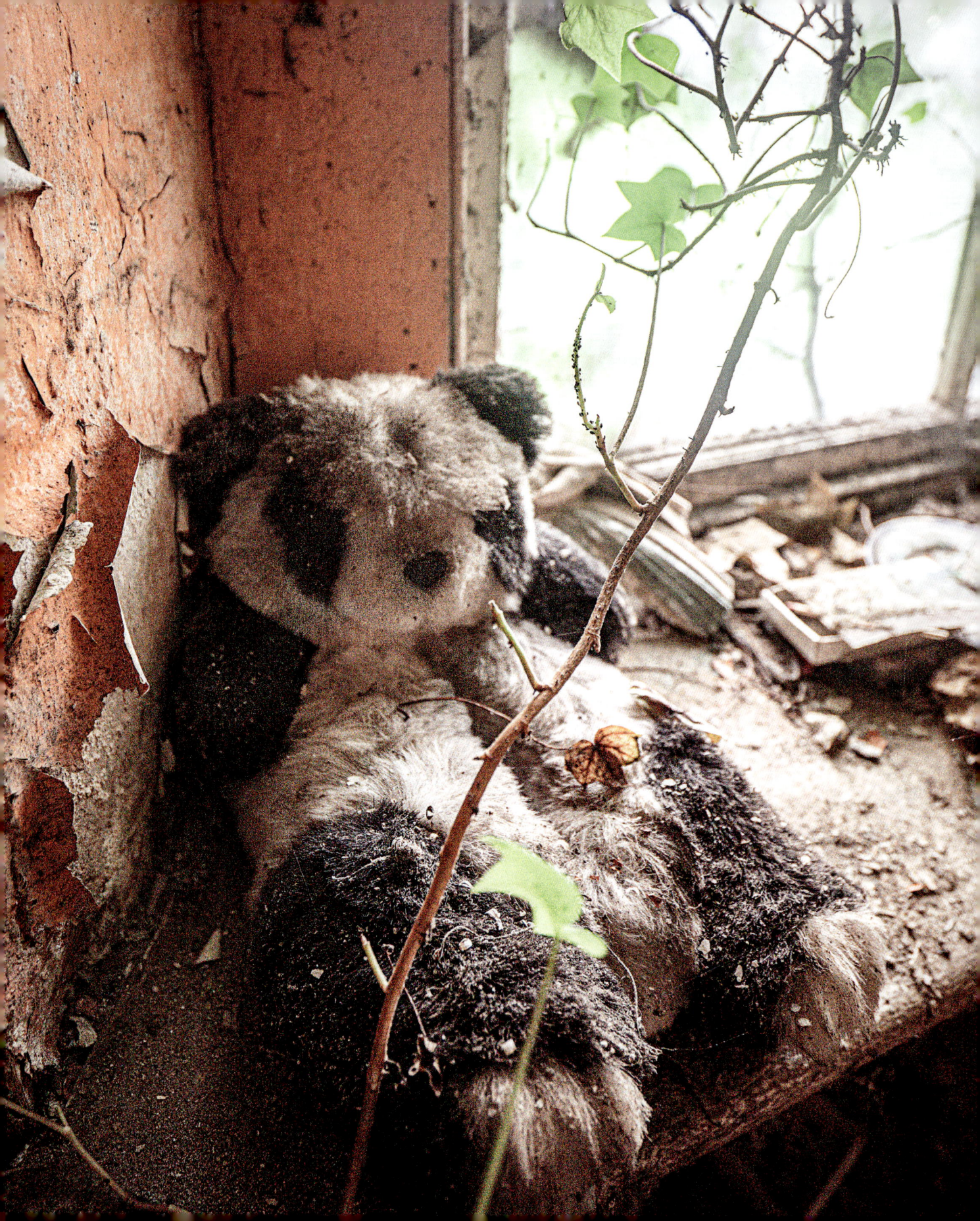

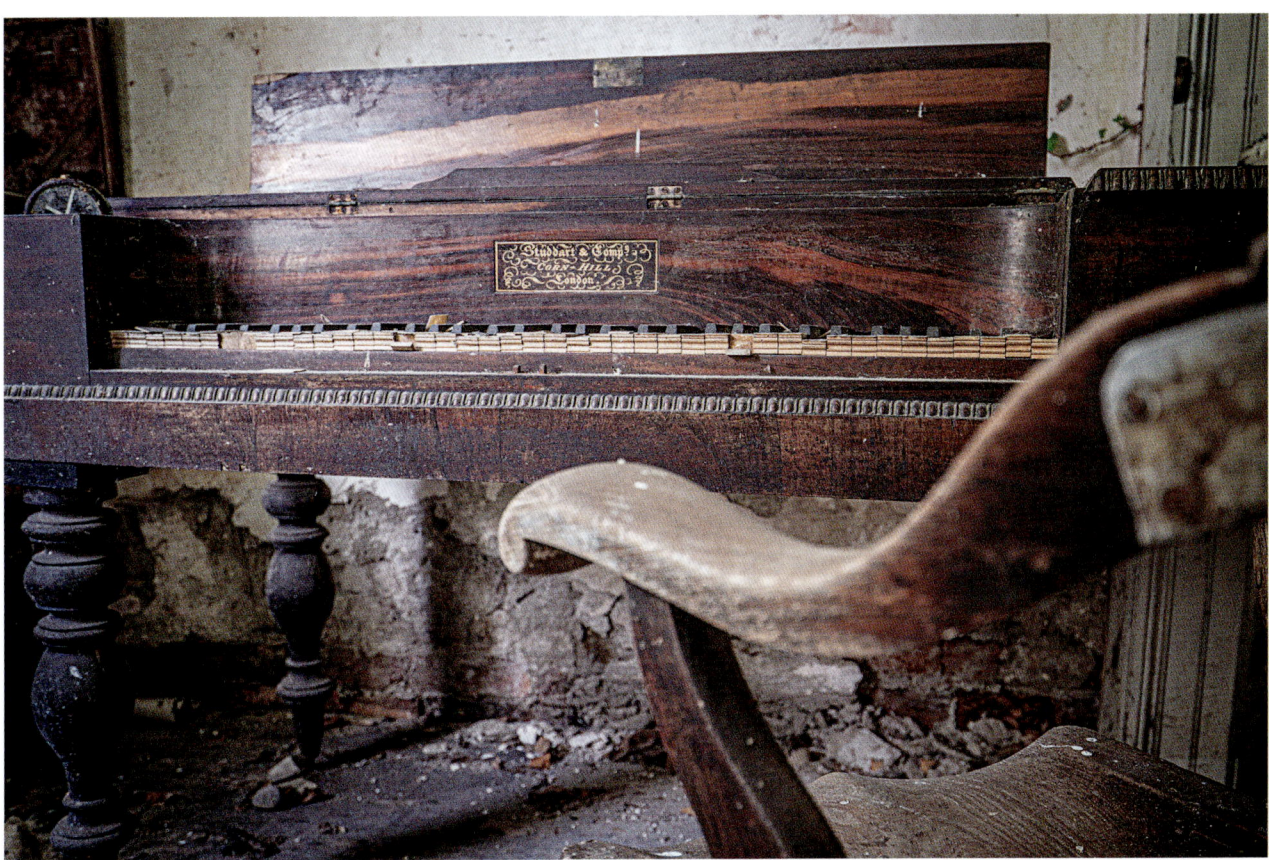

stacked suitcases and a table filled with old books – it looks almost as if the reader has just stepped out of the room to put on the kettle. It is scenes like this, with their prevailing sense of mystery, that drew me into this kind of photography all those years ago.

The bedrooms upstairs that I was able to reach are each brightly coloured, one in pink and the other in yellow. Clothes still hang in the wardrobes, serving as a reminder of the previous occupants, Peter's aunts. Since they passed away, the house has lain empty.

Peter tells me even though the house was grand and his ancestors lived comfortably, it didn't come easily. It was all down to sheer hard work and determination.

Peter and his wife, Marita, now farm the land around this house. They grow asparagus and garlic, both of which can be found in shops under the Drummond House label. On the conclusion of my visit to what I dubbed 'Garlic House', I was sent home with some produce to try and I can testify that the asparagus was the nicest I have ever tasted. They also produce a scape sauce that is out of this world!

Peter has no plans for the house and, for now, is simply keeping it as a family museum.

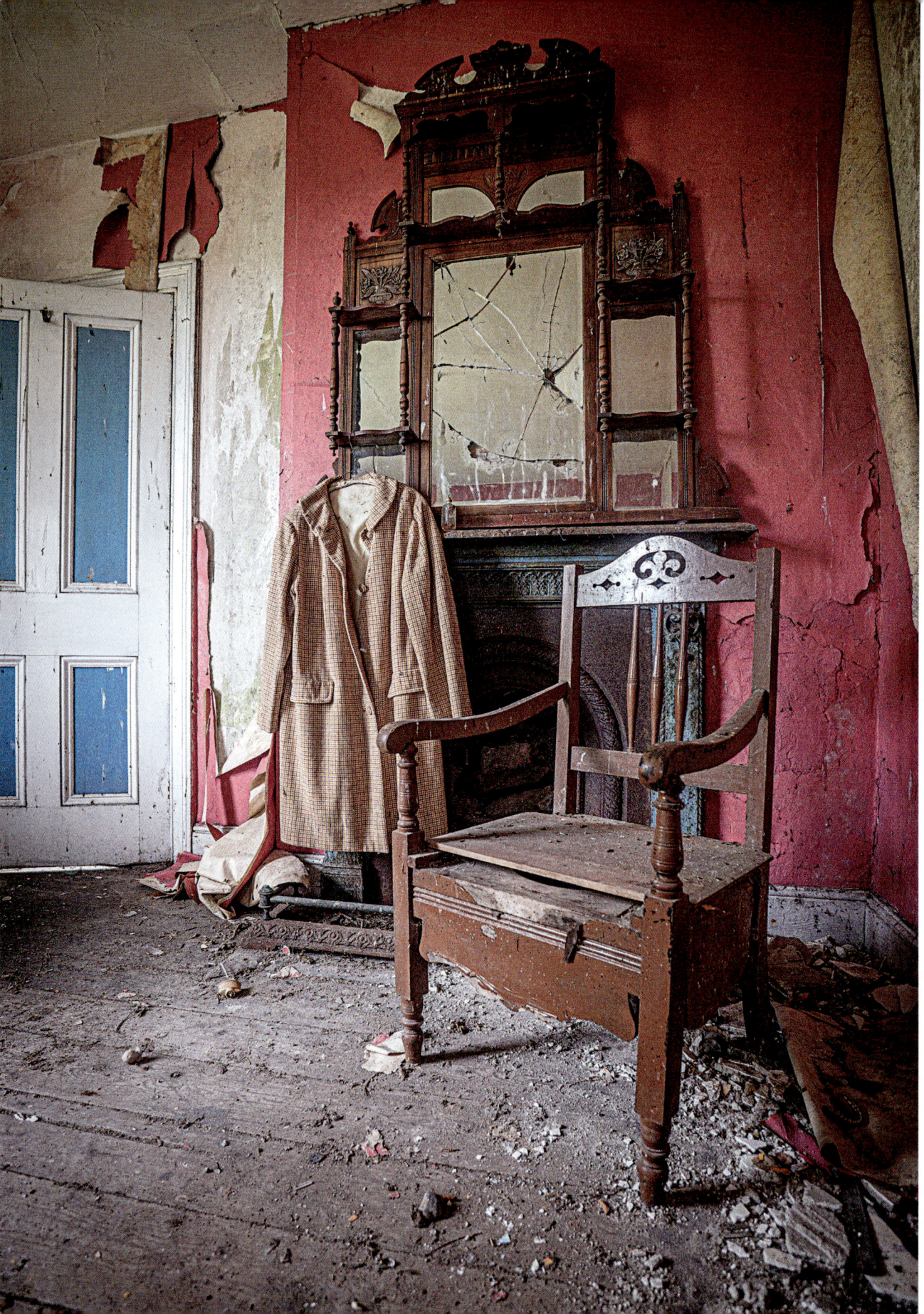

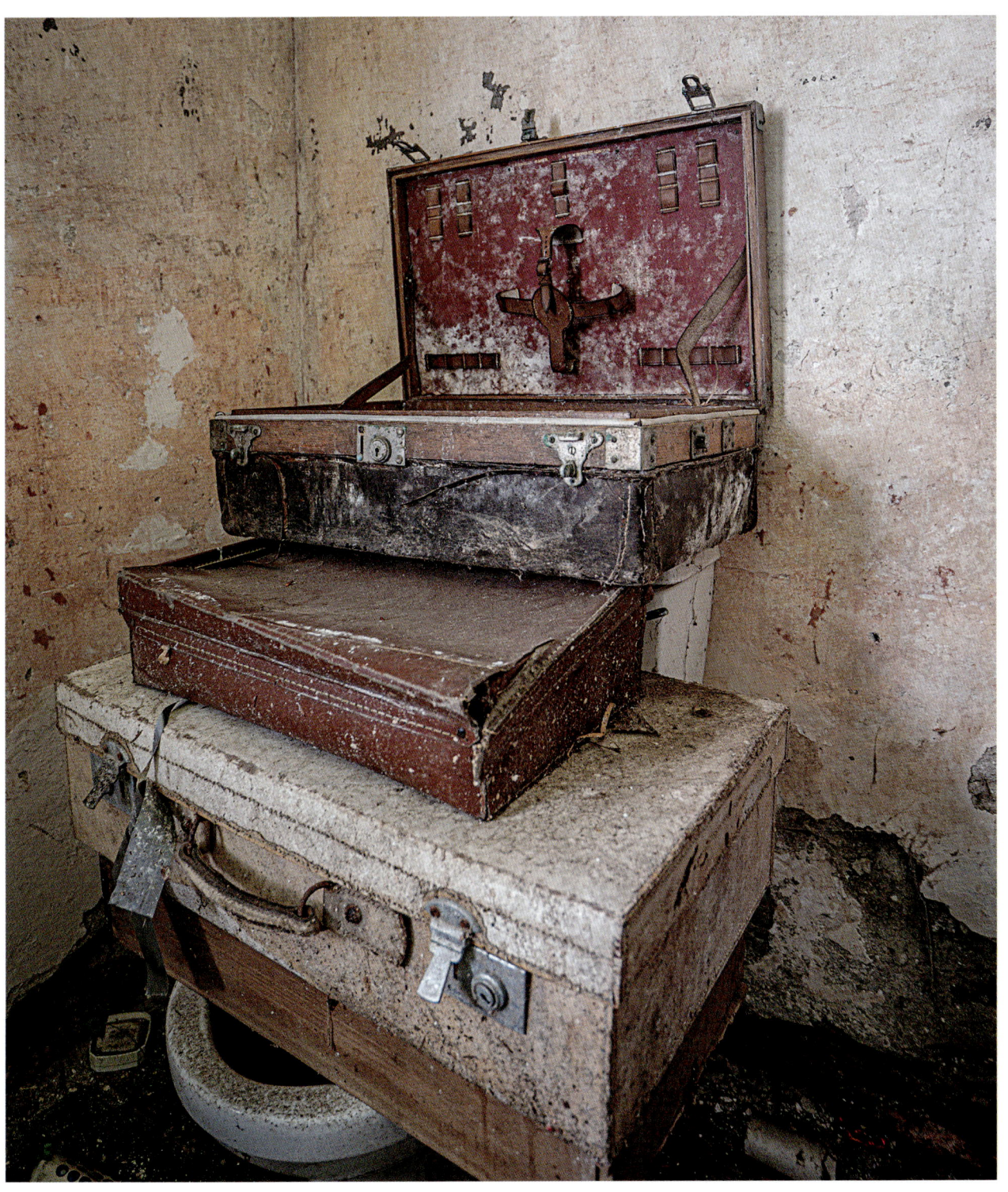

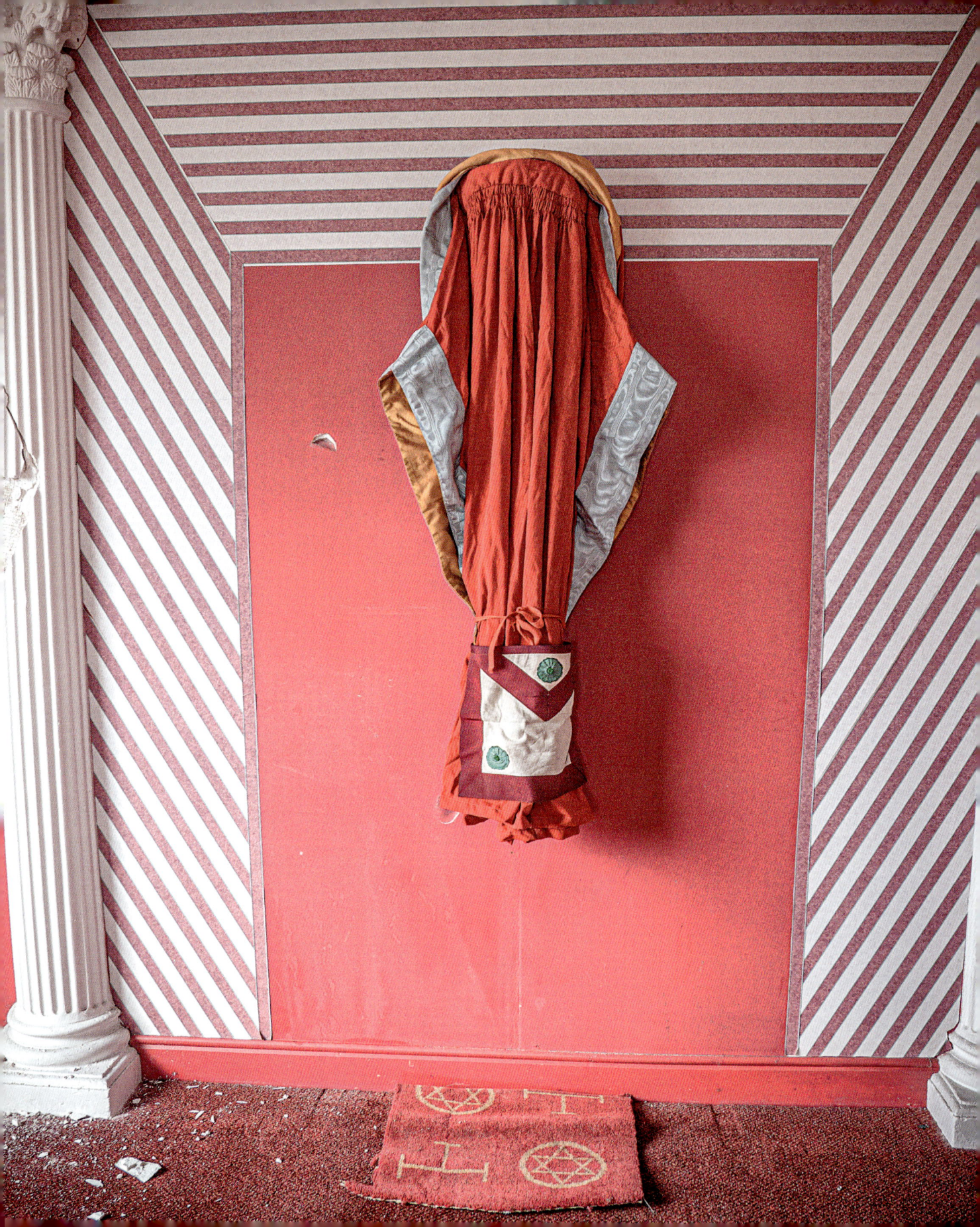

# FREEMASONS' LODGE

Although this lodge has only been closed for four years, the vandalism has been extensive. Despite this, I wanted to see if there was anything symbolic left that I could document and, to my surprise, there was.

The history of Freemasonry in Northern Ireland dates back to the early eighteenth century, when the first Masonic Lodges were established in the region. The exact date of the founding of the

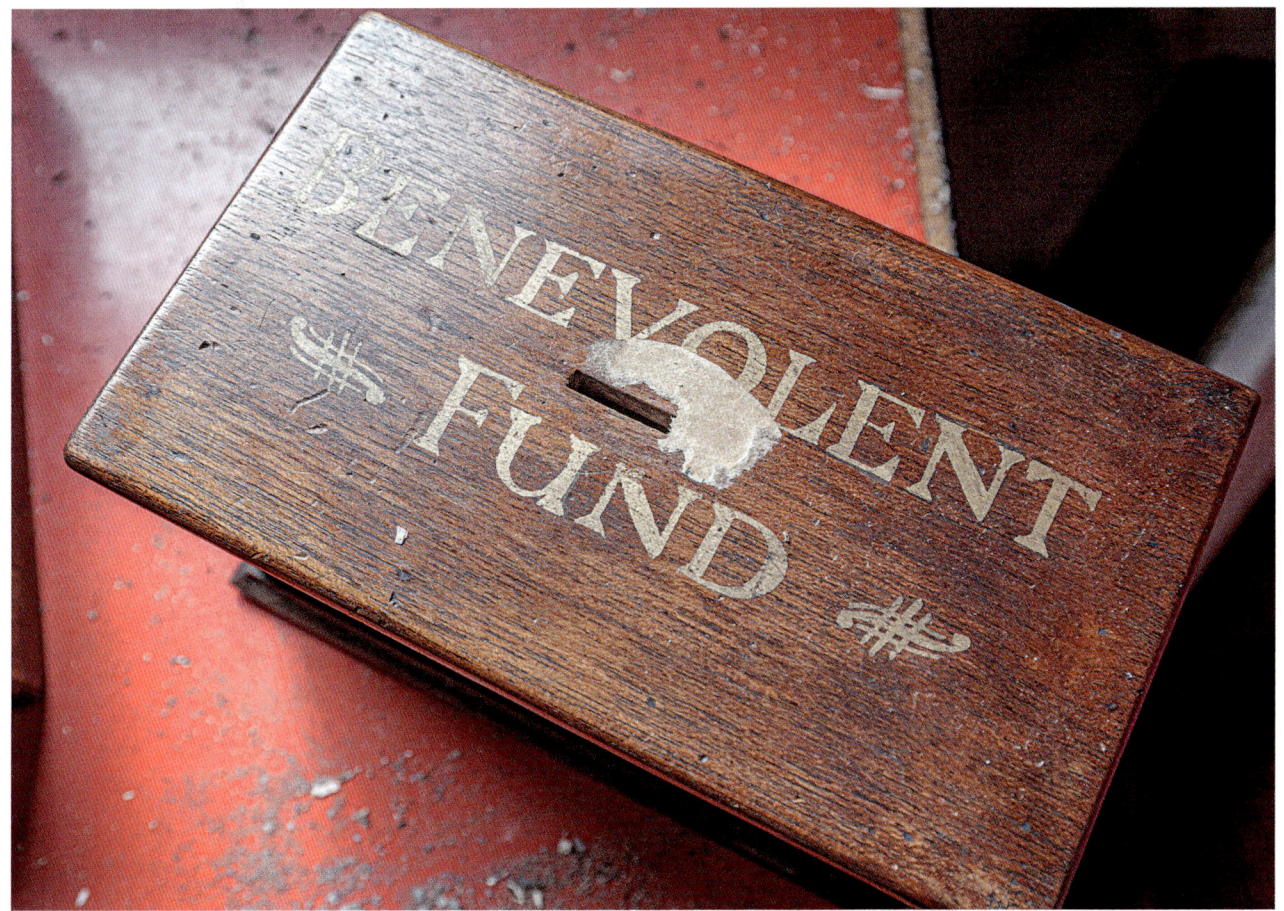

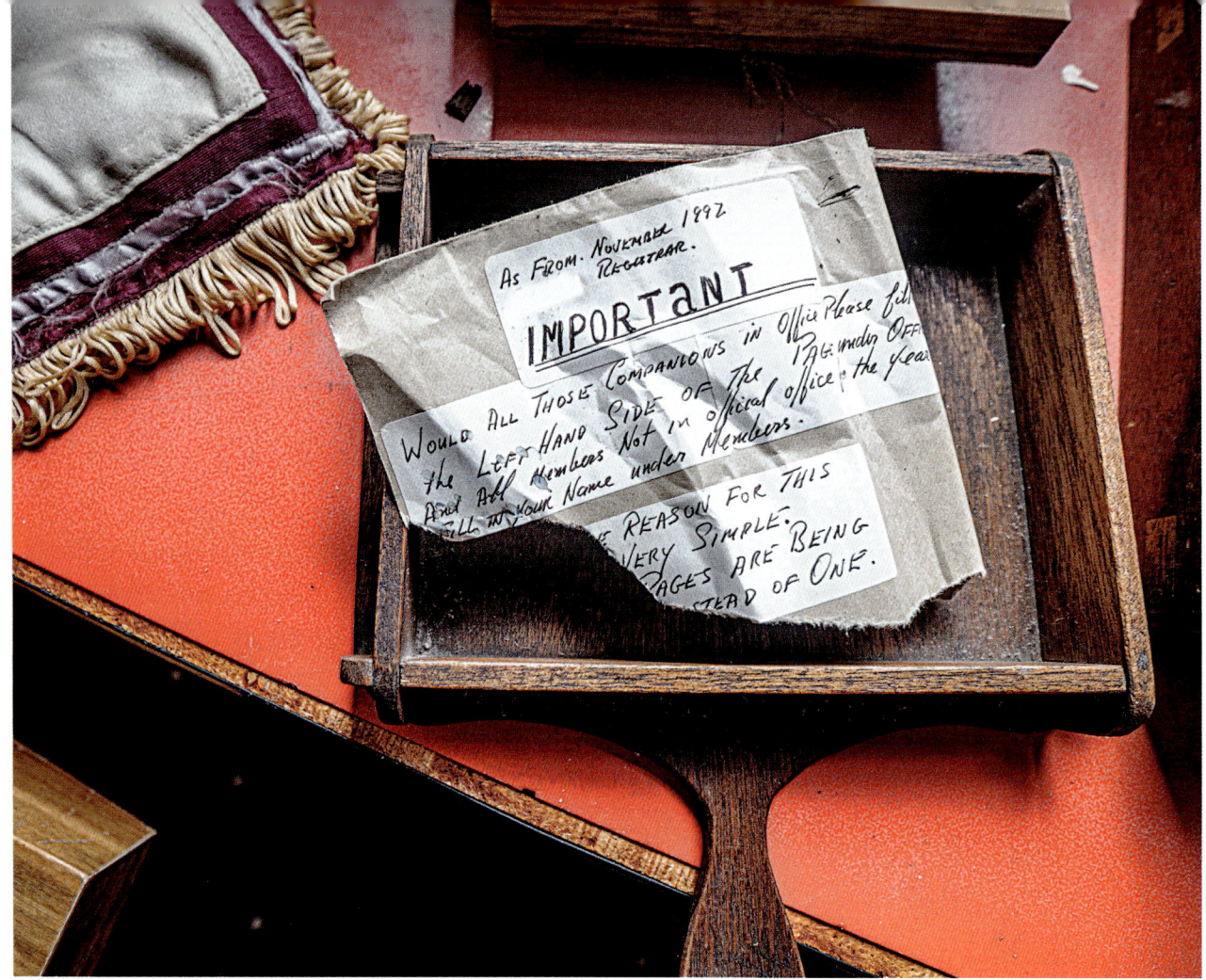

first lodge is unclear, but by the mid-eighteenth century Freemasonry had become an established and influential presence in Northern Ireland. As in other parts of the world, it is an organisation that has always been shrouded in secrecy and mystery, with much of its history passed down through spoken tradition and ritual.

Throughout the nineteenth and twentieth centuries, the Freemasons in Northern Ireland grew and expanded, with new lodges established in towns and cities across the region. These lodges played a significant role in the social and cultural life of Northern Ireland, with many prominent individuals in government, business and the arts becoming members of the fraternity.

The Troubles, a period of sectarian conflict in Northern Ireland from the late 1960s to the 1990s, had a significant impact on Freemasons in the region. Despite being a secular organisation, many lodges were targeted by paramilitary groups, leading to a decline in membership and a sense of fear and insecurity among members. However, they persisted through this difficult period and today the Freemasons still have a large following in Northern Ireland.

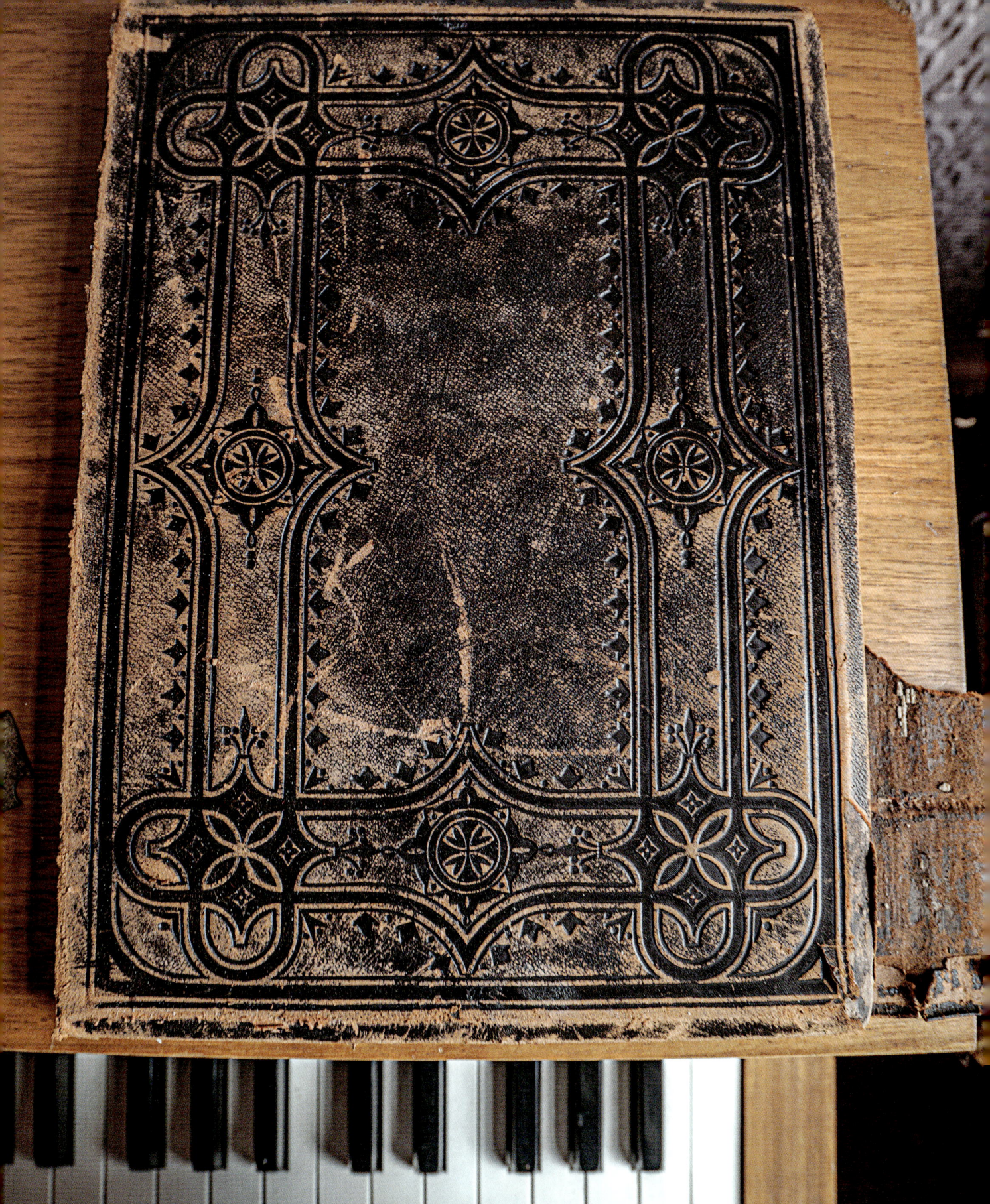

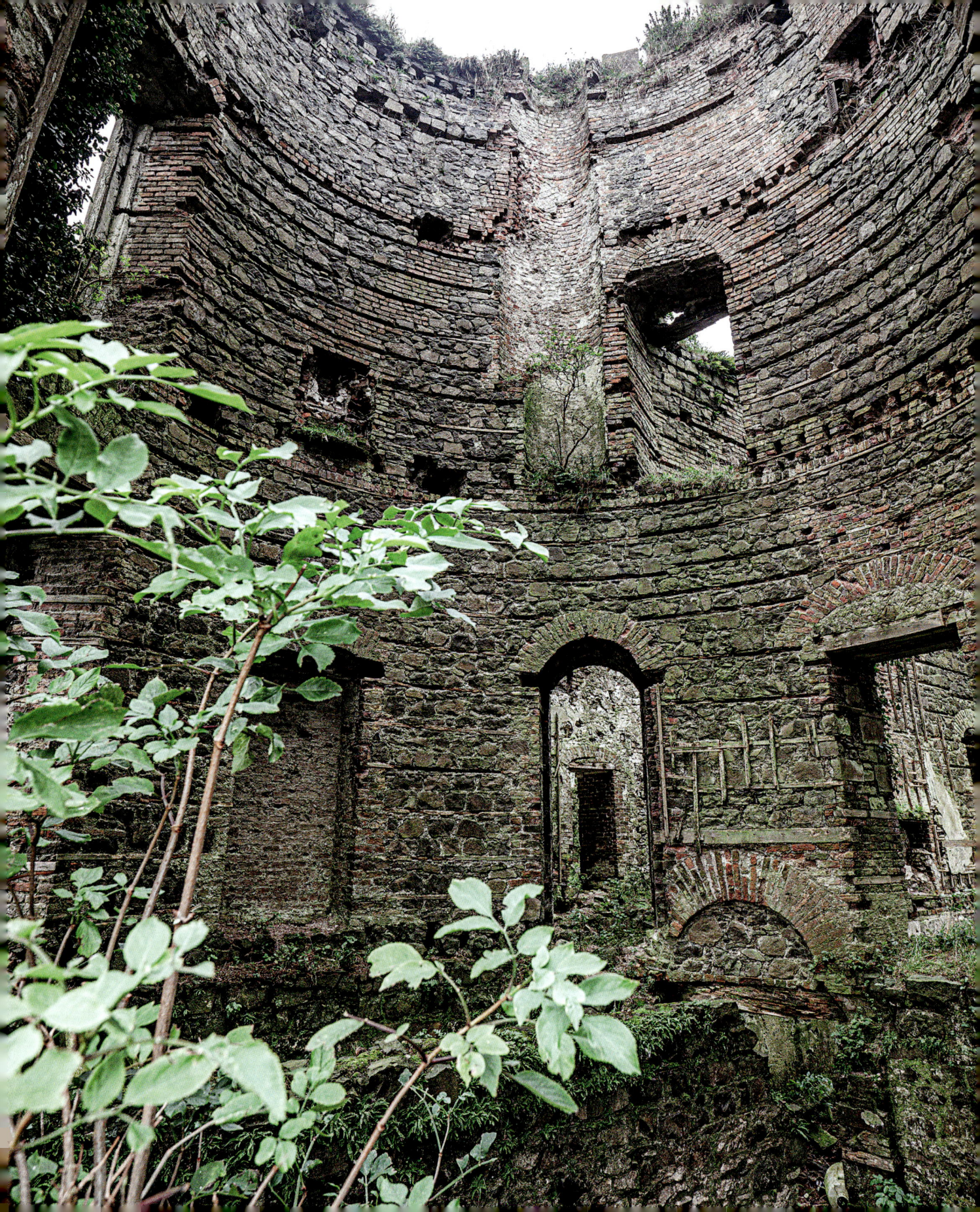

# KILWAUGHTER CASTLE

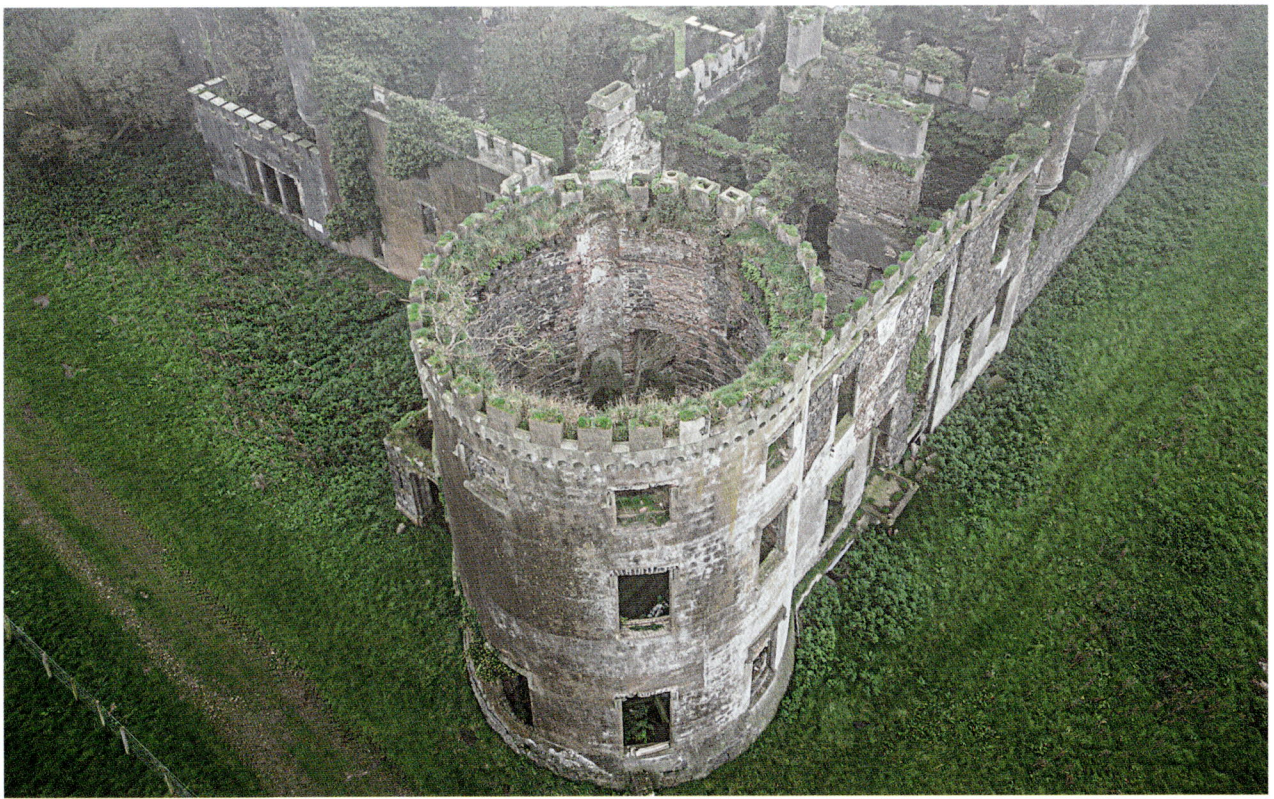

Kilwaughter Castle is the perfect example of how a building that may appear as just a ruin at first glance can have a rich history and fascinating stories waiting to be uncovered. I visited this castle one misty morning, which made for some very atmospheric photographs.

The original structure on this site was built in 1622 for Patrick Agnew, but it has undergone some changes over the years. In 1806, at the age of ten, Patrick's great-grandson Edward Jones Agnew inherited the estate. The estate was managed by agents until he reached adulthood and it wasn't until then

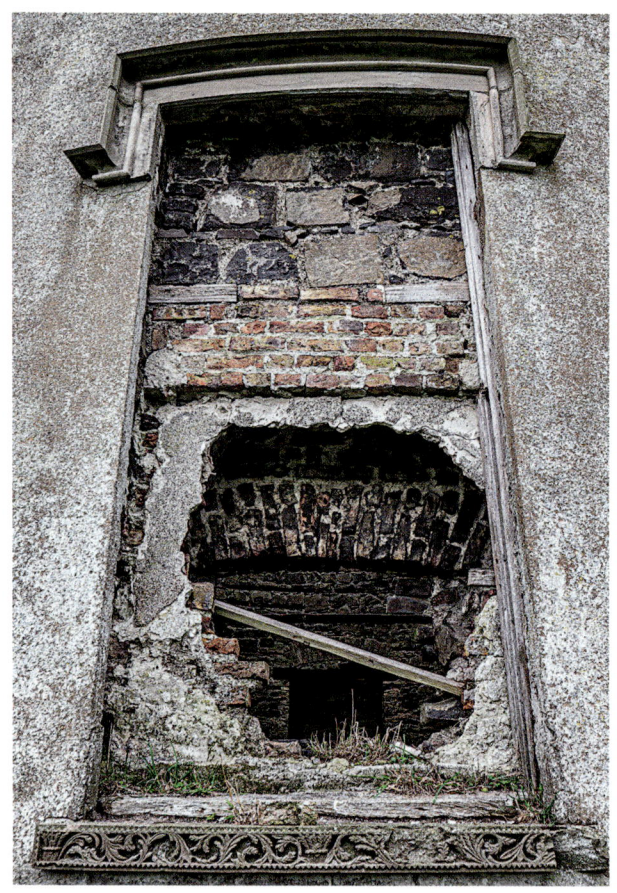

that he finally moved into the castle, accompanied by his sister Margaret. When they arrived, they were shocked to find the castle all but empty. There wasn't even a tablecloth, let alone a spoon, knife or fork for eating. The building was outdated and in need of major refurbishment.

Edward decided to hire architect John Nash to renovate and expand the castle. The project transformed Kilwaughter into an imposing castle, and the grandest feature was a castellated tower with breathtaking views of the artificial lake and surrounding parkland, which still can be appreciated today.

In 1834 Edward passed away, leaving the estate and castle to his son William. He expanded his holdings to 10,000 acres by purchasing additional land, making Kilwaughter one of Ireland's largest estates. William, who spent most of his adult life in Paris, never married and passed away in 1891. Upon his death, the estate was inherited by his niece Augusta, who was married to an Italian count named Ugo Balzani, a highly respected historian. They had two children and split their time between family homes in Italy, England and Kilwaughter.

In 1891 the castle was rented to John Galt Smith, a linen merchant, and his wife, Bessie, for the next thirty years. They had left New York and initially settled in Belfast before deciding to lease Kilwaughter Castle. Bessie played a crucial role in modernising the castle, putting her own unique touch on it. Renowned for their extravagant dinner parties, the couple were well-known entertainers. Tragically, John passed away in 1899, just eight years into their lease.

During the Second World War, the castle was deemed 'enemy property' due to its owners residing in Italy. It was seized by the British government and transformed into an army training camp for British and American soldiers. Following the war, it was purchased by a scrap dealer, who stripped the furnishings and even sold off the lead from the roof.

The castle is now managed by the Kilwaughter Castle Restoration group, established to ensure its future would be protected.

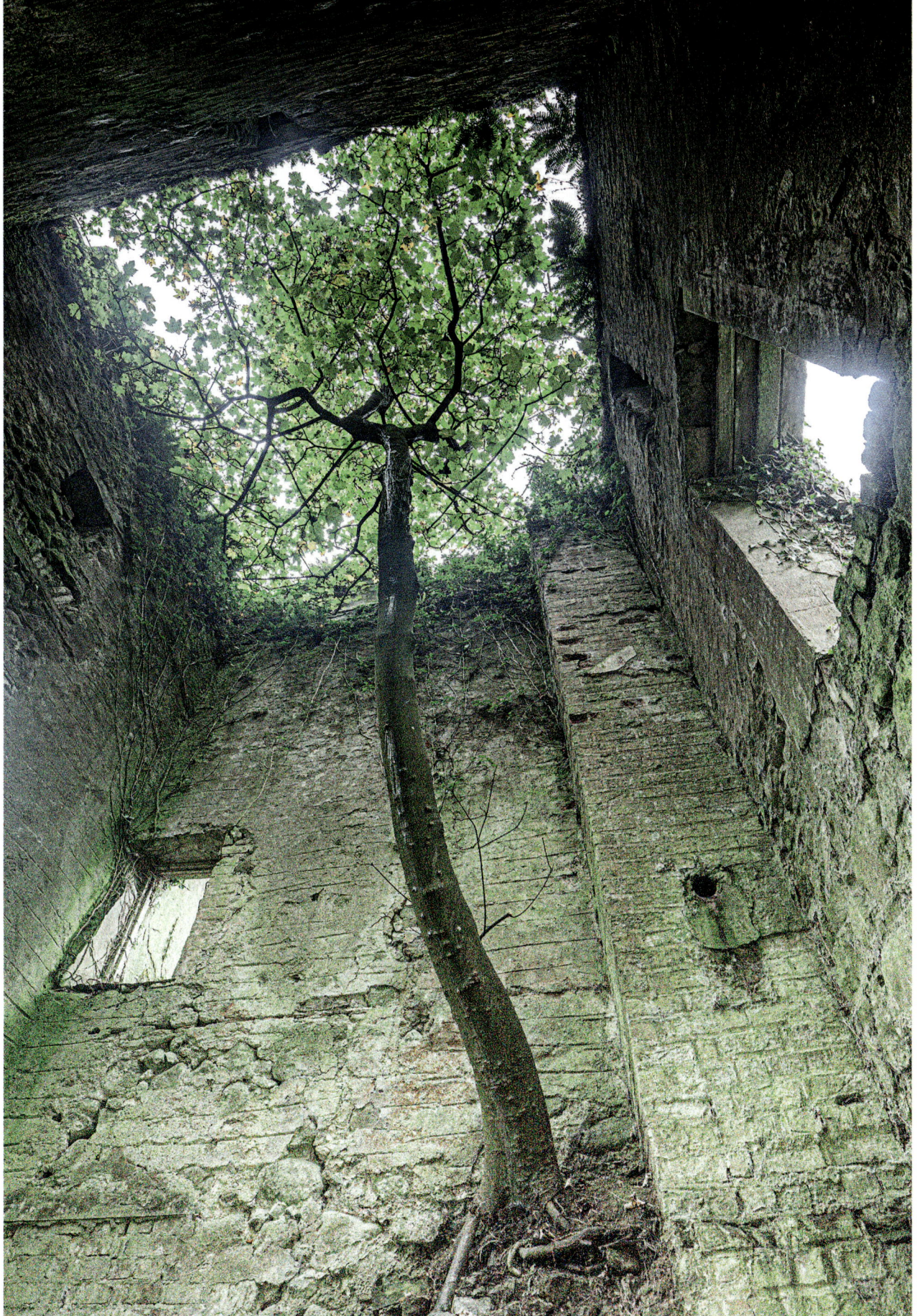

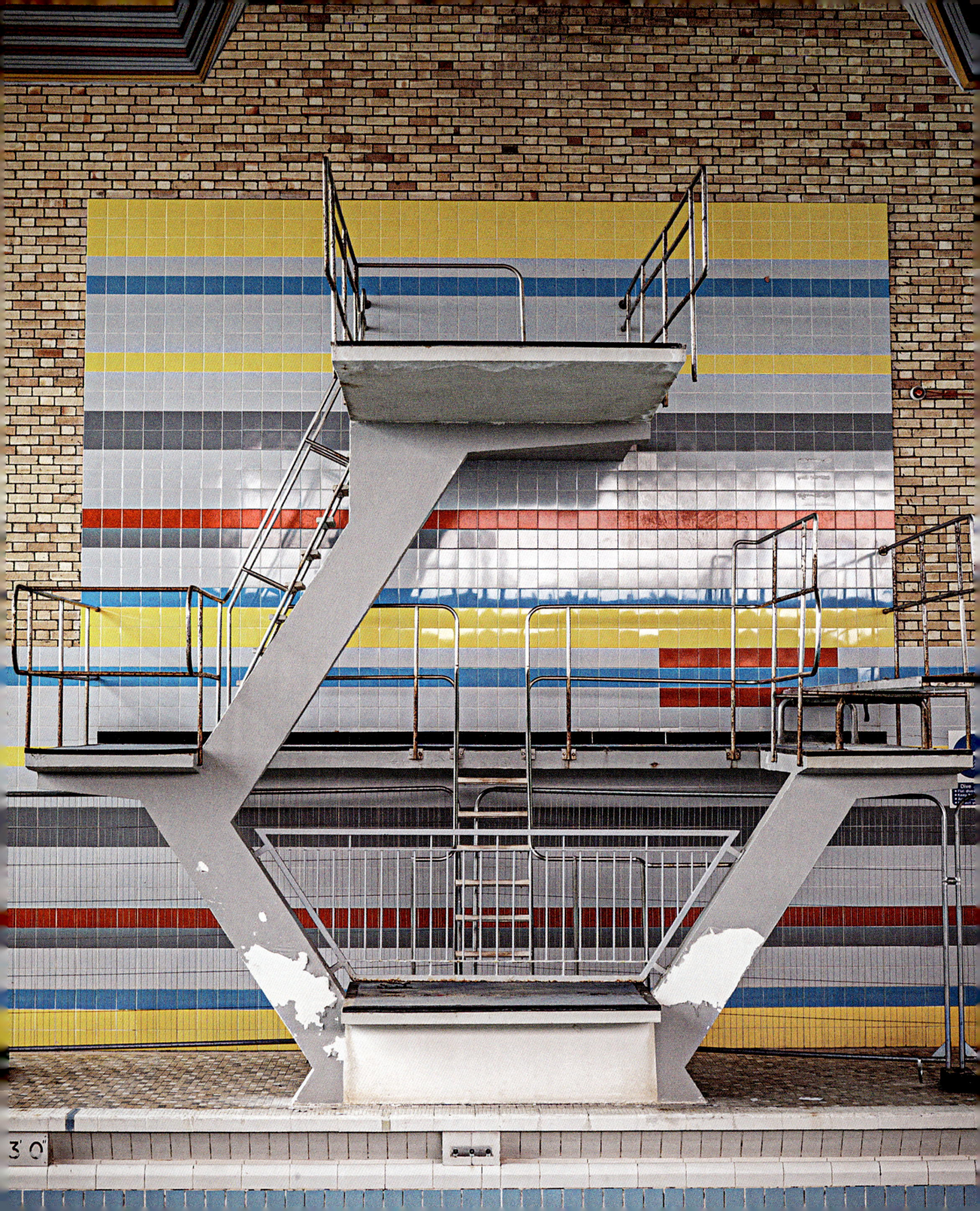

# CASCADES LEISURE CENTRE

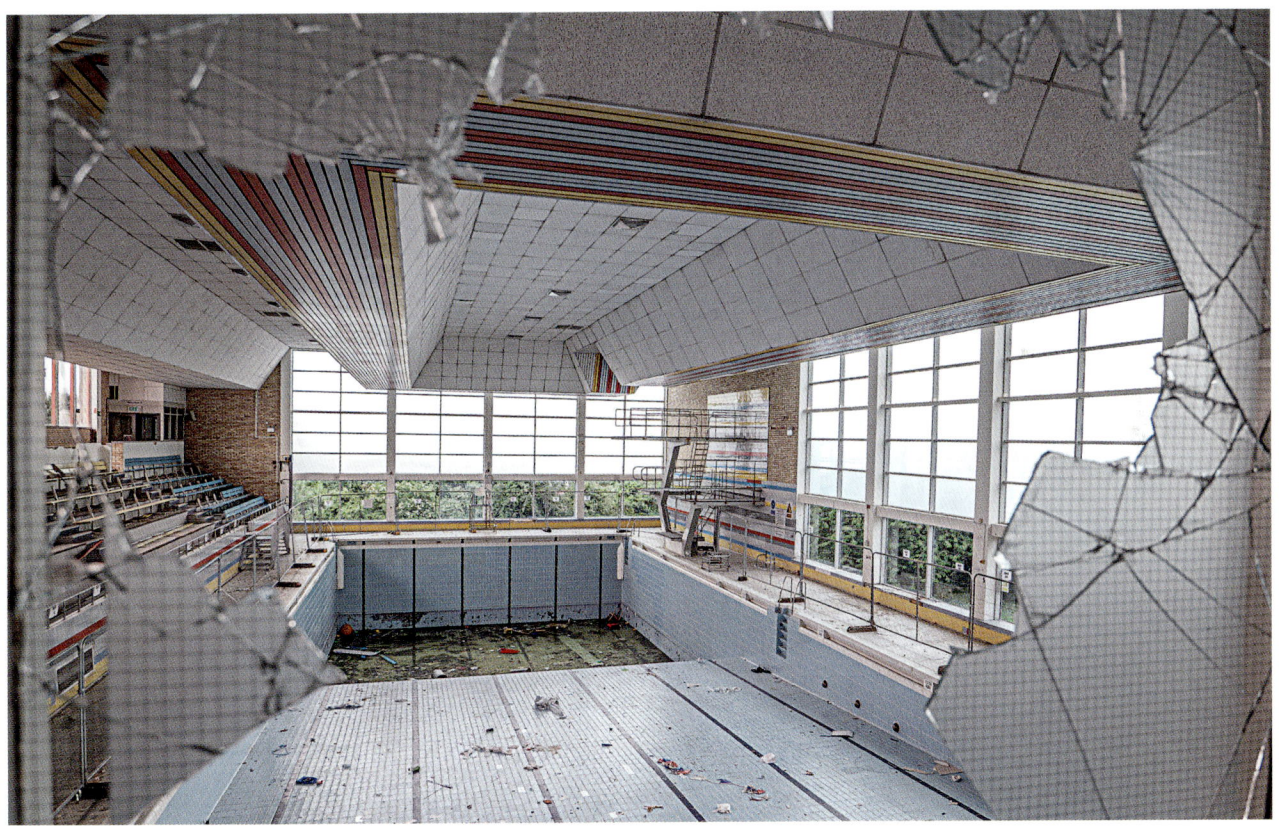

I have visited some derelict hotels and homes that have had old disused pools, but I had never before been to a completely derelict leisure centre. Recently, I heard of one that had shut down due to the construction of a new £30 million leisure centre nearby, so I reached out to Gareth Wilson, who was lord mayor of Portadown at the time, and he put me in touch with the council to arrange access, for which I was very grateful.

The leisure centre closed in 2020 and has experienced a lot of vandalism and broken windows since then. As a result, the council has now secured

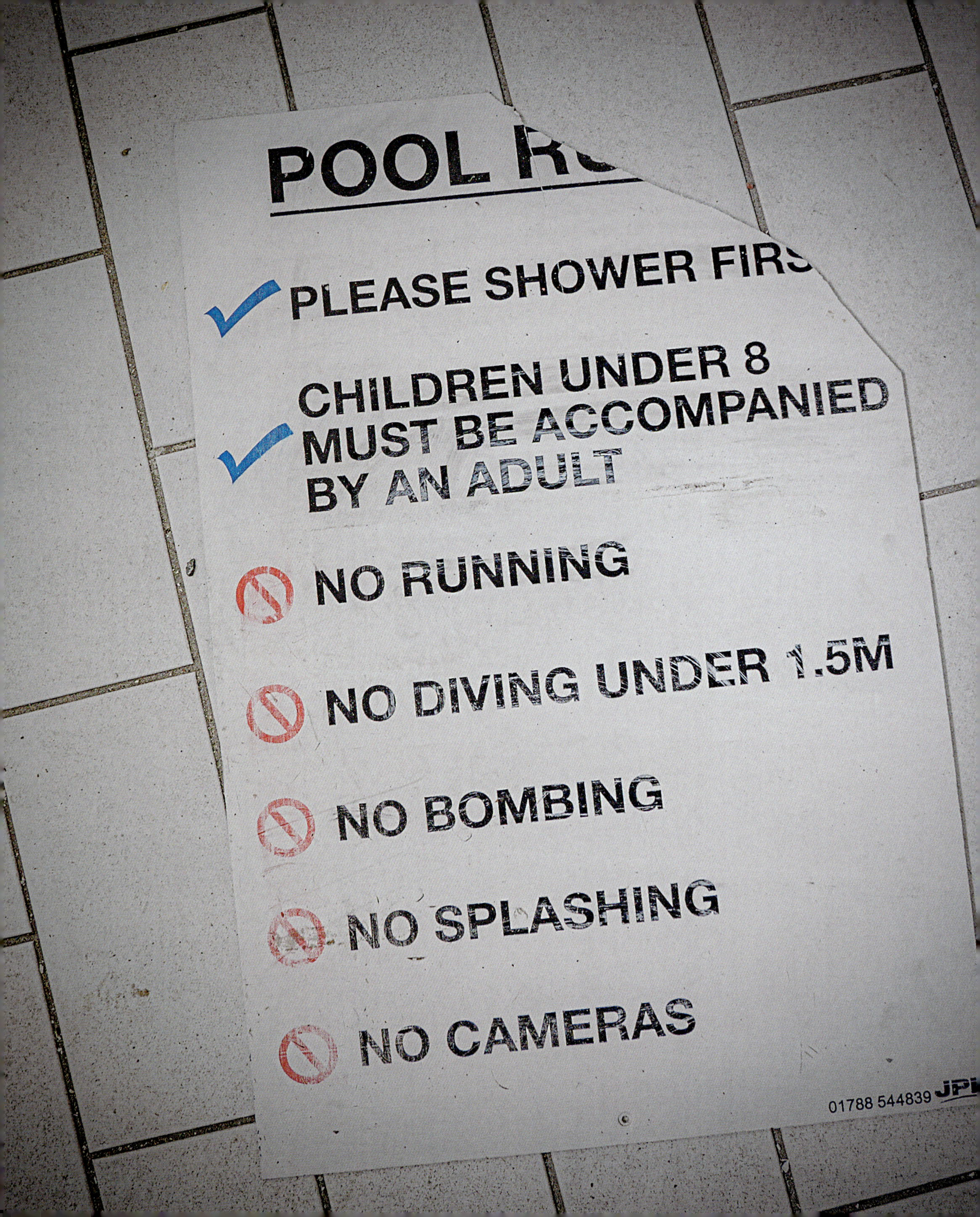

# POOL R[ULES]

✓ PLEASE SHOWER FIRS[T]

✓ CHILDREN UNDER 8 MUST BE ACCOMPANIED BY AN ADULT

🚫 NO RUNNING

🚫 NO DIVING UNDER 1.5M

🚫 NO BOMBING

🚫 NO SPLASHING

🚫 NO CAMERAS

01788 544839  JPL

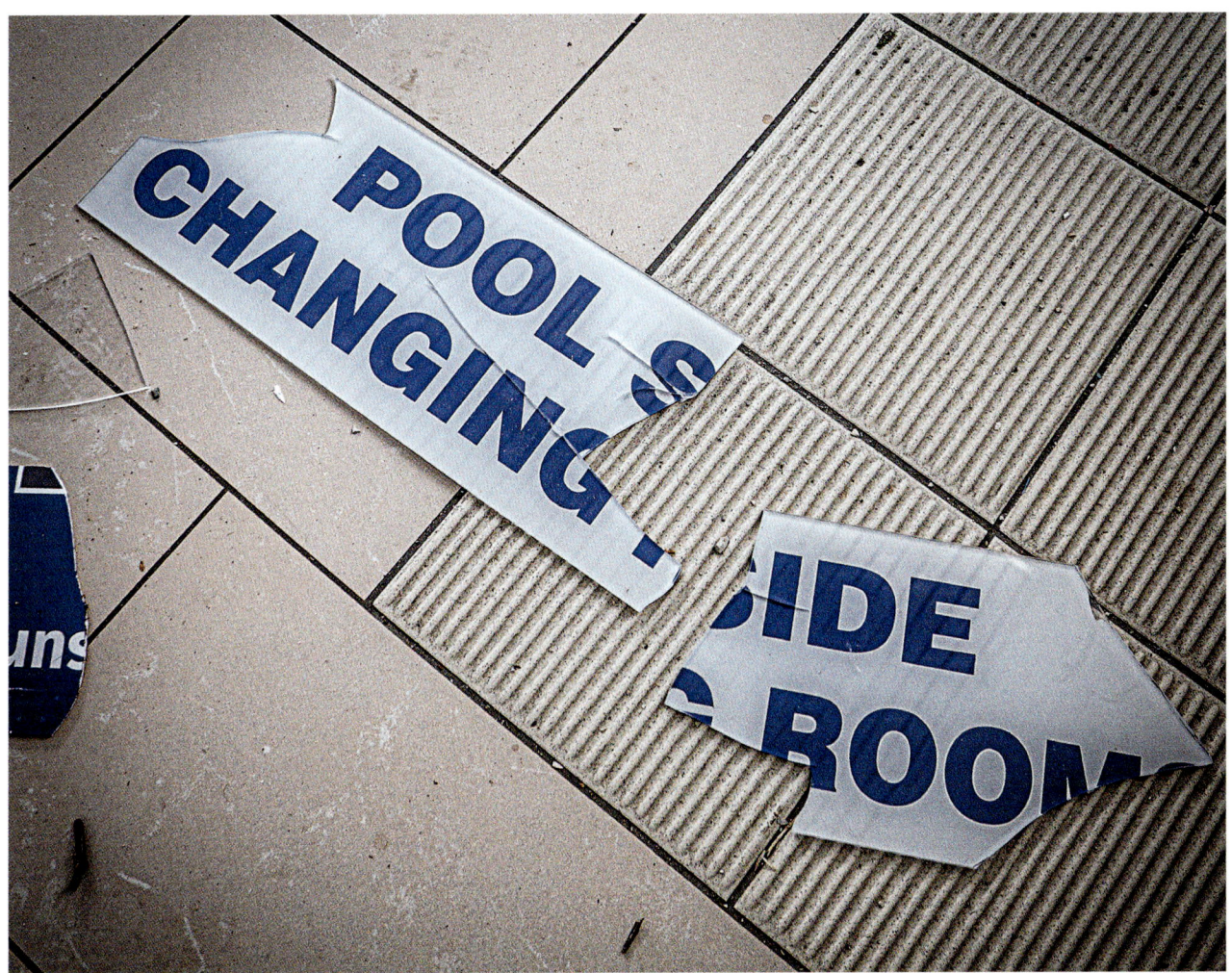

the site well and installed active CCTV. The main pool is 33 metres long and has a 13-foot deep end, along with 1-metre, 3-metre and 5-metre diving boards. It was one of the last remaining pools of its size in Ireland.

When I walked into the main pool area, I could see the vivid red, blue and yellow striped decor, which reminded me of the many 1980s-style pools that I visited and swam in growing up. There was

also an upper viewing gallery, remains of an old café and a cleared-out gym space.

The pool and its car park are now on the market for a modest £500,000. There have been various petitions online to try to reopen the leisure centre, as the new one built at Craigavon Lakes cannot accommodate the vast numbers that attend it, although I think this is very unlikely due to the condition the Cascades is now in. But never say never!

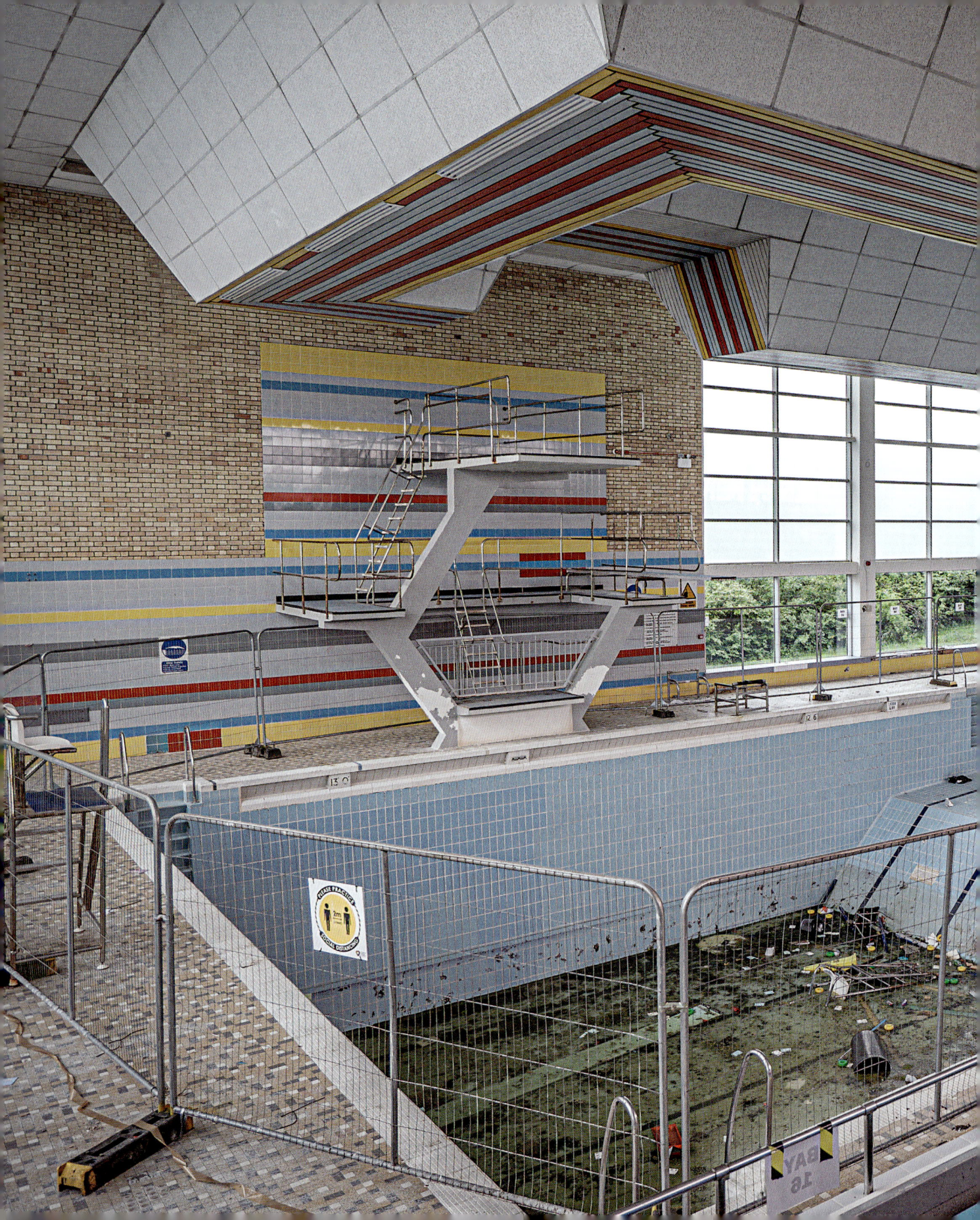

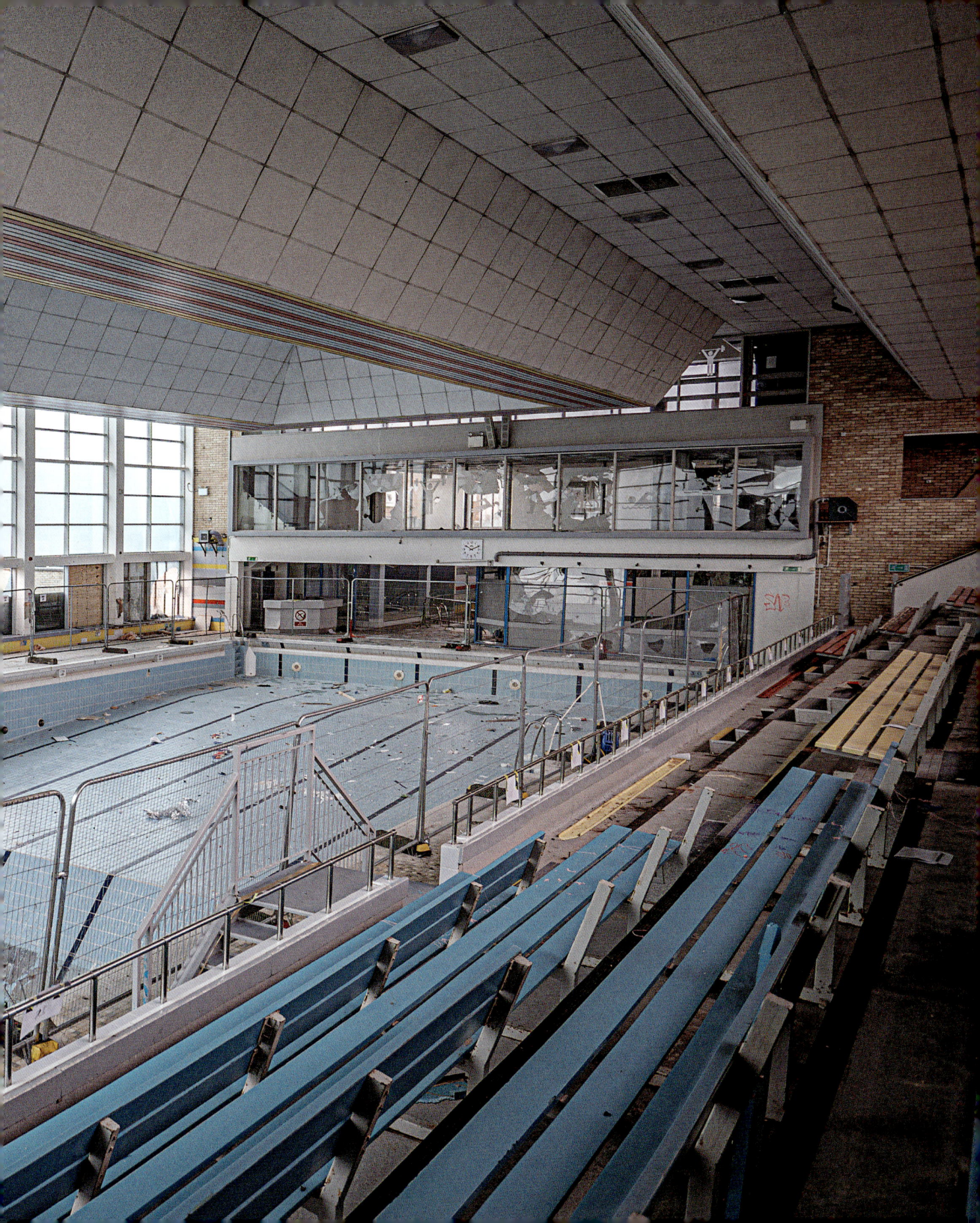

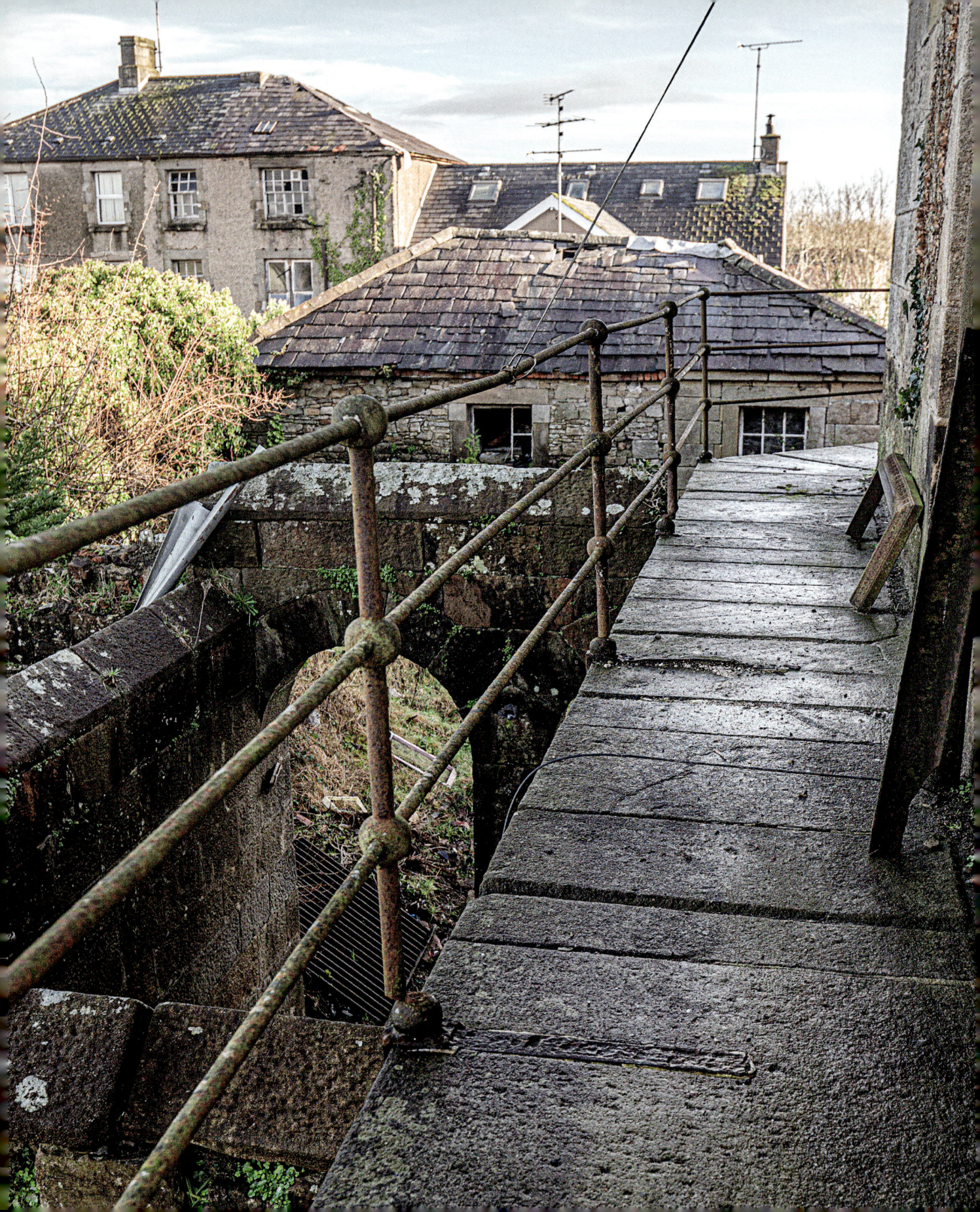

# THE GOVERNOR'S HOUSE

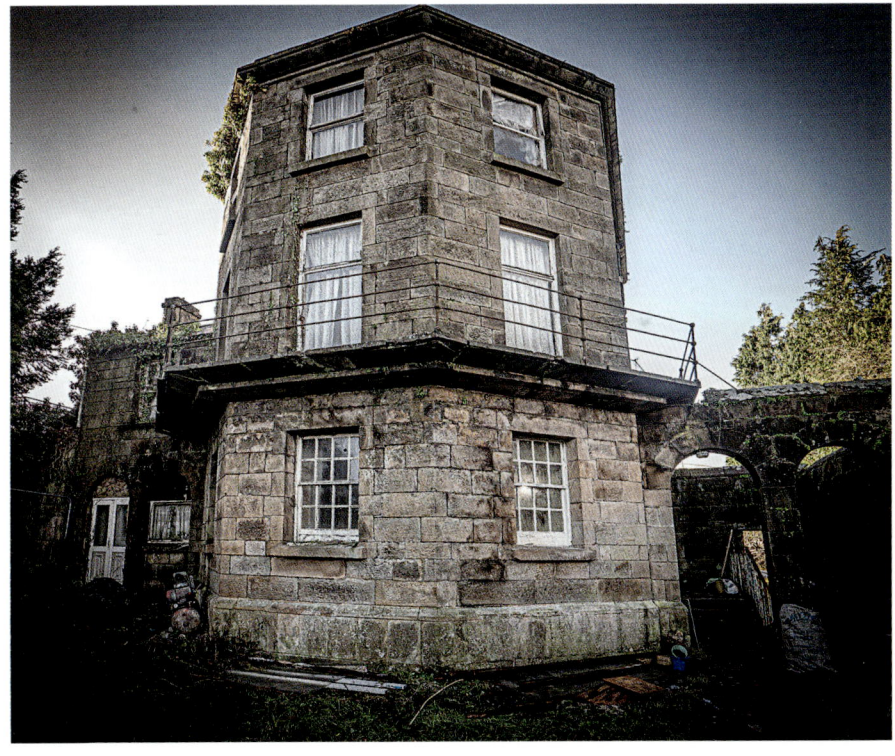

I first visited the old Governor's House, part of the Omagh Gaol complex, in 2017, hearing that it was up for sale and feeling compelled to see it for myself. At that time, I had little knowledge about the place other than its distinctive octagonal shape and that it had been the residence of the gaol's governor.

Upon walking up the driveway and into the garden, I was struck by the overwhelming amount of rubbish and debris scattered around. The previous inhabitant of the house seemed to have been a hoarder, piling up scrap cars, metal, tyres and trailers in the garden. Some of the debris reached heights of over 5 feet. On that day, I decided to throw in the towel and head back home without the pictures I had hoped to take.

Then, in late 2023 I heard that the Governor's House had been sold. This presented another chance for me to gain access to the property. Eventually, I managed to connect with the buyer, who was happy to let me to visit and photograph the house before any significant renovation work commenced.

The Governor's House was constructed in 1790 and the gaol was operational from 1804. Historical records show overcrowded conditions within the gaol

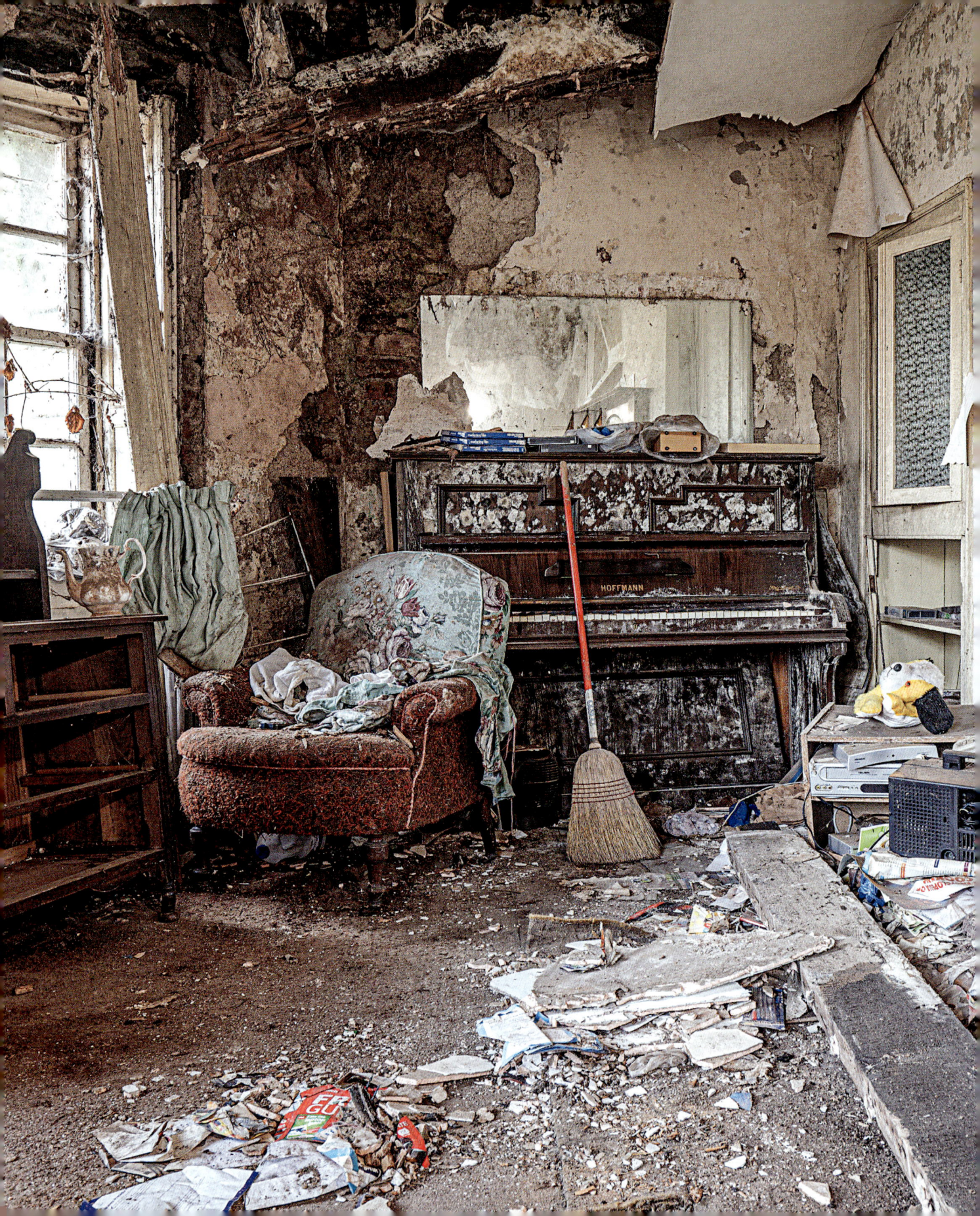

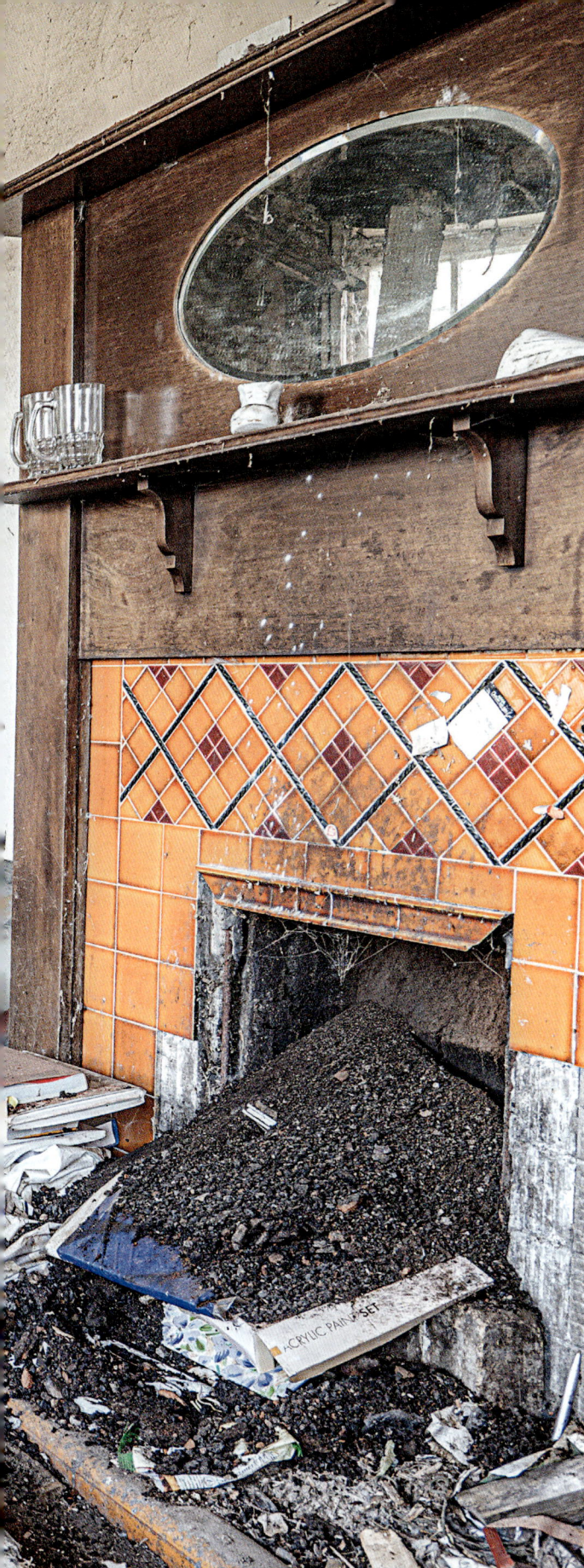

from the outset, with 145 inmates recorded, including fourteen classified as insane. Initially designed as a debtors' prison, the cells accommodated fourteen prisoners per cell with just two beds between them. The prison's sanitation and hygiene standards were reported to have been of a very poor standard.

This is confirmed by a fascinating piece of history I learned about the gaol. As I delved deeper into its past, I discovered a tragic story about one of its governors: Mr Disney. When he took up his new role, the house's sewage system was in dire need of attention, and Disney took it upon himself to improve this. Unfortunately, the work was unsuccessful and raw sewage began to leak freely throughout the gaol complex. This led to a devastating outcome for Disney and his four children, with all of them succumbing to fever, likely caused by their exposure to the contaminated environment.

In 1823 architect Thomas Hargreave expanded the prison with new wings, enabling the segregation of prisoners into different wards based on their classification. Following the expansion, the gaol could house up to 300 inmates. The new section allowed for separate blocks for men and women, with enclosed work spaces in front of the original building. A tread wheel was operated by prisoners to supply water to the complex from the nearby Strule river. The prison was enclosed by a high stone wall with the Governor's House at its centre, giving the occupant a view of both yards and allowing him to see what the prisoners were doing at all times.

Punishments within the gaol were severe, including executions that were conducted at Gallows Hill.

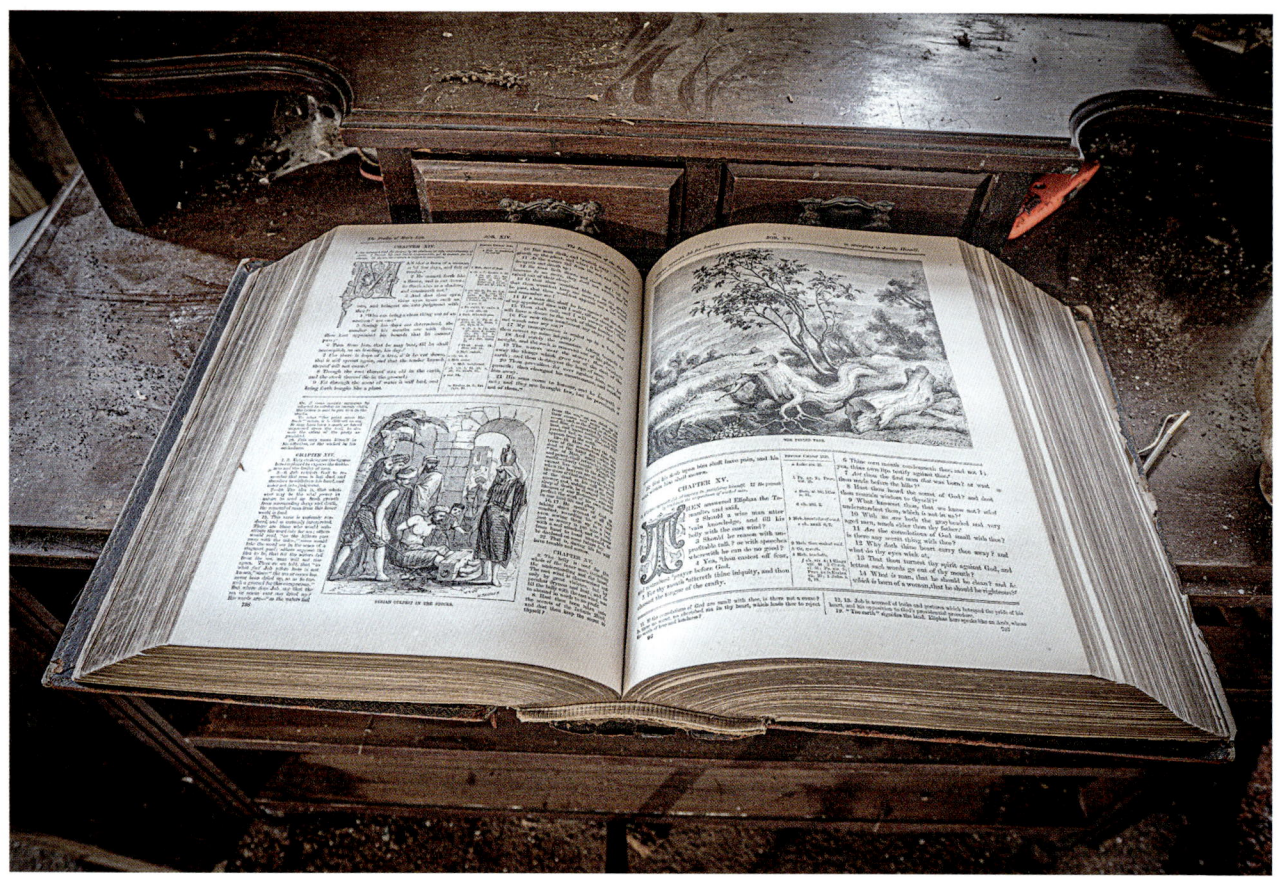

There were no actual gallows, hanging was done by simply attaching a rope to a tree. One infamous incident involved a man who miraculously survived his punishment. The hangman clearly miscalculated, and when the 'corpse' was being transported to nearby Fintona for burial, the man jumped off the cart and made his escape. He wasn't at liberty for long, though, as he reoffended and landed back at the gaol. This led to him being the first inmate to be hanged in the prison, after executions were moved within its walls. This time, the authorities didn't take any chances and had him buried at the gaol.

One of the gaol's most notable inmates was Thomas Hartley Montgomery, a local policeman who was hanged there. Montgomery robbed a bank in Newtownstewart after getting into financial trouble arising from gambling debts. During the robbery, he fatally wounded bank teller William Glass, stabbing him in the head with a filing spike. Despite using his position as the local inspector to attempt to deflect suspicion away from himself while investigating the murder, Montgomery was eventually found guilty after three trials (the first two were mistrials). On the morning of 26 August 1873, he

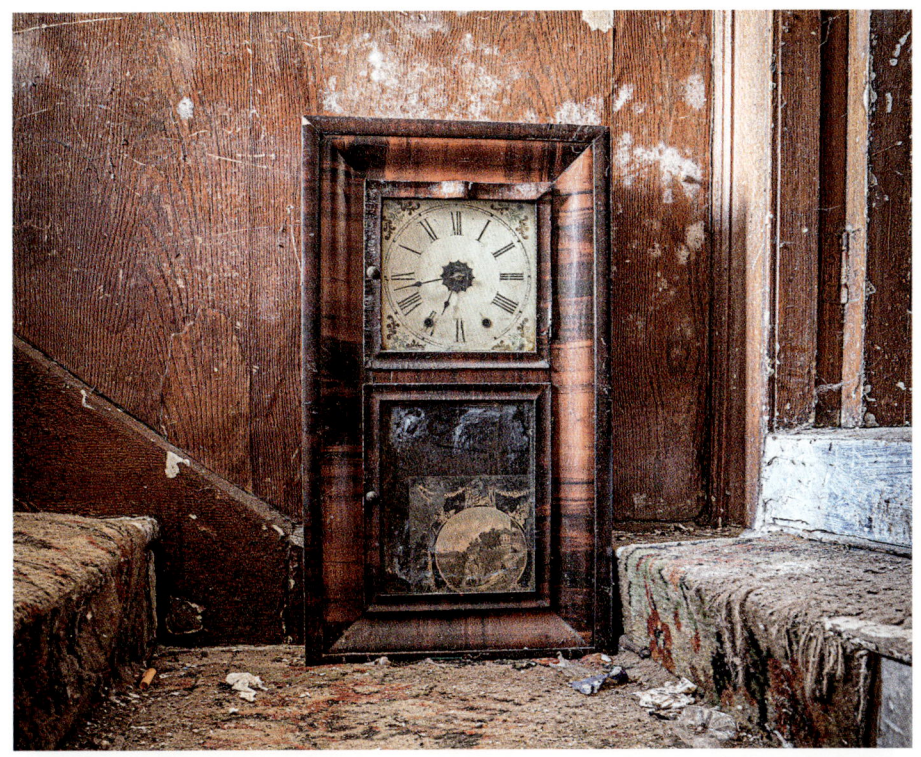

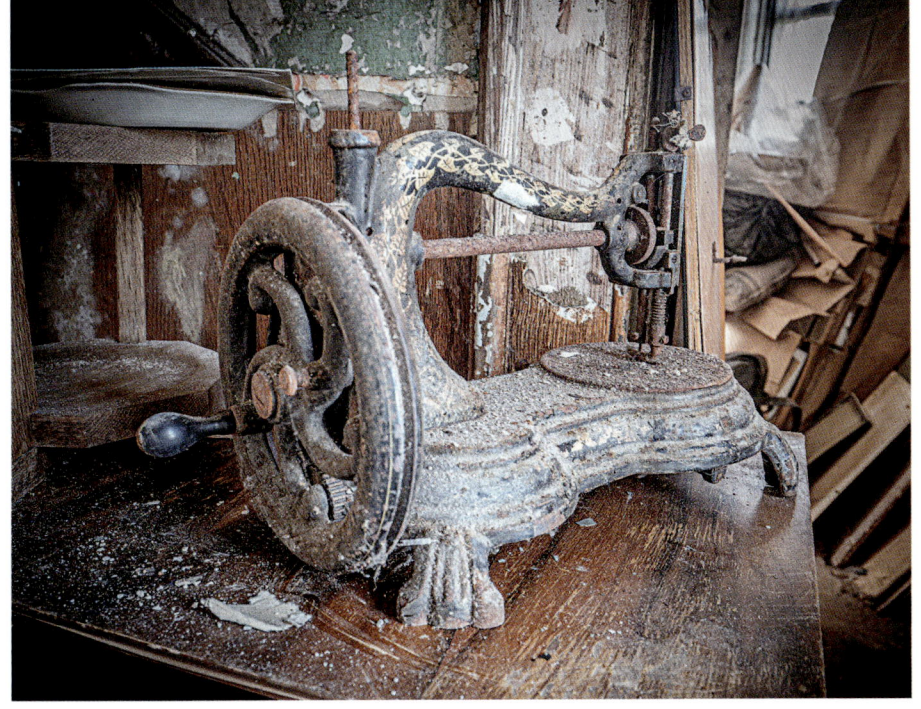

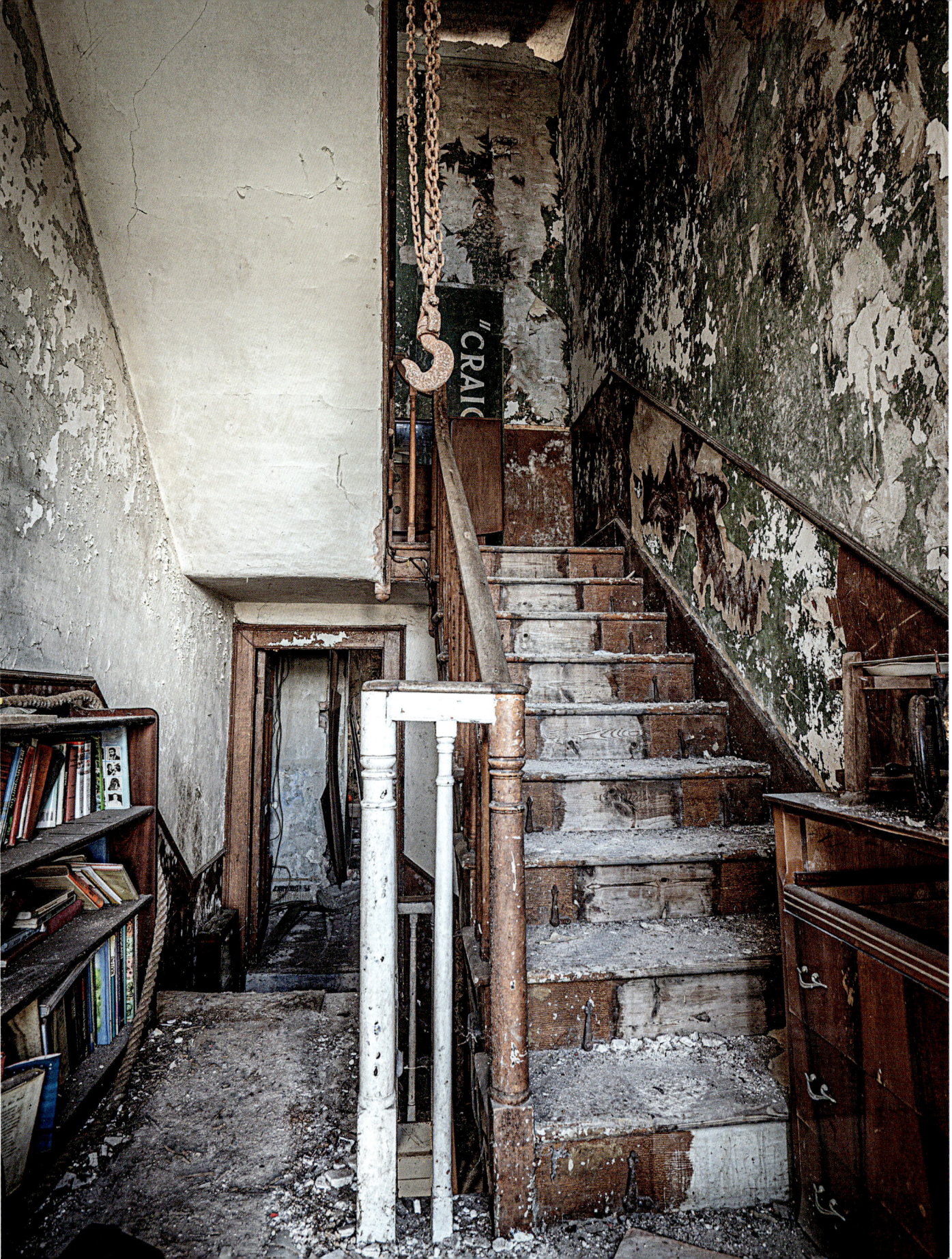

met his end on the gallows, becoming the only Irish policeman to be officially executed. He was laid to rest in the governor's garden. It was recorded that he asked the hangman, seconds before his execution, 'Is hanging a painful death?'

The gaol closed in 1902 and the house came into private ownership in 1960. It has changed hands a few times since then, but the owner is now clearing out the house and surrounding site and plans to repair the building. He is undecided what he will use it for at this point, but it will be restored sympathetically and to the correct standards. I can't wait to follow its new journey.

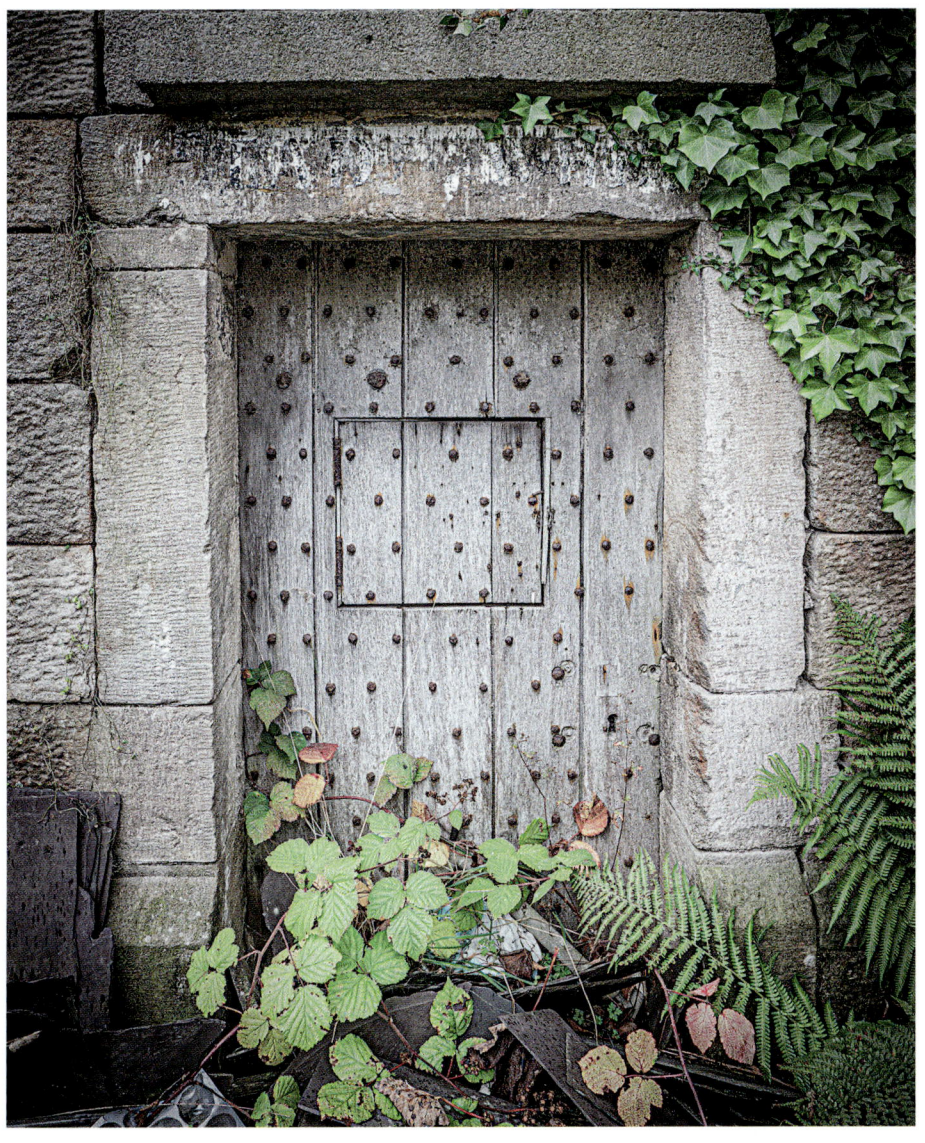

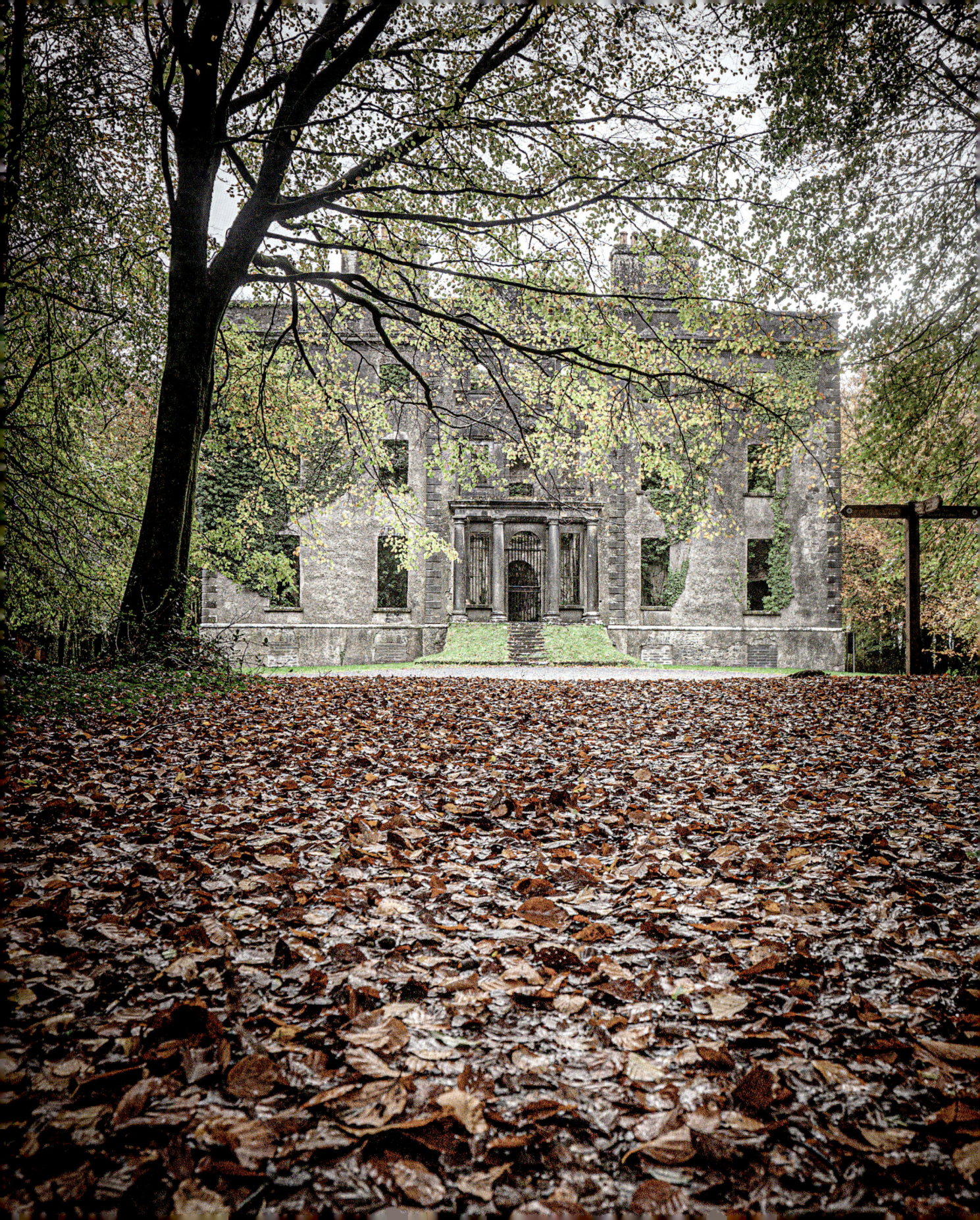

# MOORE HALL

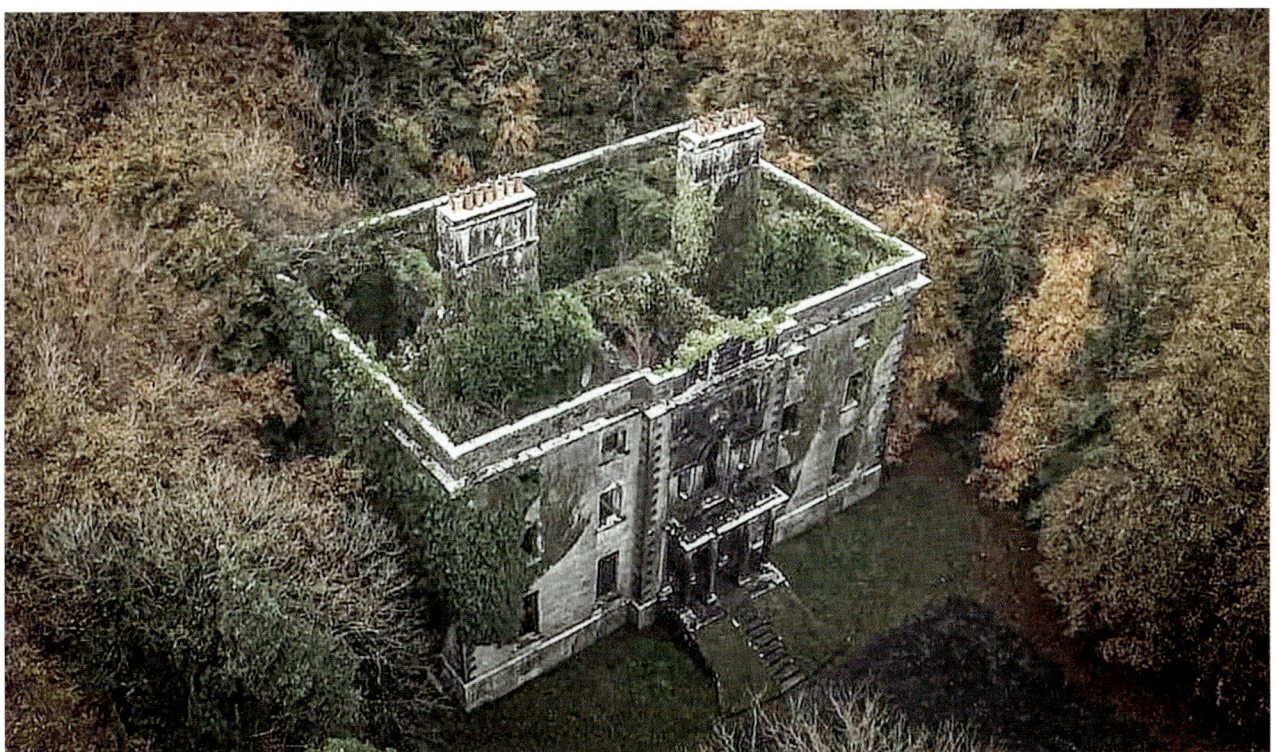

I had seen pictures of this colossal ruin online and to me it appeared incredibly mysterious, sitting in the heart of a wood. It was one of the reasons I decided to invest in a drone – I really wanted to capture an aerial view of the house, especially during the autumn months when the trees were at their most vibrant. Unfortunately, during my visit, the weather was very blustery, with heavy showers, and my drone did not survive.

The history of this dilapidated mansion is fascinating. It was constructed by the Moore family between 1792 and 1795. The family was advised against building on this site, high above the shores of Lough Carra, due to its supposed unlucky past –

legend has it that an ancient druid was killed there around AD 400 – but they proceeded regardless. At the top of the building, I noticed an inscription in Latin on the stone which read *Fortis cadere cedere non potest* – The brave may fall but never yield.

Some incredibly significant historical figures have graced the halls of this house. George Henry Moore (1810–1870) stands out as a particularly beloved figure among the locals. Co. Mayo was one of the hardest-hit regions during the Famine period, with many landlords evicting and mistreating their tenants. George, however, was very different. He had a huge passion for horses and horse racing and in 1846 entered his horse Coranna into the Chester Gold Cup. When Coranna won he pocketed a whopping £17,000 (equivalent to €2.5 million) but didn't keep the money for himself. Instead, he imported thousands of tonnes of grain to feed his tenants and also gave each family a cow. Thanks to his generosity, all the tenants of Moore Hall were able to survive the Famine and none were evicted for not paying rent. He was a remarkable individual.

Two of his sons were notable in their own right. One, George Augustus Moore (1852–1933), became a famous author, and notable writers of the time, such as Oscar Wilde, Lady Gregory and W.B. Yeats, were regular visitors to Moore Hall. The other, Senator Colonel Maurice Moore (1854–1939), served as a lieutenant in the Connaught Rangers and fought in the Second Boer War. He later became a senator in the newly established Seanad Éireann of the Irish Free State. When the IRA began targeting houses belonging to senators, Moore Hall was one of them, despite the fact that the house belonged to George and not Maurice. One evening masked men arrived, and James Reilly, the steward of the Hall, was witness to what happened.

A few weeks after the attack, George penned a letter to *The Morning Post* giving an account that he received from James: 'I had no option but to give up the keys, and suspecting what was on I pointed out to the leader that the house was not Colonel Moore's property. This had no effect. I sat up all night, hoping that when all would be clear I could save even a portion of the library. At four o'clock, I heard four loud explosions. At five I went to the place and found the whole house a seething mass of flames. I at once saw that all was hopeless. A fire brigade would be powerless, so firmly had the flames gripped the entire building. I could do nothing but stand by and await the end with the same feelings one has when standing by the open grave of a very dear friend. I do not say this in the "Uriah Heepish" way, for I really loved that old house. To me, it was a modern edition of King Tutankhamen's tomb. At six o'clock, the roof fell in with a terrific crash. When the fire died down I got ladders up to the library windows, hoping to save even a few books, but nothing living could enter, so fierce was the heat.'

Since then, the house has been abandoned and left as a burnt-out shell. The property is today owned by Mayo Council and access is restricted. But if you ever do visit Moore Hall and find a drone, it's probably mine!

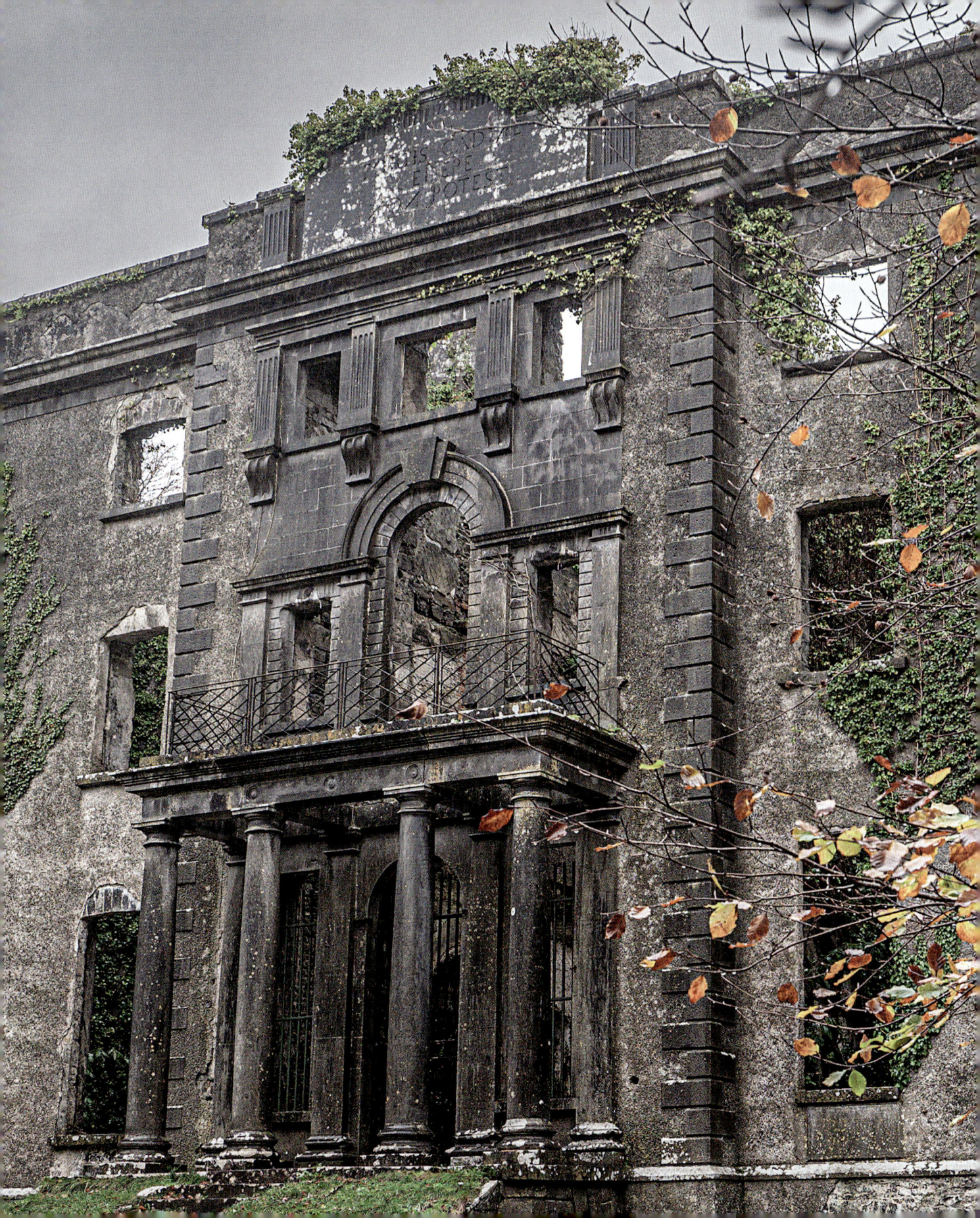

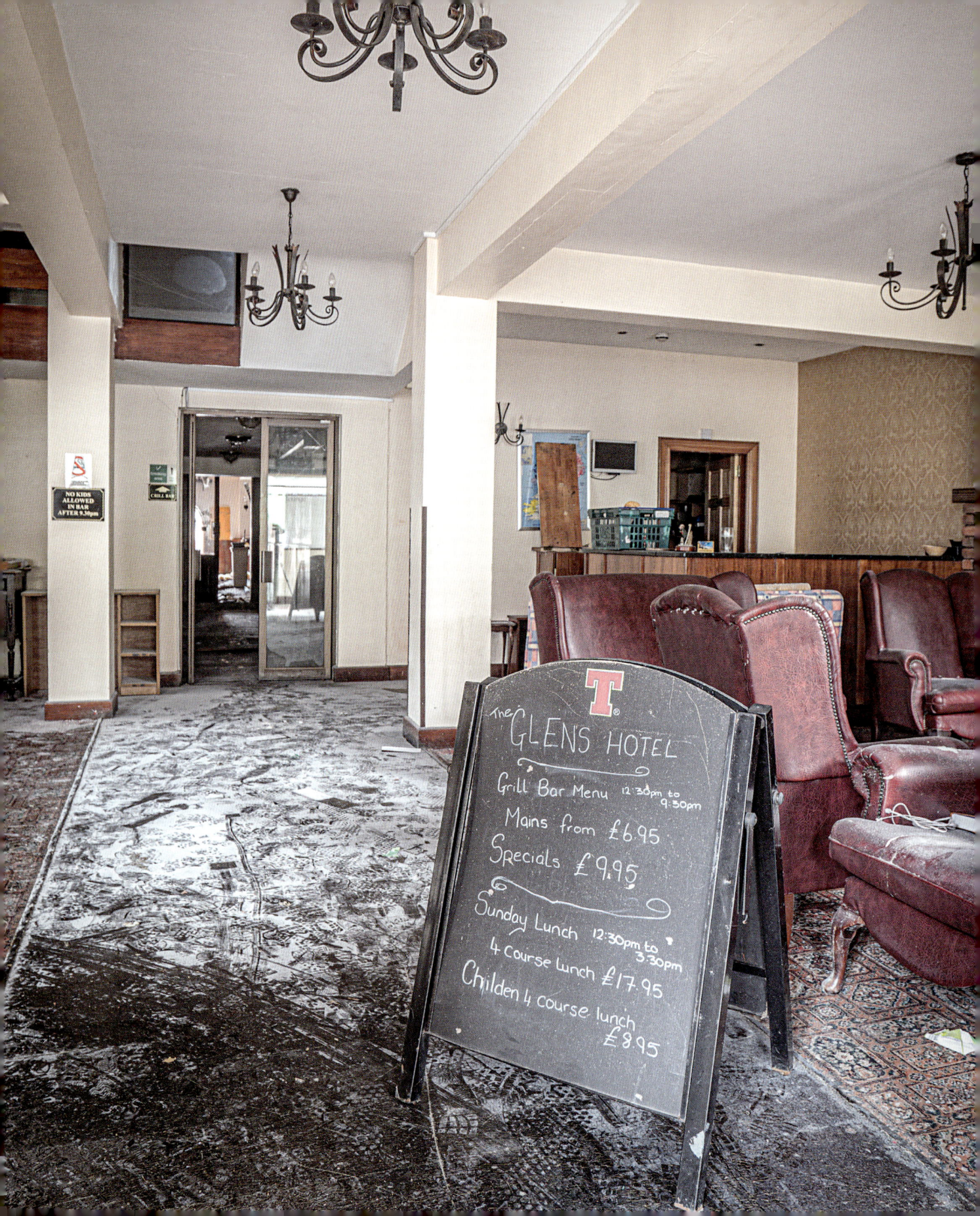

The GLENS HOTEL

Grill Bar Menu 12:30pm to 9:50pm

Mains from £6.95

Specials £9.95

Sunday Lunch 12:30pm to 3:30pm

4 Course Lunch £17.95

Childen 4 course lunch £8.95

NO KIDS ALLOWED IN BAR AFTER 9.30pm

# THE GLENS HOTEL

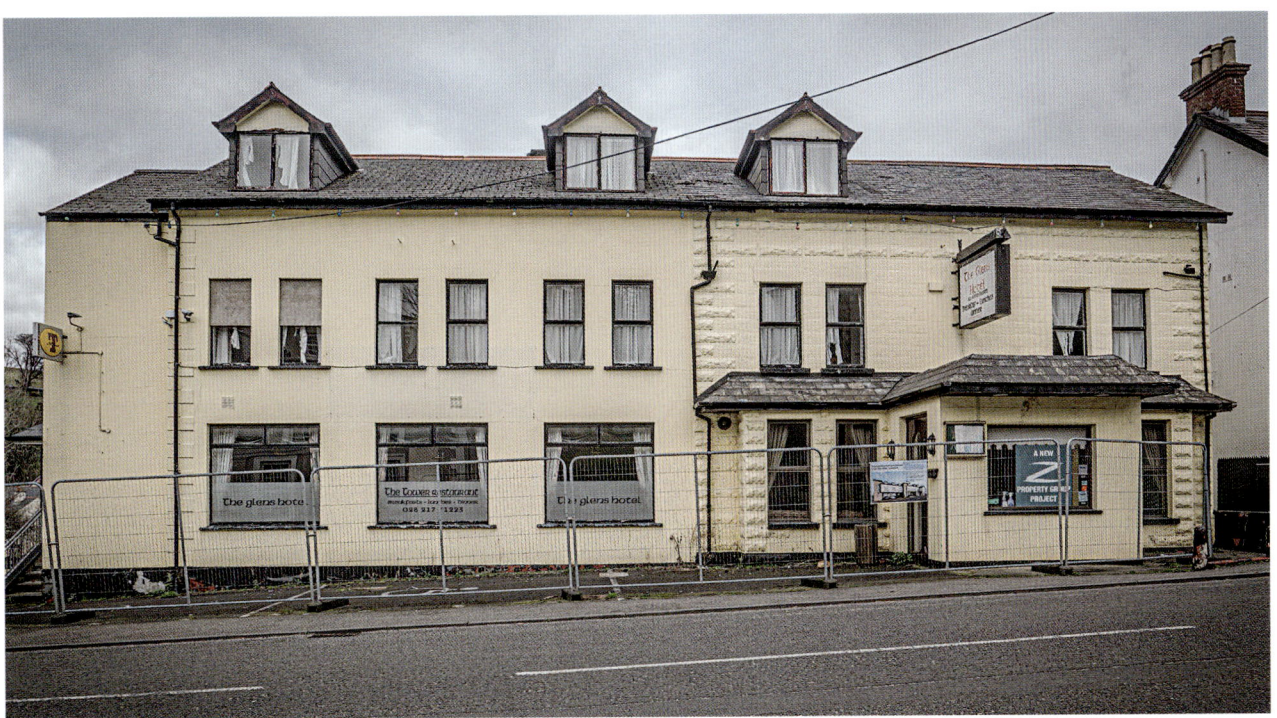

The Glens Hotel has a rich history that dates back to the early 1900s, when it was originally built as a country house. In 1913 it was transformed into the Thornlea hotel. During the 1940s it was a bustling seaside hotel, with many people coming to stay from Belfast and its surrounding towns. One of these visitors was local TV presenter Eamonn Holmes, who has recalled fond memories of staying in the Thornlea during his summer holidays. The property was owned by the Faulkner family until 1974, when it was purchased by building contractor Jim O'Neill, who undertook extensive renovations and expansions to create the hotel as we know it today.

Throughout the 1980s, the hotel changed ownership multiple times. Like most rural hotels it had busy times with weddings and local parties, but it

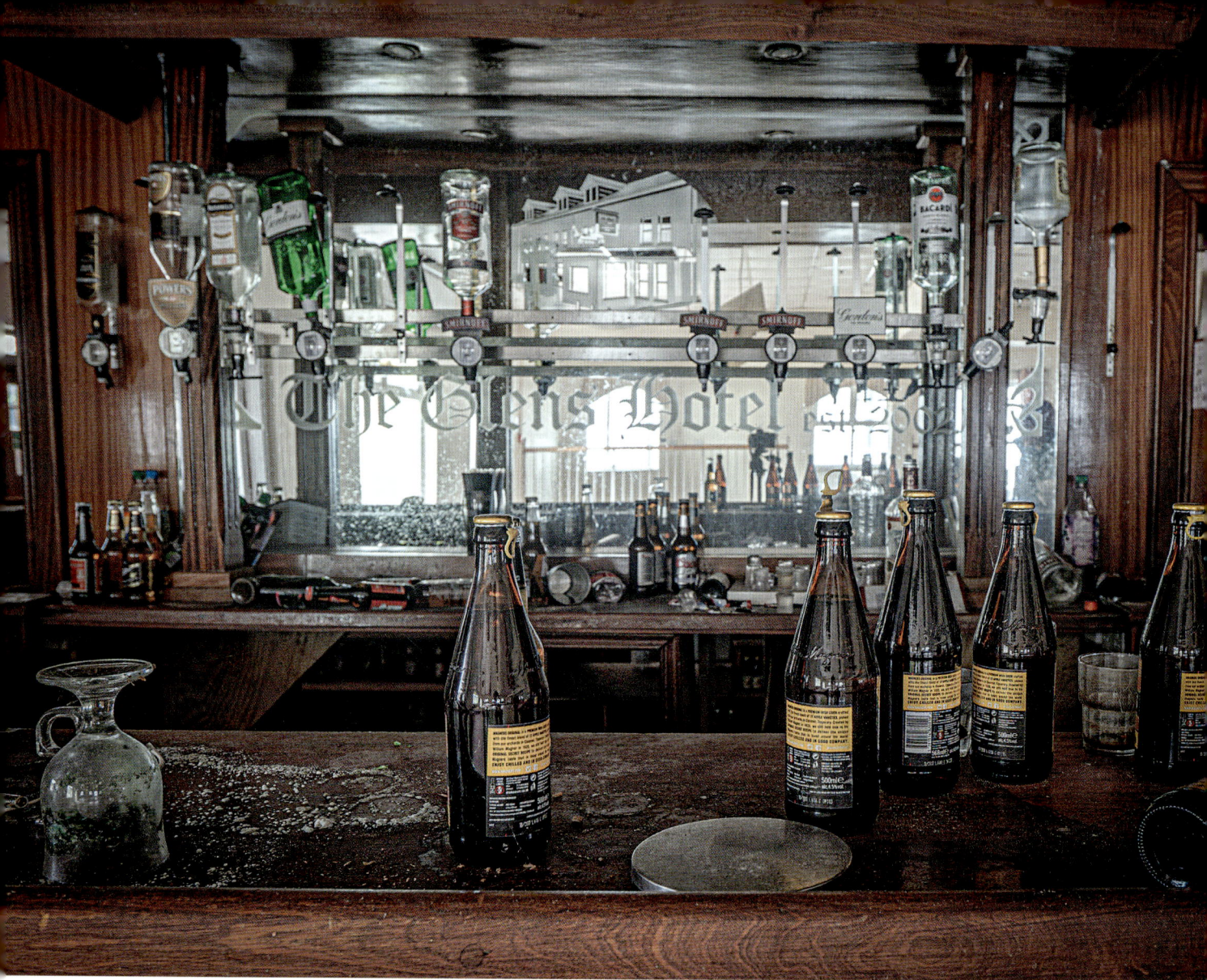

closed its doors for good in 2016 when the owner retired and it was acquired by a Donegal business-man. Now it is under the ownership of Z Property, who have exciting plans to renovate and enhance the property. These renovations will include an extension to accommodate thirty-nine bedrooms, a 200-person function room, spa facilities, a bar and a restaurant.

These new developments are sure to make The Glens Hotel a must-visit destination once again, and I am eager to return when it reopens, perhaps even for an overnight stay!

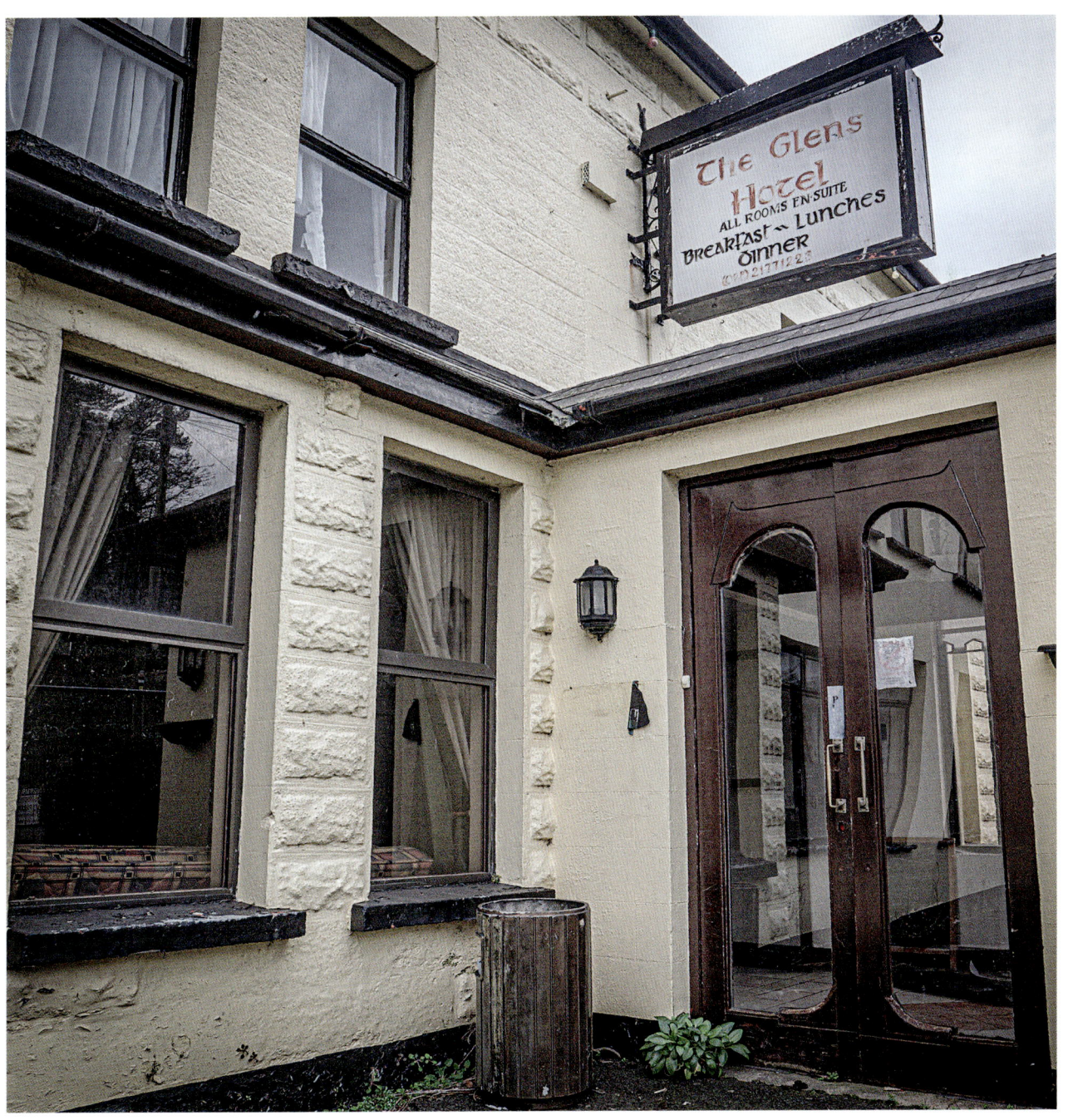

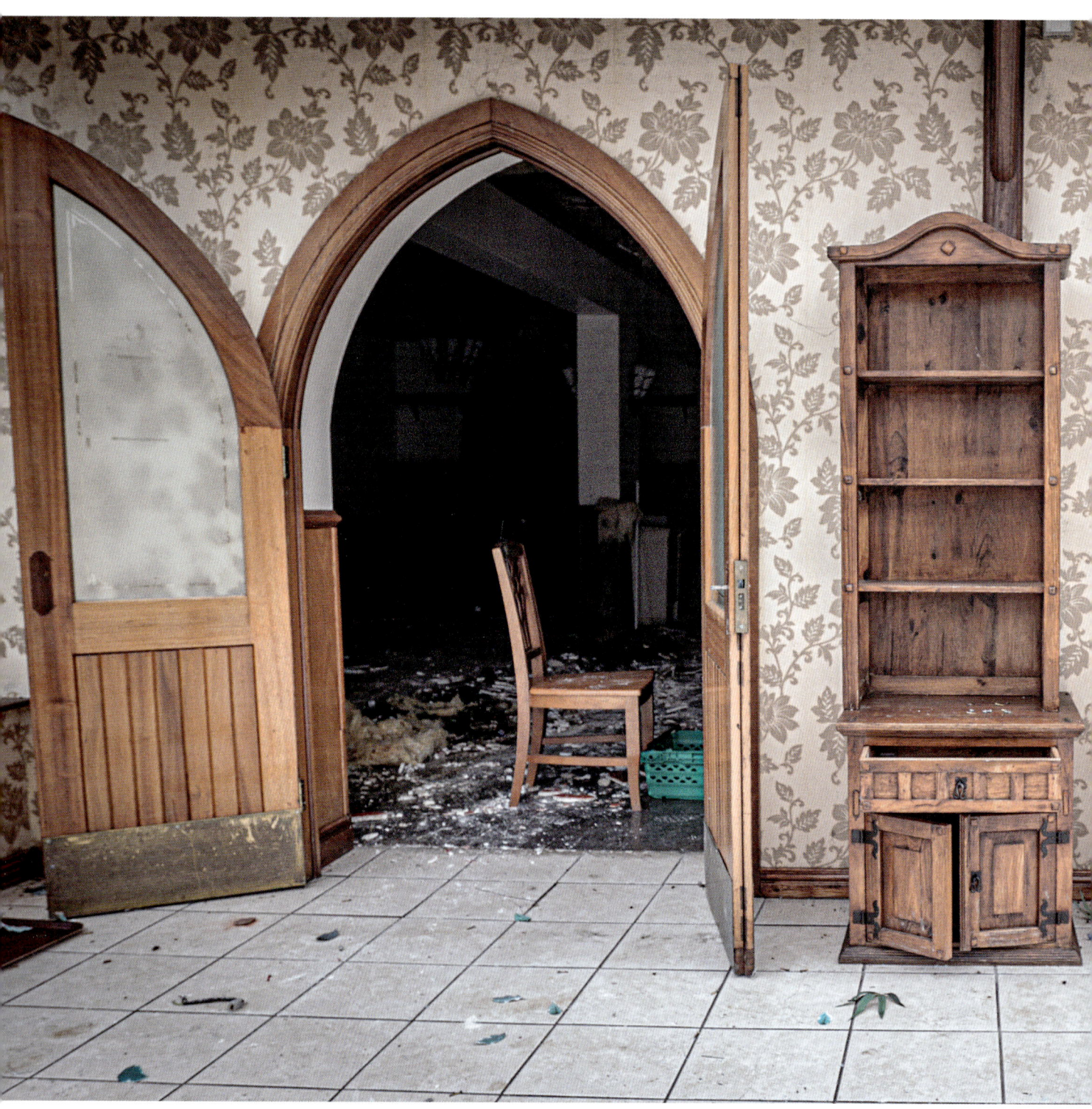

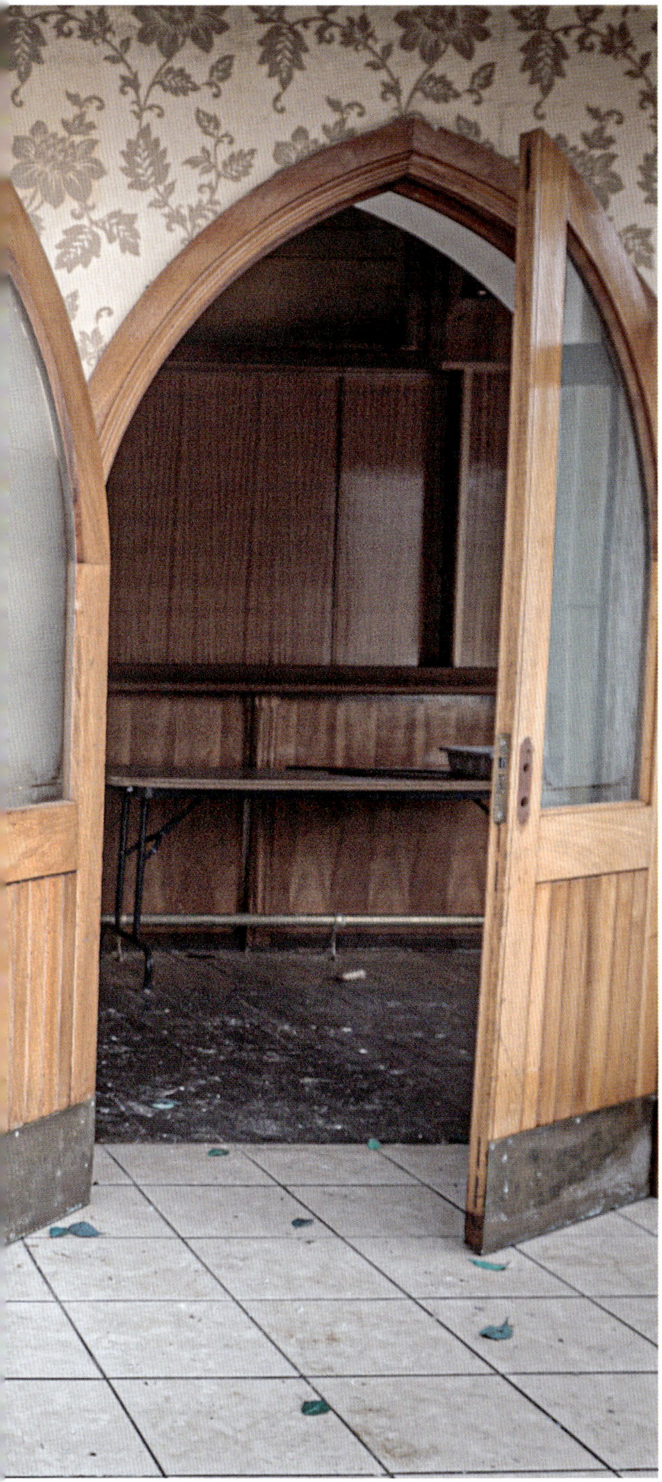

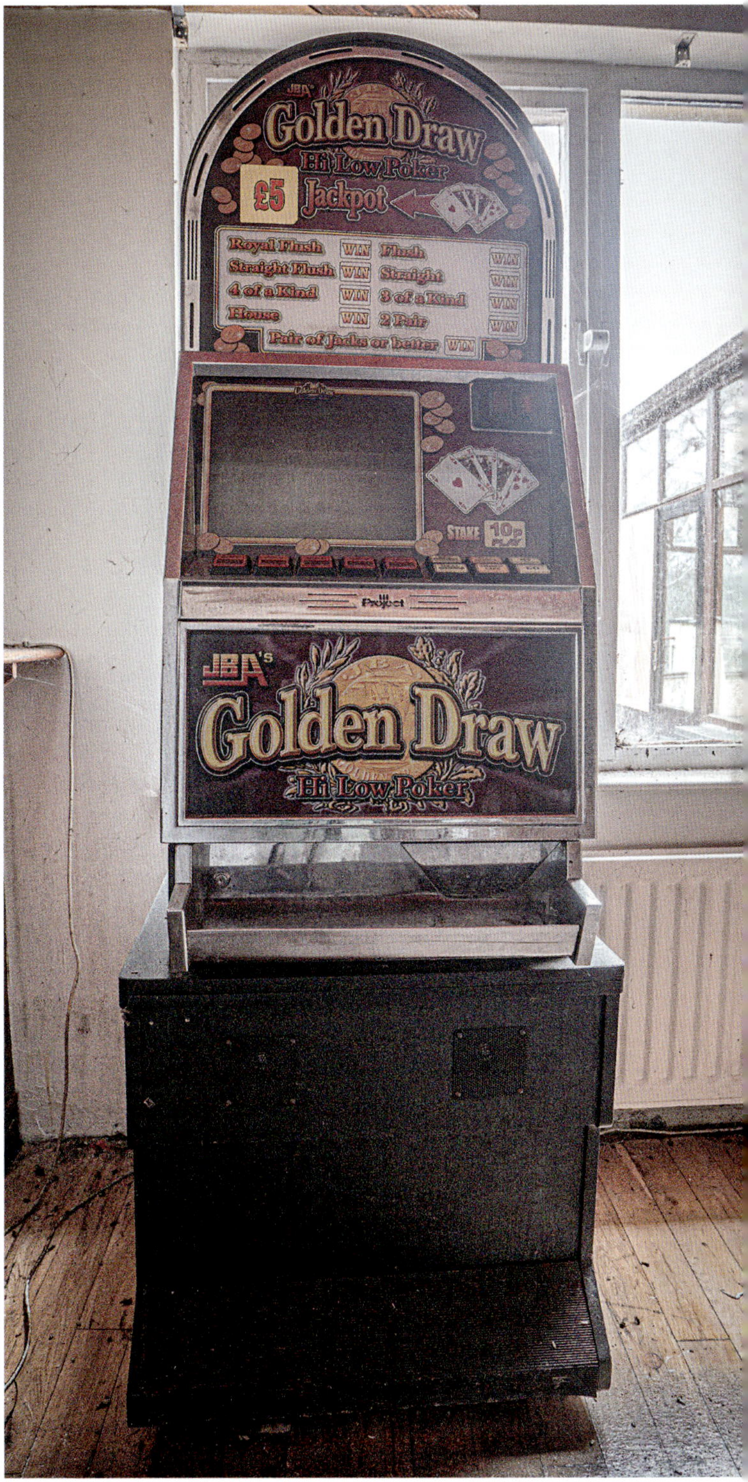
Golden Draw
Hi Low Poker
£5
Jackpot
Royal Flush WIN Flush WIN
Straight Flush WIN Straight WIN
4 of a Kind WIN 3 of a Kind WIN
House WIN 2 Pair WIN
Pair of Jacks or better WIN
JBA's
Golden Draw
Hi Low Poker

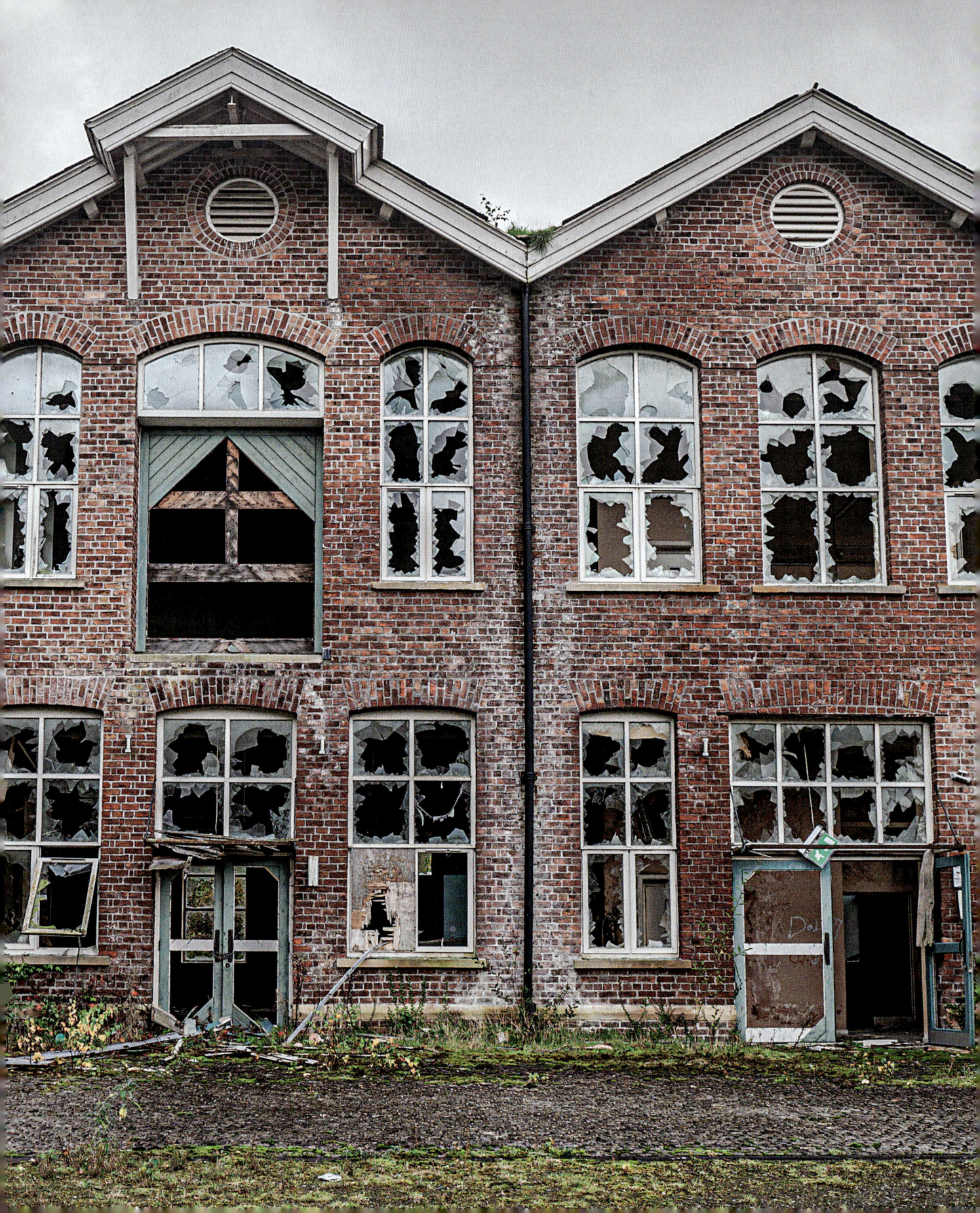

# HERDMAN'S MILL

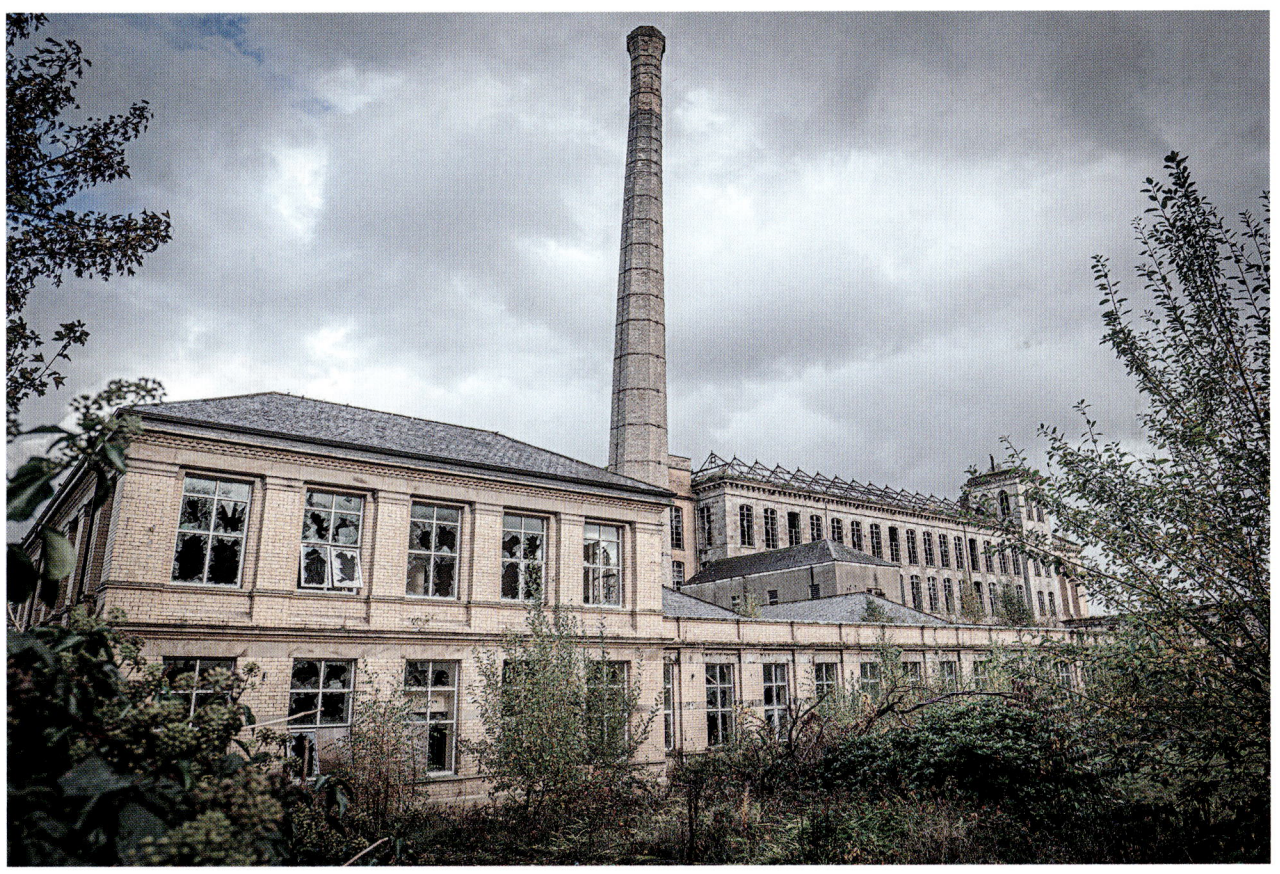

At this point you're no doubt aware of my love for a derelict mill, and this was one that truly lived up to my highest expectations. Its story began when three brothers from Belfast – James, John and George Herdman – purchased a site on the banks of the River Mourne near Strabane, in a place formerly known as Seein, but which eventually became Sion. The site already had a history of corn mills dating back to the 1600s, and the Herdman brothers were drawn to it because of the potential for harnessing the power of the water from the river. They hired the renowned architects Lanyon, Lynn and Lanyon, who were responsible for designing Belfast Castle and other notable Irish buildings, to design, extend and upgrade the mill buildings.

The new flax mill opened in 1835 with seventy-five employees, but the Herdmans were not solely focused on linen production. They aimed to create a model village for the workers and their families, providing schools, places of worship and recreational facilities, such as a cricket pitch and football club at what would become known as Sion Mills. (Tennis courts and a bowling green were added in 1935 to celebrate the town's centenary.) The consumption of alcohol was prohibited (the first pub was not built until 1896 and only after a successful legal challenge to the enforced temperance) and this became a God-fearing, non-sectarian community.

Over the years, the village expanded, with 118 dwellings built by 1866, increasing to 240 by the late nineteenth century. The mill had a gasworks that enabled it to provide lighting for every house in the village, a luxury at the time. The shop boasted four lights, and even street lights were installed. Later, turbines were installed to power the lights for the mill and village.

The quality of the linen produced by Herdman's Mill earned it a global reputation as the Rolls-Royce of the linen industry. By the 1850s the mill had expanded, employing 1,500 people who worked up to seventy hours per week. Payday for the workers

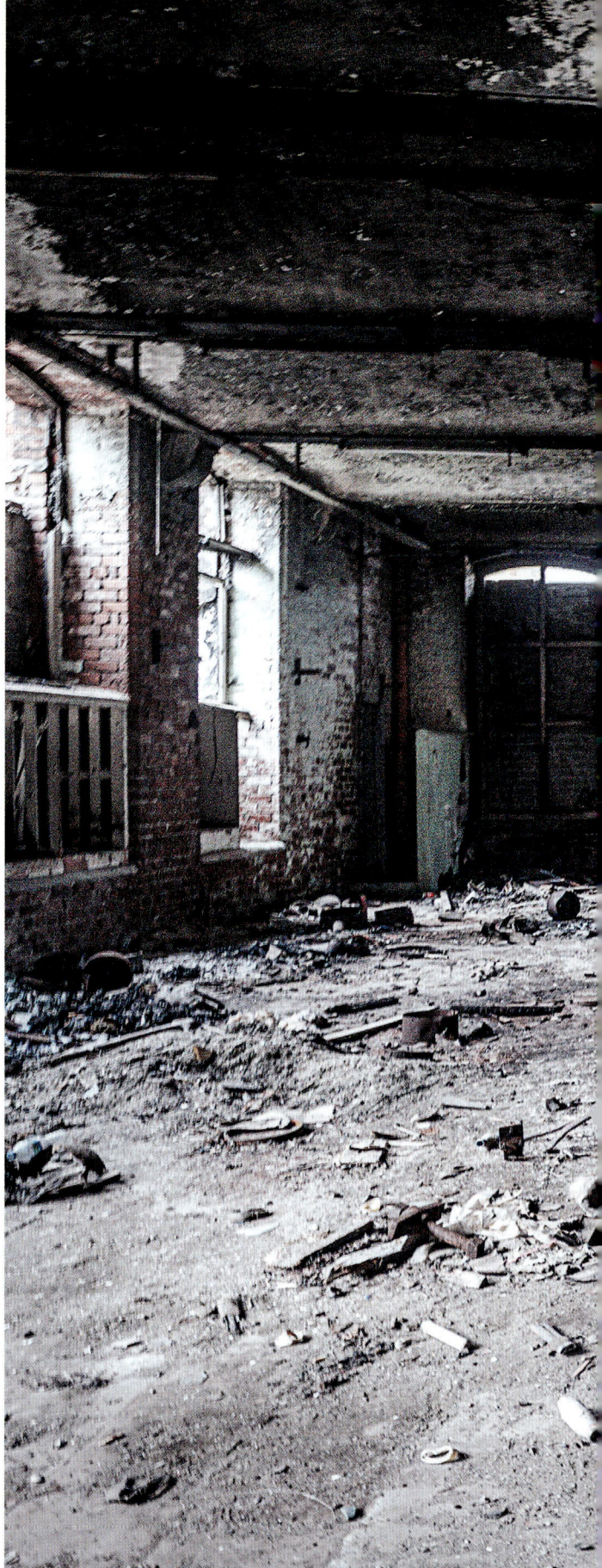

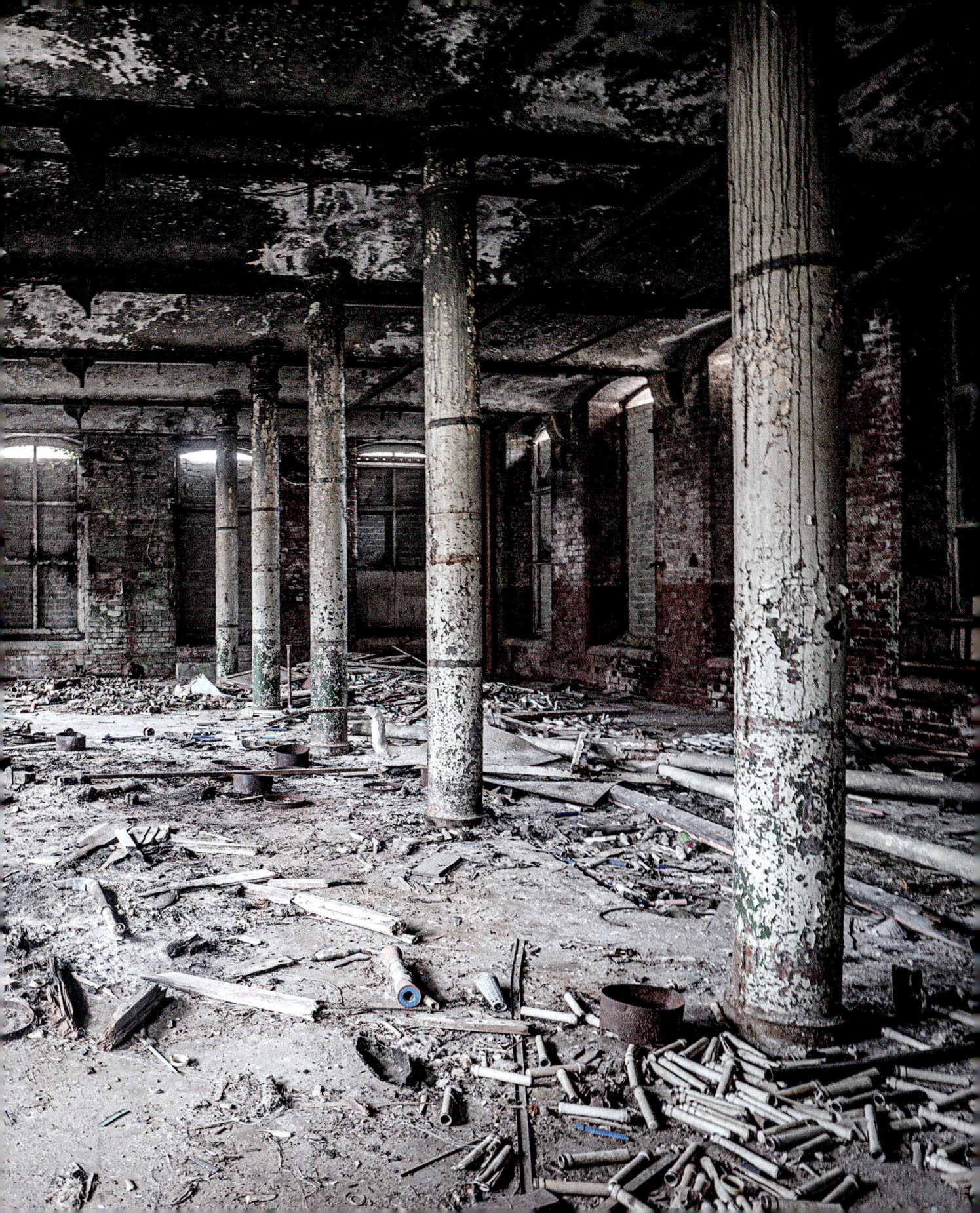

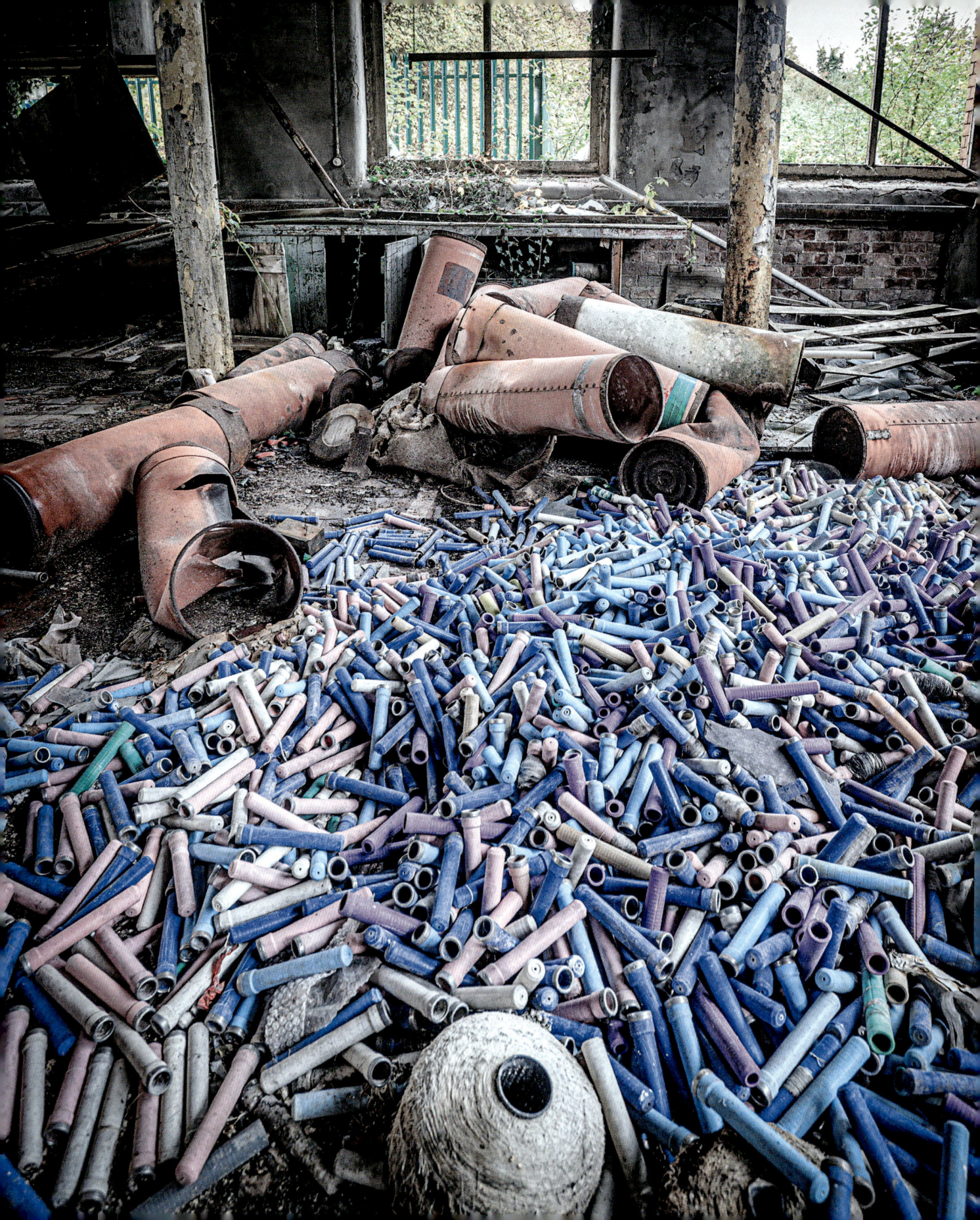

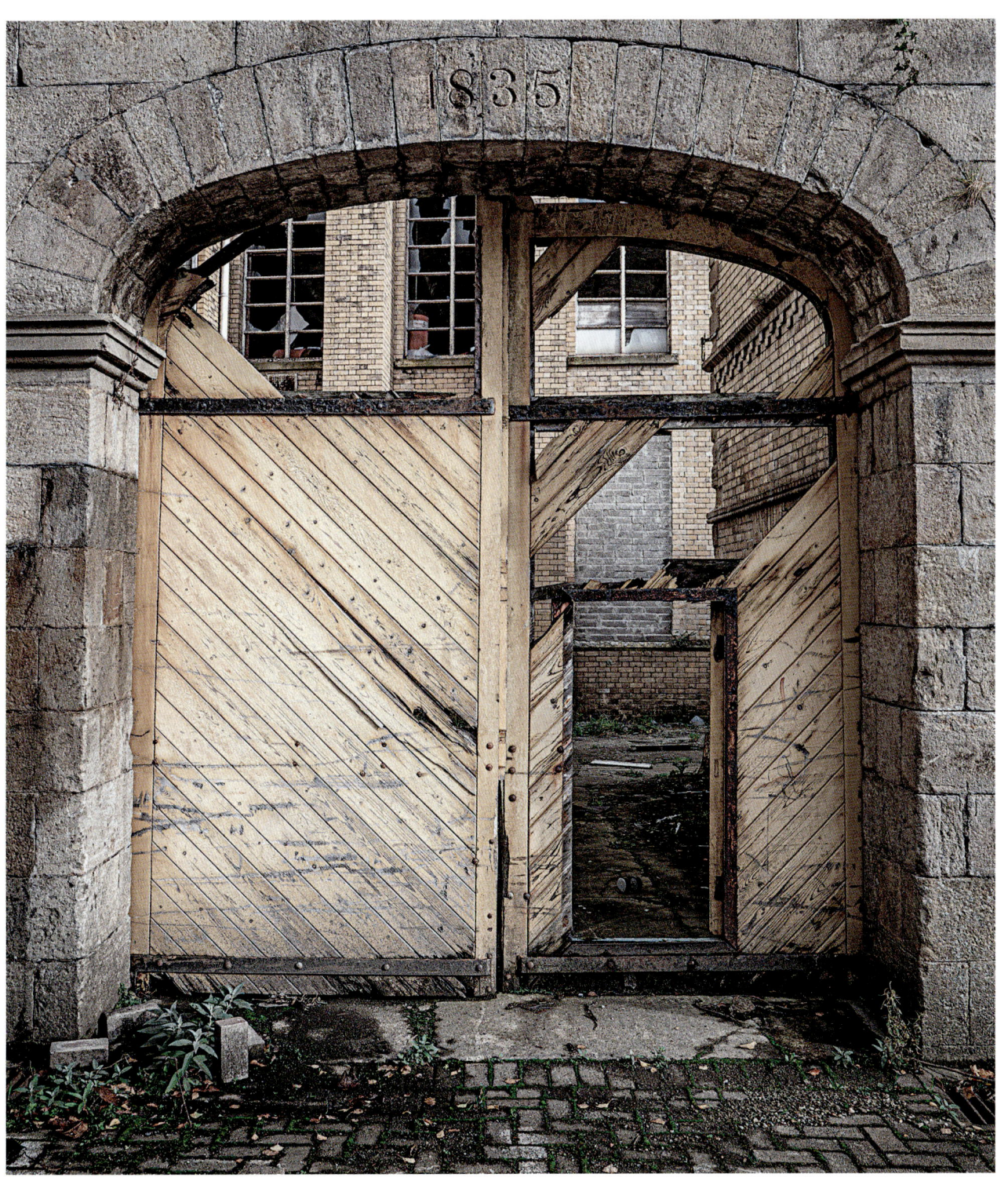

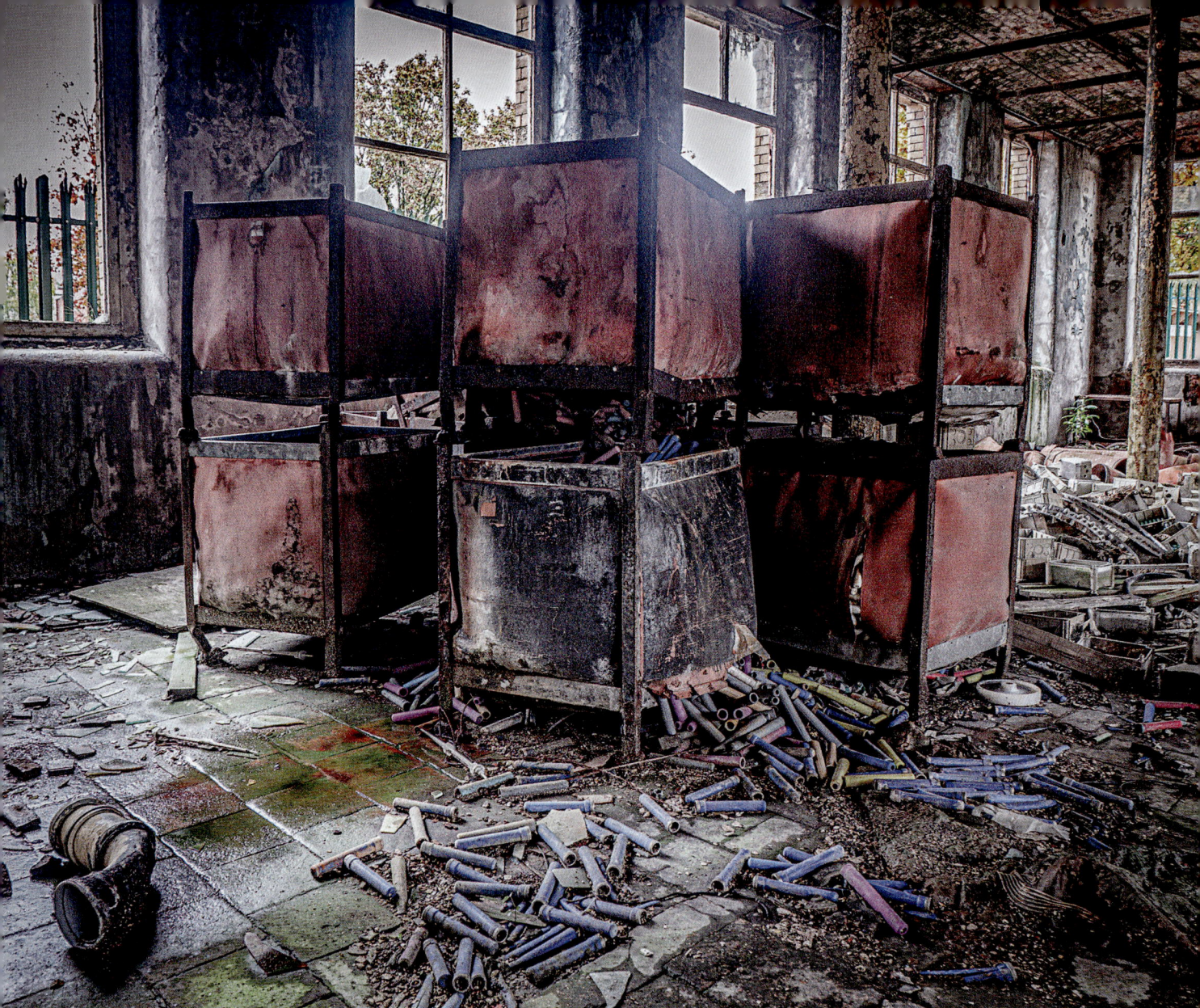

involved them receiving their wages from a numbered tin box. The mill operated twenty-four hours a day, with 60 tonnes of linen leaving the gates weekly and being distributed worldwide – America and Italy were the biggest customers.

The mill and village were integrated, with Protestants and Catholics working and living alongside each other. This unity allowed it to survive decades of political turmoil in Ireland. Unfortunately, the decline of the linen industry led to Herdman's Mill ceasing production in 2004, when the gates closed for the final time. In 2014 the complex was bought by a local lottery winner, but has suffered from arson attacks and vandalism, leaving it abandoned and desolate.

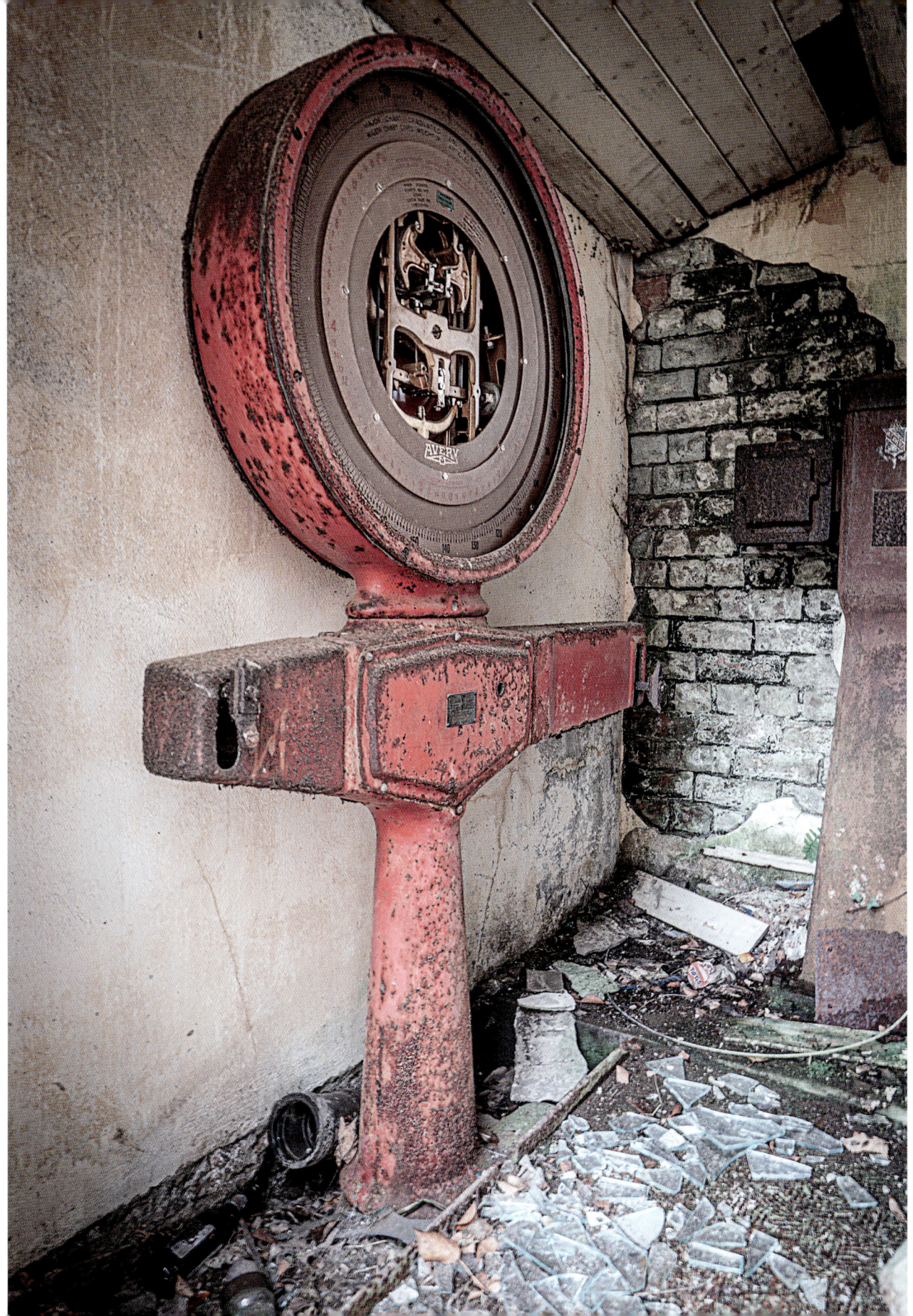

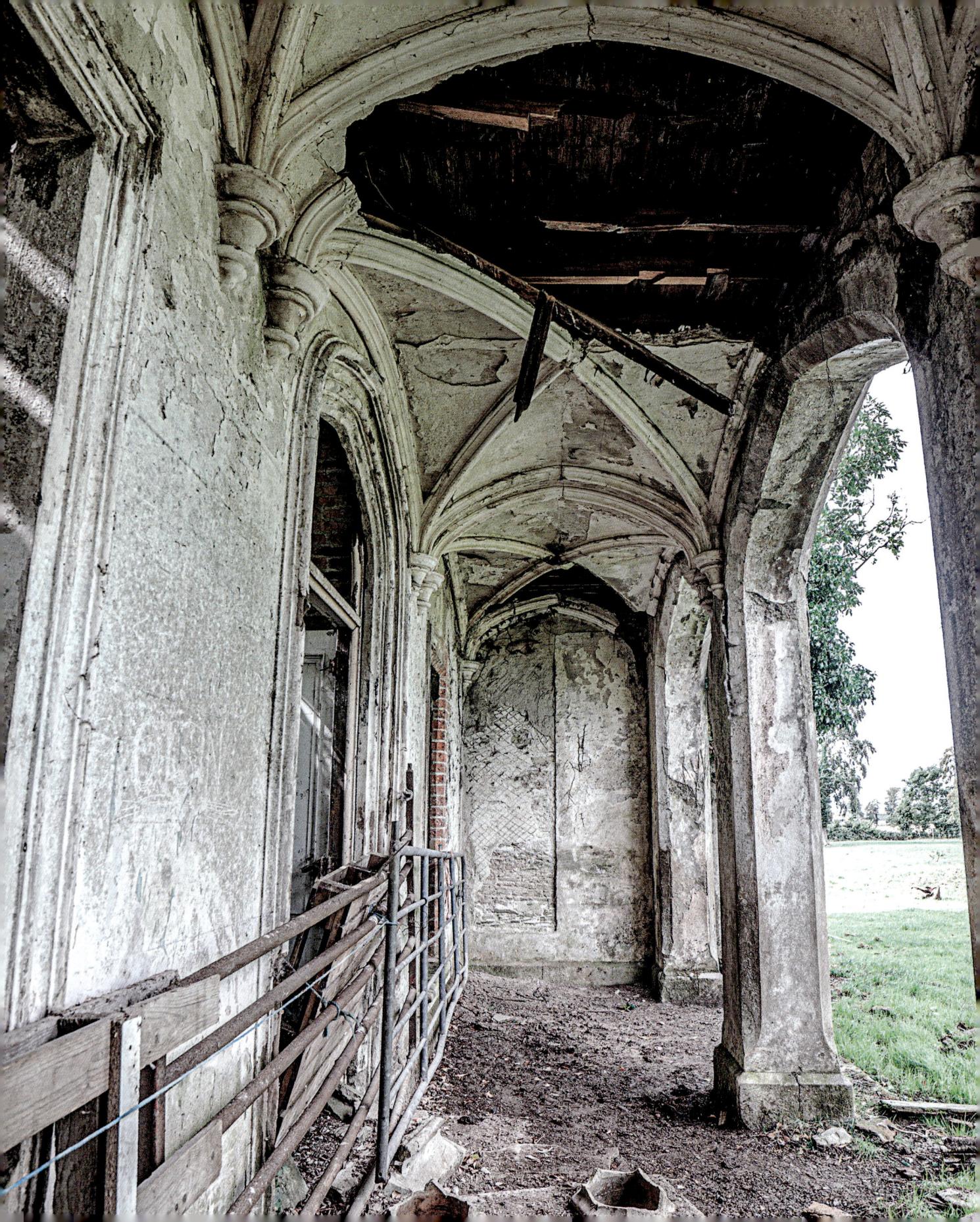

# GLYDE COURT

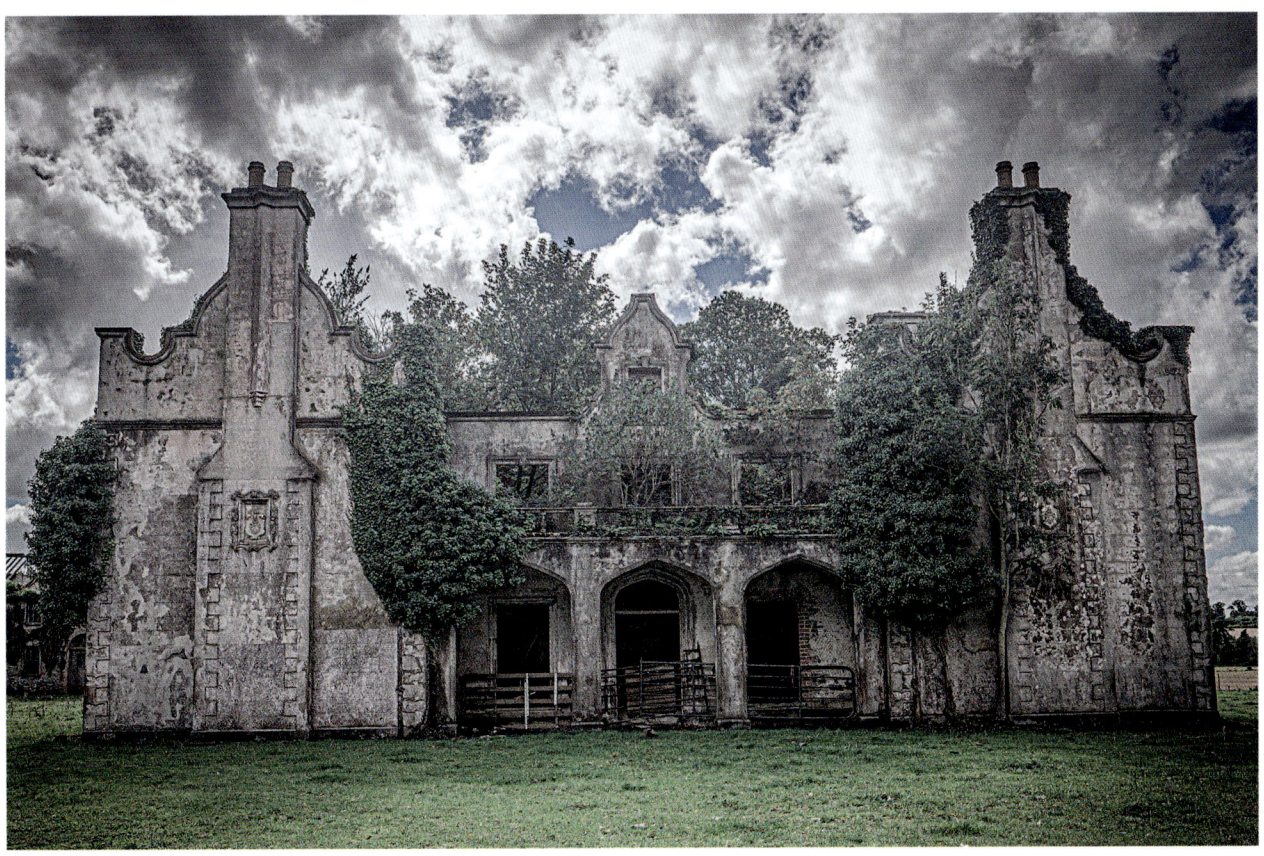

This period mansion sits proudly on its own in the middle of a field. The surrounding grounds and estate are still very impressive to this day. As I walk down the drive, I can almost imagine the sound of horses and carts passing by.

Glyde Court was built in 1780 and then remodelled in the 1860s in Jacobean style to suit the contemporary architectural fashion. In its early days the house was known as Rosy Park and was home to John Thomas Foster, his wife, Lady Elizabeth Harvey,

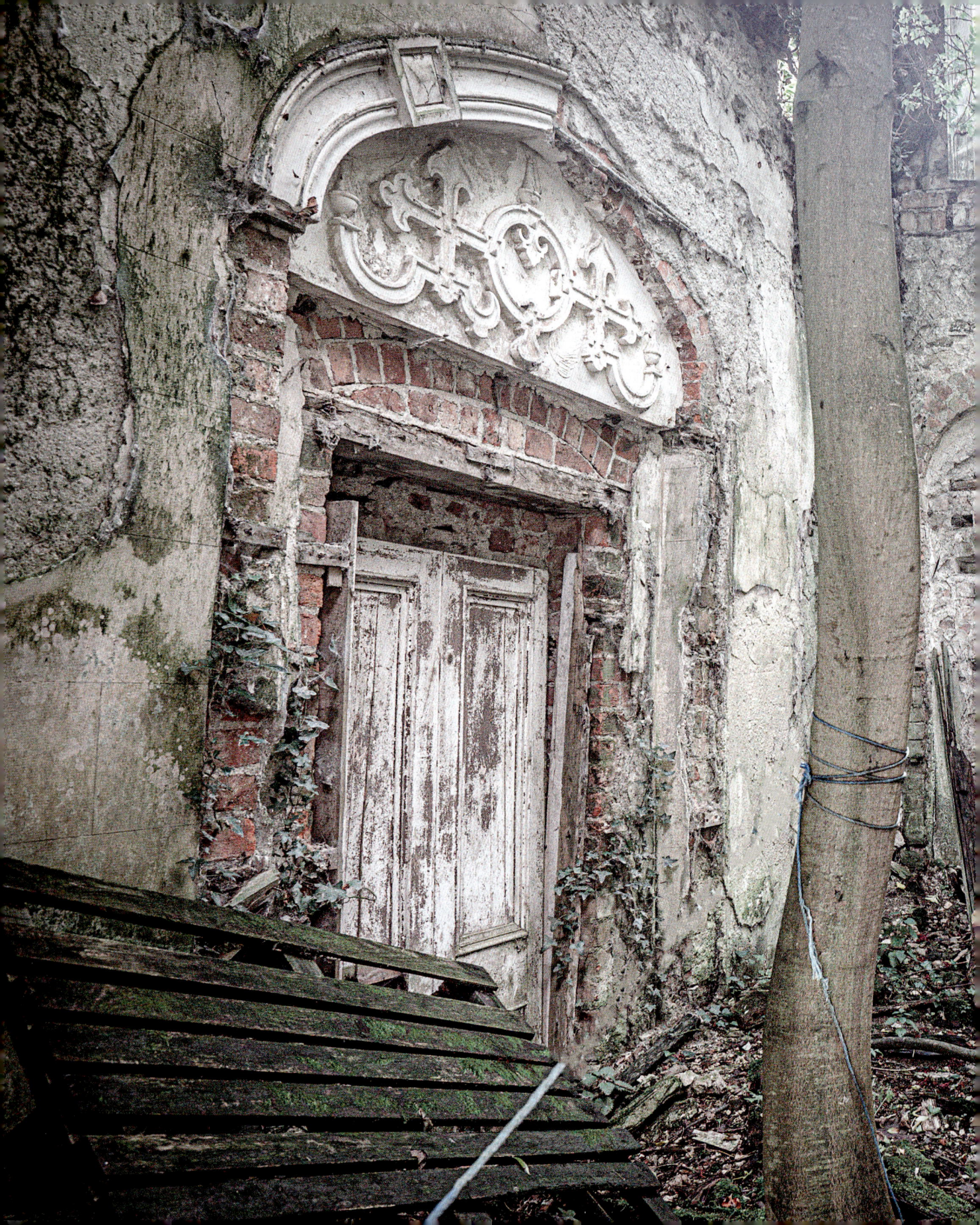

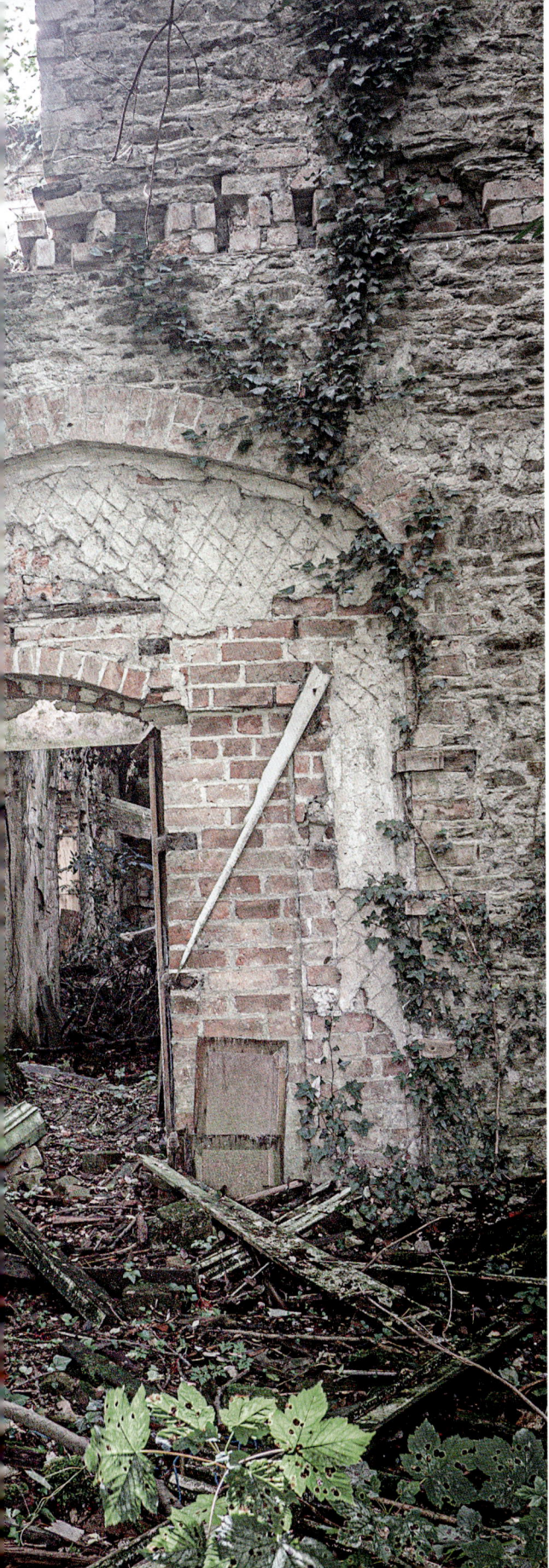

and their three children, only two of whom survived into adulthood. Unfortunately, the marriage didn't last and John and Elizabeth went their separate ways – Elizabeth to England, where she remarried, eventually moving to Rome.

Augustus John, one of their two surviving sons, became a diplomat and by 1811 was a Minister Plenipotentiary to the United States. He returned to Britain on the outbreak of war in 1812 and was elected to the House of Commons. In 1814 he left again, this time for Copenhagen, Denmark, where he served as British Minister Plenipotentiary. He married Albina Jane Hobart in 1815, going on to have three sons: Frederick George, Cavendish Harvey and Vere Henry Louis. They stayed in Denmark until 1824 before moving to Italy, where Augustus served as the Minister Plenipotentiary to Turin, Kingdom of Sardinia, staying there until 1840. During this time, he was knighted by King George IV and named Baronet of Glyde Court, Ardee, Co. Louth.

Augustus died in 1848 after cutting his own throat. He was suffering from delirium due to poor health and his death was ruled a result of temporary insanity. In the 1930s his 'Notes on the United States of America', written in 1840, were found in a cupboard in his family's home and published posthumously.

Vere Foster, the youngest son of Augustus, was a Victorian philanthropist and educator who has been described as an 'English Gentleman and Irish Champion' by author Brendan Colgan. He began his

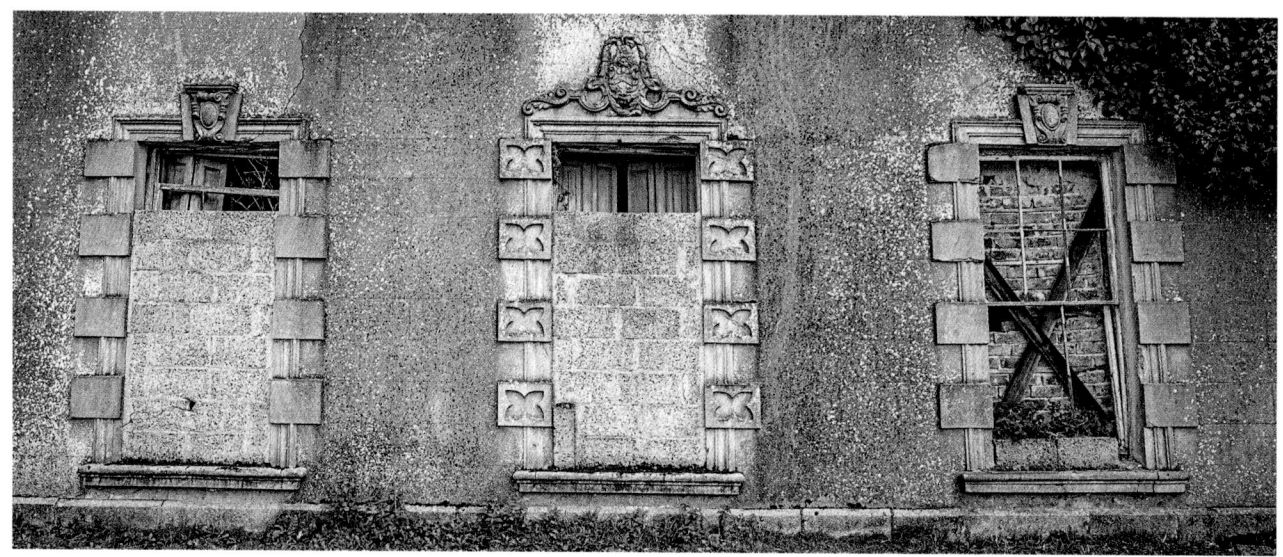

career as a British diplomat in Rio de Janeiro. He did a tour of Ireland, including his ancestral home, in 1847 during the Great Famine, and was moved by the poverty and hunger he witnessed, dedicating the rest of his life to the social betterment of the Irish poor.

Emigration to the United States from Ireland at this time was very high, and the only means of escape was on disease-ridden 'coffin ships'. Vere made three trips himself on these ships, masquerading as a pauper in order to experience the ill-treatment and appalling conditions first-hand. Afterwards he wrote a report and presented it to the Houses of Parliament, leading to reforms in the Passengers Act (1851).

His work did not stop there. He went on to build new schools for both Catholics and Protestants and paid for the refurbishment of thousands of others all over Ireland, all at his own expense. He even created and published a series of school instructional books to improve literacy among the poor, which were printed in Belfast and remained in use until the 1950s.

Vere made a valuable contribution to the people of Ireland, including founding the Irish National Teachers' Organisation. He spent the last thirty years of his life living in an attic on Great Victoria Street in Belfast and died in 1900 virtually penniless, having spent his immense fortune on charitable causes to better the lives of the Irish people. He is buried in the City Cemetery, Falls Road, Belfast.

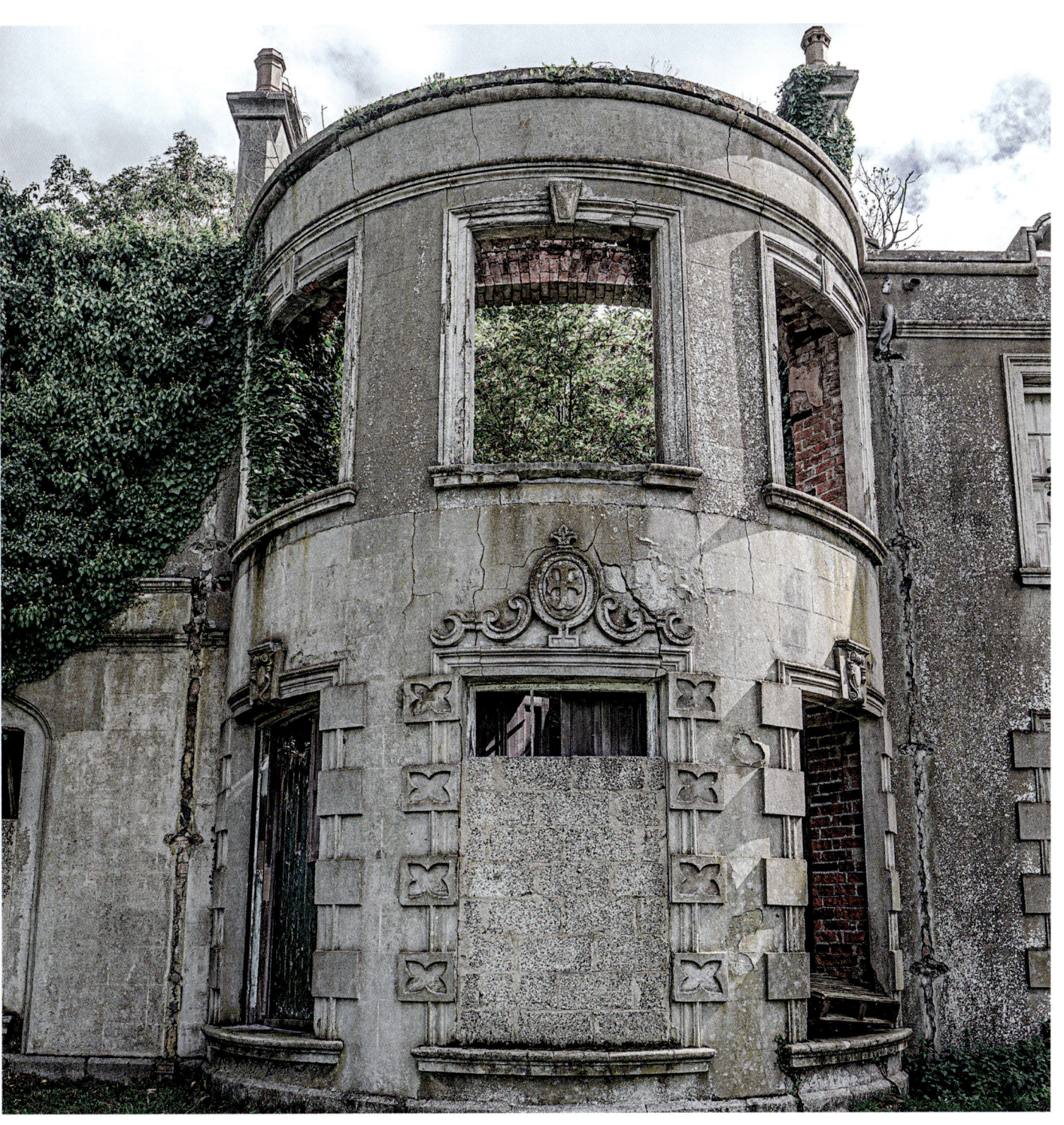

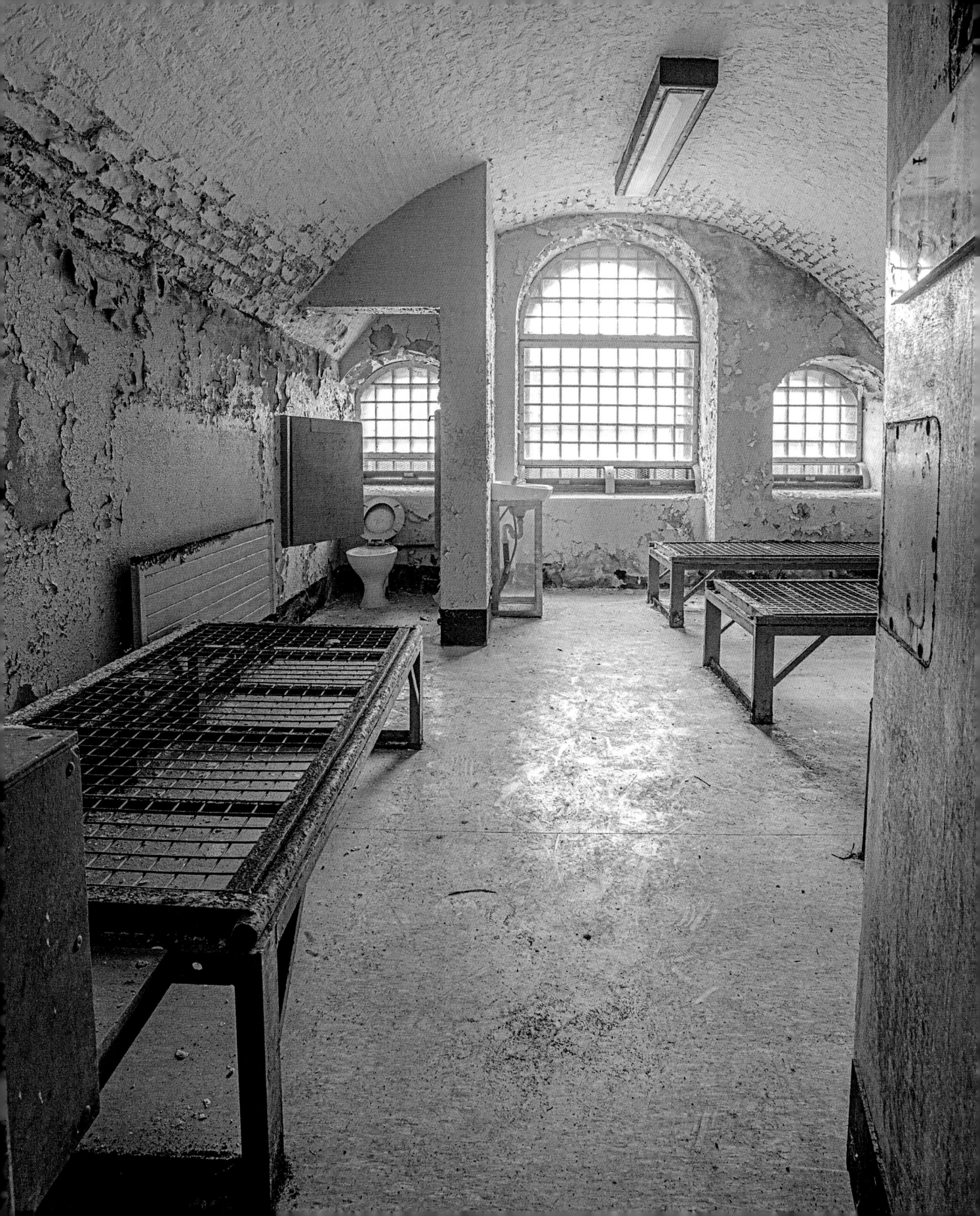

# SPIKE ISLAND

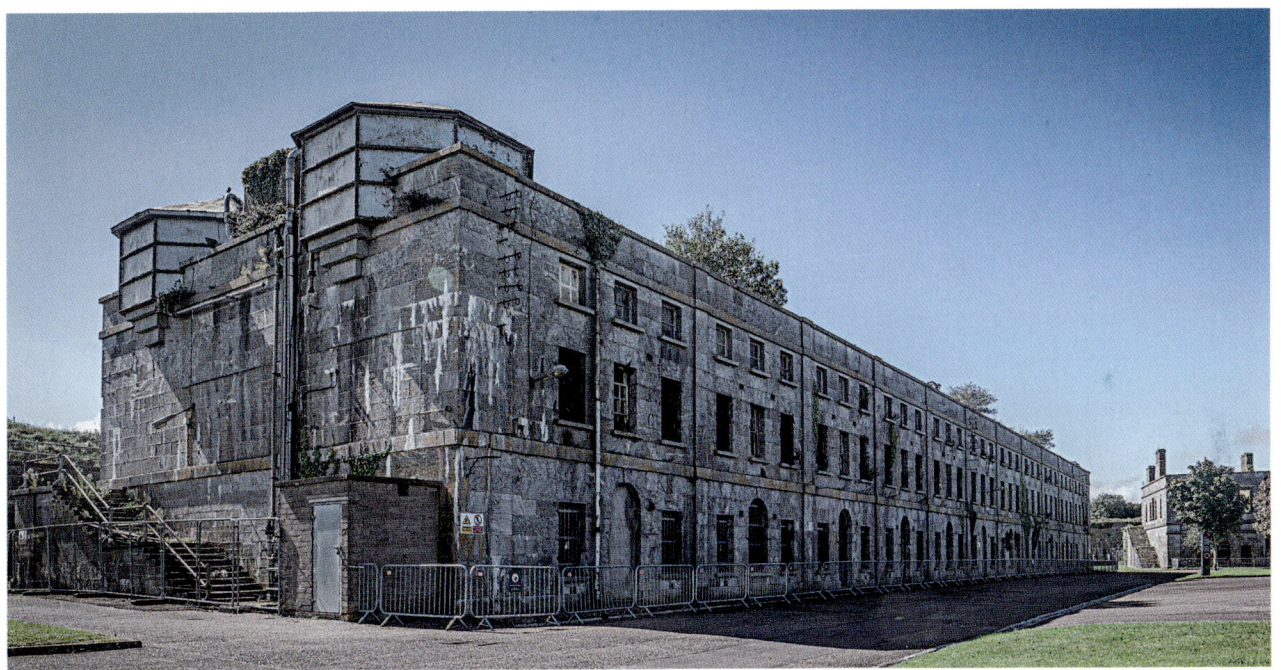

Now an internationally recognised tourist attraction, Spike Island may seem like an odd inclusion in a book called *Abandoned Ireland 2*. However, not all of the site has been rehabilitated, and when I contacted those managing the island and asked if there were any 'unseen' or abandoned parts of the prison that I could document, they told me they had an old prison block that is not included in tours and some very old tunnels that people do not get to see.

The history of human occupation on Spike Island began over 1,300 years ago when St Mochuda founded an early Christian monastery on the site. Despite being ravaged by Vikings in the ninth century, reports indicate that a monastic settlement persisted on the island until the sixteenth century.

Better known is the island's long history as a place of confinement, punishment and defence. Originally known as Fort Westmoreland, it was used

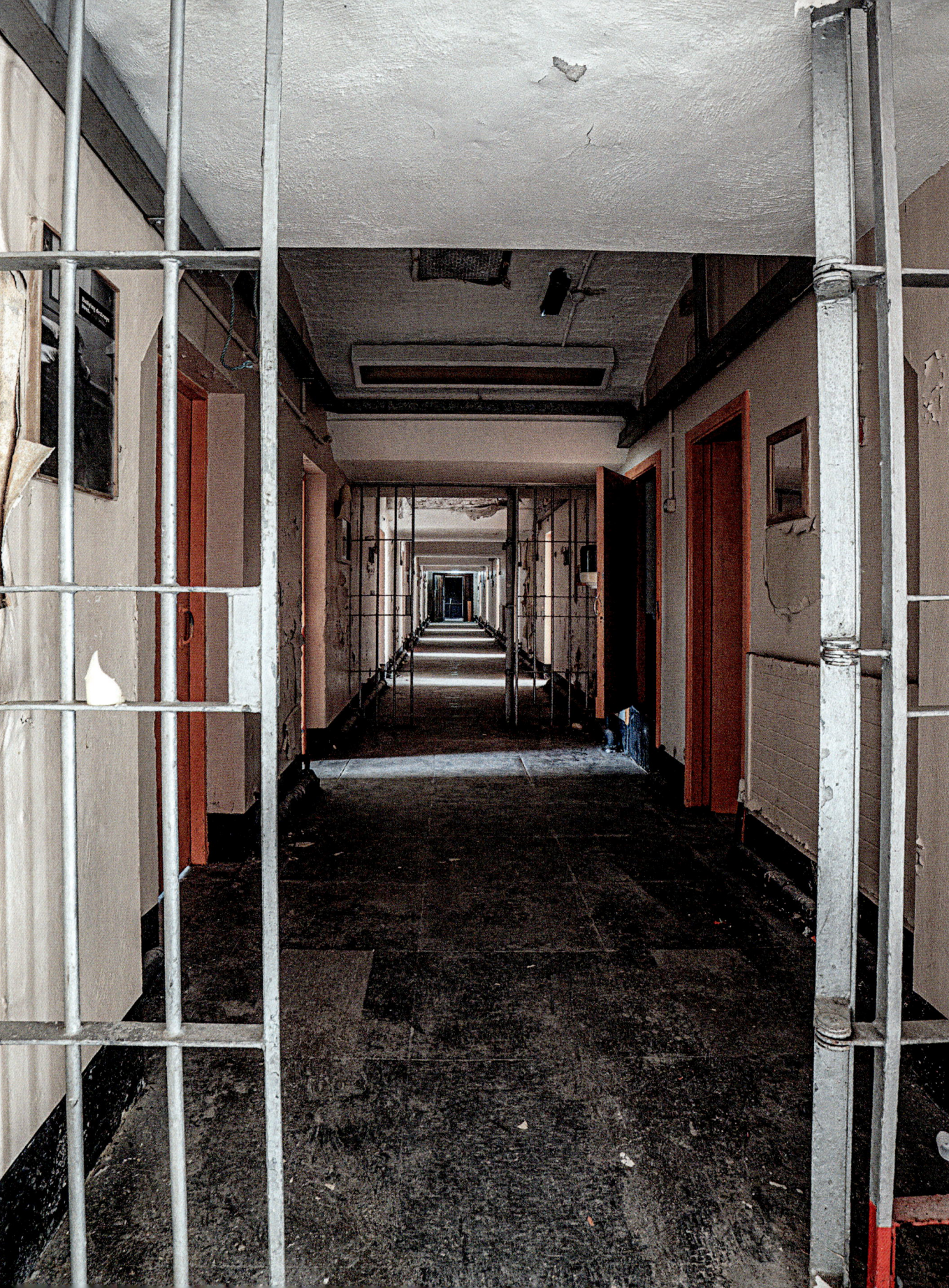

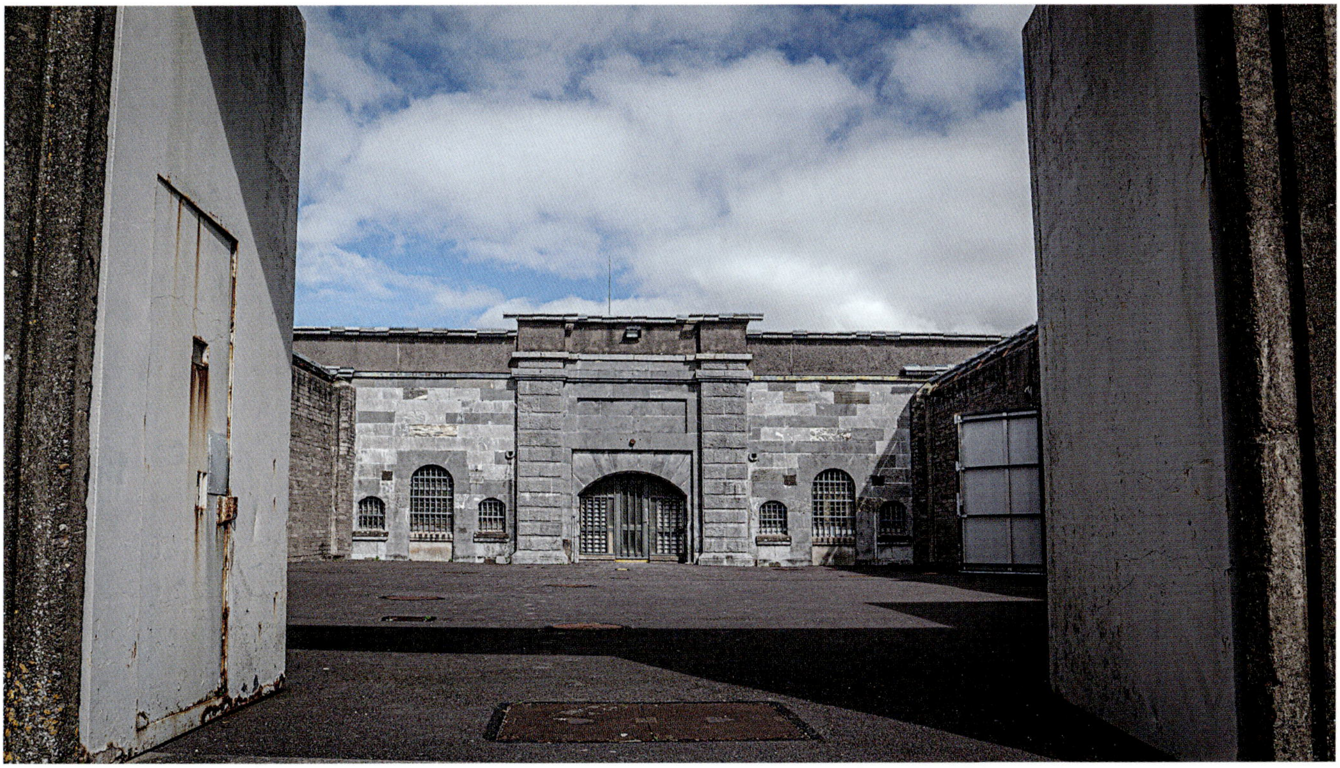

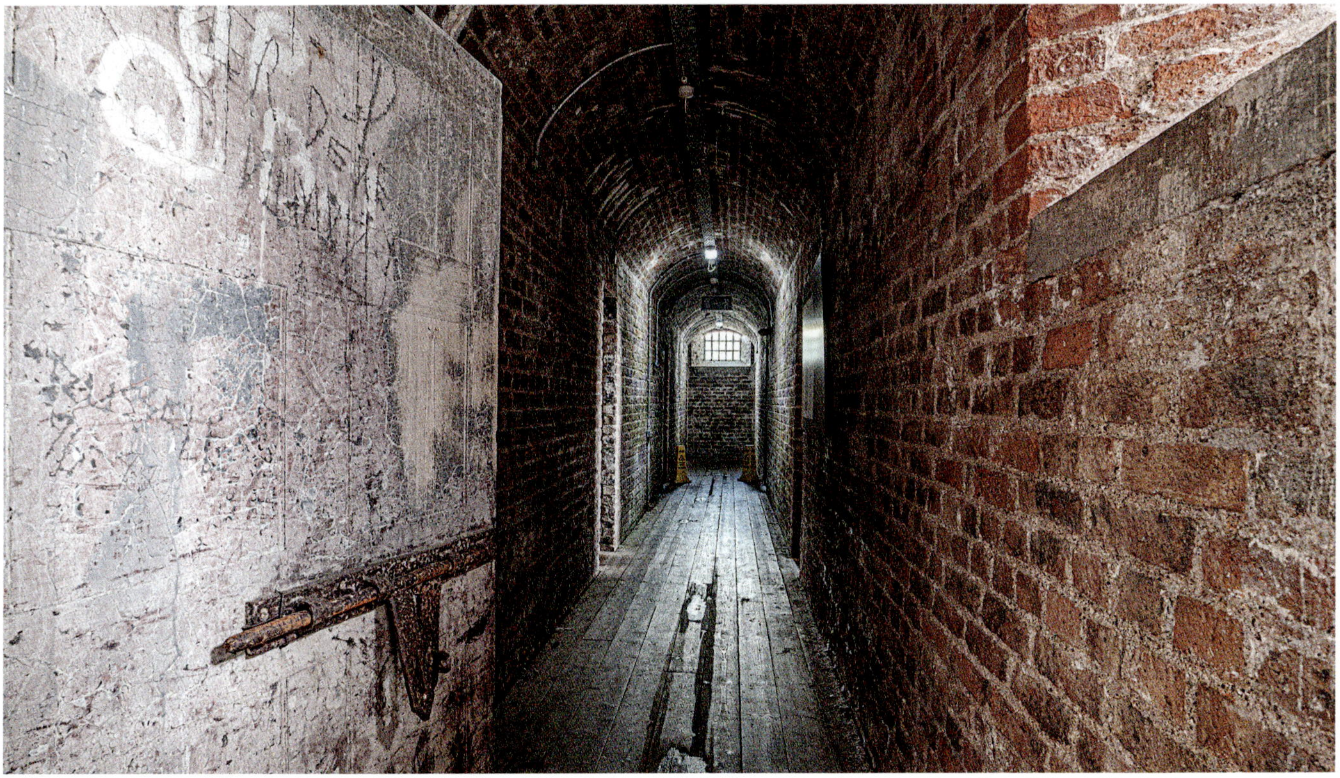

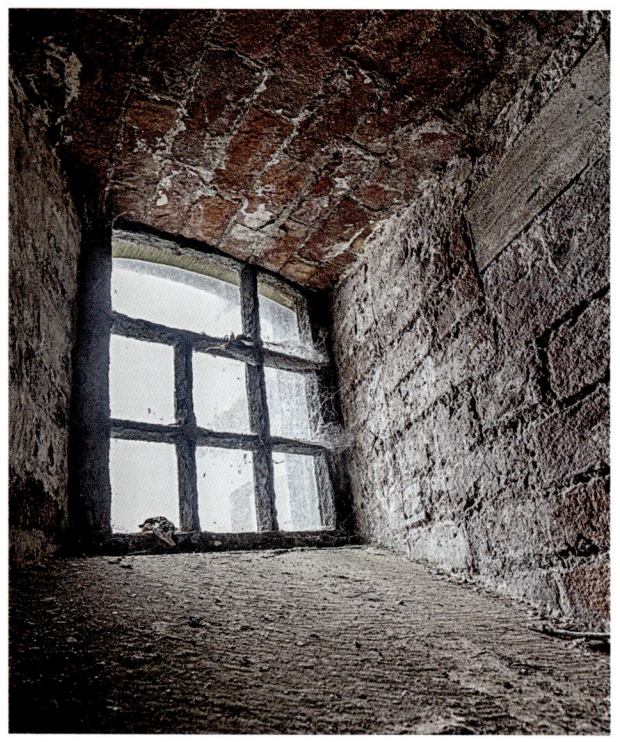

During the Irish War of Independence, in the early twentieth century, Spike Island once again became a place of detention, this time for Irish republicans and other political prisoners. It was also used by British forces as a base of operations against the Irish Republican Army. The prison on Spike Island became a symbol of British oppression and resistance for many Irish nationalists.

This was only exacerbated by incidents like the death of Patrick White in 1921. Prisoners were allowed a certain amount of time outside, which often involved the playing of Gaelic sports. One afternoon some inmates were playing a game of hurling when the ball went into the barbed wire surrounding the yard. Patrick, from Meelick, Co. Clare, had run over to fetch it when a sentry on duty shot him. The soldier then reloaded, ready to fire again. The camp commandant arrived and had the soldier removed. Paddy's comrades went to him and said a prayer, but he died soon afterwards.

After Ireland gained independence in 1922, Spike was taken over by the Irish Free State and continued to be used as a prison. In the years that followed, the prison population on the island fluctuated, with periods of overcrowding and unrest. The island was also used as a military base and training facility for the Irish Defence Forces. In the late twentieth century, the island was decommissioned as a prison and visitors can now explore its rich history. But at least one small part of its story remains abandoned and out of their reach, at least for now.

by the British Army to defend Cork harbour from potential invaders. The strategic location of the island within the harbour made it an ideal spot for military fortifications. The island's iconic star-shaped fort, constructed in the eighteenth century, still stands as a reminder of this military past.

In 1847, during the height of the Great Famine, the island was used as a prison to house convicts and political prisoners. The conditions at this time were harsh, with overcrowding, poor sanitation and inadequate food and medical care leading to high mortality rates among the inmates. The prison population swelled as the British government sought to quell dissent and maintain control over the Irish people.

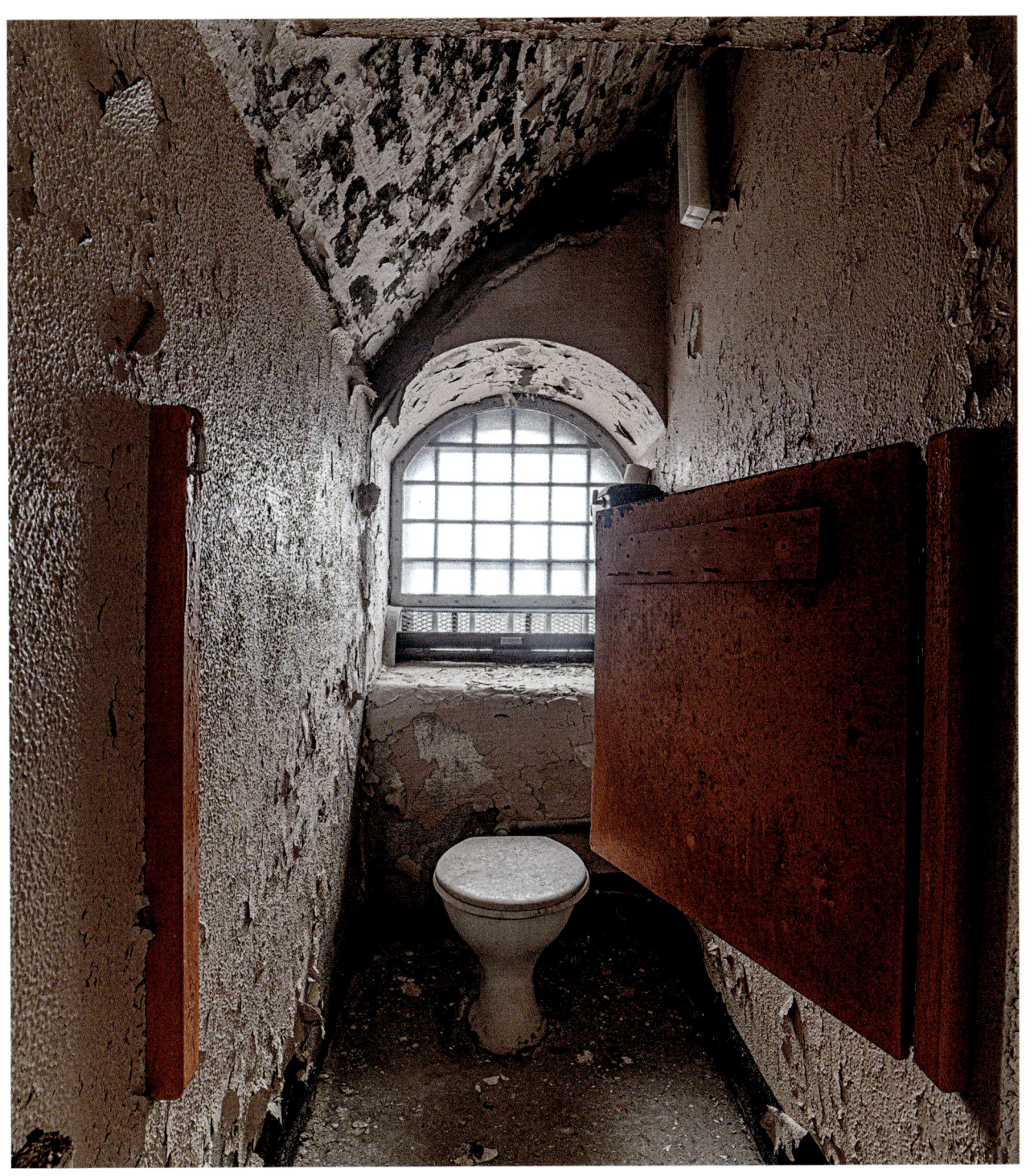

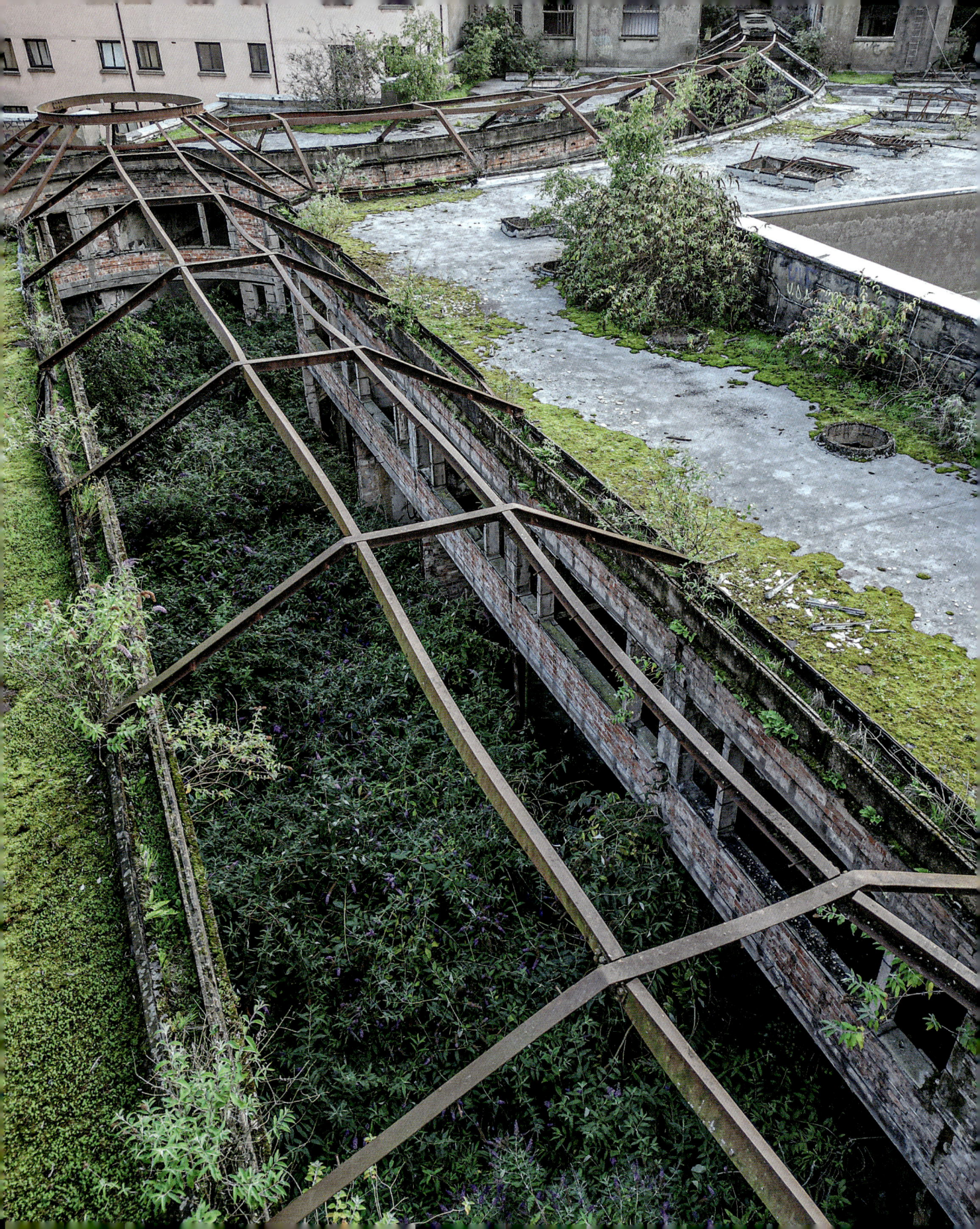

# NORTH STREET ARCADE

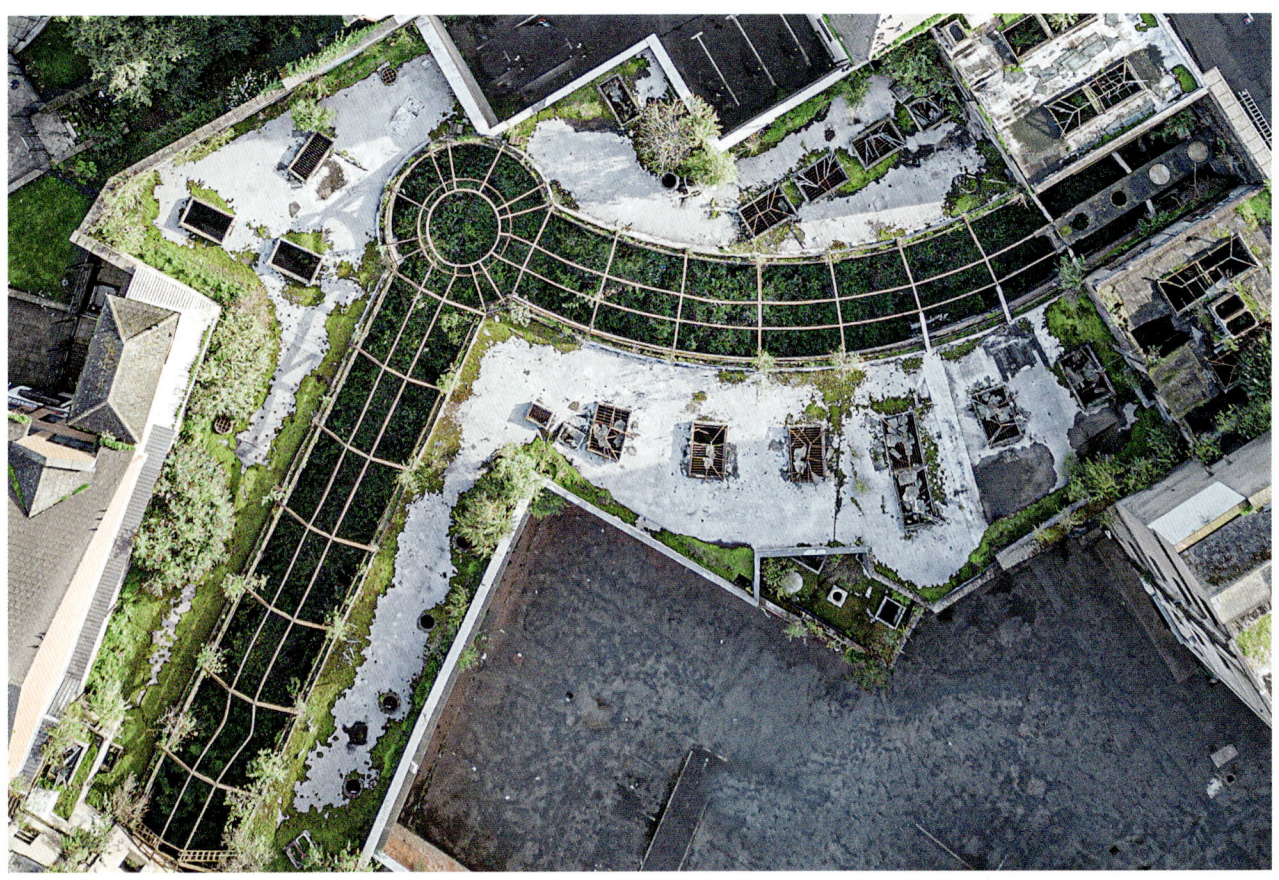

This Grade B1 listed art deco shopping centre was built in the 1930s on North Street in Belfast, making it the only one of its kind in Northern Ireland. Before it was constructed, the site housed various retail premises, with the most notable being the Brookfield Linen Company warehouse, which was there from 1869 to 1881. Some remnants of this warehouse can still be seen within the arcade today.

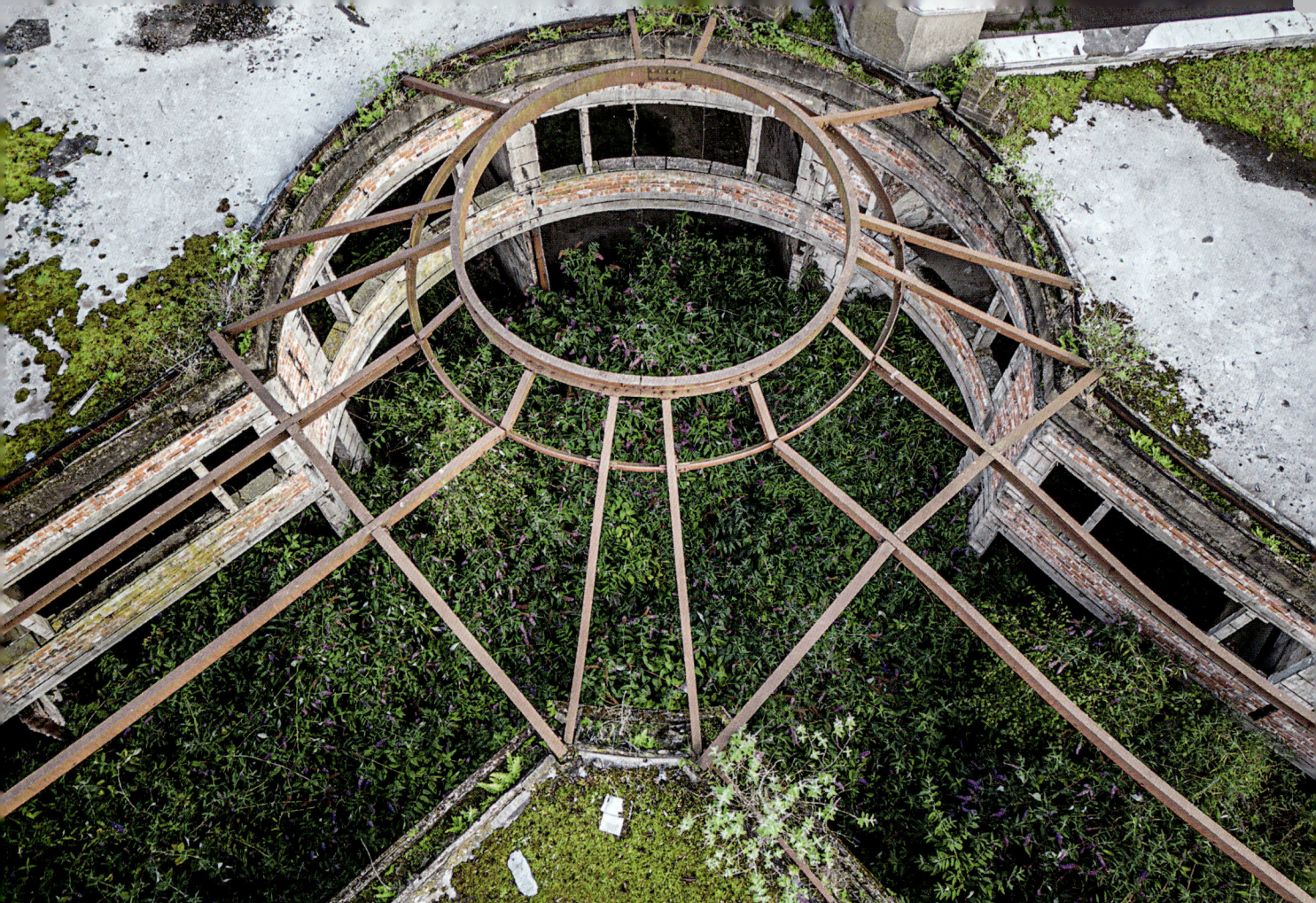

Other smaller shops, such as shoemakers, leather/iron merchants and haberdashers were also present, as well as a pub.

The traditional shops and warehouse were torn down to make room for the arcade, designed by architects Cowser & Smyth. It was a high-end shopping centre covered with a glass roof. Initially, the arcade struggled to attract businesses due to high rents. However, after the Belfast Blitz of the Second World War caused a loss of retail spaces in the city, it began to thrive.

During the Troubles the arcade was targeted in two bomb attacks. One, in 1976, killed two civilians and the two IRA bombers after the bomb they were planting went off prematurely. In 1990 the arcade received listed status, leading to lower rents and attracting artists and creative businesses to establish themselves there. Notable spaces like the Arcadia Café, RIP Off, Skin Works and a recording studio were among the businesses set up in the arcade.

Then, in 2004, a deliberate fire completely destroyed the arcade. Since then, it has been abandoned. Proposed redevelopment plans have yet to materialise, but to me it would seem beneficial for the City of Belfast to restore this unique art deco arcade for future generations.

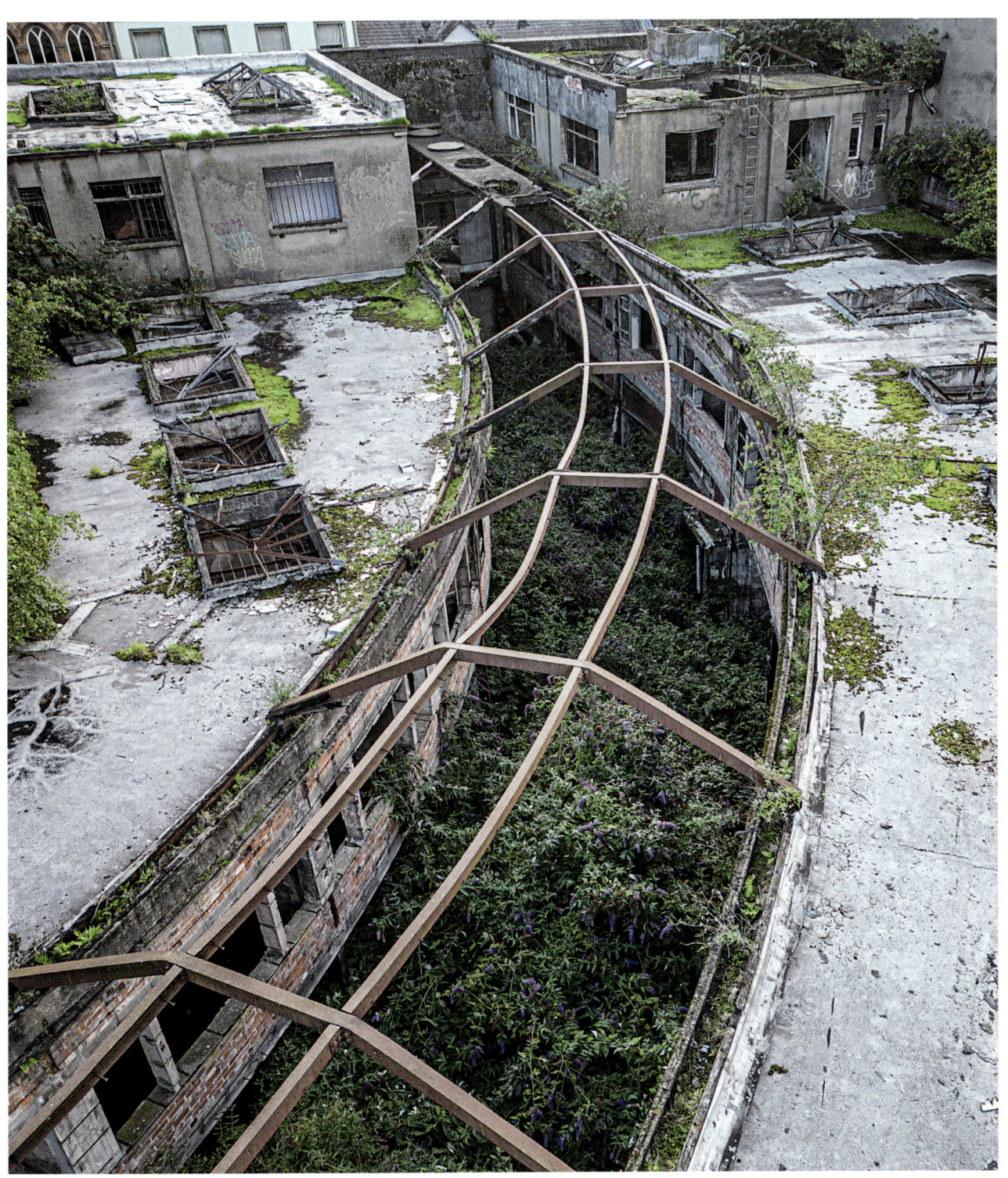

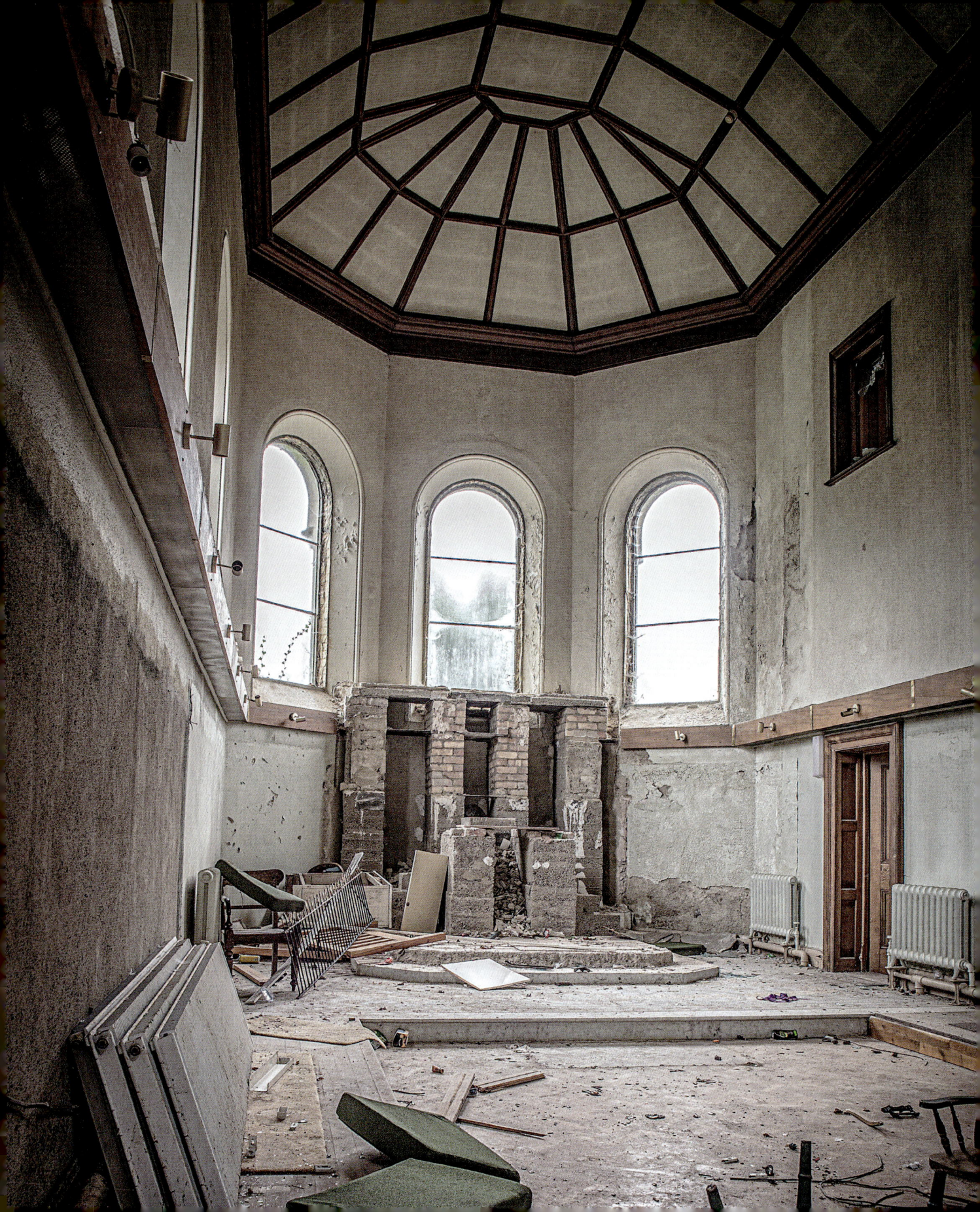

# SISTERS OF MERCY CONVENT

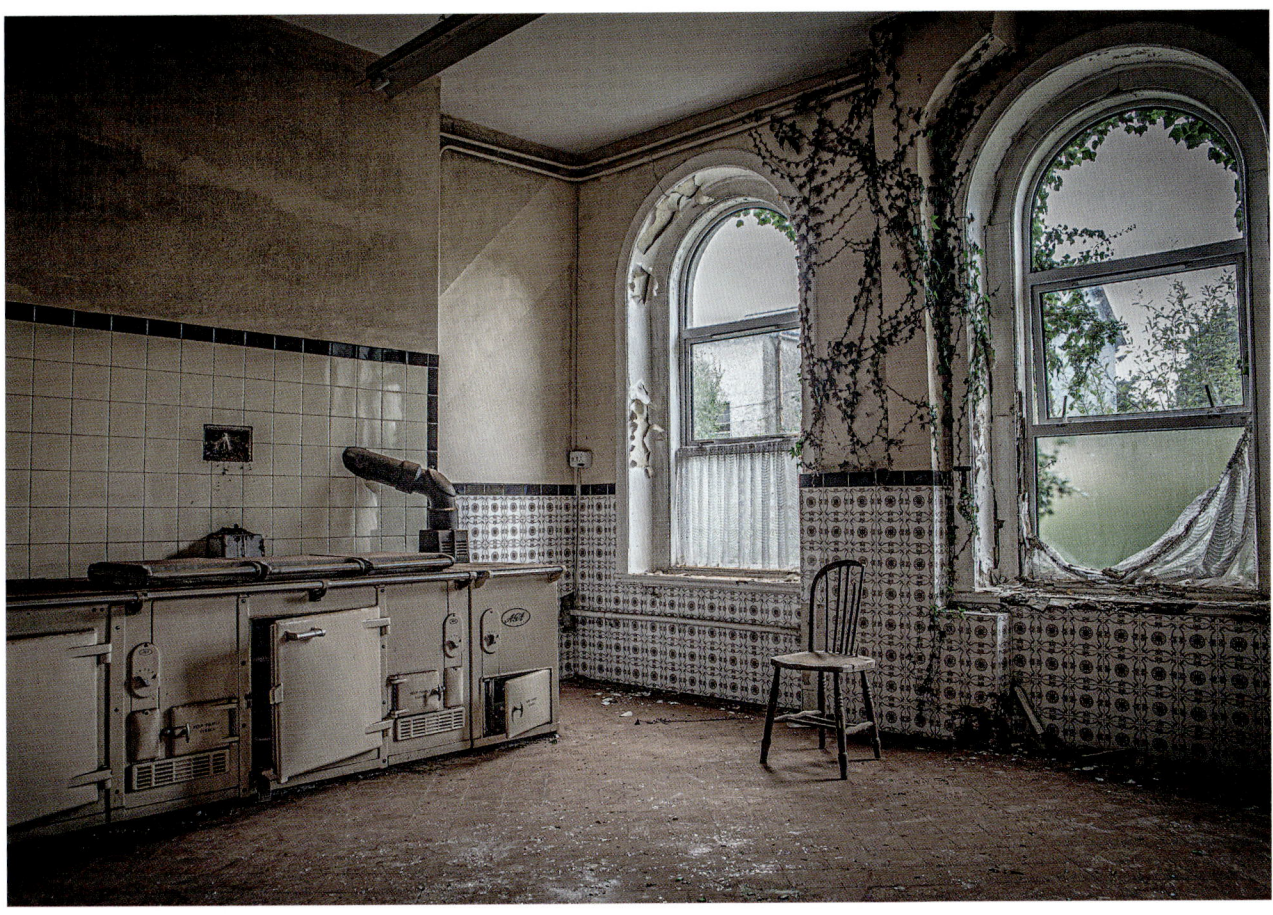

I always find photographing convents to be an interesting experience, as there is just something about them that makes for a good photographic subject. This particular one, built in the late 1800s, was renowned for its musical legacy, with its nuns teaching music to local children along with their regular teaching duties. The nuns also started a lace-making business to support the community and help

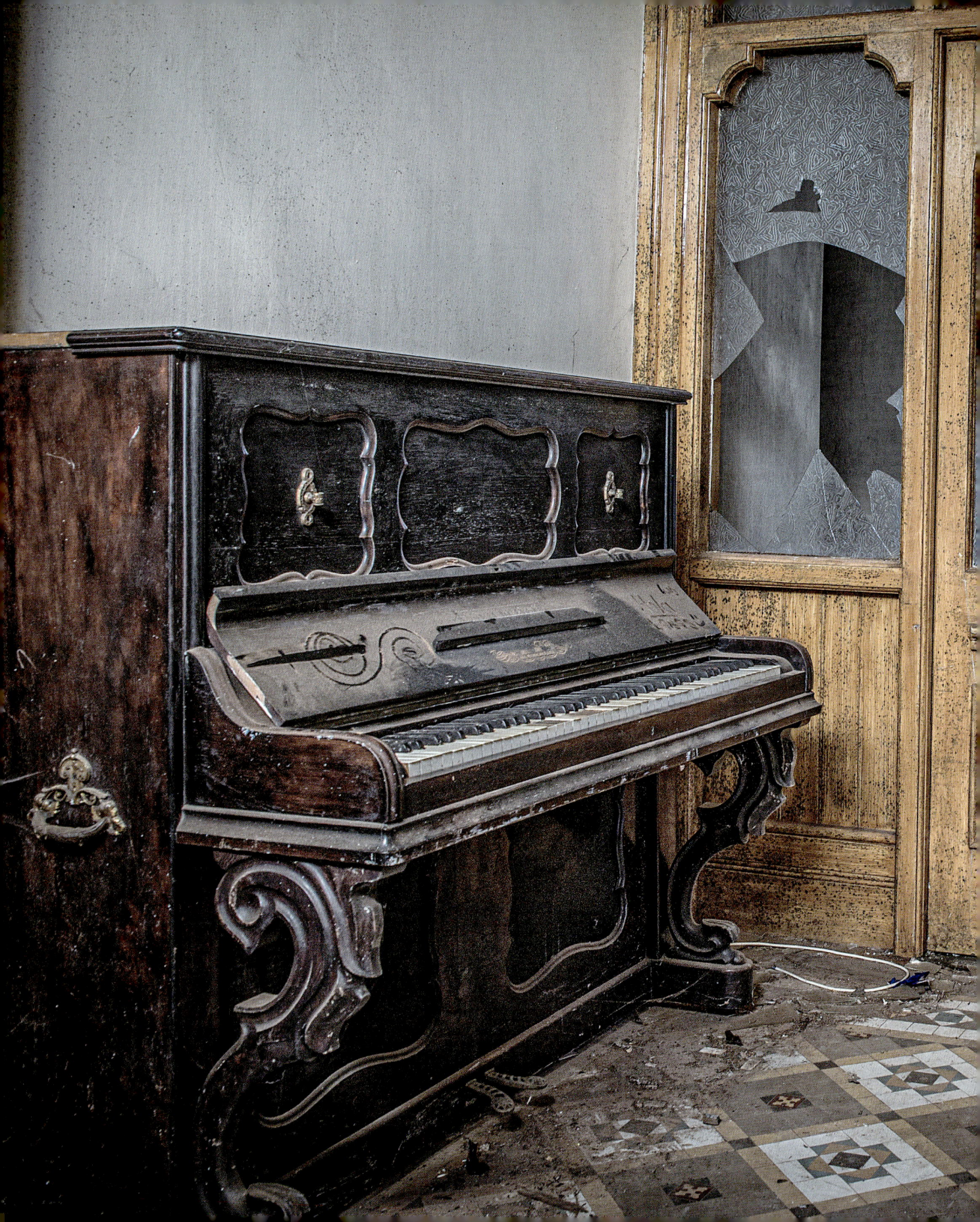

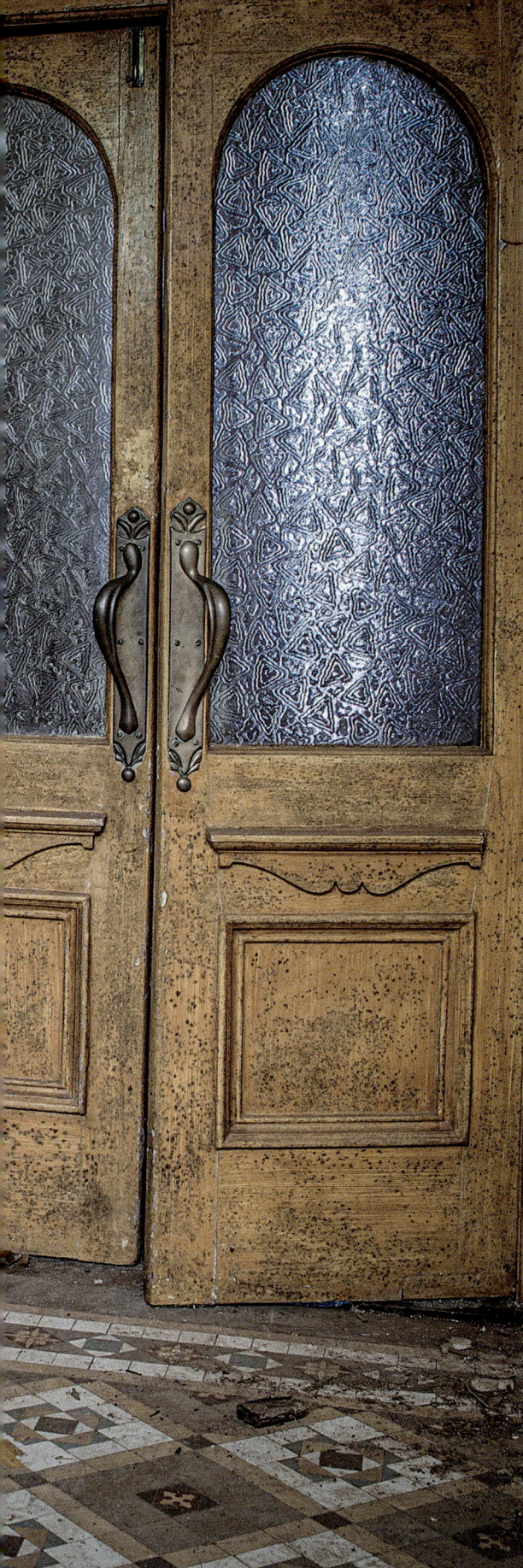

hard-up mothers earn money. The success of this business led to the establishment of a lace factory within the convent, where the craft was taught and the lace created and sold. Additionally, a secondary school was later added, furthering educational opportunities for local children.

Faced with decreasing numbers taking on a life of religious vocation, the convent closed its doors in 2005 and has remained vacant ever since. Situated in a built-up location, and despite being featured on television shows such as *Don't Tell the Bride*, it has since fallen victim to vandalism. The top floor has become inaccessible due to a collapsed staircase, which is a real shame, as I could see that the balcony would have provided me with a unique view overlooking the main chapel.

After its closure, grand plans to transform this twenty-bedroom, four-bathroom building into a boutique hotel fell through. The convent is now back on the market and I eagerly anticipate its sale to someone willing to take on the challenge of restoring this historic building.

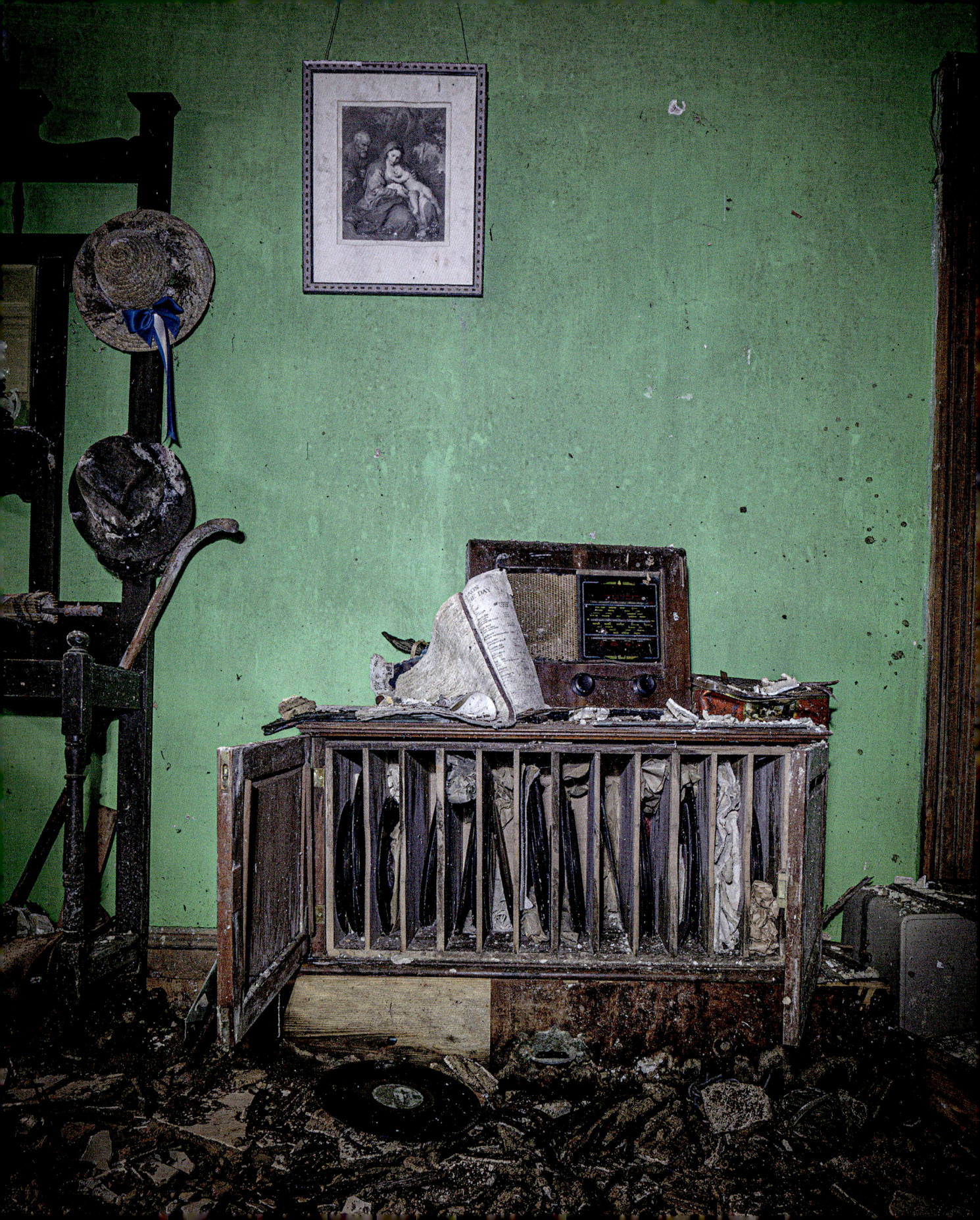

# GENTRY MANOR

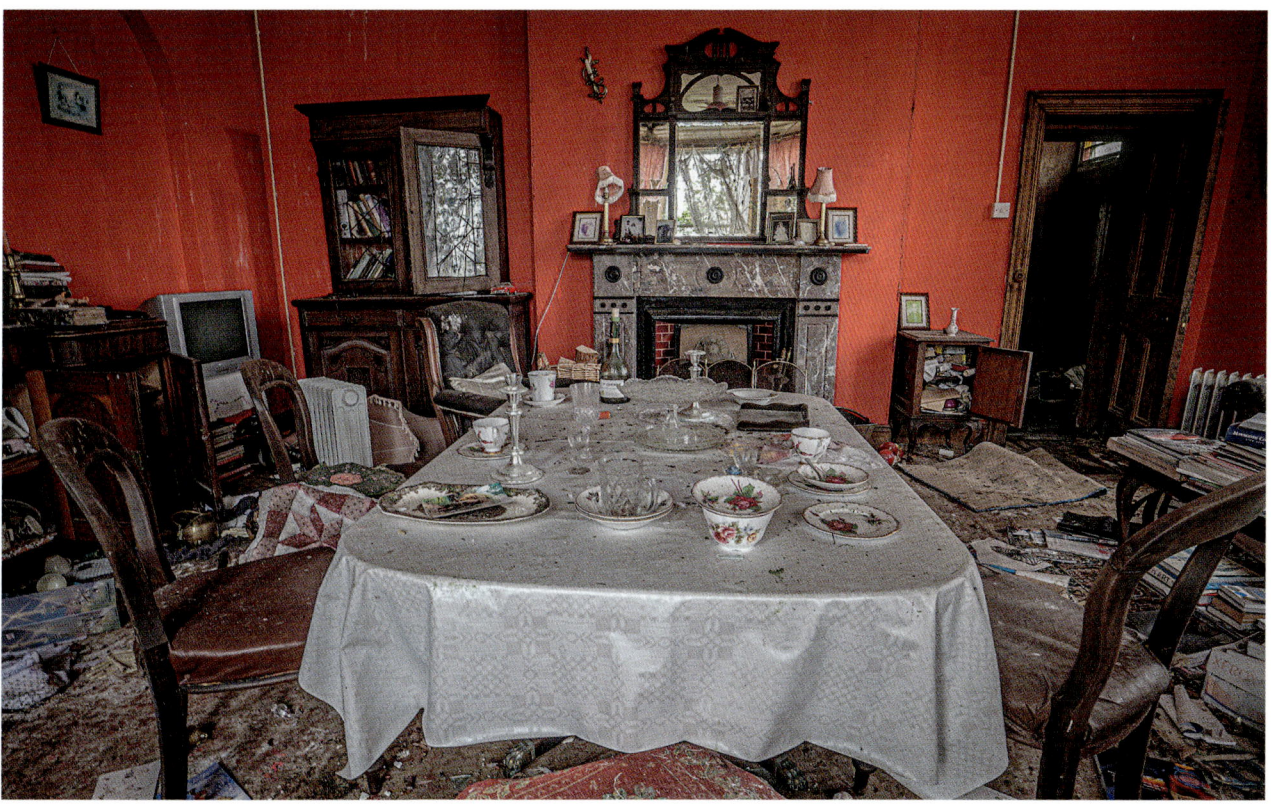

I first heard about this period mansion from a resident who lives nearby. The property was constructed in the 1830s and has been unoccupied since the late 1990s. According to local legend, the family who lived there suddenly vanished in the middle of the night during the Christmas season. The reason for their abrupt departure is a mystery and no one has seen them since. Naturally this piqued my interest and I had to visit.

Reaching the house, located deep in the countryside, requires a trek through a forest. As I approach, a glimpse of the ominous structure peeks through

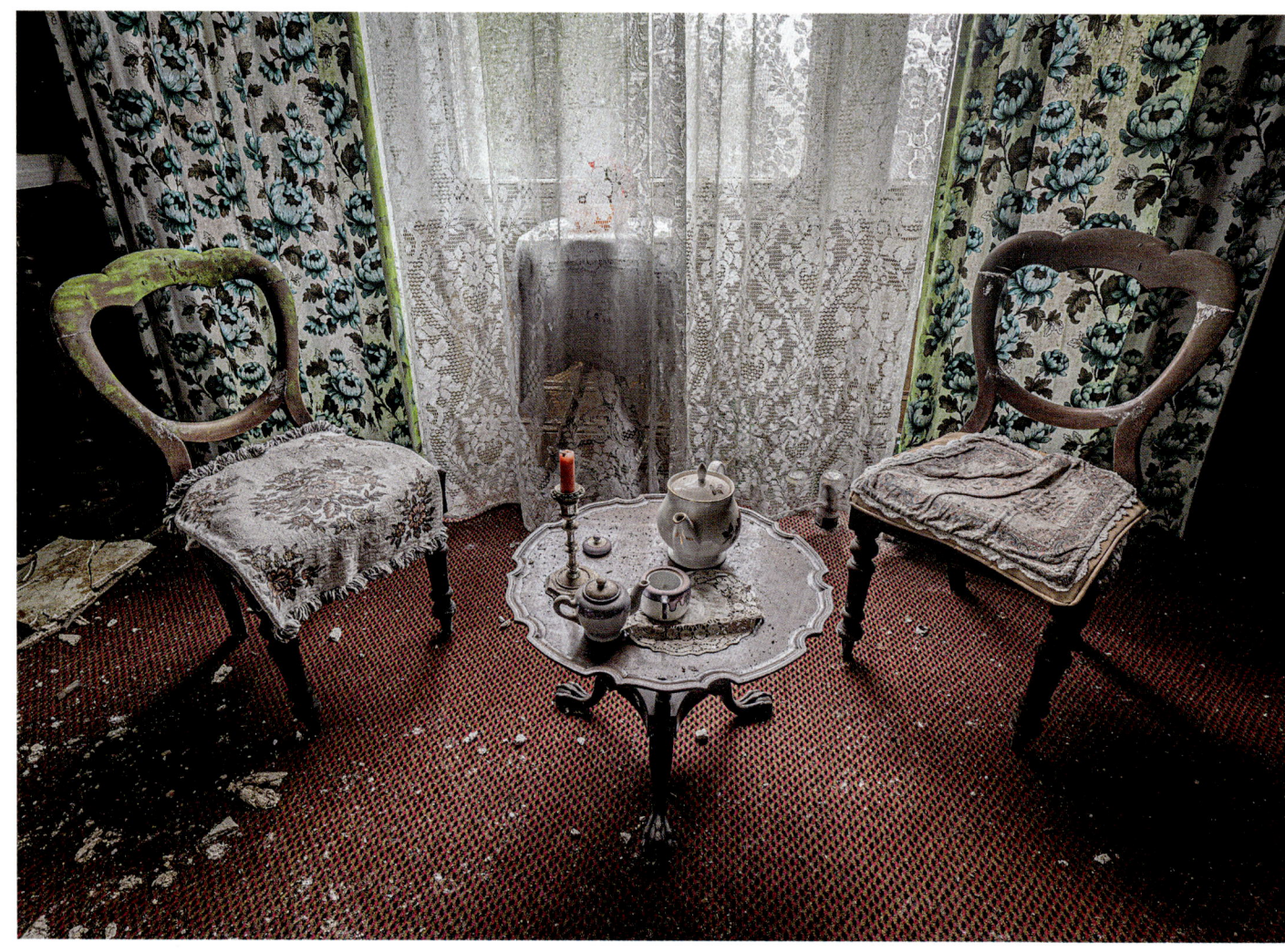

the trees, enhancing an already eerie atmosphere on this typically gloomy Irish day. The unsettling feeling only grows as I near the door, with the mysterious departure of the owners lingering in the back of my mind.

As soon as I enter the mansion, it becomes evident that Christmas was being celebrated by the family, with festive trees and decorations still adorning the halls. The table in the dining room is elegantly set with china teacups and tableware, and candlestick holders wait to be filled with flickering lights, as if the residents departed abruptly in the midst of preparing for a meal. The atmosphere is creepy, as if time froze in that moment.

Each room is painted in vibrant shades of red, green and blue, while the walls are adorned with elaborate religious paintings. The sideboards are still filled with exquisite ornaments, numerous tea sets

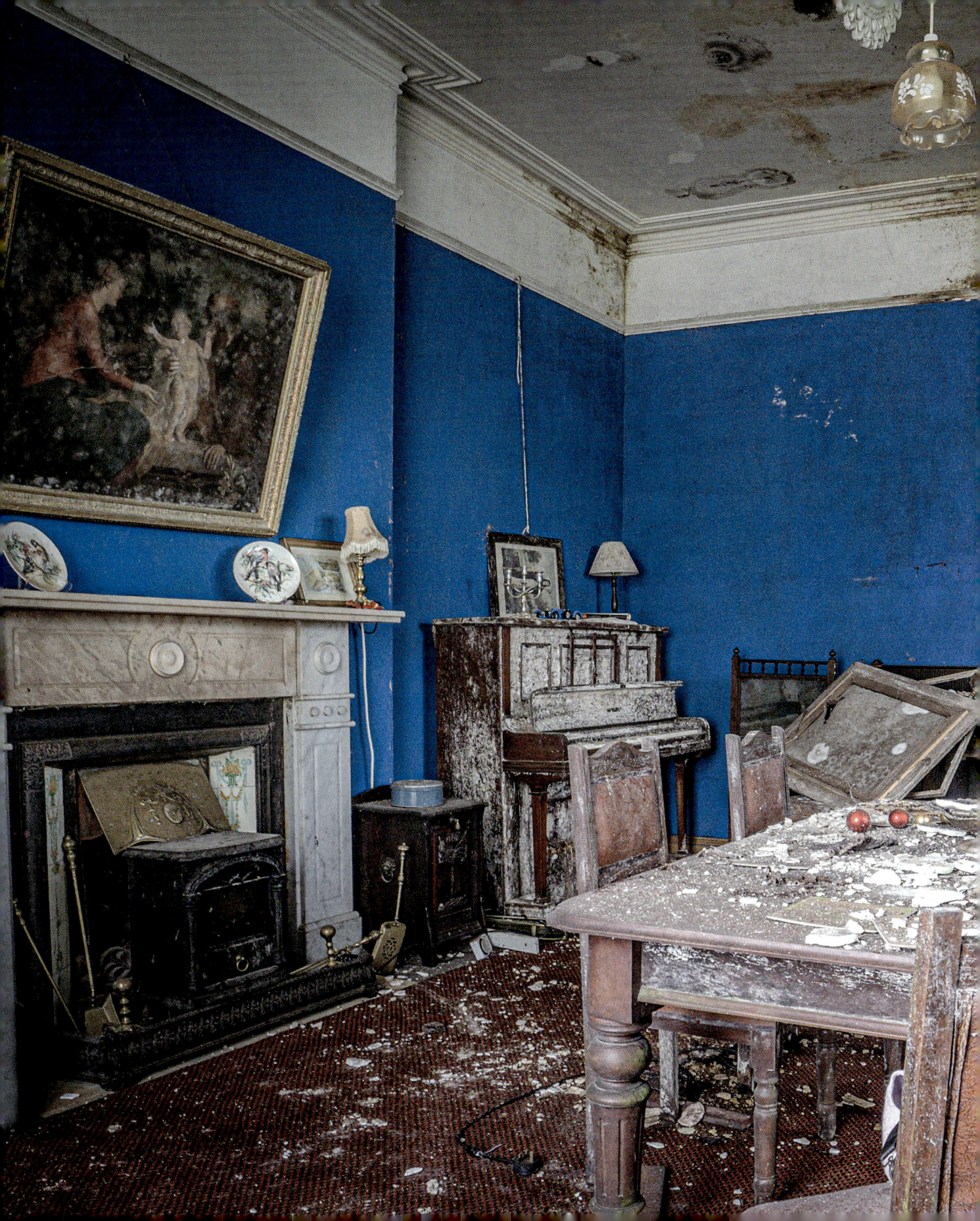

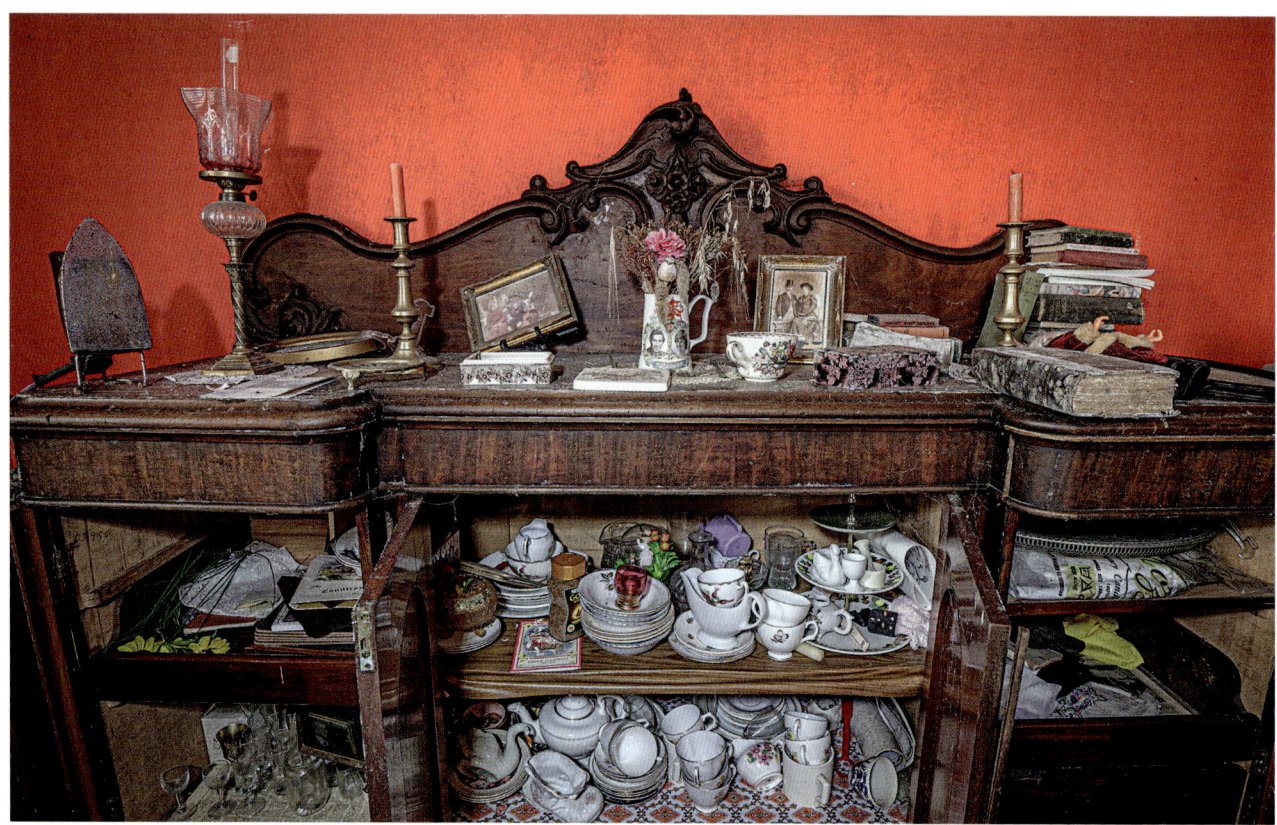

and an abundance of old black-and-white photos. In the corner of one room sits a piano, its keys covered in a thick carpet of white mould. I could picture the scene – guests being entertained as music fills the air, drinks flowing and lively conversations and laughter all around. The opulence is evident, raising a multitude of questions as to why such wealth was abandoned to decay.

With the house being quite large, it strikes me as odd that the kitchen is so small – all it possesses are twin Belfast sinks and an Aga. There is an adjoining room with a sideboard and another small dining room. Servants' bells are visible on top of the door frame, hinting at a time when there would have been staff here. It is almost like a mini Downtown Abbey.

The three-storey house has a top floor that is partially collapsed, making access impossible. Water is seeping in through the roof, streaming down the walls and ceilings. It seems like only a matter of time before this once grand structure is reduced to dust.

The number of grand mansions and humble homes scattered across this country that are simply left to decay continues to amaze me. The abundance of memories and history being abandoned and forgotten is truly disheartening. At least by photographing these neglected buildings, I feel like I'm making a contribution to their memory by creating a visual legacy for future generations.

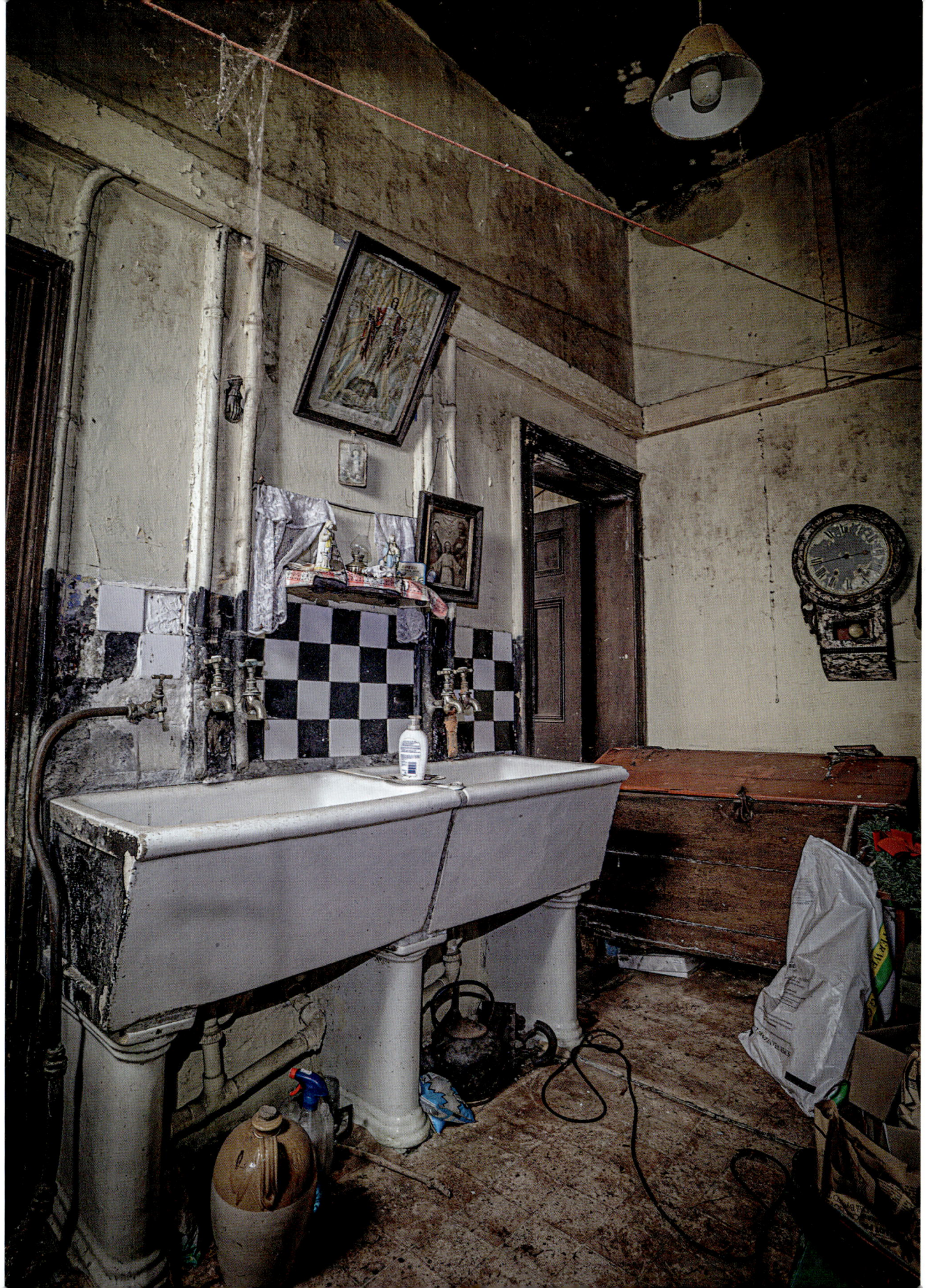

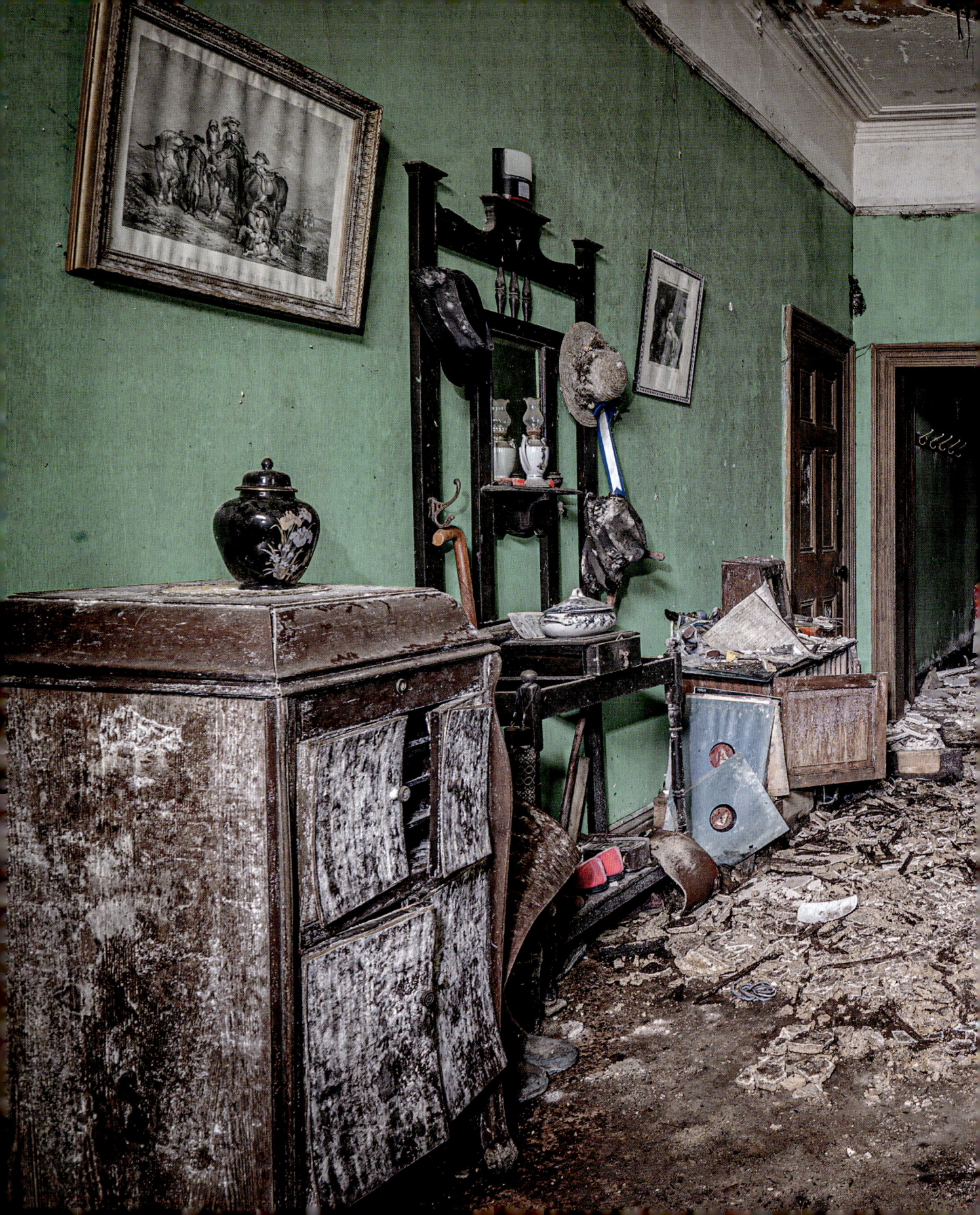

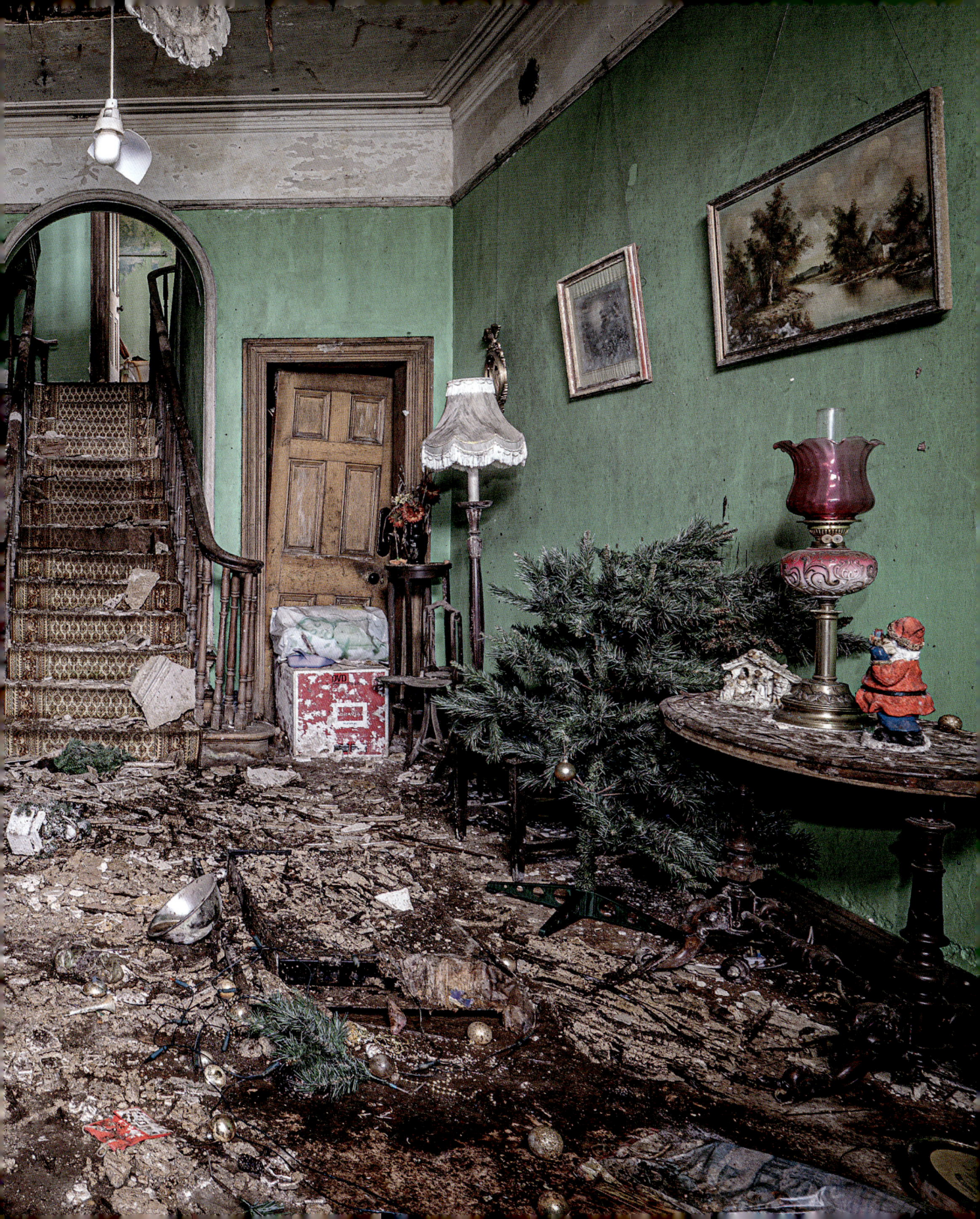

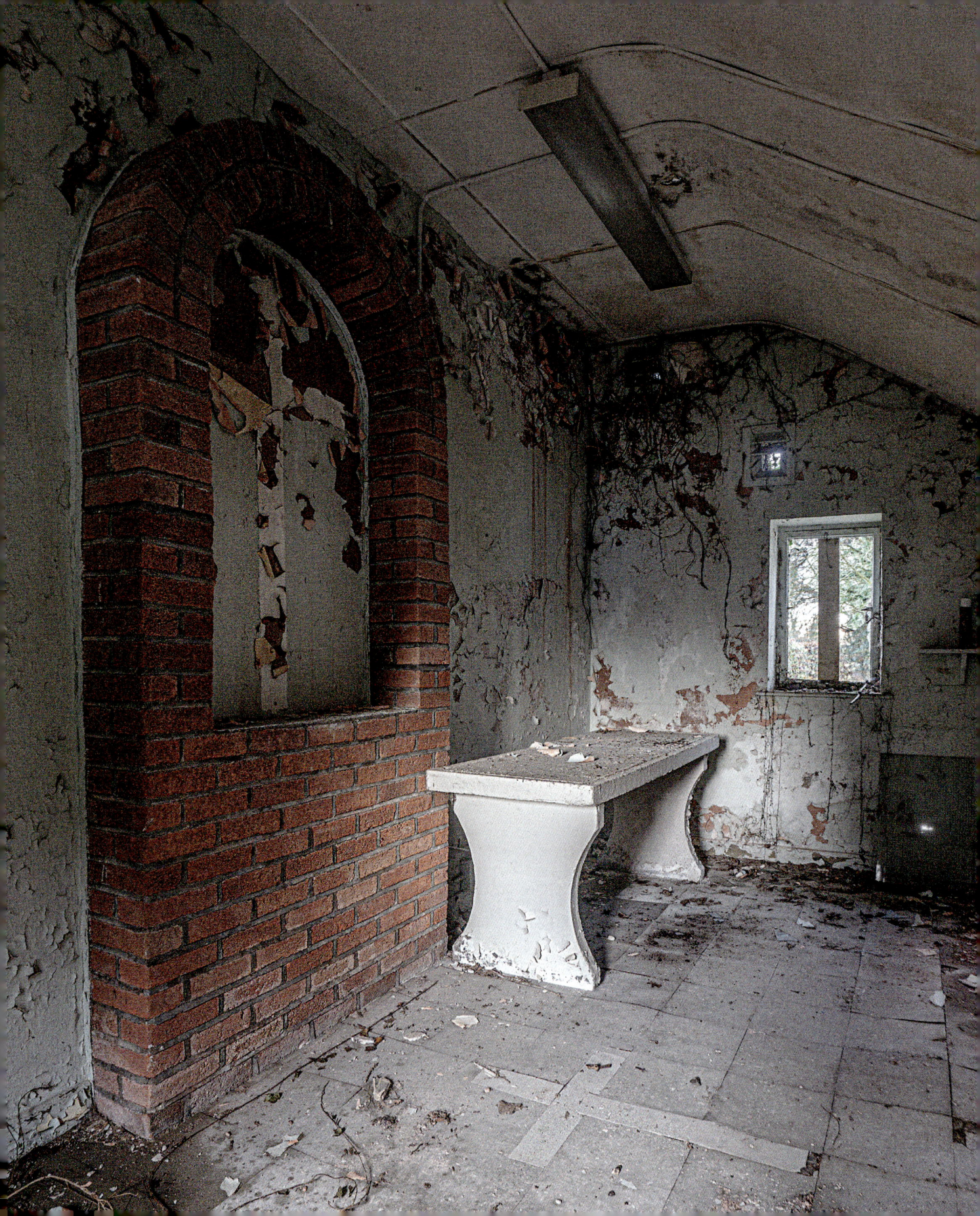

# THE COUNTY HOSPITAL AND HOME

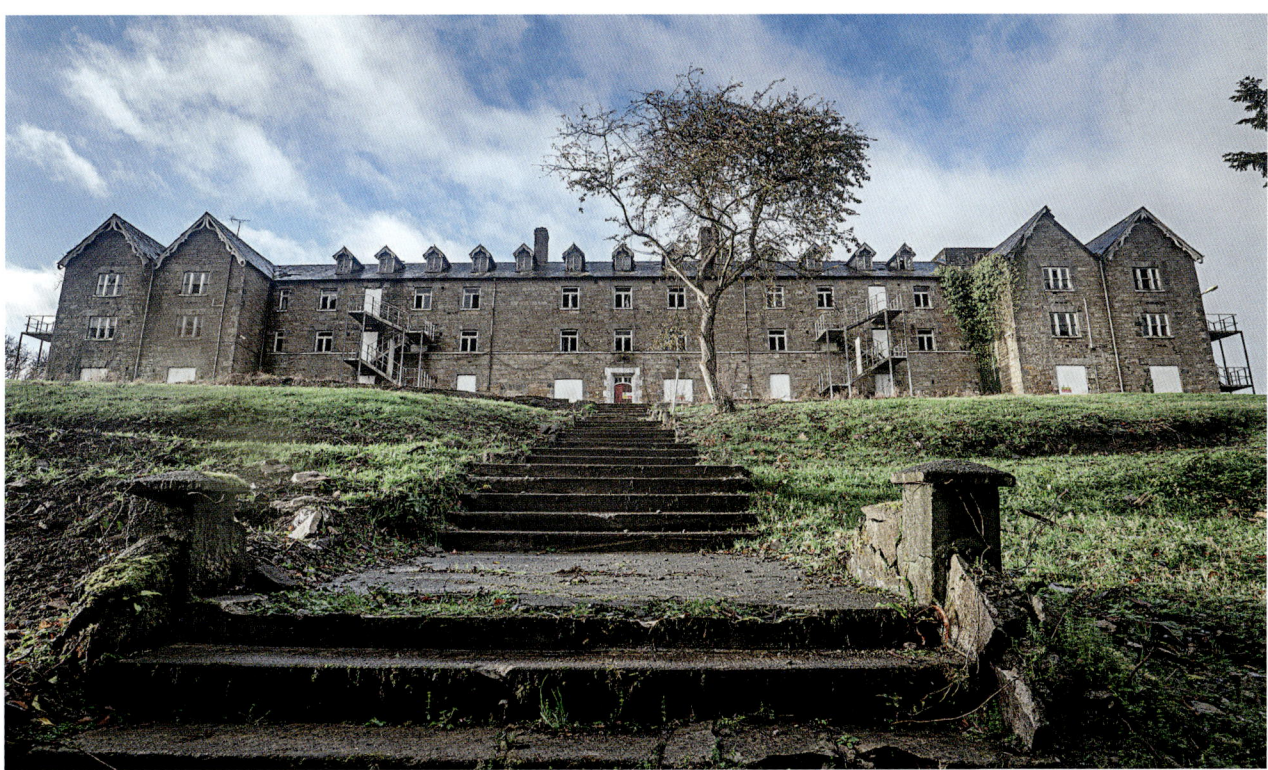

Like most hospitals in Ireland, this one began as workhouse, also known as poorhouse. Built in 1842, it was one of the earliest and could house up to 1,200 inmates, making it Ulster's largest. All the workhouses of Ireland were designed by the architect George Wilkinson, who worked for the Poor Law Commissioners, and they all have the same Tudor Gothic design. He had strict instructions to keep the buildings durable, cheap and plain, in order to make them as cold and as much of a deterrent to potential inmates as possible. They certainly all present a sinister appearance and must have instilled great fear in those who had to resort to their unforgiving regimes.

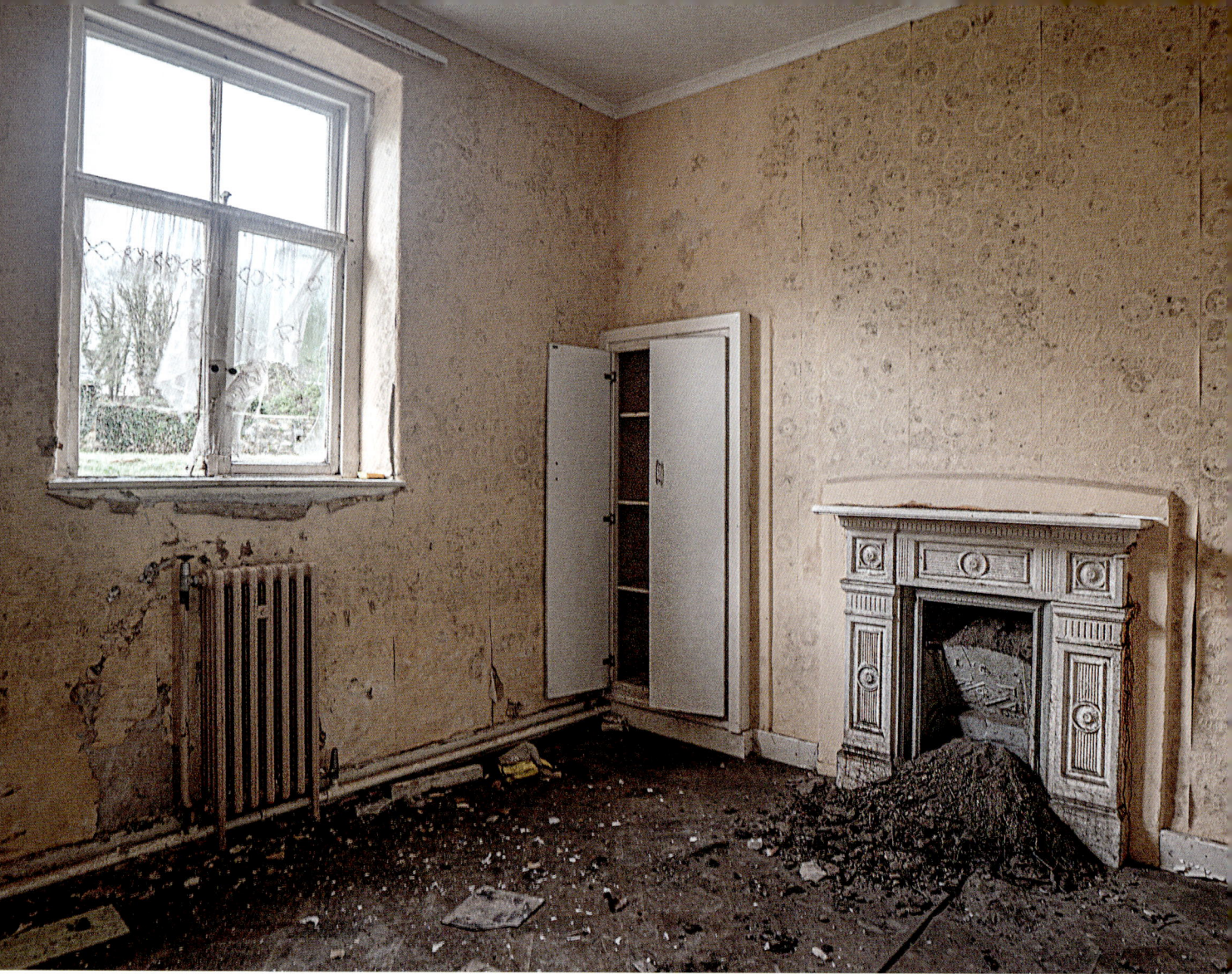

This workhouse opened just three years before the Great Famine started and it has a famine graveyard located behind it. Like all examples, the sexes at this particular institution were segregated, with separate blocks for men, women and children. The master's and matron's quarters were located in the middle. In addition to the living quarters, a kitchen, laundry and bakehouse were connected to a dining hall and chapel. The infirmary and 'idiots' wards were situated at the back of the complex, with a morgue on site and a fever hospital added in 1847. Reports from as early as the 1890s show the hospital was not fit for purpose. One records horrendous conditions there, with no trained nurses in sight. Patients were instead under the care of other patients, who were prone to providing inaccurate diagnoses and incorrect medication.

After the establishment of the Irish Free State in 1922, the workhouse was transformed into the Cavan County Hospital and Home, following the

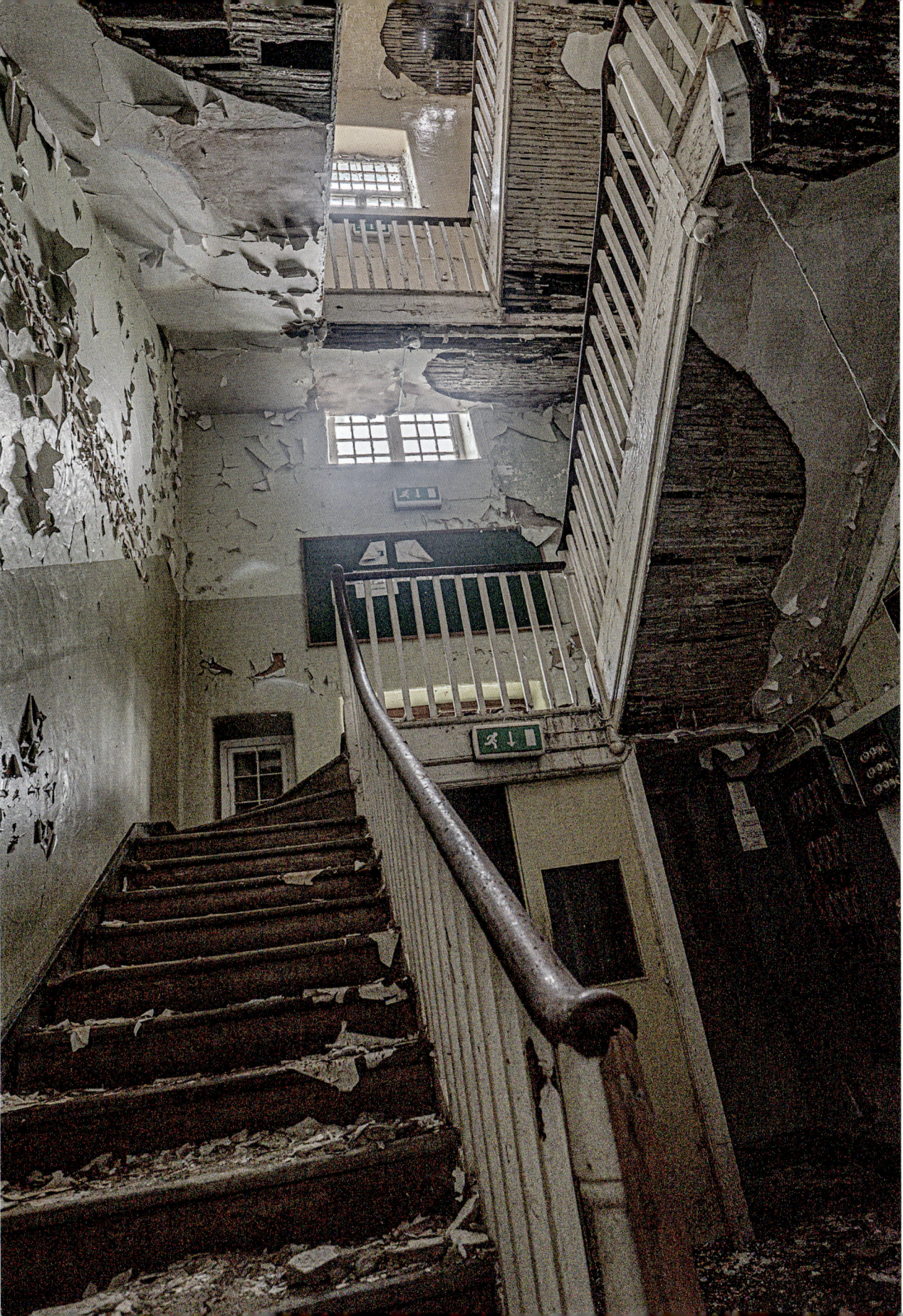

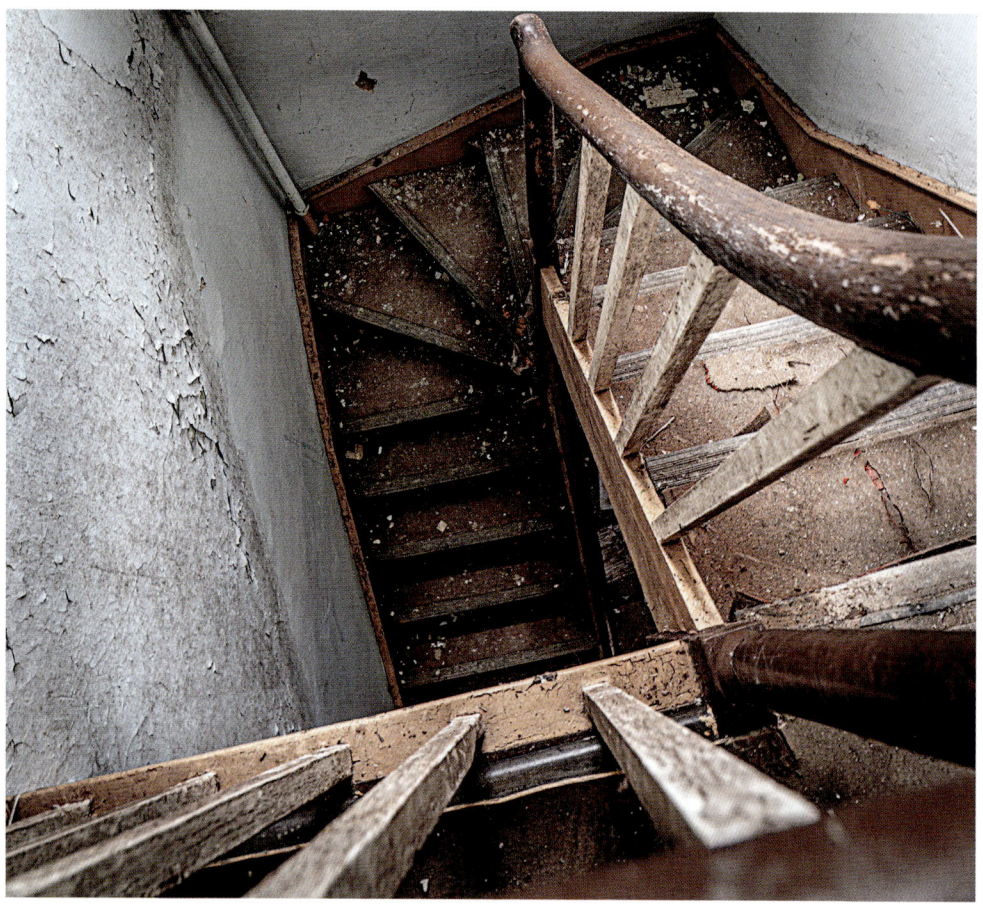

abolishment of the workhouse system. A 1927 report described the hospital as bleak and cold during the winter months, with insufficient accommodation for patients. Moreover, the fever hospital was recorded as not having a proper disinfecting chamber. The County Home, located on the ground and first floors, was also in need of improvement. It would have been used to house a wide variety of largely poor people: the elderly, the chronically ill, the mentally ill, the intellectually disabled and unmarried mothers. In the 1950s the complex was renamed St Felim's.

The hospital closed in 2003 and has lain derelict ever since. Its history is now being investigated as it has been accused of being used as a mother and baby home until 1962. Since its closure, the buildings have endured severe vandalism, with holes in the walls and smashed sinks and toilets. The destruction seems senseless, and I often wonder why someone would expend so much energy on such activities. I guess I will probably never understand.

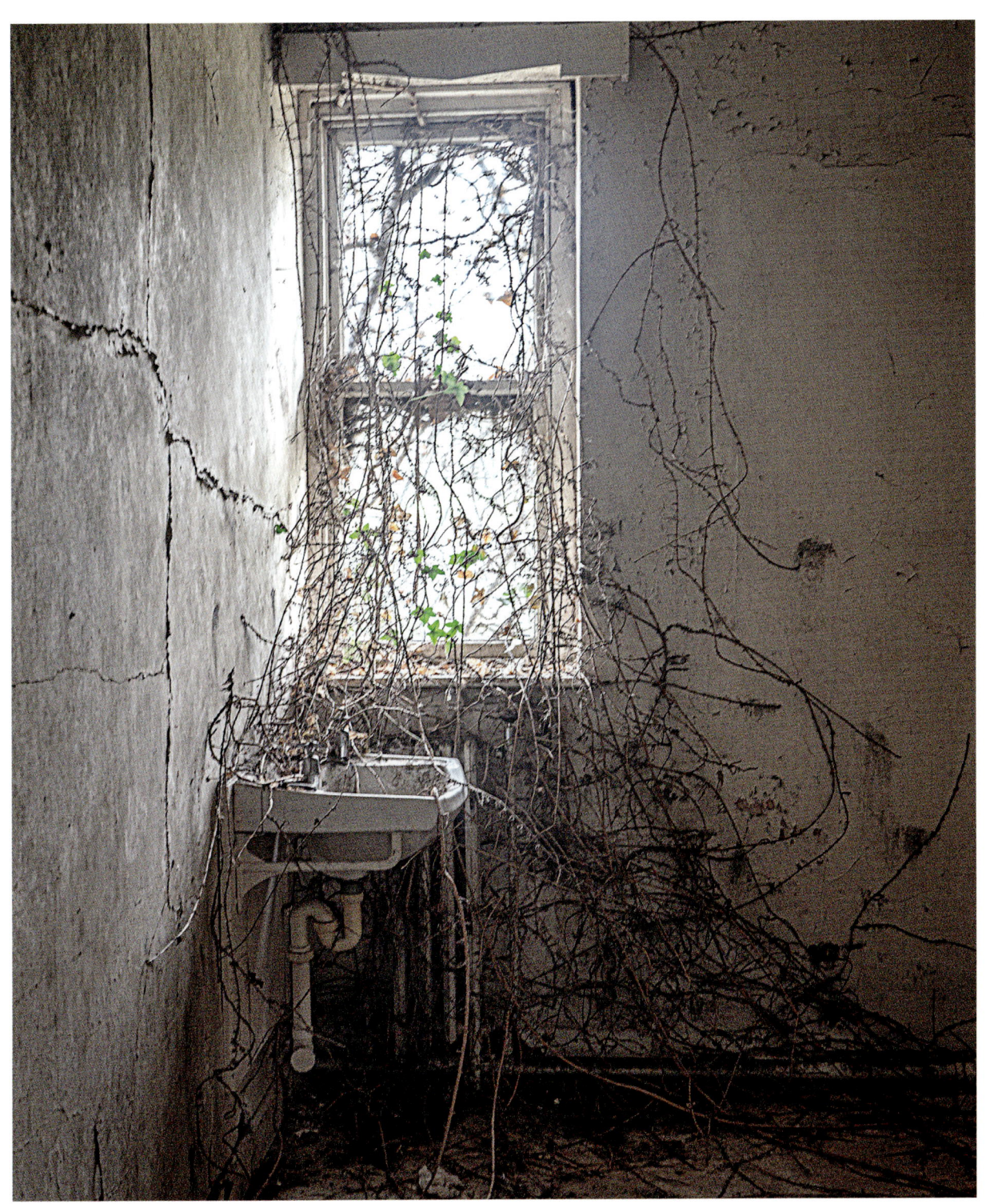

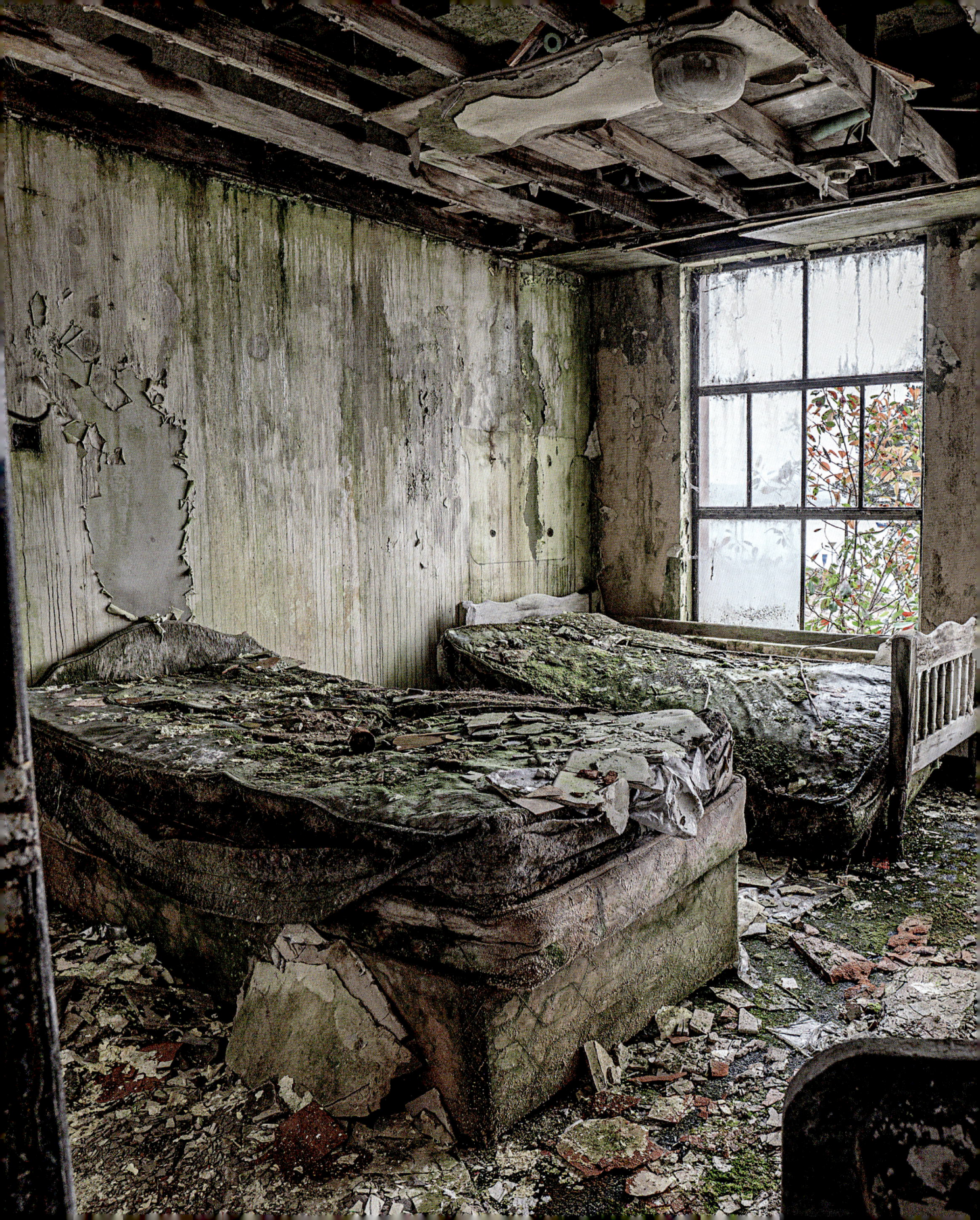

# TÁIN ADVENTURE

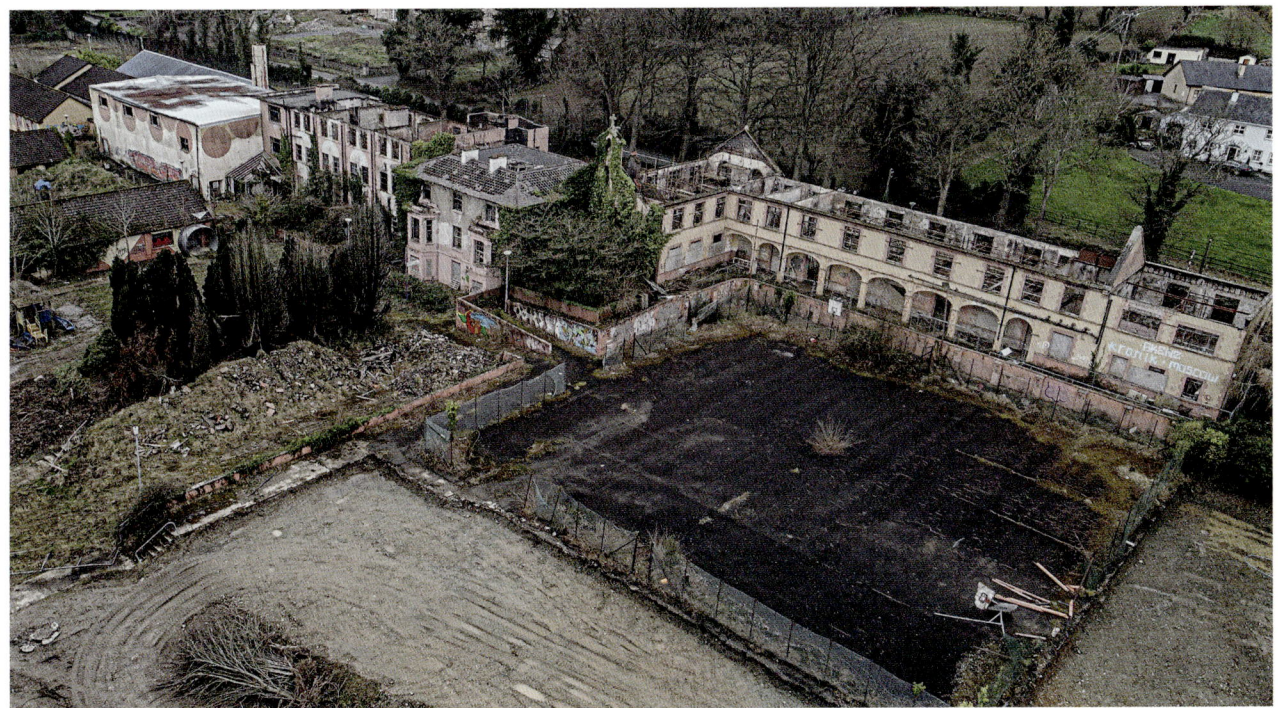

This place was one of the first I explored photographically back in 2012. By this point it had already been abandoned for a few years.

The story of this site starts in 1840, when a retired Protestant clergyman named Rev. Robert Greer had a large house built there for his retirement. The house, named Ballyoonan House, was set in 15 acres of land. Rev. Greer was a kind and charitable man, who was always helping others. He was influential in the fishing community and even had a pier built in the village, which is now known as Greer's Quay. However, his peaceful retirement was disrupted when a new railway line was installed through his back garden. As a result, he decided to move, and sold the house.

In 1880 Edward McCreanor, a retired school

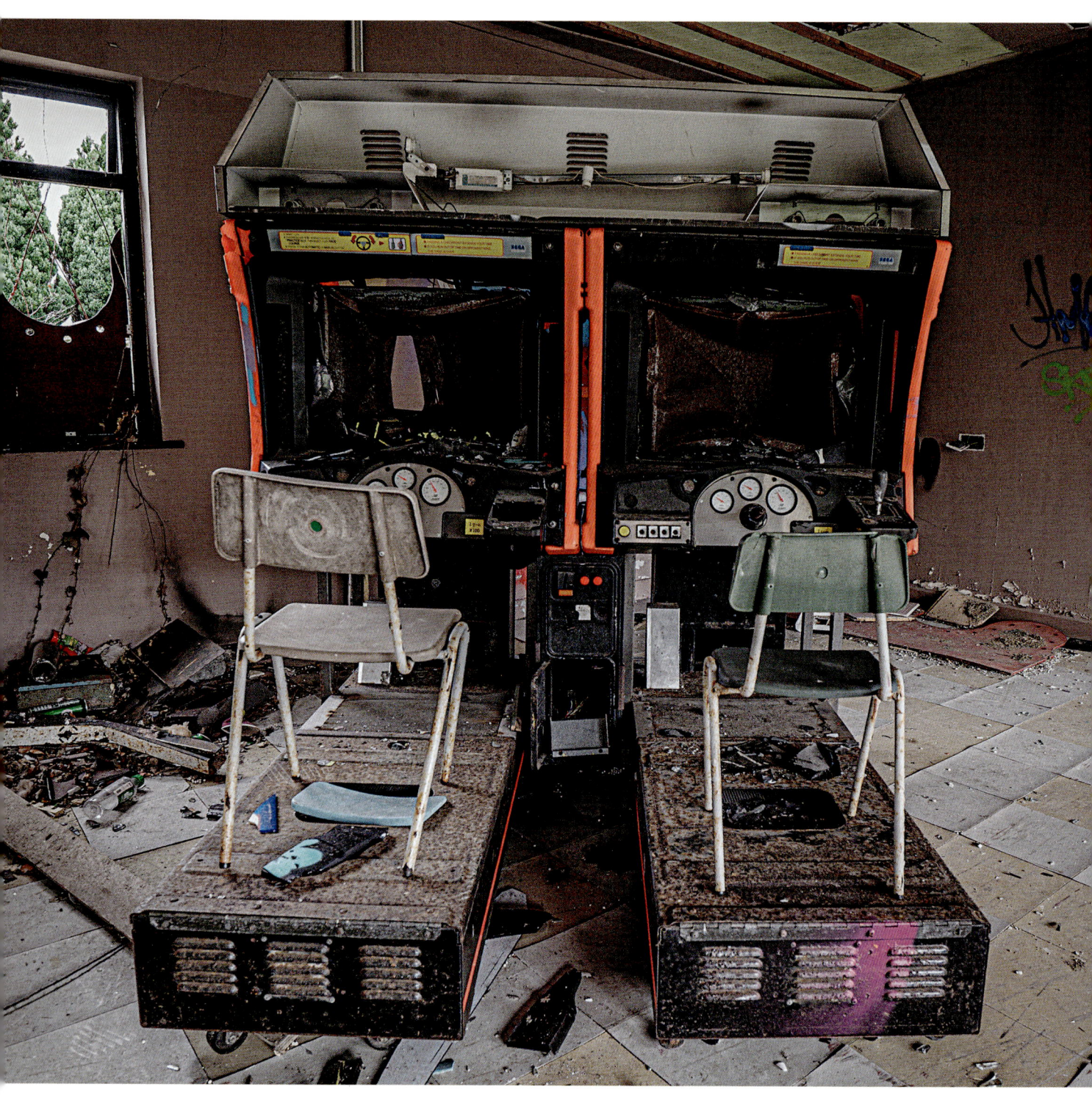

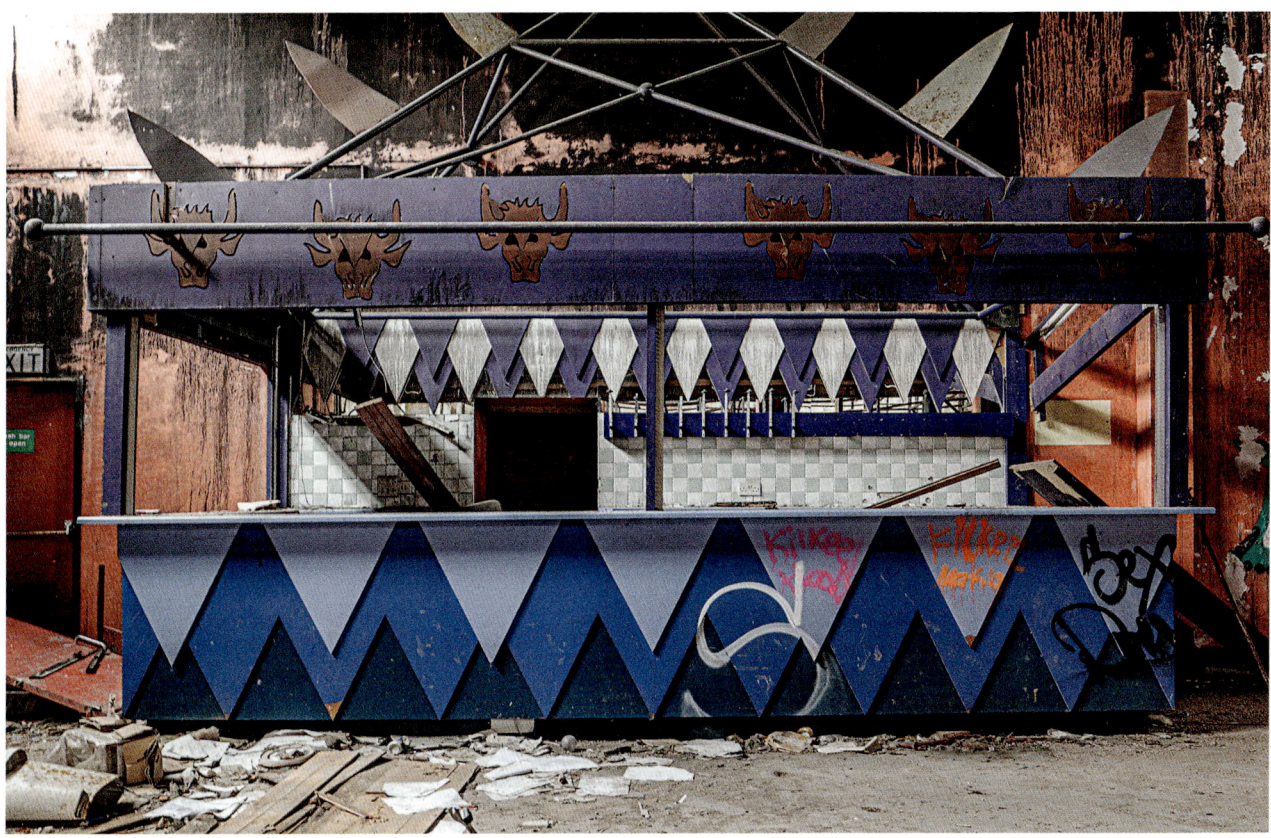

inspector, made the decision to settle in Ballyoonan with his daughter and niece. However, his health began to decline, leading him to relocate to Belfast, and he expressed his desire to leave the house to an orphanage or religious order. In 1901 the Rosminians acquired the property and rebranded it as St Michael's. Over time the house was expanded and transformed into a training school for priests. At its peak, it hosted up to 100 priests in training, but in 1986, faced with financial challenges and a decrease in enrolment, the decision was made to close St Michael's.

In 1994 the site was transformed and opened its doors as a holiday village for the public. It offered a wide range of outdoor activities, and its location on the shores of Carlingford Lough provided breathtaking views. The centre boasted amenities such as a swimming pool, restaurant, basketball court, games rooms and even a Laser Quest arena. Kids would visit here on school trips for week-long stays. However, it was not just for school groups, and families and individuals from all corners of Ireland flocked to the village for short and long breaks. The site even had facilities for touring caravans. Unfortunately, over time, the once-thriving holiday village experienced a decline in visitors, leading to its closure in 2007.

As I mentioned in my introduction, my initial

curiosity about places like this was aroused when I was part of a group exploring the paranormal, and on this site my two interests collided. During my visit I was accompanied by my sister, and as I took photographs, she recorded video on an iPad. We walked through the entire building and finally reached the dormitory section with its long corridors lined with rooms of bunk beds where the kids would have slept. Upon opening the last door, we distinctly heard the sound of a male voice as if standing right beside us. Startled, we left and then played back the recording on the iPad in the car. We could hear the voice, which had an Ulster accent, saying, 'You're crazy.' I've shared this eerie encounter on social media multiple times, but some people don't seem to hear anything, while others hear different words. If you're curious, feel free to check out my social media.

After our visit, the condition of the site continued to deteriorate, with vandals setting fire to the main building and destroying much of the original structure. In early 2023 the adventure centre was demolished, and plans are now in motion to transform the site with a nursing home and tourist accommodation. When I think about it, I can't help but wonder if the male voice still perceives me as crazy.

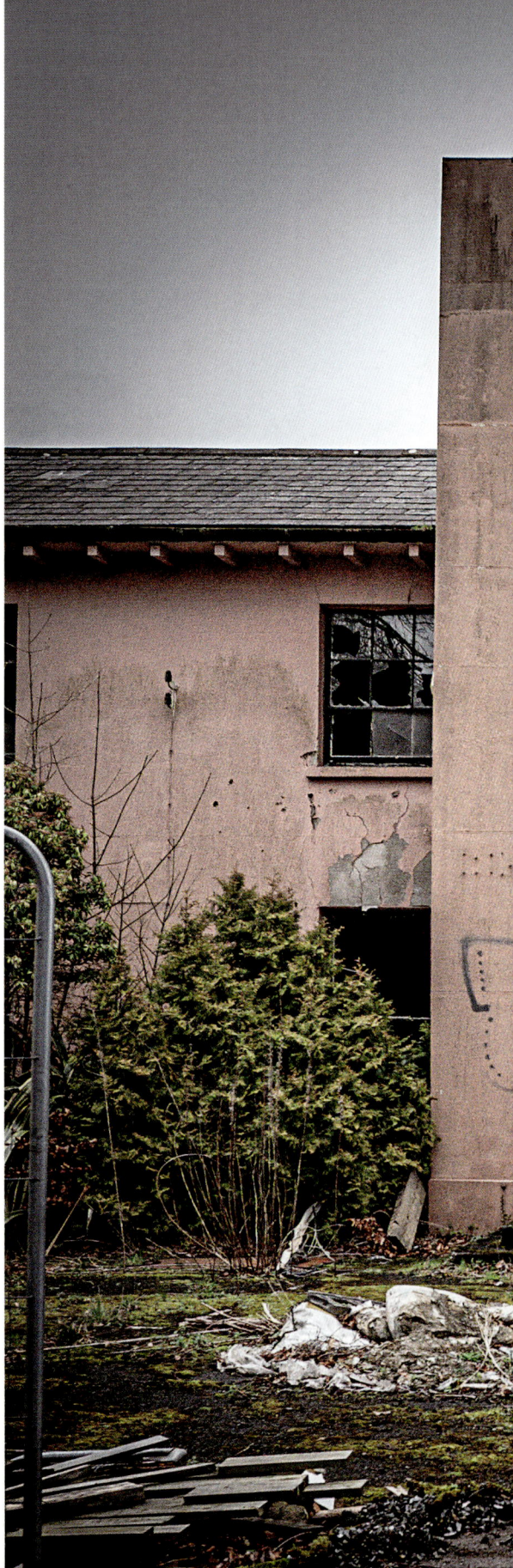

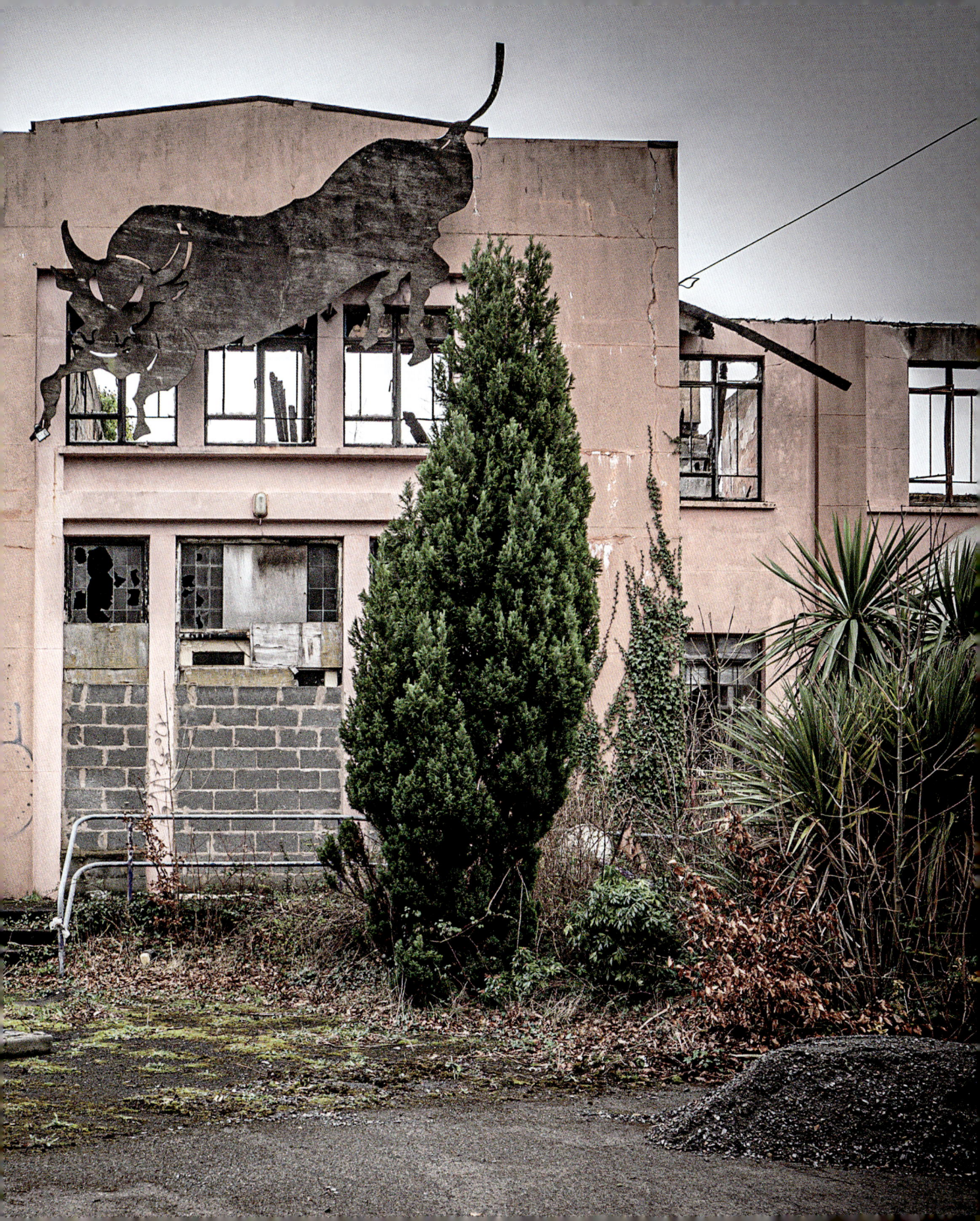

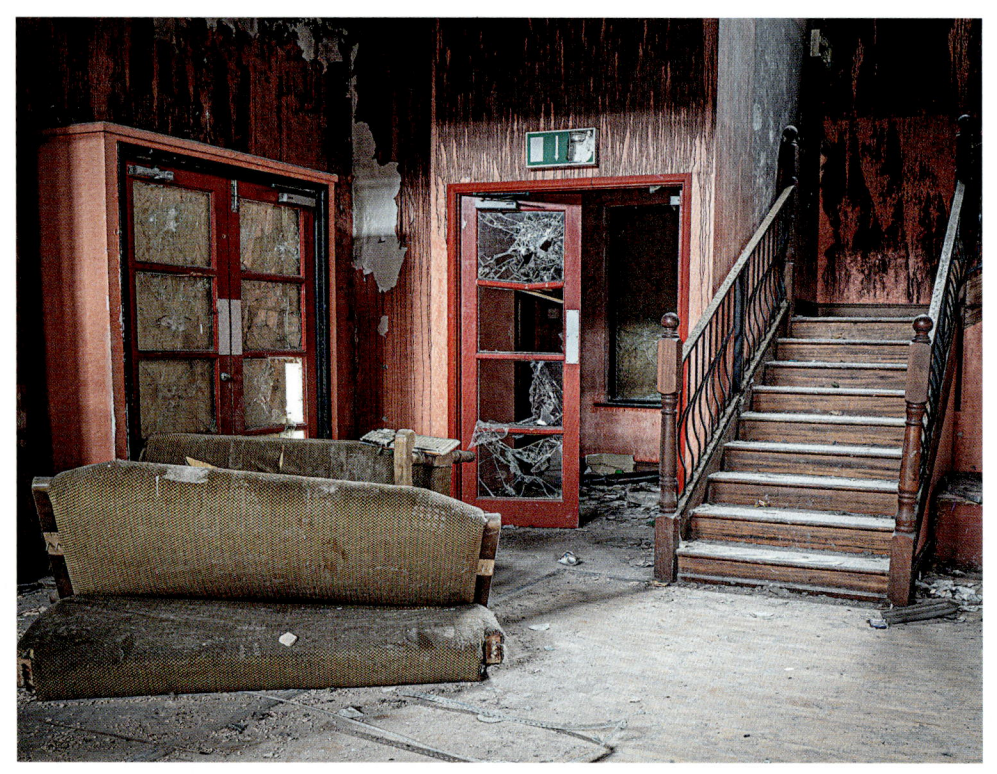

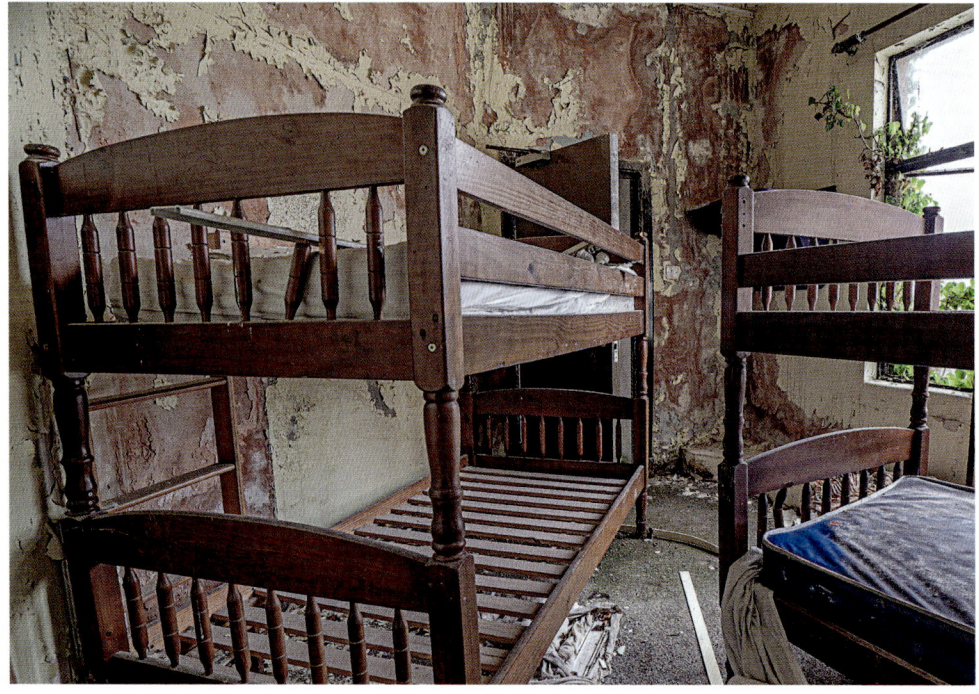

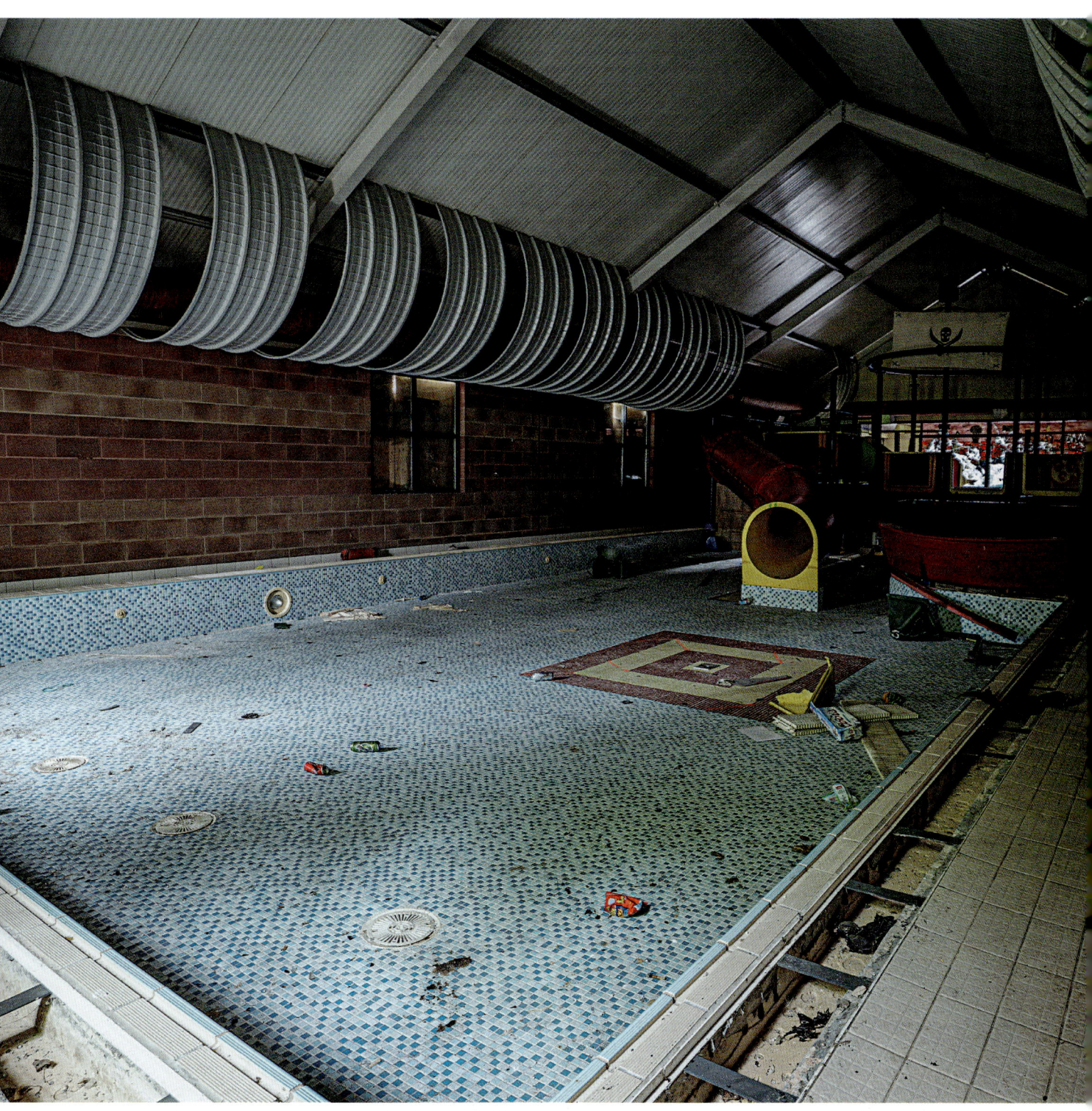

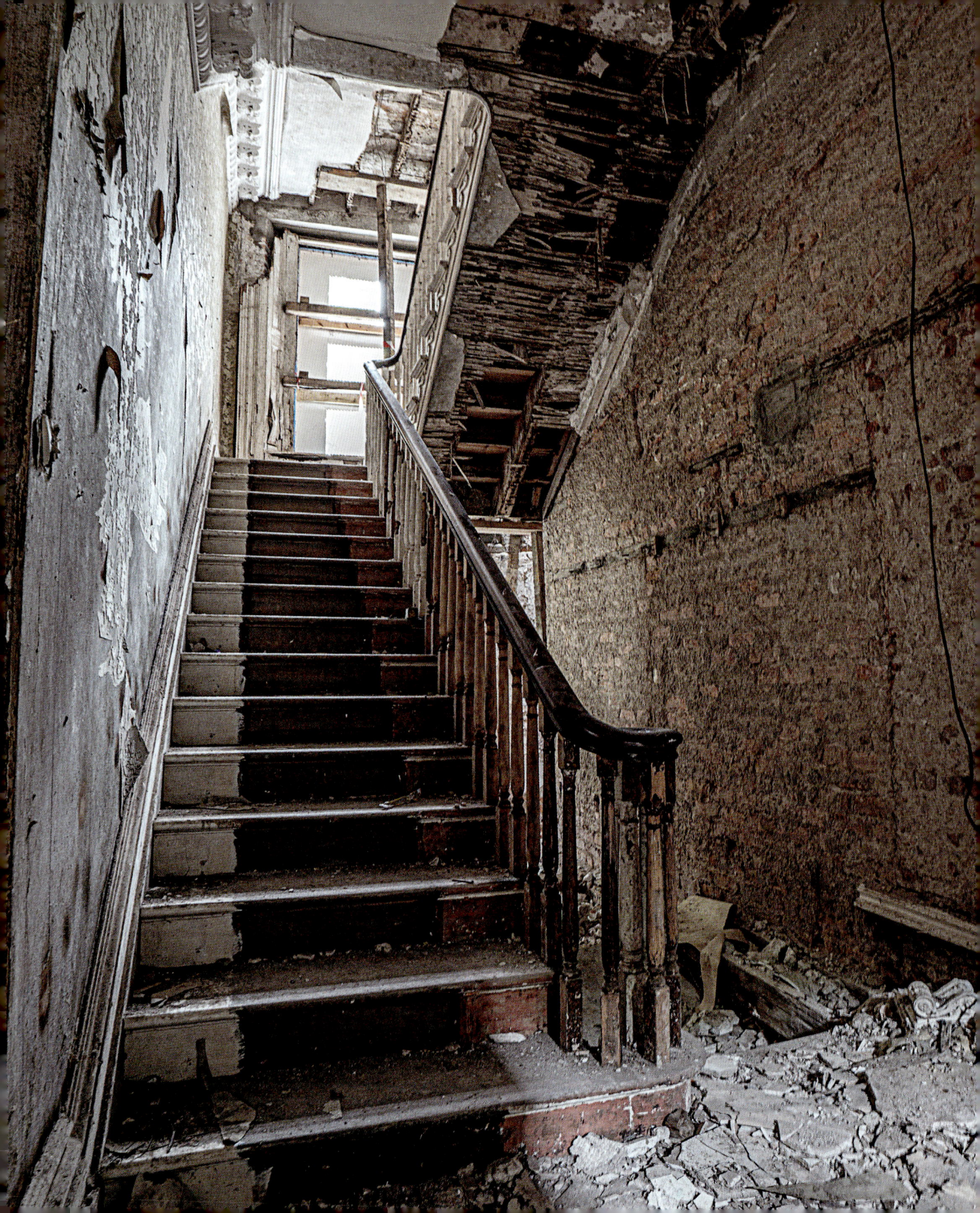

# BALNAMORE HOUSE

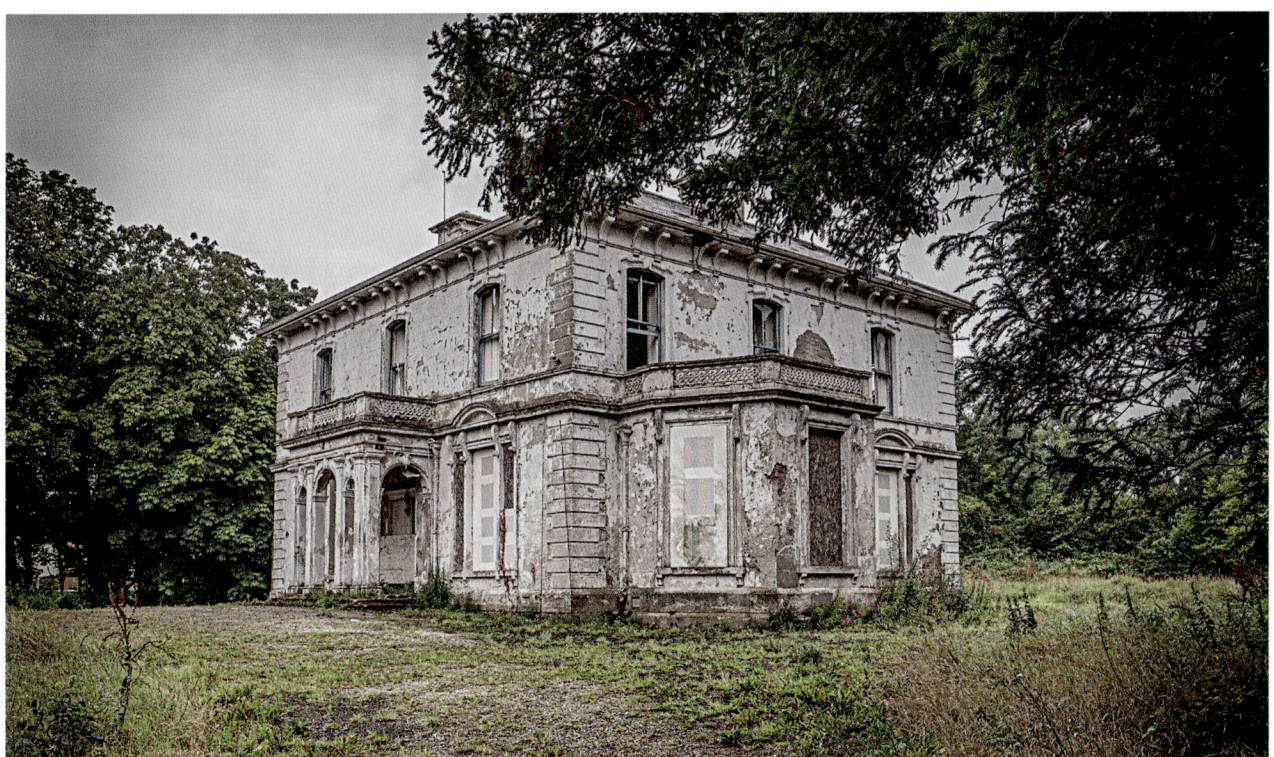

I had received lots of messages regarding this house over the years and one day I was in the area, so I arranged a visit. I was glad I did. Although there wasn't much left of it, due to fire and repeated vandalism, there was still enough to tell its story.

Constructed in the mid-1800s, this grand manor house was once part of an extensive mill complex.

It was not the first structure to occupy this site – a smaller dwelling named Millburn Cottage was demolished to make way for what we see today.

John Caldwell, a captain in the Ballymoney Volunteers and well-known linen merchant, purchased the manor house and 40 acres of land, which included a corn mill, for his family residence. He

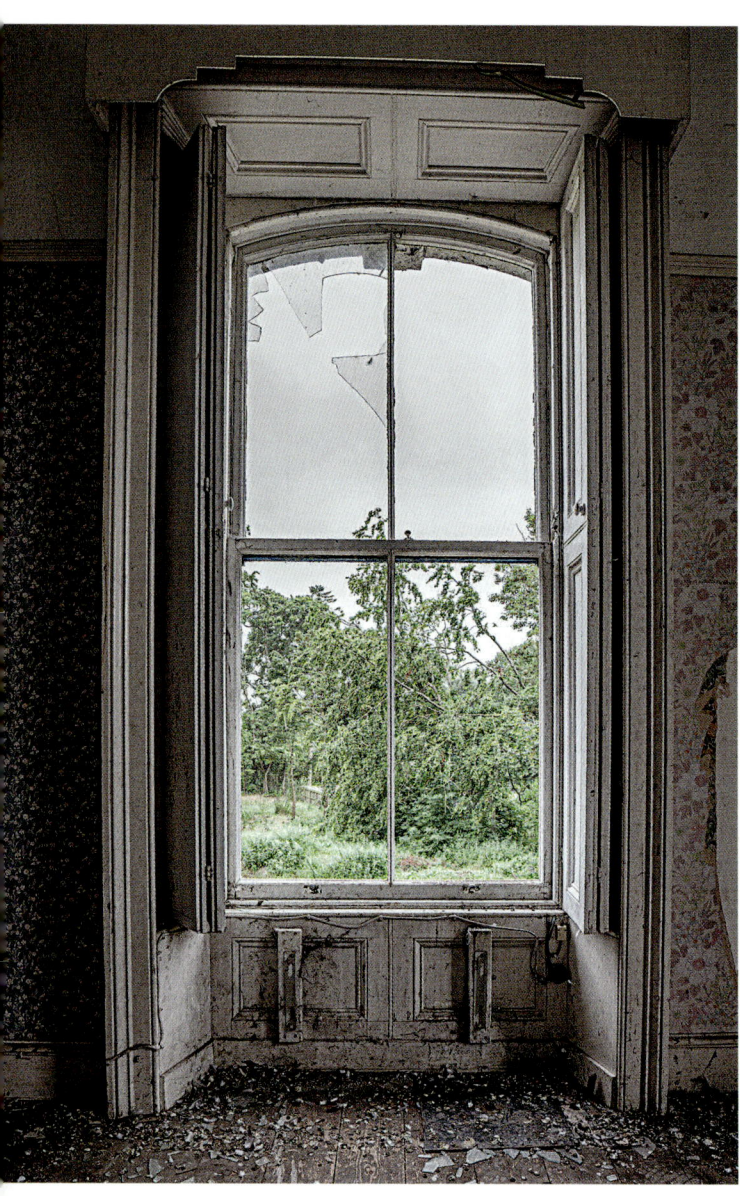

its peak, and the community flourished around its operations.

Trouble arrived when John's sons, Richard and John, both became prominent figures in the United Irish rebellion of 1798. This caused some tension in the area, and one June morning a local lord and major arrived at the house with orders to set fire to both it and the mill. The family was given just five minutes to gather their belongings before witnessing the destruction of their home. In shock, they sought refuge in a nearby hedgerow under a makeshift carpet shelter, until kind neighbours assisted them in relocating to one of the mill's bleaching houses.

Richard was brought to court, where he initially received a sentence of execution for his involvement in the rebellion. However, thanks to his father's connections, the sentence was commuted to deportation. This decision was not well received, leading to a review by the courts and, ultimately, the family's voluntary exile. Richard departed for America, followed by the rest of the family, and they reunited overseas.

Subsequently, the house found a new owner, who rebuilt the mansion in its present form and invested heavily in the mill, buying over 400 water-powered spindles, making it one of the largest spinning mills outside of Belfast. The mill eventually closed its doors in the 1960s, while the house has been unoccupied for the past two decades.

The building changed ownership not long after I photographed it and then suffered another huge fire, causing extensive damage. Its future is now extremely uncertain.

then built a bleach works beside the corn mill and, not long after, a small beetling mill was added. This processed the brown linen cloth being produced in local homes. In a short time John had created a mill complex employing over 400 individuals at

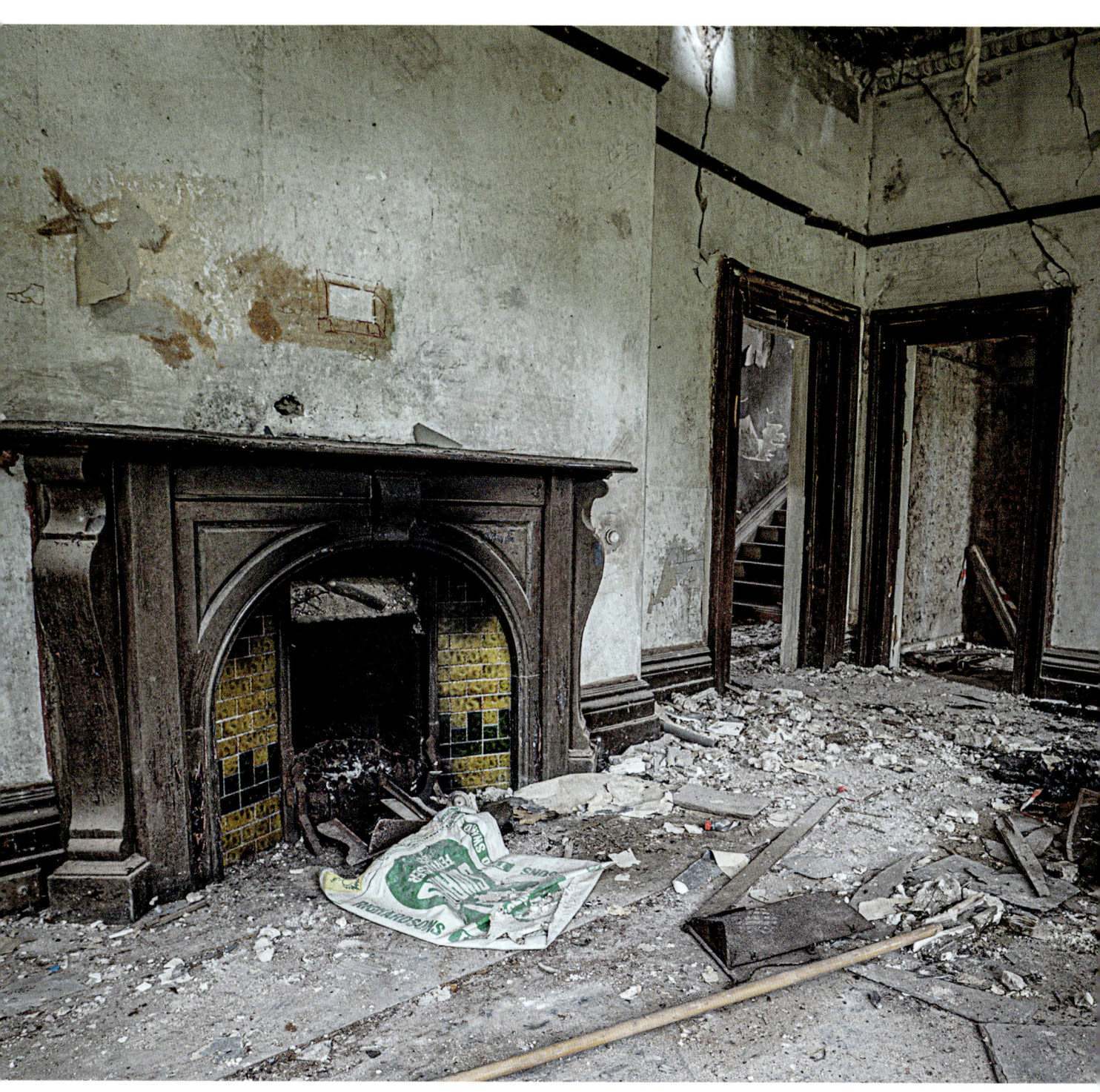

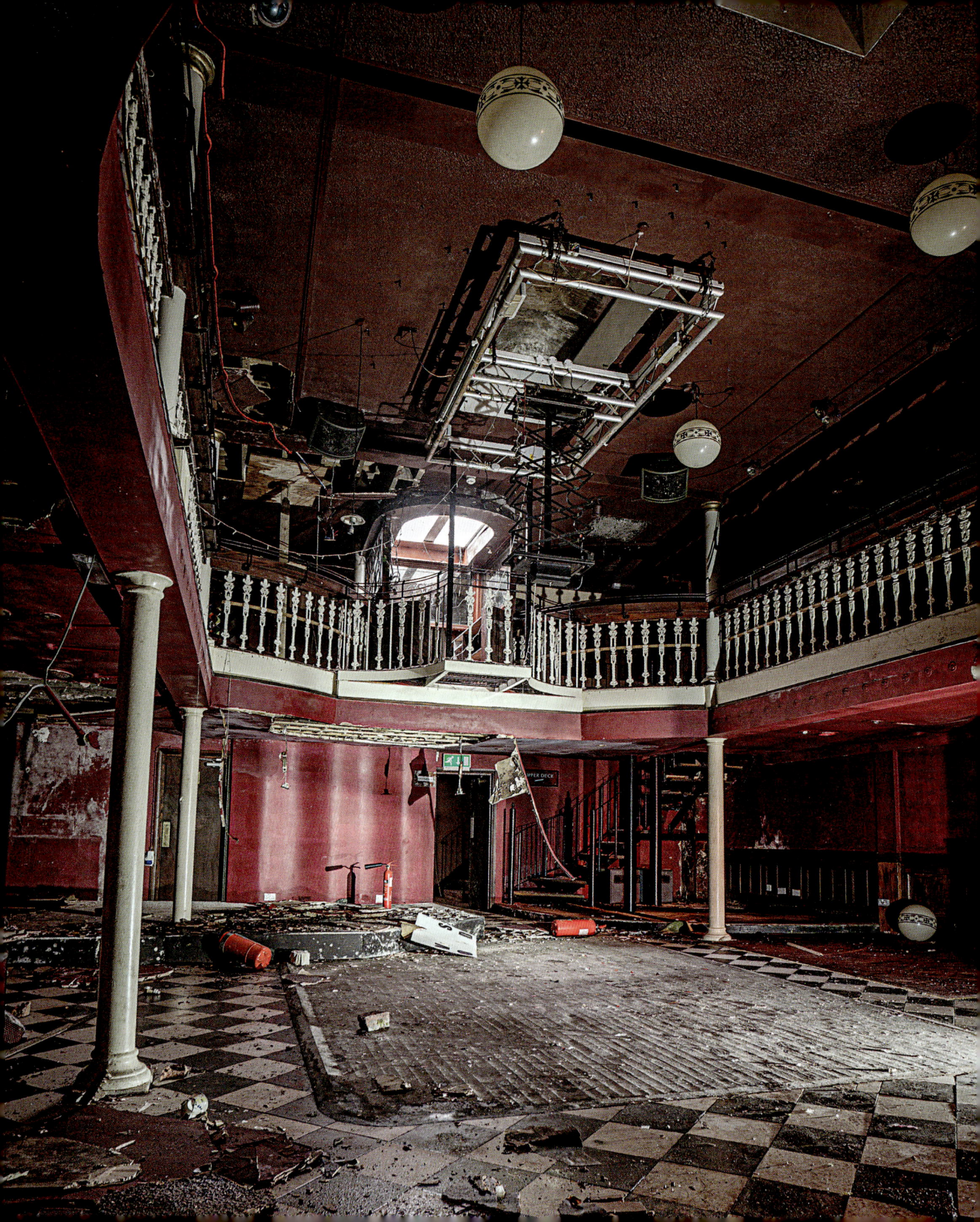

# THE ROYAL HOTEL

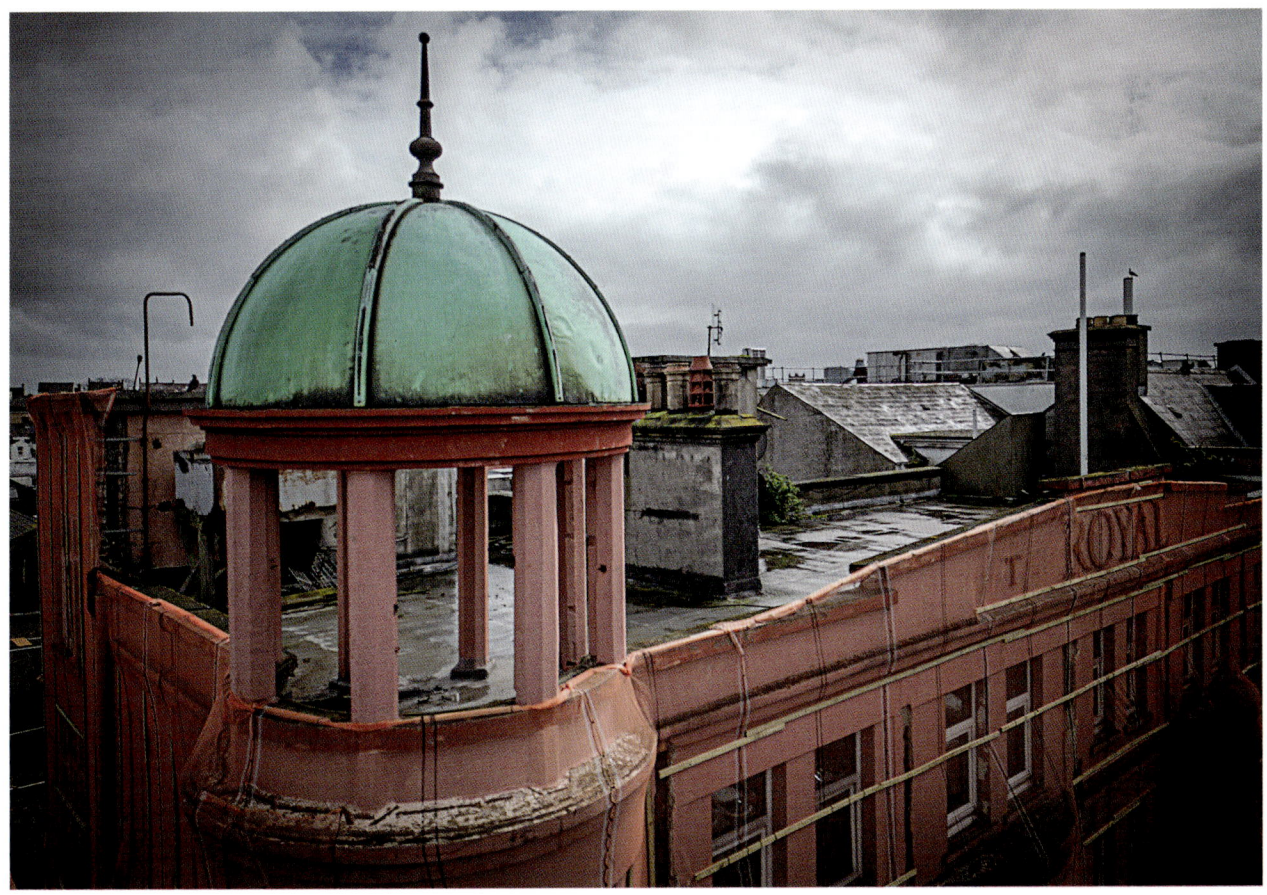

Located on the seafront of Bangor, County Down, a charming seaside town that has long been a popular destination for a day out by the sea, this iconic hotel has always been a familiar landmark. I remember it from childhood visits and I have also attended a few weddings there, so you can imagine my delight when the owner, Colin, invited me to document the hotel. By that point, it had been closed for nearly

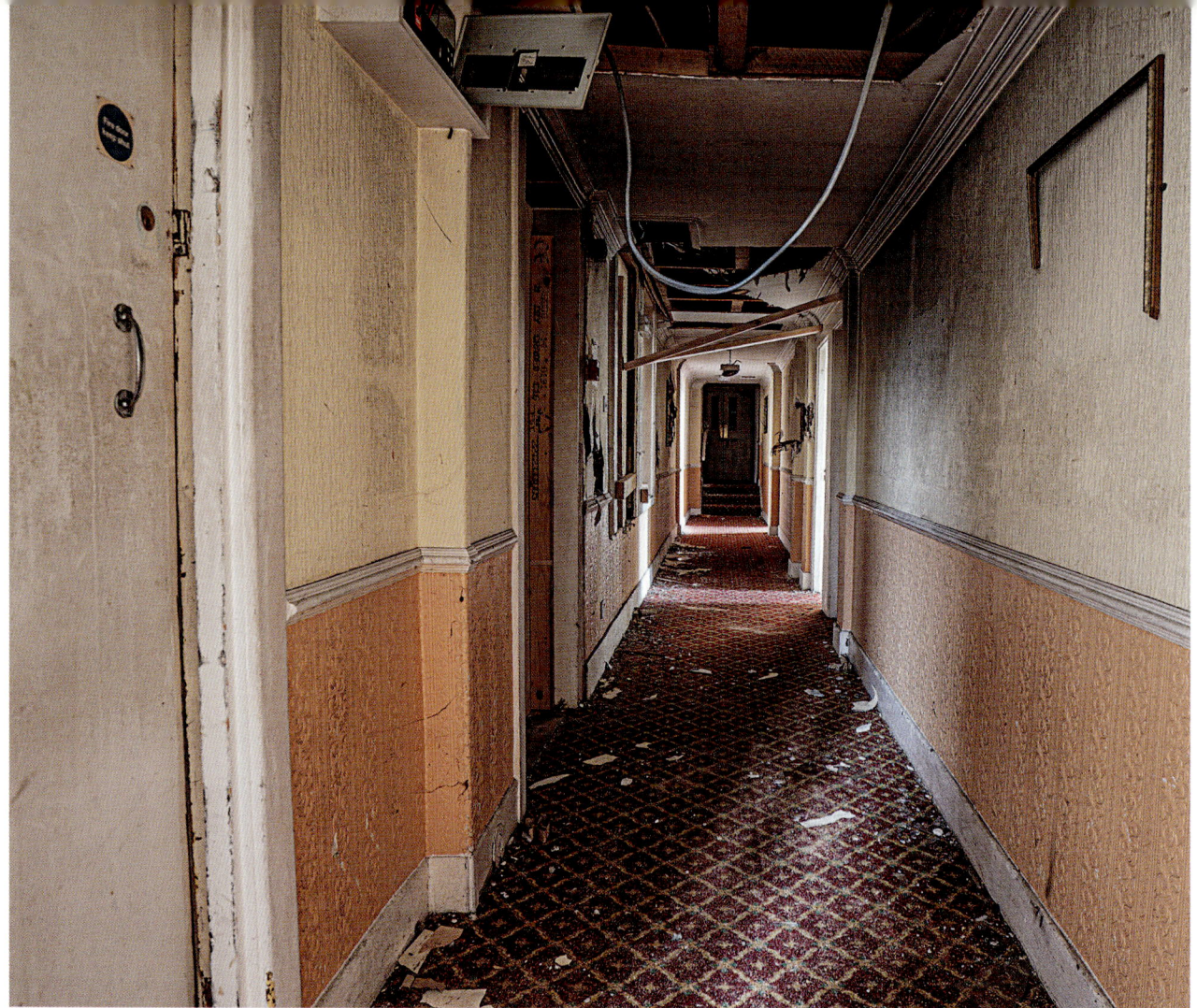

a decade and I had always wanted to feature it in my photography collection.

The hotel was originally constructed in 1773, but it was rebuilt and remodelled by the O'Hara family in 1932 to create the structure we see today, with its distinctive corner turret. The hotel remained in their ownership until the early 1990s.

While researching the hotel's history, I came across an article in *The New York Times* from 1 April 1972, which described the scene in the Royal Hotel at night, where you could see lights shimmering across the quay and hear the sounds of cocktail glasses clinking and laughter mingling with Tom Jones' powerful voice singing 'Maria'. The journalist interviewed Bill O'Hara, the owner at the time, who extolled the virtues of life in Bangor and how it was a wonderful place to raise children.

During the Second World War, Belfast Lough was bustling with warships, and the top floors of the hotel were initially utilised by the Royal Navy, which set up a signal station on the rooftop, and then by the US Navy. In preparation for the D-Day landings in Normandy in 1944, General Eisenhower visited Bangor to inspect 30,000 American soldiers

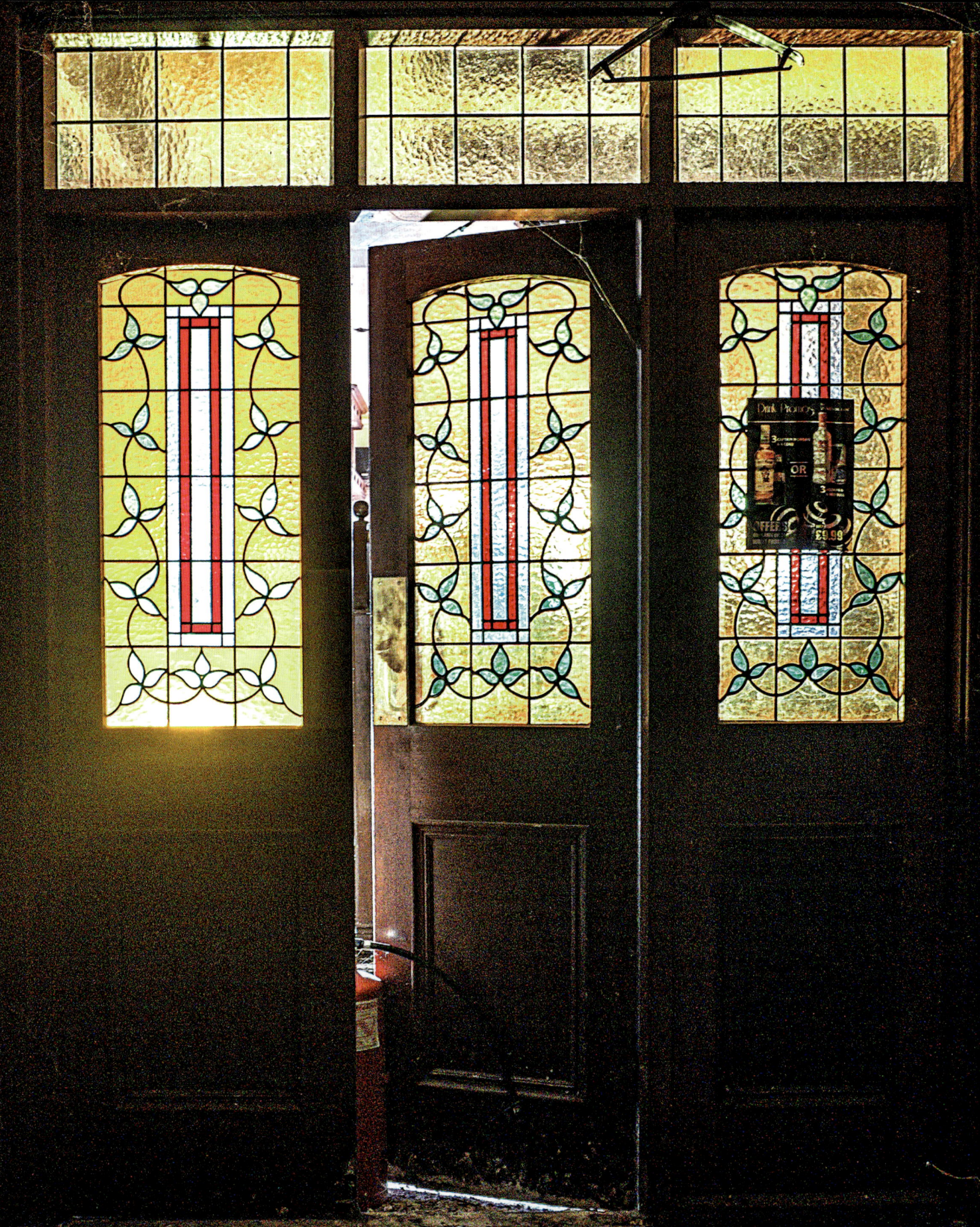

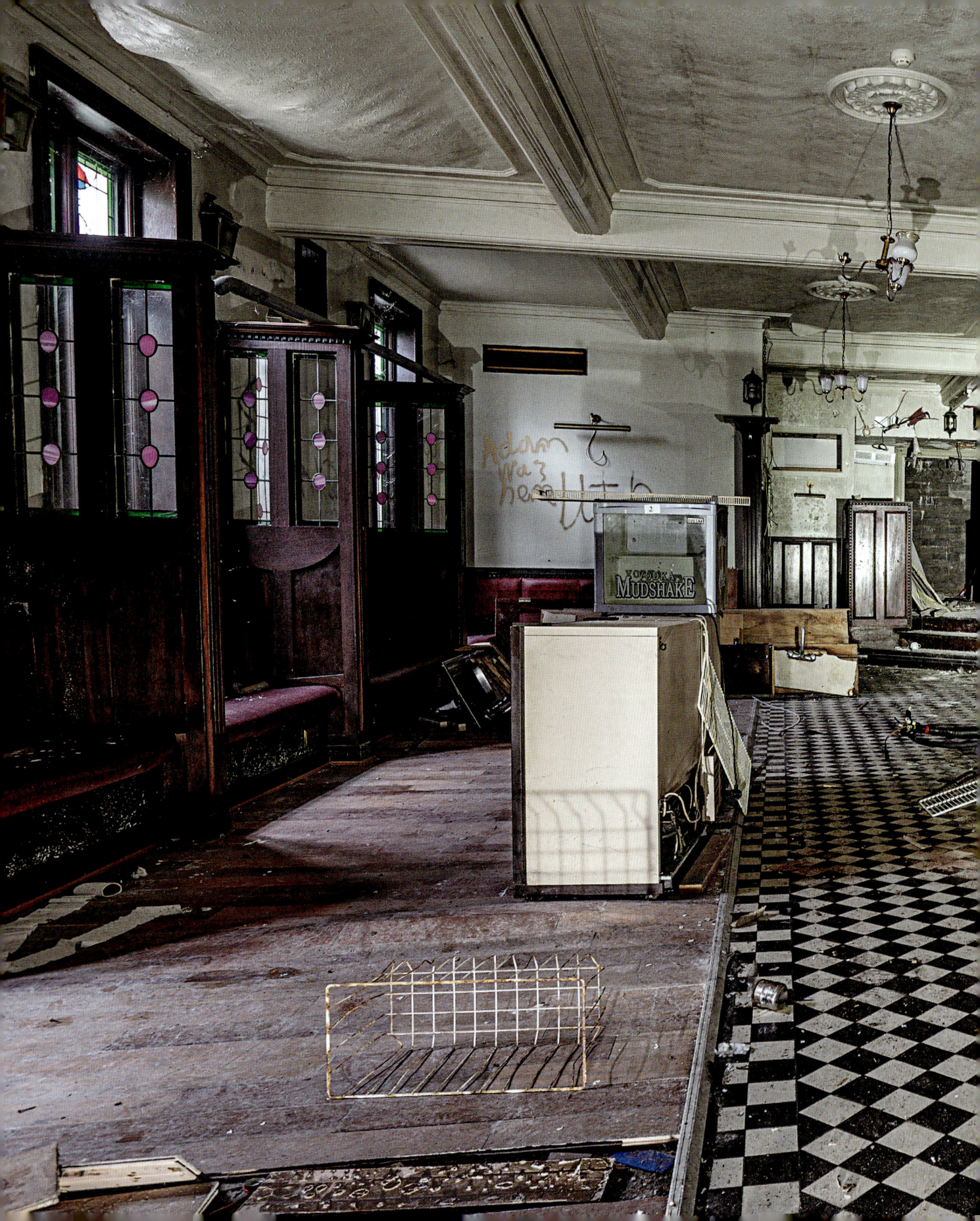

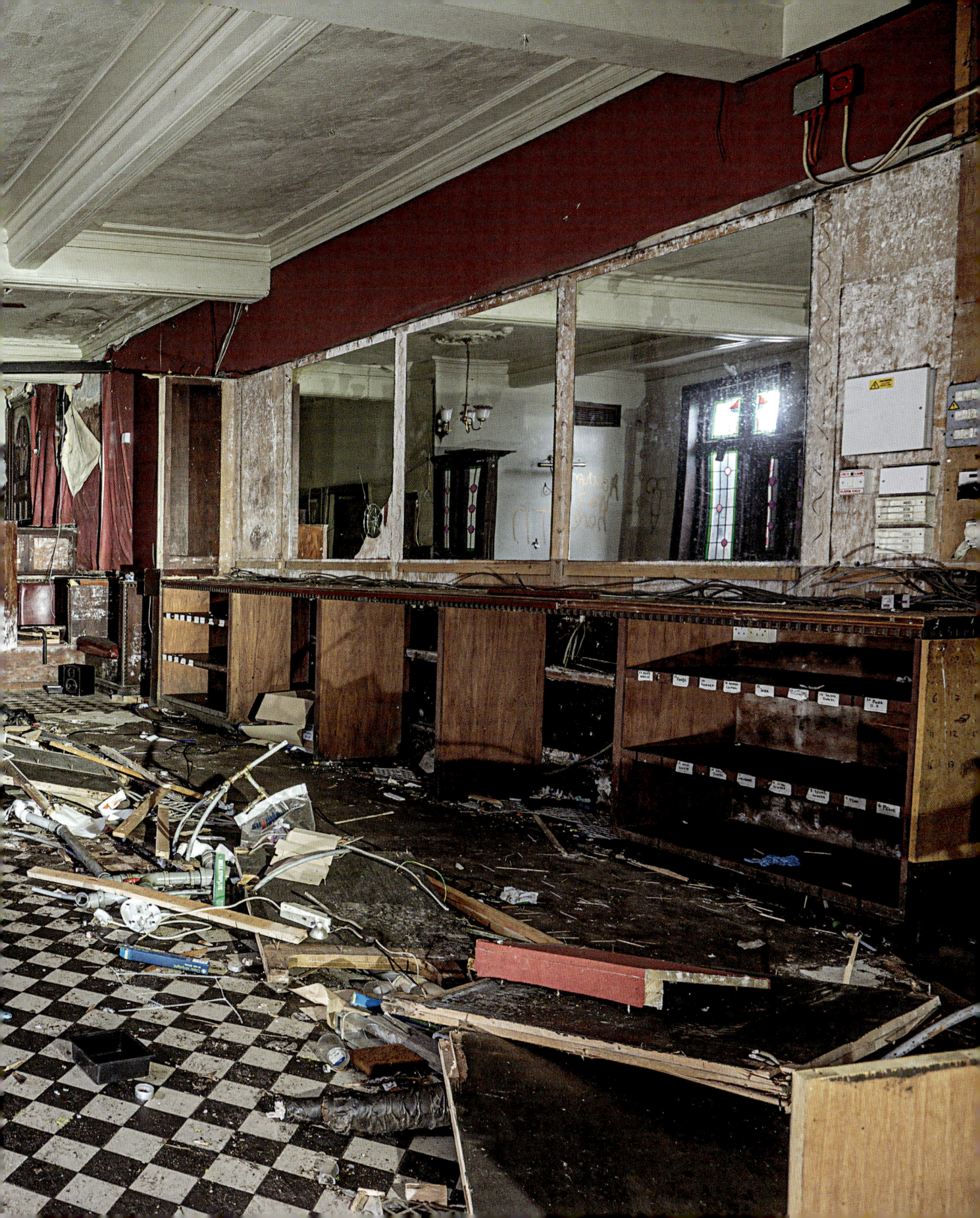

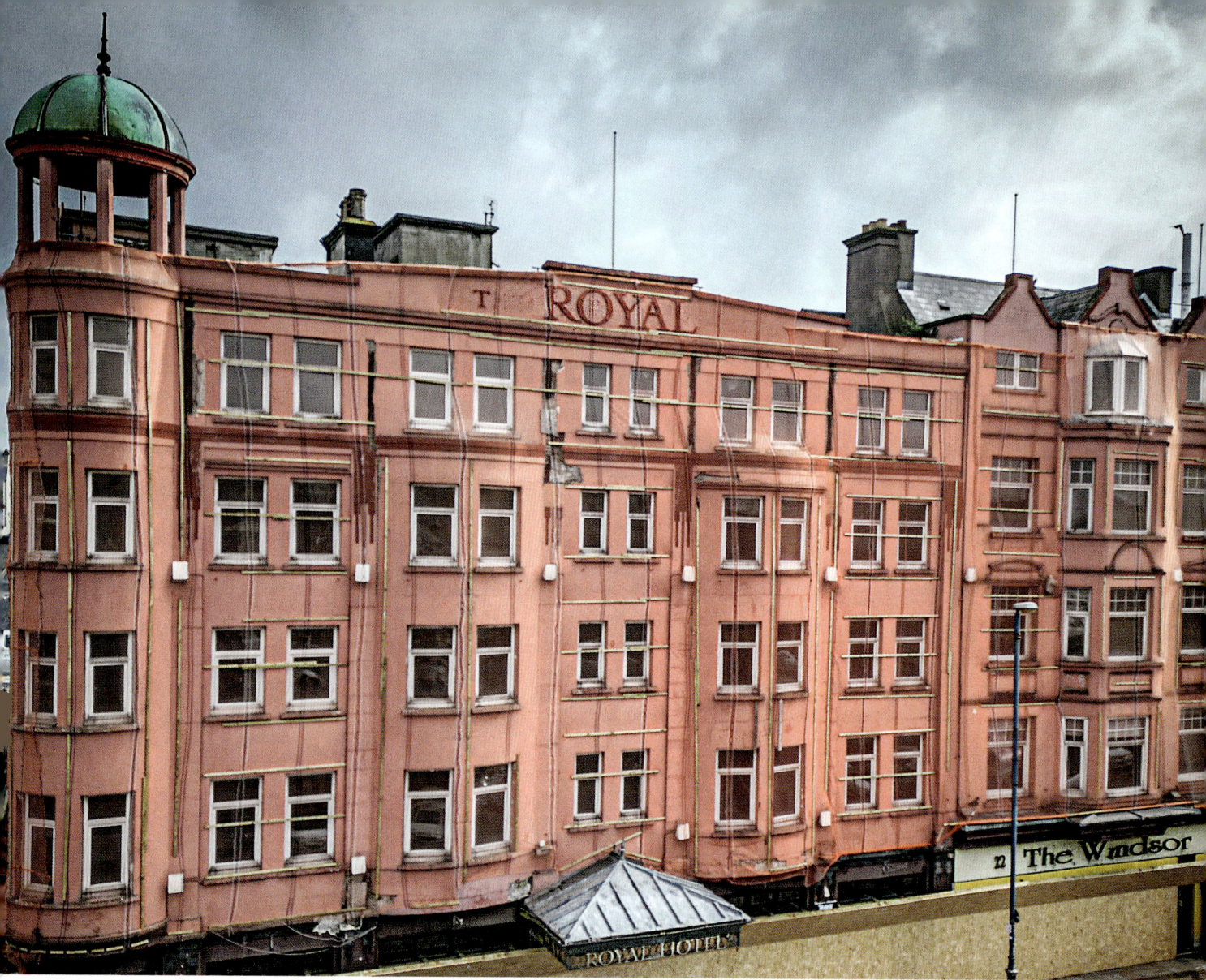

and sailors who were stationed on three massive US Navy battleships (the *Nevada*, *Texas* and *Arkansas*) in Belfast Lough. During his inspection, he also stopped by Naval HQ at the Royal Hotel. There is now a pier named after Eisenhower in Bangor that is a popular fishing spot.

Throughout the years, the establishment has welcomed numerous other famous guests, with Van Morrison making frequent appearances there.

Another notable visitor was Giant Haystacks, a prominent figure in the 1980s wrestling community. Standing at an impressive 6 feet 11 inches and weighing 31 stone, he was quite the sight to behold. Staff members shared stories of his visit to the hotel, recalling the challenge of accommodating his size and having to adjust the famous revolving door to allow him entry. They even had to create a custom bed for his stay.

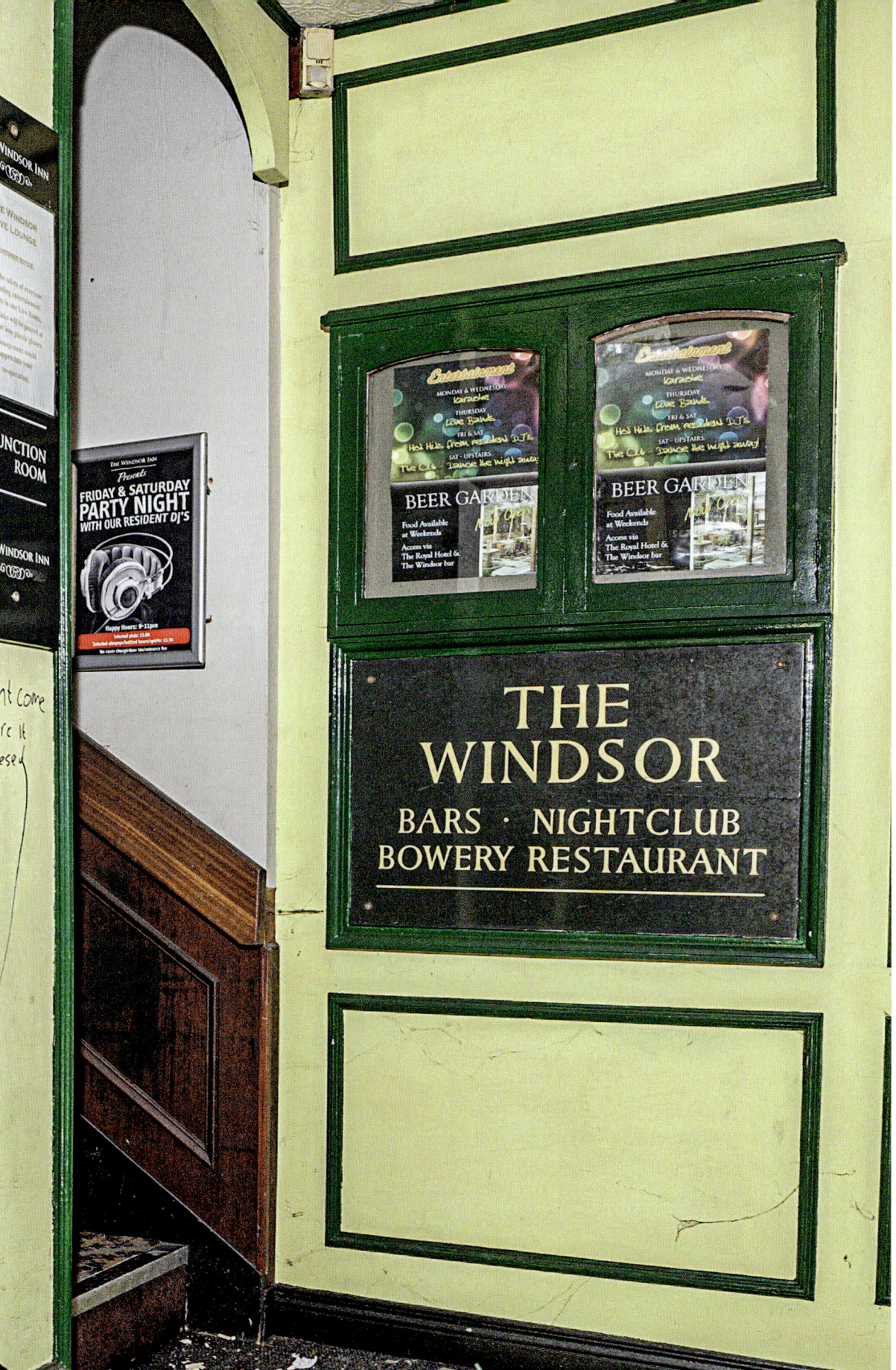

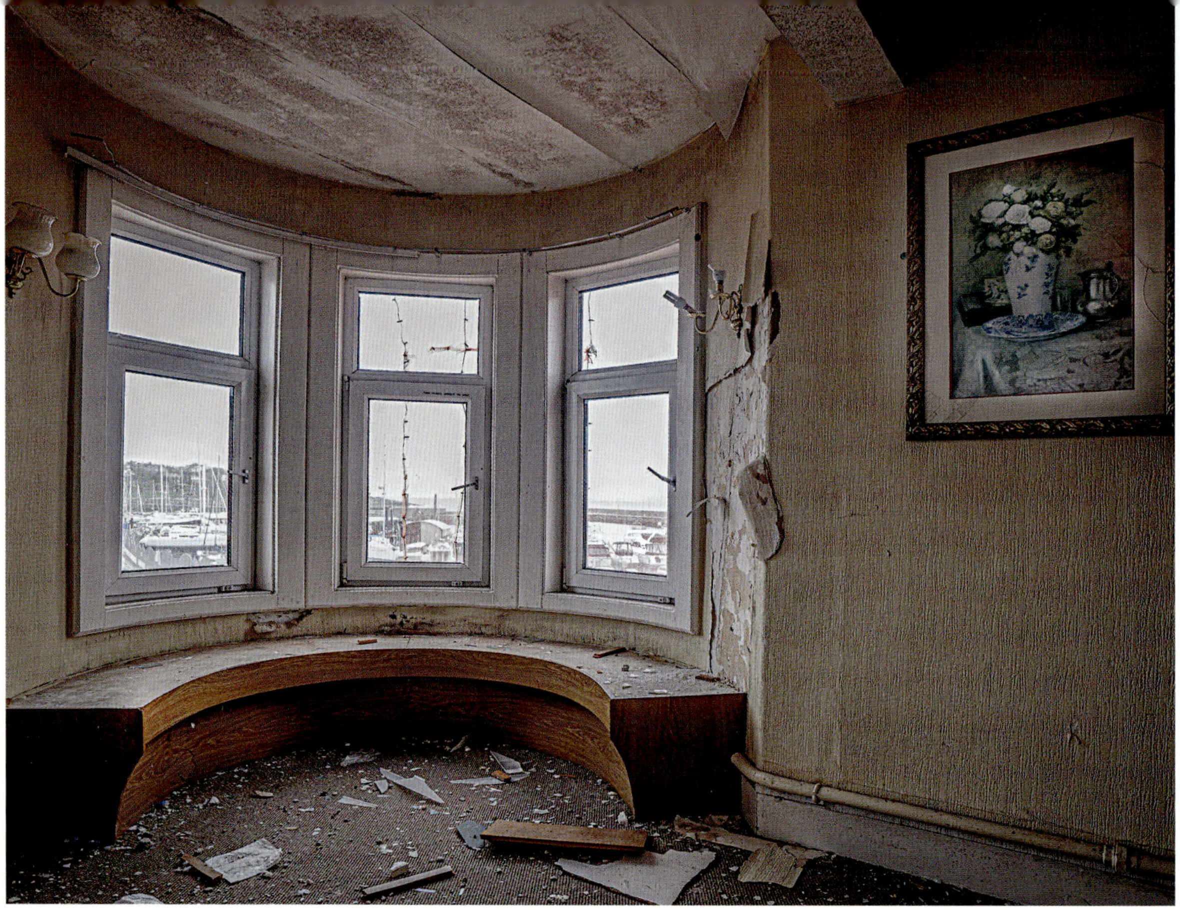

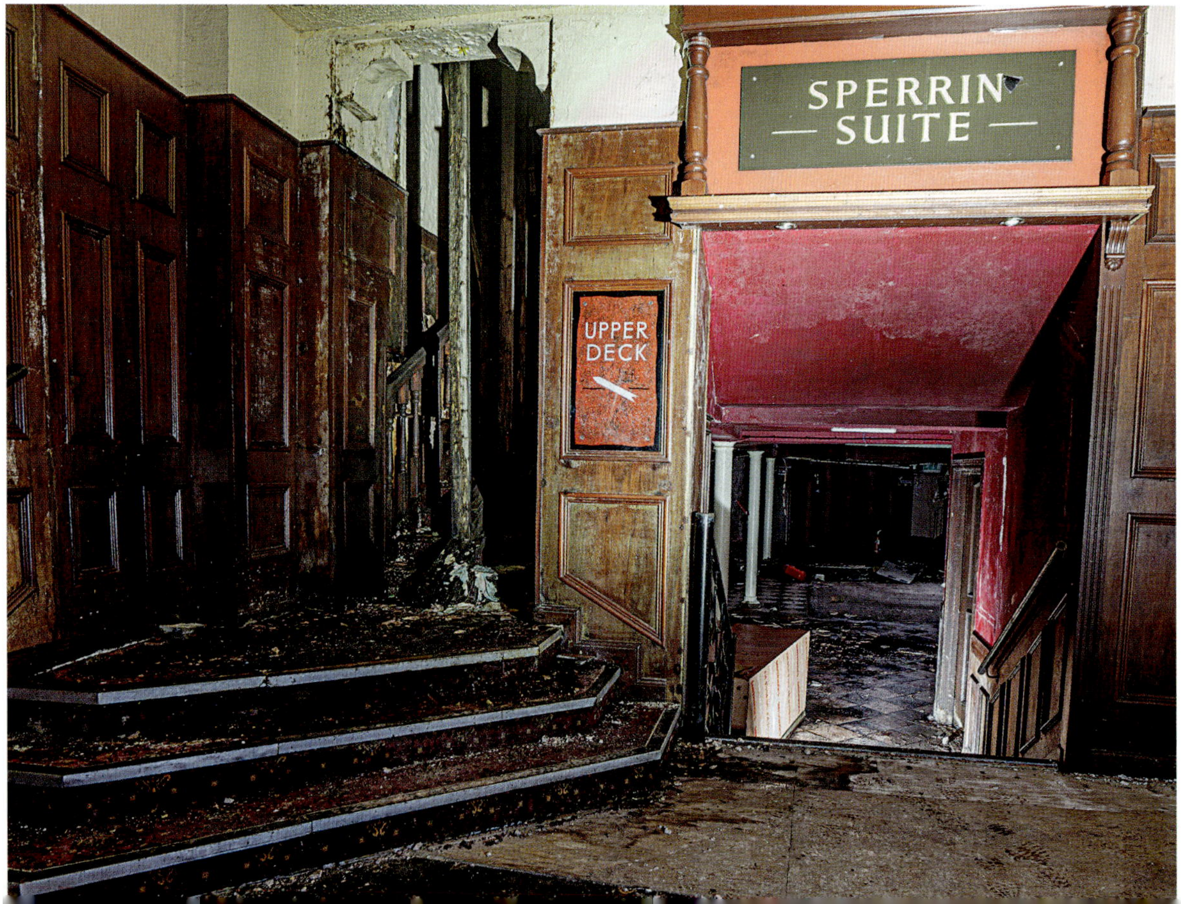
SPERRIN
SUITE
UPPER
DECK

Adjoining the hotel, and part of the complex, was the Windsor bar and nightclub, which was a major success and drew crowds from all over Northern Ireland. The nightclub hosted performances from popular artists such as Otis and the Elevators, Nicki French (best known for her hit cover of 'Total Eclipse of the Heart') and New Atlantic (known for their hit 'Sunshine after the Rain'). These names evoke a real feeling of nostalgia in me for times gone by.

In the early 1990s the Donegan family bought the fifty-room hotel from the O'Haras. Unfortunately, however, due to declining numbers visiting Bangor, the Royal and the Windsor closed their doors for the last time in October 2014, after operating for over 200 years. Not many businesses can boast such a lengthy tenure!

Sadly, the hotel is currently in poor condition structurally, with corroded steel columns causing decay. As a result, the new owner has proposed demolishing the hotel and rebuilding it while maintaining its historic facade. The revitalised building will serve as apartments, with restaurants and shops on the ground floor. While I always hate to see a building torn down, in this instance I believe it is necessary. The new design will honour the legacy of the hotel while modernising its functionality.

I can't wait to visit once it is reopened.

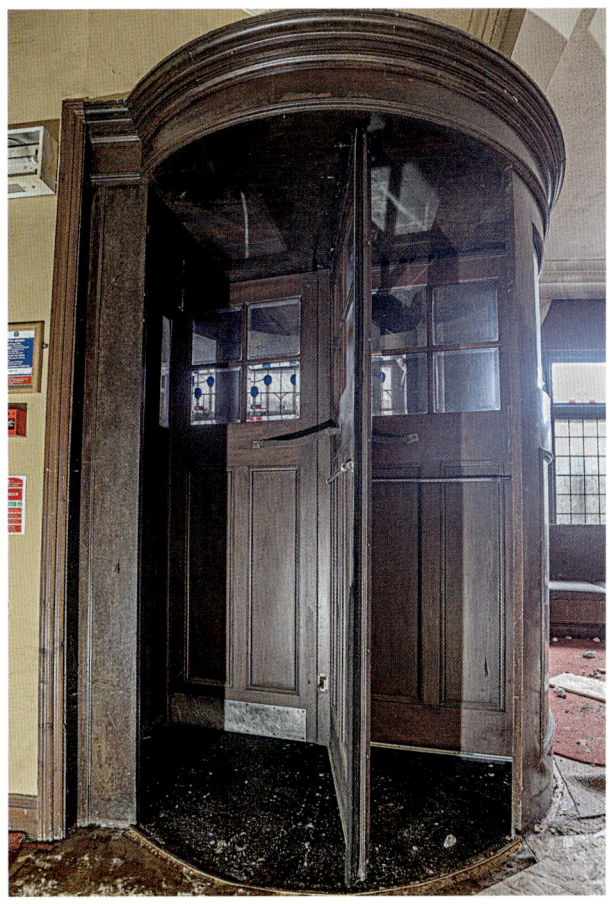

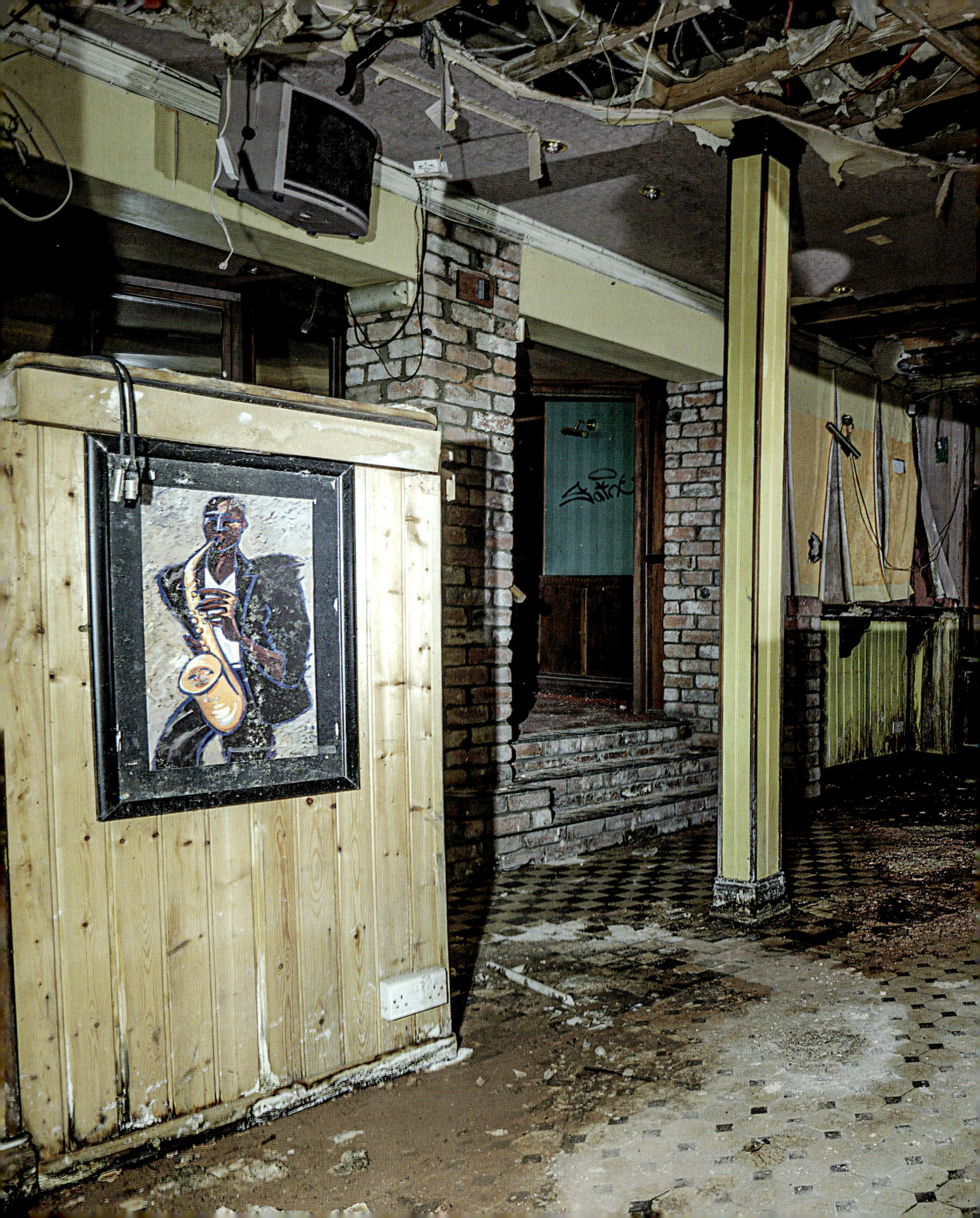

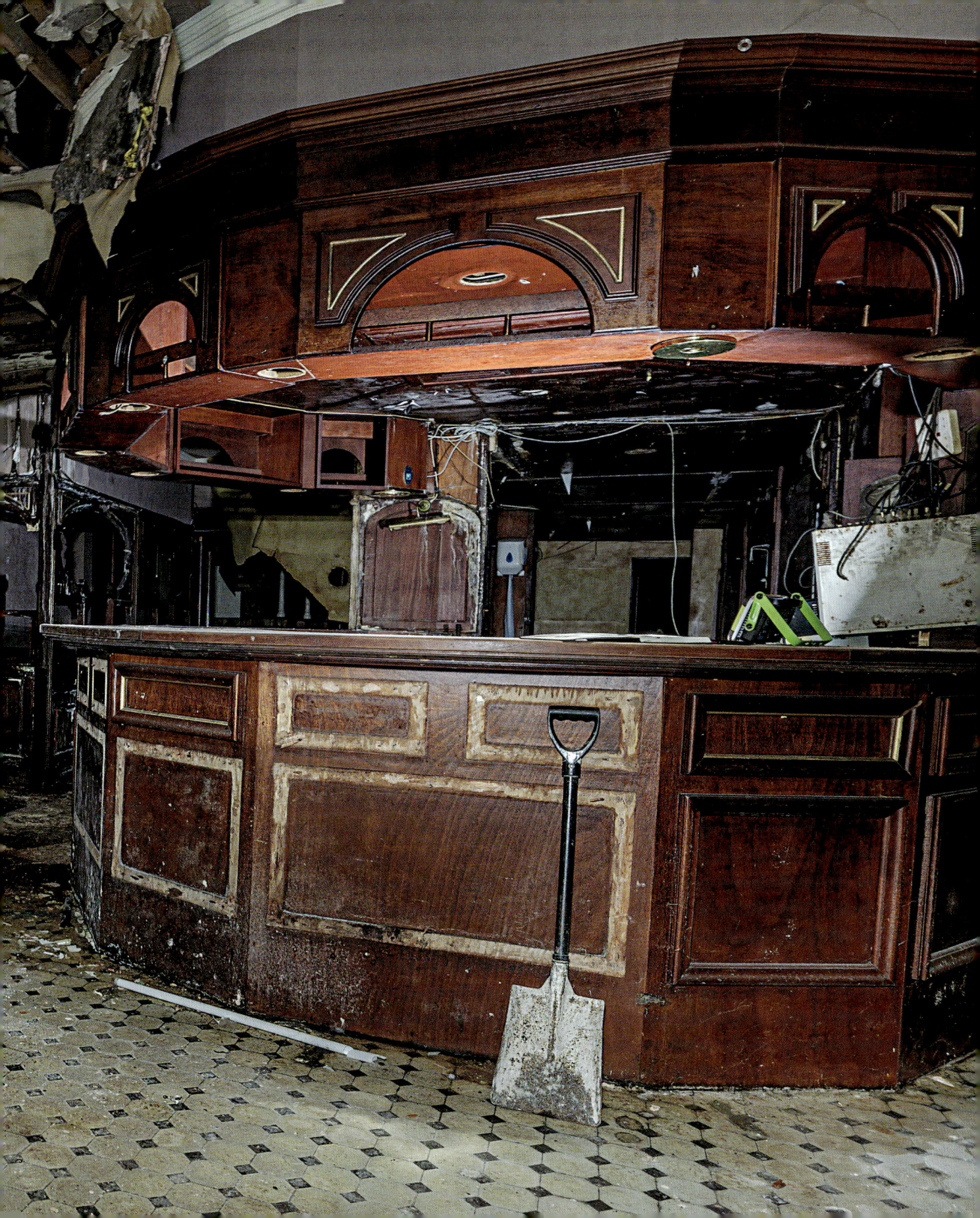

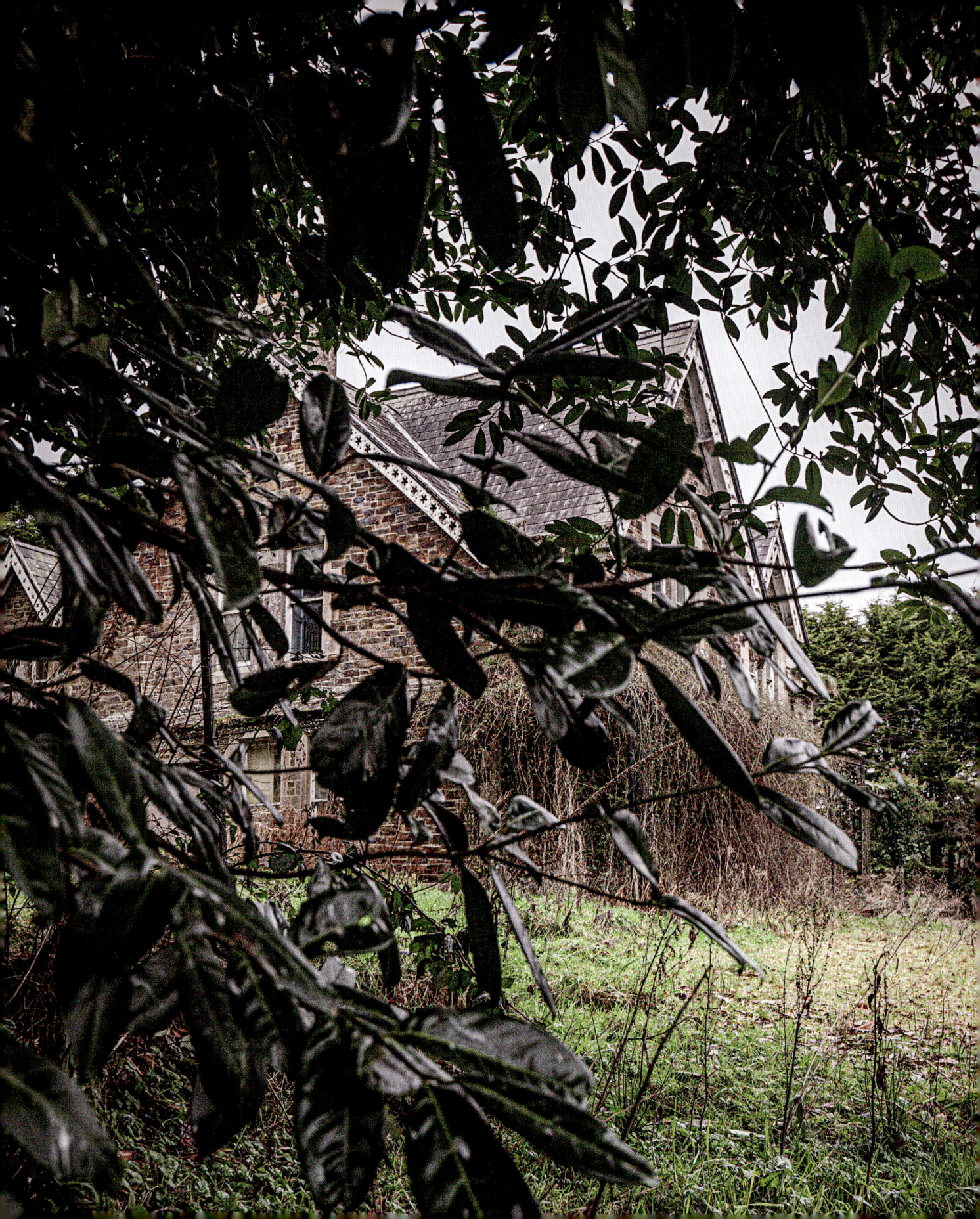

# TRAGEDY MANSION

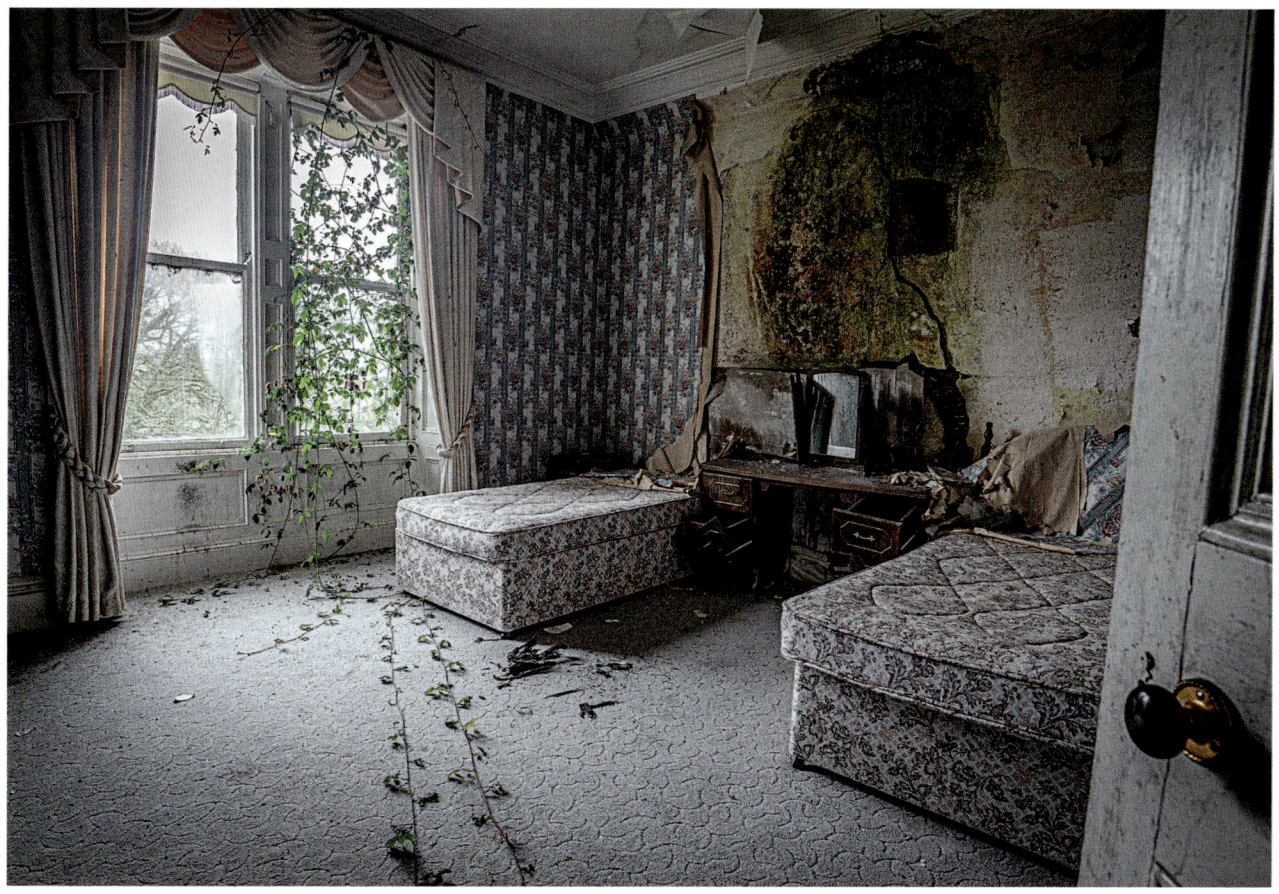

I had heard about this house and the terrible trage- dies it had suffered at various times over the years. The more I heard, the more I doubted whether I should pay a visit, as I realised its history would make it a very affecting place. However, in the end, I decided that it deserved to be chronicled.

Upon arriving at the property, I noticed a huge tree in the front garden with a rope tied on a branch.

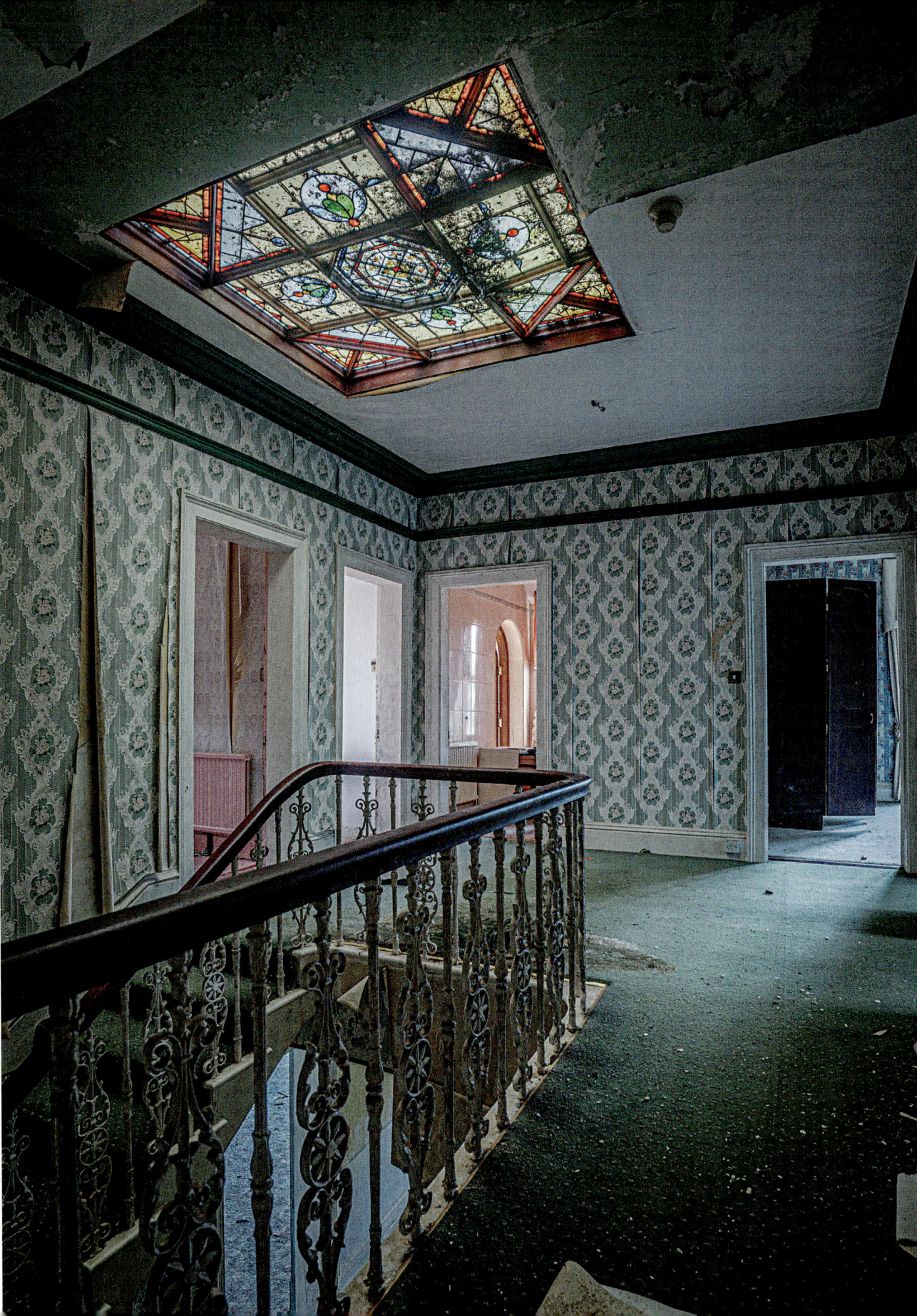

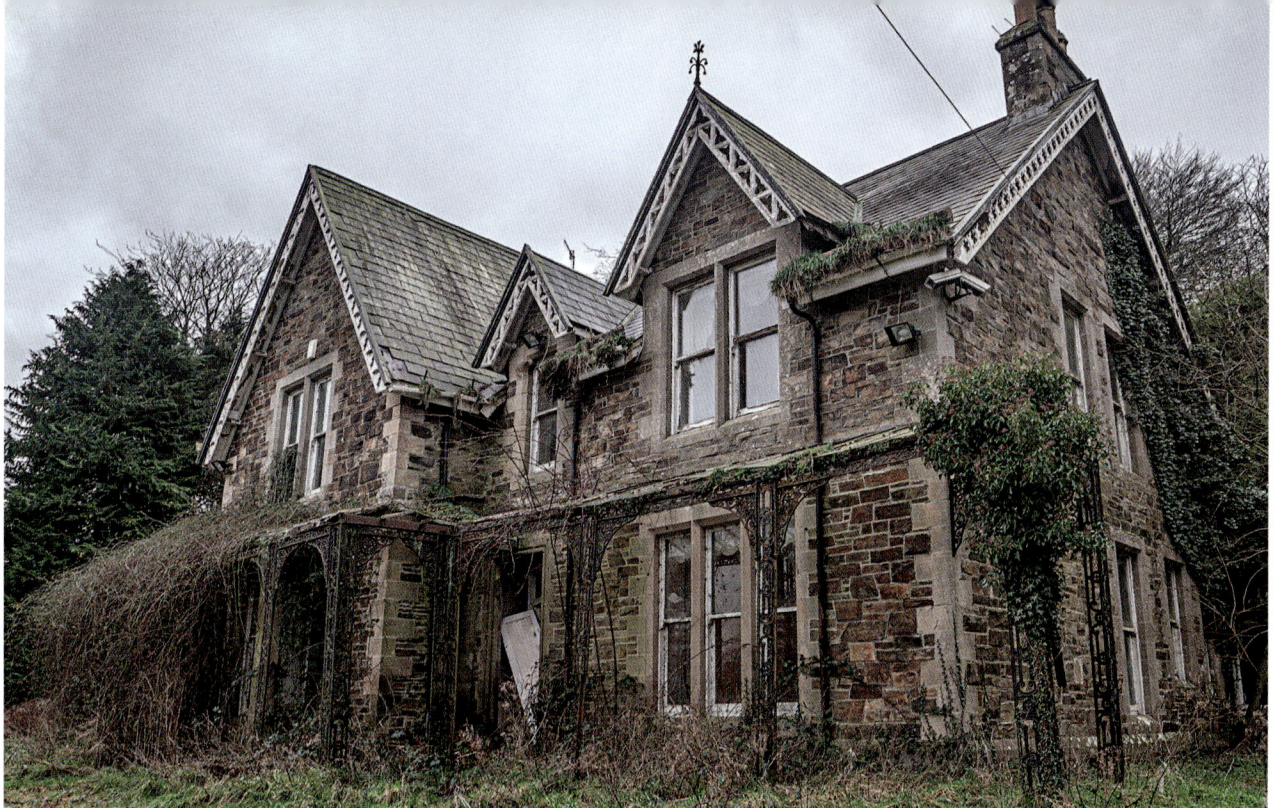

It was probably just my subconscious playing tricks on me, but I was instantly reminded of a scene from *The Conjuring*. I tried to ignore this connection as I made my way through the overgrown garden.

When I reached the front door of the house I was greeted by the most beautiful iron wrap-around veranda I had ever seen. Despite its stunning appearance, the veranda was in really bad shape, with sheets of glass hanging from the roof like ready-to-fall icicles.

Once inside the house, the sinking floors immediately caught my attention, prompting me to tread carefully. The interior still contains a multitude of furniture and personal items left behind, including wedding photos, paperwork and records. Even the dishwasher in the kitchen was filled to the brim, as if someone had left abruptly.

According to a local resident, no one has wanted to live in the house for over ten years due to the series of tragic events that have plagued the property. These started with the mysterious suicide of an army captain in the sitting room in 1952. His obituary stated that he was discovered on a Sunday evening with a bullet wound behind his right ear and his revolver lying next to his chair. Then there was the death of a small child, who reportedly drowned on a nearby water wheel. Another tragic accident resulted in someone losing an eye and there was another death, this time by electrocution. On hearing all this, I start to wonder if the house was built on cursed land or near some unmarked graves.

I quickly documented the house and did not linger any longer than necessary. I believe this house to have the saddest history of any that I have visited to date.

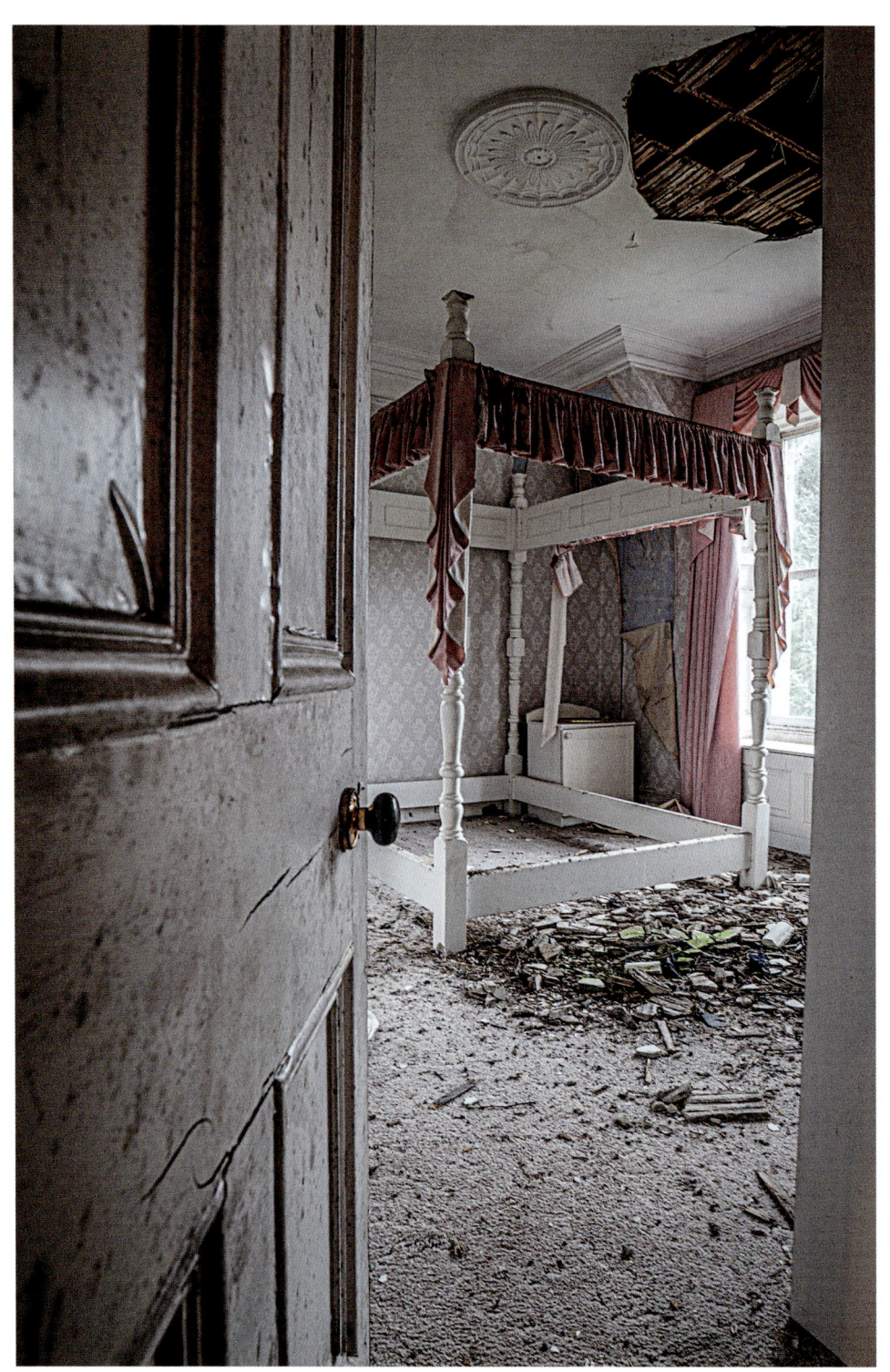

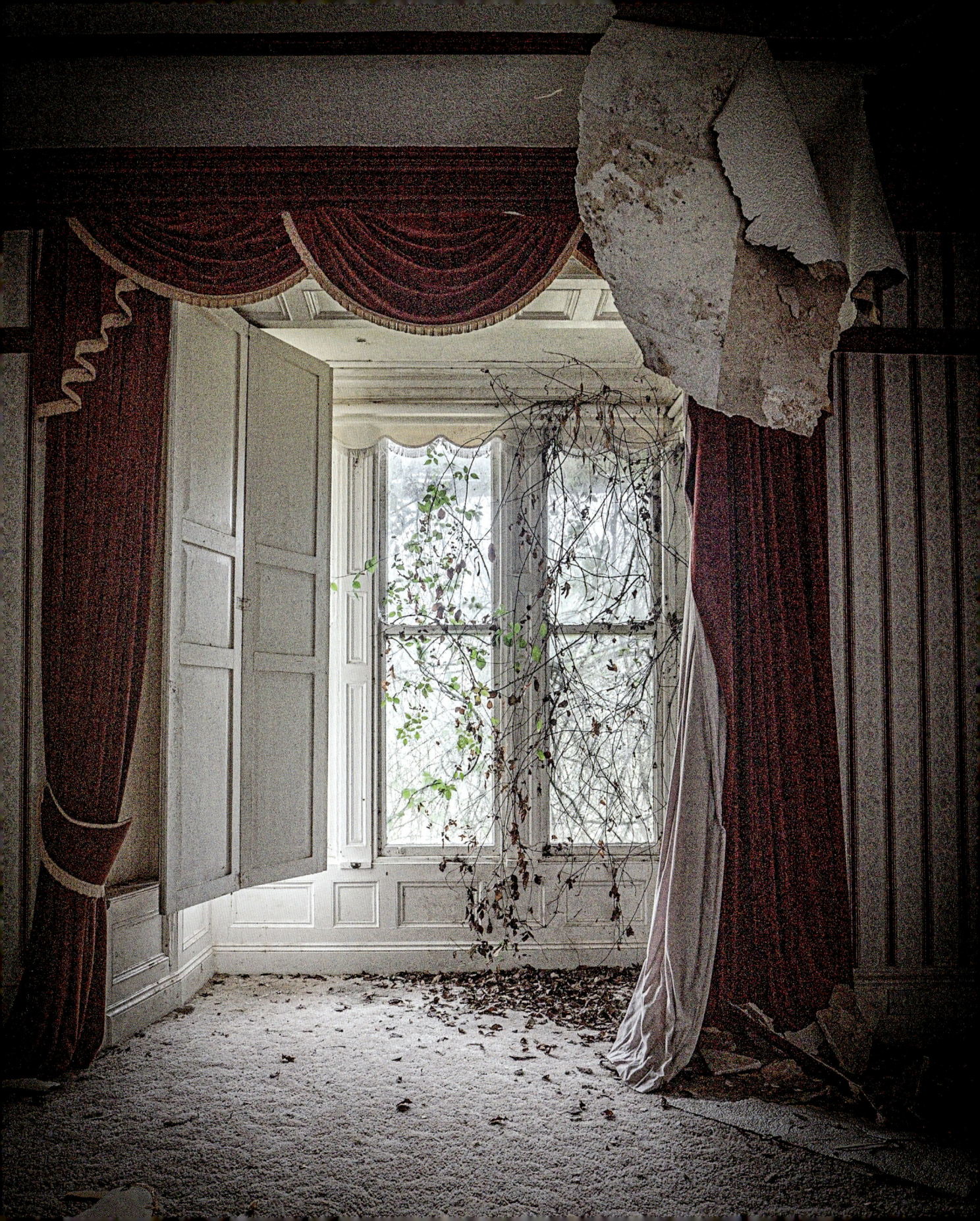

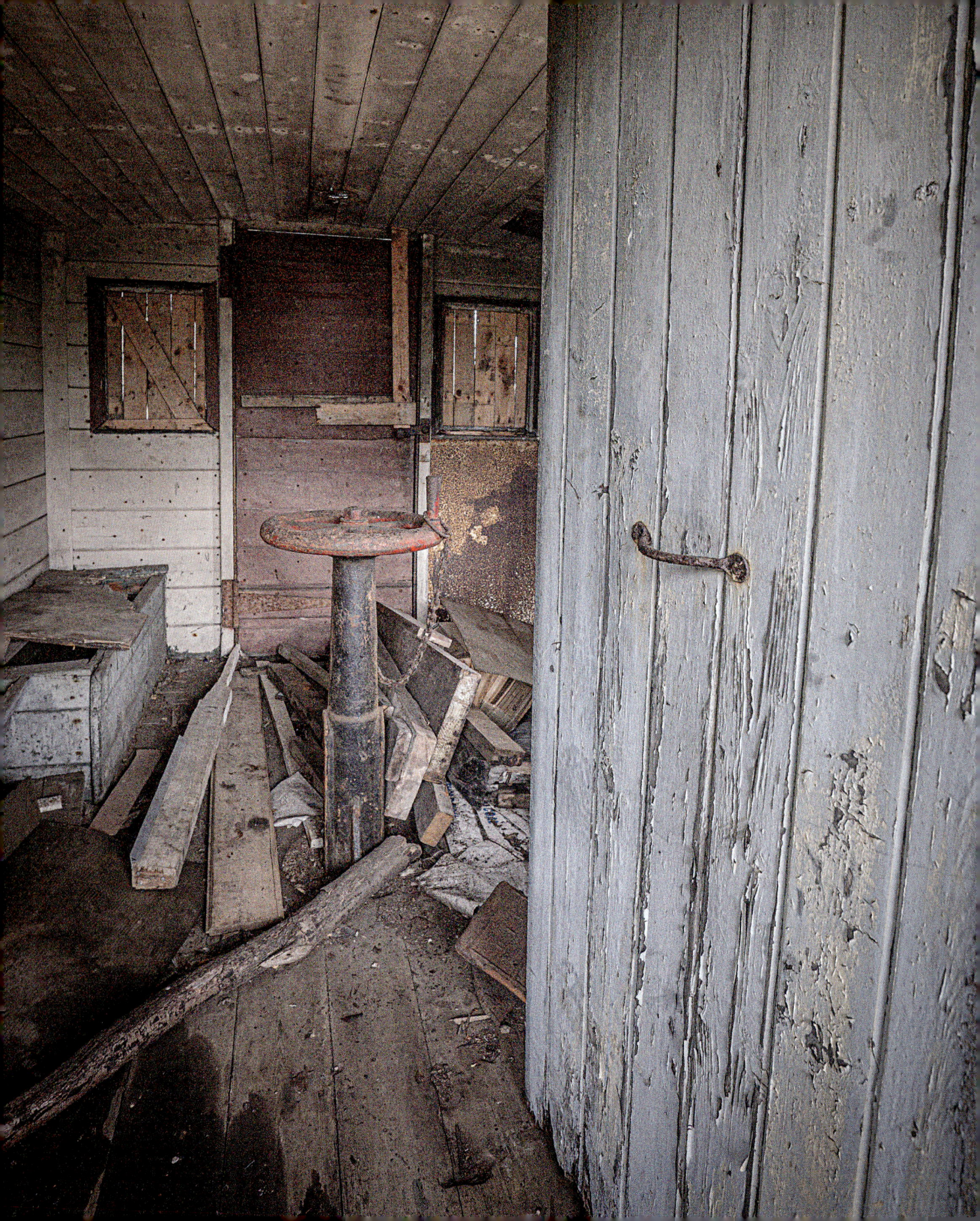

# THE LINE ENDS HERE

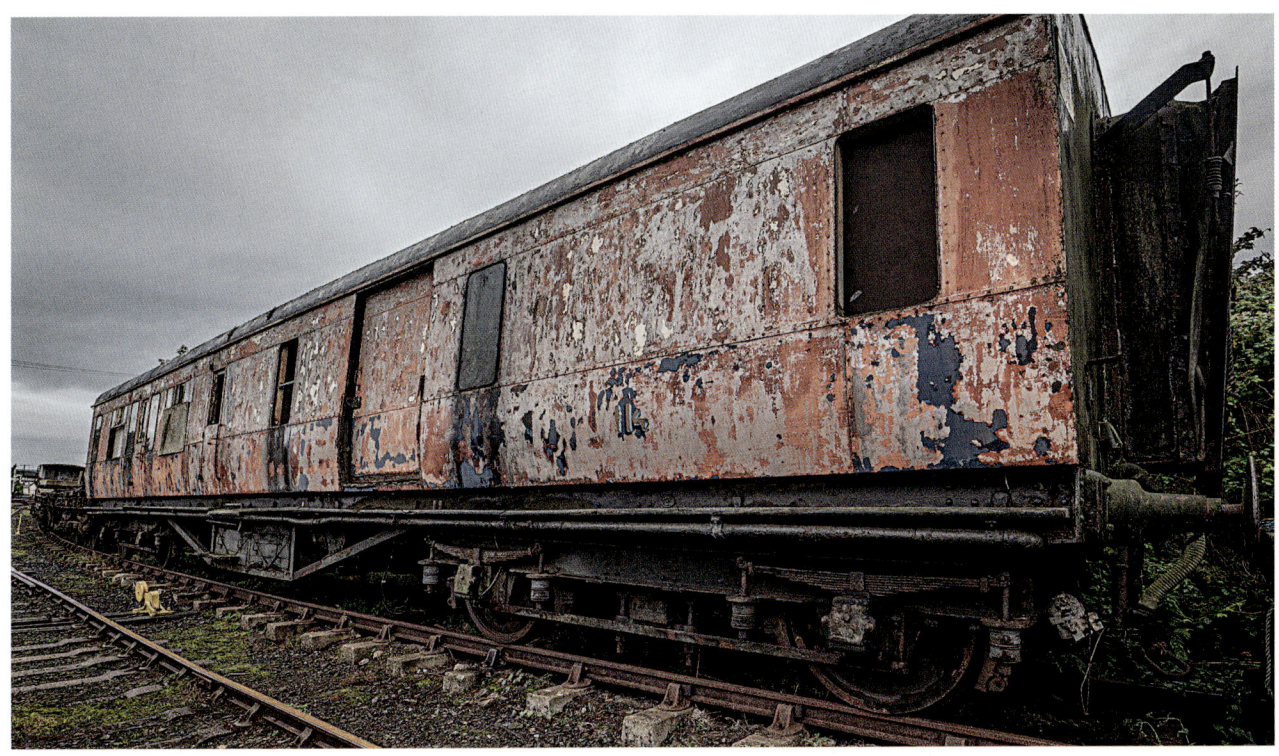

It was a pleasure to be invited to the Whitehead Railway Museum, where the team said they had a few carriages that needed renovation that may be of interest to me. They were right. From the moment I stepped onto the museum platform, I knew these were going to be great subjects. They had all those elements of peeling paint, rust and muted colours that make great pictures, not to mention the old signage on the walls, which really took me back to a time forgotten.

In Whitehead, there are two stations: one still in use by Northern Ireland Railways, which serves the Belfast to Larne line, and one originally used as an excursion station which opened in 1907. It

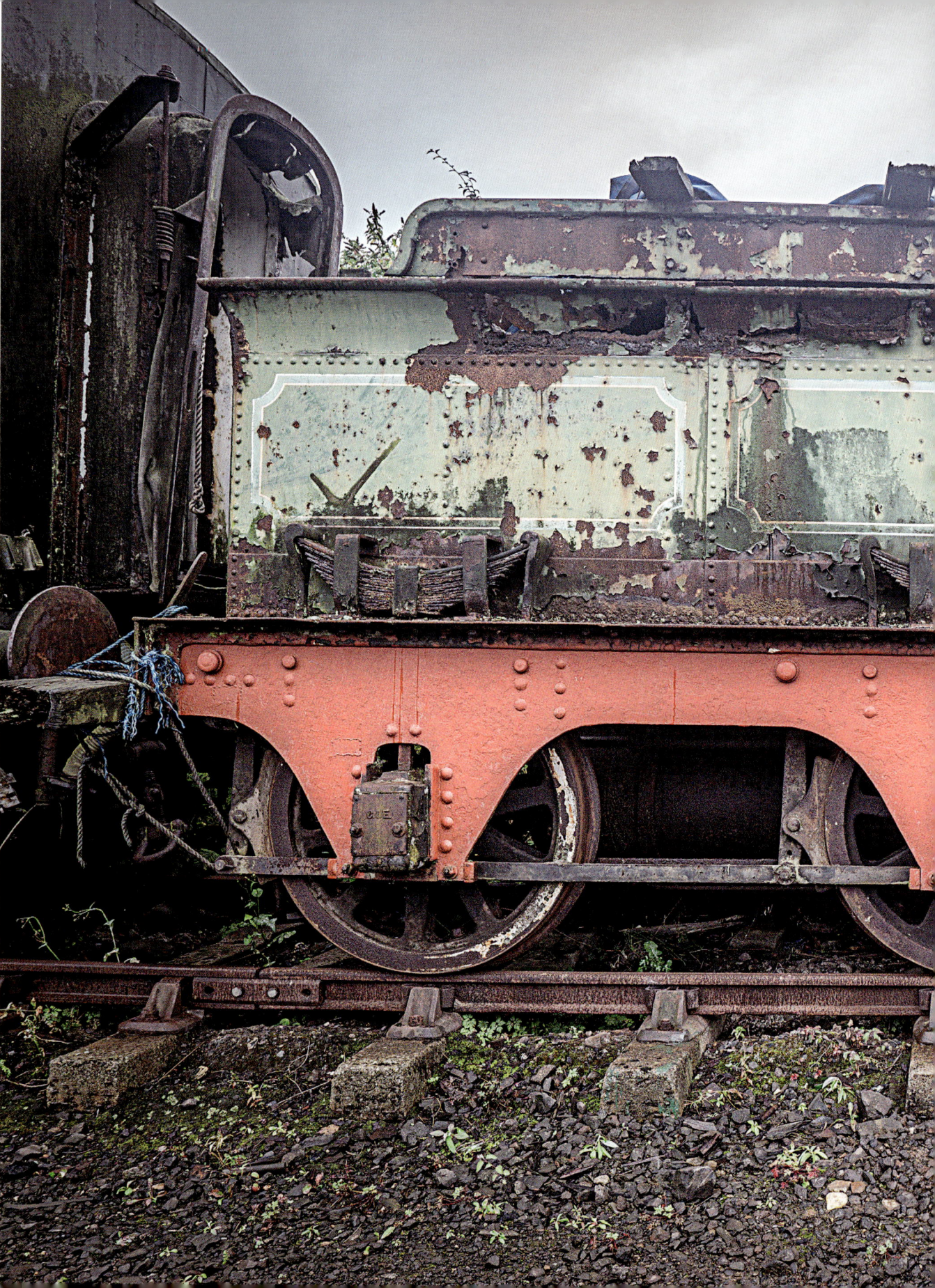

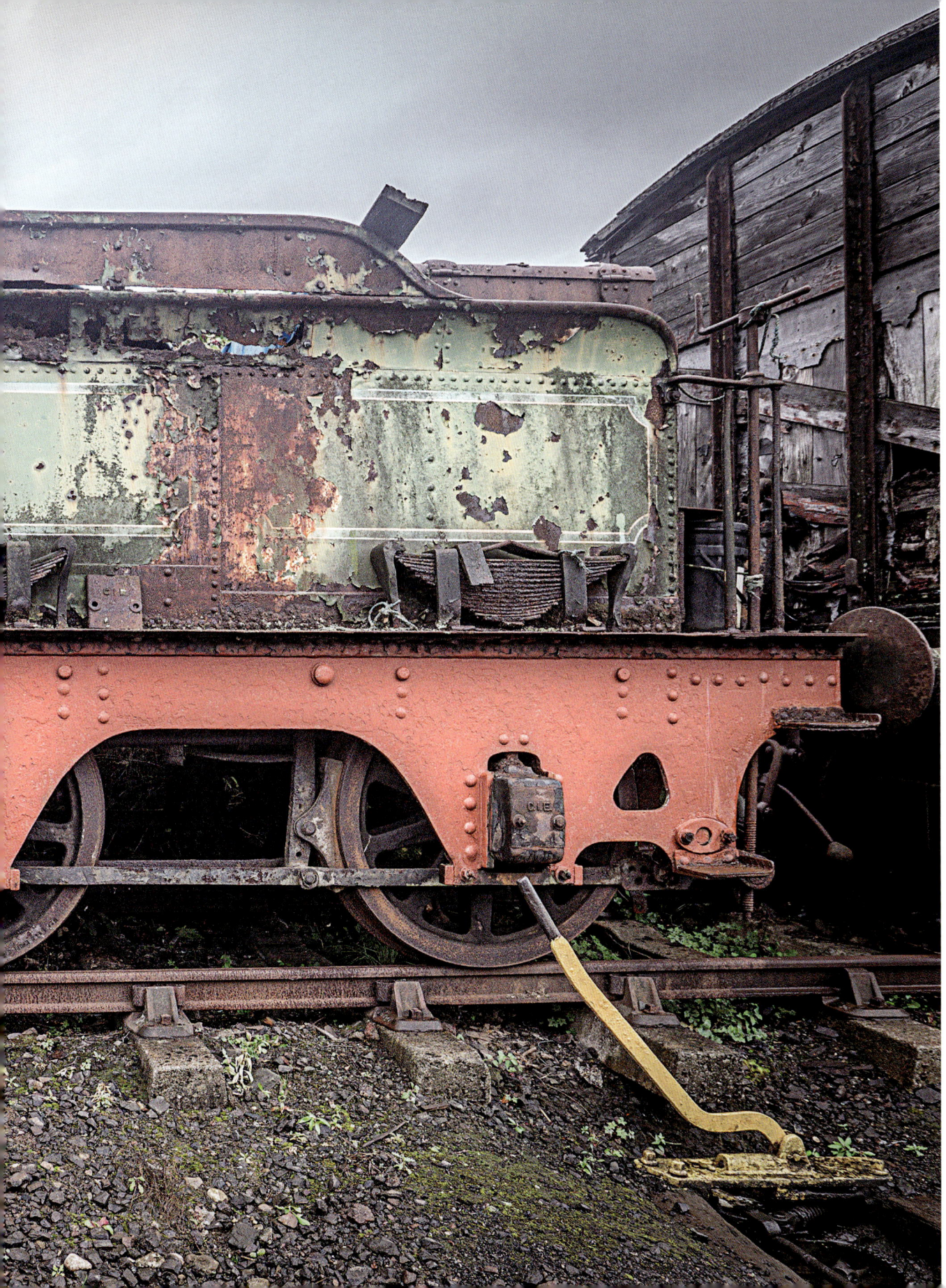

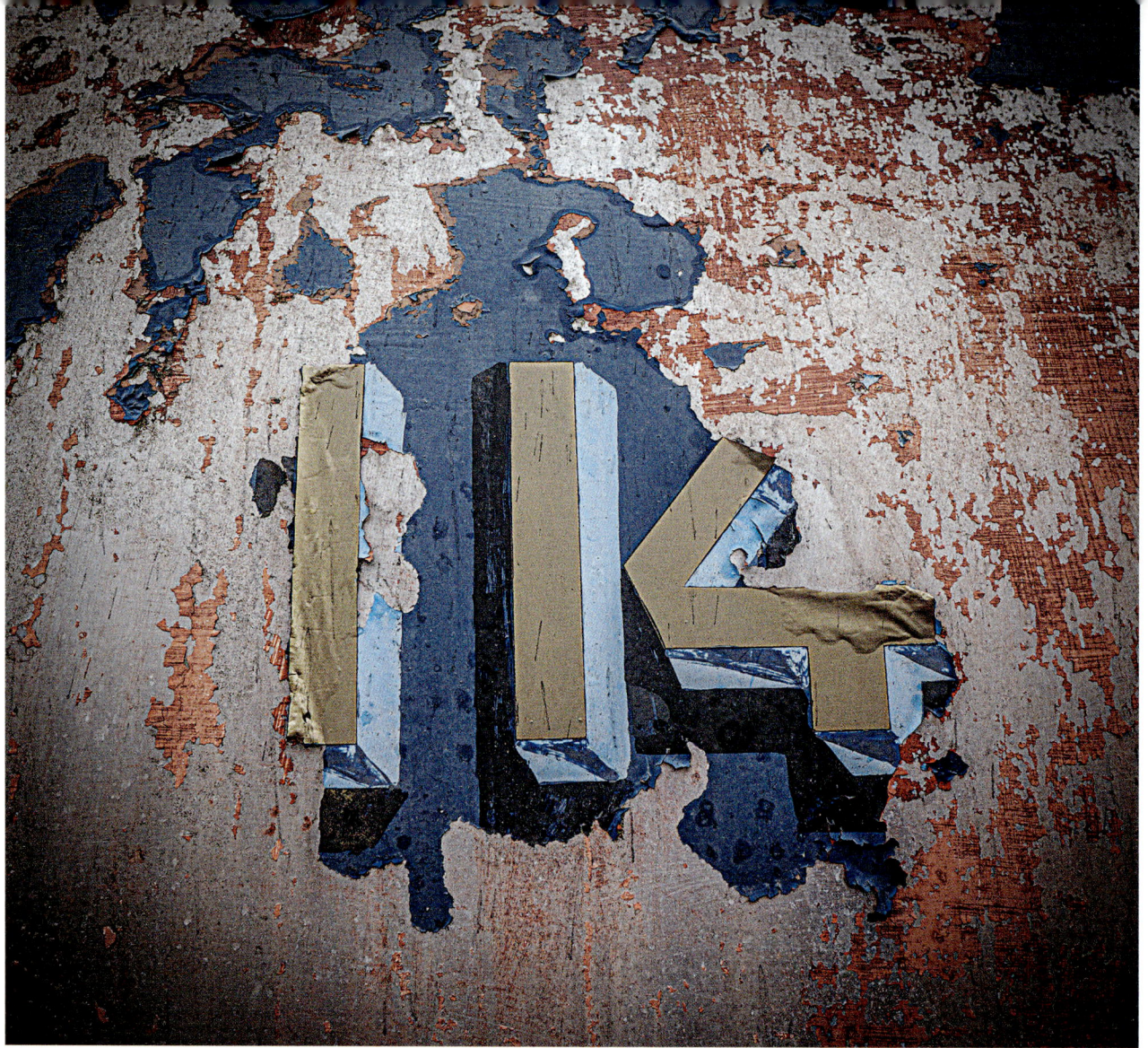

was designed to serve day trippers who came for the man-made beach and sea air. Currently, it is home to the Railway Preservation Society of Ireland and has been for over fifty years. Here they restore and maintain engines and rolling stock.

Several of the restored trains and carriages have appeared in films and TV shows, such as *The First Great Train Robbery*, *Michael Collins*, *Angela's Ashes* and *Remington Steele* to name but a few. However, my interest was in those not yet restored. Mail and goods would have been transported on some of these carriages. The passengers would have been at the front of the carriage, with the goods to the back, along with bunks to allow the workers some rest on long journeys.

These carriages are on the road to restoration. There is a plan to turn one into a space that will be used for events and talks, with a small bar at the back, a job that is expected to take up to two years to complete.

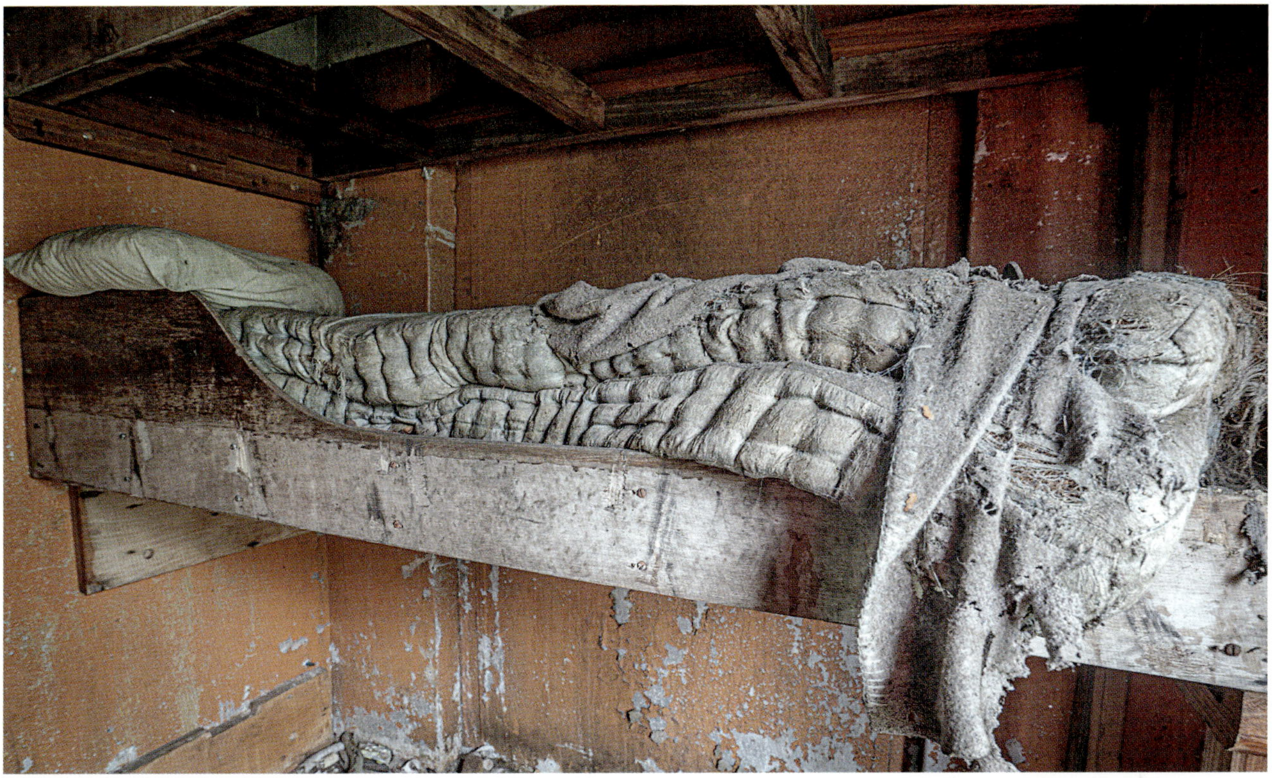

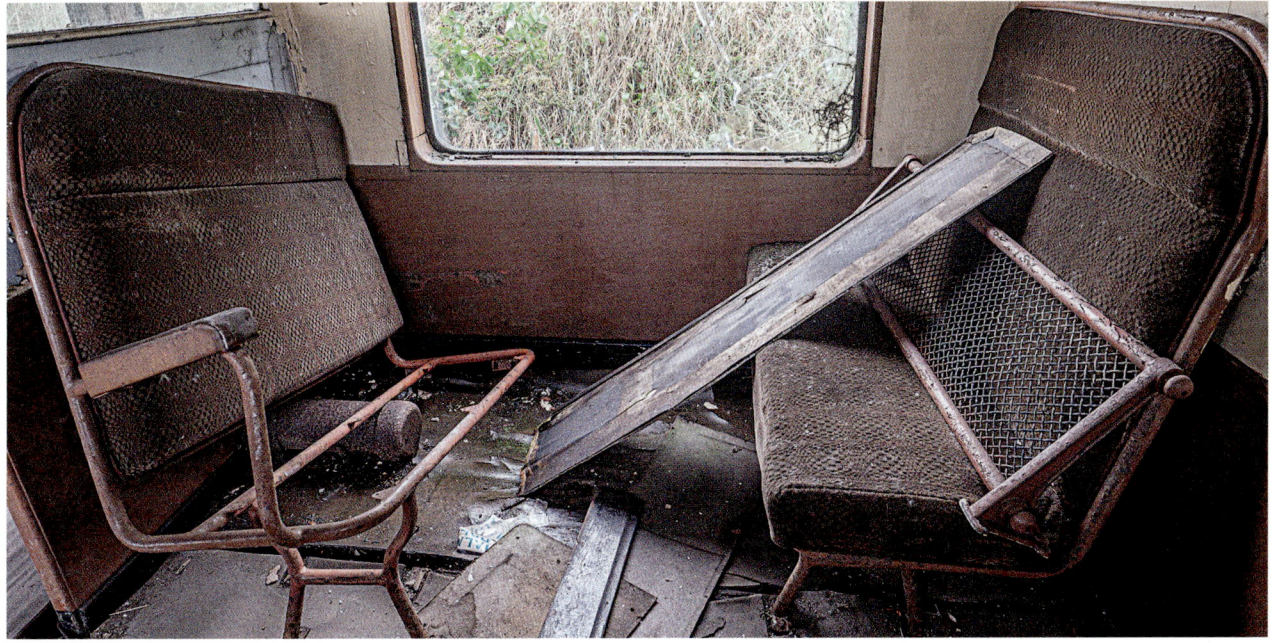

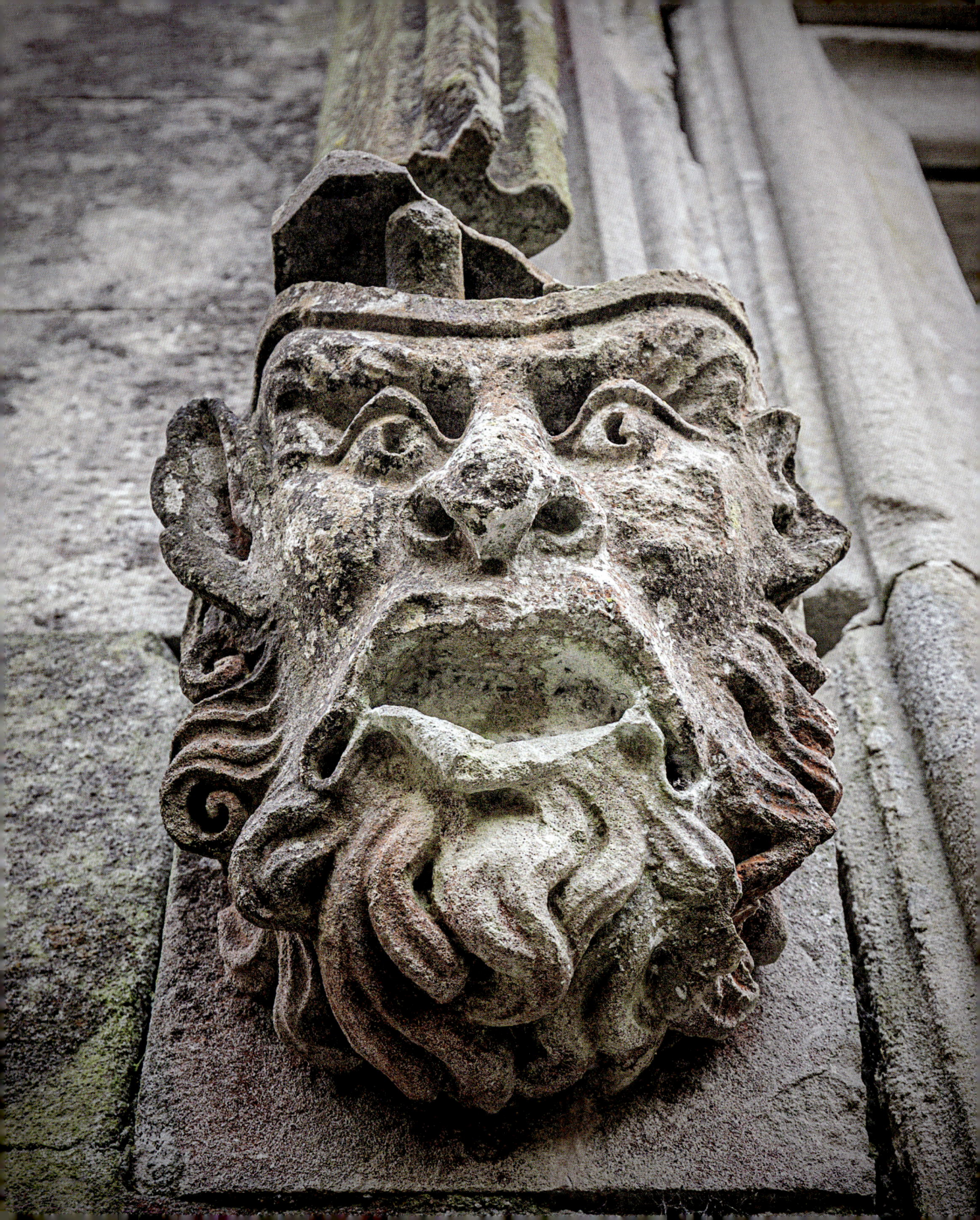

# LEARMOUNT HOUSE

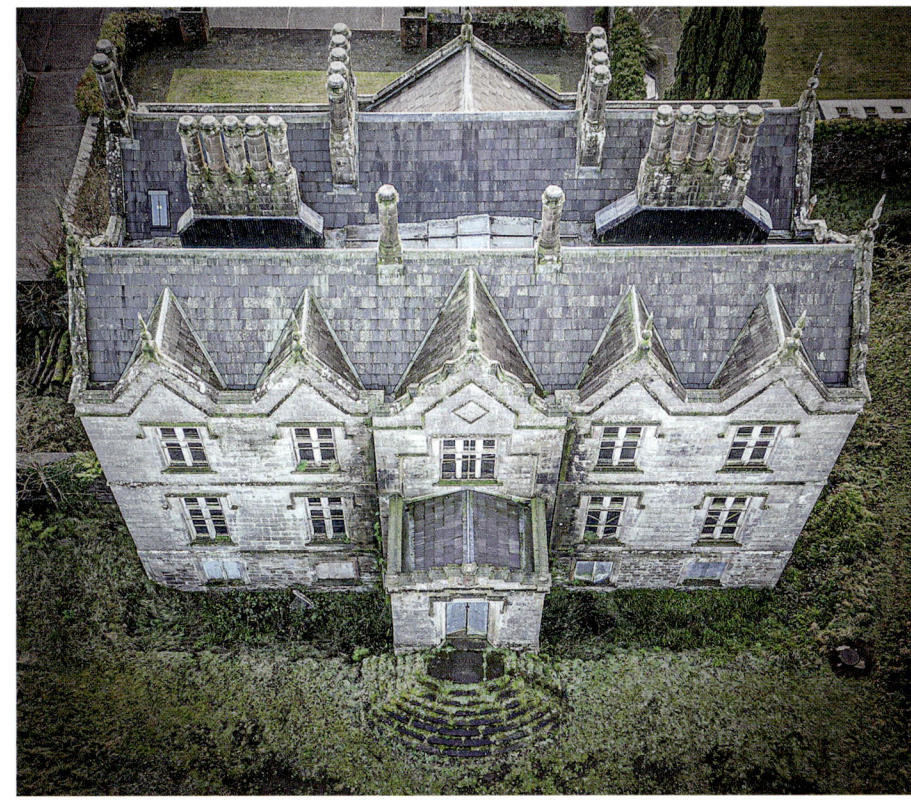

This Tudor Gothic-style mansion is an extension of an older building from 1710, originally built by a Captain Montgomery. It was extended in 1830 by Henry Barre Beresford, who was a land agent for his cousin George, the 1st Marquess of Waterford. The estate includes various gate lodges, a coach house and a large walled garden that provided vegetables for the house and workers.

The last Beresford to live on the estate was Henry Ralph, who was only eleven years old when he inherited. By 1924 he was the High Sheriff of Londonderry. When Henry died in 1925, the estate began to fall into disrepair. The house remained in the family and was rented out by Colonel Marcus John Barre Beresford to the Osgood family for about four years.

During this time, they brought the house and estate up to modern standards, installing electricity, a telephone and a water wheel in the grounds.

Despite owning the estate, Marcus Beresford never lived there. After the Osgoods left, the house

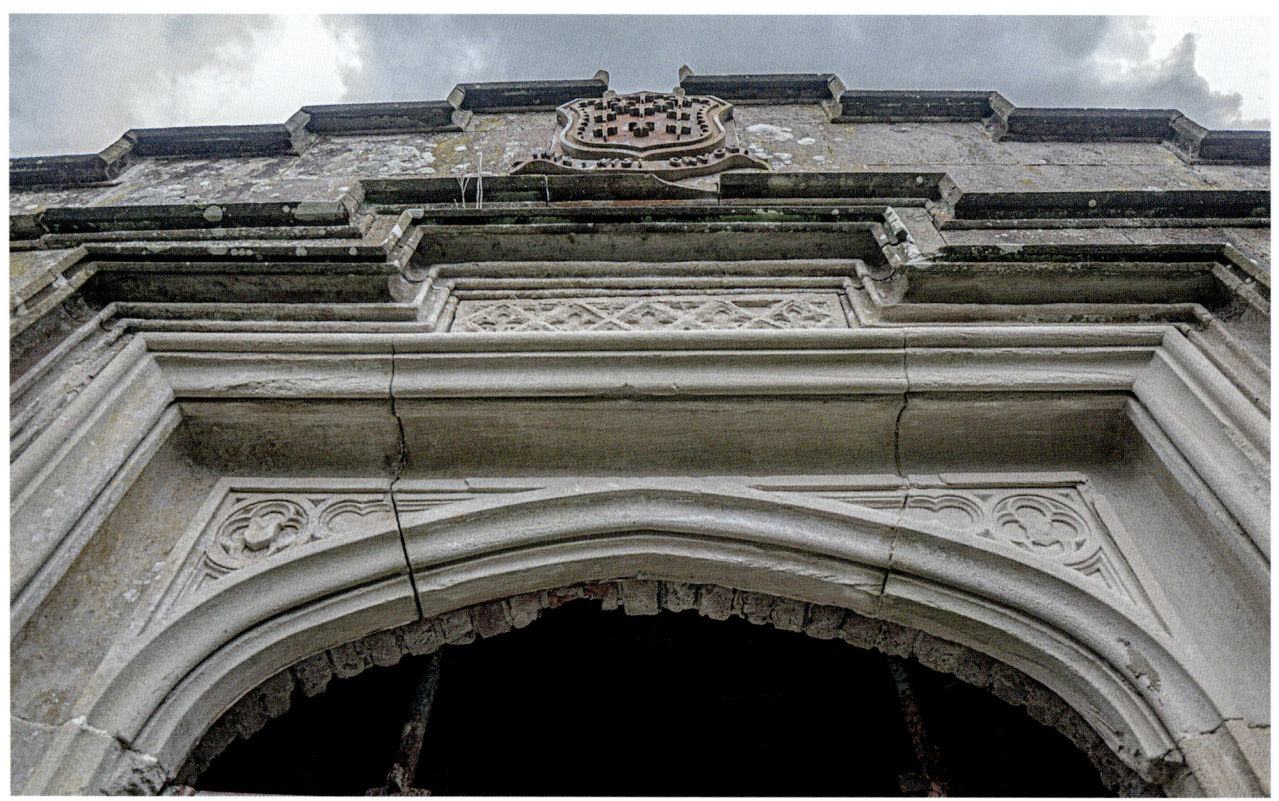

and estate were unoccupied until the Second World War. During the war, the house was used for the girls of the Ashleigh House School when they were evacuated from Belfast due to the risk of German bombing. The war had another impact on the history of the house – in 1944 Marcus was killed in action by enemy forces. As a result, Learmount passed to his daughter, Patricia, who decided to sell it.

The Northern Ireland Forestry Service purchased the house and surrounding estate. The Youth Hostel Association then rented the house and grounds. However, their lease expired in 1983 and they vacated the premises. Currently in private ownership, the coach house in the estate is in use as an Airbnb, but the old mansion house is derelict. Nevertheless, its beauty remains intact.

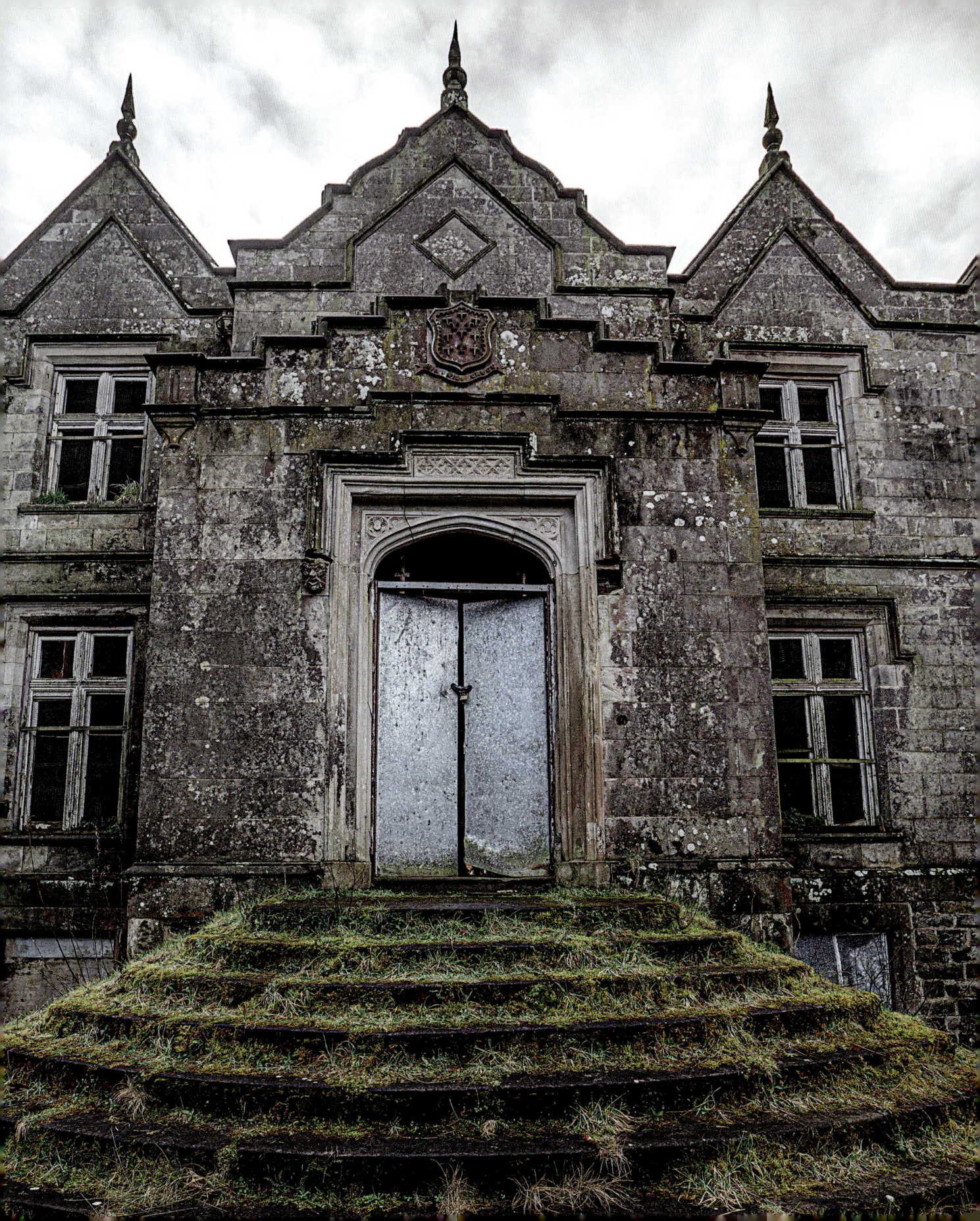

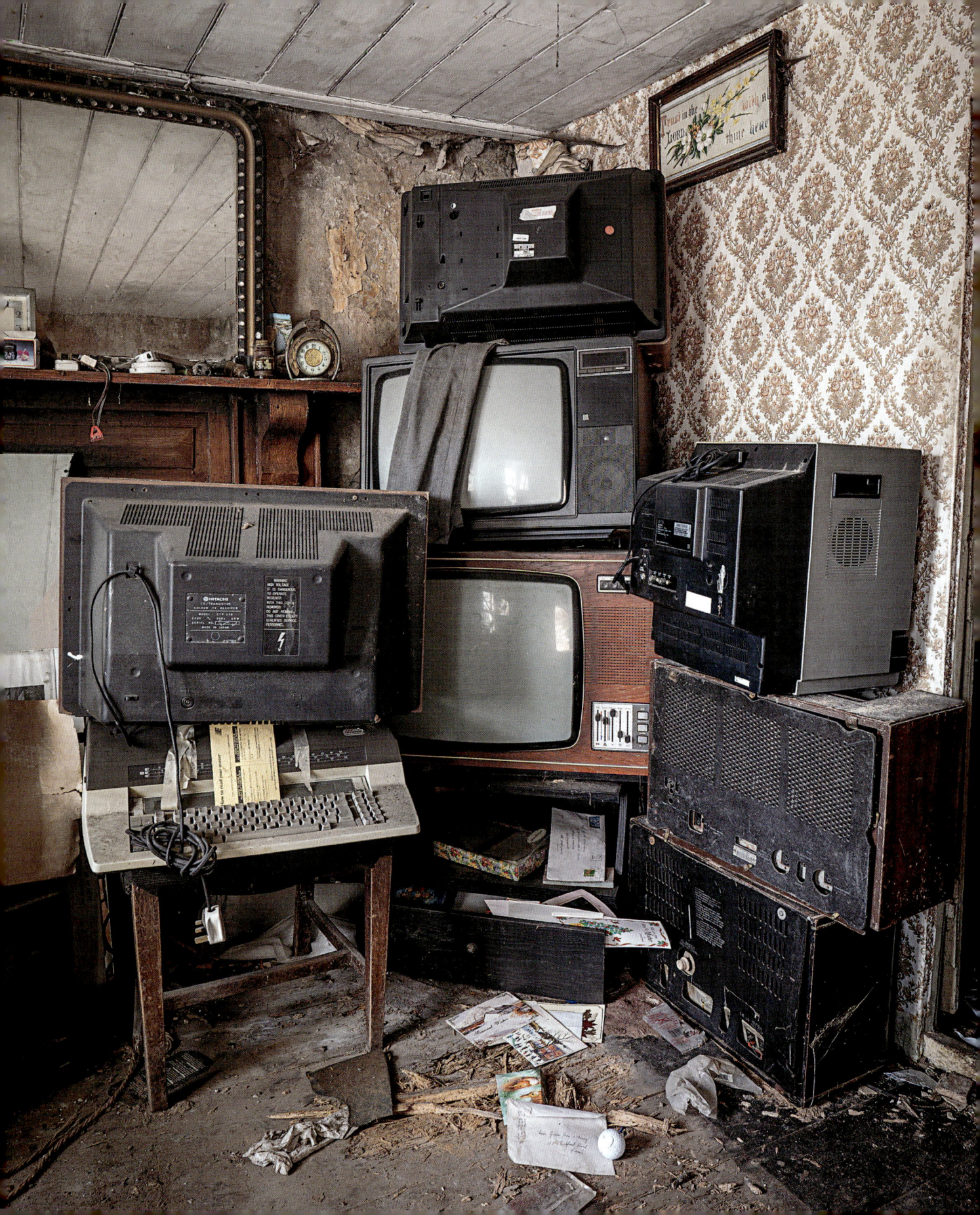

# THE TV REPAIRMAN

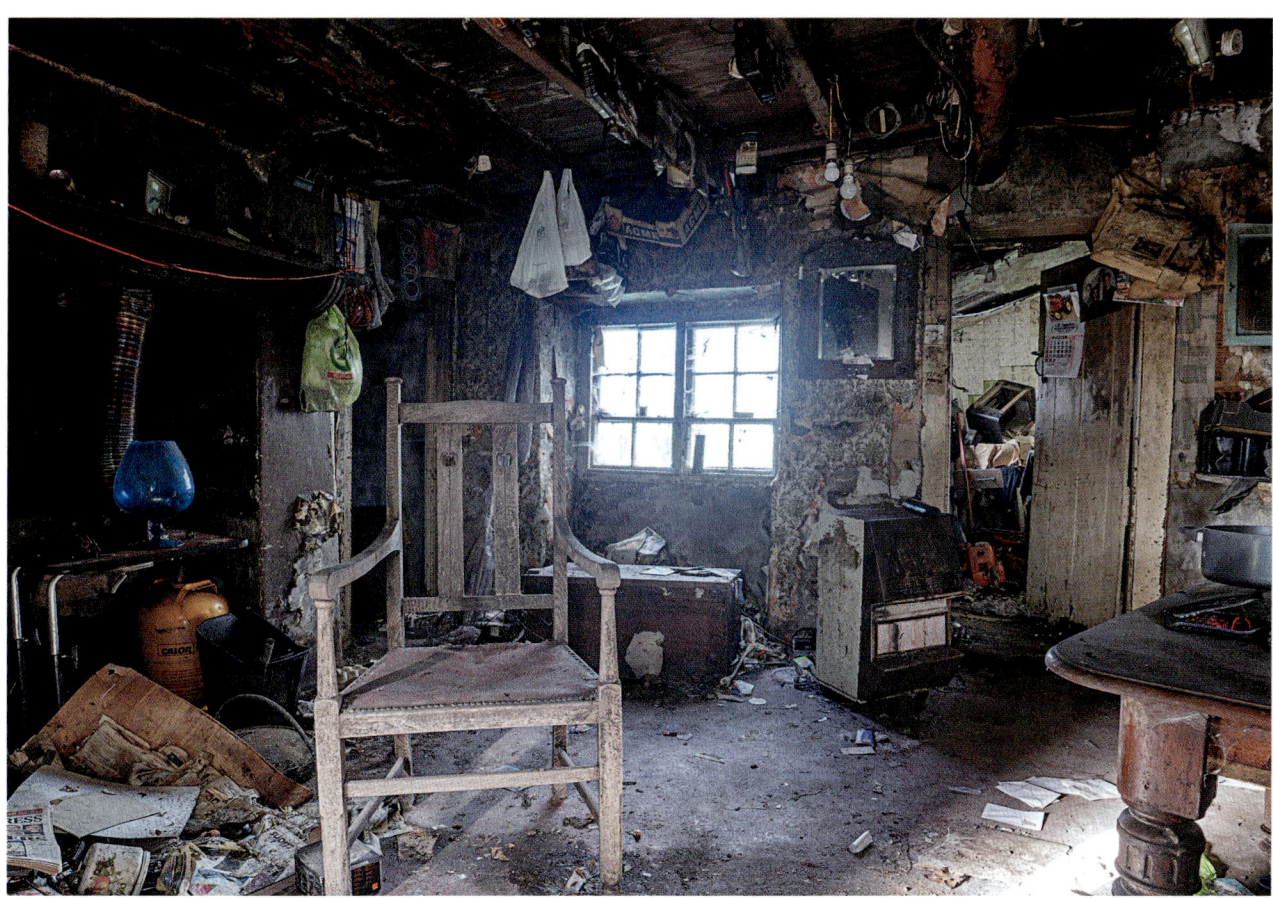

I always say that the smaller homes I visit have the most interesting personal stories associated with them, and this house was no exception. Elaine, who had reached out to me about Ashfield Store, also connected me with the owners of this charming little gem. The couple who purchased it, James and Nicole, are currently building a new home next door, and they have fond memories of the previous owner,

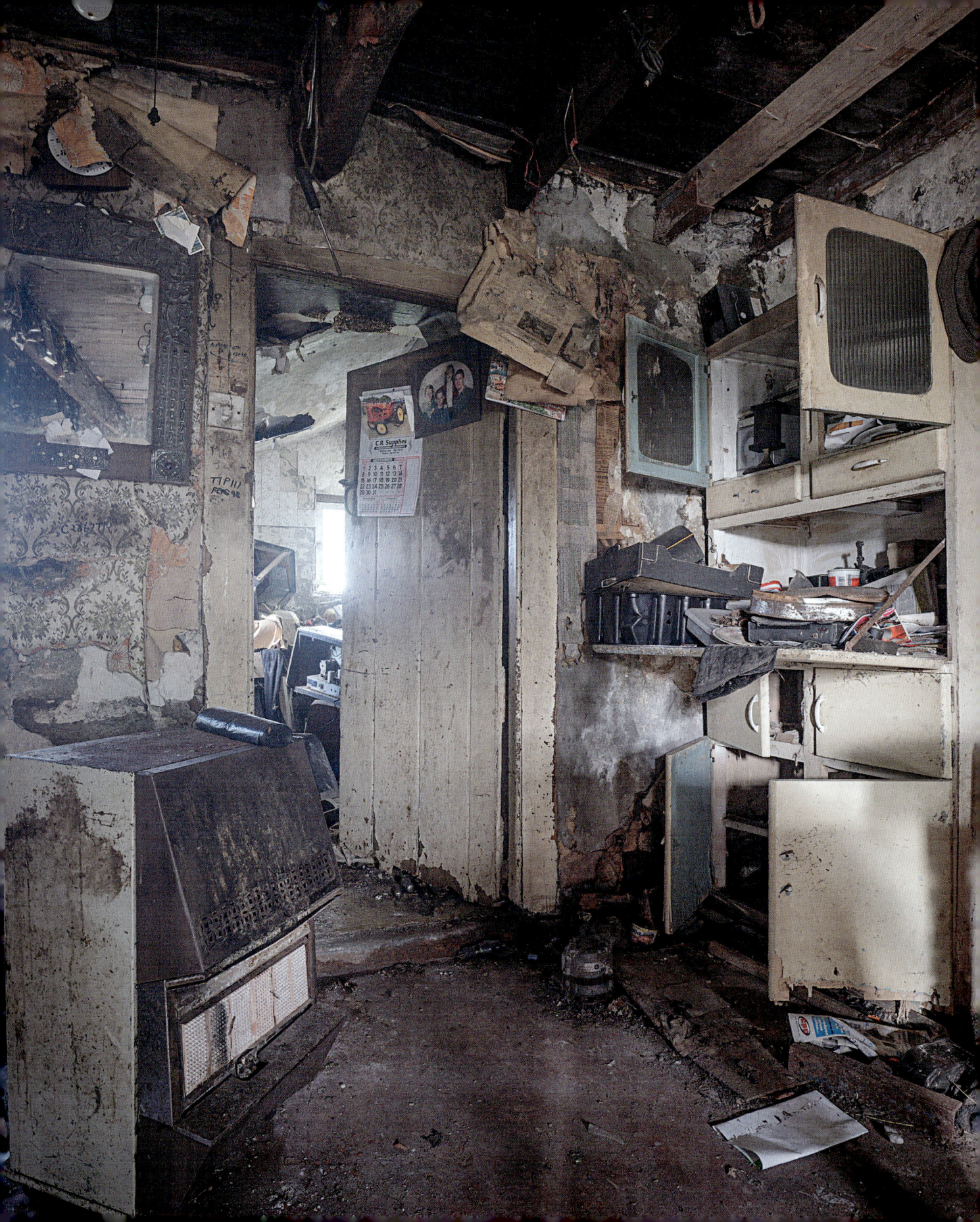

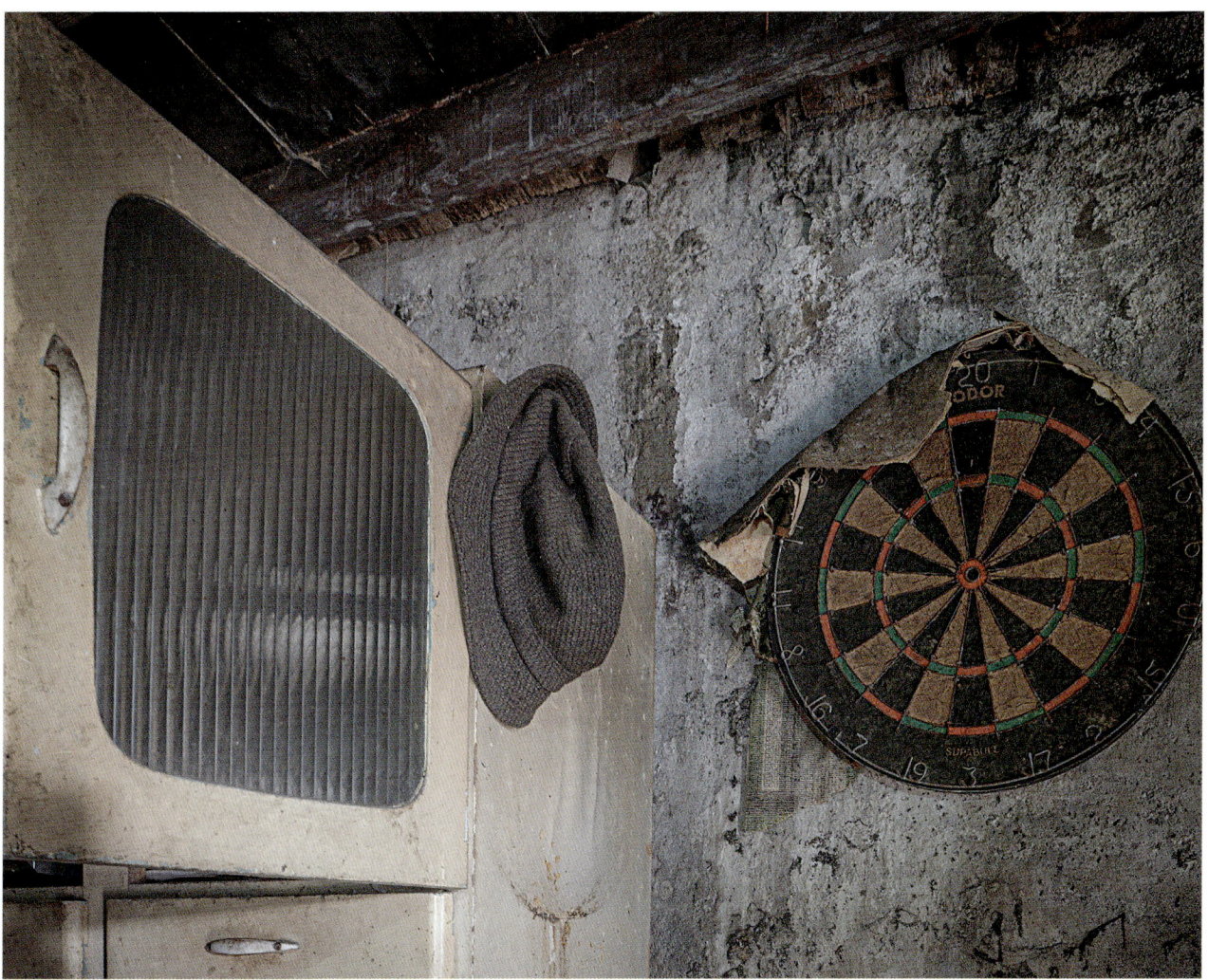

Andy, from their childhood. I always find hearing people's first-hand memories heart-warming, and the nostalgia is truly infectious.

Andy's story serves as a gentle reminder of how a quiet, simple life can hold a wealth of history and character. Upon entering his unassuming bungalow, I was greeted by a collection of vintage TV sets. These bulky, old-fashioned models are reminiscent of a time when TVs were a luxury item, with just a handful of buttons for channels and volume control. I would wager that most of them are black and white. Andy worked as a TV repairman, and locals would bring their sets to him for repair. The TVs that remain in his home were no doubt beyond repair, which is probably why Andy held on to them. The collection also includes old radios, phones and clocks – a testament to his skill with all things electrical.

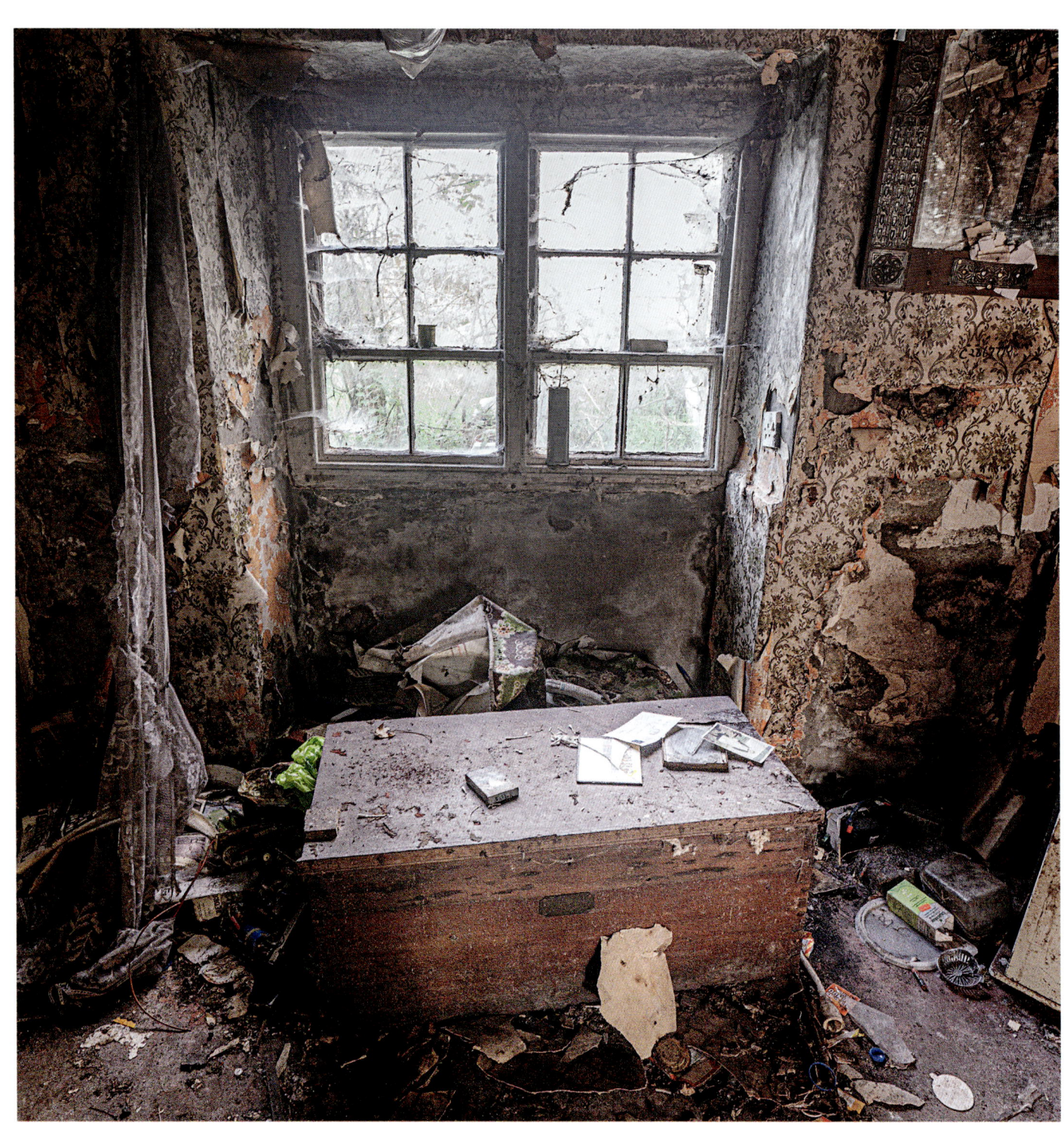

Andy never married and lived with his mother in a nearby house for some time. After her passing, he moved into this bungalow. Despite his solitary existence, he had a tight-knit circle of family and friends who would visit regularly. James, the current owner of the house, would often bring him dinner, as Andy was not known for his culinary skills. The kitchen saw little use, other than boiling a kettle for a cup of tea. He was a dedicated darts player, evident in the two dartboards with darts still in place in the room.

Every surface in the house seemed to hold spare bulbs, batteries, screws and various tools for his everyday tasks. I noticed his coats still hung on the back of the kitchen door – a poignant sight. A small set of stairs led to a small attic, likely once used as a bedroom. Carefully making my way up, I discovered more old furniture and belongings, a treasure trove of memories.

One particular picture caught my eye above the bedroom door – a painting by a child with 'James' written at the bottom. This was the current owner, who had painted it for Andy when he was very young. The fact that Andy had kept it up on the wall for so long showed that he treasured it as a meaningful gift.

James and Nicole have plans to preserve the cottage and begin renovations once their own home is finished. I'm excited to see what they do with it.

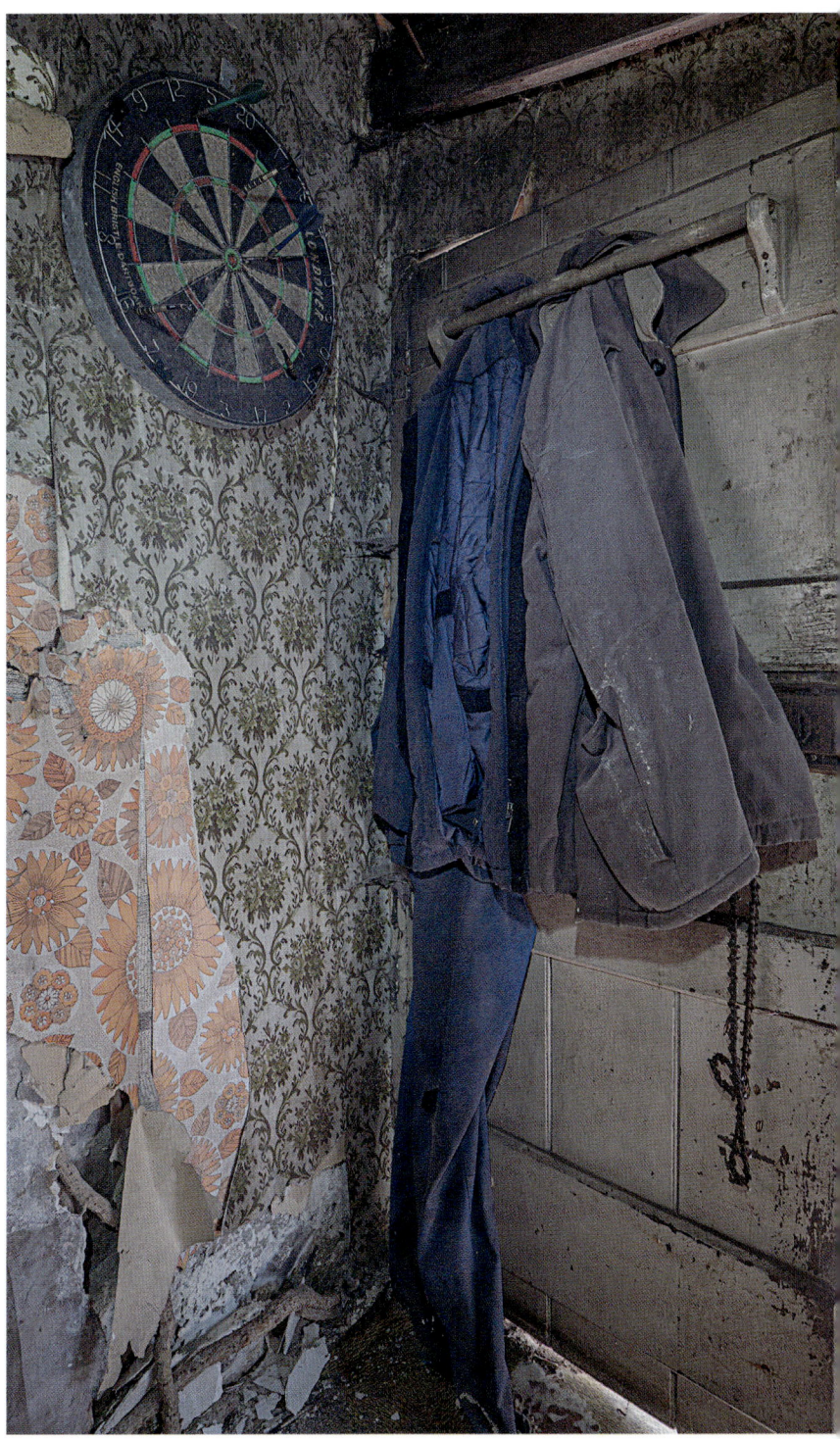

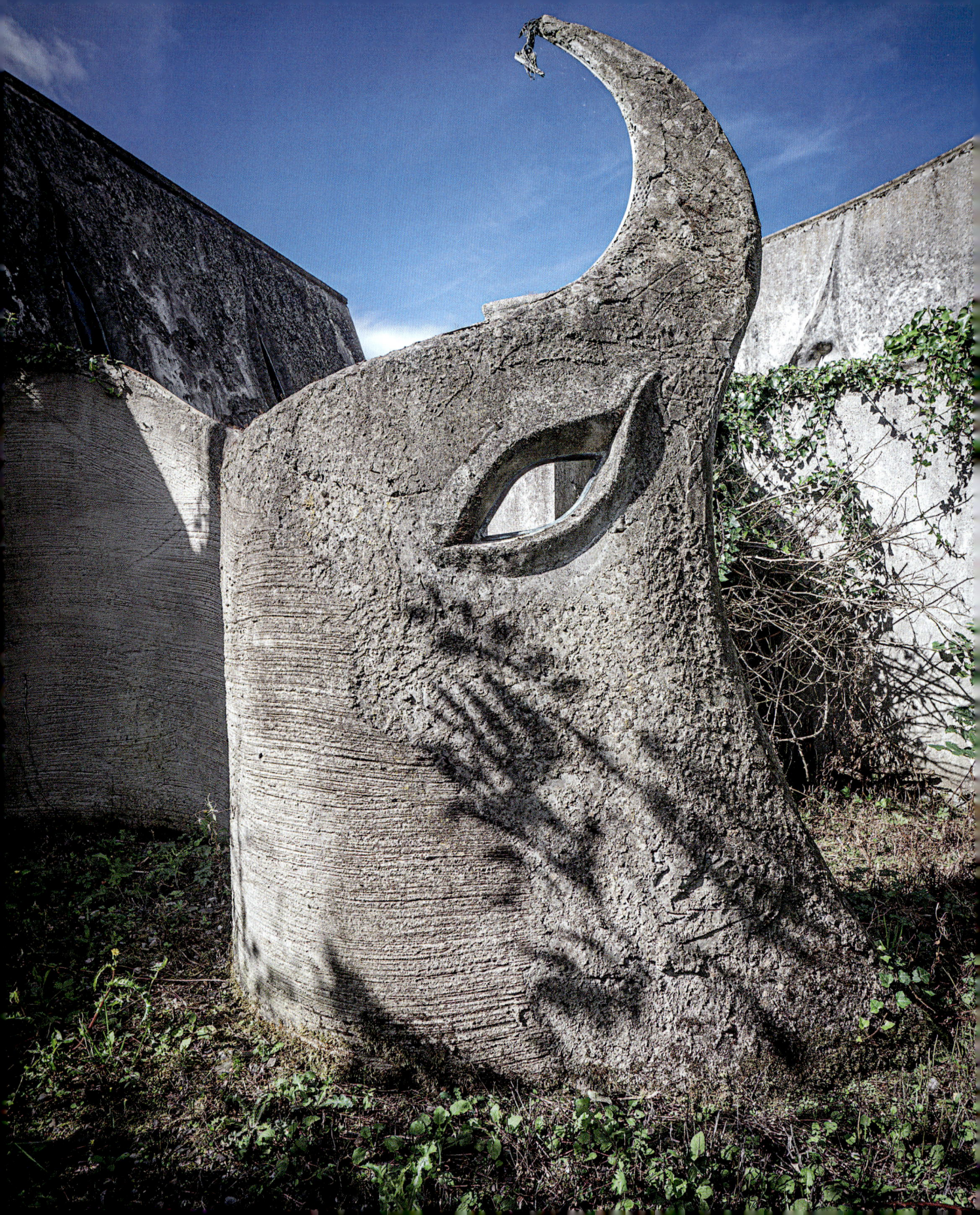

# A CULT VILLA?

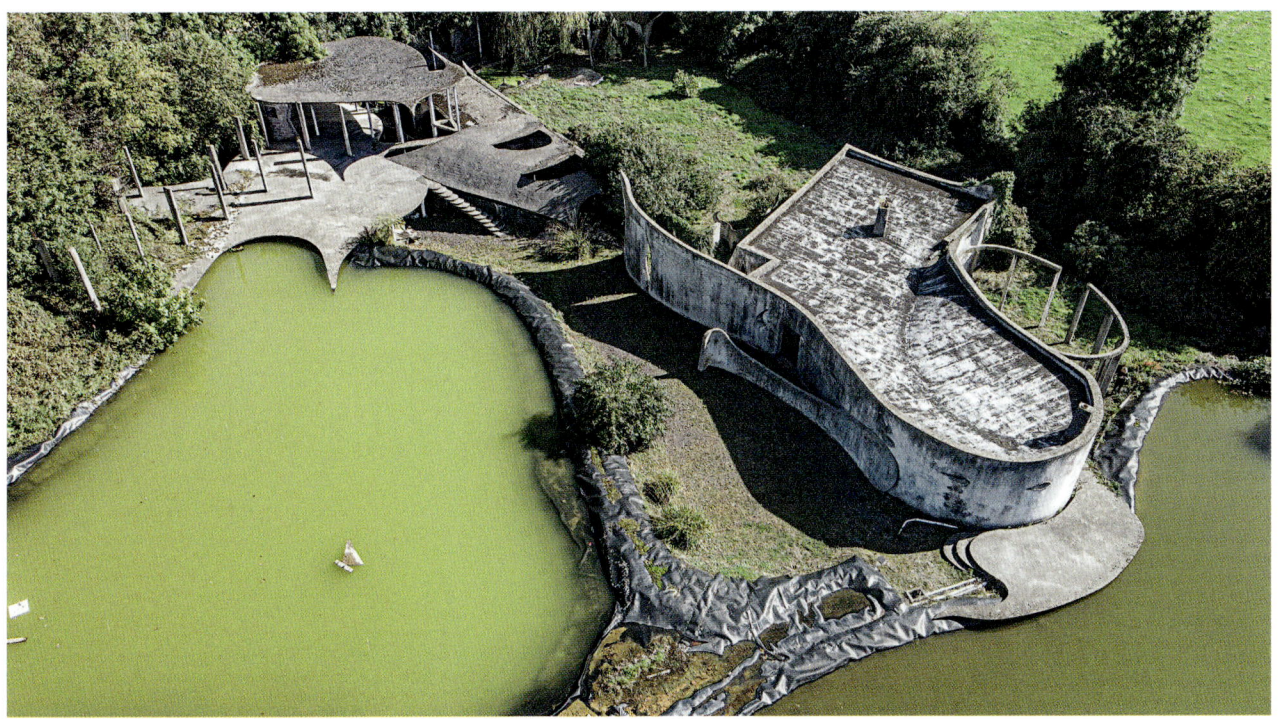

Without a doubt, this is the most bizarre location I have ever visited. No one will discuss the villa, not even the locals, who keep quiet about its history.

Rumour has it that it was built by an artist without proper planning permission, leading to construction being halted and the building left incomplete. Whispers suggest it was used for cult rituals, a possible explanation for the unusual features, such as the eyes, birthing pools and fireplaces resembling parts of the female anatomy. There are also stories about the owner returning in white robes, which neatly fit the idea of ritual use. Other stories are even more salacious, alleging that murders took place here. Of course, all these claims are unverified and more than likely just hearsay.

This concrete creation was never lived in, nor

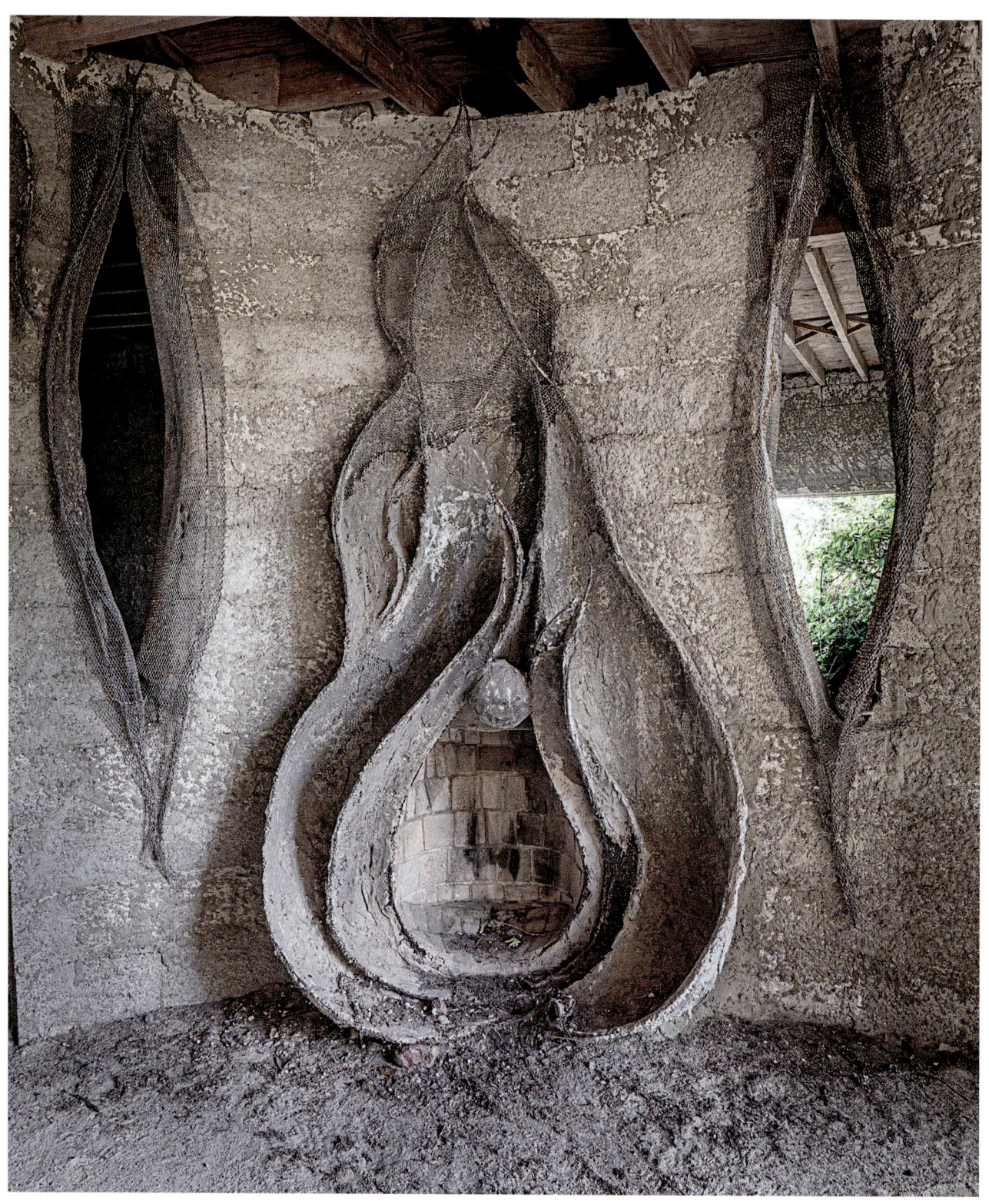

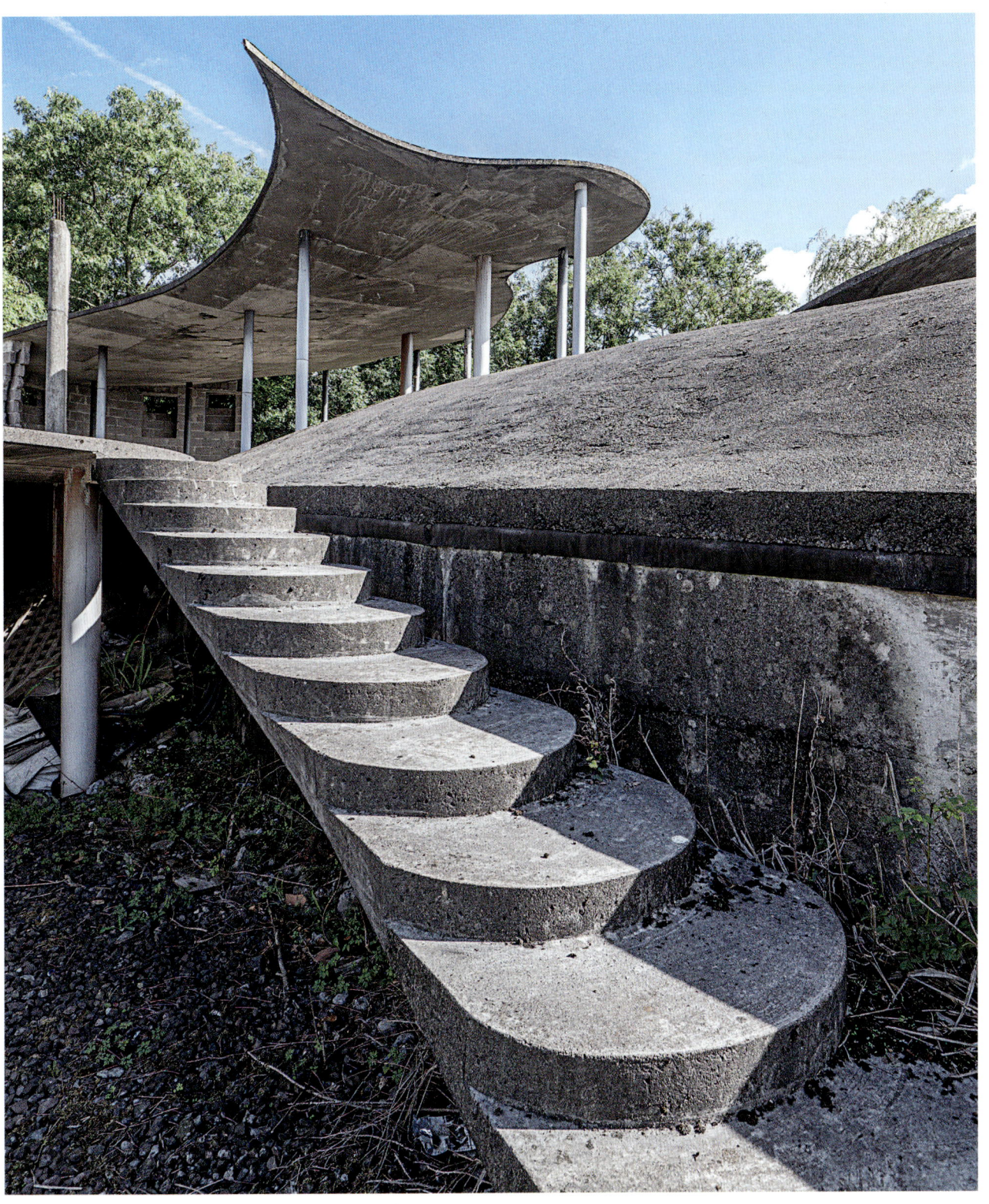

does it seem that there were plans ever to do so. The large rooms flow seamlessly together, but they don't look as if they were designed for habitation. Rather this seems more like a place to gather and meet. There are steps that glide up and down, some disappearing into pools of water. I wonder if there are lower rooms and chambers that are inaccessible. The only piece of furniture left in the building is a piano, now unplayable.

All that I can confirm with any certainty about this building is that it is incredibly mysterious and was constructed by a very creative mind. I doubt I will ever see anything quite like it again.

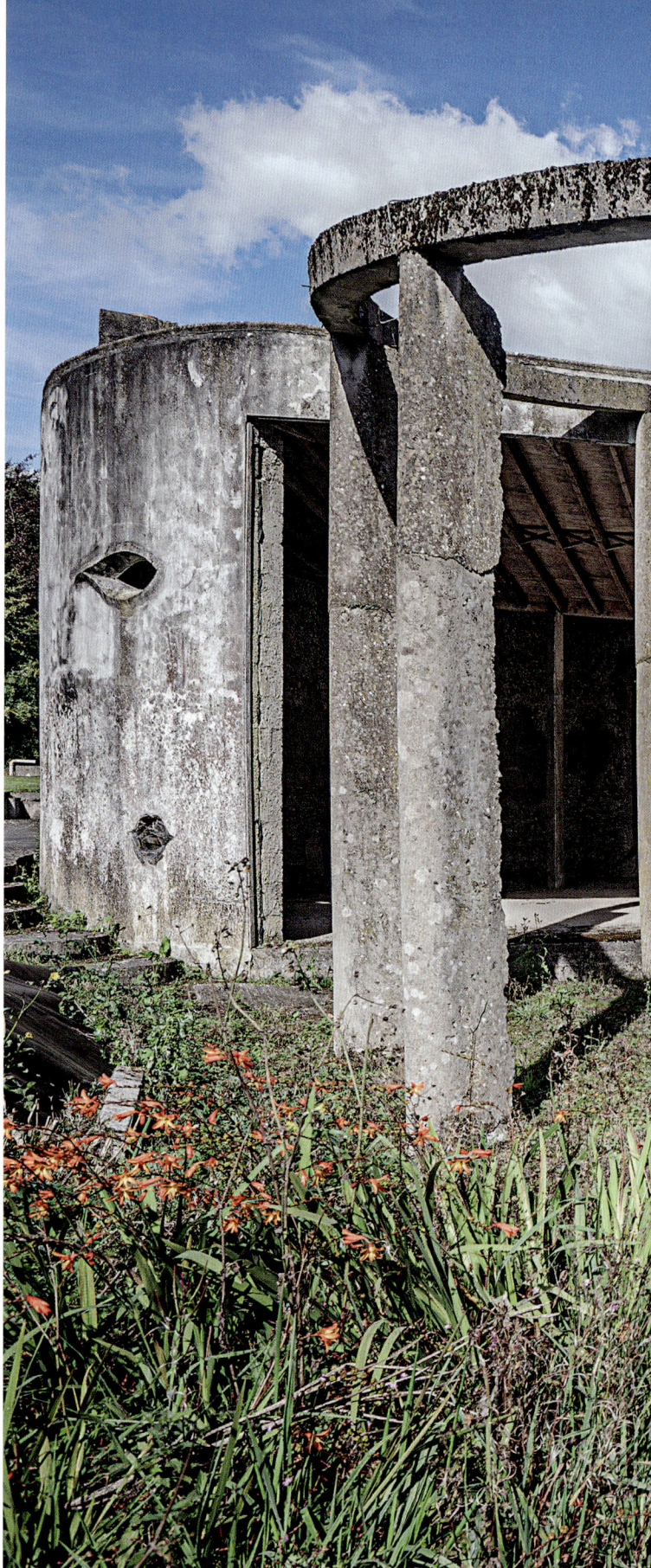

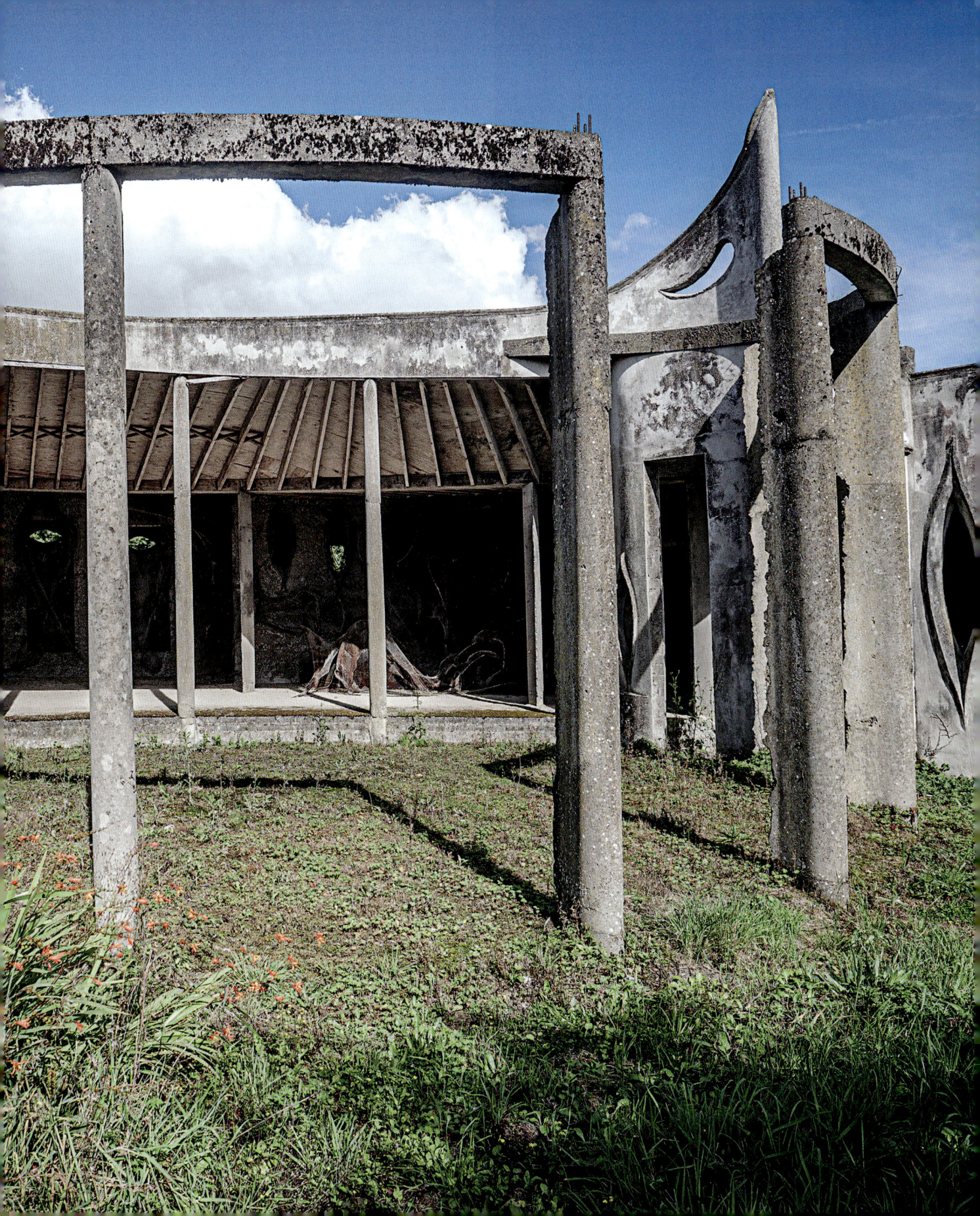

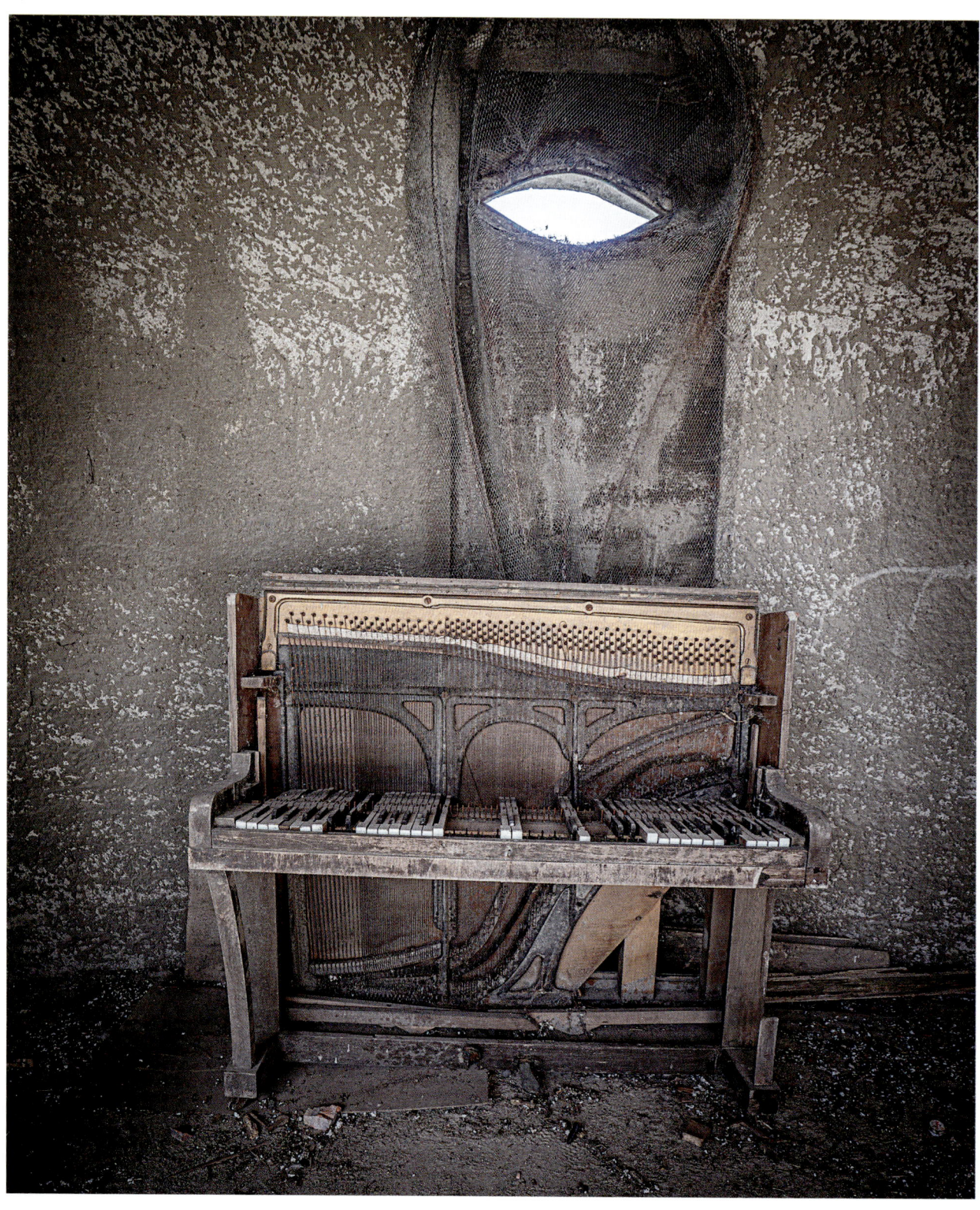

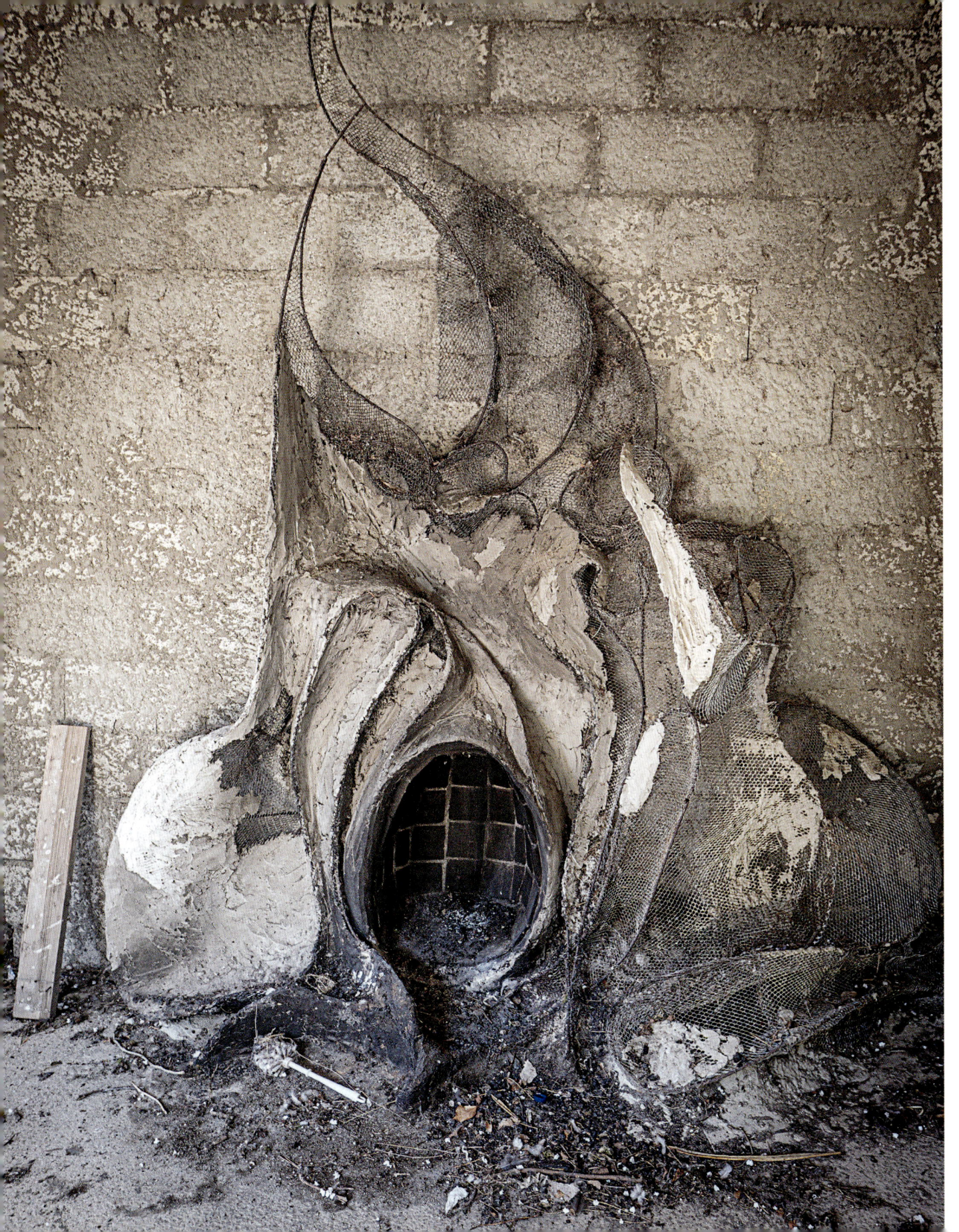

# ACKNOWLEDGEMENTS

I'd like to take this page to thank my followers on Abandoned Ni for supporting me throughout this wonderful journey. You're all amazing and you give such positive encouragement, it keeps me going. Especially on the early Sunday mornings when all I would rather do is lie in!

I'll take a moment to thank Julie and Ines Perez for joining me on some recent memorable trips and visits – 'viva la fiesta'. More of these to come, I hope! Catherine Willis who has been on many of these trips with me, some from the very beginning, is the best. I know I thanked my parents in the first book, but I'd like to give them another huge shout out for being so supportive.

Also, a big thank you to all the owners (you know who you are), especially Tony Dunlon. We need more of you to preserve these precious buildings.

Finally, I'd like to mention my two children, Oliver and Rhea, who continue to inspire me every day.

Thank you for reading and sharing my passion.

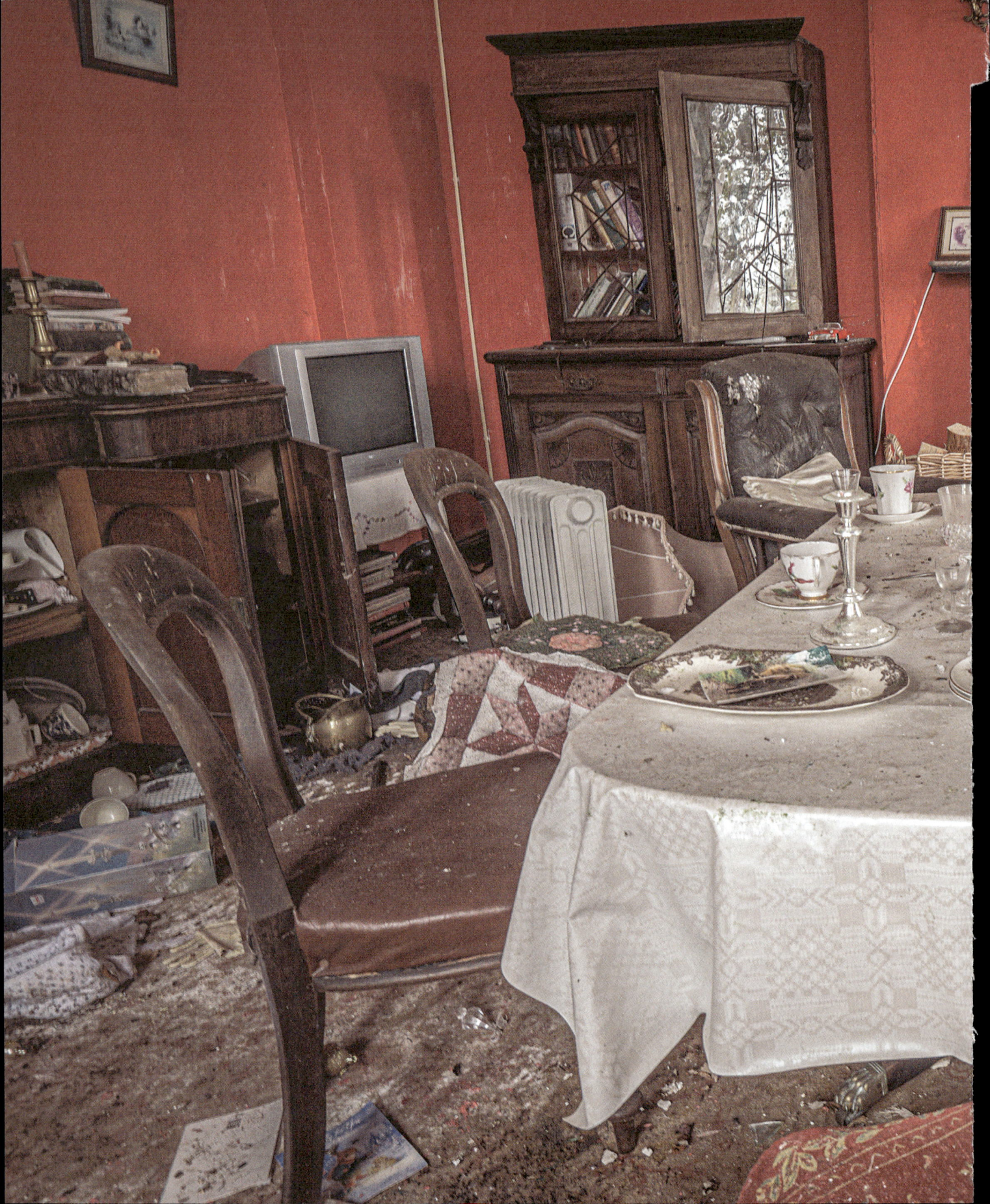